THE COSMIC SPIRIT

THE COSMIC SPIRIT

Awakenings at the Heart
of All Religions, the Earth, and the Multiverse

Roland Faber

CASCADE *Books* • Eugene, Oregon

THE COSMIC SPIRIT
Awakenings at the Heart of All Religions, the Earth, and the Multiverse

Copyright © 2021 Roland Faber. All rights reserved. Except for brief quotations in critical publications or reviews, no part of this book may be reproduced in any manner without prior written permission from the publisher. Write: Permissions, Wipf and Stock Publishers, 199 W. 8th Ave., Suite 3, Eugene, OR 97401.

Cascade Books
An Imprint of Wipf and Stock Publishers
199 W. 8th Ave., Suite 3
Eugene, OR 97401

www.wipfandstock.com

PAPERBACK ISBN: 978-1-7252-6069-6
HARDCOVER ISBN: 978-1-7252-6065-8
EBOOK ISBN: 978-1-7252-6070-2

Cataloguing-in-Publication data:

Names: Faber, Roland, 1960–, author.
Title: The cosmic spirit : awakenings at the heart of all religions, the earth, and the multiverse / Roland Faber.
Description: Eugene, OR : Cascade Books, 2021 | Includes bibliographical references and index.
Identifiers: ISBN 978-1-7252-6069-6 (paperback) | ISBN 978-1-7252-6065-8 (hardcover) | ISBN 978-1-7252-6070-2 (ebook)
Subjects: LCSH: Cosmology. | Spirituality. | Religion. | Religions—Relations. | History—Religious aspects.
Classification: BL48 .F20 2021 (print) | BL48 .F20 (ebook)

Manufactured in the U.S.A.   MARCH 1, 2021

"The Cosmic Spirit"

I am a single Self all Nature fills.
    Immeasurable, unmoved the Witness sits:
He is the silence brooding on her hills,
    The circling motion of her cosmic mights.
I have broken the limits of embodied mind
    And am no more the figure of a soul.
The burning galaxies are in me outlined;
    The universe is my stupendous whole.
My life is the life of village and continent,
    I am earth's agony and her throbs of bliss;
I share all creatures' sorrow and content
    And feel the passage of every stab and kiss.
Impassive, I bear each act and thought and mood;
    Time traverses my hushed infinitude.

—Sri Aurobindo

Contents

Why You Should Read This Book xi

What Is in a Title? 1

Preamble: We Are All Poets of the Spirit 7

    Theosis 7
    Nine Paths 14
    Differentiation 21
        Meditation I: Nothing, but Light 26

1: The Small Flame in Everything 29

    Space 29
    Fire 35
    Heart 42
    Epilogue: Suffering 47
        Meditation II: The Inner Fire 50

2: Crossing the Infinite Sea 52

    Ocean 52
    Horizon 59
    Mariner 67
    Epilogue and *Meditation III: Dying Sea, Dying Spirit* 70
        Meditation IV: The Raft, Vanishing 74

3: A Finger in the River 76

    Flow 77
    ΧΑΩS 80
        Meditation V: Mind the Flow 87
    Passage 89
    Epilogue: Manaus 95
        Meditation VI: Let There Be Life 98

4: Falling from the Tree 99

    Life 100
    Knowledge 107
    Garden/Forest/Wilderness 115
    Epilogue: The Throne of God 120
        Meditation VII: Becoming Wood 124
        Meditation VIII: Becoming Life 127
        Meditation IX: Becoming Worlds 129

5: The Show from Backstage 131

        Meditation X: Prospero's Magic 133
    Prologue: Theatre 136
    L'Orfeo 139
    Moses und Aron 142
    Akhnaten 150
        Meditation XI: The Sun, All in All 156
    Epilogue: Epiphany 164
        Meditation XII: Koan 168

6: Fata Morgana 171

    Desert 172
        Meditation XIII: Monad, Nomad 180
    Mirage 186
    Epilogue and *Meditation XIV:* Vibration 196

7: The Mountaineer 201

    Numen 201
    Ascent/Descent 206
    Summit 216
        Meditation XV: Mirrors 222

8: Staring at Stars 226

    Heavens 227
    Interstellar 234
    Light 243
    Epilogue: Immolation 250
        Meditation XVI: The Stellar Blanket 254

9: The Life of Other Days 257

    Prologue: Matrix 258
    Polyphilia/Multiverse 262

Meditation XVII: Other Lives 269
Awakening—Detachment—Compassion—Peace 271
Meditation XVIII: One/All No/Self 283
Love/God 286
Epilogue: Extinction 293
Meditation XIX: The Placeless 302

Epilogue: The Great Numenaries 311

Bibliography 321

Index 367

Why You Should Read This Book

ARE WE MORE THAN stardust? Is the appearance of the fragile Earth in the vast universe more than an accident? Does the capacity of the cosmos to produce immense manifolds of shapes of energy and light, of forms of life and the reflections of the mind, beings able to enjoy and question their existence and that of the multiverse in which they seem to be thrown, have any meaning beyond the moments in which they witness these wonders and suffer their own passing? Are we not only children of the stars, but of a Spirit that pervades the dust, rejuvenates life, and embraces the ever-evolving universe—a Spirit in which the All shapes the bewildering manifold of heavenly bodies, our globe, and our lives as our home? Is there a cosmic Spirit that wants us to awaken to a consciousness of universal meaning and sacred purpose, of freedom of diversity and mutual friendship with all beings, of deep insight into the divine nature of existence and to the hope for a future in which a universe will communicate in peace?

This book answers these questions with a spirituality of the numinous in our relation to the elements of the earth in the matrix of the multiverse by taking you on a journey through nine paths and nineteen meditations of awakening. Not bound by any religion, but in deep appreciation of the religious and spiritual heritage of human encounters with the divine depth of existence in our Selves and in nature, they invite you to become co-travelers by engaging the most profound embodiments of the intangible Spirit by which it facilitates its own materialization in the cosmos and our spiritualization of the cosmos—a process by which we become participants in the realization of the ultimate meaning of our Selves, the living earth, and the unending multiverse. Use—says this Spirit—the stardust that you are to become a spirit-faring species in an eternal journey of the cosmos to realize its ultimate motive of existence—the attraction of love!

Spirit manifests in cosmic becoming, but is not of it. In the wheel of births and deaths, Spirit is the birthless and deathless. The cosmos itself is a spiritual reality, inexhaustible by its merely material or energetic or informational states. In the mutual foldings of the cosmic Spirit and the spiritual cosmos, the nine paths of awakening of this book will present you with a spiritual landscape of human religiosity as means for communicating our common earthly and cosmic existence, expressing itself in the realities of space and time, interiority and exteriority, mind and matter, soul and body, life and love, mystical experiences and cosmological understandings. They want to take you into the interior of becoming-divine and the exterior of becoming-cosmic, becoming Spirit and becoming cosmos. They want to document and facilitate spiritual awakening in the recognition of the transreligious poetic patterns by which the spirit seekers in their passageways through the heart of the material and symbolic embodiments in which the cosmic Spirit expresses itself—such as the ocean, the rivers, the mountains, the stars—and by which we become travelers of oceans and rivers, mountaineers and star-farers—may find life unborn and deathless.

Throughout the nine paths of spiritual awakening to cosmic depth in appreciation of our fragile life on Earth, a philosophy of the Spirit addresses questions of religious multiplicity und spiritual unity; divisions in theistic and non-theistic accesses and answers to God and ultimate Reality; the deficiencies of spiritual materialism and naturalism; the becoming and meaning of diverse forms of pantheism, panentheism, and trans-pantheism; implications in the contact between scientific and philosophical cosmology as well as their religious counterparts; current research on the historical roots of Abrahamic monotheism and its interaction with the non-theistic complements of Daoic and Dharmic nature; the difference of monism and dualism from a dipolar and non-dual understanding of God and ultimate Reality; the implications of pre-axial, axial, and post-axial religious identities in conversation with postmodern philosophical thought; diverse philosophical constructions of the process of cosmic impermanence in the search for the unconstructed and undeconstructable Reality in its midst and as its origin; multiverse theories and ecological spirituality; and many multireligious themes around spiritual cosmology and cosmic spirituality. Yet beyond any romantic simplification of the spiritual blindness to the reality of suffering, perishing, and violence permeating all of these themes, awakening to the cosmic Spirit can only claim to release or exhibit spiritual authority if it also leads into, instead of hiding, the questioning of its own ambivalence in all cosmic realities, from exploding star-matter to life as food and gross inhumanity. In the end, cosmic spirituality must ask the question of you, the reader, pondering on its matters, whether you see the light in the darkness and can feel your spiritual home in the immense interstellar expanse of space and time.

What Is in a Title?

THERE IS REALLY NO good reason why a book should be named *The Cosmic Spirit*, except that there is really no better title for what this book wants to propose. I will explore the implications of its meaning within the current spiritual landscape in the preamble. Here, I want to foreshadow the following text with a disclaimer: there are many things that I don't mean to invoke with this title, and there are many potential connotations it may trigger in anyone's mind or on diverse backgrounds of experience, knowledge and patterns of spiritual interest and search that are problematic. Nevertheless, important reasons have hindered me to avoid the confusions that the title may signal.

The term "cosmic Spirit" has undergone many metamorphoses. It appears in very diverse areas of thought and commerce. It is the name given to a figure of a virtual playworld, a code for the experience with certain entheogenic drugs, and, in the plural, a euphemism for alcoholic spirits. It appears as a title of various pieces of music and art but also as the theme of a tarot deck, and it can represent astrological considerations. It is used as an apostrophe to characterize certain artists, writers or musicians, lacking any other form of expressing the overwhelming grandness of their mind and intentions as well as the impact of or universal desires enshrined in their work. In religious connections, it functions as a synonym for the ultimate object of desire of diverse forms of theistic or non-theistic spirituality; or it signals biblical or alternative non-western forms of personal, impersonal, or transpersonal encounters with God. It may stand for the essence of the universe as well as for the essence of its becoming.

Although relatively few books are titled *Cosmic Spirit*, they exist. And if it is not a book title, we may find it heading chapters or presenting us with one of the central concepts propagated by such books. Without appealing to any details of the general direction and suggestive implications they want to convey, we can still say that such books direct our attention toward a higher kind of consciousness at the heart of our existence—a consciousness that expands far beyond our ego-limitations and even any sense of Self to the vastness and depth of the universe as a whole, to that by which it is supposed to be held together: some kind of cosmic consciousness, be it ours or that of the cosmos or some divine reality. It is our close companion but cannot be reached without a change of perspective. In some religious contexts, it has become synonymous with cosmic or universal Christ- and Krishna-consciousness. In related contexts, it may stand for the Spirit of God or of Life, or it may refer to a specific way of life of a community that follows a certain religious or spiritual path.

When "cosmic Spirit" is evoked in religious literatures, it often represents an evolutionary view of a deep reality that must be reached through certain forms of training or by levels of mystical ascension, or it may be accessed by maps and plans of certain steps one must take in order to obtain its experience. In certain spiritual corners, it becomes a means of selling some kind of twelve-step program or the like by which, one is promised, one may attain spiritual peace or meaning in life. Alternatively, it can be connected to similar notions or associated meanings extracted from sacred literatures, scriptures of the religions of the world or the oral traditions of primordial religions and their current representations, mostly in order to build a case for alternatives to organized religion. It can stand for a new religiosity that is ecologically sensitive and planetary in scope. It may have feminist connotations or indicate windows into the recovery of lost dimensions of human existence as well as future reconfigurations of human life, consciousness and existence on Earth and in the cosmos. Or it may intend to devise "cosmic religion" as a natural development of, or alternative to, the checkered past of dogmatic religious interests and the small-minded religious imaginations regarding the world as a whole.

I am not inclined to argue against any of these incarnations of the meaning of the term "cosmic Spirit." They are just not exactly what this title and concept means in this book. My use of the term does *not* imply that a development of religiosity or spirituality beyond past instantiations of religions necessarily needs to overcome the religious diversity of the past and present—either in the form of departures from nature (natural religion) and humanity (revelation religion), transforming itself or being transformed into cosmic dimensions (universal wisdom religion), or in the form of oppositions to organized religions, indicating free spirituality. On the contrary, the impulse and desire for a movement of "transcending" might just be about the awakening of the heart *of* these religions and spiritualities. Further, the search for the "cosmic Spirit," here, is likewise *not* about adding experience to doctrine, or exchanging theory with practice, or reconnecting our humanity with the world around and beyond humanity—as the ancient religious patterns might already have been closer to these transcending universals and ecological integrities despite the distortions of the later memory of humanity. While I value the undiscovered, suppressed, or lost dimensions of religiosity that the "cosmic Spirit" can evoke or remember, in my understanding, it is more about an *affirmation* of these ancient patterns and forms as limited elements of the *vast multiplicity* in which the Spirit of life addresses itself in its *cosmic* dimension. Even if these worn perspectives may seem to be limited ways of addressing religiosity (that is, the value of any form of religious consciousness, theory, practice, or character), it is precisely such "liminality" (bounded, but in excess of meaning) that makes a certain path valuable. The cosmic character of the "spirit" of any limited religious expressions releases its depth and breadth in its inherent transgressions of meaning, thereby intersecting and interacting with the diversity of such self-transcending processes. So, widening *our* horizon rather than that of the ancient paths to a global view of their interaction means becoming aware of the inherent spiritual character of the very *multiplicity* of these mutually diversified but related religiosities.

What I *mean* to say with the combination of cosmos and Spirit is but an insight that is, presumably, as old as religious consciousness itself: that consciousness and reality resonate. *Cosmic and spiritual consciousness are mirrors of one another.* In fact, as far back as we can recover ancient religious and mystical literatures, even in their most mythological and symbolically distorted forms, we find a *correlation* between spiritual stations and cosmic states to be an *essential* feature of religiosity. While the old astrological stratification of spheres of planets maps cosmic reality onto spiritual states, so many spiritual traditions relate their experiences of spiritual, mystical, divine, or alternate realities to either a mirage of the mind or a mirror of higher realities that are invisible but powerful, that pervade and transcend physical reality, and that even create reality for some mysterious reason. Moreover, the diversity of heavenly realms in many religious traditions have been interpreted as cosmic *and* symbolic realities, that is, as cosmic manifestations of spiritual realities *and* as states immanent (only) to the human mind. While, for instance, Buddhist traditions variously interpret ultimate reality (*nirvana*) as both objective state and as subjective experience (and the fixation on either to be nothing but samsaric imagination), Baháʼí scriptures, conversely, affirm both perspectives as necessarily transgressing into one another.

"Spirit," then, is a *cosmic reality*—the *immanent* reality of the cosmos beyond its becoming and perishing. Spirit manifests *in* cosmic becoming, but is not *of* it. In the wheel of births and deaths, Spirit is the birthless and deathless. The cosmos itself is a *spiritual* reality, inexhaustible by its merely material or energetic or informational states. While for the skeptic this may all be a figment or an expression of our consciousness, it may also be *that reality through which the world becomes a cosmos* of harmonizations of multiplicities of realities of which our consciousness is only one element. It is in a landscape of such vibrations, oscillations, and mirrorings that the mutual foldings of spiritual and cosmic realities render the cosmic Spirit interchangeable with a spiritual Cosmos. Their mirroring appears to become *present* precisely at the points at which religious intuitions become meaningful, new religions appear, old religions become inspired again, and at which our understanding of the cosmic reality that we live in opens a window into the essential implication of *our* spirit to populate it. It is in this sense that I will pursue modes of *awakening in* this cosmic Spirit to a spiritual landscape of human religiosity as means of communicating our common cosmic existence, expressing itself in the resonances between macro- and micro-realities, interiority and exteriority, mind and matter, becoming and being, space-time and everlastingness.

The epigraph to this book, from a poem by the Indian sage Sri Aurobindo (1872–1950), captures some of these themes and dimensions of the interference of the Spirit and the cosmos in a way that does not simplify it to either a mere limitless and unproblematic harmony—without acknowledging dissonances as part of any interesting and realistic harmonization—or some merely vague hope for such a harmonization projected onto the painfully missing simplicity of the perceived nature of the cosmos in and from which we live and find our suffering, and to which we die. Although, in Hindu fashion, the poem preferences a universal unity of the cosmos that, simultaneously, pervades it as it embraces its limitations, that is, the *brahman-atman* unity that transcends any limited entity of a merely private and often possessive nature, it also resembles the detached and disinterested-compassionate *dharmakāya* of Buddhist philosophy and experience.

I am still struck by the pervasive character of a spiritual "presence" of this embracing and pervading unity of detachment-compassion in Sri Aurobindo's poem that, rather than just being a witness or a register, feels much more like a transforming power. Not the kind of "power" that we might project onto it—that of desire, interest, agenda, self-aggrandizement, or even atavistic self-affirmation through selflessness and service—but rather a "power" that reveals something that the philosopher Alfred North Whitehead (1861–1947), a contemporary of Sri Aurobindo, has poetically described as "brooding presence." Interpreting a poem of William Wordsworth (d. 1850) in his book *Science and the Modern World* (1925), Whitehead speaks of Nature as the aesthetic process of birthing, bringing forth, as the matrix of generation, even being Creativity itself—the ultimate principle in Whitehead's philosophy. But that which senses and lives the birthing process—the "Self" of this becoming at the heart of its (Nature's) self-transformation—is the Spirit *of* the transformation of the cosmos.

This Spirit is the Spirit of the earth and the cosmos, indicating a spirituality of Mother Earth in the matrix of the multiverse. This Spirit creates by brooding, by sensing its birthing process. It is a power of letting be and of attraction to become. It also perceives what it releases. Its listening silence speaks without syllable and sound. It is the spirited vibration that receives all words/worlds and that recycles their value in infinite living variations and connections. Endlessly playing the chords of cosmic multiplicity in its own "space," the cosmic Spirit emanates and receives the vast cosmic expanse through an "open mouth." The cosmic Spirit is not a mere "mystery" that is accessible only to mystics (from the Greek *muein*, with "closed mouth") but a *polyphilic* Spirit who *loves*, breathes and lives *the manifold* that it births, senses, receives and creatively transforms.

And, in concordance with Sri Aurobindo's evolutionary expectation of the ultimate Spirit to "involve" itself in the progression of the universe, the Spirit that breathes in us and the cosmos, that broods, births and drives the cosmic becoming, is *that* reality *in* us and everything that is both birthless and deathless. As such, it is the sign of the *ultimate value* of cosmic becoming beyond itself, but also *the impulse to value cosmic becoming itself*. The cosmic Spirit names the motive "power" of the process of the spiritualization of the cosmos in which the cosmos both *becomes from* the birthless and, in the process, becomes *deathless* itself.

Preamble: We Are All Poets of the Spirit

> God's role is not the combat of productive force with productive force, of destructive force with destructive force; it lies in the patient operation of the overpowering rationality of his conceptual harmonization. He does not create the world, he saves it: or, more accurately, he is the poet of the world, with tender patience leading it by his vision of truth, beauty, and goodness.
>
> —A. N. WHITEHEAD, *PROCESS AND REALITY*

> At that hour will the Mystic Herald, bearing the joyful tidings of the Spirit, shine forth from the City of God resplendent as the morn, and, through the trumpet-blast of knowledge, will awaken the heart, the soul, and the spirit from the slumber of heedlessness.
>
> —BAHÁ'U'LLÁH, *KITAB-I-IQAN*

Theosis

WE ALL LIVE OUR lives, if we are lucky, without asking, Why? If we are "lucky"—but what kind of luck is this? Is it the luck of being born into a family that can afford to feed itself? Is it the luck of a having been born at a given time or place in this world we did not invent? Would I like to be born in, say, the 1400s CE in Europe amid the bubonic plague sweeping through the lands and killing up to two-thirds of the population? Or would I like to live during the Spanish conquests of the New World, witnessing the slaughter of up to 90 percent of the indigenous populations there? Certainly not! But why are people born at these times? Why? The question of luck and fate always arises in times when we are robbed of just living our life in peace

We seem to experience the gravity of the meaning of life when its very "spirit" seems to have gone missing. Yet that is not the entire truth. We also experience the "spirit of life" when we consciously avoid *just* to live our lives. When we, instead, begin to *wonder*: Why are we *here*—here, in time and space, on this continent, at this time, on this earth, in this cosmos? When we are not content with things just as they are, we begin to ask for the very "spirit" of it all. Whenever we are not just doing what we do, we become aware of a "spirit," or its absence, that makes what we do or feel or think *meaningful*. We become, then and there, right then and there, not only aware of the spirit of life or its lack. Rather, such situations impress on us something essentially human. We become *spirit-faring*. By transformative experiences of fullness or lack, pain or joy, injustice or liberation, contingency or eternity, we become the *poets* of our spirit of life.

Let me first say what I don't mean. I don't mean to say that we "create" this spirit. It is not that we experience meaning as *our* creation, at least not exclusively. We find ourselves—if we are lucky—already in a world that conveys to us by its very existence a profile of meanings (or the painful recognition of their lack) when we become conscious of it. But we feel that we, in being born into a world—into its contingent "situatedness"—are not its creators, but actors in a play that is always already on its way of working itself out. Nor, at least deep down, would we accuse our parents of being the "creators" of our part in this play. They would, if you asked them, admit that they too have just appeared on that stage, seemingly from nowhere, becoming participants in a scene by a mysterious reason other than *their* parents. We are *here*, no reason given, no reason found.

The questions whence and why are smoothed over by our consciousness, rounded, closed, foreclosed. Like our continuous field of eyesight, we normally don't see or miss the blind spot. The blind spot of "whence" and "why" is squeezed out by the seamlessness of our consciousness. Neither did we "create" this consciousness or manufacture its "well temperate" roundedness. But we know of its createdness. Especially if we begin to ask "why," we are bound to encounter the "spirit" of this contingent life. Then, we become liberated to become "poets" of this spirit.

Let me give you an example of what I mean by "poet" here. Imagine that you read a poem: You recognize it *as* a poem if suddenly all the words, the intersection and clash of their images, the restlessness and strangeness of their symbolic interaction—all that becomes *significant* in new ways, in ways far beyond the materials used and the meanings translated. Unlike a set of instructions for building a piece of furniture, unlike a report in a newspaper, unlike even the page of a novel, now every word and its position in the text, on the paper, the form it takes, the sound and rhythm it reveals when we recite it, the contour it releases when its polysemic images confront each other—all that and more we may feel to be a gift of *placement*. This serendipitous togetherness in the poetic composition may urge us to ask deeper questions, such as, Is this all coincidence or destiny? It is with such questions that we not only become aware of a text *as* a poem but also, in a true sense, *become* its *poets*. No one else can replace the way the poem becomes a poem for *our* feeling and in *our* mind. Not that we "create" the poem, if we are not its author. And even if so: Did we really create it or was it *felt* by, and *fall* into, our awareness? In the poet lives the poem, but it arises, appears. We become poets as much through the poem as the poem becomes a poem through us as poets.

The poet does not create, the philosopher once said, but *saves* the world in a poem—so the epigraph of this preamble. In the poet's vision, the world comes together in its very *spirit*. In this sense, we are poets of our spirit.

Yet the spirit of life is not *our* spirit. We do not "possess" this spirit. It always *arises* as a *gift*, in between things, because of their excess or lack of aesthetic appeal or existential meaning. This appeal or meaning does not gather by a willful act, but neither is it a mere passive given. It comes like "a thief in the night" (Matthew 24:43; 1 Thessalonians 5:2; Revelation 16:15), without warning, always unexpected, and in ways unanticipated—if we let it compose itself. We *suddenly* become poets when our life's *becoming* converges as a poem. Yet we "become" its poets only by sensing its *convergent* spirit. Not by manipulating it, nor even by steering it willfully, but rather by mediating and meditating on the gift of its spirit. Only in this sense are we poets of our lives, do we become a poem of the Spirit. In the experiences of our lives, the Spirit arises as *the event of their meaningful togetherness.*

The passages from the New Testament invoking the poetic image of the "thief in the night" indicate something else, too: that this experience may not just be one of unexpected appearance, even suddenness, but of some kind of a *shock*. It is inherent in this experience of the spirit of our lives that it may happen when we are sorely and acutely missing its meaning, when we are thrown into the low strata of animal existence, when the bare bones come out. When the spirit seems to be missing like in the prophet Ezekiel's vision of the field of bones, without flesh, awaiting some kind of divine action, we sense, we hope, we awaken to the desire for a revivification. Indeed, this image of a field of bare bones awaiting awakening has become one of the original poetic renderings for the spiritual figure of "resurrection," collectively as a people or individually from a life in the shadows, on the border of death, or even after death (Ezekiel 37). What the dead bones are hoped to be clothed with is not just "flesh" but *spirit*, meaning, life. The spirit of our lives is always the spirit *of life*, a life that is given as (a gift of) the power that overcomes death, figuratively or literally, collectively or individually, in this life or beyond its confines. As the Gospel of John so decisively states: It is only the Spirit that bestows life; and the one without Spirit is without life, whether living or dead (John 3:6; 6:66).

We *all* are seekers of the spirit. We are a spirit-faring species. This seems to be a steep statement. Why? How can I claim that? Because when we receive the gift or shock of the spirit of our lives, as indicated in the epigraph of Bahá'u'lláh (1817–92), the prophet-founder of the Bahá'í religion, it is with our sudden awakening to the wonder or lack, the wondrous or dreading contingency, of meaning in our lives that we become spirit-seekers. We begin feeling alive or dead, seeking life or more life.

The Cosmic Spirit

We want to gain or regain meaning, or we seek to understand its wonder or disappearance. We may wonder how we could ever have lived just so, without consciously experiencing its wonder. Or we may wonder how we could have ever missed to be thankful for the wonder of our life as long as it *was* in our "possession," and we did not really feel this to be a big deal until we found it missing. We may, indeed, become weary of our life if it does not release more than a sigh for a vivacity either *beyond* the one that vanished because of a loss of love, friendship, a lover or friend, or *beyond* the very life we already lived because of its thrownness into stern times, among war, hunger, and homelessness or creeping meaninglessness.

We all are *seekers* of the Spirit—whether we want it or not—because we are always already "out of luck." Not that we cannot be lucky, possibly, for a moment in time, to live our lives without the shock of the spirit; but the luck that this luckiness indicates is not really great. It is either the luck of the unaware or it will always become the luck of the sedated. This luck is the anesthesia of the ones who have not yet experienced the roughness of life or who have become numb to it because of the hardship it brought. This luck is in no way more satisfactory than the lack of luck one dreads when it has gone. Such luck is rather unlucky, because it cannot find "a spirit" in life. It has either lost it, lost the opportunity to find it or not been given the opportunity to seek it. If we have not become *a question* ourselves, we will not set out on the quest for, and the encounter of, "the spirit" in, of, and for our lives. Yet as long as we have not become "spiritual," in *this* sense, we waste our lives either for ourselves or for others: for ourselves, because we have not become aware of our Self yet; for others, because we waste others' lives that we leave untouched, ignoring them or impacting them only like lifeless objects.

The Spirit of life impacts by *touch*. Seeking life, seeking the Spirit of life, is seeking to touch and be touched by *all* life, whether ours, others' or that of this world: of the beauty of nature, of the relief of the thirst or the release of the imprisoned—much like Jesus wanted us to seek *the* Spirit of Life, of resurrection, of a new life, of offering life to others, in our touch of the excluded (Matthew 25).

Seeking the Sprit in everything is seeking its *inner* life, vibrating with the Spirit— like two instruments that are close enough to pick up each other's vibration. It is like becoming a *body of resonance* that synchronizes with a world fine-tuned in the cosmic Spirit of life. In the Spirit of life, we become *spiritual beings*. Not that we ever were without "it"—life or Spirit. We always *were* spiritual beings, even before we noticed it. Nothing is without "it."

The Spirit hovers like an eagle, effortless and still in the wind of our Self, or moves like the wind over the waters of our inner being, churning up vivid patterns of foam and contours where surface and depth meet like the waves of the ocean and the air into which they pierce their forms. This is the *cosmic* Spirit in the image of the initiation of creation as it appears in the book of Genesis (1:2): the mysterious *ruah Elohim*, the divine Spirit that is *just there*, placeless, *before* the act of creation, *before* light and darkness part, and land and water retreat to their own realms. Is it (like) a wind, a bird, a power, a presence? Maybe pure potential or creativity? Is it personal or more? Is it singular or plural, a relation or a web, maybe?

The cosmic Spirit of life is, well, *cosmic, universal*. It is *not owned* by any religion. Its reality appears in *all* religions—for instance, as the dynamic and creative presence of God in the Hebrew Scriptures; as the Spirit of pure life in the New Testament; as the Great Spirit of indigenous American tribes; as *brahman*, the essence of Reality in Hinduism. All of these religions mean the vivid Spirit inherent in all existence and in us. It is in this recognition that the cosmic Spirit stretches us to be released beyond any splintering differences and limiting boundaries. In the excess of the cosmic Spirit, we should measure "its" gift of life only by the intensity by which we give ourselves to others.

The cosmic Spirit is *not* a spiritual *reality*. It is that *by which* there is "spiritual reality," that is, a reality that awakens to the vividness of life and its unbounded meaning. *We* become spiritual reality *in* the Spirit. In seeking the Spirit, we become what we are—spirit seekers, poets of our life on a world and in a cosmos that is moved by the process of becoming spiritualized.

If we say we are "spiritual, but not religious," we miss the point here. With the "deep empiricist" (relationality) and pluralist philosopher William James (d. 1910) in his book *A Pluralistic Universe* (1908), we should be intent to see the opposition between spirituality and religiosity as an aberration imposed by materialist reductionism and secularist concessions to its "spirit" rather than an empirical insight. It is *in* the cosmic Spirit that we are spiritual; but it is the *religions* that remind us of the empirical *accessibility* of the Spirit: that the cosmic Spirit *cannot* be possessed either by religions or beyond their limitations. Since no religion possesses the Spirit (as does none of its deniers), their fine differences should not be a means for conflict, which often was and still is the case, but a warning: In the Spirit, there is freedom; in the Spirit, all are only *possessed* by the Spirit *if they are empty* like a reed or a flute for the wind, the tone that the melody of "it"—Spirit, life—creates in them. Yet the Spirit only "appears" in the *manifold* of all the melodies it poetically instills as a gift, and differently so in all of them, *including* the pleroma of religious paths.

"The spiritual" is *not* a reality different from "the material." Rather, the Spirit rises in "its" and our passages through *matter*. "Matter" is not in a dualistic opposition to anything other than that which avoids or negates "the spiritual." But even then, the Spirit that is negated is the *one* Reality on the basis of which such a negation is granted. What is more, the Spirit of life *seeks the dead*, to vivify them. The patience of the Spirit is the power of persistence. Maybe continuity and constancy are the characteristics of "eternity"; but, then, eternity may be the characteristic of the patience of the Spirit, offering space and time for seeking "it" out, inviting to a life of adventure, momentum, and activity. The Spirit of life never reaches (for) a final resting place. It always seeks revivification, overcoming any grave. That, here and now, may be "resurrection," the coming to life in the Spirit of life.

Matter *is* spiritual; *materia* is the birth that the *mater* gives to life. It is the Mother Earth and the cosmic Matrix of becoming-Spirit. It is nothing fixed, as we might think if we were (still) limited by old categorizations imagining matter in terms of inert things or particles, operating like billiard balls in a universe of collisions. Rather, as newer physics has recognized, we live in a universe of touch, between forces, energetic potentials, and forms of fields that coalesce, that relate, that communicate, that mutually influence one another, become, or move into each other. We live in a universe where "things" are clouds of activities and potentials, of events and processes, of energies in exchange of characteristics. Everything moves, relates, is present in one another in dynamic ways. The spiritual connotations of this universe are endless, of course. But the one important connotation, at this point, is this: the cosmic Spirit indicates the *vividness* of these movements and exchanges, of these mutual ways of being immanent to one another beyond any abstract characterization in isolation, be it that of "matter" and "mind," "form" and "content," or "activity" and "potentiality."

The ancient and venerable philosophers and sages of diverse spiritual and religious traditions, whether in the east or the west, knew that. The Stoics rendered *pneuma* a refined "spirit-substance"; *brahman* could be understood as the most rarified "material of existence" (*Chandogya Upanishad* 6.13); and for Aristotle (d. 322 BCE), *materia* is nothing but a "sphere of potentials for activation." This is not a bad image for the reality of the Spirit: the *field* of a multiplicity of infinite *potentials of activation*; the *attractor* of all potentials to be realized according to beauty or goodness; and the *infinite movement* that seeks such realization. Matter, here, appears as the spiritual *milieu* seeking "its" multifarious realizations of touch, beauty, and mutuality. The first spirit seeker is the Spirit! It is the Spirit that sighs in us (Romans 8:25–27). Spirit is the true movement at the heart of, the urge for, and the desire to actualize *love* within the elementary "matters" of life.

As the *Spirit* is the seeker "in us" for infinite actualization of spiritual potentials, so is *God* the first poet of the Spirit of life—or that is what I, with A. N. Whitehead, will name "God." While *we* might be the poets of our life's spirit—dispossessed by its gift—it is a gift *only* in the saving view of the Poet. Why? Because it is only God, or that *is* God, who or that can save everything to life, who or that *is* the Spirit of life, who or that *becomes* God in all that becomes, who or that realizes the spiritual potentials of their lives, and who or that becomes alive in them. This is the God who or that becomes "all in all" (1 Corinthians 15:28). Did you ever ask yourself, What does "all in all" mean? To be *all* in all things does not seem to leave any space for anything else besides this reality. What besides God is everything, then, if it indicates the "all" in which nothing else "is" but God? We could call this "pantheism," a becoming-God of everything, or a partaking in God's nature (2 Peter 1:3–4). But we should rather talk about spiritual seeking as *becoming* that which we already *are*: spiritual potentials for the realization of divine Life. It may be an infinite process of becoming, but it is a "becoming-God." The ancient ones have called it *theosis*.

There is too much in this little word "theosis" to be excited about. Yet, at least, it should be pointed out that it is not only a profound Christian notion, venerated by its Eastern traditions throughout the centuries. It is meant to indicate the highest aim of human existence as such, independent of specific religious connotations. It is also imminently connected to another term used here, namely, the "poet." Indeed, *theosis* is a short version of this term: *theopoiesis*. It announces that we are "God in the making." However, *this* "becoming-God" is not signaling *our* hubris—like the one suggested to Eve by the snake in the garden of Eden (Genesis 2–3)—but the self-gift of *God* the Poet in which the giver becomes the gift and the gift becomes the giver.

Like the mystics of medieval times, such as Meister Eckhart (d. 1328) and Nicolas of Cusa (d. 1464), this "becoming-God" suggests *unio mystica*, the mystical union in which God expresses Godself (the Self of God) as "all in all" (1 Corinthians 15:28). Alternatively, as Islamic mystical language suggests, in this spiritual "state" nothing remains in this union but the Face of God (Qur'an 2:115). The *theopoetics* of this "becoming-God" is the poetics of the spirit seeker: becoming a *spiritually awake* being "in the Spirit." Let the Spirit seek "in" us the very realization of the infinite potentials that indicate divinity in humanity and humanity in divinity. Spirit is not opposed to matter, but the "incarnation" of matter *in* the spirit—yes, I mean that: not the realization of the spirit in matter, but the realization of matter in the spirit, of the awakening of spiritual potentials toward their actualizations, of the poetics of humanity in divinity, of becoming-human in the Spirit.

While the Spirit is *formless* or *pluriform*, allowing for many forms of realization and actualization of its potentials and powers, its poetic force adopts modes of *imagination* that can be meaningfully differentiated in their *materializations*. I will lead you through *nine* such "materializing forms" of imagination or *poetic matters* of the Spirit self-realizing itself (its Self) as you become the "imaginal" poet of the spirit of your life. One can understand them as "paradigms." In the meaning of Plato, who introduced us to this concept, this term indicates "a perfect potential," a "heavenly image" that gathers all of its potential actualizations together like *folds* in *one* poetic imagination (*Republic*, 592b). In religious terms, this translates into a manifest "image of the invisible God" (Colossians 1:15), that is, *a poetic materialization of the Spirit* seeking its realization in us. They are not "imaginative," but rather, in their profoundest appearance that constitutes these poetic "matters" as potential or powers of the actualization of the Spirit, they are "imaginal" in the sense of the subtle realms of mystical experience, as explored in the work of Henry Corbin (d. 1978) on Shi'i and Sufi sources.

While the potentials of realization are infinite in their modes but also in their combination, such paradigmatic images or *clouds of imagination* can release the different types of spirit seekers to variegated resources within and outside of religions for their awakening to the awareness and realization of purpose and meaning in their lives. These paradigm-clouds allow for *spiritual patterns* to arise that are sufficiently different from one another so as to resonate with diverse materializations of the Spirit or with different "potentializations" of life-matters in which the cosmic Spirit may indicate its presence in our lives. They each actualize *different poetics of spiritual awakening*.

These image-clouds are *poetic* in the sense that they "save" the *matter* of spirituality—again referencing the epigraph of this preamble. They are "material" in the sense indicated above: concrete, embodied images of the invisible infinity; and they are "materializations" in the sense of being lived through by merely living in this world. They are spiritual due to their aesthetic immediacy of imagination—that is their poetic nature. These *poetic forces* are taken from different immediate bodily encounters with the world before education takes them away and exchanges them for abstractions: *concrete encounters* with the world of *nature* and *aesthetic*, of *sense* experiences and *primordial mental* operations "before" any reflections.

These image-patterns lead us back into profound *vibrations of inclusiveness*, of the primordial includedness of our bodies in a world of elements and temperatures, evoking explorations in haptic, visual, auditive, and olfactory sensations, of moods and temperaments in such encounters, of activities and feelings before mind takes over. Yet these experiences *don't* become poetic through the *exclusion* of mind and reflection, language and communication, abstraction and construction, either, but rather by seeking, *through mental* processes, the release of the primordial *potentials* of these embodied life-forms and -forces to concrete actualizations. It is this *potentialization* that makes such imaginations universal paradigms of the spiritual.

Nine Paths

The book consists of *nine* paradigmatic and poetic *paths* of seeking the cosmic Spirit of life. Alternatively, these paths of potentialization of life highlight patterns that traverse spiritual landscapes without fixed boundaries. Couched in their valleys and hills, we can trace various passages meandering through some of the most elementary forms of the "matters" of our life—luminating them in the light of the cosmic Spirit that rises in them and releases us as vortices of their conjugation in the evolution of the cosmos, this earth and humanity. Alternatively, we may say that these paths are the clouds of images representing nine modes of passage spirit-farers may want to *recover* as potentials that they have already encountered, inherent vibrations of life to be vivified, or inert folds of potential life to be unfolded.

Postmodern writers on religion, such as Luce Irigaray (b. 1930) and Ellen Armour (b. 1959), have indicated that we might, at a time of feminist, racial, and postcolonial intersectionality as well as global consciousness and ecological integrity, dare an important shift in our spiritual perspective by moving away from abstract concepts and doctrines, upholding limited religious identity, and, instead, find spiritual satisfaction and nourishment in the "elements" of existence, such as water and air, fire and earth, that are fundamentally shared with all beings. Yet, since ancient times—in the west and the east—these "elements" were not simply physical appearances of our human-size mesocosmic world, but, contrary to the materialist assumption, the *intangible reality* of which the "material" is a symbol—and as such they are not "constituents" (ingredients) of material reality, but their spiritual "universals."

Indeed, *as such* these elemental forms of nature appear in virtually all religions and are used in many spiritual traditions, physically and symbolically, as means of action and of imagination and as sensible envelopes of the divine born from the spiritual earth. In these elemental encounters, the most primordial expressions of the sacred character and perception of the numinous "power" of the cosmos and the earth dawned on primal and indigenous consciousness and ways of living, and it still reminds us that these universal experiences of the Spirit have always been a companion in the human encounters with the mystery of existence, divinity and Reality. In fact, to the extent that this spiritual encounter with our common material existence actually makes us human, in the first place, it may well be precisely the *elemental* engagement with the numinous divine or spiritual Reality that awakens us to the avoidance of religious striving. We all share this treasure by means of which deep spiritual conversation between many traditions, religious or not, have been and can be facilitated. By invoking their all-pervasive, constitutive, and healing presence, we may consciously begin to understand that "we," that is, *all* of humanity and *all* other beings we touch through these elements, are—as another feminist and poststructuralist religious thinker, Catherine Keller (b. 1953), remarks in her *Process and Difference* (2002)—united on our *only common ground*, this earth, and its diversified but interrelated Spirit. The impression that the whole planet Earth (with all of the enabling cosmic constellations that gave birth to her and sustain her, such as the heavily bodies, the physical forces, evolution, life, mind, and so on) is the minimal "undivided unity" or smallest "entity" of meaningful existence—quasi the "atom" of meaning in the "cosmos"—was not invented by the sensibilities of eco-theories such as the Gaia hypothesis of James Lovelock (b. 1919) and Lynn Margulis (b. 1938), but reflects our most ancient human spiritual knowledge and experience.

In this sense, the following nine paths or patterns or modes or forms or clouds of images may be understood as a kind of *transreligious* impulse for *awakenings* of our existence "from the slumber of heedlessness" to a spirituality of the numinous at the *sensible heart* of *all* religions and non-religious sensibilities to the sacred—not only of the natural integration of humanity in the rhythms of nature, but of the Spirit as an expression of an ecological integrity that *transcends* all boundaries while imminently remaining *essential* to all of these traditions. So, now, these are the *nine transreligious poetic patterns* that spirit seekers, in their passageways through the heart of material existence in which the cosmic Spirit expresses itself, may employ, concurrently or successively, actively or reflectively, in the search for life unborn and deathless.

The Small Flame in Everything draws us into the realm of the small and large. As a matter of magnitudes, we realize that the Spirit is not only in everything, but everything is in the Spirit, placed in it as its all-embracing space. It is the encounter of the heart of things, of that which matters when everything else is said and done. It evokes the images of life as fire, of life under fire, of the burning sentiment of life, the ineradicable thirst for life, and what this means for seeking the Spirit in all things, small and large, important and negligible, found and lost, picked up and thrown away. The Spirit of the All makes its appearance in the minute, the minor, the excluded, the undiscovered, the small voice. Here, the irreplaceable voice of God's Self, the *vox ipsissima divina*, manifests through the heart of our Self in the form of a vibration between hearts, in modes of truths that cannot be expressed except in the language of the heart. The spirit seeker who follows this path will want to become minor to become everything. This path stands for a theopoetic emptying—as is suggested by the invoked images and gestures of the self-emptying Reality (*sunyata*) in Mahayana Buddhism, but also by the christological hymn in St. Paul's letter to the Philippians (2:6–11), one of the oldest, if not *the* oldest, of the texts of the New Testament.

Crossing the Infinite Sea employs the image of an ocean cruise. Danger, adventure, and trust meld to create the image of an extraordinary reality, of a situation of high alert, of the perpetual renewal of orientation and purpose. One can be lost in the open spaces of the sea, drowned by its violent upheavals, miss one's port of exit, disappear in its endlessness, but also find peace in its calm waters and the infinite horizon that offer us places to linger. The ocean has a presence like nothing else and a depth with an impenetrable life of its own; it hides monsters and treasures. It may be traveled but cannot be drunk. Why are we crossing it? How do we stay alive? Not whether, but when does its own vivacity become too much to bear? The spirit seeker who travels this path will be in awe of the primordial, grand and inconceivable *otherness* of Reality and its Spirit, a Life so alien and yet so familiar that it reminds us of the sensation and multifold powers of the ocean waters, of their salty strangeness, of their transcendent depth and width, of their patience in carrying us and their seeming indifference swallowing us. Like the Leviathan of old (Job 41), no one has created this ocean (Genesis 1:2). A poetics of chaos can only lend the power of chaos to healing by persuading it to calm down long enough for the spirit-farer to find a harbor (Jonah 1:12; Mark 4:31–45).

A Finger in the River references the moment when we encountered moving waters, their flow, and the urge to touch them. A river of life streams by, presenting life to an embedding landscape, while a dry river indicates death to the whole land. By touching the river, we create a change of flow. Flow upon flow! We cannot cross it without being changed, moved away, transported downward, dislocated. Yet we cannot avoid crossing it, either, if we don't want it to be the end of the world. And we know it is not. Bathing in it, eating of its fish, using it as means of transport and release, seeking its origin and end, waiting for its yearly flood, in fear or anticipation—all that and more binds us into the rhythms of nature and imprints on us an image of life and transcending movement. Sit at the river and follow its flow! Movement and stillness at once; flat and deep places; eddies and rapids; waterfalls and meanders—all that may indicate to the spirit seeker a path of crossing boundaries, of the permanence of flux, of constant change, of the unity of opposites in the face of impermanence. As with Ecclesiastes (1:9) there is nothing new under the sun, except that the sun comes up every day to grant us a new day; so, here, nothing stays the same, but no change is permanent either.

Falling from the Tree evokes an image of childhood: climbing a tree; but maybe also: falling from a tree. Why do we climb trees (some of us, at least)? It is higher up; we must trust the tree to hold us in its arms; we hide in the crown among the leaves. All that—and: the tree is in all spiritual traditions a symbol of life. The Tree of Life (Genesis 2:9). The Tree in Heaven. The Wishing Tree. The World Tree. The Sacred Tree. The Qur'anic *sadrat al-muntaha*, the Tree of the utmost boundary beyond which only God resides (Qur'an 53:10–18). Trees have their own language, the language of the spirit-wind, of the leaves in the wind. They have their own mysterious life, as forest, the rain forest or cloud forest, as jungle or the redwood forest. They can be beautiful ornaments in gardens and unexpectedly resistant inhabitants of a wilderness. Ancient forests, groomed gardens, and the inhospitable wilderness harbor the most extraordinary and oldest living beings on Earth, thousands of years of age. But it is also a "tree" that reminds us of "the fall," the insight into good and evil, the ability to be morally responsible (Genesis 2–3). And we should not forget that humans come from trees. We have "fallen" from trees, walking on two legs instead. We abandoned trees as haven in order to live under trees and from their breath. In many cultures, trees house spirits, wisdom and fate. The spirit seeker who treads the path of the tree will be aware of the "other life" we depend on. With the Jewish philosopher Martin Buber (d. 1965) we may encounter a "Thou"—a companion that speaks not through leaves of books but in leaves of trees, and not in words and sentences but in the rhythms and songs of birds; it tells not the story of our little sorrows, but the story of the evolution that brought us about.

The Show from Backstage will, for once, depart from the images, and imaginations, of nature. Instead, it thrusts us into the poetics of art, of imitation, of drama and tragedy, of culture and the mirroring of humanity to itself. It is a strange place to be in or around: the stage, the world as stage, the stage as world. In one sense, art becomes the mirror for our spiritual being. In another sense, however, we become isolated from spiritual meaning, as we are mirroring only ourselves onstage. We claim our mind to express *our* existence without, outside of, despite and in oblivion of nature. Backstage, we even begin to see the whole drama only as a human construction. The only meaning we glean from the perspective of backstage lies in the mechanisms of its production. It is not "theopoetics" anymore, the "making-divine," but the making of ourselves. *Causa sui*! Are we the cause of ourselves? The spirit seeker who follows this path will become aware of the shadows of existence, the construction of its categories, purposes and meanings. Eventually, the seeker will not find meaning in humanity, but only the cry of meaninglessness, the mirror of nothingness, that makes the constructedness of our concepts of the divine obvious. It is a way of deconstructive darkness and questioning, doubt and hollowness, but also of the clarity not to confuse the ultimate with the penultimate. This path will lead into the desert, the free space of emptiness, if it is traveled without attachment to either meaning or nihilism. If it fails, however, one might get stuck onstage or behind stage, and go like a Ferris wheel round and round.

Fata Morgana happens at sea and in the desert, mostly. It can appear anywhere if the right conditions are met: heat and sun, a flat space, long distances, a certain perspective. It *happens* to you. And yet, you *co-produce* it by the way you relate to the constellation of the sun, temperature, landscape and your position in them. It is a matter of relation and illusion. Where there is only the "hermetic" relation of these things, we imagine the water of life, an oasis of rest, palms of nourishment. Not that those perspectives are illusions, but they superimpose a lack on global integrity. They carve something out for themselves that "fits" a certain interpretation of reality but that "in reality" is just a relational integration of constellations of reality that produce an illusion. This is a peculiar process: reality creates illusion by nothing but real constellations of itself. Think of the cycle of day and night: sun and moon fly around the earth, or do they? Spirit seekers of the desert path (the sea path was already addressed) will be exposed to dryness, spaciousness, emptiness, and a host of illusionary presentations of lushness, of the water of life, of the refreshing rest in an oasis just in front of their path. Yet it is in this environment that we may encounter the Spirit, in the midst of the primordial *tohu wa-bohu* (Genesis 1:2), the empty plain of a deserted place awaiting a new creation.

The Mountaineer is a paradigm of majesty. Glancing upward at the slopes and walls of a true mountain, vast and expansive, disappearing in the clouds above and grounded in an unimaginable gravity from below, reveals the Earth as living being in its most gravitated but still lofty protuberances. To climb a mountain through the biospheres and temperaments of stratified but continuous and continuously changing landscapes, over terrain rough and challenging, over rivers and waterfalls, crossing woods and wastelands, exposed to the moods and whims of rain and wind, walking among clouds and ice—this is the path of the spirit traveler into rarified areas where even air becomes thin . . . how much more so all support systems of life. At these heights you can freeze and fall. All ways seem to end. The peak stops all ascent. The end of a journey impresses a final transformation on the traveler: all ways lead down into the nether life, paths so diversified that none of them will ever repeat the same descent. The contrast between the one peak and the many paths is the image that will remain vivid to the seeker of this path. Highs and lows will reverse: oneness is not an aim, but a beginning; the multifariousness of ways is not a danger, suggesting that we have become lost in relativity, but the truth of the Spirit arising from the All it fills and descending into the All it sustains.

Staring at Stars is an abduction, a skyjacking, lifting not only our eyes but our souls beyond, and the essence of our life out of, any murky messiness that we live in day by day. Just lifting up our view may lift up our lives, too, out into the clarity of the blue carpet above, but also into the heat and blinding light of the sun. In the midst of the impenetrable darkness of the night sky, however, we awake to the immense but gentle lights of the heavenly bodies granting us the gift of their sparkle. This light of the stars, without any reason or purpose, seems just to be spent on anyone or anything that wants to recognize them. The spiritual seeker of this path will embrace both rest and infinite distance—at once expansiveness and locality, perspective and wholeness, finiteness and infinity. Light in the form of patterns and constellations will be the leading waymarks for orientation. But no orientation is final. All constellations are there and are not there, real and illusionary, penetrating imagination and instigating it. Everything is laid out like treasure. We may only glance at it, but we cannot own it. This treasure is always too far away to be grasped. In the end, the stars are the light that reaches us with an intimate call, but without leaving their transcendent palace. And if they "fall," if the apocalypse is on us (Matthew 24–25), it is only to reveal the renewal of the cosmos, a new creation, a new eon (Revelation 21–22).

The Life of Other Days is the path of time. While all other paths were more spatial than temporal, this path is about the seeker's journey as the becoming of time. If we believe Ecclesiastes, the Wisdom teacher who has no illusions, all has a measured time (Ecclesiastes 3:1–8). Impermanence is essential to this path, as well as eternity, the indestructibility of life, the permanence of movement, change, renewal, of other times to come or that have happened, of memory and forgotten feelings, of forgiveness and forgetting. Have you ever had the impression that you might have lived in another time and wondered how life might have been given all the different restrictions at that time? Have you ever imagined a future world, far distant from ours, and how it would be to live life then? Have you ever imagined living on another world, being another being, looking from one strange, unnamed star up there down to our Earth, being of another world and another eon? Have you ever encountered someone randomly and imagined who they are and how it might be to live their life from now on instead of your own? The spirit seeker on this path will encounter the wheel of fortune, the randomness of one's life, how and when it is, the finiteness of its realization confined by numerous parameters so as to be coming together only as a bundle of temporal strands of fate without deeper reason. Or is there? The spirit seeker on this path will confront the dark depth of purpose and reason, the Why of everything in its finiteness, but also the inescapable beauty of this finite fusion of unanswered Whys. So, we will end with the question of destiny and fate, necessity and contingency. Must things happen, as the gospel writers suggest? Is there a divine *dei*, a "must be" (Luke 24:13–35)? Is there a randomness of becoming this or that? Is there a grand scheme that escapes the chaos of new beginnings?

In this spiritual search for meaning, two trajectories, pervading all nine paths, will coalesce, at this point, summoning the whole spiritual journey to a choice: between the way of *multiplicity*, of a *multiverse* in which to develop self-transcendence through ultimate spiritual virtues and in which their cosmic realization approaches the convergence of peace in the translucency of trans-personal Reality, and the way of *love* that finds the self-transcendence of Reality "itself" to realize ultimate relationality as that by which we become *persons*, in the first place, and for the expression of which *God* remains a meaningful category.

The relationship between the nine paths follows several *overarching patterns*: at first glance, their arrangement is somewhat *symmetrical*, making available resonances between the first four and the last four paths, with the central path being a reflection on all of them. So begins the first path with "space," as the last one ends with "time." While the second one invokes the "ocean," the penultimate one reflects on the ocean of the "starry heavens." As the third path reflects on the flow of the "river," so does the third-to-last one evoke the permanence of the "mountain." And as the fourth path presents the diversity and lushness of "trees" and "woods," so does the sixth path invoke the emptiness and subtleness of the "desert." A second dimension, however, transforms this center-periphery axis into an axis of *progression* and *retrogression*, pervading the linear chain of the appearance of the nine paths: from (one account of) spaciousness to (another account of) spaciousness; from (one account of) light to (another account of) light; from (one account of) flux to (another account of) flux; from (one account of) disillusionment to (another account of) disillusionment. A third dimension, finally, emphasizes the axis of *descent* and *ascent* in the chain of paths by which their magnitudes shrink to human dimensions and expand back out of them.

These connections between the nine paths reflect *diverse movements*: First, there are four *spiritual* movements—that of concentric *circles* or revolution of spheres; of *oscillation* of tides; and of *layers* of mutually inclusive magnitudes. The fourth movement of the middle path, finally, is that of the *radiation* and *absorption* of the unconstructed ultimate transcendent reality of the Spirit *into* the constructed manifold of "realities"—cross-culturally presenting spiritual experiences of the cosmic pervasiveness and immanent embrace of the numinous Spirit. Second, the *cosmic* movements of the natural *elements* involved in the nine paths transit from fire to water and from earth to air, and backward. Third, the *human* involvements with these elements exhibit a movement from *internalization* to *laterality*, and from *downward* to *upward* gestures.

The nine paths are surrounded and interspersed by the following *explanatory dispositions*: each chapter is introduced by short but culminative epigraphs, essential to the explored images in the respective chapters. They are not mere ornaments but modes of explanation evoked and interpreted in due course. Further, the nine chapters are surrounded by this preamble resonating with an epilogue that will summarize the spiritual elements and their understanding during the unfolding of the book as media of the encounter with, and as expressions of, the numinous. As "luminaries" are as manifestations of the luminous, the nine paths harbor nine great spiritual "Numenaries" of the *numen*, the Holy, the divine Spirit of the earth in the matrix of the cosmos.

Finally, the nine paths are infused with nineteen meditations that want to experiment with their "spiritual matter," related either analytically to aspects of these paths or intuitively to the gist of the whole. While all of them have their own pace and complexity, often introduced with some contextualization, in the end they want to transcend the reading process and lead to the edge of boundaries potentially triggering the sudden experience of its imaginations as realities. And since imagination and intuition appear embodied only in varieties of experiential and experimental resonances with diverse types of human minds and environments, their modes of approaching such boundaries are themselves of quite diverse nature: evoking imaginations, guiding visualizations, provoking intellectual processes, appealing to heartfelt feelings, and demanding action.

Differentiation

Be aware that "spirituality" in this book is *not* a doctrine, say, of the Holy Spirit, such as that developed in Christian pneumatology, *nor* is it an elaboration, for instance, of Hindu schools of (the Duality or Nonduality of) the Spirit (*brahman*) and the Self (*atman*). Neither are the nine paths meant to "introduce" you to methods of experiencing the Spirit or cosmic consciousness; nor should these nine paths or passageways or spiritual patterns mislead you to confuse them with a nine-step procedure. Finally, neither is the Spirit authoritatively talking to you, here, nor are its nine paths nine simple steps of becoming spiritual, or more spiritual, or more religious—nor are they suggestions of how to remain non-religious while claiming the label spiritual.

So that is it, then? A series of nine "inspirations," if you will let them. In the form of imaginations of multifariousness, the nine paths seek poetic *traces* of the Spirit in our mind and life, as they uncover the realities that already, before we seek them, are invitations in the world around us and in our body of *transcending* movements of that Spirit that flows through our embodied existence. In other words, the nine paths are *mirrors* of the divine in the flow of cosmic matter: rendering tangible the intangibles at the heart of the world of becoming and offering a diversity of poetic images of and for the awakening to the deathless in the midst and at the heart of all religions.

However, while this *transreligious* approach doesn't seek a foundation in any of these religious traditions in their more set identities or orthodox expressions, the transgressive impulse of the clouds of spirit-matters appearing in the nine paths does, of course, *not exclude* deep resonance with the less constricted trajectories of diverse religious traditions. While, in other words, the *universally transgressive relationality* inherent in the nine paths undercuts the doctrinal limitations of religious differences, it still connects with the spiritual terrain of these religions, either touching elements of their ancient memory or mediating some of their diverse connective facets in a constructive way.

The Hindu *brahman*, for instance, could be translated with "cosmic Spirit." Resonances drawn throughout the text will exhibit its "attributes" (*saguna brahman*) and "attributelessness" (*nirguna brahman*) (as they are not dualistically differentiated) as well as its congruence with the cosmic Self (*atman*), insofar as, in these conceptual images, we are pointed to an important insight in the current context: the "indifference" between the cosmological vastness *and* the mystical immediacy of spiritual awakenings beyond any dogmatic limitation. And the spirit-matters of the nine paths will be inclusive of one of the most profound splits running through this vast religious tradition (as well as many others), namely, the divergence between personal and transpersonal characteristics of this ultimate Reality.

Resonances with a Christian context, but transcending its dogmatic limitations, will arise where the opposition in its theistic thinking and experiencing of the split between order and form, on the one hand, and life and formlessness (even materiality), on the other, is projected onto divine reality. This opposition has itself worked out in the difference between *logos* and *pneuma* and the related doctrines of the Christ and the Spirit. The developed doctrine of the Trinity has tried to hold these divergences together. However, this fusion succeeded only imperfectly: it was not possible to suppress the remaining differences between these two strands, as has become obvious by the vastly divergent "limits" proposed for the divine mystery in later and current Christianity by the bifurcation of Logos-Christology from Spirit-Christology and their respective subordination or universalization of the function of the divine Spirit. As can be witnessed, for instance, in the work of theologians of the Spirit, such as Geoffrey Lampe (d. 1980) and Roger Haight (b. 1936), if one forgoes the former's doctrinal taming of the Spirit that insists on the superiority of Christianity because of the alleged exclusivity of the event of the Incarnation of the Logos, then the latter approach amounts to a universal release of the Spirit from such limitations. Then, the expression of human spiritualization becomes exemplary in figures *such as* Jesus, but never exclusionary. This latter view is, therefore, much more in tune with the understanding of the cosmic Spirit as it will unfold in the coming chapters (not because Christ must be sidelined or relativized, but rather because the inclusive character of the Spirit will affirm *universal* spiritual transformation rather than exclusive opposition between an eternal, perfect "being"—the Logos—and us, the deficient, imperfect, undeserving images).

However, while such resonances may be revealing, the invitation to experience and experiment with the cosmic Spirit in the nine paths doesn't follow such abstract concepts. It rather *materializes* itself in symbols and images that are literally *universal* in, and symbolically *immediate* to, all of our experiences, all of them taken from our existential, ecological, organic, and metabolic interwovenness with the earth. There may be many other symbolic patterns that one can choose instead, in and beyond nature; but besides the restrictions that characterize *all* paradigms (so as to make them specific and limited figures of the formless creative energy that encloses the earth and pervades the cosmos and, hopefully, our lives), the nine chosen image-clouds here will be tracing patterns in which we may sense the divine within a *sacred relativity of possibilities*. They transcend religious traditions, don't exclude non-religious sentiments, and are inclusive of other potential doctrinal divisions, such as the ones just mentioned. While they are expansive and exhibit an internal infinity of variation and inclusion, they remain also *contingent* on a profound level. The spirit seeker must be aware of this profound *arbitrariness*: that there is no "ground" or "bottom" to this process of seeking the Spirit of life. All nine paths embrace this "groundlessness," that is, they remain ways of *seeking*, never coming to rest on any ground or bottom. They indicate a fountain of life, releasing us into a stream of infinite modes of realization as we "flow out" from the effervescent treasure of gratuitous life.

Before I invite you to explore these nine paths of poetic imagination of the cosmic Spirit that pervade our lives, at least three warnings must be given here. The first warning is related to the use of concepts such as Spirit, Poetics, Life and Cosmos. While these concepts have a long, variegated and diversified history in religious, cultural, artistic, and philosophical contexts in the east and the west, as already mentioned, they have also been implicated in a storyline of *suspicion* that they might have contributed to justifications of religious, political, racial, environmental, and psychological forms of *violence*. Mostly, I suspect, because the misuse of religious and spiritual, philosophical and inspirational images and imaginations manipulates language and "creates" ideologies so as to serve the interests of the rich, the powerful and the perverse—as, for instance, indicated by the attack of the French philosopher Jacques Derrida (d. 2004) on the German philosopher Martin Heidegger (d. 1976) in his book *Of Spirit* (1987), in which Derrida pointed at the underlying fascist tendencies of the related language and spiritual terminology in Heidegger's work. Yet we are in a *perpetual* situation that *any* language we might use for the seeking of the cosmic Spirit of life will, at any point in history, already have been misused in this sense. I don't want to be blind to this fact. But I do believe that because of the *liminality* (or inherent excessive polysemy) of these terms, misuse cannot completely foreclose the appeal to fresh imaginations in these images. We should not fall into the opposite trap of avoidance. We may just give in. But, then, we let these expressions of manipulation and violence take away our ability to articulate ourselves in a language, any language, that we "share" with "the better ones." Then we are damned to the silence of graves by the ones that dug them for us.

The second warning is directed against the misunderstanding of the use of the language of Spirit, Poetics, Matter, Cosmos, Life, and the like, as another form of the *privatization* of religion. A whole industry of spiritual literature may, indeed, play into a late capitalist form of consumerism that is guided and manipulated by the "invisible hand" of the market and the not so invisible but seemingly untouchable "hand" of its financiers. "Stay away from the political arrangements of the powerful, the playground of the 'better ones'!"—so says the invisible voice using spirituality as a pacifier. However, it was the great Catholic theologian of the twentieth century, Karl Rahner (d. 1984), who insisted that the future of religious identity will be mystical *and* political, or it will not be anything. I think this is true for any religion or spiritual tradition, or any secular ethical and aesthetical impulse for the humanization of humanity. It is the imperative of the Spirit to be *both at once*, existentially transcendent *and* universally embodied. Yet I also think that no "theopolitical" embodiment will ever be able to substitute the "theopoetic" imagination that is necessary for the overcoming of the limitations of the political sphere. There must be something better than politics (at least, so I hope)! We should not let anyone take away the power of the poetic imagination inherent in the images that the Spirit of life touches in us and around us in all spheres of life. Especially in our daily life as bodies among bodies, as living organisms among living organisms, as minds among minds, as spirits among spirits, of which this world is populated far beyond humanity, we *know* with every fiber of our existence that spiritual transformation is never less than, but also never bound to be exhausted by, the political impact it might have. Humanity must learn to grow beyond such child's play (1 Corinthians 13:11).

The third warning must engage the postmodern condition—as diagnosed, for instance, by the French philosopher Jean-François Lyotard (d. 1998) and many others after him—that, in today's context, no "grand narrative" can keep up with the *fragmentation* of reality anymore. Well, besides being itself a new grand narrative, albeit invisible, we may just give up altogether thinking in such limited categories of grand and small, overarching unities and diversified multiplicities. Instead, as the French poststructuralist philosopher Gilles Deleuze (d. 1995) and the psychiatrist Félix Guattari (d. 1992) in their book *A Thousand Plateaus* (1980) have warned us, we ought to think from the perspectives of *minorities* that are excluded by smooth foreclosures invented by the rich and powerful, and the manipulators of history, if they were to arise in the formulation and formation of the exploratory terms such as "cosmos" or "Spirit or Life," or preference of "the poetical" over "the political," and so forth.

Yet we should not succumb to the opposite narrative that only "a minority perspective" is the right one, either. Why? Because these perspectives are *always multiple*, and they *only* continue to be minor *if* they remain multiple. Otherwise, they will always degrade into only *my* perspective, that of *my* real or imagined "minoritarian status." Limited imaginations often pervade such depleted attitudes toward "myself," which, then, react sensitively to presumed universalizations of other views, but are often *themselves* just that: universalizations that re-colonize. Instead, I believe, the flow of the cosmic Spirit of life through, among and beyond any limited foreclosure and any magnifications of parochial perspectives, with "its" power of poetic imagination that reaches far beyond any limited reactive life of the fear of exclusion, will free us from both self-serving accusations and undeserved possessions. Let us find this Spirit of the earth that unites us in our fragility and as moments in her evolution, and maybe in her purpose to give birth to a spirit-sphere that can mature like the biosphere from which it springs. Let us find this universal poetic flow of life that connects us to the globe of the earth and that vibrates through the deep matrix of the cosmos before all else, in us, among us and beyond any limited "us," before we settle again for less, spirit-less!

So, while spiritual images *can* be misused for (or even justify) violence, terror, suppression, fascism and dictatorial rules, they can also always be awakened again to new life, new poetic imagination of resistance, a new spirit transcending shallow pacifications. While they *can* be seen as an indication of theopoetic negligence of the theopolitical dimension of religion, the impact of spirituality in its existential dimension is always about the transformation of society into something new and fresh, a *spiritual civilization of the earth*, an *eco-spiritual civitas* transcending any self-serving *polis*. And while the imaginations inherent to the images used here can be misunderstood as upholding grand narratives that sustain methods of exclusion, their *inevitable multiplicity* is their reserve against, and remedy of, such simplifications. In other words, these images and the overboiling energy by which they provide us with a relentless unfolding of their inherent imaginations—released for human transformation, the transformation of heart and mind and body—is so wedded with our life on a *primordial level* that no misuse can exhaust their meaning, as we already always live *from* them. Rather than waiting to be accessed, we have merely forgotten that *we live through their reality* that surrounds and pervades us and everything, that binds us together with everything else, this world and the cosmos beyond. These are the adventures they promise.

The poetics of the imaginations used in the nine paths are but another attempt to trace the promise to a spirit-faring species for its *cosmic awakening*, an awakening that cannot be facilitated by star-faring alone but must be accomplished by the reconciliation of spiritual interiority with the cosmic adventure, of the outer and inner spheres, of mind and matter, of potential and event, of memory and consciousness—by according the cosmic Spirit with the emergence of a spiritually maturing cosmos.

Meditation I: Nothing; but Light

Interspersed within and between the chapters, I will record meditations, practical and intellectual, per visualizations or imaginations. They are best attempted after reading the text of a chapter up to that point or, in relation to the whole chapter, as an entry to their spiritual sphere or as their fusion. Place yourself in a quiet state of mind, undisturbed from any outside noise, and try to quiet down the chaos of the racing mind. Take a few deep breaths in and out without intention and thought. Calmly only listen to the sound and feeling of your breathing. Then read the whole meditation and memorize its steps of visualization. Take your time to establish the images and your Self in every step, completely, before you move on. Or, alternatively, read one line of a mediation at a time and visualize it. Then follow with the next line the same way. When you have reached the ultimate image and have situated yourself fully in it, remain in it as long as you can without feeling pressured. Of course, you can also use these instructions for a guided group meditation.

> *Imagine. Find yourself in a meadow, midafternoon, a mild sun shines on the land, you hear the sound of the grass in the calm breeze and feel its breath on your skin . . .*
>
> *. . .*
>
> *You can fly . . .*
>
> *Lift from the meadow and feel the movement of lifting . . .*
>
> > *to the height of a tree . . .*
> >
> > *look down and take in the landscape within which the meadow flows . . .*
>
> *. . .*
>
> *You are free from gravity.*
>
> > *Glide higher . . .*
>
> *feel the movement of elation . . .*
>
> *look down and survey the land of the whole continent . . .*
>
> *. . .*
>
> *You are free from any environment.*
>
> *You can sail through space.*
>
> > *. . .*

Preamble: We Are All Poets of the Spirit

Speed up, and you see the whole planet Earth under your feet . . .
    water, earth, clouds . . .
    the fragile small band of the atmosphere smoothly veiling the face of the globe . . .
. . .
As you speed up, you gain a view of other planets . . .
    the earth becoming a small spot in the dark of space . . .
the sun becomes a spot among bands of stars . . .
. . .
There is no stopping now.
You speed up and leave the Milky Way . . .
Can you see its brilliant shape? . . .
    shrinking to one of the spots among the bands of galaxies . . .
    galaxies over galaxies all around you . . .
. . .
Imagine. You are free from movement or rest . . .
Are you still speeding? Or are you still, in empty space?
. . .
You have gone far beyond the universe of sparkling lights . . .
    only dark space remains . . .
. . .
Realize. There is only empty space . . .
    no lights . . .
    Where are you?
    What do you see?
. . .
You are free from everything . . .
    Imagine that there is no Earth, no galaxy, no universe . . . nothing . . .
    What do you see?
. . .
Imagine. You are free from anything . . .
Remove your Self . . .

1

The Small Flame in Everything

In the middle of the living creatures there was something that looked like burning coals of fire, like torches moving to and fro among the living creatures; the fire was bright, and lightning issued from the fire.

—EZEKIEL 1:13 (NRSV)

It is precisely because [the Spirit] is infinitely profound and punctiform that God is infinitely near yet present everywhere. It is precisely because [God] is the center that [God] fills the whole sphere.

—TEILHARD DE CHARDIN, *DIVINE MILIEU*, 75

Space

WHERE TO BEGIN? WHAT about this question: How to enter the space of the spirit? What kind of space is it? Or is it a "space"? Can we even "enter" it? Is that even a question? Should we not begin with experiences, examples, characters, rules, stages, or forms of the spiritual—rather than with its "space"? Let me try this: Spirituality happens in a space, or rather it *is* a space to be in, to become within, to move about even before we know it. Much like the "unknown divinity" of St. Paul's conversation with the philosophers in Athens (Acts 17:23) "in which we live and move and have our being" (Acts 17:28), Spirit is the space in which we live, are, become. Not that we *become* spiritual; rather, we *are* expressions of a certain space. That space is "the spiritual" in everything, because everything becomes, moves, and is already in "its" space. When I say "its" space, I mean: Everything has its own *place* because of the *space* in which it is situated or located. Everything is spirit-located.

The Cosmic Spirit

What kind of space is the spiritual space? First of all, it, Spirit or spirit-space, is *not identical* with any physical space. Its "spaciousness" is, as in the Buddhist "identification" of space with ultimate reality (*nirvana*), only a symbolic expression of the intangible transcendent reality of the Spirit in terms of its manifestation, appearance, or way of approach when we awaken from the "illusions" of a spiritual materialism that identifies spiritual realities with or as material entities—as we will see soon (see ch. 4). This is what A. N. Whitehead has called a fallacy, that of "misplaced concreteness," of confusing abstractions with concreteness, splitting the world into realities and appearances and investing the appearances with even "more" reality—which actually degrades them to illusions (see ch. 6). Space, as is true for all other "elementary" universals, is only a "sign" of divinity, if we use it to express divine Spirit and spirit-space. However, as we will see throughout the book, Spirit is also *not different* from such symbolizations, but rather *indifferent* from/to them or, in the deepest sense, *beyond* the differences, unfathomable by them, and, hence, paradoxically inherently *immanent* in them so as to allow us the experience and conceptual approximations of the Spirit through such "elementary" symbolizations or "imprints."

So, how to understand the divine reality of this spiritual space in its "material" symbolizations? As the epigraph from Pierre Teilhard de Chardin (d. 1955), the paleontologist and influential Catholic spiritual writer, imagines: it is an *open* space. He also used to say that it is "the divine milieu" (1957) in which everything is and moves, becomes and develops. Everything, all that exists, has already always entered this space just by "being," but also evolves by becoming its own Self, by always moving toward what it is and is meant to be: a unique expression of this open space. What is this open space like? Frankly, it is somehow scary to imagine its openness: It is a space without underside or backside. It has no other side, no hidden beyond, no transcendent other; it is everything. Yet, it is also the opposite: only hidden places, folds, mountains, and valleys, moving like waves in a storm; it is impenetrable, infinitely complex if you come closer, and just simply "one" if you zoom out. It is formless and folds all forms together. It is the space of all potentials that like a cloud of ghosts or a halo, a hive of light, circles all happenings, all worlds, all places and times, all becoming and characteristics in it. It is the figurative *coincidentia oppositorum* of the mystics: no opposites are excluded; rather than being opposites anymore, they have become shades of similarity and dissimilarity. In this space, if we gain consciousness of it, a pleroma of potential developments and missed opportunities seethes in intense light and heat and protuberances like the surface of the sphere of the sun. This sphere, this perfect space, is of infinite movements, like colors smoothly melding into one another, *and* incompatible alternatives striving for realization over against all others.

Many images have been devised for this space of the Spirit. In the *Bhagavad Gita* (second century BCE), that most revered synthetic text of the Hindu epic *Mahabharata* (chs. 23–40), Lord Krishna, in the avataric presence as the charioteer of the prince, Arjuna, at one point in his teachings in the middle of a battlefield reveals himself to

Arjuna as the very *space* of spiritual existence, that is, as the Spirit that is *brahman*, ultimate reality, in its unity with *atman*, the universal Self of everything. It is one of the famous theophanies of religious world literature, besides the appearance of Yahweh to Moses on and around Mount Sinai (Exodus 3–33) and the transfiguration of Christ in the company of Moses and Elijah in front of his dislocated disciples Peter, John, and Andrew (Mark 9:2–8; Matthew 17:1–8; Luke 9:28–36). In this theophanic space, all things, the cosmos, appear(s) transfigured, as Krishna reveals his "cosmic manifestation" (ch. 11), a form that is not only formless but also includes all forms. In this space, the universal Spirit and the Self of all things are uncovered to be *one*. It is less important whether this is to be understood as unification or sameness, as interpretations in Hindu philosophy range from monistic and pantheistic (Adi Shankara, d. 820 CE) to diverse shades of nondualistic (Ramanuja, d. 1137 CE) and dualistic views (Madhva, d. 1317 CE); rather, what is important here is that the Spirit (*brahman*) is everywhere, in everything, the space of everything to be, and, in an important sense, closer to the self of everything than that self is to itself. In this form, the interiority of the Spirit appears also in Abrahamic traditions: in the Qur'an, God is said to be closer to our self than our own jugular vein (Qur'an 50:16), and Saint Augustine of Hippo (d. 430 CE) understands God to be in the interior of our interior (*Confessions* 3.6.11).

What is so unique in the vision of the *Bhagavad Gita*, chapter 11, is that it not only describes the experience, awesome and bewildering, of this naked open space, but also interprets this space for us in a divine voice. This whole theophany is so comprehensive, it warrants a few more details with regard to its presentation of the divine space we live in if we were ready to awaken to it. I will concentrate on three elements of the text: the experience of the spirit-space as infinite unity and multiplicity; the *Gita*'s interpretation of this space; and the "prophetic" projection of the meaning of this space in the voice of Lord Krishna himself. This is how the *Gita* describes and interprets Arjuna's vision:

> Arjuna saw in that universal form unlimited mouths and unlimited eyes. It was all wondrous. The form was decorated with divine, dazzling ornaments and arrayed in many garbs. He was garlanded gloriously, and there were many scents smeared over His body. All was magnificent, all-expanding, unlimited. This was seen by Arjuna. (11:11) If hundreds of thousands of suns rose up at once into the sky, they might resemble the effulgence of the Supreme Person in that universal form. (11:12) At that time Arjuna could see in the universal form of the Lord the unlimited expansions of the universe situated in one place although divided into many, many thousands. (11:13)

What a space! A space of infinite forms, imagined as infinitely many eyes, all seeing all from all perspectives, infinitely many perspectives in mutual viewing and perception. But also, infinitely many mouths, breaths in everything—everything breathing in and out everything else in mutual inherence, inhalation, in-taking; and all mouths divulge the sacred sound (Om), the letters and word (AUM) that—according to the *Mandukya Upanishad*—is (of) God. *One* space folded in infinitely many places without losing its oneness. Dazzling ornamentation, not just emptiness. Magnificence, beauty, infinity, expansiveness. The supreme expression of God, a "personality" that is nothing like us. But still, this "personality" being not just less than a Thou, "it" rather indicates a space you can trust amidst all of its strangeness, and of unbearable complexity. Arjuna, overwhelmed, begins to pray and interpret what he experiences:

> O Lord of the universe, I see in Your universal body many, many forms—bellies, mouths, eyes—expanded without limit. There is no end, there is no beginning, and there is no middle to all this (11:16) . . . You are the origin without beginning, middle or end. You have numberless arms, and the sun and moon are among Your great unlimited eyes. By Your own radiance You are heating this entire universe. (11:19) Although You are one, You are spread throughout the sky and the planets and all space between. O great one, as I behold this terrible form, I see that all the planetary systems are perplexed. (11:20)

Infinite arms and eyes, suns and moons in everything; everything consisting in its interior of these innumerous lights and perceptions and activations; infinite creativity in the smallest of places. A fire of a thousand suns in every being! The greatest of beings in the universe, as it were, like planetary systems and galaxies, but also the universal substructure of the fine-grained foam of space-time, move and shine from the perplexity of the wonder of being in a space filled with divine fire and light, and activity and breath, and song and beauty. In Arjuna's interpretation, the *personality* of God is the *Spirit* in everything, the *radiance* in which everything shines light on everything else, and the spread-out *space* in which everything is what it is in relation to everything else. Spirit, fire, space. Finally, this is how Krishna portrays and enacts his theophany to Arjuna:

> The Blessed Lord said: My dear Arjuna, . . . behold now My opulences, hundreds of thousands of varied divine forms, multicolored like the sea (11:5) . . . Behold the many things which no one has ever seen or heard before. (11:6) Whatever you wish to see can be seen all at once in this body. This universal form can show you all that you now desire, as well as whatever you may desire in the future. Everything is here completely. (11:7) But you cannot see Me with your present eyes. Therefore, I give to you divine eyes by which you can behold My mystic opulence. (11:8)

Not only are all things interior to themselves filled with the opulence of a divine manifold of light, heat, activity, breath, perception, and creativity. What is more, Krishna projects this spirit-space outward to include all possibilities, all potential directions of the realization of cosmic differences, and, most importantly here, all desires, all imaginations, all that *could* be. But to be able to perceive and awaken consciously to this infinite mutual relationality of interiority, Arjuna needs a new view, *the eye of*

God, as it were. This is also a wild spiritual truth. Bahá'u'lláh, for instance, in sync with Sufi mysticism and the tradition of the Persian mystic-poets, relates, as recorded in the *Gleanings* (1935) of his writings (#127), that we can only spiritually know (*irfan*) God in everything and our Self if we "see" *with the eyes of God*. And the second chapter of the important Buddhist *Lotus Sutra* (between the first century BCE and the first century CE) discloses that only a Buddha knows (can "see") a Buddha, which, in the Mahayana context, means that we must discover the space that is the Buddha-nature as the space that we *are*, by which we are surrounded and which is the essence (the heart of the heart) of everything.

This is the *poetic gift* of the spirit-space, our *theopoetic* becoming, our *theosis* among the *theosis* of everything. It indicates not only an external space in which we or anything is placed, but an interiority *in* our Selves and everything from which that exterior space springs, a patient space that lets everything be external to one another although everything is mutually interior to each other. In his book *Adventures of Ideas* (1933), A. N. Whitehead has called this all-embracing space (beyond the opposition and even the differentiation between "the physical" and "the spiritual") the "medium of intercommunication," modeled on Plato's *khôra* of his influential late monologue *Timaeus*: the infinite "place" of all beings and the "third genus" of "grounds of being" besides the Heaven of Ideas and a divine Harmonizer. It is a "Wherein" in a twofold sense. In one sense, everything exists *within* it as it has a place in this space in relation to everything else; it is the *placement* of all forms and activities, allowing patterns of being to emerge, contours to rise and to disappear, and the becoming of things to happen. In another sense, however, there is no exterior space in which everything exists like in a container, but the "contained" *is* the "container" of that space that is its own interiority, as the *relationship* of everything to itself and everything else. Imagine, become aware of, awaken to this experience of mutual inherence! This is the spiritual space to which I am trying to attach words here: infinite interiority in which we can access everything else; it is us and it is not; it is a wholeness that is beyond anything that expresses it, but it is nothing but that relationality itself.

This may be the meaning of the Hindu "yoking" (*yoga*) of the Spirit (*brahman*) and our spacious Self (*atman*). But it also arises from the Buddhist image of the essence of being as *spaciousness*. "Space" is an ancient image of the essence of reality, the true nature (*nirvana*) of becoming (*samsara*), their mutuality or nondual unity in Buddhist understanding—as in the *Heart Sutra* (seventh century CE) and the work of the philosopher-saint Nagarjuna (d. ca. 250 CE). It is the *emptiness* (*sunyata*) that indicates the co-arising of *interrelation* without surplus or remainder such as a god-figure (*pratitya-samutpada*). In the Tibetan tradition of the Dzogchen master and poet Longchenpa (1308–64), "spaciousness" is the expression of the utter emptiness of reality, the universal Buddha-body, the *dharmakaya*, which is empty of *itself* (is self-transcendent of Self, which *is* its "Self") in the sense that it is pure creativity, the potential pleroma of all things. And the same nondual unity of emptiness *and* creativity is one of the most profound insights of the *Dao De Jing*: In its first chapter, famously, the Dao named and unnamed "is" one, one of one another, one as differentiated into the nameless apophatic ultimate *and* the creative mother of all things—a "dipolarity" that will become important later (see ch. 5).

Returning to the image of "space" in the epigraph of Teilhard de Chardin above: the spiritual space, the space insofar as it is empty *as* Spirit, indicates that it is *formless* like an "infinite sphere." This quasi-mathematical but really all-transcending image can convey four important insights. First, a "sphere" consisting of an infinite multiplicity of points that are dimensionless makes the space an emptiness of infinitely many points. Second, its "center" *coincides* with its "periphery" *if* the circumference of a sphere is infinite; then, what seems to be the center of the sphere has, in an imaginative, surreal movement, become spread out over the whole volume of the space that is *infinite*. Third, since nothing is "*in* a point" except that which is in *any* point, the whole infinite multiplicity of points has become an expression of all other points, which makes a *smooth* space. As the German philosopher and mathematician of infinities (one of the inventors of differential and integral algebra) Gottfried Wilhelm Leibniz (d. 1716), in his *Discourse on Metaphysics* (1686), has reasoned: if some things cannot be discerned—like points, which in their dimensionless "existence" are indiscernible—then they are indifferent, *except* if they were established by relationships. In other words, the space of the infinite sphere is the expression of the *relationships* of its infinite points but hides this interiority of the points away—a differentiation also important to Nicolas of Cusa and Gilles Deleuze, as we will see later (see ch. 6). However, in reality the seamless continuity of the external space is constituted by their *internal multiplicity in mutuality*. Fourth, the *interior* of the interior of the infinitely related but empty points is nothing but the *Spirit* itself, *God as space*. We literally are positioned "in" God, as "God" means the interior of all points that we are occupying as place in the open space that flows through everything without moving, thereby being the Spirit in which we live and move and have our being.

Two other related implications arise from these renderings of the spiritual space: first, spirit is not opposed to matter, and, second, it is both invisible and visible. As with Plato's *khôra* or Teilhard's punctiform divinity, all "matter" is nothing but the *interrelationality* in which things can *appear* in order to exist from that "matter." In a sense, *the cosmos is the primordial theophany, as it is the material that in its inwardness is nothing but the Spirit*. While Plato's *khôra* represents his notion of "matter," the "situatedness" of forms and activities as a world of becoming, Aristotle's *materia* signifies the *potentiality* of the actualization of these forms. In process philosophies from the pre-Socratic philosopher of becoming, Heraclitus (d. ca. 475 BCE), to A. N. Whitehead, this *formless space of potentials* transforms into the invisible aura of the manifestation of choices, of activities, of events: form and matter really become alternative versions of the spirit-matter, the space of the actualizations of such choices. Paradoxically, then, the invisible spirit of the interior life of all things is, *simultaneously*, the manifest wholeness of anything of which *materia* (potential) is just an abstraction, as it is the *manifold space* that becomes in the theophany of the Spirit the *mater* (mother) or originating oneness of that space of everything.

This is the spirit-space, the spirit-matter, I am talking about here: relationality, mutual interiority, pure formless and creative activity, omni-potentiality, universal patience and perceptive compassion, and, as western religious traditions say, pure love, that is, love overflowing, without ulterior motives, as a pure gift, at once poem and poet, Spirit. In this sense, the space of the Spirt is really, essentially and in our theopoetic becoming (*theosis*) explicating the "all in all" of 1 Corinthians 15:28. Indeed, there is nothing "in" all things but the interior of the interior, namely, the punctiform God who or that is the heart of all-relationality. It is in this God-space of punctiform but seamless multiplicity that everything "is." It is by this hidden (enfolded) divine space that everything exists as a multiplicity (as many folds) that harbors "its" eternity in their heart, and it is by the relationality of this multiplicity that everything manifests the smooth space of the exteriority "in" which it then seemingly moves.

Fire

If we could "see" the world and ourselves in it with the divine eyes of Krishna, our body as organism woven into, and growing out of, the extensive web of mutual patience, as this space of "letting be" and of infinitely manifold "suns" in the process of uncontrollable movements of life—what comes to the fore? We may discover, in it and us, *a world of fire*. Indeed, "fire" is a pervasive image of the Spirit (Matthew 3:11). Think of the fire of the burning bush (Exodus 24:17), the fire of revelation (Ezekiel 1), the flames of Pentecost (Acts 2), the overflowing spirit-life of the new creation, the eternal fire of Zoroaster, the creative fire of Heraclitus. But wait! What about the fire-sea of the second death (Revelation 15:2; 21:1)? What about the fire of hell (Mark 9:43; Matthew 25:46)? What about the fire testing spiritual worth (Malachi 3:3; 1 Corinthians 3:13)? What about the rhythmic conflagration (*ekpyrosis*) of the cosmos in several ancient philosophical and religious traditions, not only of Stoics like Chrysippus (d. 206 BCE) but also, for instance, of Platonists like Plutarch (d. ca. 120 CE)? What about the fire of desire that, in the Buddha's Fire Sermon of the *Adittapariyaya Sutta* (in the *Samyutta Nikaya* of the Pali Canon), perpetuates *samsara*, the cycle of an ever-new inflammation of the suffering of impermanence? Indeed, in the image of fire, Spirit is an *ambivalent* symbol: It relates some kind of light, but is burning and exuding heat rather than mediating clarity of sight. It is creative unrest. It is formless and untamable light in a nascent state of perpetual becoming. It is chaotic but shining; vivid but burning what it touches; granting heat from a distance but devouring what it engulfs.

In the spiritual space, *the inside is turned out*: what is the hidden becomes the obvious. While fire may be the experience of life in the punctiform view of the spiritual space, if it appears "outside," as the external, global character of the inside, as veiled theophany of the innermost Spirit that not only penetrates everything but is its very "center," then Spirit-fire will "materialize" in experiences that feel like a *word-burning apocalypse*. Cosmogonies expect the end of the world in water or fire, a deluge or a sea of fire, drowning or burning up. Traces of both are still present in the biblical stories of an "ancient eon" before the all-drowning water (Genesis 6:9—9:17) and a new eon after the word-devouring fire of the end (Revelation 15; 21–22). Remnants of ancient prehistoric cosmogonies remain visible in mythologies from around the world: the world is often born from water (Genesis 1:2), even before light appears (Genesis 1:3), and it often dies in a global conflagration, when all light-emitting bodies, like the sun and the stars, fall (Matthew 24). Or, as registered as the ancient wisdom of Egyptian priests in Plato's dialogue *Timaeus* (ca. 360 BCE), humanity was "known" to have repeatedly been destroyed by water and fire.

Yet the regularity of a rhythm of such conflagrations indicates a spiritual principle of creation, rather than of apocalyptic definiteness. Fire burns and grants life. Fire is the image of the cycle of life that is wedded to change, impermanence, becoming and perishing. Nothing stays the same, but the universal rhythm instills a hope against all hope (Romans 4:18)—a hope for re-creation, renewal, and new life out of destruction (Romans 4:17), because this image of the rhythm is only an expression of the innermost spirit-space of permanent renewal, of revivification, of death and resurrection, of an ever-new spring following the winter of death. In the *Purusha Sukta* of the *Rig Veda* (X, 90), the fire-energy of creativity yields even the shocking image of the world being created by the sacrificial self-immolation of the primordial divine Person (*purusha*)—is it the fire of love (see ch. 8)?

An old symbol for this process of renewal through fire is the *Phoenix*, the bird that finds death in the fire but cannot be annihilated. It is pure spirit; it is fire itself; it rises out of fire. It is life immortal, but *through* a process of becoming and perishing. In this image of the winged creature, Spirit is not an apocalyptic harbinger of death, but of a life that does not know of any static point of rest or final state. Rather than indicating a definitive apocalyptic dissolution, the Phoenix stands for the universal *process of renovation* as the principle of life, as *its* very spirit. Like the Spirit over the waters (Genesis 1:2), the dove over the receding deluge (Genesis 8:11), and the dove over the waters of the river Jordan (Mark 1:10; Matthew 3:16; Luke 3:22)—all relating to Spirit-water—the Phoenix, the Spirit-fire, reveals a *process* of life at the heart of existence: as the process of renewal. Represented by the *firebird* of Slavic mythology, the Phoenix is the spiritual sun that manifests the rhythms of its rising and falling, of day and night, of the most basic rhythms of life on Earth that the physical sun permits. And in Kabbalistic stories, the Phoenix was granted immortality because it was the only creature that did not eat of the fruit of the forbidden tree in paradise, but rather nests in the tree of life—in the double sense of the mythological tree of the book of Genesis (2:9) and the kabbalistic representation of the *sephirot*, the divine powers of creation and revelation (see ch. 4). The flaming swords of the *cherubim*, the fire-angels that guard the access to the tree of life (Genesis 3:24), cannot hold back the Phoenix, who is born from fire, who is fire, rebirth itself, and who nests in the arms of the tree of life. Becoming cannot be stopped.

In this image of the *cosmic* Phoenix, spirit-fire is the process of rebirth, renewal, return, resurrection and unbounded creativity of the universe. It does not exclude but embraces death, destruction, disintegration. In the image of the Phoenix, immortality is not beyond anything that is or becomes, because it always changes or disappears, but is at the heart of this universal cosmic process. Apocalyptic imagery, in this symbolism, is put back into a much wider context of a rhythmic, universal process of renewal. This process has no beginning or end; it is in its own way eternal, the eternal process of the Spirit. If we, in the spirit-space, encounter the Phoenix, the invisible power of life that we seek in this image will make us become seekers of immortality at the center, and in the face of, relentless becoming and perishing, not beyond it. Beyond this cycle that the fire reveals "is" really nothing, not any heaven or hell, not mere death or life after death, only illusion. Resurrection needs to unite itself with death. The universal return or renewal, the *apokatastasis* of all things, is a rhythmic process of conflagration and rebirth (as in Stoicism), of restoration (Acts 3:21), and of recapitulation, the *anakephalaiosis* (Ephesians 1:10), in the creative universal manifestation of the immortal in and as the space and light-life of creation (Colossians 1:15; John 1:3–5). This spirit-fire has become the symbol of universal "salvation": of salvation not from, but *of* the world; and not of any individual, but only of the collective *multiplicity* of being; and not beyond the world, but *into* it for its renewal. As all things are in their innermost "center" the spiritual space of infinite and infinitely related "divine points," the spirit-fire that this internal divine punctiform multiplicity reveals is the eternal renewal *as* that which unifies the spirit-space.

Several related images have been stirred up in the cauldron of imagination about the Phoenix, rounding out the spirit-space of fire: the rhythms, the light and heat of the *sun*; the flaming *angel*; the S*p*irit-*bird* in the twigs of the tree of life. The "sun" has, of course, not only always been a symbol of life and death, of allowing growth and proliferation of life, but also of burning heat and dryness, thirst and loss of land to the desert. And it has always been a symbol or even a representation of the nature of the divine reality "in the sky" or "in heaven," radiating light and heat, or warmth and clarity, or love and mind. The sun-god Aten was the literal and highly symbolic overflowing gift of life for Egypt in pharaoh Akhenaten's interpretation (see ch. 5). The Zoroastrian sacred, eternal fire, *atar*, is the origin of light and heat, the manifestation of Ahura Mazda—God as goodness and wisdom, order and light, and life. The Greek sun-god Apollo was an image of the victory of the intellect over the chaotic world of feelings represented by Dionysus. The linguistic interpretation of Plato, in the dialogue *Cratylus*, relates Apollo to *apolysis* and *apolousis*, salvation and purification, respectively. It was the answer of the oracle of Apollo at Delphi, according to Plato's *Apology* of Socrates (d. 399 BCE), namely, that Socrates is the wisest human being, that set Socrates on his quest for wisdom beyond any state of answer ever reaching the point of "unknowing" that is true wisdom. This "sun" resembles or expresses the Stoic *logos*, the wise order of things—much like the light of the Logos in the Prologue of the Gospel of John (1:4–5). But other Greek etymology allowed the word also to be deduced from *apollymi*, indicating a destroyer. The whole multiplicity of imagery around the sun is ambivalent, indeed: it gives and takes life. In the end, it stands in for the *divine* Wisdom (John 1:1) that is far beyond our understanding of measure, justice and mercy, as it grants its light and warmth to good and evil (Matthew 5:45). And the ethical implications of a spirituality of the ambivalence of the fire-Spirit are probably nowhere worked out in more clarity than in the Sermon on the Mount of which *this* omni-patient image of the "sun" is at the heart of an understanding of the invisible but all-engaged God.

The solar imagery of light and heat is also the background for the fiery character of the *splendor* and *gravity* of life and death exuded by divine appearance or revelation, epiphany, and theophany. Not only does this splendor pervade the universe as the visible manifestation of the invisible God or Wisdom (Genesis 1; John 1); *all* images for the invisible God are light-infused, blinding and inaccessible, illuminating and all-knowing, intellectual and loving. In the visions of the Hebrew prophets, God appears in such a light and fire, simultaneously revealed and hidden, or as the source of light and life. The visions of the book of Daniel of the light-radiating divine presences, angelic presences, and divine beings of the court of God have had a long-standing influence on the whole genre of apocalyptic (revelatory) "journeys of the soul" to the divine throne; of the representation of the cosmic Christ in the gospel scene of the transfiguration; of God, Christ and the living beings surrounding the throne of God's Glory; of the divine light and fire appearances in the book of Revelation (1:14; 5; 22:5); of the *mi'raj*, the heavenly journey of Muhammad, as he meets the half-fire, half-snow angel leading him to divine closeness; of the Angels of Death and Hellfire as well as the Cherubim, the Angels of the Throne, in Islamic traditions; or of the *Paradiso* of Dante (d. 1321) where the seeker in the spiritual journey of the soul to the ninth sphere of heaven perceives God in the form of intense light, the light of innumerable angels, that hides rather than reveals God.

The mystical experiences of the great Hebrew prophets mirror the same imagery. When Isaiah and Ezekiel are struck with divine presence, what they visualize is fire and light, the living beings around the thrown of God, the *cherubim* (Ezekiel 1) and *seraphim* (Isaiah 6:2–6). In the *First Book of Enoch* (20:7; 61:10; 71:7; Jude 1:14–15)—another archetypical journey into the divine presence—both classes of angels appear as closest to the Throne. In the *Second Book of Enoch*, the seraphim, the burning angels, appear as Phoenixes: they alone can "see" God while they burn away. Their immortality is a gift out of death, the death that every living being must go through, as none can see God and live (Exodus 33:20). In this tradition, the seraphim burn with the fire of the love of God so that nothing else can be seen by them, in them and as them other than God who is hidden in the fire of that love. They are really the "living symbols" of mystical union and the "materialization" of the human aim of theosis.

In Ezekiel's initiation vision, we encounter the "four living creatures" of the book of Revelation (4:6–8) for the first time. Around the divine throne, they appear like "burning coals of fire" or like "torches" (Ezekiel 1:13). And when these cherubim move, as the throne of God is a chariot like the chariot of Apollo, they are like a multitude of winds and voices (Ezekiel 1:24). The Spirit of God as unfathomable *divine manifold*! And on the throne appears the glory of God (Ezekiel 1:26–28), the splendor and gravity, the *kabod Yahweh*, in the form of a human being, but all brilliant radiance and fire and light and ornamented with the spectral colors of the rainbow (the sign of the divine covenant). It is this vision of the divine manifestation of the invisible God on the throne that will be leaving its traces throughout tradition. Prominently gravitating, in the book of Daniel and in its later Jewish and Christian renderings, toward the image of "one like a son of man" or (in its hypostatic rendering) *the* Son of Man, and culminating in the claim of the fulfillment of this imagery and its promises in the mouth of the Jesus of the gospels as well as the watershed contemplation on this declaration with the becoming-flesh of the Logos in the Gospel of John—all that is but a "reflection" of the presence of the *kabod*, the glory of God (John 1:14). The influences of this glory in the ancient "material" imagination of the Hebrews and the prophetic images of the being on the throne reach into the depth of the divine light-symbolic of primordial human encounters with light and fire, splendor and gravity of an ultimate reality of life and death, but also perpetuate their unabating power through the adaptation in the creative and all-encompassing figure of the Logos of Christianity and the Light of Muhammad, as they become, for instance, in the imagination of the great Andalusian Sufi philosopher Ibn ʿArabi (1165–1240 CE), but also in Islamic mysticism more generally, expressions of the primordial manifestation of the Mind of God.

Following the traces of this fire-light back to one of its ancient roots, we find ourselves again caught up in the scene that became of such pivotal importance to the whole evolution of the tree of Abrahamic religious traditions—the Sinai event (Exodus 3–33): the firebrand, the bush or tree that burns of God (variously interpreted as God's Self and an angel in the Hebrew Scriptures, as Christ in Christian interpretations, or as a cherub, or even the cosmic figure of ʿAli ibn Abu Talib, the cousin and son-in-law of Muhammad and the figure of origin for Shiʿism, himself in Islam) but is not consumed; the revelation of God in God's unique name, the Tetragrammaton, YHWH; the repeated visions of God on the mountain in a column of fire; the quest of Moses to "see" God and the devastating "view" it would be and is to whom or that on which divine light-fire may fall, so that Moses cannot "see" the glory of God except from its backside, hiding God's unbearable face; the presence of the *kabod* in the tent of the covenant and, later, in the temple of Jerusalem; the dynamic presence of the wandering of God's glory, the divine "presence," the *shekinah*, with the people into the Babylonian exile in later interpretations of the Exodus-events in later rabbinical literature—all that marks one of the paradigmatic trails of divine fire and light, of the Spirit-fire, through sacred histories and the experiences and imaginations of diverse religions and communities to this day, appearing and reappearing in the "incarnation" of the Logos in Christianity; in the primordial light of Muhammad in Islamic mysticism; in the Manifestations of God in the Bahá'í religion; and even in contemporary interpretations of *avatars* of Krishna in the Hindu *bhakti* tradition, the way of divine love-worship.

In all of these fiery solar manifestations of the *invisible* divinity, it has become one of the archetypical mystical "forms" of experience of this divine light-fire that it expresses a profound dialectic of presence and absence, inaccessibility and revelation, unmanifest formlessness and manifest forms. One may only invoke the biblical images of God *as* light (1 John 1:5), yet will find that it indicates but the inexorable hiddenness of infinite divine life wrapped in "inaccessible light" (1 Timothy 6:16). Or one may invoke the beautiful Islamic images of the Qur'anic Light Verse (Qur'an 24:35), that God is "light upon light," yet will find that it is cloaked in a niche, in a lamp in which it glows as a flame fed from the oil of the olive tree neither of the east nor of the west without burning up or touching the oil; and that according to Islamic tradition, God's life is wrapped in seventy thousand veils of light.

In this dialectic, two directions of spiritual transformation can be realized: one will enfold the spiritual space into its hidden dimensionless interiority; the other will reveal the hidden interiority as the true universal reality that becomes manifest to the spiritually awake eye. The latter tendency can be witnessed in one of the most interesting transformations or reversals of the solar images of spiritual light-fire in the Islamic tradition attributed to the fourth Sunni caliph and first Shi'i imam, 'Ali ibn Abu Talib, the *hadith al-haqiqah*, the tradition of Kumayl, of Kumayl ibn Ziyad al-Nakha'i (d. ca. 85 AH/704 EC). It presents the solar image of divine fire-light in the open spirit-space, in which the hidden becomes manifest reality. Imam 'Ali, on a journey, is asked by his close disciple the all-important spiritual question: What is (ultimate, divine) Reality (*haqq*, *haqiqah*)? Imam 'Ali answers with five characteristics that, in progressing intensity, reveal the divine Sun as its primordial image: the uncovering of the worthlessness of images of splendor (vainglory); the effacement of superstition hiding in knowledge; the uncovering of the veil (of illusion) by mastery of the mystery; the attraction to divine uniqueness (*ahadiyyah*) by way of divine oneness (*wahadiyyah*); and the insight that *Reality is a light shining forth from the morning of eternity over the temples of unity*. While multitudes of interpretations have been, and can be, given to this complex tradition, the fifth answer of Imam 'Ali reveals the dawning of the divine Sun over the spirit-space as the beginning of a New Day: the divine light shines so brightly that it covers all other lights; it rises to rend asunder all imaginations of divine Reality, as it "erases" the starry lights of the spiritual night.

The former tendency, namely, to enfold the spiritual open space into the infinite points of existence, is, indeed, but a version of this latter insight: that the sense of the public space of apocalyptic transformation in fact happens always and only as an infinite process of permanent transformation, not as one-time final blow (as already discussed in the previous section); that the Day of God is imminent in spiritual regenerations within creation and in the renewals of the Spirit in new religions and renewed enlightened expansions of consciousness. In what may be his boldest interpretation of a biblical image, the spiritual teacher Richard Rohr (b. 1943), in his book *The Universal Christ* (2019), transforms the spiritual fire of retribution (as classically conceived in exclusivist contexts) into the fire of renewal. While the frightening apocalyptic warning that the Son of Man has come (and publicly will come) "to cast fire upon the earth" in the hope that it may be "blazing" soon (Luke 12:49) anticipates the great day of judgment, the Day of God, when the Son of Man will appear in a terrible Glory of cosmic conflagration (Luke 21:25–27), Rohr, conversely, interprets this apocalyptic image as an ongoing universal process of spiritual change in the cosmos and us that always folds back onto itself. The apocalyptic scenario, with this shift in perspective, now loses its stigma of a destructive end of the world and becomes an image of the internal transformation of everything, a renewal of universal dimensions (not only human particularity) that sinks through death, but indicates a resurrection of life from death as a universal pattern of cosmic life. This is the fire-energy of love.

Like the rhythm of day and night and the seasons, this Fire-Light indicates renewal, a new revelation, even a new religious reality, a new divine revolution of the wheel of life—at least that is how Bahá'u'lláh, in his *Kitab-i-Iqan* (*The Book of Certitude*, 1861), has understood this eschatological charge, namely, as a radical transformation of the understanding of "salvation" into the universal coming of a *new* Day of God: resurrection as *return* and as the *renewal* of creation; as an *eternal* renewal of religions and spiritualities; as multiplicity of spiritual transformations of humanity into a future that we cannot even imagine yet—one in which humanity will become "spiritualized," but, without end, infinitely approximating the spiritual Sun and the apophatic Reality of which it is the Light-Fire. And it is the same infinite rhythm of divine engagement of the world of becoming that leads the *Bhagavad Gita* to the declaration that the "all in all" only happens as a *process* of approximation in the ever-new attraction of all spiritual paths to a unity of Reality, of Spirit and Self (4:11; 7:19; 9:25) *through* the endless repeating "incarnations" (4:8) of the divine Person of Krishna from eon to eon (6:13–14; 18:54).

With this *transreligious* reality of Spirit-fire, we are asked to look beyond the intra- and interreligious strivings and all multireligious separations to the *uniqueness* of Reality and the *one but manifold* Spirit-sun that shines in and over *all* of them. Especially with the coming of a new Sun of God, a new Manifestation of the invisible Reality, the divine fire burns away all veils. *If* we could see with the all-pervading eyes of God, the Spirit-fire would be revealing ever anew the way in which the eternal mysteries transform the world of becoming without beginning and end. This is a truly universally ecumenic message of the one Spirit in which all life burns only for God or Reality, much like the seraphim and the Phoenix who only know God and are immortal in this knowledge and "spirit" of the renewal of life. Apocalyptic fire has been transformed into an eternal process of spiritual revival.

Heart

There are three markers of divine identity in the New Testament. These identifications are mentioned without reserve, as absolute statements. They are best understood as essential substitutes for the word "God." Instead of using "God," these alternative demarcations are not just "characterizations" of God who would also have other attributes aside. Rather, they are in their absoluteness close to another all-inclusive *naming* of divine reality. These markers are Spirit (John 4:24), Light (1 John 1:5) and Love (1 John 4:8)—all three of them from the Johannine writings. We have encountered already the first two—Spirit and Light; this section is about the third one: Love. It appears in the Shema Israel, the central creed of Israel, as the unconditional love we are to give to God; and it was unconditionally confirmed by Jesus (Deuteronomy 6:4; Matthew 22:37). Yet if we seek the Love of God, we seek its "place"—our *heart*. Divine love, any love really, is poured out in the heart by the Spirit (Romans 5:5). And in order to sense it, we need to prepare its place, make the effort for a *pure* heart (Psalm 51:10). It is really the reality "at the heart" not of just some human individuals who happen to encounter it, but of human *essence* itself and, beyond that, at the innermost reality of *all* things. Like Spirit and Light-Fire, Love is the heart of the spirit-space. It is the flame at the heart of all beings by which they are expressions of the Spirit-reality, which is light and love (see ch. 9).

Teilhard de Chardin contributed the same two motifs to this spirit-space—Light and Love. As *Light*, Spirit is in the heart of all beings, but enfolded in a fragile form, as a flicker, a ray of light, slight and easy to overlook. This "ray of light" reveals the "incandescence of the interior layers of being" flooded by the "divine milieu" so that every point, event or being is the revelation of this interior flame of the Spirit, in its consistency as well as its fragility. The Spirit-fire is the little flame at the heart of everything. As *Love*, Spirit is the magnetic force that draws everything together to a synthesis, as a process of cohesion, of gentle correlation, and as the expression of a profound mutuality of existence. Through this process of unification, internal correlations to everything else become "complex," that is, they express a togetherness of diversity. The more things are united, the more they realize the inner multiplicity of the universe that they unite. They become ever more *many* folds of the One, mutually immanent and perceptive of one another. The more they become focused to express the internal "point" that is their very heart, the point of unity, the more they also become the place of the *pleroma* of everything they embrace without destroying it. They become "all in all" from the inside out. This unity of love is the internal growth of the love of *everything* beyond all limitations of lesser unities, such as family, tribe, ethnicity, race, sex, and all other forms of identification. Light and Love are the expression of the *internality* of the Spirit, the *folded* spirit-space, being at the heart of all things.

For Teilhard de Chardin, this process of unification is *evolutionary* and directed toward a "point" in which everything will reach this internal cohesion with everything else so that the All, in fact, transforms all externality into internality such that the external space of the universe would be transfigured into the very spirit-space that simmers ever in its heart. This final "point," given the name "the Omega Point" in his book *The Phenomenon of Man* (1955), would be the resurrection of the whole cosmos into a new creation; there, internality and externality have lost their meaning, as they are, then, one and the same: *the cohesive pleroma of divine multiplicity.*

Generally, Teilhard has been interpreted as following a simple scheme of development and fulfillment (tentatively typical for the linearity of Abrahamic salvation history) such that this Omega Point represents the final eschaton, the real end of all things and the universal transformation of the creation into the reign of God. I do not share this view, for two reasons. First, like any evolutionary scheme, it must be set into the context of the infinity and indefiniteness of divine creativity, which must not be thought of as having an end or any state of fulfillment such that the divine mystery was at this "point" reached. Rather, the Omega Point is always beyond the reach of realization; it is an approximation, a view from the eternal becoming of the spirit-space. Second, as the whole process has neither beginning nor end in either time or eternity, since it is always a manifestation of the infinite unfolding and refolding of the divine values and virtues, attributes and characteristics, this "point" is not an expression of a state, but of *becoming*, the divine process of manifestation *itself*—think again of Krishna's promise in the *Gita* to return. Hence, whenever we enter the spirit-space or begin to feel, see, or sense the inner divine flame at the heart of all things, we enter the love that has already overcome any need for fulfillment, as it "is" *in this moment* what it always has been and will be: the heartbeat of existence, the heart-to-heart vibration of love.

And it is this *alternative* view of things, this spiritual space beyond the oppositions of internal and external, one and many, I and Thou, this or that, this *nondual becoming (as always anew becoming nondual)*, in which we connect to the flame of love at the heart of all things. Through its focal "point," we connect beyond all external categories and divisions with the "all in all" that reveals itself in this space not as an outcome of an evolution but as the very motor of the whole process. In *Science and Christ* (1919–55), for instance, Teilhard calls this inner motor the *Christus evolutor*, the cosmic Christ that (since even biblical times) was understood as the origin, pervasive force and encompassing unity of the whole process (John 1; Ephesians 1; Colossian 1; 1 Corinthians 8). This is the heart of and in "all in all"—the Image and Manifestation of the invisible Spirit-Light-Love in which all is "at heart" a manifestation of spirit-light-love.

The fire of love at the heart of every being is the sense by which all things know one another *immediately, intimately* from the inside, as if there was no external space. No distance differentiates things connected through their heart, and the magnetism of love on the outside is just a remainder of the veils that still distance things from one another. This external distance has its important meaning for the reality of evolution and freedom—Whitehead calls this external space the "elbow room" of creation. It allows the internal vibrations to play melodies from heart to heart, but per *expression* in a cosmic process of ever-new harmonization. Ancient philosophers and spiritual masters, such as Pythagoras (d. ca. 495 BCE), Heraclitus and Plotinus (d. 270 CE), knew of these harmonics as movements of proportions and the measure of beauty, of living tensions or vibrations, and as correlations of cosmic sympathy.

In the Pythagorean view, all beings are proportions of vibrations, like those of the harmonies played on instruments, but in cosmic dimensions of planets, star systems, and all other potential magnitudes of cosmic music. All beings are related by the internal feeling of these vibrations to contribute to a composition directed at beauty. This is concomitant with an important insight: that the meaning of existence is *beauty*, that is, that it is fulfilled in itself and its harmonic and harmonious relations to everything else. A. N. Whitehead has summarized this poetic view by declaring that, if the infinite process of the universe tends toward anything, it is not any state of fulfillment but the realization of beauty. In this view, the universe is directed toward *itself*, its own process, that is, at (the development, unfolding, and evolution of) its internality, where it must "listen" to and "articulate" its own *potential pleroma of life*—always anew in ever new harmonies and intensities.

Heraclitus is known as one of the primordial process thinkers, emerging from the ancient, pre-Socratic philosophical landscape of Greece. Philosophy, at that time, was not yet (in opinion and reality) reducible to an intellectual reflection, if it ever was, but named a serious engagement in a whole way of life and the attentive expansion of one's consciousness and conscience regarding the world we live in, and then a program to live in a way convergent with the gained understanding. The fundamental insight of Heraclitus was so revolutionary that it would need many generations to reach this radicality of insight again—as in G. W. Leibniz, William James (d. 1910), Henri Bergson (d. 1941), A. N. Whitehead and G. Deleuze. Many others followed another philosophical direction based on a vision of his antipode, Parmenides (ca. mid-fifth century BCE), that seems to have at its center the fear that Heraclitus faced head-on: that the world of becoming is disgusting, should not be at all and, hence, is a mere illusion. Heraclitus challenges the Parmenidean eternalist view that there is only "being" beyond which there is (only) "nothing," that in reality there is no becoming, no process, no evolution, not temporality. Instead, he claims that becoming is *all* there is. The All is in becoming. Not only is becoming real; it is also the only permanent reality. In fact, since at the heart of all things burns a fire, a spirit of life, an unrest of movement without which there was only death, the fundamental reality of the universe is *Fire*. He called this fire *Logos*. What a grand vision! When others called on the Logos, such as the Stoics, they were thinking of (rational) order, that the world is based on a specific order that represents the eternity of being for which becoming is basically an illusion. Instead, Heraclitus insisted on *Life* as the permanence of change, of life and death, of becoming and perishing, of impermanence. Fire is the *image and activity* of the invisible Logos, the *cosmic* fire that burns with life and movement at the *heart* of all things. It is not that through the Logos the All is in competition with itself, as Heraclitus is sometimes interpreted. Rather, the All is in a mutual *tension* of challenge, the challenge to live more intensely, more in the fire, more from the divine. As a bow (*biós*) only works if its parts are held in tension, so is life (*bíos*) the *mutual relation of otherness in process* (*Fragments*, B48).

We know today that "no movement" would mean the death of cosmic existence; zero degrees Kelvin is the point of absolute freezing. Life is temperature, heat, movement. But no movement can live without change, tension of mutual influence, mutual challenge, and the inner fire of life. That this fire may also include suffering, death, and imperfection is not an anomaly here, but rather similar to the expression that *in the divine view* the spiritual sun rises over good and evil.

Plotinus is his own universe. His collected works, known as the *Enneads*, have become influential in philosophical, religious, spiritual, and mystical traditions second to none. The aspect that interests me here is how he understands the internal relationship of the All to itself—which is an emanation from the One, which again is beyond all categories but manifests as both an intellectual (intelligible) and a sensitive (feeling) character. This triad of the One (*hen*), the Mind (*nous*) and the World-Soul (*psyche*) expresses a world in which all things are internally related through "sym-pathy," which means: coming together in the mutual feeling of one another. On this view, not only is everything one in the One, the nameless God beyond all categories. Rather, since the *One is nothing for itself* and *all for the All* that emanates from it, it is the *All-One in which* all things are "all in all" such that in it all things are related through mutual sym-pathy, mutual feeling. The implications are extraordinary: If all things are related in their heart to everything else, then all movements of one thing are reflected in movements within all others. The world is a grand organism of *mutual implication*. "God," the One, is not in competition to this sym-pathic organism, but is not different from it either. Transcendence and immanence coincide. At the heart, all things are one and, in this mutuality, the expression of the One. If you meditate and pray, it is not an external Godhead that answers, but the whole organism that feels and reacts to the desire of the heart.

A. N. Whitehead, reflecting in his own way these three insights of the masters of old, has found wonderful expressions for these heart-to-heart vibrations of Spirit-Light-Love. The motor of the process of universal becoming is what Whitehead in *Adventures of Ideas* calls the "harmony of harmonies." Its activity is that of a divine *attractor* by which everything in its own becoming can express its inherent potentials more intensely and harmoniously or less harmoniously and intensely, but always in relating to (and with implications for) all other things. Everything is already an expression of the potential harmonies and intensities it can become in concert with all other things at any moment. The heart of all things actuates *their* very becoming as the realization of their ideal potentials that God suggests in view of the divine feeling, knowing, and imagining of all other things. God here "presents" Godself as this attractor, the divine love of mutual inherence in every moment of becoming. Thereby, when he introduces divine harmonics, Whitehead directs us not away from the heart-to-heart relationships of the All in all things to something external, an external Godhead. Rather, he *expands* the divine creativity, the process of harmonization, to *all* things. Everything has in its own heart the fire of creativity; nothing is a lifeless puppet of a general law or order. In Whitehead's magisterial book *Process and Reality* (1929), the divine Spirit in its receptive aspect (the Consequent Nature of God) is the compassionate harmonization of universally inherent creative activities of *all* events, processes and things, which are based on *their* very own inherent fire of life, not any fixed or pre-given order, among themselves, but *by way* of God's initial, imaginative, and creative aspect as "Logos" (the Primordial Nature of God), the universal immanence of divine appetition to the realization of this vision of the divine Wisdom.

Ultimately, Spirit-Reality, here, is neither God nor the World, neither Creativity nor Harmony, in isolation, but their *mutual Immanence*, that is, a *mutual sym-pathy*, by which everything is part of the becoming of everything else. This mutuality must not be confined to or confused with causality, even mutual (a-temporal) causality. It is rather similar to the Buddhist notion of mutual conditioning (*pratitya-samutpada*) that, as in Whitehead, allows for novelty, syn-thesis, reversal (of ignorance, *avidya*), creativity in the process of becoming (against mechanistic causal relationship). It is also closer to the mutuality of the influential *Avatamsaka Sutra* (first century BCE to fourth century CE) and the ensuing Hua Yen Buddhist understanding of every being as a multiplicity of facets of enfolded relationships, imagined in the form of jewels that mirror one another brilliantly. It also appears in the mutual enfolding of everything in everything in the thought of Nicolas of Cusa. Yet in the Whiteheadian context it is (despite all potential temporal paradoxes) central to the creative *process* of becoming (coming together in novel ways). Everything exits in the creative tension of a multiplicity of relations that become united and, again, contribute themselves to a new multiplicity for new processes of unification. Harmonization is an infinite process of *aesthetic appreciation of otherness*.

This understanding of the spirit-space and spirit-fire, if it is taken seriously, harbors fundamental spiritual insights that will change our perception of the reality in which we live. Divine encounter happens in the sym-pathy with the things that generate us and that we generate, that are our environment and of which we are the environment. The divine dimension of this encounter lies in the attraction to beauty, harmony, intensity, and mutuality. In this view, God is the *Eros* of mutual appeal at the heart of all things, ever so gently suggesting itself as the ever-greater respect for, preservation of, transformation with, and liberation to the little flame of creative life in all things. In the spirit-space, there is no external force of compulsion, only the compulsions by which *we resist* this process of the embodiments of spiritualization.

Indeed, if the heart makes itself the spirit-place, there is a great power in this little spirit-flame. At the heart of everything is the place of the encounter with the infinite "suns" of the Spirit, the place of the revelation of God in an infinity of creative power. But only in the awakened conscious space of such a spiritual perception can we perceive the power of this *mysterium tremendum et fascinans*—in the famous description of the numinous by the German philosopher and comparativist of religion Rudolf Otto (d. 1937) in his book *The Idea of the Holy* (German 1917/English 1923).

It is the grace of this mystery that its infinite "suns" are enfolded in the little flame that must be accessed in humility, in sym-pathy and with compassion to all things. To access this spiritual flame in modes of altered consciousness and with a pure heart in states of contemplation and through actions of love and compassion transfigures our view—if only for a time, until impermanence prevails, a process of enfolding veils the heart again and "seamless" exteriority takes over the punctiform multiplicity of the inner heat and light. These are the moments when we can see the heart of another being and act in sym-pathy and in a creative harmonization with it. This is the state in which we might experience God in all things (like St. Francis of Assisi), or release and realize Christ in the excluded (Matthew 25), or find Krishna in the overwhelming cosmic multiplicity (*Bhagavad Gita*, ch. 11), or encounter the Buddha as our nature, or be struck with the Sinai experience (Exodus 33) that might shock us with a force that, in the Qur'an, caused Moses to faint (Qur'an 7:143).

We may experience the Day of God (Joel 2:31) in such moments, the apocalyptic transformation of all things. It is real, but it is not an external reality. Only in a humble approach can we withstand its power. In Sufism, the "heart" (*qalb*) and its "interior interiority," the "secret" (*sirr*), is the seat of the revelation of God. In it, in the love of God, *only* God appears; everything else disappears in God's presence. In this ecstatic state of contemplation and utter alterity, which is *the heart of the heart* of our being, we become extinct in God (*fana*) and are resurrected in the life of God (*baqa*). Nothing remains in the heart but the Face of God (Qur'an 28:88).

Epilogue: Suffering

In this chapter, I have not gone into several other aspects that we face when we name the Spirit as space and fire and locate it in the heart. I mean associations of fire with hell and the intolerable pain that humans inflict on one another with fire, symbolically and literally—one is reminded of the horrible burnings of "the others" at the stake, or the use of napalm bombs in the Vietnam War, or the cremations of the dehumanized in Auschwitz. Or one may be dumbfounded by the fact that humans take it on themselves in situations of an utter impasse to protest with arson and self-immolation. Additionally, I mean also the "other sides" of spaciousness here, the experience of emptiness and nihility, for instance, of that of the utter meaninglessness of life—so eloquently stated by the Japanese philosopher Keiji Nishitani (d. 1990) in his analysis of the western "space" of nihilism. And I mean the unbearable, unhinged bottomlessness of mourning that the heart experiences with the loss of loved ones, or when facing the nearness of death, or through that imposition of inexplicable heaviness that quenches the flame of life from our heart when it experiences deep sadness—not the sadness of any particular loss or lack, but that shallowness or shadowy disappearance of a fading world.

It would not be hard to dwell on these experiences to which we all, in this or that form and with diverse degrees of gravity, probably can relate. I have elected not to do so, mainly for two reasons. There is really no rationale replicating these pains of existence with or without the symbolic or literal reference to space, fire, and the heart in textual form, as it would not add anything to their (missing) meaning or (hoped-for) remedy. Conversely, if we believe that any language of reflection will elevate the suffering (to some kind of heroic existence or imagined worth), we may have a fairly unrealistic expectation: the best you can ("aspire" to) do in any situation of suffering is to act or to listen. Every superfluous word may be, well, superficial; and any concept trying to capture its character in order to somehow control its effect is nothing but a form of magical procedure that may have convinced itself of the unhealthy illusion that manipulation would be the right reaction to suffering.

The second reason not to exploit the symbolic and literal realities of the Spirit for their ambivalence of the good and evil they can illuminate in us to highlight the suffering of the world is that the negativity that is needed to view them as means of negation is a state of mind and things that the Spirit may tolerate, but tries seducing or convincing us to leave and transform. The ironic, sarcastic, or even nihilistic mode of the human mind in embracing the inevitability of suffering in the world easily becomes the "natural" state or zero-point of consideration and action. This cannot be countered by adding poetic images to them.

The only way, really, still to use language for such situations in order not to fall into a silence of hopelessness or embarrassment is by way of prayer to, or of the divine verses attributed to and pursued in, the Spirit (Romans 8). It can be the language of lamentation as that of the Psalms or the Wisdom literature (for instance, as captured in the book of Lamentations) or it can be the language of supplication or remorse. In any case, it must be the language of transformation, of *metanoia* (Mark 1:15), of going beyond (*meta*) the grasping mind (*nous*) and of falling into the mystery of powerlessness and poverty—as advised in the Beatitudes (Matthew 5). What we should not do, instead, is to use the symbolic or material expressions of spiritual realities for their poetic power to gloss over the powerlessness of suffering, as if we could heal by denial or merely by covering the wounds with excuses in the form of images or some magical remedies solicited from contact with the sacred vibrations of related material elements.

Not by shedding light on the suffering and its reasons, but by lifting us from them and, thereby, by burning their pain in a self-sacrifice skyward, are we liberated, become divine, become human—*theosis*. It is in such movements that we may become aware of our *soul*, the principle of life in us that *is* us and is *more* than us, which is the power of awakening in us, but cannot be captured within our conscious horizons of knowing and feeling (see ch. 9). It appears as the flaming horizon from which we "burn" up our possessions and the possessiveness by which we are possessed, that which seems to hold us in its grip: the attachment to the forces of destruction in and around us. Only if we realize that such spiritual flames do what they are supposed to do, namely, to deconstruct our attachments, thereby breaking down the grip of destruction, suffering, and evil on us, are we relieved of the pain this grip, this possessiveness, asserts in us.

It is movements of spiritual dispossessing that conspire in awakening us to the little flame in all things. In the openings of the spirit-space, this flame may become a collective rushing of a world-burning desire for transformation. Apocalyptic imagination in the face of oppression and suffering is really but a participation in the suffering of the God of relationality in us, of the *heart of God* in turmoil that burns with our pain but that also burns it away, transforms it into (spiritual and mystical) insights of a loving embrace that sheds light on both the good and the evil, but carries not only its joy but also its burden. It is this love that is enfolded in the heart of all things. And the only way, really, to avoid falling into the silence of hopelessness or embarrassment is to admit the sighs of the Spirit in us (Romans 8).

And when the veil of externality again impresses on us the hiddenness of these realities of fire and space, we should not use the symbolic or material expressions of spiritual realities by exploiting their poetic power, but we should try to remember their burning desire for transformation. It is in the powerlessness and poverty of the burning heart of the Spirit in us that we may begin to feel this transformative power in all the realities in and around us.

Meditation II: The Inner Fire

The heart is the space of divine revelation, of the revelation of wisdom and compassion, the impulses of love and desire, and the space that can embrace the world, if it is opened. Deleuze and Guattari in *A Thousand Plateaus* use a term for the infinity of the movements that can form in the heart as the creative space of infinite variability based on a vision of a state of altered consciousness: Imagine that your body is only skin, and is empty inside, without any organs. This "body without organs," then, can become a poetic symbol for the freedom of a creative space in which we are not bound by absolutes, but are their creators. A. N. Whitehead calls the same phenomenon an "entirely living nexus" of events—life, free in its movements and embracing all streams and characteristics and forms in a gracious spaciousness. We become "apophatic bodies." Perhaps "Spirit" names this *apophatic space of pure Life*—wherein we have burned away everything except the flame itself.

> *Imagine. You sit calmly in a dim room, comfortable, near the floor, grounded. You have no concerns right now.*
> *Everything is quiet, maybe asleep . . .*
>> *only you are awake, a sentinel, watching over the dreams of the sleeping . . .*
> *In front of you, a candle, lit . . .*
>> *you follow its flicker, its rhythm of sacrifice of light, skyward . . .*
> *. . .*
> *Imagine. You lift the candle to the height of your heart . . .*
>> *leave its flame—there . . .*
>> *lower the candle to the ground, but the flame does not move . . .*
> *Extend your hand and with your palm gently invite the flame into your body . . .*
>> *it does not touch anything, or burn . . .*
>> *it is only light . . .*
> *. . .*
> *As it enters your body, approaching your heart, the room around you has disappeared.*
>> *Your body has become the space around . . .*
> *. . .*

The Small Flame in Everything

The flame lights up the body from the inside . . .
    but you see only empty space . . .
    feel it . . .
. . .
A flame in the midst of infinite space . . .
    inside you, the universe . . .
. . .
You can move around the flame in all directions . . .
    what do you see, feel?
. . .
Now blow out the flame . . .

2

Crossing the Infinite Sea

God is a Sea of infinite and measureless essence
[*pelagos ousias apeiron kai aoriston*].
—GREGORY OF NAZIANZUS

God is even as a Sea of infinite and, in consequence, indistinct substance
[*Est enim deus pelagus infinitae substantiae et per consequens indistinctae*].
—JOHN OF DAMASCUS

But the trees also commingle their roots in the darkness underground, and the islands also hang together through the ocean's bottom. Just so there is a continuum of cosmic consciousness, against which our individuality builds but accidental fences, and into which our several minds plunge as into a mother-sea or reservoir.
—WILLIAM JAMES, *ESSAYS IN PSYCHICAL RESEARCH*, 374

Ocean

WITH INFINITE VARIABILITY, THE ocean is literally and symbolically reminding us of all kinds of infinities, dangers and the awe of grandness, depth and unfathomable distances. The gravitas of an incalculable mass, the lively play of its surface, the uncontrollable hyper-dimensionality of its boundaries and contents, its movements and secrets, together are second to none to any image that can impress on us the depth of the recognition of the formless and inexpressible reality of existence. That we easily drown in the realities these images convey is, of course, an ancient memory in collective human consciousness and mythological accounts of destruction and the utter uselessness of human technologies to secure civilization against natural events such as earthquakes, tsunamis, volcanoes, and other catastrophic forces of nature that have moved masses of water and oceanic forces into fertile lands.

In all of those characteristics of alterity that in a profound sense archetypically accompanied human experience throughout its millennia of evolution, migration, historical recollection and impact on any understanding of the material, mental and spiritual (aspects of the) universe have also become the images of divine unapproachable alterity, ambivalent presence, and super-rational, unpredictable activity in the world. It is the Spirit over the waters of an infinite, alien ocean, touching the unimaginable depth under its face, that is the privileged image of the genesis of existence in the ancient Hebrew cosmogony. This constellation indicates the state "before" creation (Genesis 1:2) and the unfathomable ground of being "after" creation (Genesis 6). While later apocalyptic prophets envisioned the future in terms of fire (Revelation 21–22), the antediluvian Noah cycle stands for the same prophecy in the form of the dangerous power of the waters to return creation to a state of chaos, a state *before* creation, and a state of *indistinction* and *formlessness* as the *pluripotentiality* for a new creation (Genesis 6–9).

In a sense, the ocean is one of the most alien and alienating impositions of the omnipresence of Reality to the human mind that might always seek reason and understanding, wisdom and personal address in the natural events supporting and endangering its need for security and meaning. The ocean stands for the uncontrollable, the irrational, the unfathomable, the end of the world in both the spatial and temporal sense, its permanent endangerment from chaos, the monstrous side of the world humanity cannot escape living with (see ch. 9). While the ocean can never be mastered, it can be experienced as a challenge to the world or its forces but also as a promise to its vow to hide and defend its secrets from human exploitation. While the ocean can be navigated to the extent that it grants shortcuts and access to foreign lands and riches, refuge to the persecuted and advantage in tactics of war, exploration, commerce and love, it can never be subdued and remains alien to human motivations and purposes.

It is not hard to believe that the ocean could become a symbol of both divine and anti-divine forces in the universe, but always of a power that seems not to be able to be pressed into neat ethical categories or clear-cut existential differentiations between good and evil, or even meaningful antitheses between aesthetic feelings of beauty and horror, or adventure and madness. It is also not really surprising that the profound ambivalences und uncontrollable abilities of the ocean to upset any human familiarity with Reality were projected onto all that which seemed to be in need of control by social forces of a civilization, making the ocean the literal and symbolic enemy especially of the patriarchal structures of early societies organized around agriculture. The identification of the ocean with the mother of the gods that in her madness ought to be slain by her own son, as the myth in one of the oldest documented epics in human history, the Babylonian *Enuma Elish* (first half of the second century BCE), says that the king-god Marduk (male warrior-king) did to Tiamat (ocean or saltwater), is just a caricature of the emotional need of an agricultural society to control the elements that always befall and betray it, and—as Catherine Keller has demonstrated in her book *Face of the Deep* (2003)—of the male hierarchy of that society to control women and all lower classes so as to hold all else but the reigning religious and political elite in check. It never worked; however, this recipe is still in place and tirelessly tried out. Chaos cannot be controlled! The more control, the greater the downfall and depression. We can try, again and again, but oppression doesn't work forever. Naturally, chaos will deconstruct forces of oppression. When will we learn that?

Chaos is a friend of freedom. It is the freedom of creativity, originally, eventually, or in principle, not to be bound by any pre-given law, be it natural or divine (see ch. 3). Images of "the chaotic" have become partners of the desire for liberation from oppressive structures. Liberation movements are never energized by the punishments of an oppressive order alone, but rather by a just order, an order that does not take away the power to be free and self-defining of one's destiny. Chaos is the means to creatively facilitate this transformation, to not only imagine a new creation, but to initiate an apocalyptic novelty that will establish the convergence of freedom, justice and a life that is worth living. This liberating chaos turns against the false chaos of oppression; its anticipated just order turns against the order of destruction and alienation, misogyny and patriarchalism, classism, sexism, and really any limited ideological exceptionalism. But even more than of just "order" (even "just" order), the chaos that always hides in *any* order reminds us of the immanent creativity of Reality that is not an accomplice of our schemes and biases, ulterior interests and manipulative self-serving aims. It is both inscrutable and indifferent to any interest and limited meaning-making. Like the Roman goddess Iustitia, chaos is blindfolded, or we perceive it as such, either as unbiased or as indifferent; and like the Greek goddess Pallas Athena, chaos mediates wisdom and war—the ambivalence of freedom and order. In its profound ambivalence, the images of chaos, Reality remains inaccessible.

It is in all of these senses that the oceanic imagery has become a symbol of either a force that God alone can master and release, with all the effects of divine retribution that made the ocean a matter of existential fear, or an anti-divine force that is permanently independent of divine order or must be subdued by God in an epic struggle between good and evil. It is in this image of *monstrosity* that the religious and social elites have used this imagery as justification for their own assurance of power over any deviating views and motivations for divergent religious and social activities and for alternative forms of religious and social organizations. But the dangers of the alien ocean have also become the characteristics of a God who or that cannot be swayed by human manipulation and who or that is always independent from the evil schemes of humanity. In this sense, the ocean is a prophetic warning against human hubris and a memorial to the independence of God from any religious authority of elites and their claims legitimately to destroy human life if it does not submit to their limited understanding and perpetuation of status and existence.

Yet, then again, oceanic chaos and divine aura stand for the divinity of uncontrollable life and utter beauty. It is in this image that the divine nature of oceanic life is one of the three partitions of the world order in Greek mythology. Poseidon relates to his brothers Zeus and Hades as the "third space" between the divine fire of will and purpose and the living death residing in the underworld, namely, as the life that is neither good nor evil and is beyond categories, but is not identical with death, either. And it is in this image of oceanic chaos that beauty becomes beautiful, because it cannot be manipulated. It is, like Aphrodite, born from the chaotic movements of the foam of the waves on the beaches, the interfaces between the ocean and the lands of human habitation. As life is not rational, so is beauty beyond any categories of control. This life is beyond any fixed forms—formless, even—but is also, as such, the breeding ground of innumerable forms of creative becoming. This is a beauty beyond any fixed categories. It is utter relativity, but not subjectivity. It is a pleroma of modes of beauty that cannot be limited by any divisions, ideologies, or interests. The oceanic pleroma of life and beauty is what is divine here, not its dangers, as they are only consequences of the misunderstandings or failed misappropriations that are their own harbinger of death and evil, meaninglessness and the mirror of human monstrosity.

The ocean is a *paradox of limits in the midst of infinities*. There is the oceanic boundary of its *margins*, the shores, by which the ocean seems to be confined, but always ready to transgress these boundaries. Poseidon as the earth-rocker imprints still the image of earthquakes and tsunamis that ignore such limitations. Yet, conversely, in ancient imagery it is the earth that swims in this ocean. So, the shores are rather the limitations of the dry grounds than of the ocean that sustains them. Then there is the limitation between water and air, the boundary of the *surface* between the realm of birds and fish, navigated only by humanity's fragile ships and barges, rafts and artificial platforms, permanently and imminently exposed to the inscrutable movements of its waves. Yet again this boundary is an expression of the power of the ocean to transgress rather than of any limitation on its ability to upset control. And then there is the boundary of its *depth*, as we can only dive so far into its expanse without being crushed or running out of air. The ocean's depth is inaccessible, but the creatures that populate it appear as transgressions of this boundary—deep-sea monsters and prolific alien life forms, on occasion spotted at the surface, were always a symbol of a pleroma that subtracts itself into the hidden darkness, away from the reach of human access and understanding. All of these boundaries, however, only appear as *ours*, not that of the ocean. It rather seems to graciously allow something else to exist besides, in, or under it—the floating earth and the gliding atmosphere; and it seems only indirectly and imperfectly limited by any power higher than itself. Then there is the boundary of its *open horizon*—nothing but water all around, no end in view. It is the most unbarred boundary, endless and without hindrance. While it might also have contributed to orientation and the feeling of being enveloped by infinity, this boundary is but the physical expression of the limitation of everything in it by nothing less than infinity itself, the boundary of the *unbounded*.

The ocean is the home of adventures and treasures, islands and ever-new discoveries, but also of profound disorientation. It is the playground of the wild biblical monster Leviathan, which "sports" with God (Psalm 104:26) and which much later, in the social contract theory of English philosopher Thomas Hobbes (d. 1679), in his book *Leviathan* (1651), becomes a symbol of the warlike chaos of nature in need of a state under the absolute control of a sovereign. It is a space of indirection but also a forbidden or forbidding territory. It is always formidable as enemy and enormously gratuitous if it, on occasion, appears as friend. It is the home of what is beyond human life, but life nevertheless. Its boundaries are always open, but still impenetrable. While we may ride its waves and navigate its tides and currents, we remain subject to their moods. While we may dive into its shallows, we always remain in view of (and are invited to probe) its depths. While we may always forge ahead into new areas of its expanse, we always are left exposed to the sudden changes of the weather above and the surges below. While we may always find something new above, on, or below its surface, we may just disappear without a trace. The character of the oceanic being is its *formlessness* by which it can become whatever it wants: a calm place of sunset or a raging monster, the provider of sustenance or the taker of life, hungry to devour all who dare to trespass its body. Or it will starve the hungry and parch the thirsty whom it leaves to perish on its back. Its power is a reminder that it will transform all "on, in, or below" it in unexpected and dramatic ways if they expose themselves to or transgress its four boundaries: its margin, surface, depth and horizon.

It is fascinating to encounter *this* ocean at the beginning of, as the state before, and in the position of primordiality in the biblical account of creation. It is *this* ocean, the ocean that is named by its depth and surface, the face of chaos, of life and beauty as well as inscrutable and uncontrollable wildness, that the Spirit of God is facing—not by creating it, not by controlling or limiting it, not by any power struggle descending from above, like Marduk, not by condemning it or warning of its awful force, not by scrutinizing it or avoiding it . . . none of these. Instead, the Spirit lingers above the ocean, respecting its pluripotential indifference, gently (like a breeze) aware of its boundaries, but ready to absorb any of its transgressions—just *hovering* (Genesis 1:2), *being* in-between, *being* (at) the boundary. Neither touching its surface nor violating its depth, nor being exposed to its tides, the Spirit is perceptive and receptive of its potency, life and beauty. It has nothing to add to it, nor does it subtract anything from it. The act of creation (1:3), then, is "light upon light" (Qur'an 24:35), not light over or against darkness. There is no source of light yet except the creative act or word of God (Genesis 1: 17); there is no rhythm of day and night yet (Genesis 1:4), and no division of domains into land and water (1:10), or saltwater and freshwater (1:6), or water and heavens (1:7). Sure, these are all sovereign acts of "division," creation by limitation and differentiation, but they are not "out of nothing"—to which the later mythology of omnipotence shifts the paradigm of enlivening to controlling. They are "out of the ocean" and "the bare land" and "the darkness" and "the Spirit of God" in the midst of all of them. The Spirit "gives time," "makes space," and "infuses enlightenment." All of these elements of water, earth and air are like the halo of the Spirit in which the spark of divine fire (Heraclitus), the world of light or the light of the world (John 1:3) ignites diversity, but never the disappearance of its spiritual aura. The pre-creation elements remain the *numinous companions* of the Spirit (see both preamble and epilogue). The life of the ocean, its depth and face, its mysterious darkness and the formidable chaotic bareness in the form of "the waves" of the desert, are the signs of the Spirit whenever it sparks life beyond any limitation, whenever it appears as the transgression of life itself.

So, finally, consider *all* of that—and now read again the epigrams of Gregory of Nazianzus (d. 390 CE) and John of Damascus (d. 749 CE) with which this chapter began: that God in God's innermost *essence* is of *that* nature, the nature of *that* ocean; even more: that God's primordial *substance* is that of this ocean! In a sense, then, the ocean, of which the image of the physical ocean that we literally experience and which is symbolically imprinted onto the collective unconscious mind of human memory, is only a sign, a weak expression, of the *potency* of the Ocean that is God—"weak" in the sense that the material ocean, in this identification of God with the primordial ocean, is only a hint of that which we can just barely comprehend in our fragility, of the primordial potential of which there is nothing similar we could ever imagine in physical experiences and mental images, limited as we are. The image of the ocean here stands for the uncontrollable transgression that any category will suffer when it is related as an announcement of the mystery of God. Again, we end with the *mysterium tremendum et fascinans* (see ch. 1 and the epilogue). Whether in the form of "space" or "fire" of the infinity of the "heart" of all things, or the "ocean"—all imagery here is only a gift of transcendence, shocking us out of our settled routines of perception and ratiocination, out of our settled categories and images, out of the limitations of our mind and body, to open us to the inner space of an infinity that we can only touch if we give ourselves up to it.

Like the spirit-space and the spirit-fire, the spirit-ocean is a symbolic transgression between all categories holding us apart, holding apart realities and beings, regions and forms of creatures, in this cosmos in oppositional or antagonistic categorizations. Here, Spirit escapes our warring ability to set one against another, one category over another, like spirit and matter; or one kind of being against another, like humanity and all living beings; or even God and the world against one another, as in a bodiless divinity and a bodily creation. Instead, like the Stoics, developers of the art of living in ancient Greece, we may find an enlightened insight in thinking of the Spirit (*pneuma*) not as opposed to matter but as the *essence* of matter. Perhaps, then, *matter is the substance that in its essence is spirit.* Then the whole universe, in all of its expressions and through the plethora of its beings, becomes spiritual at heart. Matter, as Karl Rahner (more on him in the next section) has reasoned so imaginatively, is but "frozen spirit"—not of a different kind (than spirit), but of a different temperature, mood, mode, grade of movement and heat. It is in such a transgression of categories that we may learn to become ever more at home in this universe of impermanent and always multifarious movements of life, of becoming and perishing, without fear of this, its *oceanic* character. This does not mean that we cannot express or seek the deathless in the perishing or the eternal in the temporal; but we will, concordant with the movements of the ocean, have learned that this also means to seek the temporal in the eternal and the unique worth of the finite moments of becoming in a sea of death. In fact, this might be the essence of "oceanic feelings": not the feeling of mere dissolution in an undifferentiated One, but the loss of fear of the unpredictable and uncontrollable connectivity of all existents in their mutual instigation of forms and moods and surges of life *as* the One, the One of which we now know ourselves to be part.

It is all the more a profound insight, then, when several traditions of religious history—specifically, in the mystical modes of those traditions—even refer to the divine Ocean as that of which the world is nothing but its play of waves. In the Hindu tradition, Paramahansa Yogananda's prayer-song to Ishvara, the ultimate personality of God in the form of Krishna, which is of the universal and universally shared nature of Spirit-*brahman*, expresses this transgression between divinity and humanity with the supplication "I am the bubble, make me the sea." Christianity has known of mystical union with God in the image of the ocean since at least Evagrius Ponticus (d. 399 CE) and has, throughout the complex relationship it exhibits to the tensions between biblical and doctrinal expressions of the divine-human nature of Christ, on occasion made the same advance: that we are all of the *nature* of the Logos who becomes human to make us divine (*theosis*)—in the tradition of Duns Scotus (d. 1308 CE); that our soul is the place where the Logos is born, in which birth we reach beyond the difference between God and the world into the Godhead, the ground (*grunt*) of both God and soul beyond such differentiations—as in the work of Meister Eckhart. And the diverse religious traditions have found their own radical formulations for this thought: that everything is a vibration of the emanation of the Tree of Life with its ten emanations (*sephirot*) from the undifferentiated divine unity (*Ein Sof*)—as in Jewish Kabbalah; that the whole creation is the emanation from the original light that God created, in the form of the Self of the Prophet Muhammad, the Muhammadan light (*nur Muhammadiyah*)—as in the Islamic tradition of Ibn 'Arabi; that we are all waves of the one ocean that is the primordial Manifestation of God (*mazhar-i-illahi*)—as in the Baháʾí tradition; that we all are of the same Buddha-nature (*tathagatagarbha*) as the Buddha (*tathagata*).

This transgression between the ocean and the waves of its surface or even the substance of its body is only poorly understood if it is feared as a form of "pantheism," as a simple "identification" of God or ultimate Reality and the world. Not even "monistic" versions of unity proposed, for instance, by many of the Indian schools of thought, such as Advaita Vedanta, are ever that simple. Its more subtle thought pattern that arises as the basis for such unitary formulations is nondual (*advaita*). The difference lies in principle in the intention: monism might seek some identity or identification, for instance, by claiming that God and the world share the same material substance or metaphysical essence. Contrarily, a nondual view tries to avoid *any* identification. Instead, it would make any approximation of categories dependent on the insight that categorizations *always* fall short because of their inherent complexity, which expresses itself often by way of oppositions: either this or that. The message, then, is not that the ocean and its waves are identical in substance or essence but that the divine Ocean is beyond any category that we could use as a means of identifying or differentiating it from its waves. But even in its simpler form such a "unitarian" thought would not dare simply to identify the whole Ocean with *any* of its waves: what about all other waves; what about its depth; what about its global movements far beyond the ability of any of its local waves, and so on? And finally, one should not forget that the non-difference of the ocean from its waves is irreversible to the extent that it is the activity of the ocean, not the wave. In this sense, even a seemingly monistic formulation upholds the transcendence of the ocean over its waves, of God over creation, without, however, implying a "distance," which would be more fitting to any anthropomorphic sovereignty of power-greedy kings and Machiavellian princes.

The spiritual seekers, in this mode of awakening to the Spirit-ocean, will be drawn to the complexity of life and beauty that begins to stream through them. As they realize their vibration as or with ever-greater unison emanating from within this divine Ocean, they experience both the empowering and humbling power of the oceanic pluripotential transgressions at once. They will, if they are honest, find themselves on a journey in the midst of a multitude of infinities and infinite boundaries in which every spiritual move brings life and death, nourishment and starvation, purification and pollution, swimming and drowning. They know that they will only "be" this Ocean if they "disappear" as a particle and become a wave, that is, acknowledge that they have ever been a wave of the divine Ocean—that they are the waves through which the Ocean flows.

Horizon

At sea, look up in any direction: sky encircles the view! Whether day or night, with the sun, the moon and the stars, or without them in complete darkness, whether in calm or fierce weather, cast in clouds pregnant with rain or haunted by lightning—the horizon always fills with anything but itself. The horizon is always seemingly *untouched* by what appears on its empty scroll. At sea, especially if there is nothing else to hinder its completeness, nothing that disturbs its self-similar vastness in any direction, the horizon is the limit to nowhere, a limit without limitation. It is everywhere, but is nothing itself. It is like a boundary to the waters below or the stars above, as intuitive imagination taught humanity over millennia; but it is nothing the like: it is really *infinite space* in the form of a *formless surrounding*. It appears to us like a protective cover of blue and black, or shades of gray; but it is nothing the like: it is mere *unimaginable openness to an infinite universe* that encircles the globe. It only *seems* like a protective sheet, because it is "filled" with a thin, fragile layer of air that allows us to breath and stay alive while we are really in deep space.

Horizon—it does not impose anything, as everything is allowed to happen in it. It does not force even its own recognition, as all that happens can ignore it. It is a sign of existence: *the letting-be of becoming*. Always coming-to-be within it, nothing is compelled to follow any direction or course. However, survival at sea depends on the recognition of the potential directions it provides. It imposes itself only as far as we admit it. It is in this sense *the image of transcendence*, of the movement of letting-be within itself, but always escaping any grasp. It is this infinite space beyond the sea that, as horizon, provides us with the insight into *consciousness*—consciousness of itself and of the horizon as being that in which we are conscious of ourselves and reality. *In the image of the horizon, God appears as infinite Spirit of and beyond any embodiment within it.* Perhaps no one more than Karl Rahner, in one of his great theological insights, rare in the twentieth century, has fused four characteristics of the spiritual image of the horizon more intensely: the difference between consciousness and reality; God as open horizon; freedom as dialectic of concrete universality; and true pantheism. Let me touch on all four of them.

With the image of the horizon we can, as a perennial question about spiritual reality, or reality as such, ask, Is reality "itself" without *our* consciousness of it? Is our consciousness that which registers *or* creates reality? Is reality perhaps that which is in its very essence consciousness, or is our consciousness that in which anything that appears can be named and unnamed as real? These are age-old questions central to both the western doubt about reality or even its atheism, and the eastern, especially Buddhist, search for ultimate salvation in "the deathless" beyond the turns of perpetual becoming and perishing. Both views are dependent on the presumed *indifference* between consciousness and reality—as the most sophisticated position one can take regarding these matters. Both react against the dualistic differentiation of both, as if they were different worlds or built one upon the other like an asymmetric enclosure by which reality includes consciousness, or vice versa. In the first case, one assumes a (bottom-up) material evolution that produces consciousness; in the second case, one spiritualizes this process and, conversely, understands reality to appear (top-down) from consciousness. Against this mutually "reconstructive" dualism, we find the western mind seeking *either* to secure a basis for the human mind and its consciousness by ultimately identifying consciousness as a divine reality, as in the two "modern" philosophies of the consciousness-tilted dualism of René Descartes (d. 1650) or the pantheistic monism of Baruch Spinoza (d. 1677), *or* to prove this identity to be the illusion of a mindless reality (there is no mind or consciousness), as in the atheistic and scientific materialisms of the last few centuries—especially guided by simplified "objective" perceptivity of physical facts organized by astronomy, classical physics, the so-called Newtonian universe of mechanisms, the clock, the steam engine and the Industrial Revolution. The eastern mind, conversely, *identifies* ultimate reality with consciousness, either as that consciousness that is beyond the duality between reality and limited consciousness, as in many forms of Hindu and Buddhist philosophy, or as consciousness in which "reality" only appears as an illusion of spontaneous dreams of this consciousness taken seriously, by which "reality" becomes an illusion of formless consciousness, as in the "mind only" school of Yogacara, but especially in later Buddhist schools of Dzogchen and Atiyoga, the Tibetan forms of the search for the "original mind" behind all phenomenal reality.

The German philosopher of the "Copernican turn" to a philosophy of the mind pattern "generating" reality, Immanuel Kant (d. 1804), tried to avoid both the simple dualism as well as these forms of reductive or expansive monisms or nondualisms by differentiating between transcendental consciousness and transcendent reality. What this means is that we can understand things in our consciousness by the *form* this consciousness applies to the phenomenal world—this is *transcendental* knowledge of "epistemology," of *how* we know and by what patterns we know reality. But this also implies that we cannot know reality *itself*, in itself, which always transcends the ability of consciousness to experience independently from the forms by which it is restricted to experience. Think of a unicolor glass though which you only see grey; now imagine that this is not due to glasses but the fact that your eyes are color-blind; now imagine that you cannot know how it would be to see without eyes. The implication is, for Kant, that we cannot know God or any spiritual or *metaphysical* reality, as they are *transcendent*, that is, such "realities" cannot be captured by our transcendental consciousness; they remain unknown if we don't want to naively project our phantasms onto reality.

Karl Rahner takes this insight a step further by *nondually uniting both* transcendental consciousness and transcendent reality in transcending the limitations of Kant's differentiation. He accepts the transcendental consciousness of Kant as an *immediate space* of knowing anything, but expands it in the sense that it is really an immediate experience *of* the infinite movement of the mind *beyond all categories*. Therefore, mind is able to perceive and understand *any* reality, *any* form. Mind is in this sense *formless* or, better, of the "form of God," that is, an *infinite* movement beyond any limited object of knowledge in its horizon. This is so because this transcendental consciousness is moved and, thereby, created *by* the transcendent infinity of reality *itself*, which is God, and which signifies God as the movement of the infinitely consciousness-opening

Reality itself. Transcendental consciousness and transcendent reality now are *one*, but not identical; they are different, but *one movement*.

What does that mean? God is the movement of the infinite horizon in which consciousness of reality is itself an infinity of allowing any object of experience and knowledge to arise and disappear. Our Self, if we seek to concentrate on our consciousness, is like the retreating *horizon* encompassing the open sea. But while it sees everything in itself as limited in its infinity, it is self-limited in understanding the infinity of the space beyond the globe or the sea that is actually the horizon that from its own limited perspective still seems to be a "boundary." God is the *boundless boundary* in which we are conscious of anything and everything, because we are beyond any boundary, but experience this beyond *as* a boundary. The Spirit not only hovers over the sea but is *this* infinite horizon in which it appears itself open and infinite.

Rahner's second image regarding the horizon of the sea has already been mentioned: that God's being in *relation* to the world is rather like this horizon. In fact, God is *the* horizon of everything. God exhibits the characteristics of this horizon: it is infinity; it moves as infinite retreat to let anything be in itself; although it cannot be touched, this horizon is constitutive of what exists in it; the closer you seem to come to the horizon, the farther away it seems—at least we seem not to come any closer to it, although it is always the horizon of our very movement in any direction we choose. This is God's transcendence. But it relates even more the character of God's immanence. God is not infinitely far away but the *immediate* horizon in which anything can come to be; because of the infinity of the horizon, its boundlessness, any boundary appears *in* it. Its immediacy is what has been called "panentheism"—that the All is in God. While this being "in" God can mean different things to different people, in the meaning as the horizon of existence, it includes everything such that nothing *is* God, but *in* God has the potential to arise and becomes *itself*—or would not exist at all. It is an expression of freedom and openness that does not fit any interventionalist view of a petty God that controls and regulates everything and is concerned with the micromanagement of everything. This small view of God is really nothing but an exchange of the transcendent horizon with a merely transcendental pattern, but one that has rigid boundaries and dead structures at its heart, not the Spirit of *life* with its infinite patience of the God of the infinite horizon that encourages infinite possibilities and variability of directions, as well as creates by creatively letting be.

It was the enormously impactful German philosopher of relativity and the arrival of postmodernity, Friedrich Nietzsche (d. 1900), who made an argument for the overcoming of this petty God. He understood ordinary religion, represented (in his Eurocentric reductionism and superiority pyramid) by Christianity, as robbing human infinity of its vitality by projecting it onto a transcendent God who controls all "becoming" by "being," by having a certain law-like form of essence that all in existence must fulfill or end up vanishing in retribution or annihilation. Instead, by giving up these limited categories, he found himself in an infinite world without any controlling "transcendent object." Like Kant, Nietzsche saw such religious connotations as a confusion of transcendental consciousness with transcendent reality, projecting our limitations onto God, but declaring them divine. The interest behind such a move, however, is in no way innocent. Rather, it is based on the power of the masters over slaves, as oppression and regulation of humanity by elites that justify their power over them by such a limited object "God" that represents the power characteristics they employ for their plots and trials. As Nietzsche does away with such limitations, he finds himself (again) where humanity with its infinite consciousness should be: in an *infinite* horizon. He celebrates this revolution with the image of the freedom of a *journey through the open sea*.

Nietzsche's antireligious temperament is matched by Rahner's transformation of the infinite transcendent horizon of human transcendental consciousness into the infinite reality that it is and from which it is: *God* as this infinite movement of such a horizon of opening freedom and consciousness—not any limited, projected, possessive and oppressive "object." Freedom is, now, not one in which nothing can be said of this future—something that in its frightening openness led Nietzsche to seek an anchor in an "eternal return," the present state of things as inevitable potency of existence. Rather, Rahner understands the potentials of this infinite horizon of the human mind as based on self-less love, namely, of the self-communication of this God-horizon in itself. As movement of self-less love, it can give itself without reserve, without ulterior motives, and in such a giving *becomes immanent in its own horizon* in any (by it limited, but also infinitely opened) consciousness, at its heart, as revelation of Spirit in the midst and at the center of all becoming and existence.

This *freedom* is the third element. It draws on the second, namely, that in such a self-less self-communication of transcendence into its own immanence, divine reality is less like any order of being, but rather like "nothing," empty of self and of formless inclusion, like the "sea" itself. The freedom that such a self-less nothingness or emptiness of itself opens is one of liberation *to* one Self, but also of the insight that one's Self *is* of the same selflessness as that of the horizon's movement of retreat and letting-be. Our Self is being bounded only by such an infinite horizon, but also being aware of one's Self's *boundedness* within such an infinite horizon. That is, we are aware that we do not create our Self, but are already born into its infinity as bounded by it, as finite in penetrating its infinity. Like the infinite of the cosmos beyond the earth that appears as blue horizon but is really without boundary, we cannot expect to have traveled the infinite beyond in which we awake. Our freedom is *concrete*, however, that is, it is *limited*, as the horizon of finite decisions, actualizations, movements and directions never forces them, but also never suggests them. Like the steering of a ship on the open sea, we never leave the sea *into* the horizon, but its retreat and making-space remains the condition for any of our limited but undetermined movements.

We are reminded of Martin Heidegger's "riddle" that being and nothingness "is" the same; that this is freedom; and that it also liberates us to the selflessness of the

Self. He makes the observation that we are living in such a horizon of consciousness that appears to us as a unified world in which we become conscious of things. Yet instead of differentiating between such *objects* of perception and consciousness and us as *subjects* of such perceptions and consciousness, we experience our "existence" as being beyond these categories, as being open to Being (*Sein*). We *ex-sist*, we stand out into an openness that is without form and definition, and in its infinity empty—nothingness. This experience is the reason that we always also experience our finality, our eventual death, as threat (*Sein zum Tod*). Yet in a wider Whiteheadian context, the fear of such an experience of open-ended ex-sistence *also* includes that we may have lost the immediacy of meaning that we may assume animals have, as they do not show this fear of death; that we mistake everything else besides our Selves, as "objects" of manipulation, function and power, as if they were not open to Being, and us, in light of this inanimate world, as isolated subjects.

To some, philosophers or not, this freedom seems to be absurd—as the French "existentialist" thinkers Albert Camus (d. 1960) and Jean-Paul Sartre (d. 1980) assumed: that the price of this freedom is utter meaninglessness not just of our own human existence in this world, but of the existence of a world as such. But for others, like the Buddha, this experience of freedom is rather a sign of our opportunity in this present moment of freedom to gain an insight into the limitations that bind us to the categories of subjects and objects, of desires of clinging to the oppositions by which we make this world not a bit more meaningful. And for thinkers like Whitehead, this freedom must even transgress the anthropocentric limitations that the "humanism" of Heidegger still upholds, by setting it in its cosmic context: that all beings are open to being and nothingness, emptiness, and relationality in maybe different modes and degrees, but nevertheless, profoundly. The infinite horizon is the *unbounding* freedom in *all* beings, not only humans. It is "incarnate" in all beings and works, as for Teilhard de Chardin, from the inside out, as the very Spirit of freedom. It is the Spirit that *ex*-sists at the heart of *all* beings—in the epigraph of William James—as a connected "mother-sea" without beyond. Always transgressing any boundaries of disconnection, it escalates the *immanent* movement of a *transcending* that flows *from the inside out* rather than from any external reality pressing itself on anything.

Karl Rahner adds, however, this element by insisting that this selflessness or emptiness of the infinite horizon in which we become Self is itself a sign of *love*, and not of the irrelevance of existence or mere meaninglessness. This love makes the horizon a sign of the *Spirit*. While Spirit is infused in any direction such freedom may take, for better or worse, the Spirit always seeks the direction that recognizes its freedom *as* love, as creative freedom of offering life to its most intense realization: that of selflessness, as the gift of letting-be, harboring life rather than death, opening horizons of novel existence rather than limiting them.

The fourth element in Rahner's envisioning of the horizon follows from the third: a completely transformed understanding of the divine *nature* of the Spirit. Like the

Spirit-ocean, the Spirit-horizon *transgresses all categories of opposition*. It even ventures beyond our simple differentiation between God and the world, or, conversely, our simple identification of them! Not that this means that their "relation" is more complicated. It is rather much more *simple*: simpler than both simple differentiation or identification! While the infinite horizon is itself not a boundary, as the gaze into the sky may insinuate, it is *as such*, as infinite, still a boundary. Think of it: the horizon *has no* boundary, but that is what is the essence of its *being* a boundary! It is in this sense that Rahner ventures the extraordinary claim that God and the world are *not two* beings or realms, as if they were "objects" that we envision or project in our minds: like two apples, a world-apple and a God-apple, or an apple and an orange. But if they are not just objects in the mind of subjects, are they then beyond subjects and objects *identical*? No, says Rahner, with the long-standing mystical tradition not only of Christianity: they are *not* the same, but also *not different*! *God is*—beyond subject and object, mind and matter, and beyond God and the world, really beyond *all* categories of difference and identity—*the difference from anything itself*! Like the infinite horizon, God is not different *from* anything in the horizon, but the difference *itself* in which anything "is" as limited being different from anything else and identical with itself. God is the "unbounded boundary" in which anything is bounded, but the boundary is itself nothing but infinite beyond-ness itself.

In this sense, there is no difference between ocean and horizon either. Spirit-ocean and Spirit-horizon are not different, but not identical either. Beyond these images, however, if we imagine the essence of God as infinite ocean, the ocean itself *becomes* the horizon *in which* anything can exist—as it was captured in the ancient mystical image of all existents as sea-creature bathed in, and surrounded by, the vast life-giving ocean. It is neither identical with God nor different from it. God-spirit is beyond all of these oppositional categories. God cannot be captured in our differentiating and oppositional categorizations by which our mind always makes the imagined an object of itself. Hence, God is not about theism or atheism—this is, as the German-American theologian Dorothee Sölle (d. 2003) so clearly states, a wrong alternative or ultimately irrelevant antagonistic opposition. And also: God is not about theism or pantheism, as this also presupposes the same antagonism. In a sense, we can say that pan-*en*-theism comes closer to the insight Rahner wants to convey: that God as infinite ocean is that "nothingness" from which anything is different without being outside of it, as it is the infinite horizon in which all existence is made possible and can become actual.

Of course, not forgetting the "existentialist" impression of infinite freedom, but also following the flow of love through the veins of its emptiness, we should ask: If we leave the substantialization and objectification of God in theism and venture toward panentheism, are we not still supposing a relationship of "being in" like objects in the mind or monsters in the ocean or stars in the night sky? Would not a pantheism of identity be more adequate and honest—a pantheism that may express itself as atheism or as reverence for the universe as an integrated whole of relationality without any beyond: no God-object inside or outside? And shouldn't we, then, not expand this movement even further in a direction that can only open up if we did, in fact, face the *loss* of any difference that any concept of God as different from the world would be able to make? Only then, if we accept this "collapse," I suppose, are we able to understand the move *beyond* pantheism as the move that does not remain in the illusions of theism and pantheism: that although God is not an object different from anything, God is not identical with anything either, but *who or that from which everything is different because God is not different from it*. Since *this* "in," here, is not one of the oppositions of immanence and transcendence, or that of container and contained, I prefer to name the *avoidance* of "identity" and "difference" alike trans-identity (and trans-difference), and this "panentheism," hence, *trans-pantheism* (see ch. 6). This trans-pantheism is beyond categories of alienation, opposition, and antagonism. It is a hint for the Spirit-seeker not to desire *any* image to "represent" the Spirit, but in the *multiplicity* of images to find the adventure of infinite ways to address its mystery.

Multiplicity is our last spiritual sign in this section on horizons. The night sky opens our view to a sheer unimaginable assortment of heavenly bodies, stars and planets, comets and asteroids, galaxies and other strange objects. If we think of the world as the earth and of unenumerable worlds beyond, or even as a cosmos and of inexhaustibly many universes beyond—what are we in this sheer expanse? Think of God in relation to such an expanse, such an interstellar vastness, such an unending proliferation of universes (see ch. 8)! How can we in a multiverse think of God in the same way as some of our ancestors who might have believed that the world ends with the ocean and who presumed that above the "horizon" water is bounding the world? No small God will fit anymore. The Spirit seeker will eventually come to the insight that in such a multiverse only these three criteria may justify trust in a divine ground or a divine friend: that we are not the center of attention; that there are higher goods than our existence; and that whatever is important about us and maybe our earth, existence is not about petty issues of morality for which we think God will end this world in an apocalypse in the demand for justice. What, then, may be *worth* the divine attention of humanity on this anonymous planet somewhere in the side arm of a nameless galaxy in a star cluster in which this galaxy is not of particular greatness, in a sector of the universe that is not more or less significant in any way than any other, and maybe in a universe that is just one of indefinitely many without special characteristics?

Rationality may demand a "principle of mediocrity": that we live in a universe or on a planet that is not exceptional in any way because the probability that it is otherwise is always smaller than the medial position on a scale. Conversely, that we live in a universe and on a planet that allows for life may in fact be *exceptional*. We may be a rare breed in the universe or in a rare universe of all universes, most of them hostile to the development of life. Yet in any case, if this universe has a *spiritual* ground permeating nature or a purposeful drive toward the realization of spiritual virtues and consciousness, are we not, nevertheless, to assume that we are not here to follow any little book of laws rather than become ever more an expression of this precious expanse with all of its freedom and greatness? The Spirit seeker should not be the last one to recognize the importance of this insight for the way of life of a being that has been granted even to entertain such insights. On the contrary, this should be the "prime directive" of that being in which, despite all odds, the Spirit can break through and break (us) free. Are we not responsible, then, for performing this breakthrough if we realize that only the long, arduous and precious evolution of life and mind in a multiverse has given us our position of opportunity in it? And what kind of God would it be who or that we may seek or even worship in such a universe? Would it not be a God who or that values or is the motive force of the realization of the values of universal ecological awareness of connectivity and responsibility? And would it not be a God who or that becomes a "friend"—as in Persian mysticism—precisely and only when we value such breakthroughs with sym-pathy to the spirit-nature of all things?

Mariner

We know what it means to be "in between" something: to be between times, past and future; between individual and collective; between Self and Other; between generations and cultures. We are travelers without a fixed map. The images of the ocean and the horizon symbolize this being-in-between even more intensely: between two infinities, we can only survive if we do not get lost in either of them. We can always drown from storms that blur these boundaries between above and below; we cannot dive or fly away either, as we will soon run out of air in both directions. We are bound to stay right in between, as on a ship or bark, navigating the in-between, free only along one of its dimensions, but without boundary of our direction. We are the mariners who travel the waters and must trust the weather and the stars. This is the place over which the Spirit hums. Or it is the place in which the Spirit arouses life like death: storm and rain and waves and dark clouds that remind us of the fragility of this existence in between.

The French novelist and aviator Antoine de Saint-Exupéry (d. 1944) is supposed to have said that when you seek to build a ship, the first thing you must do is not to cut wood and collect nails and the like, but to awaken the longing for the infinite sea in the builders and travelers. In his book *The Wisdom of the Sands* (1948), the first thing he wants us to do if we want to travel the sea is to develop a taste for, or maybe to get a taste of, the ocean in which all contradiction resolves into a community of light. Such is the trust of the mariner.

We know the biblical stories of trust related to ships: the trust in full fishnets (Luke 5:1–11; John 21:1–14); the trust in calming the winds (Matthew 8:23–27; Mark 4:35–41; Luke 8:22–25); the trust even to walk on water (Matthew 14:22–33). We also know of the sign of Jonah (Matthew 12:38–42), the whale, the resistance to prophecy (the book of Jonah), and the identification of symbols of water with death (Genesis 6:9—9:17; Revelation 21:1) and life (Isaiah 12:3; 1 Corinthians 12:13; 1 Peter 3:21). Sailing the sea, we are exposed to death, its water that cannot be drunk, and we will drown if we cannot sail to safe harbors. The ocean is not a place to dwell. It is dangerous and empty like the desert—while it hides its own fullness of life we live from and the life we cannot reach, alien life, so different from ours that we may question our own existence in light of its beauty and strangeness. Sailing across the sea is like challenging death; arriving in a haven is like escaping sure death, like rebirth. There is no place for us to live at sea; even pirates need islands on which to rest. And yet, we know it is the womb of life—a life it gave away and to which we cannot return. We are expelled from it and yet cannot escape it.

Can we be mariners sailing the sea of God?

The great Plato, at times, employed these immortal images, allegories, and metaphors that shed light on such a question: the question of whether Spirit can be "navigated." One of them features fire (*Republic*, 514a–520a), the other water (*Republic*, 488a–489d). In the former, we—humanity—sit shackled in a symbolic cave with our back to a fire and see only shadows of movements in the light it projects on the wall in front of us: the total distortion of perception of reality that we "think" is real. Philosophy, in Plato's understanding, and maybe spirituality in a profound synergy, indicates the process of liberation from such illusions, and the dissociation of reality from illusion, by turning toward the fire—who cannot associate the *metanoia* (turning around and beyond the limited mind) of the message of Jesus here (Mark 1:15)?—and realizing it for what it is, an *artificial construct* of petty light in a cinema of deception. Plato was *not* a *relativist* in the sense of the rival Sophists of his time, such as Protagoras (d. ca. 411 BCE), but he was a *deconstructionist* of perception. In this realization, the cave becomes a cave and loses the status of being identified with the world. Walking out of the cave, we discover the *true light of the sun* (see ch. 1). But beware—its fire blinds the onlooker! We must safeguard ourselves against its intensity. What is the sun here? It is *the Good*, the *idea* of the Good, that which is *beyond any form, shape or limitation*, the *true light* that exudes itself, that is, emanates reality free of interest and deception (*Republic*, 507b–509c; 508e2–3).

The other metaphor is that of a ship at sea. It is a problematic image, not "politically correct" in terms of the current understanding of the status of liberal democracy, since it imagines democracy as a failure. Why? Because, says Plato, if every sailor on the ship contributes to the decision of where to go, how to steer and how to navigate, then what will result is chaos and poor decision-making. Deception and all forms of mutual manipulation will reign, the navigator's authority will be degraded to that of an idle stargazer, and the captain become a mere nuisance. With this allegory, Plato wants to instill in his readers the necessity of a unifying agency in the decision-making process—a state needs a navigator who knows the stars and a captain who can decide when to set the sails and where to steer the ship. The commander is the philosopher-king; the necessary expertise is nothing but the intellect of the light of the Good. Minus the last conclusion, one is reminded of Capitan Kirk of *Star Trek*: the decision-maker.

I add a third Platonic allegory, that of the charioteer, that is, the *soul* that holds the reins of the harnessed team of horses, the body (*Phaedrus*, 246a–254e). In fact, this triad of sun, chariot and ship might just be part of the old Near Eastern, Egyptian and Greek mythological heritage of Platonic tales, in which we find the sun cast in the image of a divine chariot and of a bark that travels "the sea of the heavens." So, then, the following picture arises. Whether in collective or individual contexts, regarding the unity of one human being, that is, what is called its soul, or the unity of the state, that is, what is the intellect of the philosopher-king, we gain an interesting picture of spiritual perception and effort. It is only the *true mystic* that should lead, navigate, and direct the world of activity. The mystic is the one that has seen the sun, the Good, and knows how to navigate the sea.

So, who is this "perfect mariner"? The perfect mariner is the mystic that not only *knows* the uncontrollable, dangerous, immense and uninhabitable beast that is the sea, but also *how to survive* on it. Note: the mariner is as expelled from the sea and as exposed to the forces between sea and horizon, and as veiled from the infinite horizon, as anyone. The assumption is that the horizon gives with the sun and the stars the instruments of survival, but not the insight into the nature of the ocean. The mystic passes through the divine ocean, but neither the sun nor the stars *are* the divine ocean. Despite all knowledge of truth and goodness, and despite all the skills in making the heavenly movements a map for decision-making, the mariner will remain exposed to the unpredictable forces between sky and sea, weather and waves, to the point that it is not the mystical insight that becomes decisive in the journey through the Spirit-ocean but the insight in the absolute contingency of all features and skills and insights, and the experience with the necessary ingredients of the spiritual journey.

Leviathan never sleeps! It is only God who can sport with the monster. The divine ocean is the monster. The divine substance cannot be sailed! It is uncontrollable, unpredictable and unknowable. This is the insight the Spirit seeker will ultimately find to be not the end of a journey but the new beginning of a different journey: one of fragility and uncertainty, of skillful unknowing of any security, of losing the illusion that the sun and the stars will save one from the moods of the sea.

In a different setting, the Polish author Stanisław Lem (d. 2006) has given us a metaphor that, perhaps better than Plato's allegories, demonstrates my point here. In the novel *Solaris* (1961), Lem transports the reader into an alternative cosmos in which humanity has found a planet, Solaris, "who or that" is its own enigmatic life-form. It encompasses the whole planet as an ocean of a psychophysical "substance" without any form, or of infinitely many forms, appearing and disappearing without fixed patterns and in sheer creative rejuvenation beyond any intellectual restraints. All means of study employed to understand Solaris fail; they only fill new volumes of research publications and encyclopedic reports. And human attempts to contact Solaris lead only to reflective images of deep secrets and desires suppressed in the minds of the expeditioners. In Solaris's world, humanity becomes caught in its own illusions, its wishful thinking and unresolved conflicts. Yet "it" also grants immortality, a life beyond this world *in* its own universe or mind-ocean. In a strange sense, Solaris grants wishes of innocence and love, while it remains itself utterly alien to any methods of understanding and to approaches other than with the touch of pure contingency, pure surrender and acquiescence.

This is the journey of the mystic, as the mariner exposed to the sea: like one on a raft tossed by the forces of fate, to surrender to its face, its depths, its waves and storms, its clouds and thunder, burning sun and meaningless stars. The wisdom of the mariner is the knowledge of navigation *and* the release of Self from navigation. No, you cannot navigate the Spirit! You can only be *exposed* to it in moments of defenselessness. To be spiritual in this sense, approaching or touching the divine ocean, is to become anaphylactic, that is, extremely sensitive to this divine substance, but simultaneously avoiding the shock. It is in this tension of life and death, exposed to the elementary *dynamis* of the *pneuma* (Acts 1:8), that we may sail the Spirit-ocean.

Epilogue and *Meditation III*: Dying Sea, Dying Spirit

The Sargasso Sea is an area in which the rotation of the currents of the Atlantic Ocean create a gyre that houses the *Sargassum* weed. It is often calm and presents the onlooker with a blue sea—or, in the language of children's book author Ruth Heller (d. 2004), "a sea within a sea"—and a mystery of its own. The weed is a gigantic organism floating, rotating, and full of sealife seeking rest in their migrations across the expanse of the Atlantic waters. Yet it is human existence, although absent from this habitat, that has polluted and endangered the life cycles of this extraordinary environment. Because of the proliferation and waste of plastic, the Sargasso Sea now shows the wound of human litter: it is in the process of being transformed into the North Atlantic garbage patch. Though plastic-devouring bacteria have been found to nourish themselves from this "plastification" of nature, are they helping to restore the organism, or are they just messengers of a worldwide distribution of its prophetic message of doom?

If there was a meditation on this double layer of the patience of nature and the seemingly "gentle," slow-motion violence of the lack of sustainability, it would perhaps be this "auditory vision":

> *Imagine, you drift in the Sargasso Sea with eyes closed . . .*
> *The sea lies calm.*
> > *You feel the* Sargassum *beneath your body,*
> > *both slowly vibrating in sync . . .*
> > *Listen!*

> . . .
>
> *You only hear the sound of the ripples voicelessly clapping against the seagrass . . .*
>
> . . .
>
> *Imagine, you drift in the Sargasso Sea with eyes closed . . .*
>
> *The sea lies calm . . .*
>
>> *You feel the soft touch of plastic bottles against your body,*
>>
>> *both slowly vibrating in sync . . .*
>>
>> *Listen!*
>
> . . .
>
> *You only hear the sound of the bottles voicelessly clapping against each other . . .*

Although I would love to lose myself in the imaginations of the "nature" of the ocean, it would be dishonest. It would be to deny that no spiritual search today can avoid taking into account our inability to become gentle sustainers of our earth. In fact, wherever you look you will find pollution, poisons, litter, the unsustainable wounding of waters, lands, woods, rainforests, rivers, air, and even the space around our planet. What is even more disturbing is the *hopelessness* with which we must recognize that we all are part of a worldwide system of destruction that we sustain, even those of us who want to escape it. The only sustainability, it seems, is that of perpetual destruction! And nature is patient! "Gaia"—the earth-organism (see the preamble)—seems to plan its vengeance with prophetic signs and culmination points, of punctuations, of sudden shifts of its own equilibrium of patience. We all know it. And still, we all seem to live in the grip of the Borg: resistance is futile!

> *Imagine, you drift on the divine Sea, blinded by its splendor . . .*
>
> *The Ocean of God lies calm.*
>
>> *You feel the infinity of the divine substance around your spirit-body,*
>>
>> *both feverishly shivering out of sync . . .*
>>
>> *Listen!*
>
> . . .
>
> *You hear only the sighs of mourning of the wounds of ignorance and wasting voicelessly clapping against each other . . .*

Spiritual maturity would demand our action, but also our insight—and our compassion with nature. But more than anything, I think, it would need the recovery of the *beauty* of that which we are in the process of destroying. And one definition of "humanism" would be: perpetual destruction. This perpetual perishing is not, as it is in nature, life cycles of impermanence, but instead cycles of death. Death upon death instead of light upon light! Rather, the perpetuation of this human process is the use of our creativity to erase the roots of our creativity. Humanism is division instead of diversity, opposition instead of variation, antagonism instead of cooperation, the Darwinian struggle of mutual death instead of the Heraclitan fire of mutual support of life (see ch. 1). So, how to be "spirited" in such a claustrophobic down-spiral into the ninth sphere of Dante's hell? How to avoid its freezing point, Dante's devil? Perhaps it is the insight that you cannot kill the Spirit; that the divine Ocean cannot be crossed, but will always alienate all alienation by its monstrosity of alterity. And isn't that its beauty, the beauty of the Spirit and the beauty of the Spirit-body of nature, of the profound depth of the sea and of the infinite horizon of the heavenly bodies beyond? That we cannot make them part of our petty interests; that any wasting of their splendor is to them nothing but a transformation that will devour all traces of poisonous coagulation.

I see this shift of perspective in the answer that Sir David Attenborough (b. 1926) gave when he was confronted with the criticism that his presentation of nature in its extraordinary beauty—as narrator of the TV series *Blue Planet* (2001), *Planet Earth* (2006), and *Our Planet* (2019)—never left the impression of a wasteland of human destruction. He insisted that instead of doom and gloom, or at least a greater emphasis on the ecological catastrophe that leaves its ugly marks everywhere we look, it will be the fascination with and interest in the beauty of life on our planet earth that will motivate us to support change and facilitate transformation. Preaching doom only has the effect of desensitizing us to the horror, of hindering our ability to perceive, of blinding us and making us look away, change channels and discourse, and disappear into our small worlds, the bubbles that sustain the perpetual destruction. Spirit motivates by attraction.

There is another aspect to this "humanism" of destruction: while it may be true that the fruit of the Spirit is love (Galatians 5:22), humanity concerned with itself suffers from the inability to extend compassion beyond the smallest perspective of interest and love. We love our own life; we may love another person; we may love our family (at least partly); we may love our ideologies and possessions—but we rarely love the world, the planet, the selfless, the holy, the unattractive, the excluded, the oppressed, the liberated, the other, the alien. In an interview, the Slovenian philosopher Slavoj Žižek (b. 1949) once characterized "love" as ugly, as it only divides, selects, prefers and hence destroys. A. N. Whitehead avoided "naming" ultimate reality with "love" for a similar reason: love always seeks the smaller interests; he chose instead "harmony of harmonies" as a less dividing and more integrating metaphor. This is the "humanism" that draws its boundaries around human beings over against nature, especially animals, and that can become the decisive ideological factor in divisive outbreaks of xenophobia, racism, sexism, classism, ethnocentrism and ecophobia.

It was in this context that the French philosopher Jacques Derrida (d. 2004) wrote his book *Of Spirit* (1987), on Martin Heidegger, who, in avoiding "spirit" in his philosophical terminology but in reclaiming "the Spirit" as a "history of Being," had fallen prey to racism and justification of the Shoah. The "humanism" behind these complex movements of avoidance and acclamation is one of the limitation of the openness of Being (*Sein*) to humanity (*Dasein*) over against nature, and the closedness of the *community* of being (*Mitsein*) to the evolutionary history of the Spirit that selectively and specifically issues in the peak of the cultural axis between ancient Greece (the origins of philosophy for Heidegger) and (Nazi) Germany (the fulfillment of the Spirit). It is in this sense that "Spirit" has been misused to justify genocide and the technological instrumentalization of humanity and nature in the interest of the elites that are the true representation of the equation that Being is Nothingness—the Nietzschean identity of creativity and nihilism in a "will to power" of the chosen ones. This has, of course, a long history: the history of religious superiority of Christianity over all other religions, and especially Judaism, the "murderous pack" that brought the seat of the Holy Spirit, Jesus Christ, to the cross (Matthew 27:25). The evolutionary superiority connects the expectation of a realm of the Spirit in the visionary projection of the future of humanity by Joachim of Fiore (d. 1202) with the philosophy of the Spirit (*Geist*) of G. W. F. Hegel (d. 1831), who rationalized the consummation of the history of the Spirit (*Geist*) in himself and the German people. Yet while Joachim's Spirit was a new age of liberation from oppressive orders and the downfall of religious authority (as legitimation of state structures) and church structures, Hegel's vision was more like Plato's philosopher-kingdom: a "state" of fulfillment; a state beyond history; the State as the end of history and total dictatorship of the "Spirit"—Hitler called it "providence."

The question then is, Can we avoid using "Spirit" to justify racism and biologism, fascism and elitist thinking? Can Spirit be or again become an expression of universality *beyond* humanism, seeking a *posthumanism*, without denying the human impulse of Spirit-seeking? How can the Spirit seeker denounce the misuse of the terminology after the Shoah and the lost innocence of any spiritual language? Can the insight in the universal community of the ecological and cosmic Spirit-body save us from the humanism of division and superiority? Can the images of the Spirit-ocean and Spirit-horizon avoid any "fall" into the ignorance of the necessary division between the affirmation of the Good and the annihilation of evil? Note: this is the opposite move from the biblical allegory of the Tree of Good and Evil (Genesis 2)! "In the Spirit," as this figure of speech and thought has lost its innocence, we cannot avoid any longer, or ever again, to differentiate between good and evil. The non-difference beyond all categories that the Spirit-ocean and Spirit-horizon intimate *must not* become equivalent to a moral disinterest in such a differentiation. With Whitehead, we could say that this indifference would be nothing but anesthesia, loss of consciousness, loss of sensitivity, loss of compassion. Compassion, that which Whitehead called the sympathy of *feeling the feelings in others* and the ability to discern the best, most intense and most harmonious possibilities in these feelings in order to give them the greatest aesthetic future—this *alone* is the Spirit, the spirituality of the mature Spirit-seeker.

We must never lose the ability, sensitivity, and insight to differentiate between the Sargasso Sea and the plastic poisoning that befalls it in the name of humanism. The Spirit appears only when human self-interest vanishes.

Meditation IV: The Raft; Vanishing

For Teilhard de Chardin, matter and spirit are not substances or opposing kinds of beings but *directions* in all things: the direction downward toward darkness and sheer multiplicity, the material direction, and the direction upward into the light of unity, the spiritual direction. These are also the directions of science and religion in the human mind, and the directions toward disintegration or death and integration or life. Yet the more we become unified, for Teilhard, the more we also differentiate or complexify, become mind and light, become spiritual. Spiritualization is the movement of "creation" (whether human or not) toward the creative transformation of the whole cosmos. In this divine movement, all simple multiplicity reaches a point of freedom in which its spiritual inside becomes the externality of all being, the spiritual body of life and freedom, difference, and unification. This whole evolutionary process is made possible by the divine plunging into the ocean of matter (the aspect of sheer multiplicity), by becoming its inherent evolutionary motor, the *Christus evolutor*, who, for this reason, must absorb the ocean of suffering that this vast evolution of the cosmos toward the Omega Point, the point of no return, of critical cosmic transformation, takes (see ch. 1). From the ocean of suffering to the ocean of light; from the ocean of simple manyness of blind unconsciousness to the ocean of a complex community of conscious and awakened freedom (see ch. 9).

In order to find the Spirit inside matter, inside the body—which, for Teilhard, is the *divine body*, harboring the "Spirit of fire" in the "spirit of the earth"—we must also trust its movements as being inherently spiritual, though uncontrollable and on occasion, in our perception, monstrous. Yet as they are part of the Christ-movement of Spirit-liberation, they cannot be our enemy. They are rather our companions, as we are not (identical with or possessors of) our Selves, but the ocean that surges in us. We must listen to this ocean. Like the Dao, we must let it flow through us, unobstructed, unobstructing.

>   *Open your eyes and find yourself on a raft—on the open sea . . .*

>   *. . .*

>   *It is morning . . .*

The sun is just over the calm waters, leaving a trace of glitter bursting toward your raft . . .

Indulge in the reflections of the light—points, circles, lines, interfering, converging, jumping here and there . . .

. . .

The day goes by. Night . . .

. . .

Dark.

Water slapping the raft; wind whispering through the wood, swaying . . .

No stars. No land. No birds . . .

. . .

Another day . . .

No land. No direction.

Slapping. Whispering. Swaying . . .

. . .

Another night . . .

. . .

No change. Only change . . .

. . .

Don't think: Where am I? Will I be found? How can I make myself noticeable? I am just a speck on the fast fields of water . . .

Don't feel: I am thirsty! I am hungry! I am wet! The sun burns! No shade . . .

Detach from yourself. From your place and time! . . .

Fly! . . .

. . .

Look down on your raft in the middle of nowhere . . .

Speed up the sun: sunrise, sundown, day, night . . .

Look down: No change; only change . . .

Blink. Look down . . .

Where is the raft? Where am I? . . .

All sea . . .

Day and night . . . waves . . . traceless . . .

3

A Finger in the River

Heraclitus, I believe, says that all things pass and nothing stays, and comparing existing things to the flow of a river, he says you could not step twice into the same river.

—PLATO, *CRATYLUS*, 402A

No thinker thinks twice; and, to put the matter more generally, no subject experiences twice.

—A. N. WHITEHEAD, *PROCESS AND REALITY*, 29

Many a casual reader has concluded from the simile of the raft simply that the Dhamma is to be let go. In fact, one major Mahayana text—the Diamond Sutra—interprets the raft simile as meaning that one has to let go of the raft in order to cross the river. However, the simile of the water-snake makes the point that the Dhamma has to be grasped; the trick lies in grasping it properly. When this point is then applied to the raft simile, the implication is clear: One has to hold onto the raft properly in order to cross the river. Only when one has reached the safety of the further shore can one let go.

—THANISSARO BHIKKHU, ON THE RAFT PARABLE
OF THE *ALAGADDUPAMA SUTTA*

But if it is by the finger of God that I cast out the demons, then the kingdom of God has come to you.

—LUKE 11:20 NRSV

Flow

STREAMS AND RIVERS ARE inextricably linked to human expectations for and hopes of life. Other than the salty ocean, the river is the water of life for the thirsty. Names of grand streams immediately trigger memories of the birth and sphere of civilizations, but also adventures, exportations, expeditions, remote mysteries, remote lands and religious imaginations. The Nile, the Amazon, and the Indus; the Yangzi, the Danube, and the Mississippi; the Niger, the Volga, and the Mekong; the Orinoco, the Euphrates, and the Colorado; the Loire, the Dnieper, and the Tigris; the Río de la Plata, the Seine, and the Shatt al-Arab; the Rhine, the Congo, and the Yukon; the Thames, the Rio Grande, and the Jordan; the Ganges and the Zambezi. Rivers are nothing but personalities in the native cultures and primordial religions of the world. Rivers figure in creation myths and define continental landscapes, they restrain and release, become borders and waterways. Yet, in any case, if you make your way through any land and you reach a river, the first thing rivers impress on you is—they flow.

Rivers are themselves elemental, nonhuman states of meditation. Rather than inviting any further instructions, the flow of a river is itself enough to transport any onlooker into its essential movement of flux. Quietly drawn into the great stream, majestically passing our spot, or dragging us into its loud screaming, surfing impassable rapids or crashing over resistant rock formations and, pulled by gravity, plunging to the depths—we are being excused from our little selves, invited or dragged into taking leave of our lives and problems. Literally and symbolically, this flowing mass of water draws one's consciousness beyond itself into *its* Self as the true state of consciousness beyond any limitation of mind, beyond any categorization and conceptual framework. It is as if it just catches us and shares its own heart of existence: flowing—the most elementary expression of nature, life, awareness, and sentience. It whispers without sound—indeed, it practices right before our eyes—that life is an everlasting movement and the relentless churning of momentous inexorability. In *its* view, it convinces us of a nontrivial truth: not just that everything flows, but that to flow *on* is to flow *by*; that the power of flowing is the flux of *impermanence*; that the flow of impermanence is *all* there is.

No surprise, really, that this open secret of the life of flowing waters has found words of profound wisdom with its friend and prophet, Heraclitus, who deeply felt that the nature of this world reveals itself in its *becoming*: that there is no being that is not in becoming; that Being is not nothingness, but neither is it its opposite. The only truth is Becoming. With the "logos-fire" and the "bow-life," the "river-flow" belongs to the rarified images that Heraclitus uses to make us understand that the world we live in is not just an illusion of something else but, in its core, exactly what we experience: movement is more fundamental than any static images, concepts or constructs; wherever you may look for ultimate truth and reality, you will find this flow of reality to be already there, already being the river at or on which all other things, concepts, insights and wisdoms are only guests, floating, transforming, traveling, passing.

Other than Plato, who, if you consult the related epigraph of the dialogue *Cratylus* (402a), well knew of Heraclitus' insight, we should not seek any permanent reality beyond this flow. Rather than "more real," such "higher reality," Plato's realm of permanent forms of being of which any specific being is just an object of execution, is really only an abstraction from the flow of becoming. No permanent reality is more real than the flow itself, which is permanent as movement. Eternity is movement, as is time. Plato's tremendous (influential) eternalist understanding of this flow as the moving image *of* (from) eternity (by which passing actualities are variations of eternal ideas) can be reversed into a Heraclitan axiom of flux without changing anything: now, becoming *is* the flow of images *of* (which) eternity (consists) (eternal ideas are constituted by the flow of actualities). Nietzsche found another, more technical than poetical image for its demonstration: "being" is just a dam that holds the waters of becoming back. That which is *real* is the river of things flowing. The dam is only an *obstacle*, a kind of futile resistance against the energy of the flow.

The question is, Why do we think that Being is more profound than Becoming? Why should eternity be more attractive than the flow of time? Why is permanency more desirable than change? The honest seeker after truth will answer: It is the fear of death! It is the messiness of concrete happenings! It is the horror of perishing! It is the uncontrollability of encounters in space and time! It is the dismay of loss and the dread of impermanence!

How many theories, philosophies, religions, and prophecies have sought to act on this fear and in seeking the self-abstraction from becoming have hoped to find salvation in "arrested" states: states of heaven, of nothingness, of being, of eternity, of rest, of constancy and permanency? How many crimes have been committed and justified in the name of such religious, psychological, social, political or cultural permanence? How many deceivers of humanity have looked to convince their followers of the promises of such permanent states of perfection? How many religious adherents would give everything not to taste impermanence anymore, because it seems to overwhelm us with pain and suffering, loss and moaning? But what about the urge for renewal, rebirth, resurrection, life from death, growth from the death of a grain, novelty and creativity? What state would *that* be that has lost these vivifications of what we feel life is about?

Spiritual consciousness might just "be" this insight: *that it flows*. Rather than being swept away by time, perhaps *Spirit is the offering of a time of becoming*. Consciousness itself may be this *flow that connects* and, alive in the flow, has permanence in this flux of becoming across the hiatus of things flowing through it. Something like this was the great insight of the American philosopher of consciousness and experience, William James, from his book *The Principles of Psychology* (1890) onward: that deep awareness is a duration of presence in which a present moment moves into another interruption, like a "stream of consciousness." This insight is matched by that of his admirer A. N. Whitehead, referred to in the epigraph, that no thought can be repeated and that no thinker thinks twice "the same"—that, in fact, no experience can be repeated, but that every experience (and related conscious state) is always a new, emergent moment of this flow of thought and consciousness.

Where *creativity* is at work, not just in artistic expressions but in nature—are we not persuaded to transform (or be transformed by) our perception and conscious registration of the flow of things so as to recognize them as somehow so wondrous that no explanation whatever, whoever gives it, will do justice to its relentless power? I will come back to some of the implications of this transforming and transformed perception and awareness in the next section. But what I want to highlight here is that such an insight of the ultimacy of the flow of things has profound spiritual flavors not to be missed: If this flow cannot be reconstructed by something else, then *some kind of vividness must penetrate all (notions of) permanency; eternity cannot be devoid of flow* either. In fact, if flow is ultimate, could we not say that there is nothing more ultimate than this flow: that *becoming is ultimate*; that *creativity is ultimate*; that it cannot disappear into a Platonic heaven? What is more, even Plato, who became famous for the heaven of archetypes that do not change, in his later works became wary of this problem and discovered a different view: namely, that even Ideas, archetypes, are rather like *living* beings. Consequently, some Platonic mystical philosophers began to compare them with angels. And then there are the universal, transreligious images of the rivers of paradise, the waters of life, the images of pure flow in heaven as on Earth—how could we ever miss that they indicate eternity as divine and mundane conviviality instead of "unmoving" and "unmoved" permanence?

If this flow is infinite: is God flowing, too?

There are several profound approximations to this thought in the diverse religious and philosophical traditions of human imagination. Of course, there is the Infinite Sea of the previous chapter: the sea of God, the oceans of divine substance or essence, the waves of *brahman*, the primordial sea of the book of Genesis. But the idea of "flow" is directly expressed in the Platonic coincidence of mystical and ethical, philosophical and cosmological, theological and pedagogical thought: the Idea of the Good. The Good is good because it cannot hold back its goodness to *overflow*, naturally, without ever losing anything that rushes downward from it or that, through this flow, begins to exist and is tolerated in its existence because of the patience of this flow to allow it, even if it cannot live up to this flow. For Plato, the overflow of the Good is its *nature*, to the extent that it cannot ever be grasped except *in* the flow of things that it allows to come into existence: the ideas, the living beings, the world-soul, the living cosmos, the souls and living beings in it, the sentient nature of all material beings. The flow of the Good means that there is nothing beyond this flow. It is ultimate.

From this flow, the profound medieval religious thinker, poet and mystic Meister Eckhart (ca. 1260–ca. 1328) imagined the divine essence to be a *boiling sea that boils* over (*ebullitio*), creating the world from its overflowing energy of creativity. In a deep sense, God is not changeless beyond flow, overflow, emanation, creative exertion, but beyond this flow to ever change. A. N. Whitehead has called this ultimate flow *Creativity* and has understood God to be the *characterization* of this flow by the Good, the values and attributes the realization of which would be creative of ever new forms of goodness and worth. Rather than timeless and changeless, Whitehead understood God to consist of a twofold movement of life: *everlasting*, that is, perceptive of all change in the flow of things, and *eternal*, that is, always offering the most beautiful and valuable, intense and harmonious potentials (which are independent of their actualization in the Mind of God) for the realization of anything that *becomes* in the infinite cosmic flow. In this sense God *becomes*, but does not change.

God touches change. God is the finger in the river.

If God's overflow (or, we might say, God's revelation) is as infinite as the creative process that it expresses, then another implication becomes available: namely, that *the flow of revelation never ends, as it has never begun* in time either. Doesn't that mean that no religion can claim to be either the first or the last? Doesn't this mean that all religions may only be viewed as events in the process of this flow, a flow of infinite spiritual becoming that might have phases, layers, velocities, areas, spheres, and other forms of differentiation, but that never ends in any final fulfillment? No claim of finality and superiority will *not* be swept away by the cosmic flow: the end of a religion, the end of an era and area, the end of a world, of a cosmos, is *never* the end of the process itself, the process of the creative overflow of the Good. Religions are moments of the river of rebirth. The flow of rivers mirrors that of the earth and the moon around the sun, and of the seasons throughout the year.

But the river of life can "overflow." It can flood the land. In this sense, we might not always be able to *bear* the revelation of the divine flow. Religious adherents might drown in the flowing, overflowing, flooding of revelation beyond their "dams of being," of alleged finality and superiority. But their particular rivers, creeks or ditches may run dry, while the water remains flowing in other channels. This is hard to accept. One may sit at the dry bed of a particular river and pray for water, while the next river carries these life-giving waters. What to do? No predictability can stabilize the becoming and disappearing of phenomena of creativity, be they religions or cultures, worlds or cosmic epochs. Creativity remains alive, seemingly arbitrary, but rather what we could call, with Daoism, *spontaneous*.

ΧΑΩΣ

Spontaneity cannot be taught; yet, we can learn to detect the spontaneous flow of things. Spontaneity indicates a flow. But not from point A to point B. It is not a substance that is on the move through space-time. Even the flow of a river is not such a substantial movement. Rather, we detect the flow of spontaneity as arising on its own, without effort, at any moment as *event* of arising. The flow of the river is *that*: not a moving substance but a production of energy from one event to another, from moment to moment and from spot to spot, arising and disappearing, revolving in this process so as to give us the impression of a substance that flows. In fact, in spontaneous flows, nothing flows; everything just arises and disappears. Like the waves of the sea, which are not movements of particles from one place to another but transfers of energy from one spot to the next, so the river of things flows from nonexistence into existence and back. While doing so, the river moves on an energy of transfer, yet nothing, "no thing," is transferred.

The Chinese philosopher Wang Ch'ung (d. ca. 100 CE) says of spontaneity: it appears in that which arises without work or effort. It is *reality* arising if we do not work against it. It is nonaction (*wu wei*), a central Daoist and Confucian philosophical term, in which spontaneity operates naturally (*ziran*)—or, as translated by western transmitters of this wisdom, such as Alan Watts (d. 1973): it is self-so. And for Wang Ch'ung, of the triad of plateaus of existence—namely, heaven, earth, and humanity—it is *heaven* that operates spontaneously because it has no desires, no needs that create the urge to act. Its offerings are free from desires and urges, and hence truly spontaneous. This energy of heaven, this Spirit-energy, flows through us or releases its energy (*qi*) if we let go of all urges and desires. It is a different kind of freedom if we reach the point of spontaneous "letting go," and "being for," and "flowing with." Pure pro-existence, it seems, has left us with nothing but an embedding into the universal flow of fields of energy and value, virtually directing nothing but that which *wants* to arise in any situation given its locality in the space in which it forms from everything else everywhere else. This is the freedom of emptiness, and emptiness that generates everything in its due place and time and importance.

With Nietzsche, and in the understanding of Deleuze, this is *the power of becoming one's own potential*; but a potential that is not possessed or isolated or administered or confronted in clashes of mutual movements of expansion. If it were, it would become antagonism, not freedom; oppression, not liberation—and (unfortunately) some have understood or misused Nietzsche in this way. Rather, we are talking about a "power" that can *receive* its own becoming in the universe of which it is a local expression, a spatiotemporal moment of the whole movement—at least that is an understanding arising with Whitehead's event-processes as fields of mutually interpenetrating and coinhering movements. And if we could "hear" it, this universal spontaneous process would intone the sounds of the Dao.

Like the image of the flowing river—if we take it to be an expression of ultimate reality and of the spiritual nature of our existence—the spontaneous movement of arising and disappearing may create in us anxiety: the fear of impermanence; the urge for security and permanence; the hope for an end to all suffering that is always (if not outright evil) related back to a world in becoming. What should we think of a world the "ground" of which is really nothing but the spontaneous arising of existence from nonexistence at any moment and the folding back into disappearance in any event, but, thereby, unfolding an energetic flow of expansion and contraction, propagation and resonance, oscillation and recurrence, spanning a world or universe?

You must give up all grasping reflexes to hear the Dao! The sound of the Dao oscillates in the resonances of everything in every moment of movement. It is hard to do, and yet so easy: If I say that this means "not doing anything except floating with the flow of things," or "surfing its waves" and "riding" its purposeless direction—I don't want to invoke the simplification of a substantial movement of "everything flows," but, again, that of *momentariness*, of spontaneous arising and perishing in every moment. Its direction is clear, exceedingly clear: If I say, "it runs down," I mean to say its resonances always close in onto the vanishing point of arising and disappearing, toward the deepest point, humble, just being where we try to avoid "to be" or dwell, because we will only find *Becoming* there. The *Dao De Jing* knew it as the path to the purposeless liberation of the Way (the Dao): It is the flow to the lowest point of service; it means being, in humbleness, with the lowest of the low, the excluded, the ones that can only be conceptualized as the Others, outside any scheme of being, status or importance; resurging in the truly important ones, the ones that have nothing to lose or gain, but *are* the flow, the flux of emptiness, we empty ourselves in nothing less than the grand place of gathering: the ocean of God. These are the waters over which the Spirit hovers and which, therefore, have a "face"—a face that forms in the face of nothing but the divine; a face of emptiness and fullness; a face that is not possessed anymore of desires and urges.

What is the Dao? The wisdom of the flow! The river, the sea, the sewer.

The Dao is not a thing or an image; it does, in fact, not even exist. It indicates that which "is" when we take everything else away; and that is the empty space in between, that which lets things be by being spacious. Although it has been understood as ultimate reality, it rather appears as the *web of things* themselves: there is nothing beyond all that is, and what is, is in permanent becoming. The Dao is the Way itself, the river itself, the rhythm of becoming and perishing, the revolution of the up and down, the weak and strong, the scream and the whisper. Its weak *yin* relents and gives way; its striving *yang* wants to create and build a world. The insight it releases to the spirit seeker is twofold: one impression must be that there is really nothing to gain, to seek, to find, to have, to be, that is not already *latently there*; that the unity of the world in all of its unfathomable diversity is already the *basis* for its movements and flows apart and together. And the other impression should always be that no state can be established even for a moment that does not have in itself already its decay, and its movement beyond itself or even into its opposite. Self-transcendence! Do not fight it! Do not flee it! Do not ignore it! Do not force it! Let it become!

The Dao is not the Logos of the Stoics or the Gospel of John. It is not "order"; it is pure *life*. So, the Dao may appear to us as mere *chaos*—spontaneity, in a sense, always is. We fear becoming; we fear chaos. Many do. It seems to be the opposite of any positive achievement, even worse than emptiness or nothingness. Chaos is a state, it seems, of the pure lack of any meaning, order, form or purpose. In a way, it is all that: meaningless, unordered, formless and purposeless. However, we should rather say that this chaos is an *activity*: liberating from any limited meaning (like freeing us from a cage); "unordering" that which freezes and stabilizes "order" to oppression or boredom; "unforming" any fixed and irreformable idea and ideal; "reversing" all energies and structural patterns into their limits of mutual otherness; "transcending" any purpose if it has been transmuted into a mere function, the functions we fulfill in social environments or the expectations of our character or the shapes of our identities.

We mistrust chaos for the same reasons that we abandon the groundlessness of any flow: it seems to unsettle our urge for eternity, immortality, established meaning and identity, success, final achievement. Like the Dao, chaos does not allow for these emotions to be seen as more than emotions, or as abstract concepts that will shatter in the surf of the waves and the always changing cover of the river of life. Bahá'u'lláh even poetically relates the power of the overwhelming, unsettling *revelation* of divine reality with the image of a flow that rushes over everything like a mighty, surging stream. Divine presence is like death: no one can see God and live, says the Torah (Exodus 33:20). God's presence is like the "angel of death": you will drown in the river, as you will not be able to withstand its onrush. Either you will experience death and resurrection, dying and return, *fana* and *baqa*, as the Sufis say: dying to the self and living in the eternity of God; or you will be swept away, unreformed, drowning with dismay, bewilderment, and without gaining understanding.

Revelation is such a chaos, the chaos that disturbs all settlements, and fixed riverbeds, and the dams of Being that we build to hold back Becoming and change or to try to control and contain them within our limited directions of that which we think is bearable and thinkable. But no! It is the *unthinkable*, always; and it is the *unbearable*, the *beyond*. It is, in fact, *the Alpha and the Omega* of all happenings and processes, organizations and universal patterns. If God *is* the Alpha and the Omega, as another revelation claims (Revelation 1:8, 21:6; 22:13), *the* Beginning and *the* End—literally and semiotically the first and last letters of the Greek alphabet, of language, of the possibility of articulation—it is *the* Word beyond which there is only silence. Yet its boundaries transcend "the Word" and indicate the origin and dissolution of Becoming itself, the becoming-becoming, the whole of the cycle of becoming. The "boundary" that the A and Ω of becoming indicates or symbolizes is itself *boundless ultimate spontaneity*: ΧΑΩΣ. I have "chaotically" changed the original Greek for "chaos" from ΧΑΟΣ (using the omicron) to ΧΑΩΣ (using the omega) for this reason: to indicate that the boundary of becoming is the essence of its origin and end; that its ground is its spontaneity; that its divine immanence is the transience of that which is beyond simple order; that it is the unity of novelty and order, of patterns and events, of the groundless joy of becoming and the fathomless pit of dissolution; that it symbolizes the chaotic "sun" shining over good and evil (Matthew 5:45), the Good that rushes out over everything—the Good the nature of which the ancient ones have seen in its rushing outward, its unnarratable flow, its gracious diffusion: *bonum diffusivum sui*.

The Jewish Prayer of Manasseh envisions the creation process not as a process of invention or division through the divine Word, but rather as a process of *limitation* of infinitely *chaotic powers*, as symbolized by the primordial ocean of Genesis 1:2. It envisions the inexpressible Name of God, the Tetragrammaton, as the *seal* of the primordial chaos. Even in this sense, we could say that the understanding of God as the Alpha and the Omega not only conveys the nature of divinity as that of the enclosure of creative chaos, but also, as in the book of Revelation, makes this chaos part of the divine Name itself. Note that the A and Ω are letters of the inexpressible Name of God in Greek rendering, such as IAΩ (YHWH). Here, the Name of God is the boundary of XAΩS.

Chaos is not necessarily merely chaotic. It is rather a *metastable boundary between repetition and difference*: that which cannot and will not be repeated and that which drives toward or desires repetition or affirmation. Several theories have accreted around the "chaotic" movements by which these negations and affirmations are bound together. In the chaos of chaos and complexity theory—a mathematical-physical theory of the "classical" sort, that is, not infused with quantum freedoms—spontaneity only arises for grand numbers and stochastic spaces that we cannot compute but that seem in principle to be computational. But if we add the quantum mechanical factor, namely, the field-theoretical probability space of happenings that is covered *at once* in every event (nonlocal), not one after the other (nontemporal), not one against another (noncausal); and if we understand the "breakdown" of the wave function (the superposition of these potentials) as the actual happening out of this spooky space of possible and probable distribution, following a certain historical trajectory out of this probability space and "erasing," as it were, all other potential histories (or banning them into "another" universe)—then *spontaneity becomes indiscernible from divine intervention, that is, creative attraction to the realization of divine values.*

What I mean is this: Divine activity was on occasion "demonstrated" as if it were operating in and on a "classical" universe devoid of relativity and quantum patterns. Take the idea of God's "finger": Jesus driving out demons with "God's finger" (Luke 11:20). This "act" is like Michelangelo's fresco *The Creation of Adam*: the finger of God, touching humanity, releases life. It is a symbol of the creative Spirit released to awaken to life, granting the breath of life (from *nasham*, "to breathe") to the dust of the earth (*adamah*) to become "living dust" (*adam*), a living being (*nephesh*; Genesis 2:7) or, perhaps, spirit-earth. This life is (released and bound by) the breathing of the divine Spirit (Job 27:3; 33:4). Or, in the case of "deathless life," Jesus becomes the archetype of the theopoetic "life-creating Spirit" (*pneuma zoopoioun*) beyond the "living soul" of the spirit-dust of humanity (1 Corinthians 15:45). So, the "finger of God" that heals the poison of death is but the Spirit of life (Matthew 12:28). It is this Spirit, which is the divine Wisdom (Wisdom 9:17; Proverbs 8:15–16), that is the divine map (Proverbs 8:22–31) or, we may say, the Spirit-space in which creation is not only created but *creative*; and that is the creator herself (Wisdom 7:22; Sirach 24:4–6).

In the "classical" macrocosmic world of rivers and riverbanks, if we stick a finger in the flow of water, it will create disturbances, turbulences, rotations, and counterflows—subject to chaotic movements and fluctuations. *Divine* intervention figures as *chaotic* intervention, of creating life in the flow of death. In the context of the microcosmic *quantum* world, however, such turbulences are questions of realizations of matter and energy in which *the Spirit of life appears as spontaneous constellations of novelty and creativity*. In fact, if one believes that there is any interaction between mind and brain or consciousness and body with no reduction of mind to matter, as current empirical research unmistakably has established and as was quantum-theoretically explored by, for instance, the renowned physicists John von Neumann (d. 1957) and Henry Stapp (b. 1928), then it would be of the same kind: it looks like a *natural* process in which spontaneity (of material quantum action) *cannot be differentiated* from acts of will (of the nonmaterial mind) and, hence, may seem "mindless" while they are not devoid of the teleology of mind, consciousness, will and soul. How, then, do we expect *God* not to act "naturally"—but without the need to reduce the happenings to "naturalistic" (mindless, godless) activities of mere chance?

The ancient Fathers of nascent Christianity used to characterize the Beyond of becoming, *its* divine boundary, not only as that which transcends birth and death but also as a kingdom of life, which can only be named as being/becoming *without origin*. The God of this "kingdom" appears, as does it, in the chaotic-poetic image of the postmodern theologian of phenomenology John Caputo (b. 1940), as *an-arché*, the anarchical Spirit; the divine kingdom is pure anarchy. The Spirit of life, the living God (Deuteronomy 5:26; Daniel 6:20; Matthew 16:16; 2 Corinthians 3:3), the God of the living (Mark 12:27)—is this the "king" of a kingdom, or the horizon of a sphere of life, that is not about law and order but about creativity? Is *that* the kingdom or sphere "to come," to be realized in the heavens as on Earth (Matthew 6:10)? Is it the marriage of spirit and matter (not that they were ever apart)? Is it the coinherence of becoming and being, chaos and cosmos, a *chaosmos*? Is it the *translucency* of micro- and macrocosms, an interfusion of classical and quantum reality with one another and with the creative Spirit that expresses itself through this unison? Is it the "finger of God" in the flow of the river, creative of the births of the multiverse and of the permanent transitioning of the chaosmos?

The Heraclitan flow of things reminds us of the vastness of the birth and death of universes in an undying *multiverse*—be it of the quantum kind of differentiation of universes in any actualization (breakdown of the wave function), fulfilling all possibilities of the probability space in another parallel universe (as in Hugh Everett's theory); be it through the birth and rebirth of ever new universes in a process of eternal inflation (as in Alexander Vilenkin's theory); be it just in the form of ever new causeless eruptions of a universe through the properties of the wave function (as in the Wheeler-deWitt equation); or be it in the ever new eruption of universes, like the bubbles of a bubble bath, within a cosmic landscape of ever new energy states (as in Leonard Susskind's theory). Or be it, as in A. N. Whitehead's philosophical cosmology, of the eternal becoming of events and nexuses of events, ever new organizations of organized environments birthing ever new universes as cosmic epochs in a deathless process, but living from the life and death of all of them (see ch. 9). We are left, again, with the question of the meaning of it all: If there is no final state and no beginning, but ever new realizations of potentials in an "eternal" flow of things, of becoming and perishing, of creativity and exhaustion—what is the meaning of this very constitution of the All as becoming, and what can be the meaning of human existence in such a vast process in which we seem to be nothing more than, or even much less than, a bubble in a bath? If there is a "finger of God" touching the flow, adding chaos to it, instead of order or a halt, creating eddies rather than berms, life rather than being—how does that make any difference? Is XAΩS (with the omega) really different from XAOS (with the omicron)? Is everlasting creativeness in the face of massive loss worth it? Where is the healing in this process?

Whitehead answers with a surprise: not only is *Creativity* (XAOS) touched by God as the mind in which all possibilities are *valued* according to the Good and Beauty, Intensity and Harmony, Mutual Immanence and Coinhabitation—that is, the *Alpha* of XAΩS rather than that of XAOS (although there is only one letter to tell us that they are not dualistically opposed or simply different from one another). What is more, the flow of things is touched by God in a more mysterious, indirect way, namely, by the *memory* of God by which the flow of things becomes the experience of God's life in which all in the All is related to everything according to the Good and Beauty, Intensity and Harmony, Mutual Immanence and Coinhabitation—that is, the *omega* of XAΩS rather than the omicron of XAOS. It is in this *flow of touch* between the creative river of the chaosmos (differentiation) and the cyclical rainbow of divine valuation and transformative memorial (repetition and affirmation) that meaning arises. This is *the touch of the divine Spirit* (finger) inhabiting the flow of things by which this flow is not meaningless, but (in another of Whitehead's great images) full of a future in which novelty does not need to imply loss.

Meditation V: Mind the Flow

In your mind: Sit down at a small stream in the woods high up in the mountains . . .
You have just climbed it in the shade of the trees . . .
The atmosphere full of the fragrances of the trees, flowers, and bushes . . .
Sounds of birds fill the background of deep silence . . .
. . .

You hear the murmuring of the stream as, in seeming idle slowness, it covers the rocks and moss of the bed.
Listen! . . .
. . .

Hold your finger in the flow . . .
    Lower your hand.
    Feel the fresh, cold body of the water running across your hand . . .
    Taste the life of the water in your hand . . .
. . .

In your mind: Stand at a grand river, vast and wide.
    A massive flow of water.
    The other bank almost too far away to discern its vegetation leaning toward the waters.
Observe . . .
. . .

You feel the desire to touch the water, to feel its power as it flows, unimpressed by your presence . . .
    Lower your hand into the flow . . .
    Feel the passage through your hand, unimpressed by your disturbance . . .
. . .

In your mind: You become a witness to the birth and death of universes . . .
    They flow in your presence . . .
Observe . . .
. . .

The Cosmic Spirit

Feel the awesome vastness of the millennia and unimaginable distances this flow covers at every moment as they flow, unreachable in their beginning or their end . . .

. . .

Where do they come from, where do they go?

. . .

Do you dare to touch the mighty stream of worlds upon worlds passing by?
Try! . . .

. . .

Now dive into it . . .

Passage

Rivers are symbols of survival and abundance: the annual flooding of the Nile, say, and the fecund land such overflowing creates or sustains. But survival can also become a matter of escaping the deadly power of the water's flow, the swelling of rivers after torrential rain, the floods that unsettle the banks, ignore the berms, move houses and human artifacts, and transform the surrounding landscape. Rivers not only present lively and deadly passages, but are used for rites of passage, like the baptism associated with the river Jordan or the annual submersion of millions of devout Hindus, naked ascetics, and curious tourists in the river Ganges. Rivers have become symbols for passages of *bridging*: symbols of physical, political, or spiritual crossings, like the Greatest Builder of Bridges, the *pontifex maximus*, the high priest of Roman religion and later the Christian pope of Rome. And rivers are passageways of goods and ideas, connecting vast areas and foreign cultures. Such "passings" have different directions: with the flow; against the flow (using eddies to travel up a river against the flow). Across the flow; avoiding the flow (using ships, ferries, or bridges). On the (surface of the) flow; into the flow (diving below the waters). Obtaining what flows in it; avoiding what flows in it (like fish and alligators).

The *cosmic passage of things* that these alternatives in the encounters with, or exposed vulnerabilities to, the powers of this flow symbolize exhibits all of these dimensions, too. Overflowing is the nature of existence, as nothing that is can be without being in relation to something else. So, it is the nature of the Good to overflow and of everything to be good, that is, of worth and of meaning. A symbolic river that just "stays" in its riverbed, unimpressed by the weather, thunderstorms, and rains in the mountains from which it originates, does not give to the land that is patient to its presence. Although philosophical positions were tried to think through the unrelatedness and passivity of things, such a disinterest in connections remains utterly self-occupied and unproductive of any good besides self-interest, making it irrelevant to anything. Not even Darwinian evolution can rely only on competition—but competition would at least be *some* relationship of things. Sure, an overflowing can be a flood. It may be dangerous and destructive, but it constitutes the passages of the becoming and passing of things: they become by giving themselves away, they pass by offering themselves. It is the same process.

And the flow of things lives from the *participation* in it of all things being *invited* into its flow. One must dive into, float on, or cross the stream in order to be alive. Becoming is not only an overflowing; it is even more so an invitation to the world to participate in it, in every one of its processes. The All constitutes all events entering it as a measure of patience of the All for this event to carry the universe along in its moment of existence, bringing together all of its forces and emotions, streams of desires and pollinations, to its own point of creative culmination, the mark it will leave on the process beyond itself in ever new processes. As we must overflow, the world always leaks into our lifeblood.

The flows of things are *passageways of life and death*. They convey to us what our lives through time reveal about our identity: even if we were a certain stream with a certain name and a defined environment that we could not just abandon without changing the surroundings, nevertheless we would not remain the same. We are a passage of becoming, and, through all of our changes, we still retain our identity as a *particular stream of life*. It is a gift to look at a river's flow and, at the same time, to see in a grand vision our life laid out in that way as a stream of experiences and events, situations and forces of flow, and to transcend in such a visualization the simple illusion of personal identity as some kind of thing or substance or fixed essence. Instead, if we *become* the flow we visualize (that which we always already *are*), contemplating the whole life we have lived and are in the process of living as such a stream, then we will also realize the deep implication of this grand passage: that *all* we are, are the *events* in which we *overflow*, stream on, and invite the world to become floating, swimming, surfing, diving into us. But we can also see that we thereby mirror the life and death not of ourselves alone but also those of all who or that "trust" to enter it. In a way, we become conscious of our life that lives without the possibility of halting, streaming away its life. What, in this image, can it mean to be persons? We come from wells or rain; and at the end of the stream, if you are lucky and do not percolate in the desert, is the ocean in which we disappear before we rain down again on a riverbed waiting to be filled with life.

The flow of things does not spare religion, too. *Religions are such streaming pathways of spiritual transformation. Spiritual paths are such rivers of life and death*. We can only be transformed if we let go and enter their stream, dive into them, indicating the death of self and resurrection to a new reality toward which they transport us. But we cannot follow such spiritual paths without being transported to *other* places. They are *streams of change* through space and time, cultural and historical relativities, and the relativities of their truth in relation to other such paths. Here, one of the deep meanings of the *transreligious nature of religious paths* becomes tangible: that no religious tradition or spiritual path can exist only in its own identity, as even such an identity is defined as a flow, a permanent change. No mind sharpened by the memory of history and an eye for the emerging processes of religious becoming can avoid arriving at this insight. Nothing stays the same "in itself," even if one path is different from another, like two rivers that are not the same.

Also, no path can exist without overflowing and inviting the world into its stream, thereby creating its identity in the first place. All religious paths are in such *constant and deep communication* with the world and the whole ecosystem of the religious, spiritual universe, as well as with all other "spirits" besides. And religions are passages in another sense: they are born and they die. They rain down like divine revelation or a gift of the universe, always giving birth to new life when the Spirit of life replenishes the cosmic landscapes in ever new springs of becoming. It is these landscapes that produce the different religious traditions and spiritual paths as passageways on their course to either grace the desert or the ocean, where they again disappear into the arid earth or the salty pool from which they will be returning as clouds, rain, and dew, feeding springs and vegetation.

No religious or spiritual path is "better" than the others, even if some of them are mighty like the Amazon, or fecund like the Nile, or holy like the Ganges, or known for religious events like the river Jordan. But why has the mountain brook less value—may it not be closer to the source, the spring, and responsible for mighty rivers to gather together? And there must always be many such streams flowing through a fecund landscape in order to water it or to drain it of its excess and in order to create the ocean from which they all begin as clouds and rain. And while large rivers may carry all the poisonous influences of their territory, of religious or human history, small creeks may be clear and refreshing, fragile but simply enlivening and healing. Eventually, the spiritual seeker, as she gains consciousness of the vast world beyond any limited environment, some kind of universal consciousness, will come to this insight: that the paths of religions and spiritual experiences are expressions of the cosmic Spirit of life that circulates through the processes of renewal symbolized and expressed by the cycle of water *transfiguring itself* between ocean, clouds, rain, springs, and rivers.

Rivers are *crossings and borders*. The Rubicon indicates a border that Caesar crossed; the river Danube was the border of the Roman Empire. The Missouri (with the Mississippi) stands for a continental crossing. On the one hand, the river divides and secures difference; on the other, it connects through vast (and vastly different), seemingly unconnected landscapes. In a symbolic sense, to be a spiritual being means this: to be a boundary, *creating difference* by just existing, flowing in between worlds— and to *connect* seemingly unconnected worlds. What I mean to say here is that we are not spiritual beings in a material world, that is, we do not exist on just one side of a divide. We have not just fallen into ignorance, or through sin or fate into a world of passing, which devours our desire to evolve or unfold and thus either quenches the spiritual light or, at least, leaves us with a bitter feeling in a valley of pain and suffering where we must undergo a divine test of our worthiness before we can abandon this uninviting place of passing shadows. Rather, we *are* the divide between worlds, material and spiritual—that is, we *connect* them by flowing between and by being the life that connects the two banks, overflows into them, invites them in, and does not fear the change that makes it a boundary.

And, like temporal tentacles, like flowing roots and shoots, branches and leaves, we span worlds far apart by being pathways of the unexpected and surprising ability to negotiate various landscapes: cosmic and spiritual, material and intellectual, scientific and religious, on Earth and beyond. We are not strangers in the universe but connectors and boundaries, frontiers and horizons, edges and fringes, creating, upholding, overflowing and differentiating worlds.

The Cosmic Spirit

The Jewish philosopher Philo of Alexandria (d. ca. 50 CE) understood the Logos or Wisdom of God as the *mediator* between God and the world. Like the curtain in the temple of Jerusalem between the temple space and the holy of holies, *the Logos represents the boundary between the material and spiritual worlds.* The Logos is the manifestation of the inaccessible Godhead and, at the same time, the spiritual gate of access to this Godhead. The Logos is neither the spiritual nor the material but the boundary that differentiates them and, at the same time, connects them. The Logos is the *veil* that hides and reveals God to the world, as the world is the *clothing* in which the Logos is immanently spiritual. In our context this means: the immanence of the cosmic Spirit is *not* one "in" matter, but "between" and "amidst" and "within" mind *and* matter (and the like dualities), pervading and differentiating the material and immaterial worlds. Flowing through all of them, the Spirit "is" none of them. And so are we "in between," the *interval between worlds.*

Passage is *death*. Personally, and universally, it is not easy to avoid the impression that the permanent change of the existential flow indicates death much more than life. We may see only the birth-to-death, one-way winding down of life—or, in the cosmic context, the transition from the Big Bang to the Big Crunch, a collapsing of the universe onto itself; or to a Big Freeze, the slow freezing death of the universe in an eternal expansion in which even black holes will slowly disappear until nothing will move anymore; or, even worse, to the Big Rip, the sudden "quartering" of the universe due to the accelerating velocity of cosmic expansion. We may see only the sudden death of religions (remaining as mere artifacts) or the long, painful disappearance of religious traditions as they become antiquated or fantastical in new cultural, social, empirical and scientific contexts that constantly redefine our worldviews. In the moments of drowning, we may not be able to grasp or envision the cyclical nature of these passages: rebirth; a new spring after winter; a new life after death; a new universe after its passing; a new religion; a new spiritual transmutation. In fact, what may help here is to remember the flow of the river of life: *in every event, at any moment, we become and disappear*, as these events leave themselves as a legacy to the next moment for a new life beyond them. We may become "persons" in the river of life *and*, "at the same time" (literally), in the timeless memory of the Spirit of the universe or God. And we may in some sense, the sense of a new river or a reborn river, issue again from the everlasting flow of this cosmic or divine memory.

A. N. Whitehead created this awesome image of such an everlasting flow in which time and eternity, passage and memory, creativity and relationality, immediacy and immortality are bound together as the flow that constitutes the life of God and the world: it is as a river between worlds, differentiating and connecting them. In this flow every event in its feeling of the whole world, by which it has come into its own, passes beyond its own becoming to an existence in new adventures of its character and values in new processes. But as it performs this passage, every event in the flow of all events that constitutes the universal process of the world becomes also a moment of the divine experience of its feelings, its joys and pains, shortcomings and achievements, isolation and relation, importance and irrelevance. And transformed into God's memory, *this transfiguring flow in its everlastingness of wisdom and compassion* changes everything to its widest possible relevance for the All, flows back into the world and informs the becoming of every new event and its potential to become a deeper impression of the divine image that it is.

It is hard, as this is a process of life and death, of a passage of becoming and letting go of one's Self, to see it this way: not as a loss, but as a *cycle of love* that floods both worlds, that of divine memory and cosmic creativeness, as the very Spirit of existence itself. But this might be the spiritual insight we are all striving toward.

There is a difference between *the two kinds of crossings* of rivers—bridges and ferries—that must not be confused. While both seem to achieve the same outcome, namely, reaching the other bank, they invoke vastly different spiritual responses. The *bridge* must be built; but when it is built, it becomes a permanent crossing, accessible by anyone reaching the shore. However, bridges don't lose the memory of their construction, as they remain exposed to the flow of the river that they *resist* in order to fulfill their function. They remain in danger of being flooded and torn apart by swollen waters. *Ferries*, conversely, never resist the flow but use it to cross its changing conditions. They are more clearly exposed to the dangers of crossing, and they may fail anytime, at every new attempt. But they counter their wager of survival with the ability to flow *with* the unexpected flux of its forces, only changing direction. In "bridging" flow and permanence, becoming and eternity, we may either search for stable pathways—but risk the movements of reality away from such temporary openings—or permanently wander through the streams, rapids, cataracts, and shallows to always seek out new approaches—but risk getting lost if we misjudge the territory.

The Chinvat or Sirat bridge is an ancient transreligious spiritual image of Zoroastrian, Islamic and Bahá'í provenience. While it appears in the scriptures of the Zoroastrian *Yasna* (ch. 71) and *Vendidad* (19:27–30), as well as the *Persian Bayán* of the Báb (Wahid 2, ch. 12), one of the prophet-founders of the Bahá'í faith, it is not Qur'anic, but has a place in certain Islamic prophetic traditions (*Sahih al-Bhukari*, vol. 9, bk. 93, #532). It symbolizes the human passage from this life into death and beyond. It indicates the pathway that crosses the river of death—similar, maybe, to the Greek river of forgetting and being forgotten, the Lethe. It indicates the judgment on the values we have created in our life processes and the pain we have caused others. For the virtuous, the crossing is wide and easy; for the doomed, however, it is as narrow and sharp as a knife's blade. Only the "virtuous" will cross into paradise; the "regulars" will get a few scratches but will reach the other side; the "losers," however, will fall into the river of fire. While the emphasis of this image is judgment, a reminder to live a virtuous life, in its background is another pattern of salvation: that of justice *and* mercy, of the law of act and response (karma) *and* that of forgiveness (grace)—two widely different concepts often juxtaposed in eastern and western soteriologies. While justice may define a "natural" outcome of our life stream as one that deserves to be obliviated in the river of fire or, at least, not too easily or too soon released from it, it is also the place of forgiveness and reconciliation.

The Báb indicates that the "bridge" is the *divine presence itself* in this and any other world, in the form of the historical *Manifestations* of God who or that are the "gates" of religious traditions—such as Abraham, Moses, Jesus, the Buddha, Muhammad, Zoroaster, Krishna, the Báb and Bahá'u'lláh—and their primordial "realities," such as Logos, Spirit, Mind, Word, *brahman, atman, purusha, dharmakaya, dao,* and the like. And it is they, their "Spirit," that may *save* every stream of life from its "just" end and transfigure it *in compassionate memory and creative wisdom* into a new life in the ongoing cycle of love.

The image of the ferry appears prominently in Buddhist scriptures. In the raft parable of the *Alagaddupama Sutta* (*Majjhima Nikāya* 22), it presents us with the river between the world of becoming, *samsara,* and the deathless beyond, *nirvana*. In the long history of the interpretation of both the images and the concepts related to the two banks and the river crossing, two primary interpretations have become prominent. In the older Theravada context, one interpretation highlights the fact that in order to pass through the river of *samsara,* with its suffering and karmic forces, one must hold on to the raft. The raft represents the doctrine, the Dharma, the Reality of cosmic becoming and of eternal liberation. It can also indicate that there are different kinds of rafts, and maybe different places of crossing over, meaning perhaps that not all paths are for all seekers at all times available or useful or the same. This is the doctrine of the skillful means (*upaya*): that the Buddha teaches liberation to every sentient being in the way unique to its situation in the samsaric flow of things. The American Theravada monk Thanissaro Bhikkhu (b. 1949), quoted in an epigraph to this chapter, follows this insight, at least in the sense that one *must not* abandon some kind of limited doctrine or understanding or practice or sphere of experience that, even if limited, is a means to helping us cross over to the unlimited Reality in which we find liberation from the samsaric suffering, so that we may not get lost on the stream of becoming between the shores.

The Mahayana interpretation of the Buddhist raft is guided by a profound insight, namely, that *no simple difference into dualities is carrying the connotation of salvation or liberation*. The liberating thought or practice, habit of mind and organization of life, would instead be to understand all differences as bound by opposition and to seek the overcoming of those oppositions beyond the differences on which they are based. With the second-century CE philosopher and sage Nagarjuna and the *Heart Sutra* (see ch. 1), this interpretation "sees through" the use of the raft as presupposing that there *are* actually two different banks; that there *is* actually a movement from one to the other; that there *is* a river that divides reality; and that we *must cross* this river to find salvation or liberation. None of it *is*! There is no raft. There is no river dividing the world into two realities, *samsara* and *nirvana*. There is only *one* Reality, and it is not different from the river itself. There is no crossing for liberation or salvation. All is *here*. All is, in the language of this book, *in* the cosmic Spirit or *in* the cosmos as spiritual reality. All passage *is* Reality. Reality *is* passage. Beyond it lies only an infinity of cycles of becoming. "Beyond" lies only *the river of the cycle of love* itself, incarnating itself in infinite processes and universes and lives, in the endless protuberating of the Sun of Reality. The passage is the passage is the passage.

Epilogue: Manaus

Rivers are an important ingredient of the harmonious imagination of Reality that we feel we have lost or we have not reached yet. In the symbols of a paradise, based on Persian gardens and Zoroastrian imaginations of *firdaus*, many religious traditions, flowing from this image, have included the vision of a *divine garden of delight* in which God roams and the healed ones will wander and live: whether in the biblical garden of Eden or the Buddhist kingdom of Shambhala, the Islamic Jannah or the Bahá'í Ridván. And always, a central feature of such a garden was the river that flows through it as the most precious fluid people could think of: water, milk, honey, wine. These are the rivers of life that stand for the divine Spirit, Wisdom, Creativity or Valuation and, hence, for the flow of the Spirit, vivifying the cosmos and indicating the taste of its harmonics of perfection. They are Spirit-rivers in which all things are released and from which they spring. Only in *drinking* from these rivers will we gain understanding and life, knowledge of the secrets of creation and of eternal life, the life of the deathless Spirit.

Some of these rivers harbor the memory of names that we can identify with streams of this world. The Tigris and Euphrates appear in many of the Near Eastern myths from which the biblical and Abrahamic tradition have gained indelible marks. They harbor the memory of the early agricultural revolution in the Fertile Crescent; they appear in the record of Abraham's migration and the prophets' testimony to the Babylonian exile of the Jewish people; they appear in the visions of angelic beings of the apocalyptic text of the last biblical prophet, Daniel; they house cultural, political, religious, and intellectual centers such as Baghdad, the place of the medieval House of Wisdom and the place of the exile of Bahá'u'lláh. They have been and have become again the site of religious wars and political devastation.

And they are now almost symbols of the opposite of the vision of a paradise of which they were supposed to remind us: either they are derogated and forgotten, like Ur and Babylon, or they have become symbols of political and ecological disaster. The demise of the Mesopotamian Marshlands through damming and extensive drainage, the fields poisoned by war materials and excessive amounts of fertilizer, which run into and through the rivers, and the general levels of pollution are only standing in for worldwide *démontage* of ecological soundness and sustainability of the rivers and waterways that are the life-veins of the earth and our presence on it—motivated by economic profit, capitalism, or ideological and religious wars, and, ironically, with the same outcome: destruction.

If one follows a river to its *origin*, adventure awaits. It is as if the mystery of existence will be revealed if one can find the *source*. Such a journey is literally and symbolically the journey of life back to its roots—as if we wanted to turn and find a way back to the uterus, and even beyond. What will we find?

All attempts to imagine such a source before our consciousness began are futile. Although we can substitute such a journey with meanders, such as pre-birth impressions or reincarnation memories, they will *not* lead to the origins of our Self that is always "before" or "beyond" any regress without origination. The return to the *origins* of our Self is *veiled* by the smooth closedness of the horizon of our consciousness in which we find no blind spot. Perhaps we can find a blind spot, hinting beyond this veil of smoothness, but only if we *reverse* the direction of our conscious embrace of the world that appears in it, as we are conscious only of our Self as we engage with this world. Many meditative traditions understand this "blind spot" as the letting go of anything that appears *in* consciousness—any thought or feeling will just be resisted, or admitted and then dismissed without clinging to it. Or as, for instance, advised by the Hindu sage Ramana Maharshi (d. 1950), it is prescribed that you concentrate *only* on your Self—until it cracks and opens the veil to the beyond, the source, the origin, the beginning "beyond" the Self.

The adventures of the reversal, the upstream effort to reach the origin of the Self, have their earthly equivalent in the discovery of the Amazon. It is the largest river by water-carrying volume but also one of the most mysterious in the history of the discovery of the rivers of the earth. It harbors the greatest variety of primordial peoples; it feeds and drains the largest tropical forest—impenetrable and extremely dangerous for unprepared guests or spectators; its surrounding forests support the most diversified forms of life. It is (at least symbolically) the lungs of the earth—if the great forests burn down (whether because of global capitalistic greed or local interests of survival is irrelevant), humanity will suffocate. Its European "discovery" begins with human greed and a measureless hunger for gold. The sixteenth-century Spanish conquistador Gonzalo Pizarro sought the legendary city of gold, El Dorado, beyond its unknown boundaries and the hidden course of its waterways. And as is true for almost every river, the deeper you penetrate toward its source, the more you will be bewildered by its diversity of beginnings. Which tributary should you follow? While the Rio Negro is most famous, the most distant source seems to be high up in the mountains of Peru, near Lake Titicaca: the Nevado Mismi, at almost 6000 meters (18,000 feet) high.

And then there is, in addition to all of these complexities, a city in the midst of the Upper Amazonas: Manaus. While the city has several claims to fame—among them the fact that it has now almost two million residents, although the connecting roads in and out of the Amazon area are still often impassable—its most curious feature is an opera house, the *Teatro Amazonas*, a Belle Époque structure inaugurated in

1896 and today the home of the Amazonas Philharmonic Orchestra. Not only did fine Venetian Murano glass find its way into the décor of the building, but Enrico Caruso (d. 1921), simply one of the most famous opera singers of all time, was transported into the Amazon rainforest and graced this house with his presence. Werner Herzog's movie *Fitzcarraldo* (1982) features Klaus Kinski as Brian Fitzgerald laboring to get his boat to Manaus to hear Caruso sing in Verdi's *Ernani*. But this was all fiction. The reality may be even more strange: it is said that the opera house was built to lure Caruso to Manaus. And it was its premier presentation, on January 7, 1897, of the opera *La Gioconda* by Amilcare Ponchielli (d. 1886) that featured Caruso. Despite the deep exploration of the Amazon rainforest and the river, it still held secrets. It was only in the twenty-first century that a highly isolated indigenous population of the Yanomami (which they themselves call the Moxihatetema) was discovered to be living on the shores of the Amazon and within its rainforest.

The story of Manaus is also the story of conquest and exploitation, of the early success of the production of rubber in the nineteenth century. And the story of the Amazon is also the story of robbery, of exploitation of the indigenous people by corporations, of systematic deforestation for cattle ranching. Every year the number of trees lost amounts to four to six million! And the extensive burning of what remains is nothing short of a catastrophe. As we know, the loss of the rainforest leads not only to the reduction of the source of oxygen production but also to a worsening of the greenhouse effect and global warming.

As the flow of the river can symbolize either the human Self or the divine Spirit, it is clear that human *contamination* is mixed into the clear waters of divine grace and revelation, and that the Self itself is the outflow of this devastating turbidity.

What we may have to learn in our renewed spirit journey back upstream on the river of life and Self is this: that we are allowed to flow as "a self" by the surrounding embeddedness of the land that carries us; that in our beginnings, we are clear water and have diverse origins, confluent in later phases of our consciousness only; that we may try to decontaminate the river of Self by becoming the Spirit-river that originates our Selves before we become our Selves; and, finally, that our self-overcoming is not only symbolically bound together with our physical awareness and effort to correlate our cultural patterns of consciousness (the Opera house) but with the ecology of rivers of life, of which we are parts and on which we depend.

Meditation VI: Let There Be Life

The secret of the stream is its source. There are ways to visualize the source: One way would be to follow the cycle of the river of things into the permanent flow in which there is, in fact, no point of origin *but the cycle itself*: the rivers that empty into the ocean, the clouds that evaporate over land to rain down and feed underwater reservoirs and springs that again flow into the ocean. The other way is to follow the secrets of the river of things *counter* to its "natural" movement downward, that is, without resisting the flow or crossing it, to move upstream to the source, the hidden origin, the beginning, the disappearance of the flow into its birthplace and point of emanation. Different from other sources of water, such as a well or a reservoir, the spring is a symbol of gentle beginnings of the flow, harboring a secret of the appearance *from somewhere or nowhere*. It is never dark and dangerous (as a well might be), nor is it collected or manufactured (as a reservoir might be). It has the connotation of fragility and purity, of an exposure of the very reason of the flow to the seeker or destroyer. It is, in a sense, defenseless. It is a pure gift. It is the symbol of the gratitude of overflowing, of the emanation of things from its source.

In a religious context, such a source is very different from images of "ground" or "bottom" or "fundament" or "foundation." It does not use the strength of a rock or the power of a lion or the fixity of a dry ground or the unfathomable darkness of the deep of the ocean to make us feel the divine creativity and the origination of all things from a divine or ultimate reality. Yet it conveys that all things are, in fact, originating *within* it, without that source losing anything of its grace and overflowing plenitude. It is not a controlling power, but a gift of life. Life comes from life. What the life-giving spring gives away is nothing but *itself*. *It* flows through the river of things. It is the cosmic immanence of the source in all the flow, even if it flows far away from its origin; in its origin, it is still flowing in pure life-giving overflowing, emanating all things.

Repeat all designations and supplications incessantly (as if, like our heartbeat, their recurrence was never meant to end):

> *Let there be life . . .*
> *Love is all . . .*
> *Murmuring . . .*
> *Murmuring of the spring . . .*
> *Listen to the murmuring of the spring . . .*
> *I listen to the murmuring of the waters of the spring . . .*

4

Falling from the Tree

If a man loses one-third of his skin he dies; if a tree loses one-third of its bark, it too dies. If the Earth is a "sentient being," would it not be reasonable to expect that if it loses one-third of its trees and vegetable covering, it will also die?

—RICHARD ST. BARBE BAKER

Then came he nearer and approached, and was at the distance of two bows, or even closer—and he revealed to his servant what he revealed. His heart falsified not what he saw. What! will ye then dispute with him as to what he saw? He had seen him also another time, near the Sidrah-tree, which marks the boundary. Near which is the garden of repose. When the Sidrah-tree was covered with what covered it, his eye turned not aside, nor did it wander: For he saw the greatest of the signs of his Lord.

—QURAN 53:8-18 (TRANS. RODWELL)

Then the angel showed me the river of the water of life, bright as crystal, flowing from the throne of God and of the Lamb through the middle of the street of the city. On each side of the river is the tree of life with twelve kinds of fruit, producing its fruit each month; and the leaves of the tree are for the healing of the nations.

—REVELATION 22:1-2 (NRSV)

When I was a boy, I went into the woods alone to climb the tallest tree. Almost at the top, I slipped and fell, but managed . . . just . . . to grab a branch. It was a long drop. I hung there till my head began to burst . . . and my arms began to feel . . .

like they were being torn from my body. I can feel it now . . . the blood pounding in my ears, the terrible pain . . . and the dread of falling. . . . All I can remember now . . . is the agony of holding on . . . and the wonderful feeling . . . *of letting go.*

—FROM THE SCRIPT OF THE MOVIE
THE WISDOM OF CROCODILES/IMMORTALITY

Life

TREES ARE SYMBOLS OF life. More than any other symbol in the collective mind of human experience and imagination, it is the tree and its majesty that appears to convey a picture not only of the life we hope for, but one on the basis of which we may think our hope to be realistic. In some sense, not to settle on the worn image of the collective unconscious, we could say that in the symbol of the tree a peak of the projection of what life is has been reached based on the collective evolutionary experience of Life on this planet for (at least) the last four billion years. Becoming conscious in the human mind, hence, this image of the tree releases no less than the Spirit of Life that carries the whole evolutionary process experienced and intuited as its inner motive force: as of yet undifferentiated of its potential oppositional elements, such as a blind force of life, a mindlike purposeful lure, a divine plan of spiritualization, or a transcending elation of the whole cosmic process.

In fact, the Swiss psychologist Carl Gustav Jung (d. 1961) developed this idea of a collective unconsciousness of the human psyche as assisting the imaginative force of the natural world to be the place of human becoming. This is one of the bases for the understanding and field of action of the cosmic Spirit closer to human existence on this earth explored in the nine paths: that they are populated with profound and affecting archetypical images that convey ways of life and collect emotional and conceptual states and motions pervaded with the wisdom for their practical application to human survival and the "better" life of a cultured configuration of society in its ecological embeddedness and responsibility. These spiritual archetypes of the collective unconscious life of humanity *are* the imaginative forces or lures of the Spirit in a cosmos without linear beginning and end, as they permeate the earth and its evolutionary tendency toward life and mind (a kind of Gaia-consciousness). And the image of the tree is one of the most profound of these archetypes. It appears in the form of a Tree of Life in many cultures, as part of their memory, as part of the imagination of an alternative life, as means of hope for a coming salvation and universal justice, as warning of loss and guilt, and as sign of immanent grace and the trustworthiness of the world of becoming despite its fleeting nature.

Here, as with the other images, like that of the ocean or the river, the tree must be recovered in its "mythic," that is, *universal or transcultural structuring of human consciousness*, but today, without denying the impact of science on this process. It is not, as C. G. Jung contemplated, that the mythic imaginations, or the archetypical images engrained in the mythological storylines of diverse cultures, are a problem to our scientific access to reality; rather, it is the misunderstanding of their nature as *literal* representations. It is we, in our scientific age, who are naïve if we assume that the ancient cultures had no idea of the *symbolic* nature of their spiritual imaginations by which they understood the cosmic process to be held together. It is *our* literalism, not the spiritual power of the images themselves, that misses the inherent character of reality to be already a unison of physical *and* spiritual dimensions *before* we take them apart and decompose them into (the false dichotomy of) external physicality and merely subjective mythology. Religious literalism is as bad as scientific literalism. "Spiritual physicalism," meaning the reduction of all inner reality to external movements of matter, is as oppressive of the cosmic Spirit operative in all reality as "spiritual materialism," meaning the reduction of spiritual reality to literal physical representations of a reality that *functions* as if it were material reality but is not. Biblical literalism and New Atheism feed on this same reductionism. They both fall under the verdict of St. Paul of the deadening letter and the vivifying Spirit (2 Corinthians 3:6).

There is another necessity for *Cutting Through Spiritual Materialism* (1973), forcefully described by Chögyam Trungpa (b. 1939), from a Buddhist perspective—and influencing a whole generation of spiritual seekers in the west and the east. Trungpa laments the tendency of spiritual seekers to divide reality into "external" and "internal," rendering external reality just dead matter and internal reality the realm of a controlling ego. Thereby, he insists, not only do we in our illusions become isolated from the universal reality that is the real nature of all beings, namely, their emptiness of Self (*sunyata*) or their mutual relatedness (*pratitya-samutpada*). What is more, we use the controlling character of the (illusionary) ego to imitate the mechanisms of the (illusionary) external mind- and spirit-less world by applying it to spiritual paths as *mechanical* devices of enlightenment. Then, we end up with a "gradualism" of stages and steps, clearly prestructured forms and procedures of spiritual progress, with benchmarks and checklists. Caught in this mechanical mapping of spiritual reality and paths, we not only lose the ability to immediately sense our "sym-pathy," that is, our immediate connectedness with the world around us and the cosmos at large as internal co-constituents of our Selves, but we strengthen, instead of weakening, the self-aggrandizement of the ego, which, in the Spirit, is but its wave, vortex, or eddy, its minute event, or, in the symbolism of the tree, one in its collective canopy of leaves and branches.

It is in this sense that we are not external to the Tree of Life, as something we encounter as foreign to us, but are already always, although more or less veiled and caught up in illusionary projections, part of its life. If we take the symbolism of the image seriously and avoid reductionism and materialism, the spiritual nature of the biblical Tree of Life, as well as that of any culture, will begin to speak to us of the mystery of Life itself—as our own nature, always waiting to be discovered and embraced as that of which we are its unfoldings. This insight will greatly influence our understanding of *spiritual immortality*, "our" immortality of *the* Spirit in us (historically sometimes identified with "the soul," at other times, with "mind" or "reason"). And we will read our relationship with divine immanence in very different ways: the immanence of Wisdom (*hokmah, sophia*) and Spirit (*ruah, pneuma*), of the Word and Reason (*logos*), of divine presence (*mishkan, shekinah, memra*), or as divine Cosmos (Proverbs 8), Lure and Life (Wisdom 7; John 1), Power and Freedom (Genesis 1)—depending on the sources of Hebrew Bible Wisdom literature or diverse Greek thought patterns (such as Plato, Aristotle, the Stoics, and Plotinus). We will also rediscover our immanence in the divine Life, for instance, in the "vine" of which Christ is the life-flow (John 15:1–7) or the "tree" that is the cosmic Manifestation of God (in which the universe lives, as in Acts 17:28) and of which we are branches and leaves or fruits, as in the Bahá'í writings.

One of the important points that C. G. Jung highlights regarding the projective nature of all mythic images is that we cannot break through their illusionary character by literalism or materialism, and that their symbolic nature cannot be restated by secular images, either, if they were understood as scientific literalist protheses, but that only their connectivity itself, as it happens in events of *synchronicity*, saves us from illusion. With the physicist Wolfgang Pauli (d. 1958), Jung developed this theory of synchronicity as *non-causal* relationship of different layers of reality, only connected by a certain symbolism. While they speak to a unique situation, they actually enlighten the vast reservoir of symbolic connection in the collective unconscious like the flash of lightning in an unexpected moment of rare clarity with a purpose beyond any expectation and beyond any possibility to collapse into a material reductionism of causal interactions. As these connections in their sudden event-character form "sym-pathies" (feelings-of-the-respective-other-together-in-one), similar to the firing of synapses in the brain that may create memories of patterns strengthened by repetition, the connectivity of symbols like the Tree (and associated imageries) with Life and Knowledge and Garden, and the like, will present stabilized patterns of interaction of consciousness or mind with the world of organisms in the billion years of their co-development, and even begin to represent the evolutionary process *itself* as a *spiritual* becoming of a "cosmos" of beauty and multifarious complexity. Here, I adopt the term "synchronicity" to indicate that the Spirit is *meaningfully* expressed in event-images, as they connect symbolically, that is, *non-causally*. This synchronicity allows for the interaction of our lives and life-worlds (lived world) with such symbols like the Tree to become extractions of meaning beyond any reductionism to material or spiritual causality.

Let us begin simply again. Trees are vital elements of human experience with the world—either as present or absent. We climb trees not only for "causal" reasons, such as to secure food or a lookout, but also for fun, to measure our own strength, physically and mentally, or even more so to connect with this life-force that trees present to us: their fortitude, their age, their wisdom, their texture, their sovereignty, their majesty, their height and circumference, their stability and their patience. At the same time we can use them in many ways: for warmth, for food, for medicine, for paper, for furniture, for embellishment in our cities and gardens, for messages of love, for shade and protection—we are always reliant on their patience to serve us. Only if you touch a tree, however, feel its texture, listen to the manifold voices of its leaves and needles in the wind, probe its vigor while climbing it or hanging from it, will you be admitted to its character beyond its use: the magnanimity and equanimity, the gentle patience of tolerating us, but also the seeming immunity to time. Such experiences, then, make us look closer. How many symbolic (not least religious) realms have been associated, measured, or made accessible with the appearances of trees, their roots and stems, branches and leaves, fruits and crowns, colors and textures of bark, their healing fluids and habitats for innumerable forms of life?

Yet trees are not our servants; we are their guests. We can fall from a tree—to our death even. Wildfires can devastate human presence and reveal its fragility, being only tolerated in the vicinity of their realm. Trees are symbols of life *and* death, not bowing to human rules or projections. They are among the oldest living beings on Earth. They produce the oxygen that animal life needs to exist on Earth, but which they do not need to exist. While we might assume that they are following simple evolutionary patterns of survival, that is, competition and self-interest, as all animal life seems to exhibit, if one applies the Darwinian mechanisms of speciation and diversification, they actually exhibit also contrary or expanded features of the evolutionary forces of cooperation and sacrifice. Through root networks, trees in a forest can connect to alert their neighbors or their colony of dangers, communicate their life-situation, and, on occasion, even sacrifice their own existence for the good of the community. As with the Pando Populous colonies, they can even connect to one grand organism of roots and shoots, to a rhizome of connectivity of becoming. While, religiously, we come *symbolically* from trees, scientifically, humanity came *literally* down from trees. We humans are transformations of tree-dwellers. Does our genetic makeup and our collective unconsciousness somehow remember?

The tree structure has become a symbol of *evolution*. The *spatial* symbolism of roots, stem, and branches has always been a symbol of the diversified nature of existence, of the groundedness in the earth, of the unity of the stem, and of the necessary diversity of branches. Yet with the early notebooks from the 1820s of Charles Darwin (d. 1882), the beginning of modern evolutionary theory, and long before he published these ideas in the famous book *On the Origin of Species* (1859), the tree also became the symbol for the *temporal* process of specialization and diversification. While the tree structure was adopted before to understand diversity, it was the evolutionary application of the branching tree that re-created the symbol of the Tree of Life in the image of strange non-human and purpose-less processes, namely, of the physical generation of ever new life-forms by processes of constancy (species), variation (mutation), and natural selection (survival of the most adapted life-forms). Life is not just humanlike, human-oriented, anthropocentric, or anthropomorphic. Yet in this new application, the evolutionary Tree recovered an understanding of Life that was ancient and deeply engrained in the biological and cultural heritage of humanity and its symbolic expressions: life and death are what *is*; what *is*, is beyond good and evil. Or, in religious language: the divine ground, the origin of existence, the "sun" shines upon good and evil (Matthew 5). Like the symbolic and physical sun, which heals and burns and gives life and death by heat and fire, the Darwinian Tree of Life gives, seemingly without any purpose and in whatever direction, the fittest organisms the chance in changing environmental situations to adapt and develop, or to die off. The only "final cause," Darwin scribbles in his handwritten Notebook, is *survival*.

Great thinkers like Teilhard de Chardin, A. N. Whitehead, and Gilles Deleuze—coming from very different kinds of philosophical approaches to cosmology—have recognized this "undifferentiating" connection of life and death, but without holding on to the symbolic integrity of the Darwinian Tree of Life, either by finding a divine power operating through it, or by complementing survival with creativity, or even by replacing the "tree" with the "rhizome," respectively.

Teilhard, as a scientist deeply involved in the discoveries of the human evolutionary heritage, as a religious thinker (and, regarding evolution, in a profoundly hostile religious environment), embraces the idea of the Darwinian adaptation processes as the motor of Life, as the mutual penetration of life and death. Yet he did not give up on the divine background of those processes—a form of thought that later diversified in many branches of "theistic evolution"—that is, of a divine presence in, and purpose to, this play of life and death. He understood death in the form of mere multiplicity as the *beginning* of a process of life vivified by the divine force of unification or *synthesis* (or sym-pathy, as A. N. Whitehead would say), by which sheer manyness becomes *complexified* to ever more elaborated, refined, liberated, and intelligent organisms. While the vast process of this cosmic synthesis strives toward the Omega Point of perfect symbiosis of all reality with God, through much branching and testing of potentials and environments, many evolutionary developments die and are lost in much pain of the sentient beings they have become. But it is the divine force of unification, this divine milieu, by and in which they live and die, and become the creators of the *values* through which the whole process "will have been" worth it. The whole symbiotic process of becoming will, proleptically from its synthetic aim, namely, the unity of God and the evolved world, be of such a value as could not have reached otherwise, for instance, by avoiding the pain of becoming, the destruction and the failed evolutionary lineages that did not make it, but that allowed others to succeed.

One is remined of very old strains of the biblical understanding and experiencing of God as the power that brings life *and* death (Deuteronomy 32:39)—something we might like to overlook by a cleansed religious house of Goodness versus evil, but which is alive in many religious traditions if we dare to look closely: in Yahweh as "man of war" (Exodus 15:3) and Lord of the Host (Joshua 5:13–15); in Christ as the Word, clad in blood, with the Sword of death (Revelation 19:13–15; Ephesians 6:17), the one named Death and Hades (Revelation 6:8), the lord of heaven and hell (Matthew 24); in Krishna as the war charioteer in battle (*Bhagavad Gita*); of Shiva as creator and destroyer (*Shiva Purana*); in the Mother Kali and Tiamat, in Marduk and Zeus, in Allah, the harbinger of life and death (Qur'an 2:156), the giver of eternal life and the executioner of the eternal death (Qur'an 15:23; 19:57; 44:8).

A. N. Whitehead, himself a scientist by profession, knows well that a world in becoming is one of bloodshed and claws. His understanding of this process is captured by only three words in the form of an equation: *life is robbery*. Life feeds on other life. Every organism is an environment of other organisms or part of an environment—all of which mutually interact amicably, in cooperation, or with hostility to one another, in competition for resources or a place to live. However, in contrast to Darwin, Whitehead allows for a "final cause" to be operative through this process of the emergence of an evolutionary universe. Instead of Darwin's survival, Whitehead introduces *creativity*. For Whitehead, the driving force of evolution, of transformation, of the interaction and evolvement of interactions between organisms and the internal and external environments of which they constitute or are a part, is *aesthetic* and *affirmative* in nature. It is the *sym-pathy* (feeling together) of becoming in which intensity and harmony are the defining forces. Without such *pathos* of becoming, such feeling and awakening as ever more intense forces of the harmonization of the forces of change, there would only be the lowest form of permanence, unmoving, disinterested in change and uninfluenced by environments. It would be (apologies to the beauty of minerals!) a history of stones, but not of sentient beings, beings even of consciousness and insight, beings in which a spirit of life and mind ventures to reveal the mystery of existence in the self-reflection of the Spirit in this whole development. For Whitehead, evolution is the change by which God is immanent in all becomings as the lure toward value, intensity, harmony, and beauty. It is by this immanence that there *is* a world in the first place, that is, that there is *actualization*, which is always a process of *valuation* and of the *creation of beauty*. It is this *creativeness* that Whitehead adds to the evolutionary Tree of Life.

Gilles Deleuze, the philosopher of poststructuralist "affirmation" (instead of a Hegelian dialectic of negation), resembles Whitehead in the sense that he also believed that the more intense life becomes, the more it comes closer to death. Living organisms, for Whitehead, are the more alive the more they are creative. However, in their originality they also ravish the organization of the organisms by which their unpredictability is made possible and sustained. Novelty is like an instrument of destruction of the context from which it arises until it can either be stabilized, or it changes the environment, or it destroys it and itself with it. Similarly, Deleuze perceives of the meaning of (human) existence as the furthering of all possible processes of vivification, of intensification, instead of stabilization. Instead of settling into any structure, organic or otherwise (all the more so if one would believe such a structure to be a divine norm), life is *upsetting* any structure, *transforming* constantly such sedimentations into new life-forms by *becoming intensity* instead of remaining extensity. Such a becoming, however, if it reached the boundary of perfection, is *identical* with death, as no organism would survive to sustain such intensity and structure-less, orgiastic novelty. Instead of the image of the "tree," therefore, Deleuze understands evolution in the form of a "rhizome." Instead of the perceived *stratifications* the model of the tree indicates (the hierarchies between roots, stem, and crown) as well as the *centralization* it seems to imply (if you cut the stem, the whole tree dies), the rhizome indicates and realizes *decentralization* and *non-hierarchical democratization* of structural becoming: like potato roots, a rhizome can develop without center in different directions with different seeds; it can die off in one place and simultaneously flourish in another. It is a web of moving relationships and fluent energy distributions throughout diverse environments, a life beyond structural integrity and reduction. In the current scientific understanding of the evolutionary mechanism, *this* model would, in fact, allow the integration of *other* driving forces besides selection, namely, gene drift and surfing (random, unrelated to selection), gene flow (through mixing of diverse gene pools of different, prior unrelated populations), lateral or horizontal gene transfer (by microbic crossing of species boundaries), and the influence of human culture on the evolutionary developmental potentials and selections. Yet, the image of the tree (versus that of the rhizome) will still retain value to indicate bottleneck situations in evolutionary developments, as we will see in later sections.

While all three expansions of the evolutionary Tree of Life don't avoid the approximation of life and death, of intensity and destruction, of harmonization and pluralization, they don't exclude a *final cause* to the mechanistic models of explanation either that science seems to be methodically bound to observe, but not at all philosophically necessitates to be upheld. In adding those elements of the value of plenitude, of the aesthetic impulse of intensity, harmony and novelty, as well as the transformation of extensity into intensity, we may understand the Spirit of life as such a universal horizon, field, energy, or process that (and in which) *pure life* is the value, intensity, and harmony immanently driving *the evolution of universes toward spiritualization*. Pure life, however, is for any limited organism death: we cannot see God and live (Exodus 33:20)! Nevertheless, as Teilhard and Whitehead would add, and in keeping with the baseline of "spirit" as integrative of mind *and* matter: meaning and value are created or emerge by the *sym-pathy* of the finite becomings in its multiplicity that they comprise, and in *synthesis* with the (nondual) infinite beyond any such differentiations—and neither in overcoming the finite nor in fixating the infinite. Hence, from the Spirit *emanates* the infinite process of becoming, which is Life, instead.

Let me say this again: *Spirit is Life*. If Spirit is *pure* life, pure life will always emanate *into becoming*. Otherwise there would not be any "world" in which Spirit would be active, or Spirit would not be the "environment" (Teilhard's divine milieu) of any world at all. The Spirit is, therefore, always the *cosmic* Spirit. In the descriptions of Plotinus and many other religious thinkers: The Spirit is the One beyond all differences, but *simultaneously*, is the Spirit of a "cosmos," which can be a multiverse of worlds that are *related through* value, aesthetics, intensity and harmony, and beauty. The Spirit is the evolutionary context, the spiritual *field of becoming* of these worlds, as without such a context no *becoming* would be possible and only a fixed world would, if at all, be frozen in eternity. This field-character is otherwise expressed by "space," *khora* or *sunyata*. This spiritual field is *not* "the One" or any regional world (pantheism) *nor* "the whole" of worlds (panentheism), but the *boundary* between the infinite One beyond any categories and the infinitely many finite processes of becoming—whether on a micro-level of particles, energy packages, quanta, or their combination to fields and organisms, or, on a macro-level, of universes and multiverses or all possible worlds (see ch. 8). To be the cosmic Spirit means to be this conjunction, sym-pathy, synthesis, space and context, horizon and field of becoming that alone allows the Spirit to be Spirit and the cosmos to be a cosmos in evolution. The Spirit is the Cosmic Tree of Life, the becoming of spiritual intensities, harmonies and moving wholes of beauty—without end. The "purpose" of the spiritual nature of cosmic evolution is—beyond mere chance or sheer necessity—also not a certain structural design (the error of creationism), a best possible world of structural integrity (the error of "block universe" theories and Leibnizian holisms), a fixed state of intensity and harmony (the error of "spiritual materialism" and of postulating a divine maximum) or a peak of desirable existence (the error of linear, apocalyptic eschatologies). On the contrary, the Spirit, which is pure Life, is the final cause of the cosmic evolution in an infinite multiverse of worlds, all of which are forms and modes, varieties and the pleroma of the becoming of spiritual beings, and the transformation of worlds as organism of organisms into spiritual Life: formless, intense, always allowing for novelty, but without loss of value. Both uniqueness and the harmonization of organization, which will always be limited and finite, become the expression of this Spirit at (as and always approximating) the boundary where Life and Death are indifferent, but infinitely productive of their differentiations into and within worlds of becoming (see ch. 9).

Knowledge

Humanity has fallen from the Tree. While biologically, we abandoned the habitat living in the crowns and branches of the forests of the tropics and the savanna, the memory of the "existential fall" comes from tasting the Tree of Knowledge. But the story of *this* tree is not one of the past—how we fell from grace, as often assumed—but it is the story of the *future* of evolution. While the biblical story of Eden is generally used to mythically present us with the persistent and seemingly inexplicable as well as inescapable human reality of a (self-generated) world of imperfection, ignorance, animal desires, egotism, megalomania, crime, pain and death—which makes this story a piece of ingenious ancient psychology—such an interpretation hides, in fact, a much deeper insight, a prophetic vision of the future: that we are still in becoming, and what we might become.

Legions have been written on the Eden-story of Adam and Eve, the spirit-breath of God enlivening the dust to soul-life, the two trees, the serpent, the loss of the garden, and the state of being that it represents—I will not add to its interpretations, really, but just refer to a few counter-intuitive or ambivalent elements that demonstrate its *polyvalence*, that is, the great and exiting *uncertainty* that comes with the adoption of the symbolisms of this story in one's worldview, as this will probably be just one of a vast, diversified tree of knowledge itself. Is it a "fall" from an initial "perfect state" of existence when we, humanity, gain knowledge of good and evil? Or is this "fall" an expression of becoming *human* in the first place? And does the vision of any perfection of being human exclude such knowledge? If so, how can God be said to have planted the Tree of Knowledge, that is, that this knowledge is, in fact, *divine*? Does the serpent lie, then, when it suggests to Eve that she will be *godlike* if she knows good and evil as God does? Is to be created in the *image and likeness* of God an expression or a prevention of this knowledge? Does the law preventing knowledge of humanity indicate the dangers of innocence or the power of gained secret knowledges—much like the knowledge of the use of fire in the myth of Prometheus? Is the serpent a deceiver from truth or the opener of humanity's eyes to the truth: namely, that knowledge is always related to a transformation; but that it is ambivalent what this transformation will bear out—fire may nourish or devastate? Isn't the serpent also a symbol of the knowledge of healing—as symbolized by the caduceus of the Greek divine messenger Hermes? Is Eve a symbol of animal weakness (following the desire of the body over the spirit) or of strength, a strength of the Mother of Life (in many other ancient myths) over that of the dust-born Man?

Life and Knowledge are intertwined with the mythology of the "two trees." As it is assumed that the Eden-creatures are immortal in a well-tempered garden in which knowledge is just a temptation, it is the knowledge gain by which immortality is lost. And then there are the Cherubim with the glowing sword, defending the Tree of Life, of Immortality, from being conquered by the knowledge of humanity having become human—later a symbol of the warring Word of God (Revelation 19:30) or the Spirit (Ephesians 6:17) that can divide soul from spirit (Hebrews 4:12): Is it a symbol of divine defense against human attacks, of the image to claim its origin, the fire of purification that is needed to get into Eden, the secrets of creation and life and immortality? In any case, it is *knowledge* that, in such symbolic realms, defines human existence as one of value and ethical activity, but also one that, if it is exposed to dangerous zones, can become the destroyer of worlds, but also the conqueror of the secrets of creation and immortal life. It is not without reason that ancient "sciences" such as astronomy/astrology (without the later differentiation into quantitative and qualitative dimensions, numbers, and values) and alchemy (before its differentiation from chemistry) were in search for the patterns by which the cosmos works, either through causal or sympathic relationships, or by material or spiritual "substances" of the primordial creation process. The correlation of the spheres, the elixir, the philosopher's stone, and the like, speak of *divine* knowledges of time and creation that are unattainable without a process of spiritual (and material) purification, because without such transformations (which are the true knowledge sought) "mechanical" or merely manipulative (power-inflicted) knowledge becomes self-destructive, as it remains ego-bound.

It is also quite understandable, then, that in the process of purification, the spiritual nature of such knowledges has leaned toward *mystical journeys of the soul* to the roots of creation, *before* creation even, to the *original* Word of God in the process of creation. Many such journeys are documented in scriptures or other texts witnessing a mystical reunification of the image of God with God's original image, the Glory or Wisdom or Word or Spirit of the transcendent One, that both grants the grace of such creative knowledge and, on occasion, immortality, deification, and divine powers of creation, judgment, and redemption. As part of this process, however, they also were journeys *beyond the boundary of death*, that is, they included a process of dying and resurrection in(to) a divine realm beyond one's own power—journeys, we would say, resembling in many ways the Near-Death Experiences (NDEs) so diligently documented today—but, today, generally without more exotic elements such as deification, yet not without often dramatic spiritual transformations. They are journeys of *theosis*, of theomorphic transformations, and of the revelation of theopoetic knowledge.

The experiences of the light and fire, unbearable almost, of Ezekiel 1 in his temple vision of the Throne of God, the divine Glory in the form of a human being on it, and the prophetic mission following from these experiences, is just one of the most dramatic witnesses of a process that was also documented in the visions of the prophets Isaiah and Daniel in the Hebrew Bible, but which became common in the apocalyptic literature of the last centuries BCE and the following centuries by recourse to the assumption of the ancient patriarch Enoch (Genesis 5:22–29) and the prophet Elijah (2 Kings 2:3–9) into the divine realm while "alive," for instance, in the heavenly journeys of Enoch described in the three books of Enoch (third century BCE–first century CE). Thereby, Enoch not only gained divine knowledge of the mysteries of creation and salvation, but was transformed into the angel Metatron and, eventually, became the heavenly being of Daniel 7, the Son of Man, even the Logos. Such journeys were common patterns after the book of Daniel, appearing in many apocalypses, but also in accounts of mystical experiences. St. Paul was transported into another heavenly realm (2 Corinthians 12:2), and the visions of St. John the Divine (in the book of Revelation) became the standard for the encounter with spiritual realms and divinity. With the mystical theology of Pseudo-Dionysius the Areopagite (sixth century CE), in the Christian context, but influenced by ancient considerations of diverse cultural and religious backgrounds, such journeys were imagined as leading through a *multiplicity of stratified realms of knowledge* by which the approach of divinity was staggered regarding closeness, purity, divine power (of life and death) and the overcoming of creaturely differentiations in the face of divine unity and transcendence.

Yet this scheme of a journey of divine, hidden and even dangerous knowledge in the approach of divinity was also already a feature of *the coincidence of mystical and cosmic knowledge* in the Babylonian and Persian astronomy/astrology, and the knowledge needed for admission to higher realms in gnostic and hermetic writings and religions. Such a scheme also features prominently in the "throne mysticism" of the Kabbalah (Merkabah mysticism) and the "night journey" (*mir'aj*) of the prophet Muhammad to the "throne" of God, as recorded in Islamic traditions. Incidentally, later, Enoch became identified with the Egyptian God-messenger and inventor of script, Thoth; became fused with the Greek version of the same divinity, Hermes, creating the figure of Hermes Trismegistus; and entered the Islamic tradition in the figure of the prophet Idris: all of them expressing the idea that their heavenly visions were able to grant them *immortal life by the divine knowledge* that was revealed to them, and *the power of life that rests in the knowledge* of the secrets of the creation process itself.

What can we learn from these dense webs of symbolic and transreligious flows? There is an inherent connection between the Trees of Life and of Knowledge, meaning that *life and knowledge coincide*, or go hand in hand: one cannot be had without the other. This is true for most of the ancient multicultural symbolisms of the Tree of Life—be it the biblical Tree of Life; the Bodhi-Tree of the Enlightenment of the Buddha; the Yggdrasil of Norse mythology; the *Sidrat al-Muntaha* of qur'anic and Bahá'í provenience; the kabalistic Tree of Life; or the divine tree guarded by Gandharvas in the garden of Amaravati, the divine city under the control of Indra, king of gods, in Hindu lore. In fact, the knowledge intuited, lost and sought *is* that of Life: its mechanisms, its powers, its control, its understanding and its creative manipulation as well as the possession of secrets of immortality. This is also true for the cooperation of ancient "sciences" and religion or material and spiritual aspects of the world of becoming—and we would seek this coherence again, today, despite the mutual animosities in the "culture and science and religion wars" of the last centuries, but more in line with the new science and religion discussions and conversations of the last decades.

In this new context, there need not to be any opposition between spiritual and scientific approach to the Tree of Knowledge, especially when we follow the more recent avenues highlighting the inherent connection between physical and spiritual dimensions of reality. In such new paradigmatic discussions, we find physicists such as many of the founding generation of quantum physics: Max Plank (d. 1947), Erwin Schrödinger (d. 1961), Werner Heisenberg (d. 1976), and Wolfgang Pauli, as well as cosmologists such as Sir Arthur Eddington (d. 1944), John Polkinghorne (b. 1930), and Paul Davies (b. 1946); philosophers such as William James, A. N. Whitehead, C. D. Broad (d. 1971), and Gregory Bateson (d. 1980); theologians such as Bernard

Loomer (d. 1985), John B. Cobb Jr. (b.1925), John Hick (d. 2012), and John Haught (b. 1942); and evolutionary biologists such as Sir James Jeans (d. 1946), Michael Denton (b. 1943), and Simon Convey Morris (b. 1951)—besides *many others* who have not entered the bandwagon of animosities, simplification, or dualism. In their own way, they all understand reality not to fall apart into matter and mind, but somehow to be embraced by an integral field, horizon, or power of Spirit in which matter and energy, space and time, field and particle, on the one hand, and mind and consciousness, heart and soul, mystical insight and spiritual experience, on the other, meet or can be understood and experienced as "one" *before* they bifurcate into oppositions of epistemologies or limited perspectives such as science and religion.

In fact, spiritual insight (*gnosis, irfan, ma'rifa*), the knowledge of the mystical Tree of Knowledge, is of *this* character, namely, that it does not exclude the world of becoming, of finite structural integrities, and of empirical facts, but reorients us in a horizon in which they become available in light of the becoming of value, consciousness, life, heart and mind, and the *fundamental noetic character of existence*. It is a common trait of science and religion that they appeal to the *intelligibility* of the world, that the universe is a world of the Logos (order, logic), of mathematic patterns, of probability and structures of possible relationships that we can trust—even if this trust is itself almost of religious nature, that is, itself super-rational.

There is something to learn, here, from the *Kabbalistic* Tree of Life. Its structure of three columns of divine powers (*sephirot*), representing the ancient contrasts of grace and justice, wisdom and mercy, and their connection in a middle column that issues into the kingdom (*malkut*) below, but issues from the crown (*keter*) above (and many more intricacies, I cannot go into, here), does not only "represent" as scheme of divine life as it becomes manifest in and as a world, or many worlds, or spiritual realms, really, but indicates *a pattern of ascension to knowledge* by which one mystically *and* cosmically approximates the Godhead *beyond* any of these *sephirot*, the undifferentiated *Ein Sof*, the Void, the Pleroma—or however one wants to call the unnamable. It is this knowledge that not only holds the secrets of creation, but can only be accessed by experience, as a process of purification and detachment from all desires of Self and worldly concerns. Its "intelligibility" is not of self-interest, but of self-transcendence.

Becoming-God, *theosis*, is really becoming alive by dying of oneself. Divine Life is (accepting, falling into, and transcending) death! In Sufi mystical language, it is the process of dying of Self (*fana*) and the grace of being granted living in eternity "in" God (*baqa*).

Immortality is granted only to the one who *knows* how to die. It is for the same reason that Buddhist wisdom is that of the insight that we are not an ego, that our life (*samsara*) will only be liberated to Life (*nirvana*) if we understand it as a lifelong process of dying. Dying while alive means to leave no traces that create *karma*, new suffering, but instead to live from the insight, the knowledge, the wisdom of compassion, as only the Bodhisattva can embody and promise, and to which she vows her (eternally becoming) life.

Even in cultural references, such as movies referencing the Tree of Life, Life and Knowledge coincide. Take the movie *The Tree of Life* (2011). People strive to gain understanding of the meaning of their lives, the way their lives are interconnected, intergenerationally and in chance encounters, a knowledge that promises some kind of immortality, even if it is only for a moment, the moment of awakening to a deeper truth or the understanding of the puzzle of relationships even beyond death. *The Fountain* (2006) is a movie that features the Tree of Life in a symbolic realm connected with the frantic scientific search for a cure to a fatal illness of a loved one—again: life and knowledge, in the end even of a love in which life and knowledge must transcend death. And the movie *The Wisdom of Crocodiles*, also called *Immortality* (1998), leads us through the life story of a vampire who out of love must relinquish his immortality in order not to kill his love. It is the insight of the "gift of death" in the form of absolute trust and letting go that motivates this acceptance of death. In the passage I have pointed to in one of the epigraphs to this chapter, the moment of the existential insight of the "letting go" is symbolized by "the fall" from a tree. Imagine this to be nothing less than the spiritual depth of insight necessitated by any spiritual path and in any spiritual seeker: *giving up the dream of immortality, absolutely (without doubt and second thoughts) trusting the personal, bodily, and mental dissolution (of a loved one or of oneself), as the transformation in which one awakes to the cosmic Spirit*. We should not only imagine this "trust" to be essential to the actual process of dying, but right now, to be the *essence of the mystical journey*, as we seekers are spirit-faring the open sea.

In the *evolutionary* context, the Tree of Life, the evolutionary diversification of species, and the Tree of Knowledge, the sphere of insight by which organisms orient themselves in their environments or even begin to change them, relate by the same complexity of matter and mind. In a now classic book in the wake of an evolutionary theory of knowing (epistemology), *The Tree of Knowledge* (1992), Humberto Maturana and Francesco Varela explore the biological roots of knowledge as arising by the cooperation between human cultural creativity and boundaries and the biological makeup and evolutionary boundaries of the human species on the evolutionary Tree of Life. We know today from many scientific investigations that we cocreate reality with our cultural decisions of livelihood, agriculture, diet, area and climate of living, even, thereby, influencing our ongoing natural selection and, hence, our long-term evolutionary makeup (of genetic material). But we are also wired as animals and mammals in our way of the *perception* of the world and, as creatures of this earth, with its particular biological memory and heritage. We don't know whether such evolutionary developments of the Tree of Life on this earth is unique or not, whether evolution is unrepeatable, as Stephen Jay Gould (d. 2002) thinks, or knows convergent evolution in a wider probability space of life, as Michael Denton and Simon Conway Morris think, to arise and to sustain itself in certain cosmic environments—such as certain planets hurling around certain suns with their mutually relational characteristics (see ch. 8). But we know that this *specific* evolutionary situatedness of humanity *defines* human mind, consciousness and ways of knowledge of the world. As we also are able to creatively change our biological makeup—by cultural or technical means, such as changes of life-style, areas of living, nutrition and especially the new methods of genetic splicing. The Tree of Knowledge, in humanities future, will be about the dangerous knowledge of the Tree of Life and, hence, the future of (human) evolution.

This is what I meant at the beginning of this section: that the symbolism around Eden is a *prophetic* statement about our *evolutionary future*. Eden might symbolically indicate the ideal that tests human existence (and even of the meaning of the world of becoming) the absence of which is "explained" in these creation-and-fall texts as "paradise lost" to indicate the permanent exclusion that we feel we experience in this world as a state of what *should not be* or which can easily be imagined to be different, but in fact is unachievable. Yet it encodes not only an ideal lost, but an *ideal imagined* to be the *potential* that we are supposed to realize—if we were (to be) guided by the Spirit that gave the whole scene life. Eden encodes an eschatological, a final and definite hope of the eventual realization of what might not have been lost, but of what is "in becoming."

What is it that is supposed to be in becoming in the Spirit-infused cosmos as presented by Eden? It is the integrity of a "garden of Reality"—to use a term of 'Abdu'l-Bahá, the son of Bahá'u'lláh and leader of the Bahá'í community until his death 1921. In it, things are not only purposefully related, harmoniously meaningful and intently satisfying for the experience of its constituents, ingredients and inhabitants. What is more, this "garden" reflects the *unity* of (the tree of) life and (the tree of) knowledge, in which to be(come) "like God" (*theo-poiesis*) is the fulfillment of the human being, to be the "image and likeness" of God (*theosis*); in which the serpent is a healing presence, and in which gender is not dividing us into violent impulses of patriarchal structures, as—by implication—no difference will be divisive, be it of sex, gender, sexual orientation, class, race, or ethnicity.

It will be an *ecological elation* of all of nature on Earth through and with the same Spirit that awakens human beings as spiritual beings. It is not only eco-spirit, but eco-*spiritualization*, a *theosis* of the spirit-flow through all of "us" Earthly creatures. The Spirit-image of the Tree of the Unity of Life and Knowledge, of Becoming and Enlightenment, of Wisdom and Compassion, of Justice and Love, of Mercy and Equanimity, of Magnanimity and Servitude, as transparently realized in *all* of "us" Earthly creatures is the potential of humanity to become the image and in likeness of a God that or who is *the place in which* such interconnectivity can and wants to happen. It is like the marriage of heaven and Earth, as reported in many other creation stories, and the biblical Apocalypse. It is the *becoming-transparent* of the transient and the everlasting, of the spiritual and the material realms—like the "kingdom," the divine domain *within* the world of becoming (Mathew 5:3). And so, the prophetic impulse is not one of flight into another reality (the heavenly Eden) or just a mystical journey of the soul or an esoteric search for secret knowledge, but a "bodying" of the Spirit—which is not ever just "embodied," as *the Spirit is never without body*. Rather, Spirit, here, means, *is* the "body-space" of all becoming. The prophetic message of Eden is the public, social, and ecological transformation of the world of becoming into a Unity of Life and Knowledge, an awakening to the cosmic Spirit as that spirit in which the universe becomes Cosmos, and in which, as a tiny contribution in our minute cosmic region, the world becomes the "garden" Earth.

Yet even if we accept that the Spirit of Life has prophetically called humanity to this task of a *bodily transparency* in the spiritual transformation of our Earth—that we admit and know *that* we can transform from our states of division, oppression, war and destruction, individually, socially and ecologically—the future of humanity on Earth in light of the evolutionary Tree of Life is beset with diverse transgressive forces that might not lead in this direction. I am not referring to nuclear holocaust, multiple ecological potentials of suicide, civilizational death by too different speeds of social and technical developments, the blithe of overpopulation and food insecurity, the slaughter by religious wars, or the eventual solar death-blow to the habitat of the earth in its home star-system, to indicate the end of humanity on Earth or of the earth itself—they are all real and serious. There are *other* potential extinction-level events, at least to human endeavors of this prophetic kind of processes, already under way. Both unhinged genetic manipulation and the potential "singularity" with the arrival of artificial intelligence (AI) may initiate a "blaze," a swat into destructive transformations of a different kind: of "falling from the Tree(s)" of Eden. Both latent potentials and actual tendencies can be pictured as failing to "reach" Eden. While Eden, in my prophetic vision, is understood as the unification of the Two Trees—of Life and Knowledge—to the symbiosis or synthesis or sym-pathy that initiates and is sustained by the *spiritual* transparency of our bodily (individual, social, ecological) organizations, both tendencies under scrutiny, here, would, instead, seek a merely *physical* (reductionist) transformation and, eventually, *erase one Tree for the other*.

Genetic restructuring, now, allows humanity directly to intervene into the evolutionary development and genetic appearance or even "essence" of humanity. We may soon have exchanged the adaptive environmental pressures at the basis of natural selection and the randomness of genetic mutations with the purposeful direction of the human genome and appearance regarding particular manipulations because of interests of power, madness, curiosity, or visions of a few "better ones" with their influence and monetary backing. One may actually become appreciative of a God who is not conceived or experienced as exhibiting such ("teleological") purposes, at least that we could discern and imitate. In the best case, we may end up with purposely differentiating peacefully diverse environments of human survival and diversified habitats (say, on other planets) to diverge humanity into a mutually almost incompatible chaosmos of ever more worlds-colonizing beings. In the worst case, as most genetic changes even by means of selection, transfer, flow, drift, or mutation are maladaptive, we might finally create a viral situation of exponential expansions of forms of extinction before we can genetically so diversify as to be able to survive the changes we have initiated. The Tree of Life gives us these options. Yet knowledge will only come after the manipulative acts—empirical knowledge is risky knowledge. Here, the Tree of Knowledge is "erased" by the unknowability of the potentials, reactions, and directions of the Tree of Life.

The vision of the creation of so powerful AIs that humanity will not only have become dependent on their functioning (as it is now already in diverse areas of life), that all questions of energy production and consumption, economic distribution, the ability to work for earning a decent livelihood, all regulations of transport, communication, the flow of data and information, the contact between human beings and with nature, as well as the very ability to decide on who lives and how long, *will be taken away* from human knowledge, consciousness and decision-making and delivered into the "hands" of a new god, the almighty web of algorithms of computation machines. This "singularity," in which *humanity becomes superfluous* for the functioning of all "human" systems of energy, information, communication, and so on, as prophesied, for instance, by the futurist author Ray Kurzweil (b. 1948) and many others of the *transhumanist movement* today—even assuming the becoming-conscious of such AIs in such an event (but not as a necessary condition for its happening)—will be "the other side" in a shift between the Two Trees: the Tree of Life being swallowed by the Tree of Knowledge, implying the apocalypse of humanity.

What, then, does it mean to seek this Garden of Reality of the cosmic Spirit for humanity on Earth, as the unity of the Two Trees? And should we differentiate this "garden" from other natural and cultural *symbols* of the intersection of the Two Trees?

Garden/Forest/Wilderness

Trees can come alone or in groups. In fact, we can find trees in three archetypical arrangements: in gardens, forests, and the wilderness. These are three kinds of organisms or harmonies of organization or environments, which are, of course, not mutually exclusive, but still worth to be considered on their own.

I have already referred to "forests" in the last chapter. In all of their primordial forms, as rainforest of the tropical climates, as cloud forest in high altitudes or as primeval forest of all climes and altitudes, they are the lung of the worlds, relieving it from CO_2 and producing the Oxygen needed by most life on Earth, and of course humanity. They also hold the most amount of biomass and are the environment for most of the important ecosystems and biomes that uphold the genetic diversity, which is important for changing conditions to be the basis for natural selection to operate favorably for the long-term persistence and the diversification of life on Earth. We know this and still erode the basis of our existence and with it that of Earth's living skin. We can, of course, reforest. And no one has done more for this healing of the earth's fragile zoosphere than Richard St. Barbe Baker (d. 1982), who, from the 1920s on, raised consciousness for the necessity of reforestation, founded *The Men of Trees*—today organized in the International Tree Foundation—and planted millions of trees in Africa, the Middle East, and the Americas.

However, what happens unabashed is deforestation. Reasons are diverse, but, most of the time, relate to corrupt governments and ruthless international companies, which are only oriented toward profit. They rob the land they can get their hands on, often by occupation, displacement and other scare tactics as well as monetary potency. Such deforestation not only ruins whole landscapes beyond any recoverable level of sustainability or the potential of natural replenishment, but also contributes to the pollution of air, waterways, and lands by the methods used for clear-cutting and processing. The haze and smog in predominantly Asian cities, today, is only the most obvious "sign" of these ongoing exploitations.

Humanity has always found new ways to irreplaceably ruin whole landscapes: think of the karst mountainous areas of the Balkan states and Italy, which were human made, because the ancient Roman armies needed wood for ships to conduct wars and commerce. The desertification of the sub-Saharan savanna is as much related to generations of deforestation as it is to climate change. The disappearance of primeval forest in Europe is the result of civilizational occupations, agriculture, and domestication of animals. There are hints that a little ice age in the 1600s in Europe and America was at least influenced by the "genocide" of native American population through the imported illnesses of the Spanish and Portuguese conquests from the late 1400s on, and, by their warring and disease-infestation, the reduction of indigenous population by about 60 million people, as increased consumption of CO_2 by growing forests reduced the greenhouse effect. Yet this depopulation also contributed to the eventual economic dominance of European economy, because the exploitation of the now unused resources of South America directly influenced the expansion of European "civilization."

The symbolic use of the forest as a spiritual entity is poisoned today, as are many other symbolic images, by such wounds with which we inflict Earth. Mind the warning of Richard St. Barbe Baker in the epigraph to this chapter: that flaying the skin of the earth of its woods is but a slow torture to death, while exploiting the resources gained by this slow death inform ruthless economic expansion, other forms of exploitation and human oppression in the name of mammon and dominance of "the better ones" over the whole of humanity and the ecological harmonics of the planet Earth.

In reaction to these methods of holding humanity and the earth in a death lock grew the idea of the importance of preserving the *wilderness* of its inherent life forces prepared by the forests and their related or dependent biotopes, diversified ecosystems, and innumerable habitats of beings of the evolutionary Tree of Life. This insight is, in fact, an important "evolutionary" development of the Tree of Knowledge *for* the Tree of Life. The lovers of this idea of preserving wilderness and forests, such as Ralph Waldo Emerson (d. 1882) and John Muir (d. 1914), are well known, as are the outcomes of the ongoing process to give this idea space and body, for instance, in the vision of the national park, an idea that, today, is instantiated worldwide. Of course, with the realization of this idea, we have also inherited a paradox: *wild* nature is allowed to persist by a *culture* of preservation. Even if it is a hands-off approach, it is a symbiotic state of a certain cultural gaze of a certain worldview of a certain strata of humanity—and, hence, limited by it. And we should not forget the Native American life in the open land, the primordial wilderness as sacred space, that had to be taken away and exchanged with white "civilization" of gold and other resources, profit, and commodification, first, in order to become the wilderness that, now, must be rescued from this desolation. Hence, we, now, only gain a spiritual sanctity of forests and related natural ecologies by, simultaneously, applying a *dualism* that, in the end, will be detrimental to the Spirit that informs it: Because any dualism is foreign to Spirit, to divide the world in areas of spiritual nature and of spirit-less human exploitation is either unsustainable or unattainable in the first place!

The spiritual insight that wilderness of this kind may teach us is twofold. On the one hand, we may learn that the interaction between humanity and the earth needs to *acknowledge the wilderness as our ecological home,* rather than assuming that we must preserve some wild islands in the midst of ecological destruction. And, on the other hand, humanity must realize that it is *the contingent being* in the ecology of this earth, and *not the necessary being* "destined" to survive on the Tree of Life. Then, and only then, will we unite our existence on the Tree of Life with that of Knowledge, because, then, we will have understood that the *wilderness is of the very nature of the chaosmos,* the world of becoming, and that the evolutionary diversification of a Tree of Life may not even need this earth, but certainly not humanity, to flourish—if, in the cosmic Spirit, we may assume that Life is a *wild* ingredient of the cosmos.

As we learn to appreciate our contingency and fragile presence on the Tree of Life, we may also understand that it is a gift to participate in the cosmic Spirit; that our destiny to be spiritual expressions of this Spirit in a world of becoming and toward the spiritualization of our environment is not a guarantee, a possession or a right, but needs to be earned by the insight into the Tree of Knowledge. Only in the fragility and humbleness of self-transcendence does the Tree of Life grant "immortality" and does the Tree of Knowledge make us "godlike."

The "garden" is the *integration of nature and culture.* While this is increasingly also true for forests and wildernesses, or of forest gardens, of orchards of flowering trees and of beds for vegetables and spices, it is the "nature" of a garden to be *consciously* prepared in order to be *the* aesthetic form in which form and idea, matter and mind, human desire for beauty and natural beauty are in some harmonious and satisfying way fused to please all senses and express the spirit of that which such an integrated harmony can mean for all of its inhabitants, whether mineral, vegetable, animal, or human. The garden is spacious. It will offer areas that can harbor forests and wildernesses, but it will not be complete without clear areas of grass for lingering and enjoying the open air display of individual tree crowns and their shades, arrangements of waters and rocks, ways with surprising exhibits of colors and fragrances, intelligent temporal groupings of flowering plants giving pleasure all year long, the sound of the wind in diverse grasses, bushes, trees, or reeds, the voices of water as it flows through beds and falls and appears in springs and grottos, and the songs of birds in the branches of the trees with their own enchanting harmonies, rhythms and melodies.

It has been said that we should not give too much credit to gardens of this sort as they actually represent a social hierarchy and a privilege of the "better ones." Sure, traditionally the garden as the prerogative of the kings and queens, emperors and other leaders (not all of them deserving of so much beauty) is walled in to indicate the imperial domain and exclusivity of the noble use. In this sense, Eden is the domain of the divine king as the divine kingdom is envisioned as such a garden. It is also true that a garden of this royal kind (imitating and justifying its existence from the paradise garden) devours many recourses that could be used for a wider distribution of means. The amount of energy and "intelligent design" put into the gardens of palaces, castles, and aristocratic houses to demonstrate (at least to the envy of their peers) the extravagance of might and power in the lavishly spent spaces, the diversity of foreign and strange inhabitants, the resources and the ingenuity of presenting the wealth and treasures one can only assume to be necessary to have because one can create them, is, indeed, what makes such gardens precious and legendary. But it is not true that democratization was ever identical with the destruction of this privilege, because what gardens represent to the heart of being human is something that is deeper than the limitations imposed on the resources to create them and, hence, the assumption of their sustainability only by the rich and powerful. This is why such princely gardens were not destroyed in revolutions that shifted power to other classes or the public; rather, they became gardens of the public: the gardens of Versailles after the French revolution remained a national treasure; the Austrian Emperors opened the gardens of their summer palace in Vienna to the public including its menagerie; the gardens of the Japanese Emperors became accessible by the people. Cities either clothed themselves with gardens (think of the Gardens by the Bay in Singapore) or reserved such spaces in their vicinities (think of New York's Central Park); garden cities became the vision of the future of human living; parks became the symbol of the civilized nature of a society, and they still are. Temples and other sacred places are often situated in the midst of gardens or even consist of gardens, like Zen gardens or the Baháʼí Ridvan Garden near Akko, Israel. Indeed, gardens are the closest a spiritual memory of human worship can come to the vision of the future integration of matter and mind, humanity and the ecology of the earth. By the whole symbolic imagery of Eden, gardens are prophecies of spiritual fulfillment.

Trees in gardens, forests, and wildernesses carry their special reminders of the *spiritual nature of human perception* in their presence. Trees are places of music. Gardens invite this symphony of organisms that articulates itself in sounds of harmony and the language of peace: think of the *Turangalila Symphony* (1948) of Olivier Messiaen (d. 1992), composed of bird-songs. Trees are places of reconciliation, as in several indigene cultures, when to sit down under their crown for peaceful negotiations is a sacred expression of the vision of a unified and cultured humanity. Trees remind us of the fleeting time of human lifespans: think of Methuselah, the bristlecone pine of about 5000 years age in the White Mountains in the Inyo National Forest of California. They remain unimpressed by such perishing and the changes and chances of history they survived: think of the majestic groves of giant redwood and sequoia trees in California. Or they commemorate events long after they vanished from importance: one can still visit the tree that president Ulysses S. Grant offered the Japanese emperor in his visit in Tokyo in 1879. And they can still convey the memory of sacred events of great power and suffering: think of the garden of Gethsemane just outside of the temple mount of Jerusalem and the Bodhi-tree (*ficus religiosa*) of the event of the awakening of the Buddha in Bodh Gaya. Saplings of trees can hold us close to the meaning of the past or be a promise of a new future.

The spiritual importance of all of these ingredients of gardens, and especially their harmonious diversity, can also become a symbol for the peace between religions if their spiritual *nature* as reflected in a garden would be perceived to be their *variety* and not their exclusivity. As already mentioned, the symbol of the Garden of Reality was meant to make this point: that the variety of plants and flowers with their diversity of sounds, colors and fragrances in their harmonious coordination is the best symbol for the unity and diversity of spiritual paths. While the whole garden is the domain of one sun and refreshing rain, one divine space of mutual enrichment, the loss of diversity would equal the death of spiritual pleroma—as reflected in the inexhaustible cosmic multiplicity that the Spirit instigates without end in a potential infinite diversity of places and habitats, planets and moons, galaxies, and even universes. How can we expect spiritual paths to be less diverse than the worlds and universes that overshadow their limited value by this vast gracious manifold? Here, the garden has become, as it probably in the archetypical memory of humanity (and all beings engaged in such sym-pathic mutual perceptivity) always already has been, a symbolic reality or, rather, a *real symbol* (a symbol that "bodies" what it symbolizes) of the mystical nature of the reality of the Spirit from which all reality springs and, in all of its initiated and encouraged diversity, remains related to one another, directly or indirectly, materially or mentally, through causal or sym-pathic relations, in themselves or mediated through the naked space of existence itself. What is called "religious pluralism"—the idea that all religions carry such a truth at their heart that must be awakened, but cannot be awakened as long as it is veiled by feelings (and rationalizations) of envy, sentiments of exclusivity or a boastful sense of rightness—can be felt by entering a garden as it imbues the joy of its multifariousness as the value without which it was meaningless and empty; not empty of Self, which such harmonics always furthers, but of importance and meaning.

At the heart of all religions is the garden-Spirit in which the Tree of Life and the Tree of Knowledge are *one*, but as *diverse* as the crown of Spirit-trees can be. I will assume, here, that this insight, if it is not just theoretically known, but existentially embraced and practically acted on, will be at least as profound and important for the future of humanity as all other potencies with which the evolutionary Tree of Life and the relativistic Tree of Knowledge challenge us. And this insight may also be the correction to the dangers of the mutual eraser of the Two Trees by genetic and algorithmic transformation: not to lose the spiritual meaning of such transformations as the purpose of evolution and the generation of this or any cosmos.

Epilogue: The Throne of God

Reversing the habit of the first three chapters, this epilogue will not counter spiritual symbolisms employed in its sections with ecological realities and human inabilities, as this has been already an integral part of the body of considerations in this chapter. Rather, this epilogue will follow the religious symbolism around Eden further into its mystical beginnings or apophatic, that is, inexpressible and unknowable, divine origination. But to what avail? Well, the prophetic image of Eden is about the harmonious synthesis of the Two Trees of Life and Knowledge, exploring their mutual immanence, but avoiding their mutual dissolution (explained in the text above), especially given the fatal dangers of genetic manipulation and the AI "singularity." It follows that the divine origination of the whole symbolic web of Eden—with its trees and streams, but also lights, fruits, serpents, choruses, angels and the divine Throne—may hold hints for the spiritual *consciousness* implied in it that we are supposed to learn in order to achieve this prophetic vision of the divine garden—and, perhaps, the purpose of human existence: becoming spiritual beings, the world becoming the divine domain.

I will again begin to explore the ambivalences of the symbolisms inherent in a few visionary passages on this spiritual process of Eden. Let's begin with the "original state" of existential alienation (Genesis 3). What it expresses in this text and later Jewish and Christian interpretations is the *existential* wall that *separates* human life from its spiritual purpose. Eden as the *coming* of the kingdom of God, the dominion of Life, already includes in its "story" a *metanoia*, a *turn* toward it (Matthew 5). This means: to face the existential wall, in symbolic form of the two Cherubim with flaming swords who or that secure the entrance to the Garden with its most precious inhabitant, the Tree of Life, as that of Immortality, of the divine Life itself. This imagery connects to a plethora of other symbols of the *mystical experience of the journey of the soul into the Holy of Holies*, that is, as reflected in the "geometry" of Jerusalem's first temple. The Cherubim are the ones envisioned to carry the Throne of God in Ezekiel's vision

(Ezekiel 1). The flaming swords remind us of the purification encounter of Isaiah with the flaming Seraphim (Isaiah 6) and of the Word of God understood as the sharp sword of truth (Isaiah 11:4; Hebrew 4:12)—or the fire and flaming sword of the Spirit (Ephesians 6:17). Later Jewish texts, for instance, of the Targums, Mishna, and the two Talmuds, interpret this arrangement as referring to the construction of the Ark of the Covenant with the two Cherubim on its lid, facing each other, but leaving the empty space in the middle as that of the invisible and inaccessible (S)Word of God. The Ark forms the center of the Holy of Holies in the temple, but it is only accessible by the High Priest once a year. At the Day of Atonement (Yom Kippur), the High Priest enters through the *veil* that separates the world from the sphere of God. What is the veil? Jewish interpretation, for instance of Philo of Alexandria, understands it as the Logos, the Word, the Wisdom, the Spirit, the Son of Man, the Son of God (the Angel of the Name of God, *HaShem*), symbolizing the manifest divinity, the Manifestation of God, the divine mediator between the sphere of God and the world. Jewish Merkabah mysticism visualizes the journey of the soul into Eden toward the Throne of God *while alive* as a dangerous, bewildering, even *impossible* journey—no one can see God and live.

The *boundary*. Ascent. Descent. The Throne becomes the Tree becomes the Curtain. The Curtain is the boundary. Think of it as woven image of the Tree of Life, in the Kabbalistic form of the ten *sephirot* the Crown of which is the absolute boundary to the inaccessible transcendent, formless, nondually all-embracing One Beyond in the Holy of Holies. The two Cherubim and the (S)Word become the three columns of the Kabbalistic Tree. It is *itself* the Throne *between* heaven and Earth, which is its footstool (Isaiah 66:1) on which sits the Glory of God, God in human form, the manifest God, the divine Manifestation (Ezekiel 1:26). In the Qur'an, this tree is the *Sidrah* of the epigraph of this chapter; it is the boundary beyond which nothing can proceed, the boundary that Mohammad experienced in his journey through the heavens to the Throne of God (*mir'aj*). Bahá'u'lláh understood this *sirdah al-muntaha*, the Tree of the utmost boundary, as the manifest God, the Glory of God (*baha' Allah*), as the Word and Wisdom of God in human form, as the human being that in its transparency *reflects nothing but* the light of the Glory on the Throne—like Krishna (*Bhagavad Gita*, ch. 11) and the Christ (Matthew 17:1–8; Mark 9:2–8; Luke 9:28–36). The boundary of the Throne, the Tree, the Veil, is also a bridge—the bridge indicating the *becoming* of the dominion of God (Matthew 13) in this world as the vision of a place that has realized the return to Eden, where/when the dominion of God and the world have been mutually transgressed, as the curtain is torn (Matthew 27:50–51).

Of course, in both being a veil and a bridge, the Throne of God is a boundary that straddles (includes, saves, creates, is patient to and dissolves) impermanence. The Throne is really a *chariot*—indicating the ancient image of the specific divine movements through the heavens (the sky and all spiritual and material worlds). It is the manifestation of the divine manifold by which God's "essence" is veiled: behind the fiery beings, the Cherubim and Seraphim, and even in the human "form," that appears on it (Ezekiel 1, Daniel 7). We could press the imagery one step further and, as we must understand these veils as necessary for the protection of the visionary in the presence of God (Exodus 33), "see" the divine throne-chariot as a "construction" that under the weight ("glory") of the divine presence instantly dissolves, as it has no "unity" in itself, that is, is selfless and self-transcendent in relation to the divine charioteer. While it is the shining, but inaccessible "sun-figure" of God that holds the chariot together—as in Plato's image of the chariot and the imagery of Apollo's chariot (see ch. 2)—it also dissolves in light of the reality of its divine "fire/light"—as in Krishna's cosmic body (see Meditation IX) and the Buddhist analysis of the constructedness of any being, exemplified by king Milinda's chariot (see ch. 9).

There is another image of the Trees in the Garden, that of the Apocalypse of St. John the Divine, as quoted in an epigraph to this chapter. It is set in the context of the River of Life (the object of reflection and mediation of the previous chapter) that flows from the Throne of God and is flanked *on both sides* by the Tree of Life. Are there *two* Trees of Life! Or does the River of Life flow *through* the Tree of Life? Its/their fruits are the sanctification of time and the healing of humanity's complex social organism. The whole zodiac is mirrored in its/their crown(s); the whole universe is embraced by its/their life-stream overflowing as the River of Life and the manifold fruits of its/their multiple branches. Here, the whole cosmos appears as the Tree(s) of Life, as the manifest divinity, transgressing all distances and dualities, interfusing and coinhabiting the Spirit of Life.

Both visions taken together—that of the Tree as *boundary* and as the one *through which the River of Life flows*—can now stand for the *unity* of the Tree(s) of Life as that of Life and Knowledge, the relational process of becoming *and* of consciousness, of the evolution of life *and* mind in the physical world, of spiritual "bodying." This is the *infinitely branching* Tree of Existence, the *manifest* Garden of Reality: the *becoming self-conscious of the multiverse and its becoming self-transcendent of itself in its divine multiplicity*. In the image of the infinitely branching tree, it is only to be expected and "natural" that the cosmic Spirit generates infinite variegation of creative spiritualization into a multiverse that is only held together by the transgressive, webbed (rhizomatic) unity of the immortal Tree of Life, itself a reflection of infinite becoming.

This has two implications—one affirmative, the other negative—but both indicating infinite, selfless divine modes of overflowing goodness and love. On the *affirmative* side, such an overflow of life is *infinite*, infinitely *branching*, such that not only is there not one spiritual path or religion on Earth that can claim exclusive truth, but not even one universe to which this Divine Multiplicity is confined. How much vaster can the image be in which we may learn to humbly let go of such urges and claims and content ourselves with the feeling of trust when we let go and fall into this infinity (like the related epigraph from the movie *Immortality* suggests)? The other, *negative* side of this insight, however, is as important as the affirmative one, namely, that the infinite flow of the River of Life, flowing through the ever branching Tree of Life, demonstrates to us *the gentle power of divine creativity*, which never stops even if the creatures waste their life by inflicting suffering, and even if the tree of evolution is always one of pain and robbery, of the inevitability of the unity of life with death. Is perhaps the "river of life" that never withholds its waters but the *divine weeping* with the suffering in the flow of life through its Tree? The Spirit grows in the life-blood as it gives birth to the Tree of Life (Romans 8). In offering blood and water, it conveys immortal life (John 19:34). It is perhaps not arbitrary that blood, water and Spirit are the triad of *witnesses* to the "cosmic" divine engagement and salvation (1 John 5:6).

One interesting consequence of the sympathic synthesis of these two sides of infinite, unending, divine engagement of a world of becoming in the form of the unity of the branching evolutionary Tree of Life with the aim at spiritualization as symbolized by the Tree of Knowledge is maybe counterintuitive, but, if you think of it, rather to be expected and exciting: namely, that we, humanity, may not be (or even intended to be) the only "bodying" of the Spirit on Earth. If the earth is the eco-spiritual unity of the Tree of Life, its necessary branching may neither have begun, nor must it end, with the species *homo sapiens*. Rather, might not the *whole* evolutionary process be quite "natural" if we understand it in the context of the cosmic drive of creativity to purpose spiritualization? If evolution (the production of *cosmoi*) is, as already elaborated, meant to produce spiritual beings in a multiverse of unending cyclical or branching realizations—how could that not be also true for the limited spiritual ecology of the earth? It is intriguing to think of other branches of the species *homo*, the ones that interbreeded with us, like the Neanderthals or the Denisovans. But despite the fact that we are the only species *homo* that survived today, *we might not be the last species* expressing the evolutionary latencies of mind and consciousness in the development toward spiritual maturity—if we think of the current scientific probability of certain other species of apes, mammals, birds, and even octopods to exhibit forms of consciousness or even self-consciousness, ethical inclinations, and deep feelings of connectivity among themselves and with us. The profoundly creative and always transgressive Spirt may just be present in the eco-evolutionary Tree of Life on Earth as branching diversity of *different forms and velocities of evolving deep habitats* for the appearance of aesthetic and ethical, mental and emotional, subjective and intellectual conditions for, or conditioning, the emergence of spiritual syntheses.

Meditation VII: Becoming Wood

The transgression between humans and animals is a standard requisite of storytelling and the reflections on the essentials of human nature. Vampires and werewolves are only the most common memorials to such processes. Such transgressions are considered monstrous, but also leave the impression on us that under the divine image lurks—unconsciously and genetically—an animalic "desiring machine"—to use a term of Deleuze and Guattari. Generally, this is considered as a chaotic or inordinate realm that needs control and civilized reactions, like Plato's charioteer who, like and as the human soul or mind, must tame the horses, the biological and psychological drives, and direct them. Or such a transgression is introduced as a shock of the contingency of the human form and existence—think of *Strange Case of Dr. Jekyll and Mr. Hyde* (1886) of the Scottish writer Robert Louis Stevenson (d. 1894)—expressing an existential angst of losing one's humanity in the face of grave alienations, represented, say, by insectoid life—as in the short story "The Metamorphosis" (1915) of the Austrian writer Franz Kafka (d. 1924), echoing the existential suffering in the midst of the Great War.

It is interesting that apocalyptic biblical and extrabiblical Jewish and Christian literatures of the centuries around the turn of the common area represent human beings not as images of God, but *as animals*, and represent angels, who are considered as fully submissive to divine will and selfless in God's presence—such as the Cherubim, the Throne angels, and the Seraphim, the fire angels of divine love—*as humans*. Even God's "form" is envisioned as a human or angelic form: "like a son of man" (Ezekiel 1:26; Daniel 7:14). And even the transgressions between the angelic "sons of God" and human women are represented in human, although distorted form, as giants (Genesis 6:1–8). This indicates that the "angel" is the symbolic hope that humans *might*, one day, and through the process of spiritualization, actually *become human*, but, right now, outside of and before Eden, are not more than animals. What differentiates this prophetic view from the Darwinian Tree of Life is not the evolutionary aspect, which is actually what amicably relates them to one another, but that we could indeed *reach* such nobility that we identify with humanity as image of the divine Spirit: while Darwinian evolution may not exclude such a possibility, it does in no way suggest any directionality either.

What is more astonishing, however, is that such transgressions are more rarely reported between humans and the floral and arboreal realms. And if so, they seem to be more a question of finding peace, of transcending human desiring to a state of tranquility. (Well, there are the "body snatchers," plant-based aliens that supplant humanity from the inside, as envisioned in a series of sci-fi/horror movies since the 1950s). In Greek mythology, the nymph Daphne was, by her father, the river god Peneus, transformed into a laurel tree to be saved from the sexual desires of Apollo, but who granted him a laurel wreath that would become the sign of victors at ancient Olympic Games and the crown of Roman emperors. In several cultures, two close trees are considered expressions of eternal love. And Baucis and Philemon were transfigured into such trees by the Olympian gods when they died in honor and as memorial to love deserving everlasting remembrance.

The following three mediations are experiments in such transgressions and transformations. You should engage them only in this particular order of expansion. And you should not move on to the other visualizations as long as the one in which you are dwelling does not yield complete self-transcendence into its reality.

> *Imagine, you meditate a tree . . .*
>
> *Touch it, feel its texture, hear its leaves in the wind and the birds in its twigs . . .*
>
> *Imagine what it would be like to be a tree . . .*
>
> *. . .*
>
> *What would it mean to comprise centuries of happenings undisturbed . . . ?*
>
> *What would it feel like to survive humans in its vicinity . . . ?*
>
> *What would it be like to have survived earthquakes and fires, floods and droughts . . . ?*
>
> *How would it feel to have witnessed bloodshed and famines . . . ?*
>
> *How would it feel to see the joy of birds, animals, and humans climb its branches . . . ?*
>
> *. . .*
>
> *Now: Become the tree!*
>
> *Look at your hands and see and feel how they become wood . . .*
>
> *How your feet and hands, arms and legs lignify . . .*
>
> *Every fiber in your body . . .*
>
> > *feel it become wood . . .*
>
> *You are a tree now . . .*
>
> *. . .*
>
> *(Tat twam asi: thou art that; that art thou!)*
>
> *Feel your body, the tree . . .*
>
> *Your roots swimming in dirt throughout time . . .*

> *trusting the life feeding it . . .*

Your stem . . .

> *standing in the wind . . .*

Your skin, the bark . . .

> *pulsating fluids flowing through it . . .*

Your branches . . .

> *spreading, filtering the air . . .*

Your leaves . . .

> *praying to the sun . . .*
>
> *singing with the birds balancing in the twigs . . .*

Your blossoms . . .

> *beauty given away . . .*
>
> *desiring offspring . . .*

Your fruits . . .

> *falling . . .*
>
> *Satisfaction . . .*

. . .

Feel yourself extended throughout all of the many branches . . .

Like fingers, feel the air they touch individually . . .

Feel the life-stream flow toward the tips . . .

Feel that you grow the leaves . . .

> *and fruits . . .*

Become the stream . . .

Breath in the light of the sun . . .

> *breath out the air of the earth . . .*

Meditation VIII: Becoming Life

One of the most discussed philosophical propositions, today, regarding the ecological or even cosmic integrity of all existence in an evolutionary Tree of Life, is that such evolutionary processes of increasing complexity toward the appearance of Life (degrees of freedom), Mind (consciousness, reason, purpose) and (maybe even) Religion (intellect, ultimate reality), are not arbitrary, but are deep expressions of the urge of the universe to live, as the reason for its very existence. In the current form of "panpsychism" (which is really a group of related positions), the idea is that *all* existent physical beings express, to a certain extent, *some* spiritual characteristic—be they that of life and feeling, mind and reason, consciousness and intellect, emotional intelligence and the perception of Self—related to reality as a whole and rising from its ultimate ground or origin. While this is, of course, a contested thesis in the view of all materialist or naturalist reductionisms, its materialist denial is also fatally flawed, as the philosopher Thomas Nagel (b. 1937) in his book *Mind and Cosmos* (2012) has convincingly demonstrated, especially in light of the inability to explain the emergence of consciousness, subjectivity, reason, and ethical values. While some more conservative philosophers of science have countered this challenge with theories of "emergence" that understands mental properties to just appear on an integrative level higher than the material rules of the physical, chemical, or biological spheres of evolution (and which, therefore, remains materialistic *in nature*), others, such as the philosopher David Chalmers (b. 1966), understand consciousness as a primitive fact of this universe that cannot be reduced to any other physical reality. Others again, such as A. N. Whitehead, understand *all* events as processes in which past and future, matter and mind, fact and value, actuality and potential unite to create ever-new sym-pathic syntheses that are the basic "entities" of any physical organization and their organic evolution throughout different degrees of freedom toward (and from) a universal, but universally infused, divine Wisdom and Sprit: oriented toward ever-new forms of cosmic harmony and ever self-transcending realizations of peace, respectively.

So, boldly imagine the following transformation (as an expansion of the previous one):

The Cosmic Spirit

You are the tree . . .

    you feel yourself as one in your trunk . . .

    you feel yourself multiplied in all of your branches . . .

    and leaves, and flowers, and fruits . . .

Now—transfiguration:

    You are the Tree of Life on Earth . . .

. . .

Feel your whole tree-body becoming the body of Life . . .

Feel: Every branch transmutes into a life-form . . .

Feel: Each branch is now a species of life:

    of microbes, plants, animals, humans . . .

Feel: Each tip of a branch becomes a living being . . .

Feel: You are now the Tree of Life . . .

. . .

Feel the becoming of life over billions of years . . .

Feel the growth of your body . . .

Feel the branching into all living forms . . .

    all at once . . .

Feel the life that streams through your time-arteries . . .

Feel the evolution of new life . . .

Meditation IX: Becoming Worlds

If we widen the image of the Tree of Life to that of the Tree of Existence, it is only a small step to think of it as an *interstellar consciousness of many planes or cosmic habitats* that can harbor life and conscious beings. And it is not an impossible step to expand this vision to a multiverse, branching like a tree into many universes. While there are exceptionally many physical and philosophical theories as well as religious visions of possible versions, structures and forms of such multiverses, none of them needs to be absolutely incompatible to some of combinations of the different solutions: a branching universe can maybe also reunite to a lattice of connected universes; a successive series of universes could in a certain phase be branching or a branching one could in another phase be a successive series; branches could themselves be branching or serialize universes; branches could seem to be parallel universes at certain phases of their existence or vice versa; unities of multiple universes could be within higher unities of hyperrealities or probability spaces or abstract spaces of possible universes, which will in certain phases be actualized; and many more.

One of the most impressive religious visions of the infinite worlds that I will invoke, here, as basis of this third meditation on the tree motif, is the theophanic space in which the multiverse of all things appears as Krishna's "cosmic manifestation" in the *Bhagavad Gita* (ch. 11). It was mentioned in chapter 1 and will reappear in the next chapter. Its profound impulse is to open our limited consciousness to an infinite horizon of existence that has the form of a vast multiplicity, impossible to imagine or hold together "as one" in one consciousness, like a multiverse, but expressing an infinitude of finite forms in its formless embrace. It is a shockingly multiplicitous image, far beyond any rational grasp, but also one of an experiential revelation of a grand unity, a nurturing complexity, an irreducible creativity, and a feeling of being at home despite the shock of magnitude and strangeness. There are two reasons for this intimacy. On the one hand, this insight happens in *this* world, in the compact image of the human form of divinity, indicating all that we encounter on a regular (mesocosmic, human-level) basis as enfolded veil of that which every minute event of existence harbors in its depth. On the other hand, the intimacy is an experiential expression of the fundamental truth conveyed by the *Bhagavad Gita* and, in one form or another, most of the religious and philosophical Hindu systems, namely, that *atman* is *brahman*, that our experience of the world through Krishna is *what we are* in our innermost existence.

What better way to visualize this "revelation" (revealing us to our Selves and ultimate Reality) than by widening the Tree of Life (that we have already "become" in the previous meditation) to that of a Multiverse *itself*. I will begin this Meditation with the widening of the tree image, sliding into and ending with the beginning of the text of Krishna's transfiguration—in Gandhi's translation of the *Gita* (slightly shortened, verses 5, 7–8, 10, 12). If you want to dive beyond this "initiation," please, read the original text.

> *Become the Tree of Life . . .*
>
> *Be the Tree of Life . . .*
>
> *Feel yourself diversified into the branches of all living beings on Earth . . .*
>
> *Expand . . .*
>
> *. . .*
>
> *Every branch is a planet,*
>
> > *a whole world of life-forms . . .*
>
> *Every leaf becomes a whole universe . . .*
>
> *Feel all universes . . .*
>
> > *as leaves on your branches . . .*
>
> *Feel ever new universes growing from the life-fluid flowing through you . . .*
>
> *. . .*
>
> *Now remember: You are only* one *Tree of Universes on the body of God . . .*
>
> *. . .*

The Lord said:

Behold, [. . .] my forms divine in their hundreds and thousands, infinitely diverse, infinitely various in color and aspect . . .

Behold, [. . .] in my body, the whole universe moving and unmoving, all in one, and whatever else thou cravest to see . . .

But thou canst not see Me with these thine own eyes. I give thee the eye divine; behold My sovereign power! . . .

With many mouths and many eyes, many wondrous aspects, many divine ornaments, and many brandished weapons divine . . .

Were the splendor of a thousand suns to shoot forth all at once in the sky, that might perchance resemble the splendor of that Mighty One . . .

5

The Show from Backstage

All the world's a stage.
—WILLIAM SHAKESPEARE, *AS YOU LIKE IT*

All artforms are in the service of the greatest of all arts: the art of living.
—BERTOLT BRECHT

The theatre is certainly a place for learning about the brevity of human glory: oh all those wonderful glittering absolutely vanished pantomimes!
—IRIS MURDOCH, *THE SEA, THE SEA*

DIVERGENT FROM ALL FORMER and following chapters, this one, "centerstage," takes it cues not from the natural world and humanity's ecological symbiosis, but from human culture, art, theatre and opera, and uses the insights into the human spirit as it expresses itself in "artificial" reflections of its strange "natural" existence to uncover the *constructions* by which we understand our own *artificiality* in nature. Is all spirituality spiritual construction? Or do we find anything "natural" that is something not created by us "backstage," after we have gone through the curtain and menagerie of theatrical arrangements that comprise our self-constructions as Selves, as persons, as masks in a play of our own device? This chapter is structured differently. It begins with a Meditation of deep revealing insight into human masks of construction—initiated by one of Shakespeare's (d. 1616) last plays, *The Tempest* (1610–11). The following sections are arranged like three acts of a drama or opera, prepared by a Prologue on theatre and followed by an Epilogue that arranges this "backstage" discourse around a possible expansion: that of existence itself (beyond which there is only nothing). The "three acts" are represented by three operas: *L'Orfeo* (1607), by Claudio Monteverdi (d. 1643); *Moses und Aron* (1930–32), by Arnold Schönberg (d. 1951); and *Akhnaten* (1983), by Philip Glass (b. 1937).

Obviously, in the world of the cultural inventions of humanity there are a vast array of other, alternative forms of theatre, for instance, indigenous festivals that tell, dance, sing or perform their creation myths or history; the Indian ritualized staging of stories of the gods or parts of the national epics, the *Mahabharata* and the *Ramayana*; or the Japanese Kabuki dance drama. However, my current selection, while limiting, has certain constraining characteristics that are part of the reason to understand them as expression of *cultural constructions that chase our spiritual nature*, but *ultimately fail* as they cannot reach, but only hint at, the unconstructed Reality they seek. Beyond that, the selection is contingent and almost infinitely permutable—which is exactly what the constructedness of culture and art, as well as their symbolisms, indicate. Nevertheless, the backstage story of these masterpieces of music theatre will reveal the complex search for the origins of meaning staged in such diverse, even archetypical and still globally influential cultural, intellectual and religious heritages such as that of ancient Egypt and Greece, and Near Eastern provenience.

This central chapter is—besides the last one (the summary)—also the most complex and expansive one. As already hinted at in the Preamble, the whole book is radiating out from the middle and, conversely, from the middle reflecting images and thoughts distributed throughout all other chapters. One could read around it, at first, and approach it as the last one (after the chapter on Time). Conversely, one could have begun the journey of the spiritual wayfarer as presented in this book with it (if one would have known).

Meditation X: Prospero's Magic

In Shakespeare's *Tempest*, Prospero, the former Duke of Milan, flees his land because of a plot on his life. He becomes the sorcerer Prospero, who, after a shipwreck, now is stranded with his daughter Miranda on an island that he magically creates with his imaginations. Many things happen to them in relation to their supernatural servants, the monster Caliban and the airy spirit Ariel, including stories of betrayal and revenge, reflections on love, a marriage pageant, and, eventually, Prospero's renunciation of magic. Even the storm and the shipwreck were just magical pageantry, and the whole masquerade had to be confronted. In the end, with the abandonment of revenge and magic, stand forgiveness, restitution, and purified love.

Archetypically, Prospero symbolizes the ambivalence of a powerful man involved in the intrigues of politics and family, betrayal, and revenge, in the familial *vendetta* bloodshed cycle of violence. But he is also a man of "the book" and "the staff," a man of deep learning and insight into the secrets and powers of creation. In a sense, like a seeker who on her path has become a Kabbalist initiate or a Sufi master or an ecstatic seer or a rarified saint, after she has gone through a process of purification and has achieved *real* insight into the Spirit of existence, so is Prospero a mystic whose path has initiated him in the *spiritual* depth of the creative process. This knowledge is, as reflected in the Tree of Knowledge (of the previous chapter), hidden behind the veil of material reality, because its knowledge is in danger to mislead the wayfarer to be seduced by their own Self and self-interest instead of approaching it with, or being purified to, a self-less spiritual awakening.

This is the moment in which Prospero ends the magical spectacle and expresses an existential insight. (You can use it as a visualization. Introduce the figure and the situation, the magician and the masquerade. And then read the text of Act IV, Scene 1, three times slowly.) Prospero declares,

> You look like something's bothering you. Cheer up. Our music-and-dance spectacle is over. These actors were all spirits, as I told you, and they've all melted into thin air. And just like the whole empty and ungrounded vision you've seen, with its towers topped with clouds, its gorgeous palaces, solemn temples, the world itself—and everyone living in it—which will dissolve just as this illusory pageant has dissolved, leaving not even a wisp of cloud behind.

> We are all made of dreams, and our life stretches from sleep before birth to sleep after death.

In some way, it is the epigraph of Iris Murdoch (d. 1999) that most closely reflects the same mood of theatrical nihilism: the insight that all the magic is just that, a vain play of empty reflections. But one could also read this "wonderful glittering absolutely vanished pantomime" as the fragility of all constructions of meaning and a spiritual insight in the wonder of existence itself, which only appears when we see through the "wonders" to the *true* wonder from which they receive their reality and importance. Maybe, then, and only then, will the magic of the theatrical suspension of any laws besides the self-imposed limits of imagination be true, real, and begin to release the true myths of the unspeakable of which we have nothing else to say or know than to *follow the paths to the end of their symbolisms*—the end, where they break down.

A meditation on this moment of truth could profit from the visualization it was given by the English director Peter Greenaway (b. 1942) in his movie *Prospero's Books* (1991) in which the renowned Shakespeare actor Sir John Gielgud (d. 2000), as Prospero, walks through the whole lush scene of the masquerade on the island, upheld by his magic; and revealing itself as staging, the whole scene vanishes into nothing. When the light shining on it is extinguished, he walks towards the camera, a curtain closes behind his face, and, at this point, he announces the dream-state of the text passage above. It is this dramatic moment that not only reveals the empty staging of magic, but the profound truth of the staging of *life*: its *mortality*. Theater, art, life itself, is just a temporary escape, for a moment, from this insight of sleep/death surrounding it. The show is just a show. Maybe this is its magic: that it happens, as a gift, as a power—but only to be performed in light of the mortality that grants it.

Visualize the following scene:

> *You sit in a theatre, among an audience waiting in expectation of what will begin soon . . .*
>
> *You face the stage. The curtain is closed, lights are on its middle section, where one can assume that the curtain parts . . .*
>
> *Excitement fills the air in the room . . .*
>
> *Prospero parts the curtain, steps into the stage light, and says:*
>
> *Everything you expect to see is an ungrounded vision . . .*
>
> *It is nothing but thin air . . .*
>
> *As soon as you know—it dissolves . . .*
>
> *You know now . . .*
>
> *We are made of dreams, surrounded by sleep and death . . .*
>
> *Prospero bows backwards, vanishing behind the curtain . . .*
>
> *With a sudden move the curtain lifts . . .*

What do you see? . . .

. . .

Now imagine: the theatre is a dream . . .

    you are a dream . . .

Imagine: You are an island of magical dreams on a sea of sleep . . .

Imagine: All the world is such a stage . . .

Ask: How does this insight impact your life? . . .

Shakespeare is, of course, not the only playwright who uses not only a plot but the inventory of the theatre itself to indicate the symbolic truths of human existence in a literal way. The Swedish poet, novelist and playwright August Strindberg (d. 1912), for instance, in his drama *A Dream Play* (1902), introduces the discussion of the ultimate reality of existence with the Hindu god Indra and his daughter Agnes. While Indra is portrayed as compassion itself, listening to all human and sentient suffering, Agnes (fire) eventually burns herself in the pain of this suffering. The symbolism of a garden in which a castle appears, which, then, burns down in the suffering of the creatures, may make its play on the Eden-symbolism and the City of God (see ch. 4), but as being destroyed by the theodicy-question: How can there be a god given all the suffering?

This whole process is initiated, at the beginning of the play, when the Four Faculties of a classical university (the intellectual senses of humanity)—theology, philosophy, medicine and law—discuss the question of ultimate meaning. In the end, they open a door that will prove whose view was right. But behind the door is—nothing; nothing but the stage on which the door is situated like a surreal piece of inventory.

What is "behind" (the scene or stage) of the world?

Indra's ear, in the play of Strindberg imagined as a cave in which the sighs of all creatures collect themselves to be heard by the god, is but a stage, too. Indra is backstage. Is this divine process of listening different from, or more real than, the open door of the frustrated meaning, because our "faculties" just *construct* the ultimate reality that they defend against one another? Yet the *listening* god! Is Indra a construct of the stage *or* the very reality behind the staging, the *unconstructed* behind the constructing process itself?

The Cosmic Spirit

Prologue: Theatre

Theater is a symbolic mirror of human life, reflecting humanity's characteristics, whether good or evil, and seeking answers to questions of existence and meaning. It is about the profound parameters of living as a human being in light of the insight that human self-reflection reveals humanity's *contingency* in this world of becoming (regarding all of these questions). So, theatre may be said to have been created for, or to be the creative symbolization of, the *inevitable* human situation of having lost merely natural reactiveness to existence, but having not found any satisfying answers to these existential questions either. We can, of course, take up some language of existentialist philosophy—of the like of Albert Camus (d. 1960) and Jean-Paul Sartre (d. 1980), both of them also using theatre to express their thought on the background of ancient theatre, Greek tragedy and the Theatre of the Absurd—such as being thrown into the world, to live in face of sure death, to live in a world of suffering without secure meaning, to be not bound by any fixed essence (of what it means to be human). We *are* (to some extent, but at least biologically limited by) what we *perform* to be. Theatre may be one of the very few places that humanity grants itself to reflect communally, publicly, as an organism, and, in fact, spiritually, on these questions: mourning its uncertainties and shortcomings, but also celebrating its transformative power to envision an alternative future of escaping fate. Theatrical utopias can imagine the creation of a peaceful civilization at least by protesting all forms of simplification of the human visions and all kinds of oppressive manipulations in light of a stage that can offer possibilities for differentiation and alteration of past paths. Theatre is a human art, and it reflects the art of becoming human (or lack of it).

The epigraphs of Shakespeare and that of the revolutionary dramatist Berthold Brecht (d. 1956) at the beginning of this chapter are not mutually exclusive, although, at a first glance, they might appear contrary in their gesture. One imagines life as theatre; the other, conversely, imagines theatre just as a symbolic expression of life. In any case, both are relating art and life, culture and nature, the physical and the aesthetic, perception and affection, one to the other. Both include a reverse relationship between the *constructed* and some view of the *unconstructed*. Shakespeare *deconstructs* human life to the point that it is not more, or different from, our human artistic construction of its symbolic representation in the form of a theatrical performance. Brecht, conversely, uses the purposefully directed constructions of theatrical symbolizations of life as the transforming power to differently reconstruct human life as the art of living. But while in either case construction is central, in Shakespeare's "directedness" between art and life, the constructed stage deconstructs human life as meaningless, as all constructions are, in fact or in the end (after all analysis is done), "thin air" or a temporary credit granted by "sleep and death," the purpose of which remains opaque. In Brecht's construction, the artistic or creative change is purposed, and so, while no meaning is presupposed for life, here, it is actuated by transforming it into a creative product or performance, free from the past boundaries and, so one would suppose, the oppressions of limited and limiting cultural identities and social organization that such an art of living might like to avoid, change, and commit to oblivion.

Many elements of theatre are immediately material reflections of non-material, informative or symbolic realities of human existence. Many of these elements are also substantially involved in the development of religious practices and symbolic universes, as the ones we have already discovered, perused, or accessed: the stage as place of rituals; the curtain between the sacred and the profane areas; the masks as public functions; the figures and choruses as players in public discourse on society or private reflections of emotions and paradigmatic situations of individual human existence; the differentiation between stage and audience as real life differentiation between actors and the gaze of the silent majority; the show as entertainment; the always lingering question of illusion and reality, and the magic of blurring this difference; the performance of moral and social behavior as a place of learning to fit in or how to object social and moral norms; and, most profound of all, the integration of all sensual and intellectual means of mirroring in dense symbolic terms, but physically, the spiritual nature of humanity.

I will only highlight two thinker's reflection on the nature of theatre. In Aristotle's (d. 322 BCE) *Poetics* (ca. 335 BCE), one of the first works written on theatre, we are confronted with the problem of acting as modes of construction and imitation (*poiesis*), mirroring human acting in life and on stage. The aspect that interests me, here, is the relation of these elements of theatre to human existence in a world of uncertainty and change where it is difficult to "discern the spirits" regarding what it means to be human. The *poetic* character is that of an act of creation per language and performance of fundamental moods of human existence, such as the fate of a tragedy will transmit, like compassion and existential fear, so as to transform the audience accordingly. By the catharsis or purification that is triggered when we are connected to our raw energies of emotions and the gravity of our actions, we are reconnected to our spiritual nature. It is really theatre, and not any other art, that has the ability to correlate ideas, emotions, language and performance, in which all human art comes together with poetic power. The poet's work is less concerned with the aesthetic impression, if we mean rules of symmetry or harmony in the means of poetic creation, but rather with the deep theatrical *imitation* of human acts that trigger the *cathartic transformation*. Creation is about listening and a clear view for the deep structures of avoided or masked or revealed motivations of human actions in light of the gravity of their moral relevance, and in light of the effects of the emotions as they manipulate to avoid, mask or reveal the spiritual forces behind the veil of our human skin—the masks of our actions.

In A. N. Whitehead's philosophical universe, God is understood as the "Poet of the World," that is, the one that with utter compassion receives the acts of creatures, which in their own creativity create the web of connections that is the theatre of their lives and environments, in order to save them from the masks of their accrued limitations. God spins the poem of the world from its *material* in order to *transform* it ever anew into the *poetic vision* of the Good, Beauty and Truth. And Whitehead understands the poetic nature of *all* events to express the *inherent aesthetic internality* that cannot be reduced to material causes and, hence, is a sign of the spiritual nature of their drive to exist and evolve. In the widest sense, then, the theater of existence is the *medium of mutuality* in which all events happen as acts of a reciprocal creation of forms, structures, organisms, sculptures, and symbolisms of a future ever yet to be established, a vision of ever new realizations of aesthetic, always self-transcending realization of the satisfaction of a civilized universe.

Whitehead also recognizes the deep connection between art and human action, which is the connection between the nature and culture of human life, but really, to some extent, of all organisms, as far as they are aesthetic creatures. Art, in its most basic character, is the *artificiality* that is based on the *freedom* of a creature *from* its natural, causal, or defining environmental limitations and circuits, that is, the freedom to *imitate* this natural sphere *without* the implications of the necessities that come with it. A whole host of implications are based on this view, but only two of them will concern us here. One implication lies in the fact that the most basic *activity* of artificiality (and hence of art) is the *free energy that overflows beyond states of necessity*, that is, survival strategies, such as finding food and shelter, or initiating or maximizing reproduction, or the avoidance of premature death by falling prey to illness, accident or hostile encounters. In other words, the creative freedom beyond the Darwinian necessities of survival and reproduction allows for the formation of culture as the ritualistic imitation with the intense enjoyments of the feelings created by such Darwinian necessities *without*, in fact, being in danger of their mechanisms. Ritual gives birth to *repetition* as *aesthetic appreciation of our ultimate non-identity with these material needs*, and expresses itself in all modes of spiritual depths, beginning with the *emergence of consciousness* as such and of this process itself.

Religion is born. As religion begins in such ritualistic imitation, leading to new intensities of feeling beyond necessities; and in this freedom, it triggers questions of the meaning of existence. In such an *artificial* state beyond mere natural cycles, *symbolic* visions and projections become the medium of answering the new, human questions of existence, in the creation of symbolic webs of mythologies, cosmogonies, theogonies, creation-stories and etiologies (events that indicate why the world is as it is). Finally, such artificial freedom gives way to *rational and aesthetic feelings and models* of the world as a whole and the human performance in it. As *consciousness* is the firstborn of artificiality, it *is* the art of the conscious and conscientious reunification of nature and culture beyond any stabilized dualism.

Religion is one expression of this artistic unification, besides thought (philosophy) and experiment (science). And theatre is the artistic performance of this whole process of creative overflow, the celebration of artificiality, the symbolic vision of human existence in myths and stories, and the exploration of the natural and artificial forces that shape human existence in light of the ever-shifting understanding of the universe in which humanity seems to live. Theatre, therefore, can be understood as the realization of the boundary in which nature and culture, material causality and artificial freedom, poetic construction and spiritual ultimates act out their permanently changing interactions and transformations. This will be even more intense if we understand theatre as *music theatre*, as the unification of *all* symbolic senses with the "other" boundary, namely, that of music, of material vibrations and aesthetic feelings beyond symbolisms. (It would be appropriate, here, given that the next section's appeal to music theatre, to reflect on the spiritual import of music per se. However, in order not to "use" music as means of symbolic content—or reduce it to program music—and preserve it in its pristine mode as aesthetic art that, essentially, but not by any particular use, is purified from all kinds of symbolic projections, I will defer reflection on its importance for awakening to the spiritual journey to the next chapter).

L'Orfeo

Artistically, this opera of Monteverdi is in many ways a first. While there might have been other operas, it is the oldest that we do not only remember theoretically, but actually preform theatrically. The genre of the opera and of the whole cosmos of ingrediencies of music theater were created with this opus: actors telling a story of archetypical import; singers and instrumentalists following a complex polyphonic score; a staging with all requisites to materialize the symbolizations of the text and the emotions conveyed by the ideas and musical poetic of the score. Its theme reaches back into Greek mythology to the story of love and loss, death and attempted salvation from death—a thoroughly religious story that can be understood *beyond* the names and cultural specifics of the setting, as it reflects on *existential* human experiences: love and death, fate and desires, estrangement and salvation, hope and doom, magic and tragic, nature and humanity, and so on. It asks "backstage questions": What is behind human life, if it is the stage of the human theatre? What are the rules, the script, the score, if any? And who or what has devised them?

The story itself, of Orpheus and Euridice—well known and often since ancient times quoted, multiplied, resituated, and retold—reminds us of the question of whether we are meant as spiritual beings to overcome death, or whether we are not such beings, neither spiritual in nature nor meant to become immortal. The myth confronts us with the reality of death either to be irrevocable and an eternal loss or only to be reached in a gigantic effort of purification of desires and Self. But it is precisely such desires for love of the erotically and exclusively beloved that triggers the attempt of Orpheus to save Euridice from death *and* to lose her, as on the way out of the Hades the only rule, not to look back, not to confirm that Euridice is really following, this desire or maybe even the doubt of this love, reveals the illusionary character of the whole endeavor.

Other elements interwoven in the universe of this myth are also paradigmatic. The dead are in Hades, in Greek understanding a non-place, a tragic utopia, of the non-existence of the dead. When Odysseus in book XI of Homer's *Odyssey* (composed ca. eighth to seventh century BCE) visits the Hades, he only encounters shadows of past relationships. There is really no life after death, here. Orpheus's attempt to save Euridice *from* death, without him dying in the course of it, can really only be understood in one of two ways: The archetypical desire to save the beloved ones' life from death is futile, as there is no such thing as a life after death. The dead are really gone. They remain only as the shadow of a memory that can be resurrected in one's mind. Or, alternatively, no one can avoid death in order to be united with the beloved dead, and *only then* will we know whether the passion of love is stronger than, or as strong as, death (Song of Solomon 8:6). There is no escape from the risk to totally and without reserve "let go" of everything and fall—like the vampire Stephen Griscz in the movie *Immortality* (as discussed in the previous chapter).

There is the river Styx that divides the land of the living from that of the dead, the ferry man crossing the river, and Cerberus, the sentinel at the entrance of Hades. If it is true that the crossing over of Orpheus is cheating death and will, therefore, not succeed, then, the letting go of these egotistic desires of secular salvation or this-worldly resuscitation might indicate this boundary to be much more similar to the one symbolizing the divide of *samsara* and *nirvana* in the Buddhist parable of the crossing of the river (as referred to in ch. 3 on the image of the river). Maybe the dead are not dead shadows, or only if they are viewed from the distorting realm of desire to escape death instead of embracing it as the spiritual maturation of a life beyond the grasp of a Self.

As in the opera, so in the ancient story of Orpheus and Euridice, it is the ability of music to magically change things: Orpheus can transfix people with his music, his voice and the use of the lyre; even the ferryman can be so relaxed as to forget his duties and functions, instead just becoming a listener; and Persephone, the queen of Hades, can be convinced of the deal to let Orpheus save Euridice. The problem is not music per se—the prologue of the opera stages *musica* herself "in person" to reveal the importance of music for such a transformation—but the use of music for manipulative reasons. Orpheus has a gift, but he cannot avoid to misuse it; yet this will not give him ultimate satisfaction. This again reveals an even deeper layer of the Orpheus myth: the (assumed) historical figure of an ancient poet and musician who (beginning with the sixth century BCE) was considered the greatest in his arts, but also being considered a magician, famous for his abilities to manipulate, maybe also heal, with his gifts not only humans, but also animals and the gods. Here, music becomes a medium of enchantment and immortality, of being beyond life and death, of revealing a spiritual instrument of unprecedented importance. How fitting, then, to see Orpheus to be the subject of the "first" opera.

This leads us to the even deeper archetypical layer of the figure of Orpheus, who was probably of Thracian origin, that is, of the plains of eastern Europe, populated with Indo-Germanic tribes. It is said that he was an ancient prophet and religious figure, or at least a symbolic concentration of the forces of art beyond (and over) nature. It is not unreasonable to remember the viability of this supposition because of the archaic connection between poetic, magical and religious activity: that the world, as music, had creative power in itself. Poets were, as Plato still knows, theopoets, singers of the gods. The whole rhythm of life and death, of decent into death and ascent to new life, is one of the perennial stories told about nature, the seasons, when winter is followed by spring, and of day and night, the decent of the sun into the underworld and its miraculous reappearance on the next morning. No wonder that the Orpheus myth is connected to the life-and-death cycles represented by Isis and Osiris in Egypt—one of the oldest recorded spiritual myths (probably reaching back into the fourth millennium BCE)—and Dionysius and Persephone in Greece. No wonder also that Orpheus is said, in his later life to have rejected all gods except Apollo, the sun—the force of all of these awakenings of life in nature and for human survival, and the image of resurrection from death and to immortality.

The story of the *cyclical renewal of life* is also at the center of the religion that stands associated with Orpheus since the seventh century BCE. Orphism was an ancient mystery religion, said to have been based on poems of Orpheus. He is also supposed to have created or refined the myth of Dionysus, the chaotic god of wine and orgiastic festivals, but also the conqueror of death. While the myth of Orpheus and Euridice warns against the desires that will thwart the hopes to overcome death, the Orphic Mysteries dramatize for the initiates death and resurrection of the god Dionysius. Yet, like the Pythagoreans, which probably have been influenced by the Orphics, they were an ascetic order that might have used the Dionysian ecstasies in ritual form to mystically connect with divinity. For Pythagoras, the music of Orpheus symbolized cosmic harmonies and orders, orders that are a sign of hope to overcome the limitation of life and its sufferings. With a myth of immortality told by Plato in his *Republic* (10.614–10.621), Orphics believed in an immortal soul that, after several reincarnations, will be liberated to the communion with the gods.

We are in the middle of an ancient spiritual path of love and death, desire and purification, immortality and reincarnation, cyclical resurrection of nature and the human soul, even a religion (as well as a family of religious orders of initiates) with a prophet-seer, a poet-writer, sacred writings and ways of living, of chastity and ecstasy, of ritualization and theatrical dramatizations of nature and human life, a symbolic universe and a heavenly map of divinities. While this spiritual path might not have survived in its integrity into our time, as other ancient religions have done, it widens our view of religious diversity and human ingenuity in the construction of symbolic universes in which the development and maturation of the spiritual purpose of our existence can be generated and perpetuated. And even if the particular myth has lost its religious import, its aesthetic transition and dramatization, such as in Monteverdi's *L'Orfeo*, still can touch us with the theatrical performance of perennial existential questions that want to offer us *a view from behind the scenes* that is our fragile life in this world. Whether we accept its solutions is not a matter of intellectual assent but, at best, of experimentation with its spiritual insights.

Moses und Aron

While Monteverdi was one of the first composers successfully establishing the music theater in the western tradition, Arnold Schönberg was one of the "last generation" of composers in the "classical" sense creating operas—that is, in the sense that his musical revolution also changed the expectations of what music drama could even mean for the next generations. Of Jewish heritage and, in the growing fascist and anti-Semitic climate of the 1930s, when he lost his engagement in Berlin because of this, he reverted his assimilation to Christianity and publicly reclaimed his Jewish identity. Creating this opera at the verge of the time that marked this personal sea change, it protests the disappearance of one of the "events" that marked the beginning of the family of western religious paths, but also established a visionary problematization of organized religion, and, perhaps, hints at a counter-spirituality to them and their inescapable paradoxes.

The compositional background for this opera is the ancient tradition of relating numbers and letters. In a primordial magical or mythical world view, letters that collect themselves to words as well as the words themselves were not only composing and purveying meaning, but inviting, holding and releasing elementary cosmic and supernatural powers. Especially in languages in which words were only written with consonants (and different vowel combinations were creating several pronunciations and a great ambivalence of meanings expressed with them), such as Hebrew, Arabic and Persian, letters did not only have shapes and associated symbolic meanings as well as specified powers, but a numerical value that allowed for an exchange of words with numbers and numbers to express the meaning and powers of words of the associated value of the numbers of their combined letters. Conversely, numbers always had symbolic importance, too. So, for instance, the number of the name of God YHWH is the numerical combination of $10 + 5 + 6 + 5 = 26$. Even if Schönberg was not a follower of the ancient and medieval Kabbalistic arts of gematria, he had existential and compositional preferences and aversions for certain numbers. Thus did he avoid the number 13, which, since the Black Death, the bubonic plague, of the high middle ages, was considered the number of Death. Consequently, he changed the correct spelling of the name of "Aaron" in the title of the opera presently under discussion into "Aron" in order to avoid that the whole German title *Moses und Aaron* would amount to thirteen letters. Conversely, he thereby highlighted the number twelve, the archetypical number of the tribes of Israel, but also the basis for the revolution he inaugurated as a composer.

The musical background of the story of this opera is highly significant. At that time, the last years of the nineteenth century, the musical patterns that had dominated compositional techniques and the conventional musical conditioning of the listeners, only allowing a gradual violation of the tonal scheme of major and minor keys and their harmonious relationships as theorized on and practiced since the adaptation of polyphonic music in liturgical contexts in the 1200s, broke down. Despite grave antagonism, occasional radical pieces of "atonality," that is, music without any tonal center, appeared at that time, such as Franz Liszt's (d. 1886) *Nuages Gris* or *Grey Clouds* (1881) and the late romantic explosion of and beyond tonality, as in the symphonies of Gustav Mahler (d. 1911). Yet it was with Schönberg and some of his students, Anton Webern (d. 1945) and Alban Berg (d. 1935), collectively known as the Second Viennese School of Music (after the "classical" one of Haydn, Mozart, Beethoven, and Schubert), that the turn to atonality became a new baseline for composition. This did reflect the unhinged situation of the time, culturally, socially, and politically, and it could not better foreshadow the chaos that the time of the two great wars was going to impose on the world.

Yet this was not the end, but maybe only the prophetic beginning of a new way of finding structural and harmonic order, namely, "serialism." Schönberg began to use the whole chromatic scale of notes and set down rules that guaranteed that no tonal center would emerge, but also that, instead of chaos, this would allow all notes in the scale of twelve half-tones (the full scale on the piano) to be equally appreciated. The sound of this "dodecaphony" (twelve-tone music), however, was a far cry from the emotional states that listeners to tonal music were conditioned to, associated with deep emotional states and powers, and why they listened to this music. In other words, for such listeners, it sounded awful, shocking, disturbing, unhinged, degenerate, abnormal, "atheistic." Yet, what one was listening to, now, was a new *democracy* of notes and the structural *equality* of all of them: all had to have the same magnitude of presence—a marked difference to the dictatorial and fascist developments of the time.

While dodecaphony allowed for a new way of encoding messages, names, stories, letters and numbers into the process of composition (because of translations of "names" of notes into names of people or concepts, and of numbers into messages), it seems to be especially resonant with the *theme* of Schönberg's opera: the Exodus story (Exodus 1–40); the story of Moses, the liberator of the twelve tribes of Israel from the oppression of pharaoh; the flight from Egypt; the procession through the desert; and the concomitant momentous transformation through the encounter with God YHWH in the Sinai-event. Dodecaphony and democratic structures, the twelve tribes, the liberation motive—all were eminent counter-examples of a reality that religion and humanity should like to envision and manifest, but seems to be unable to realize. The necessity of this vision, but the inevitability of its collapse, is the story of one of the most influential "events "or myths in religious history—symbolically giving birth to the western religious traditions—as told by Schönberg in the *paradigmatic spiritual conflict* between Moses and his brother Aaron. But before I dive deeper into the implications of this conflict, of which we find a biblical outline and against which we can evaluate Schönberg's artistic, philosophical and religious counter-point, I need to go even deeper into the layers of the background of the myth on which this conflict is based.

One layer, the one that became eventually tremendously important for religious history and, hence, was also of global civilizational impact, is the "event" telling of the encounter of Moses with God YHWH in the burning bush and on mount Sanai. Not only was a new name of God revealed, a name that God gave Godself, in these three forms: "I am," "I am (will be) who/what/that I am (will be)," and the mysterious Tetragrammaton "YHWH" (Exodus 3:14–15). Their interpretation allows us to see this pleromatic Name as a mirror of the cultures it moved in and through. In the Hebrew context, it indicated a *process* of becoming, an *open* future, even a *deference* of the meaning to be filled by further *encounters* with it and its bearer; in the Greek and Hellenistic context it became an expression of the *static* eternity of Being over Becoming, a statement of the majesty of *immovability* and the *power* to create, to let be, or to hold in existence. The living, historically open experience of the passionate God of Becoming (both coming anew from the future and being passionately impacted by human reactions) transformed into the eternity of the impassionate and impassible transcendent Godhead beyond history and time.

While we might have rediscovered, today, the more original meaning of a *passionate* God engaged in history but never bound by the past, a God of novelty and surprise, a God of cosmic creativity and human intercourse, we have still not faced the even deeper layer against which we interpret the uniqueness of the YHWH-revelation on Sinai, namely, its assumed "monotheism": that you should not have another God besides YHWH, as expressed in the prime directive of the decalogue (Exodus 20:3–7; Deuteronomy 5:7–11) and the Shema Israel (Deuteronomy 6:4–5), the confessional and covenantal exclusivity between YHWH and Israel. It meaning also changes dramatically. While the *original* context was the unique *liberation experience* and its specific consequent transformation of the society, the *later* reformulation reflects a stage of reform *after* the Babylonian Exile, the Deuteronomist reform, the YHWH-only movement, and the new exclusivist and universalist monotheism of Deutero-Isaiah.

As the current state of research into the origins of Yahwism in the midst of the emergence of Near Eastern religions demonstrates: The original meaning was *not* that of the later "monotheism" that excluded all diversity of divine powers, and that concentrated all intellectual, emotional and institutional forms and reforms onto the *mutually exclusive* differentiation between the sphere of the Creator and that of "His" creation. It was rather an expression of *another profound difference*: that between the High God, the Most High, the Creator, who or that is *beyond* all categories and understanding, transcendent, and all-embracing, but *inaccessible*, called El Elyon, and that *divine sphere* of divine beings, messengers (angels) or "sons of (this) God," the plenitude of divine powers, called "the gods" or Elohim. As the rabbinical scholar Daniel Boyarin (b. 1946) in his book *The Jewish Gospels* (2012), in consonance with a host of other researchers, has compellingly demonstrated: YHWH was originally *one of* the "sons" of El Elyon, *one of* the Elohim, the south Canaanite version of the northern differentiation between El Elyon and his foremost "son" Ba'al—the eternal rival of YHWH for exactly that reason! The "exclusivity" of YHWH, then (at this point of differentiation in time), indicated the covenant of the people of Israel with *this* "Son of God" or "Angel" over and against all others, the other Elohim. Probably as the "younger" deity was related to immanence, history, war, and justice, YHWH was (in this rivalry of contenders) understood to be the *favorite* Son, the one whom the Highest God has *enthroned* over all the other court-gods or divine beings, the Elohim. Hence, the difference between the *older* and the *younger* God, the *transcendent* and the *immanent*, the *creator* and the *executor*, the *merciful* and the *warring*, the *Father* and the *Son*, triggered *another* difference: that between YHWH and the Elohim, which *degraded* to become angels, or *YHWH's* "sons."

We face the "backstage" fact that the spiritual, religious (institutionalized) and theological scenario of "two powers in heaven" was probably one of the *most ancient* Hebrew, Israelite and Jewish religious traditions that, despite the post-Exilic monotheistic reforms of the sixth century BCE, did *not* disappear. While it was only criticized by the *new* religious authorities *after* the destruction of Jerusalem and the Second Temple in 70 CE, it still textually materialized in the writings of the surviving rabbinical reconstruction of Judaism from the second century CE on. We know that this ancient tradition did *not* disappear since, *despite* the Deuteronomist redaction of the Tanakh (the five books of Moses), we find ample textual traces of this older tradition, for instance, in the exchangeability between YHWH, the Name (*HaShem*) and the Angel of God; or the pre-exilic prophets such as Ezekiel and Isaiah who maintain the encounter with the younger Son in the manifestation of the Glory of God (*kabod*) in the form or appearance of a human being (Ezekiel 1:26); but also the many passages of the Psalms that uphold this difference between El and YHWH (Psalm 110:1); and, finally, the visions of the book of Daniel from the second century BCE, especially in the vision of the *two thrones* of the Ancient of Days and the *enthronement* of the younger one with the appearance as one of the "sons of Elohim" (Daniel 3:25) or of "holy ones of the Most High" (Daniel 7:18), and in the appearance of a semblance of "a son of man" (Daniel 7:14)—*not* as one of the sons of YHWH, but a son of *El Elyon*, that is, *YHWH*.

The conflict between the *ancient* tradition of the *two* powers in heaven and the *younger* traditions of *mono*-theism, which transformed the older tradition by *identifying* El Elyon and YHWH, became the antagonistic force that created and perpetuated *two* streams of understanding of the biblical text. With the appearance of a "new star" in the religious landscape in the form of the "Son of Man" and "Son of God," Jesus, and of the Christian understanding of God and Jesus's relationship to God, this antagonism came to be the defining pattern for the development of Judaism and Christianity. Their mutual transreligious mutation into their later antagonistic bifurcation expressed itself especially in the christological and trinitarian struggles of the next six Christian centuries within and without the increasingly failing (pagan and Christian, western and eastern) Roman empires.

Not only have scholars made the convincing case that the New Testament's display of the spiritual and ontological station of Jesus is that of an *identification* with the "Son of the Most High" (Luke 1:32), that is, YHWH (*kyrios*), from the earliest pre-Pauline layers on (Philippians 2:6–11), and possibly even by his *self-identification* as Son of Man *and* Son of God (Mathew 26:63–64; Luke 22:70) *with* YHWH. Moreover, they have rediscovered this identification to have been possible because it reflects the *ancient* Jewish tradition of the two powers in heaven. It is for *this* understanding and vision for which the "first" (archetypical?) Christian martyr Stephen had to die (Acts 7:55)—reflecting the beginning and long-standing bifurcation of ancient and new theologies *within* Judaism, of which Christianity was still part for the first century of its existence, namely, between the ancient *dipolar* and the later *dualistic* monotheism. In fact, then, the becoming of Christianity reflects this *most ancient* tradition versus the reductionist "monotheistic" identification of the Most High with the *kyrios*, be it YHWH or Jesus—a recovery of the *ancient difference* that is clearly expressed in the Pauline expansion of the Shema Israel by *dividing* it between God the Creator and *kyrios* Jesus, the Mediator (1 Corinthians 8:6).

From the theophany of YHWH to Moses on, which reflects the *older* tradition, through the extensive use of the book of Daniel and related dipolar passages in the Psalms, and probably Jesus's self-understanding, in the first three Christian centuries, as can be witnessed in the writings of the early theologians such as Justin Martyr (d. 165 CE) and Origen of Alexandria (d. 253 CE), we can witness the interference with the younger tradition. It is ironic that that which contributed to the *birth* of Christianity *transformed* in the process of the justification of this dipolar theism *as* monotheism (against Jewish and Hellenistic philosophical accusations) into a confused reading of the scriptural text *as if* El and YHWH were *identical* and, hence, *erased its own origin* in a new difference: a monotheism with or without "sons of El=YHWH," Jewish and Christian, respectively. And ironically, the older tradition of the *dipolar* divinity that allowed for the *older* trinitarian understanding of God was *forcefully eliminated* in the new monotheistic condensation. While the *dipolar* theism of the first centuries upheld the *difference between the unmanifest and the manifest God*, the difference between God and Son, Logos, Glory, or Wisdom (John 1), the younger monotheism forced this difference to become one in God. The *trinitarian dilemma* was born: In discarding the older tradition, the rabbinic monotheism (eliminating the heresy of the two powers in heaven) challenged Christianity, which reacted by embracing the *same new benchmark*, but saved the older tradition by including it into a *differentiated One*, which for Jewish and later Islamic sensitivities must and did look like an embrace of polytheism (see Qur'an 112).

Yet the older tradition did not disappear, although it was weakened and ousted, it effectively became an *established alternative tradition in its own right* and with its own transreligious movements. It is in its own diversity reflected in the writings of the contemporary of Jesus, Philo of Alexandria; it can virtually without exception be witnessed in the writings of the early Church fathers, finally leading into the catastrophic Arian controversies of the fourth century CE; it appeared in the development of Plato's thinking in the Neo-Platonism of Plotinus; it survived in the mystical traditions of the Kabbalah, Sufism, and of Christianity, importantly mediated by the writings of Pseudo-Dionysius the Areopagite. In fact, in a *global* religious context, it connects with the eastern traditions insofar as they differentiate between the unmanifest, transcendent Ultimate Reality and the immanent Deity, such as in the Hindu differentiation between *nirguna* and *saguna brahman*, or between the nondual *brahman* and the personal Ishvara; in the Daoist discernment of the unnamable and the named Dao (*Dao De Jing* 1); or in the manifestations of the Buddhist "unmanifest" *dharmakaya* (the transcendent, nondual Body of the Dharma) in the two bodies of the transhistorical, cosmic Buddha and the physical, historical Shakyamuni Buddha.

Now, how does this peeling away of ancient layers of religious construction of divinity and its world-construction relate to the spiritual conflict of Moses and Aaron, especially as presented in Schönberg's opera? It is my contention that, in the final analysis, this conflict reflects the difference of these two traditions. The biblical hints can be detected in the relationship between Moses and Aaron: Moses is the one that *directly* encounters God, and Aaron is a *reflection* of Moses, the one that speaks—in this regarded imitating the difference between El and YHWH. While Moses disappears in the heights of the mountain, Aaron creates the famous Golden Calf, an "image of God" (YHWH being the image of El). Both elements are reflected and reinforced in Schönberg's opera: Moses cannot connect to the people; Aron is the communicator. Moses has the incommunicable, incomprehensible concept of God, but Aaron can translate it into miracles and the people's feeling of the presence of the powers of God. Moses is disconnected from the people, absent from the scene (in Act II)—he disappeared into the presence of God—while Aron presents God to the people in the form of imaginations, materializations, and concrete community. Moses knows only the abstract *concept* of a transcendent intangible God, which he cannot communicate; Aron, however, does not know God "directly," by experience, but is able to communicate the vision of Moses into *images*, the symbolic expressions and material representations that can be grasped by the people. Moses wants to religiously organize society by the abstract Law (statements on tablets); Aron, however, wants to organize society around the desires of the people concentrated and distributed through the image of God, the Golden Calf (which is, in fact, an old image of the High God El in Canaanitic pre-history). The *aesthetic* difference between these approaches is reinforced in the presentation of their *voices* in the opera: Moses virtually never sings, but speaks in barren voice to notes (*Sprechgesang*); Aron virtually always sings in a melodious tone.

Schönberg never finished the opera; the third act remained uncomposed. From its libretto, we can gather that, in the end, there is supposed to be the reconciliation of the two brothers that will create the new people of God. That is, the "finished" opera may have liked to convey the necessity to religiously always *harmonize* concept and image, vision and symbol, the abstract and the imaginable, or, in other words, the *transcendent* El and the *immanent* YHWH, or the unmanifest Godhead and the manifest God. Yet, in its *unfinished* "final" version, another story is told, and perhaps, in my view at least, perfectly reflecting the whole problem of being religious. The outcome of the second act imposes on the protagonists and us the profound insight *on both sides* that the connection between the transcendent and the immanent side of God *is not in our human ability to be reconciled*—both Aron and Moses admit their failure to do so! The *last words* of the second act belong to Moses, spoken a cappella: "Oh Word, thou Word, that I lack."

Here, another transition becomes available: The Word *itself could* bridge the gap, manifesting *itself*. This *was* available in the Jewish context through the *older* dipolar tradition, and that was forcefully reflected, for instance, in the figure of *Wisdom*, as she appears in the biblical Wisdom literature (Proverbs 8; Sirach 24), the intertestamentary book of the Wisdom of Salomon (ch. 7) and the speculations on the divine Logos by Philo of Alexandra, as well as the Christian claim of the *event* of "its/her" incarnation happening in Jesus (John 1:14).

However, the abrupt ending of the opera *in despair*, indicating the *impossibility* of reconciling word and image, abstract concept and symbolic materialization, of God or ultimate reality, hints at the *hiatus* that *any religious construction* of reality has to cope with or to withstand, namely, that between the mystical silence and the impossibility to express the unity experiences in any form revealing its gravity (*kabod*). And, conversely, the polyphony of images and symbolizations, materializations, and organizations of the divine reality *must* reveal their ultimate *constructed* nature by which they *cannot* reach an anchor in, or affirmation beyond, the infinite, transcendent horizon except in an experience of the *collapse* of any such attempt on finding a foundation in reality.

Yet in Schönberg's theatrical setup of the whole story and development of the conflict between abstraction and concretization, thought and image, lies *another synthesis*—besides the "harmony" that lingers unrealized with the third act, and besides the mutual affirmation of failure at the end of the second act—that may go undiscovered. However, when we discover it, almost hidden from the clamor of the adversarial energy that propels the storyline, we will simultaneously feel enlightened and disillusioned. It is, in reality (the reality of the stage) *not true* that Moses connects to God and Aron to the people (as if Moses was right and Aron wrong). The *opposite* is true: Both Moses and Aron *have fallen short of the theophany* that triggers the whole event and its consequences, because both have been right and wrong in their visionary and intuitive understanding of divine revelation. The solution to the conflict was composed into the score from the very beginning, but remained *undiscovered* by the figures of the drama and, perhaps, also by us, the audience: In the beginning, like the act of creation of Genesis 1:2, God appears not in the form of Moses' abstract concept of an immutable God and not in Aron's passionate image projected onto the Golden Calf, but in *a gentle polyphonic web of voices*, like a warm breeze of a mellow summer afternoon, almost imperceptible, but full of a multiplicity of beautiful harmonies. Schönberg composed the "song" of God with six voices, singing and speaking (*Sprechgesang*), inclusive of both Moses and Aron, and, what is more, both male and female, as well as sung through the chorus of the people.

God is already present in *all* of them as *indiscernible divine manifold* of gentle beauty, opposite to all the divisions the whole opera works out: devoid of the opposition between word and image; devoid of the violence of the impersonal Law and the self-destructive Golden Calf; devoid of the difference between revelation (to Moses) and intuition (of Aron); devoid, finally, of the hiatus between external and internal, transcendent and manifest duality. Were anyone to listen to this voice, the whole tragic drama would have become immaterial and, instead, the Spirit would have spoken: the *cosmic* Spirit over the face of the deep; the *divine* Spirit of a polyphony that embraces all oppositions as pleroma, as Elohim; and the *intimate* Spirit in which we breath and live.

The moral of the drama may be this: Only if we avoid the creation of the hiatus between concept and image, which mirrors itself into the hiatus between the Creator and the creature, will we avoid or overcome the struggles, fights and wars initiated or at least fueled by, and justified through, the absoluteness of this hiatus. It is by this measure that the Abrahamic monotheism developed its most hostile forms of mutual extinction over against heretics; the trinitarian confusions of the first six Christian centuries in which the equality of a human figure with God forced an eternal oscillation between tritheism (three persons in God as three Gods) and modalism (three persons as masks); and the Islamic war against the impression that this violates strict monotheism by assuming partners with God.

The plurality of God in Schönberg's opera and the deeper layers of the story of El and YHWH, as well as Jesus, could have been (and in a resistant alternative tradition has, in fact, been) revealing of an understanding of God as a *polar* divine. It was available in ancient Israel, in pre-Christian Judaism, and it was the *basis* for the rise of the Christian understanding of God and Christ, because this proto-trinitarian understanding of this God as acting in the all-embracing and all-pervading Spirit did not need to *divide* between God and creation. Instead, it *bridged* both in the Spirit of the dipolar transcendent and the immanent aspects of God that were experienced in theophanies, such as that of Moses and in the person of Jesus, and would have allowed a different approach to the Manifestations of the divine Horizon "within itself" *before* any divisions and *without* the perpetual violence that an exclusive abstract monotheism unleashed onto the ancient world, and that follows us like a specter until today. Here, while the dualistic monotheism appears as the unfortunate construction, the relational bridge releases the *unconstructed* Spirit of *polyphonic* unity.

Akhnaten

Neil Armstrong (d. 2012), the first man on the Moon in 1969, at some point at a White House event with his colleagues of the Apollo 11 mission in 1994 prophesied that the future development in space science and exploration by a younger generation will become possible if and when they will have pealed back some of truth's protective layers. Whatever this means in his context of space exploration, in the religious universe, perhaps, most protective layers were laid on the truth of the revolutionary change wrought about by pharaoh Akhenaten (d. 1335 BCE). The revolution he initiated of a monotheism of unprecedented rigorous exclusivity was so shocking, at his time, that after his demise his son not only renamed himself in the image of the ancient national god of Egypt again, namely, Amun-Ra—thereby recanting Akhenaten's newcomer Aten—but in accord with the priesthood of the polytheistic religious economy erased the names of the predecessor on all temple walls and places of images, pictures and hieroglyphic writing. The knowledge of Akhenaten's existence and religious reform all but disappeared into oblivion, to be recovered only in the nineteenth century.

This is the background and theme of Philip Glass's opera *Akhnaten* (this is the way he spells the figure of Akhenaten). It is in many ways situated after Schönberg's musical revolution of atonality and serialism, being an example of a new movement: *minimalism*. Less interested in harmonic experimentation (Glass can express major themes in Akhnaten, for instance, in A minor and major keys), this music permutates repetitive rhythmic patterns of slow harmony evolution and persistent structures. The effect achieved is a very energetic fusion of movement and arrested vibrating images, stabilized musical figures, and holographic sculptures, a kind of standstill of permanent patterns in intense movement. This is also reflected in the representation of Akhenaten and his story. Not in dramatic interactions and fermentations, but in rather static musical and spatial pictures, scene after scene, we witness not so much a living movement of a story from a beginning to a climax, but a series of stills that almost break up into closed but internally complex universes. They embrace *moments* that define the *timeless ideas* composing this history, such as the family-picture, the relation between Akhenaten and Nefertiti, the reform idea, the resistance of the priests, the vision of the new capital city dedicated to Aten, the collapse of the idea, and a contemporary look (from the present of the opera) back onto the past happenings, visualized as a graveyard of inconsequential ghosts.

In the middle of the opera (Act II, Scene 4), Glass situates the spiritual center of the whole story, an expansive aria that recited the *Hymn of Aten*. It is maybe the most precious theopoetic composition of the religious revolution of Akhenaten, not only expressing the deep veneration of the god Aten, the sun disc, the radiant light of life and death, of movement (day) and rest (night), the god of all gods, the creator of all things, and the father of pharaoh, Aten's son, Aten's representative on Earth. What is more, the chorus in the background of this scene connects this referential poem to the biblical context and recites Psalm 104. Herewith, Glass follows the longstanding tradition that, since the rediscovery of Akhenaton's reign, has found connections between both monotheistic traditions such as the use of language, structure, and progression of thought and imagery, but especially the relation of the effects of the sun, its movement, the light and darkness, the cycles of day and night and of time, and the like, as expression of divine characteristics. More will be said in Meditation XI; but it is remarkable to register these two cross-references: that the Hebrew transcendent YHWH Elohim is compared with the sun; and that the Egyptian god Aten is not identified with the physical sun but, as transcendent reality, is only symbolized by the sun-analogy.

The comparison with Moses (ca. thirteenth century BCE) and the Sinai theophany, generally understood as one of the origins of monotheistic thought and religions, besides maybe the reform of Persian religion by its prophet Zoroaster (between 1200 and 600 BCE), is instructive. Both figures and their monotheistic impulses are, of course, related by the fact that Moses is an Egyptian name, that the story begins in Egypt, and that it is situated in about the same time frame—the thirteenth to the twelfth century BCE. These and other resonances have led to incredible amounts of speculations of their historical and ideological, and even causal, relationship. Even the founder of psychoanalysis, the Viennese psychiatrist Sigmund Freud (d. 1939), made, in his book on *Moses and Monotheism* (1939), the claim that Akhenaten's reform was the basis for Mosaic Jahwism, that Moses was not a Hebrew, but an Egyptian, that he was an adherent of Akhenaten, and that he transmitted the fundamental idea of the oneness and universal singleness of divine reality in the face of polytheism. The exclusive relevance (worship) of just one God (henotheism) as a tribal reality was supposed to have become the trigger for the Israelite religion. Others speculated of fugitive groups of Aten-worshipers that ended up in the Hebrew context. In any case, since the surprises that the rediscovery of Akhenaten's reign evoked in the nineteenth century, many experts, such as Jan Assmann (b. 1938), who has investigated both of the cultural and religious backgrounds and developments throughout their diverse periods of interaction and their impact on the history of religions, have assumed that a deep connection between the two monotheisms was ultimately responsible for the generation and trajectory of the Abrahamic religions.

We don't really know. However, the whole scaffolding of speculation is based on a fragile and probably erroneous presupposition, namely, that the Moses-epiphany was about monotheism. At least, we must temper with such an assumption on both sides, as the "exclusivity" of Aten *and* YHWH may better be understood on the basis of an *inclusive cosmotheism* in which *monolatry* was the restraining characteristic of both reforms. It was about worship and influence, not about existence. Available sources not only show that the existence of the other Egyptian gods is not absolutely negated but rather *assumed* into the figure of Aten, which, as the physical and symbolic sun, radiates out to the whole cosmos, all subjects of pharaoh, and, potentially, all the other gods. And it is a widely accepted assumption that, in the Israelite context, *exclusive* monotheism arose only in or *after* the Babylonian exile (in the late sixth century BCE or later).

The real relationship of these figures and their religious revolutions may only become available if we take into account that the Moses-tradition was based on the Canaanite *bipolarity* between the High god El Elyon and Ba'al, with YHWH being one of the sons of El, one of the Elohim or even the equivalent of, or identical with, Ba'al (see the previous section). If we add the fact that a few dynasties before Akhenaten's reign Canaanites settled in Egypt (ca. from 1800 BCE on), and that the Hyksos, a Palestinian people with Canaanite royal ideology, worshiping Ba'al, invaded Egypt and even formed the fifteenth and sixteenth pharaonic dynasties in the sixteenth century BCE, we gain a completely different picture of the monotheistic evolution. Not only was Ba'al a known entity in Egypt, but the father-son relationship between El and Ba'al may have been the dipolar background for Akhenaten's reform. But the shock of Akhenaten's reform that led to its near complete erasure almost immediately after his reign together with the memory of the alien invasion of the Hyksos and both in combination with the explosion of a ravaging plague following from a Hittite-Egyptian confrontation in the final years of Akhenaten's kingship may have led to a traumatic transmutation. Ba'al was now an enemy-deity and became represented in the form of the god Seth as demonic force par excellence—Seth, after all, murdered Osiris (connecting to the Prometheus story) and became, in Egyptian and Greco-Roman reflections, identified with the god who was allegedly revered in the temple of Jerusalem! So, the Egyptian aversion against Moses and his counter-religion may have its historical roots in these events, but, at least, appeared in this form in the perception of the Jewish "exclusivism" of later Hellenistic centuries—as attested by the Egyptian historian Manetho (ca. early third century BCE) and the Jewish historian Flavius Josephus (d. 100 CE).

Be that as it may, the *paradoxical reversal* of these two figures and the impact of their religious reforms is astonishing. While Moses's revelation became formative for the whole religious landscape of the next three thousand years up to our days, Akhenaten had virtually no impact at all and his religion disappeared immediately after its invention from history, maybe only leaving traces in the collective subconscious, in repressed and displaced imagery, and in a traumatic memory of humanity (if it was not its expression, in the first place). However, we know nothing about the *historicity* of Moses as a human individual and not much about the making of the whole Moses-tradition before the post-Exilic monotheistic reform of the Deuteronomists and their integration of it into the emerging canon of the Tanakh. Yet since the discovery of the history of Akhenaten's reign, we know *for a fact* that he existed, what he did, and what he thought. *His* religious reform is, *in fact*, if not the oldest, so one of the oldest *historically definite statements of religious history of an individual human being* who lived three and a half thousand years ago. This is in itself remarkable! And so, we are confronted with the paradoxical situation that the oldest historical monotheistic development has had only a displaced impact of distorted projections on developments of other older forms or (by it) transformed constellations of polytheism and cosmotheism, as well as the exploding monotheistic preoccupation of religious history in the next several thousands of years, while the most influential strain of the same development, the Moses-tradition, has had no *historic* availability and only shows its *composite* face of many generations of layered evolution.

Yet with Akhenaten we know not only that such a "new" *united cosmic* worldview was not a later development, but also *not* a generally preferred solution. In its own context, its *exclusivity* might have been not just an alternative or a countering opposite, but a *radical alteration* of a concurrently emerging *inclusive* cosmotheism of Amun-Ra, the uniting, but hidden, all-embracing Godhead behind all gods and the multiplicity of world phenomena. And it was, perhaps facilitated through the traumatic rejection of Aten, by the unavoidable indirect powerful impact of this "all-embracing" monotheism of Aten that it "survived" in the increasingly expansive reformation of an *inclusive dipolar nondualism*, which manifested in *pantheistic* tendency of the later universal goddess Isis. She became considered and revered as the *una quae est omnia*, the One who or that *is all beings* (as explored in Meditation XI). This profound universality, again, remained translatable into historic forms of cosmotheistic revivals, for instance, of the *Corpus Hermeticum* (first century BCE to first century CE), its "discovery" in the Renaissance and the pantheism-discourse in the Enlightenment era.

In these events, we find an *ongoing recovery of the memory* of the spiritual universality of cosmotheism in resistance to the exclusive monotheisms of the revealed religions, which always repressed them as "paganism" or "idolatry"—in dualistic tension remembered from the exclusivity of YHWH, the first commandments of the Decalogue, and the abomination of the Golden Calf (the Egyptian god Apis), to the *la ilaha illalah* (there is no god but God) of Islamic provenience. The reason is that the relationship between unified reality and multiplicity of its expressions (or vice versa) always was an unsettled and unsettling question for the nascent cosmic consciousness of humanity. Yet, with A. N. Whitehead, we can say that inclusivist universalization in religion and cosmology inevitably developed by the transcending of any local, functional myths of social self-justification in the embrace of *the world as a whole*. Beyond any religious parochialism, humanity began to express a new question: from what *ultimate reality* is the All constructed? Yet in its problematization, the question had never *only* one solution. Because of the impact that this inherent ambivalence has for our understanding of the "cosmic" Spirit, I will return to it again (in ch. 7).

Like the other two operas, *L'Orfeo* and *Moses und Aron*, *Akhnaten* mediates—perhaps constructed over generations—(between) different monotheisms and their "prophets." *Akhnaten* is the story of a failure to reach a conclusion that gives us an insight into the "backstage" reality of the drama that artificially unfolds in reflection of important humane achievements in thought and life, religiosity, cosmology and spiritual searching. We are left with artificiality, construction, *all the way* backwards. This is in stark contrast to the heroes of the dramas who, in their historical representation, as poets, prophets and kings, construct their reference to ultimate reality through the *image of the sun*, as the *immanent* symbol of the *transcendent* divine power of creativity and governance, that they either feel or intuit, or experience, as *revealed* to them, themselves becoming the "mediators" (sons) of the divinity (Exodus 4:16; 7:1). The dramatic setting seems to allow the composers to make the *constructed* nature of all of these claims, figures, and stories of divine encounter or authority much more obvious. The artificial/artistic *representation* of their myths or histories does not distract us from the *impossibility* to mediate unconstructed reality in *any* construction; but the *artistic* representation, instead of the religious ritual, allows for our aesthetic and critical minds to awake.

In this sense, all three operas end at the point at which Shakespeare's Prospero gives up on the desperate magic of upholding "unrealities" for all reasons besides confrontation with one's Self. *In all religious dramas, the climax is an anticlimax*: the unraveling of their most desired constructs into thin air. Euridice dies, Moses loses the Word, and Akhenaten only remains an irrelevant ghost of the past. The difference between Prospero's and the three groups of proponents—Orpheus and Euridice, Moses and Aaron, Akhenaten and Nefertiti—is that they had to be forced to confront their failure, while for Prospero it was a liberation. Paradoxically, however, the historical figures underlying these artistic memories may well have contributed to, rather than resisted, the demise of the mythological forms of which they had to be cleansed in the artistic reconstructions: Orpheus *demythologized* the gods much in the way we remember from Pythagoras's immanent world harmony or Plato's transcendent Idea of the Good; Moses (the Moses tradition) helped to contribute to the *dismissal* of the polytheistic divinization of nature and the transformation of the royal mythology of YHWH from the "I am/(be)come" into the universalistic *to on/ esse* (being itself); and Akhenaten might be interpreted in a much more radical sense, as the *naturalization* of divinity in the sense of Spinoza—as were *displaced* Egyptian memories, for instance, in the *Hermetic* writings—while Akhenaten was unknown in the European Enlightenment discourses on pantheism (to which I will return later again).

These and other multiple tension and potentially ever-shifting collisions between the events and their artistic reinvention is what Whitehead has called the conscious awakening to the "motive force of the Spirit": the potential to transcend practical functions, parochial interests and evolutionary adaptations, and, instead, against all limited desires, to be freed *from* causal (karmic) repetitions and *to* the recognition of the *real aesthetic attractors*, the *deeper purposes*, and the *hidden meanings* rising to the surface of awareness and action. They offer us a choice: not just to repeat ritually, but to understand intellectually, to test empirically, and to seek mystically, the *epiphanic immediacy of the spiritual insight* that—with Prospero—only *happens* as the *awareness of the constructions* and the *search for the unconstructed* begin to *interact* in this new, enlightened horizon.

Meditation XI: The Sun, All in All

The *Great Hymn to Aten* (ca. 1500 BCE) is the expression and the only witness to the radical nature of the religious, theological, and cosmological reversal that occurred with Akhenaten's new transcending and exclusivist monotheism. It is inscribed in thirteen columns of hieroglyphs on the west wall of the courtier Ay at Amarna. The following text is a partial presentation in the translation of Mariam Lichtheim (pp. 96–100).

Meditate on it!

If you read it closely, imagine first the physical sun per se. Then, read it again, and imagine the symbolic sun, the transcendent giver of light and life of which the sun is only an image. Then, if you are bold, read both views into one: break the exclusivity of a merely immanent or transcendent monotheism and find in your *binocular* mental imagination the spiritual truth of a *dipolar* monotheism. This is the origin of a double identification that, if you consciously see and feel the layers of which it consists, will reveal to you its complex multiplicity: of the dipolar difference and mutual mirroring of the transcendent invisible Sun and the immanent physical sun. While the latter recurs *in* rhythms of life and death, light and darkness, movement and rest, the former one always shines from *beyond* these differences. While the latter one occurs in the *form* of the divine king, the Son, the former one dwells in the *formlessness* of pure light of the Father—both moving through the domain of their universe, heaven and earth.

> You rise beautiful from the horizon on heaven,
>
> living disk, origin of life.
>
> You are arisen from the horizon,
>
> you have filled every land with your beauty.
>
> You are fine, great, radiant, lofty over and above every land.
>
> Your rays bind the lands to the limit of all you have made,
>
> you are the sun, you have reached their limits.
>
> You bind them (for) your beloved son.
>
> You are distant, but your rays are on earth,

The Show from Backstage

You are in their sight, but your movements are hidden.

. . .

Darkness envelops, the land is in silence, their creator is resting in his horizon.

At daybreak, arisen from the horizon, shining as the disk in day,

you remove the darkness, you grant your rays,

and the two lands are in festival,

awakened and standing on their feet.

You have raised them up, their bodies cleansed, clothing on,

their arms are in adoration at your sunrise.

. . .

How numerous are your works, though hidden from sight.

Unique god, there is none beside him.

You mold the earth to your wish, you and you alone.

. . .

You have made the far sky to shine in it,

to see what you make, while you are far, and shining in your form as living disk.

risen, shining, distant, near,

you make millions of forms from yourself, lone one,

cities, towns, fields, the road of rivers,

every eye sees you in their entry,

you are the disk of day, master of your move,

of the existence of every form,

you create . . . alone, what you have made.

. . .

You are in my heart, there is none other who knows you

beside your son Neferkheperura-sole-one-of-Ra.

You instruct him in your plans, in your strength.

The land comes into being by your action, as you make them,

and when you have shone, they live,

when you rest, they die.

You are lifetime, in your body,

people live by you.

The Cosmic Spirit

Because of the longstanding discovery of the common patterns relating the *Great Hymn to Aten* of *Akhnaten* and Psalm 104, meditate on the following partial presentation of this psalm.

> ¹ Bless the LORD, O my soul.
>
> O LORD my God, you are very great.
>
> You are clothed with honor and majesty,
>
> ² wrapped in light as with a garment.
>
> You stretch out the heavens like a tent,
>
> ³ you set the beams of your chambers on the waters,
>
> you make the clouds your chariot,
>
> you ride on the wings of the wind,
>
> ⁴ you make the winds your messengers,
>
> fire and flame your ministers. . . .
>
> ²⁴ O LORD, how manifold are your works!
>
> In wisdom you have made them all;
>
> the earth is full of your creatures.
>
> ²⁵ Yonder is the sea, great and wide,
>
> creeping things innumerable are there,
>
> living things both small and great.
>
> ²⁶ There go the ships,
>
> and Leviathan that you formed to sport in it. . . .
>
> ³¹ May the glory of the LORD endure forever;
>
> may the LORD rejoice in his works—
>
> ³² who looks on the earth and it trembles,
>
> who touches the mountains and they smoke.
>
> ³³ I will sing to the LORD as long as I live;
>
> I will sing praise to my God while I have being.
>
> ³⁴ May my meditation be pleasing to him,
>
> for I rejoice in the LORD. (NRSV)

The "Lord" is, of course YHWH, while "God" is El or Elohim. The equation of Lord and God still rests on the dipolar difference between the invisible El Elyon and the visible YHWH, here, in the form of the identification of the physical with the spiritual sun. So, if you use the same binocular imagination from the hymn to Aten, you will discover the *dipolar differentiation* between the transcendent invisible Sun and the appearance of it "clothed in light," expressing not the physical light of the sun, but itself as the Glory (*kabod*) of El Elyon to which the heaven is like a curtain and who sits on, rides and travels with the chariot or throne of the younger immanent God (see ch. 4).

The *second* dipolar layer, the equation of the Lord-God, YHWH Elohim (son of El) with the king or messiah as son of YHWH, that is, as one of the Elohim (a heavenly figure), found its most visible expression in Psalm 110:1, in a scene of *enthronement* and declaration of divine domain. *The Lord says to my lord, "Sit at my right hand until I make your enemies your footstool."* Besides Daniel 7:14, it came to be one of the most recited scriptural texts in the New Testament to declare the *equation* between Jesus and YHWH—the Christian use of this second identification which again implies the first one. With these two Psalm texts in the background, we can study the *transformation* of the original dipolar monotheism into the exclusive dualistic monotheism, as, for instance, alluded to already in the elevation of Christ to the "name beyond all names" (YHWH) by the One who sent and elevated him (El) in one of the earliest text of the New Testament, Philippians 2:9–11.

The cosmic recovery of the domain of God *through* the Son, originally performed by the transcendent El and the acting YHWH, appears in 1 Corinthians 15:20–28, where the Father (El) has given the Son (YHWH) the domain, as already in Daniel 7:14 and 1 Corinthians 8:6. Yet *after* the equation of El and YHWH (Deuteronomist and Deutero-Isaiah), now, this also means that YHWH gave his son, the Messiah (Jesus), this domain, the kingdom of God under his footstool, as in Psalm 110:1. However, in an unprecedented eschatological move, envisioning a final unification of both layers *beyond* the promise of Daniel 7 of an eternal realm for YHWH/the divine Messiah, now, the son (of El Elion/of YHWH) *relinquishes* this "eternal" reign to the Father (El Elyon/YHWH) who then will becomes "all in all."

This extraordinary, final, eschatological "identification" per "abdication" demonstrates the transmutation of the still visible dipolar theism of the passage into an all-embracing, *panentheistic monism*. The transcendent Godhead, who or that is *beyond* the All, has become the immanent God, who is *in* (the) All, by which identification "they" have also become one *with* the world or all in (the) All. Here, a *third* identification is intended: to be all in (the) All means that in the immanence of the transcendent Godhead the *horizon* has become the *most immanent heart* of everything that exists *within* this creative horizon. However, this ultimate unification reveals its own deeper, *dipolar* implication: namely, that, in the retrograde view, the double dipolar tension (between transcendent and immanent God and between heavenly and earthly sphere) did/does always already express a fundamental form of the *nondual unity of the all in (the) All* that crosses all differentiations that the dualistic monotheism of the later Christian centuries has made impossible to understand, because it exchanged the bridge of the dipolar understanding with the hiatus of the dualistic identifications.

Nevertheless, even in this most panentheistic/monistic transformation a strain of limitation remains, namely the *patriarchal* lens of the older and the younger male king, of father and son, of the "absent" Father and the warring male figure of the younger God: YHWH as man of war (Exodus 15:3). The unshakable memory of the ancient Canaanite enthronement ritual, by which the older king transferred power to his son, was standardized and justified "in heaven" by the relation between El and Ba'al, which was, at least since the Hyksos invasion in Egypt, symbolized by the *pervasive* identification of Aten and El/YHWH with the sun that in "His" *paternal* relation to the king/messiah (also male) was impotent to include, or forcefully and equally to express, the *female* side of God as Mother. (In many ancient languages, the "sun" carries the male grammatical gender, notably with the exception of Arabic and German.)

The potential (non- or counter-parochialistic) counter-spirituality of the *Wisdom* literature in the Jewish context did not prevail. Although it allowed the dipolar monotheism to express the older Israelite tradition of the two powers in heaven, visualized and venerated even in the temple with the divine pair of YHWH and his wife Ishtar, to be even after the Deuteronomist identification of El and YHWH to be expressed in the female form the immanence of the transcendent God as Lady Wisdom, the Creatrix, the medium of creation and its divine plan, its gentle and moral impetus, identified with the divine Spirit (Proverbs 8; Sirach 24; Wisdom of Solomon 7; Ephesians 1:17).

Admittedly, we find traces in the New Testament, such as the self-identification of Jesus with Wisdom or as the prophet of Wisdom (Matthew 11:19 par; 12:24 par) and the persistent identification of Jesus with the Logos/Wisdom (John 1; 1 Corinthians 1–2) and her creative functions (1 Corinthians 8:6; Colossians 1:15; Hebrews 1:1–3). However, the transformation of this dipolar pan(en)theism of the God All in All into the dualistic monotheism of the absolute difference between God and creation (hardly bridged by the later Christology of the "two natures") reduced Wisdom to the male function of the Logos and the Son, and the Son to a warring King (1 Corinthians 15:25–27), and envisioned the King as the divided and dividing eschatological figure of exclusivist monotheism.

In the Egyptian context, a different construct developed *after* the similar patriarchal power of the divine imagery of Akhenaten failed, and for the same reason. The dipolar identification behind Aten and His Son was doomed by its monotheistic exclusivism: the only God (the Sun); the only son (pharaoh). Nevertheless, a trans-religious standard was in the process of developing by which it was understood that the different names of gods were referring to the *same* sacred objects, such as the sun, the moon, the river, the mountain or the sea. Akhenaten's shattering exclusivism pitched Aten even against the ancient identifications of/with Amun-Ra, also the sun. However, in the form of the female goddess Isis, another opposite inclusivist movement of a *panentheistic divine "All in All"* developed and began to expand internationally from Egypt of the Hellenistic and Roman areas. While Isis was an ancient goddess, she became prominent through the myth developed by the priesthood of Heliopolis, (priests of the sun god Ra), who considered her the sister and wife of Osiris, the

Egyptian counter-figure of Orpheus and Dionysus, the god of the underworld, afterlife and rebirth. Yet in this case, it was Isis following Osiris into the underworld to revive him. In Greek and Roman times, she began to embrace many of the female goddesses and was understood *as all of them* at once. In fact, she began to be venerated as "the One, that/who is All," the Creatrix and all-embracing One, a female pantheistic or panentheistic rendering of an ultimate but immanent divinity.

In this expanding, expansive, and inclusive monotheism or, as Jan Assmann says, "cosmotheism" of the first millennium BCE, Isis performed the function that the Aten-monotheism could not fulfill because of its exclusiveness. The inclusive panentheism of Isis, however, symbolized the grace and mercy of a divine manifold, non-exclusive and tolerant to a divine court of many divine figures and gods, much like the ancient Canaanite and Israelite understanding of the Elohim. In this form, the goddess Isis became also an early example of a new paradigm: that of an *all-accepting and -embracing panentheistic, transreligious and intercultural unification of religious diversity* around the Mediterranean. The Roman novelist Apuleius (b. 125 CE) in his work *The Golden Ass* (between 150 and 180 CE) described the Isis mysteries as soul-journey of death and resurrection—the old theme of Orpheus and the Dionysian mysteries. His description of Isis, however, is extraordinary (even if some Egyptologists signal that similar things could be said of other gods), as her reach was also *ubiquitous*: she is *Nature herself*, the *universal Mother*, *immanent* in all elements and time, the queen of the dead and of the immortals, the sovereign of all spiritual matters, and, finally, *the Manifestation of all gods and goddesses*—the dipolar inclusive unity of transcendence and immanence.

Meditate on this passage from *The Golden Ass* (bk. 11, ch. 47) in relation to *The Hymn of Aten* and Psalm 104—you will recognize the great resonances, but also one difference: panentheistic embrace instead of exclusive identification.

> Behold Lucius I am come, thy weeping and prayer hath moved me to succor thee.
>
> I am she that is the natural mother of all things,
>> mistress and governess of all the elements,
>>
>> the initial progeny of worlds,
>>
>> chief of powers divine,
>>
>> Queen of heaven,
>>
>> the principal of the Gods celestial,
>>
>> the light of the goddesses:
>
> at my will the planets of the air, the wholesome winds of the Seas, and the silences of hell be disposed;
>
> my name, my divinity is adored throughout all the world in divers manners, in variable customs and in many names,

> for the Phrygians call me Pessinuntica, the mother of the Gods:
>
> the Athenians call me Cecropian Artemis:
>
> the Cyprians, Paphian Aphrodite:
>
> the Candians, Dictyanna: the Sicilians, Stygian Proserpine:
>
> and the Eleusians call me Mother of the Corn.
>
> Some call me Juno, others Bellona of the Battles, and still others Hecate.
>
> Principally the Ethiopians which dwell in the Orient, and the Egyptians which are excellent in all kind of ancient doctrine, and by their proper ceremonies accustomed to worship me, do call me Queen Isis.
>
> Behold I am come to take pity of thy fortune and tribulation, behold I am present to favor and aid thee.
>
> Leave off thy weeping and lamentation, put away thy sorrow,
>
> for behold the healthful day which is ordained by my providence,
>
> therefore be ready to attend to my commandment.

Nevertheless, the emerging spiritual power of inclusivism and mutual understanding of the Queen of Heaven was thwarted by the paternalistic and patriarchal dualistic monotheism of emerging Christianity, which was responsible for the exclusivist claim of truth, the absolute hiatus between God and the world, the trinitarian and christological debates that ousted the inclusivist, panentheistic and cosmotheistic versions of the dipolar monism as heresies, and led to the successive closure of all pagan institutions of learning and temples and an exodus of their intelligentsia to Persian lands beyond the reach of the Roman agents.

It is ironic that Christianity saved the ancient tradition of dipolar panentheism, and was even made possible by it, only to leave it as an "alternative" tradition on the sidelines, and even declaring it heretical, as it shifted with the Deuteronomist party of the past and the concurrent rabbinical demand for a dualistic monotheism to an exclusivist position that it now shares with the other "orthodox" Abrahamic traditions. And further, even more ironically, while Christianity began to view its own origin in the dipolar tradition as "heretical" or "polytheist," but needed to include it within the dualistic monotheism to which it aspired with rabbinical Judaism, it was (to the same extent) viewed as "heretical" or "polytheist" by the other Abrahamic traditions of Judaism and Islam. In reaction, Christian theology created its orthodox, dualistic "two Trinities" doctrine, with the hiatus between creator and creature *dividing* the originally *bridging* dipolar divine connectivity into an immanent (God-internal) and economical (world-related) Trinity.

Eventually, the exclusivist power of Akhenaten's radical religious reform, which failed in his own polytheistic and cosmotheistic context (but, surely, not only for religious reasons), became the victor over the ancient dipolar theism of the Canaanite/

Israelite era, the panentheistic embrace of Wisdom-religion, and the pre-rabbinic Jewish and early Christian invocation of both elements in visions of a God All in All.

However, no domination of the developed "orthodox" views managed to avoid the implication of the alternative tradition within their arrangements within and without their domains: Neo-Platonism and forms of (although way too simplistically so-called) Arianism not only survived in Abrahamic contexts, but became an essential element of their developments beyond any rigid exclusivism. The complexities of these arrangements in diverse mysticisms, Kabbalah, Esoterism, Sufism and New Age, and alternative streams of spiritual and religious traditions, internal and external to religious institutions and formal associations, and recovering even older strains of matriarchal spirituality, for instance, so prevalent in Neolithic times and in Native American spiritualty, are only symptoms of the unavoidability of the relativism that unconsciously or consciously points us to the constructedness of *all* of these propositions, worldviews, cosmologies and spiritual paths—whether pantheist, theist, or panentheist; naturalist, atheist, or supernaturalist; dipolar or dualist; monist, monotheist, or polytheist; and so on.

All construction of divinity is finite, relative to alien agendas, and infested by all-too-human power struggles and desires. The question, then, becomes or remains: Can we find *the unconstructed* "behind the scenes"?

Epilogue: Epiphany

To ask the "backstage" question is to ask, What is "behind" the world? But, in a more profound sense, it is another question that hatches in the former one: Is the world necessary (that and as it is) or contingent (by chance or probability)? Yet in asking what is "behind" the world, using the theatre as symbolic expression of staging and constructing, we recognize the contingency of the existence of the world with us in it, and the constructedness of any world, really. The widest stage, then, to ask such a question from "backstage" is the universe (cosmology) or existence (ontology) itself. As it appears, in the very act of asking this question of contingency, we are really asking the question of any world, all possible worlds, a multiverse of perhaps all actual worlds, too. I will address the implications of assuming a multiverse in the last chapter of this book. In the current context, however, the "behind" is about the question of the *constructions* of religious cosmologies. So, are we admitting that all religious constructions of divinity and of the cosmos are only vanishing pantomime, vanishing in thin air (in Prospero's vein), behind the theatre of which we find—nothing, sleep, death? Or, *if* we are allowing for the cosmic Spirit to be the *unconstructed*, in the view from "backstage," perhaps, constructing all worlds, we might ask: Do we have any *reasons* to believe so? And *how* would we know whether there is a reality that or who is not constructed, if at all, but for (or in comparison with) which all worlds are "the theatre"? I will refer, here, to only two such approaches, one from the west and one from the east.

Preliminarily, however, we can say that either answer, as any answer to the questions regarding construction and the unconstructed (I would claim), will appeal to (what I will call here) "epiphany." This term, as I want to use it here, is one of immediate, internal, spiritual or mystical experience and insight rather than rational/theoretical or empirical/external knowledge. It connects to terms of the prophetic experiences of "theophany," such as that of Moses, Ezekiel, and Isaiah, that is, the "revelation" of divinity—in the western context. But it also embraces *direct* experiences and insights gained by unifications in the mystical and apocalyptic journeys of the soul beyond death and into a spiritual domain beyond ordinary consciousness and physical locality and temporality. Hence the term "epiphany" relates, especially in the eastern context, to both the encounters of Ishvara in a Hindu or Sikh context, or of the Buddha in his magical form (*sambhogakaya*), or in the sudden realization of unity of inner Self (*atman*) with the All in All (*brahman*), or the equation of *samsara* and *nirvana*, or the realization of one's Buddha-nature (*tathagatagarbha*) or of the luminous mind. In any case, the insight is one that cannot be reasoned, and even if you know what it means and what its experience would be like, as long as you don't have this *insight by immediate experience*, you will not have had an *epiphany* of this nature.

The approaches I am now exploring, therefore, can give us only a hint as to the nature of the experience that they have in mind for us to become an immediate insight. They are not taking the relativity of cognitions away that such insights might articulate and demand to be followed—as different spiritual paths would be answers to such a demand. The following propositions are only meant to demonstrate that the character of "immediacy" they invoke is *neither* naïve realism regarding, *nor* mere intellectualism over against, experience, but exhibits a *noetic* ("intelligent") structure that is developed in the awareness that, philosophically, our realm of experience is never just simply "immediate" if this means that any experience can be had without any formation throughout biology and evolution, our cultural and linguistic learning, through our social interactions, ideologies, and worldviews. However, what the noetic side of these approaches wants to convey, despite these limitations to immediacy from an ordinary perspective, is that the *layered complexity* of experience is ultimately not only a *construction* of such layers, but that this layered complexity *itself* is *nothing but* a construction.

So, we know *of what* experience is constructed; but *does* it also reveal any reality that is *unconstructed*? The pluralism and relativism of symbolisms creating a cosmic and spiritual, religious and social environment for a specific set of the understanding of Reality—such as monism and dualism; naturalism, pantheism, and panentheism; exclusive and inclusive versions of theism or panentheism; or dipolar monism or dualistic monotheism—as exemplified by the theatre of constructions in this chapter, only heightens the question: Is there in any of them a hint of an unconstructed reality? And how to approach it? The two noetic invocations of the "reality" of epiphanic *events*, here, make just the point, with several eastern and western mystical and spiritual traditions, that it is the *happening* of the immediacy of the insight in which, and only in which, such Reality is realized beyond any noetic or intellectual approximations. (I will *invoke* the immediacy of this insight in Meditation XII).

Both approaches appeal to the *solar symbolism* of the preceding sections of this chapter. However, they use it differently: they *question* the ontological insights (on Being) those approaches seem to imply and refer it to the underlying *epistemic* insight (on *how* they can be known). What is more, they answer the challenge of the *immediacy* of experience that they want to make available with a figure of thought that brings the listener to the brink of its epiphanic happening.

The eastern approach is related to one of the most influential Buddhist sutras of Indian origin, created between the first century BCE and the second century CE, but of relevance for Mahayana movements throughout China and Japan, and, today, worldwide: the *Lotus Sutra* (*Saddharma Pundarika Sutra*). It was often read together with two shorter sutras, beginning with the *Sutra of Infinite Meanings* (*Ananta Nirdesa Sutra*) and ending in an epilogue with the *Samantabhadra Meditation Sutra*—together forming the *Threefold Lotus Sutra*. The Samantabhadra Bodhisattva, already described in the last chapter of the *Lotus Sutra* proper (ch. 28), is introduced here as the perfect embodiment of the Dharma (the teachings of the Buddha), infinite and pervasive of the cosmic All and able to appear in any part of it (a kind of *avatar* or incarnation of the divine horizon within itself) in order to defend the persecuted Dharma and to save the suffering. In Vajrayana Buddhism, Samantabhadra became the primordial Buddha, the integration of the transcendent function of the *dharmakaya* and the cosmic body or the world as the body of the Buddha, being of infinite divine powers of salvation. Simultaneously being transpersonal and personal, transcendent and all-pervasive, Samantabhadra resembles the dipolar panentheism of the ancient Near Eastern philosophical and religious traditions described above. Now, in the *Meditation Sutra*, Samantabhadra is described as "the sun of wisdom."

> The ocean of impediment of all karmas
>
> is produced from one's false imagination.
>
> Should one wish to repent of it
>
> let him sit upright and mediate on the true aspect (of reality)
>
> All sins are just frost and dew,
>
> so wisdom's sun can disperse them.

Images of the "father" and the "sun" (solar, not filial) surround this statement. The *Lotus Sutra* declares that Shakyamuni Buddha is "the Father of the Universe"; and the Meditation Sutra introduces the Buddha of the future, Maitreya, as "the supreme and great merciful sun." And, as in the Near Eastern context, this imagery references the universal transcendent Reality (*dharmakaya*) and the universal immanent Buddha (*sambhogakaya*) that or who on occasion can appear as human being (*nirmanakaya*). It also, in the form of the core of the developing Samantabhadra Buddha-figure, embraces both pantheistic *and* theistic dimensions. But the important epistemic shift, here, is this: that the sun's, the wisdom's, radiation burns away all illusions of false imaginings, of karmic twistedness of insight and the samsaric veil of desire and passion. The sun of wisdom, contrarily, releases—in the act of meditation—to the existential insight of the nothingness of such illusions and liberates to an *immediate epiphany* of Reality (*nirvana*) that is free of the self (ego) of desire and, hence, full of universal compassion. What is the Reality "behind" the imaginings of the world? Let go of your Self! The sun of wisdom is emptiness (*sunyata*). It is not something, a being or a person; nor "is" it at all (has being). Rather, it is *one* in the insight that nothing will reveal "it" as the (transcendent) "beyond" that appears "in" (immanent by) the burning away of Self (*anatta*) more than that *there is nothing beyond the world* that, therefore, *is as it is* or *as such* (suchness, *tathata*). The spiritual truth is this: You *know* only if it *happens*!

The western answer that Plato has given to this same question gathers around his invocation of the image of the sun in the Allegory of the Cave (*Republic* 514a-520a) and in the apex of his theory of the Forms with the Analogy of the Sun (*Republic* 507b-509c). The cave symbolizes our ordinary reality in which we are bound to see only shadows at the wall. If we liberate ourselves from this limited perception and exit the cave, we can experience reality *in the light* of the sun, although we cannot look directly at the blinding sun. In the way the sun stands in relation to the sensible world, so does, in the Analogy of the Sun, the Good shine its light onto the reality of the Forms and Ideas, the patterns of the material world, their structures and inner immaterial reality. The Good is not an Idea, but that *by which* they exist. Hence, the Good is *beyond* existence and non-existence. This is an extraordinary claim: that which makes things good, that is, worth in themselves and desirable to exist, makes them, in fact, real. Here are four interpretations of this Platonic move.

For Plotinus, the Good is *the One beyond existence*, inaccessible by its emanations, but their transcendent origin, which mirrors itself in the divine mind (*nous*) for all existent worlds (to which I have already referred in ch. 1). The French philosopher Emmanuel Levinas (d. 1995) has made it clear, against Martin Heidegger and in rather surprising resonance with the *Samantabhadra Meditation Sutra*: the requirement of ethical imperative of the worth of the "other" is the basis of existence (ontology); but to understand this, one has to give up the Self as center of considerations (the closure of self-existence and self-interest). The Canadian philosopher John Leslie (b. 1940) ventures the argument that the Platonic explanation of existence of any world, ideal or material, is based on the imperative that it inherently *ought* to be. There is nothing else behind this self-initiating imperative of the Good: that it is better that it exists than that it does not exist. And A. N. Whitehead relates the Good (*agathos*) to the Beautiful (*kalos*), its power of by attraction, which he understands to be the *only* and ultimate justification of existence—there is no reason beyond this self-justification. In all of these applications of Plato's Sun-Good, we find the same spiritual truth: that there is *nothing "behind"* the existence of the world and, hence, that there is *no reason* for its relativity and diversity.

Ultimately, in order to *understand* this, however, we must let go of conceptual explanations and experience this reality in the "immediacy" of the *event* of insight by which we (will) "know" that this "reason" (the Good) is immanent to all that is—the sun that shines over good and evil. In this epiphany, the unconstructed, transcending (the) All but being All in All, is realized. It is in this sense that I think that the immediacy of epiphany supports the reality of the *dipolar unity* of transcendence and immanence, of personal and transpersonal divine reality. Yet this epiphany also opens to the *relativity of infinite worlds* and *infinite spiritual paths* that would, in their finiteness and diversity of journeys toward Reality, allow "its" self-realization beyond, in and among spiritual wayfarers.

Meditation XII: Koan

In Buddhist terms, it is the "characteristic" of Reality that it is beyond illusions and desires, ego-self and any arrested state of being or non-being; it is (among other connotations) "named" *nirvana*, Dharma, and *dharmakaya*; and it indicates *the unconstructed* in all constructions, the sun that burns all constructions (illusions) away, because they are nothing but constructs of the ego-self. Only the non-self (*anatta*) can realize this insight; it is the universal (unpossessed) wisdom (*prajna*) of the Buddha. This wisdom of the unconstructed beyond and in all constructs is the Reality (essence, being, nature) of all existence. The famous text *Udana* 80 of the ancient Theravada Pali-canon circumscribes this ultimate, unconstructed Reality in these terms: unborn, uncreated, unformed, unconditioned, and unconstructed.

In postmodern philosophical terms, we could say that what Jacques Derrida has designated as that which cannot be deconstructed, is of *that* nature of reality. Following his reading that everything can be deconstructed not only into a compositions of parts (ontology), but into hidden, oppressed, veiled, and excluded voices (ethics), what ought to be undeconstructable is deconstruction itself, that is, the ethical impulse to un- and recover the multiplicity of oppressed voices, and, as Derrida insists, justice. Yet, because of the inaccessibility (transcendence) *and* motivating ethical activation (immanence) of this "reality"—which also reflects the always retreating, but coming character of the name YHWH of the Moses epiphany (as elaborated in the *Moses und Aron* section of this chapter)—the unconstructed is a *messianic* force, that is, something that cannot be attained, but that *as* the unattainable is *the* motivation for action, and, maybe, if you believe the Good of Plato, for existence. The unconstructed is the unattainable—like the "river" that cannot be crossed (ch. 3). Yet, while we cannot attain it (transcendence), it is that *from which* we act (ethics) and exist (ontology).

The Japanese philosopher Masao Abe (d. 2006), an influential communicator of Zen teachings in the West, relates a paradoxical riddle or (although, here, not formulated "formally" as a) *koan* of the medieval Zen master Ch'ing yüan Wei-hsin of the T'ang dynasty (618–907 CE) in order to demonstrate the *event of epiphany or Enlightenment* at the heart of Zen practice, which is beyond all categorical and logical or other imaginative substitutes the immediate experience of Reality. In condensed form it reads,

> Mountains are mountains; rivers are rivers.
>
> Mountains are not mountains; rivers are not rivers.
>
> Mountains are really mountains; rivers are really rivers.
>
> Do you think, these three are different or the same? (Abe, *Zen*, 4)

Several complex mental operations can be deduced from this account. One can speculate, as Abe does, that the *first* phase means a differentiation and affirmation of the characteristics identifying mountains and rivers in counter-distinction from one another and of both in relation to the discriminating activity of the ego-self or the "I." The *second* phase is that of a negation of both differentiation and affirmation. In this phase we discover the emptiness of such affirmative and discriminating claims and, as they are related to the ego-self, we also discover the emptiness of this self, which, in its negation, becomes the non-self. The *third* phase, then, releases the insight that even the negation is a new kind of affirmation and differentiation, that is, an objectification of non-difference and non-ego. As this objectification (construction) must now be overcome with a negation of the negation, or a new affirmation, we will realize the reality of all phenomena just to *be* what they are (inherently), and *are* what they are *if* we are not projecting our epistemic position (of self or no-self) onto them; hence, they just are *that*, everything and nothing. The answer to the *fourth* line, the question, would then be that they are different as constructs, insofar as they are exclusive (the first excludes the second excludes the third), but from the ultimate standpoint, the unconstructed, they are inclusive (the third includes the second includes the first) and in this sense amount to "the same."

Yet the conceptual analysis is not what is intended by this and other Zen stories and *koans*. They are rather meant to lead us to the only "perspective" that would allow the epiphany, the *event* of the unconstructed, to reveal itself onto us *as our own inherent reality*. By reaching the point of the impossibility of any further reasoning, reality reveals itself to us as the *unity*—or unconstructed, uncomposed or undivided reality of—unattainability and the unconditioned, motivating existence and acting.

In this sense, I think that the unconstructed ground we seek, here, is that to which the dipolar view of Reality refers, as it expresses the unity of the transcendent and the immanent, the unconstructed and all constructions, in such a way that they do not reveal any ultimate reality "beyond" the world of existence, but only the Spirit *in which* they are let to exist. With the great medieval mystic and religious teacher Meister Eckhart, we can name this "ultimate" the *grunt* (ground) or, with mystics like Jakob Boehme (d. 1624), the *Ungrund* (groundless ground, or rather: no-ground). It means that there is no "object," a ground, beyond that which is grounded; but so is there no "non-object" such as an illusion. Neither, nor; *neti neti*, in Hindu terms.

Rather, the Spirit ("sun") is the all-pervasive but unattainable *medium* in which we experience the immediate epiphany of its nature.

With one of the most global rejections of reasonability and the use of conceptuality, the method of the Nagarjuna's Madhyamika consists of a *fourfold logic* by which he wants to demonstrate that any conceptual grasp of this immediate experience, which equals Enlightenment, of unattainable reality is unattainable. Its form follows this progression:

> Something is that
>
> Something is not that
>
> Something is that and not that
>
> Something is neither that nor not that.

In my final meditation, I combine elements of both Master Ch'ing and Nagarjuna's account of the unattainable epiphany—hinting at Zen Master Dogen (1200–1253). Perhaps, you see:

> *Unconstructed reality is that or not that*
>
> *Unconstructed reality is that and not that*
>
> *Unconstructed reality is neither that nor not that*
>
> *Leaves fall in autumn.*

6

Fata Morgana

> ... Where is the LORD who brought us up from the land of Egypt, who led us in the wilderness, in a land of deserts and pits, in a land of drought and deep darkness, in a land that no one passes through, where no one lives?
>
> —JEREMIAH 2:6 (NRSV)

> I want to penetrate to the simple ground, to the still desert, into which distinction never peeped, neither Father nor Son nor Holy Spirit.
>
> —MEISTER ECKHART, *GERMAN SERMONS*, #48

> The plane [of immanence] is surrounded by illusions. These are not abstract misinterpretations or just external pressures but rather thought's mirages.... First of all there is the illusion of transcendence, which, perhaps, comes before all others (in its double aspect of making immanence immanent to something and of rediscovering a transcendence within immanence itself)....
>
> —GILLES DELEUZE AND FELIX GUATTARI, *WHAT IS PHILOSOPHY?* (49)

FATA MORGANA IS THE Italian translation of Morgan le Fay, the fairy Morgana, the sorceress of the Arthurian circle of legends. She appears as the enchanting Lady of the Lake, the half-sister of king Arthur and demonic counterpart of the wizard Merlin. Her assumed maritime origin relates her to the kind of mirages that were named after the legendary apparitions in the Strait of Messina at Sicily. A fata morgana is a kind of mirage in which many rapidly shifting layers of inverted air produce the images of whole cities over the desert floor, or artificial objects like flying ships, or natural phenomena, like mountains over water, and the like. Although the phenomenon can be encountered at sea as well as on land, it is most famously related to the illusion of an oasis or a safe place of water, food and rest in the midst of the formidable wasteland or wilderness of deserts. It is a mirage, an *objective* illusion. That is, it is not a product of subjective, psychological imagination and desire, but an optical illusion that expresses a relationship between the elements, such as light, heat, air, surface, and the perspective of the observer. It is a *physical* phenomenon; it can be photographed. And it is independent from the projected subjective meaning humans might give it. It is itself a surface of illusory projections, like the desert itself, but it also redefines objects as shifting relations between places and perspectives, as events in mutual immanence of becoming, and as alternative potentials of the appearance of other worlds in ours. The magic of the fata morgana, unlike that of Prospero, cannot be avoided and, hence, is a reminder of the undecidedness of what we might like to be ultimately real or fear as an illusion. Like Lady Morgana, this mirage operates *in between* the fixations that we might like to name reality.

This chapter is perhaps the most philosophical. So, if this is not your thing, skip ahead of it or come back to it later (when you feel you missed something that could have been explored here; and, in all probability, it is). If this declaration has made you curious, however, know that it is an expansion of the last two chapters on spiritual and natural differentiation, and the complexity of the contrast between monotheism and monism. It addresses the question of the origins of spirituality and religion in illusions, and, conversely, treats naturalism as a mirage: not a subjective lack of realism or wishful imagination—of which naturalism would accuse religion—but as perspectival coagulation of natural conditions on which absolute reality is projected or to which it is reduced. One of the major "ambivalent" heroes of this story will be Gilles Deleuze, the French poststructuralist philosopher, who defies categorizations, but whose reconfiguration of a philosophy of immanence over against monotheism contributes important aspects to the understanding of a non-reductive, non-materialist but "bodied" spirituality of the "chaosmos" that is not (necessarily) anti-religious or, at least, closed to theistic assumptions—as they (the theistic assumptions) may be relative in their perspectives, too, that is, expressions of a mirage, a relational limitation of a relativity of many spiritual paths. However, I will commence this endeavor with the enormous fascination spiritual teachers and wayfarers exhibit toward the physical and symbolic desert, and situate the mirage of spirituality and religion in its context.

Desert

To human experience, the desert has always been one of three things: a romantic land of mystery behind the veil of heat, rocks, and sand; a harsh reality of unviability and certain death; and a wild place of spiritual renewal by way of negation, reduction, austerities, and bare necessity. The secret and sacred land. The forbidden and formidable other. The place of testing and bare emptiness. Like the sea, the desert is an expansive surface of folds in which unforeseen monstrosity seem to lurk, unconquerable. One does not stay but only crosses. Always in peril, never at rest, the desert asks the exposed "aliens" to remain on the move and expect nothing, no favor but mere survival, if one is lucky.

Like to the sea, as acknowledged on in chapter 2, the biblical myth of creation conceits to the desert pre-eternity before any assumed or imagined divine act of creation. It is the *tohu wa-bohu*, the empty and desolate place, over which not even the Spirit of God (*ruah Elohim*) hovers (Genesis 1:2). Yet it is from the desert that Israel's God comes, as one of the oldest texts of the Hebrew Bible, the song of Deborah, celebrates (Judges 5). It is the physical and symbolic land between the oppression in Egypt and the freedom of the promised land—an intermezzo of transformation. It is that which must be crossed, in which the revelation of YHWH deconstructs the people of its old identities and reconstructs it into a new creation, that of the Mosaic divine encounter, with the tent of the covenant wandering with the emigrants, steeped in the experience of total dependency on God for the path of physical and spiritual survival (1 Corinthians 10; water from the rock: Exodus 17; Numbers 20; manna from heaven: Exodus 16; Numbers 11). It is the liminal place of testing and of the holy covenant, the place of repentance and of the intimacy of divine love in light and sight of certain death. It is the original birthplace of the Abrahamic religions: Egypt, Sinai, Arabia, Syria, Palestine, Beersheba and Jerusalem, Mecca and Medina, Baghdad and Damascus—permanent reminders of the birth pangs of deep religiosity, devastating ethnic rivalry and the religious empires of the world.

Desert is not desert. Gobi, Kalahari, Sahara, Patagonia, Syria, Arabia, Karakoram, Atacama, Antarctica—their topography is nothing alike. They can be of high or low elevation; sand or rock or ice; with or without annual torrents of rain; continental or seaside; flat or mountainous; hot or cold, or both; habitable or inhabitable; hostile or connective; bland or subtle. The paradoxes of the desert haunt human imagination of dangers and surprises: while it is dry, you can find water; while it is empty, you may uncover oases; while it promises you to be parched, it might drown you; while it is a reminder of death, it may be full of life; while it seems to be abandoned, it may be the space of liberation; while it creeps towards fecund land, it warns us of wasting the mercy of the earth to sustain us; while it situates the wanderer, emigrant, nomad or fugitive into sceneries and scenarios of desolation, its formidable fierceness is patient to the travelers, offering them islands of life, water, food, relaxation, and rest.

Today, however, the image of the desert is overshadowed and tainted by the human ability to change the surface of the earth. The Anthropocene, the age of the earth in which humanity has touched all niches of its integrated ecology, has changed the romantic secret of the desert into the wasteland of civilization. While the harsh land of desolation exhibits a majestic purity, we have begun to think of it as a demonic force of expansion that takes vital space away from human habitation, pastoral and agricultural sustenance, as well as confronting us directly—like melting polar ice and swelling sea levels—with the specter of global warming. And as we imitate the desolate land in the midst of our urban, industrial and consumer "civilization" of global capitalism, ruthless profit "morality," and exclusive shareholder "responsibility," we remake the world in our worst image of the nihilism of desire and self-satisfaction. And, in the end, we begin to think that the ominous foreignness of the deserts is just an emptiness that needs to be filled with more human enterprises, that needs to be erased for more profit, that must be banned as if it was not more than the wasteland of the earth. Yet the deserts remind us always of the human dependency on the earth as one body. It may, even in the Anthropocene, resist its inclusion in human perversion and always offer us a mirror of our own futility to conquer the earth. Even in the Anthropocene, then, the desert remains a gap, interrupting human progress, the hiatus in which we unintendedly may recover the interval of the Spirit.

The desert was always, in the annals of spirituality, a special place. In the absence of distraction from imaginations and human constructs, it seems to bring us closer to the unconstructed: silence, solitude, prayer, meditation, fasting, frugality, introspection, the absence of mere ornamentation and from the clamor of human busyness and businesses. No wonder that the desert, in religious imagination and symbolic attraction, has never lost its call to exile and liberation from constraints of human organization, the city (*polis*), the state, the law of civilization, and became the intermediary or permanent place of religious reformers, prophets, holy figures, wisdom teachers, philosophers, shamans, ascetics and exiled, alien, alienated, and alternative communities, shamanic journeys and encounters with "native" spiritual guides.

The desert has also become the place of religious and cultural resistance: of the religious escape from the clamors and temptations of the city, human society or civilization—such as St. Anthony of Alexandria (d. 365) and the monastic movement breeding a new Christianity in the desert—and of the religious revival of human identity under total oppression—as with the African-American slave women who found themselves liberated from the shackles of inescapability in the image of the biblical figure Hagar, the servant of Abraham and the mother of his son Ishmael, in the wilderness (Genesis 16).

The desert marks the places of extraordinary scenes of revelation and insight, spiritual struggle and transformation, birth and death of religious paths, mystical experiences and temptations, illuminations and vain imaginings. It is the land of the desert god(s), coming again and again from the mountain or valley or sole bush or tree, coming again from the deserted place. It is the place of YHWH and of the prophets that cry ahead of God's new coming, be it apocalyptic or revolutionary. It is from the wilderness that Isaiah envisions the coming of God (Isaiah 40:3) and that John the Baptizer repeats this call from the desert and even takes his dwelling place in the desert in expectation of the coming of God (Luke 1:80). It is the place of traumatic spiritual struggles and encounters: Hagar's flight and encounter with God (Genesis 16); the transformation of the wife of Lot into a salt column (Genesis 19); Jacob's fight with the angel of God (Genesis 31:22–31). It became the place of religious renewal: the gymnosophist of uncertain eastern, perhaps Buddhist, origin; the Jewish Essenians and the community of Qumran; the Desert Fathers of Christianity; the early *ummah* of Islam. It was the place of Abraham's divine trust and of the peoples of his sons Jacob (Israel) and Ismael (Islam); of the theophany of Moses's encounter with God on Sinai; of Jesus's fasting and temptations in the Negev; of the prophet Muhammad's meditations around the mountains of Mecca and his first revelation (Qur'an 96:1–5). And so, the desert, although in many imaginative forms, remains perhaps *the* primordial space that always anew invites religious imaginations and the production of a pleroma of spiritual pathways to a desired place of otherness and divine encounter.

While the desert is a place where no one lives, as one epigraph of this chapter says (Jeremiah 2:6), it is the place of immediate experience of human contingency and divine transcendence: survival is a pure gift. In mystical topology, it is perhaps closest to the feeling of what it means that God is like the sun that shines over good and evil (Matthew 5). It is a place of *indifference*. Here, the physical experience of indifference is more than just a symbolic representation of nondualism, the indifference of Reality from all realities. Rather, this indifference is, in stark tones and colors, feelings and intuition, the impact of a real environment of the earth onto the bodily immediacy of human consciousness: of what it means to be abandoned and free at the same time; where life and death come closest together; where the absence of restrictive human laws and the contingencies of the nomad fuse on a surface that dictates its own rules for the necessities of survival. Is this the indifference of God? Not a romantic immanence in everything, not an oceanic feeling of being in the divine All that is All in All, but the *transcendence of absence*, of being *expelled* from Eden, of a *chaos* of disorientation? If it is a divine plane, we are its foreigners, housed only as alienated from it, tolerated as external to it, moving around in desperate search for symbolizations that would create meaning.

In this shock or epiphany of the realization of the desert, we discover the *pre-symbolic place*, the *u-topos*, the *Ungrund*, the groundless isolation from all illusions (*Abgeschiedenheit*)—illusions that we create in order to avoid this insight. This is formulated in such a way in brute honesty by Meister Eckhart when he fuses two tropes of the desert—both found most explicitly and articulated without any hesitation in his *German Sermons*: that we can find meaning, peace and rest only in the total acceptance of the abandonment of connection that the desert imposes on us in the isolation from all creatures that we could cling to in order to substitute God with an illusion (total contingency); and that we must withstand the audacity of the identification of God's nature with the desert itself: God is the desert *beyond* being and nothingness, the pre-symbolic *nakedness* where no one sees and lives (total necessity).

This proposition leads us back to the genial and controversial medieval thinker John Scotus Eriugena (d. 877) who intuited that the world is created out of the desert, the desert of the divine nature. Here, the desert becomes the image in which the Spirit urges the confrontation with the Self, the letting go of all spiritual materialism, the misuse of spirituality as means of self-realization, in the meaning of Chögyam Trungpa, as mentioned in chapter 4—and not to think of God as such a Self either! In fact, as the epigraph of Meister Eckhart at the beginning of this chapter states: The divine desert is *the* u-topos: beyond any image, imagination, difference, possession of personality or the procession of any difference, even that of the Trinity—how more so of anything else!

The indifference of the divine desert has led to both the renewal of theism and a justification of atheism. Indifference to *suffering* was always the argument at the basis of existential atheism—and no intellectual argument can satisfy this deep feeling of divine abandonment to the point of nihilism: the admittance that there is no ground, that the indifferent *Ungrund* is like nothingness, like meaninglessness. Yet, perhaps, this also evokes the feeling of self-creative freedom in an absurd existence—as in Friederichs Nietzsche's work. In any case, this indifference has also been a major transformative factor from any naïve theism (of a simple divine person, or even three) to a more sophisticated pantheism of the self-creativity of the universe or a panentheism of a divine Mind in which all possible and actual worlds are imagined and (somehow) realized—as in the ponderings of thinkers such as the Canadian philosopher John Leslie and the British theologian Keith Ward (b. 1938).

Yet the most interesting philosophical reflection on the religious importance of the physical place and the symbolic imaginations of desert comes, perhaps, from Gilles Deleuze, because he develops an understanding that far exceeds any simple classification of those kinds. Although he is understood as an "atheist," he is far from any protest atheism, New Atheism, or any abandonment of the subversive magnitude of past religious thinkers such as Plotinus, John Duns Scotus, Meister Eckhart, Nicolas of Cusa, Giordano Bruno (d. 1600), Gottfried Wilhelm Leibniz (d. 1716), Baruch de Spinoza (d. 1677) and A. N. Whitehead, which he all includes constructively in his work. While I will say more in Meditation XIII, let it be sufficing, here, to remind us of the fundamental character of his differential thinking that could well be called "spiritual" (although that will be contested gravely by Deleuzian orthodoxy): In contrast to many other postmodern thinkers, Deleuze has not subscribed to materialism; has not erased the ideal sphere, tracing back to Plato, that he calls the virtual; and has not given up on that spiritual or even religious avoidance of figures of thought and projection that he formulates in a language close to nondualism of the One-All and pure consciousness and immediate experience that transcends any intellectualism (of the Logos, of reason) and empiricism (of external objects as investigated by subjects), but rehearses the noetic boundary of mystical insight. In his last essay, "Immanence: A Life" (1995), he says about this reality that comes closest to Eckhart's divine desert, but exhibits encoded Hindu and Buddhist associations of religious "identifications" or "identities," such as "*atman* is *brahman*" of the important and radical philosopher and sage of Advaita Vedanta and a philosophy of nonduality (some say of monism), Adi Sankaracharya (d. 820), and "*samsara* is *nirvana*" of the equally important radical Buddhist reformer of nonduality, Nagarjuna, respectively.

> What is a transcendental field? It can be distinguished from experience in that it doesn't refer to an object or belong to a subject (empirical representation). It appears therefore as a pure stream of a-subjective consciousness, a pre-reflexive impersonal consciousness, a qualitative duration of consciousness without a self. . . . [It] is of course not the element of sensation (simple empiricism), for sensation is only a break within the flow of absolute consciousness. . . . It is not immanence to life, but the immanent that is in nothing is itself a life. A life is the immanence of immanence, absolute immanence: it is complete power, complete bliss. (Deleuze, *Pure Immanence*, 25, 27)

Pantheism? Maybe—but not materialism. Without spirit? Only if we identify "the spiritual" with a certain form of philosophy, such as that of Hegel and Heidegger, and the fascistoid implications they harbor (of ethnocentrism, antisemitism, Eurocentric and Greek/German superiority thinking), or with a certain form of established religious orthodoxy that Deleuze was sensitive to: imperial monotheism, or what I have called "dualistic theism" (see ch. 5). Yet, if we relate "the spiritual" to the *irreducibility of the creativeness of the cosmos*, to the *irreducible ideal reality* as condition for the self-creative differentiation of the All, the overflowing Goodness of the "sun" of Reality in the heliotropism of Plato and Plotinus, Meister Eckhart and Spinoza—we may find a different approach: the Spirit as the *indifference of the infinite and the finite*, the *creative process of differentiation and unification*—and all beyond simple claims of the One as the sovereign king. It all comes down to the nondualism of what I have called "dipolar panentheism" (see ch. 5), or, better even, as in my own work: *trans-pantheism*. It can be discerned in Deleuze's rendering of Plotinus's absolute transcendent One *as* the indifference from the absolutely immanent All-One, and as reflected in what Deleuze calls the "One-All." Here is an excerpt from a lecture of Deleuze on Plotinus.

> One of Plato's disciples, Plotinus, speaks to us at a certain level of the One as the radical origin of Being. Here, Being comes out of . . . the One. The One makes Being, therefore it is not, it is superior to Being. This will be the language of pure emanation: the One emanates Being. That is to say the One does not come out of itself in order to produce Being, because if it came out of itself it would become Two, but Being comes out of the One. This is the very formula of the emanative cause. But when we establish ourselves at the level of Being, this same Plotinus will speak to us in splendid and lyrical terms of the Being that contains all beings, the Being that comprehends all beings. . . . He will say Being complicates all beings. It's an admirable formula. Why does

> Being complicate all beings? Because each being explicates Being.... Treating God as an emanative cause can fit because there is still the distinction between cause and effect. But as immanent cause, such that we no longer know very well how to distinguish cause and effect, that is to say treating God and the creature the same, that becomes much more difficult. (Deleuze, "On Spinoza")

There are several things we can learn from this *trans-pantheism* in Deleuze's attempt of overcoming of imperial monotheism with the help of Plotinus: First, the *bipolarity* of the One beyond Being and beings (the divine Mind that contemplates all beings) is *indifferent*, as it does not amount to Two: it is not an external cause and effect relationship, but an *emanative* cause. The Mind of God (*nous*) is God *and* is not God, as God is really that which is beyond all differentiation. Second, the divine *contemplation* of beings is *creative*, but not externalist, that is, all beings are *explications* of Being because they are *complicated* (inherently folded) in the Being/Mind that *is and is not* God—a position, for instance, also shared with Nicolas of Cusa and Bábí-Baháʼí cosmology. This is clearly a dipolar monism, not a pantheism, rather a trans-pantheism of the One; but the One is *nothing except* the creative overflow of the All-One. Third, Deleuze's shift from the *emanative* to the *immanent* cause, or from the Plotinian All-One to the Deleuzian One-All is the decisive shift in his thinking on the Spirit: Spirit now is *pure immanent consciousness* beyond the subject-object distinction, before oppositions such as matter and mind, but best associated with the *power* and *bliss* of the immediate insight into *satchitananda*—the Hindu term for the Spirit (*brahman*) as pure Being, pure Consciousness, and pure Bliss. Fourth, Deleuze has in surprising ways revived the traditional religious and philosophical Sun of Reality (which we encountered in the previous chapter) as pure immanence of the creative self-differentiation of the cosmos, the *immanent luminosity* of which all beings are folds. He calls this a "plane of immanence," which, as the direct experience of epiphanic immediacy in chapter 5, avoids all (false) transcendence—a transcendence that Deleuze and Guattari, as reflected in the related epigraph at the beginning of this chapter, understands as a mirage of the gravest kind—a betrayal of the field pure consciousness that I have identified as the deep connotation of the Spirit. This field of pure consciousness or *satchitananda* also *is* (and is not) the cosmic Spirit, as it *embraces* the cosmos (panentheism), but is the generating self-creative space of the overflowing differentiation of all worlds *from within* (trans-pantheism). In this sense, Deleuze has restated the Plotinian view that has become enormously influential in diverse religious and philosophical traditions, namely, of all potential worlds to be contemplated by the Mind of God, by understanding it as the pure consciousness. It is the *virtual*, the generative immanent principle of actual creative differentiation of beings and worlds (more will be said in the next section).

What does all this have to do with the desert? Well, the desert is the pre-symbolic place in which the confrontation, interference, and complex mutual enfolding between the profound spiritual impulse of the field of pure consciousness and its breakdown into subject-object structures of imperial occupation happens. It is birthplace of the confrontation between immanence and transcendence, monism and monotheism, dipolarity and dualism, spiritual integration and imperial stratification. Because we can experience the desert as a place in which everything is as it is, what it is—the wind, the sand, the light, emptiness as fullness, *which needs nothing*, sacred immanence, as it were—we can also feel the *intense absence* of the sacred, the desolation, the inhabitability and the need to fill this lack with projections and substitutes that desire to gain access to the apophatic transcendence, and to draw "it" down unto the empty surface, and to transform the desert into occupied territories of power: transcendence as sin; monotheism as imperial occupation of the emptied and wasted, depopulated plane.

It is in this sense that Deleuze and Guattari in their book *A Thousand Plateaus* insist that, in religious history, the desert was the redemption of the spirit of freedom from the clamorous world, but also, as with the movement that began with St. Anthony, the locus of the reconstruction of the empty earth of the desert into the occupation machine of the spiritual territorialization of the empires of Christendom. This transition from immanence to transcendence is also the reason why the desert religions that escaped centers of power and hierarchical state-organization (the old occupied territory), in their encounter of sacredness and desolation, changed into prophetic war-machines that began to transform their desert liberation, as soon as it was reconfigured as transcendence, and expanded it by (spiritually, and often physically) erasing the ways of life that populated the old territories in order to repopulate (reterritorialize) it with the imperial forces of the conquest of the whole Earth. The holy war is a function of this transmutation.

There is a warning and a profound insight here: *If you seek the desert, seek the pure consciousness in which the creativity of the All is mirrored.* It does not oppress or occupy; it does not erase or leave a space to be occupied. Rather, it evades evacuation by externalizing the false unifications and explicating only the free movements of the immanent One-All. Don't seek power, Self or even truth, which will always need to leave or expand the desert to prove themselves, justify their own superiority and fill the seemingly empty space with imaginations that sooth the wound of desolation. Seek, instead, the mode of the *nomad*, wandering the spiritual earth as an external contingency, desiring only the inaccessible but all-pervading *poverty* of the divine desert.

Meditation XIII: Monad, Nomad

The desert is the pre-symbolic surface that allows us to understand the development and bifurcation of two very different forms of religious paths. One is geared toward all kinds of modes and characteristics only meaningfully coming together if they are the expression of *one* specific movement: that of *transcendentalizing a field* in a search for its (lack of) unity, and, then, of reintroducing this unity as the *governing embrace* of the field that was left empty by this ascent into absent, "apophatic" (unspeakable, unspeaking) unity. Deleuze and Guattari call this double movement of ascent and decent relative *deterritorialization* and *reterritorialization*. It already presupposes that the desert always ambivalently has given way to a view that understands it as desolate lack of meaning and power, always in need to be reimagined in terms of a territory with a clear (civilizational, rational, religious) law—most of the time, however, the law of possession and trade, profit, and commodity exchange, or, in one word, capitalism. This is the religious invention of *imperial monotheism*, which, as A. N. Whitehead explains, is nothing but a cosmic projection and justification of the imperial royal ideology of ancient Egyptian and Mesopotamian absolutism—in chapter 5, we already discussed the influence of the Canaanite and Egyptian royal ideology on the creation and development of historic monotheism in this regard.

Yet the ambivalence of the desert "chaos" also gives rise to another religious path that is not based on the mirage of transcendentalizing imaginations of power and possession, the "territory," but on the *integrated desert land* in which nothing is missing, and no boundaries and borders of limitation are needed, because it is the open space of the *nomad*, wandering freely through a realm that offers sustenance, but needs not to be possessed, divided, rationalized, commodified, exchanged, or territorialized. It is the path of *monism and pluralism without dualism*, valuing the multiplicity of natural creative forces and their mutual immanence that, far from being seen as lack or desolation, are the surface of open movements. While this path is closer to eastern religious preferences, it is not absent in the religious and philosophical *dipolar monisms* of the west, namely, of the differentiation between, and unity of, or non-difference between, unmanifest Reality and its Manifestation(s) as immanent creative basis of the "complication" of all things, and as the epiphany/theophany in violation of the absolute dualism between God and world, creator and creature—both of which

Deleuze discovers in Plotinus (see the previous section). Yet, in the wider context, this open nomadic space with its sacred ambivalence and its transformation in an imperial, measured space, is the tragic fate of the "American experiment," that is, the erasure of Native American life, religiosity, and the spiritual numinosity of the open land for exchange value and profit—and so is the loss of the nondual transgression of the life-force, *manitou* or *orenda*, and the great Spirit, Wakan Tanka.

Deleuze explains this ambivalence and bifurcation in relation to the pre-symbolic desert with two symbolizations of the desert space. We either situate ourselves in it as a smooth space, or we conquer it as a striated space. The difference is, in Deleuze's mind, that a *smooth space* is populated by *nomadic* movements, not in fear of loss or need of security, but in an *affirmation* of all inhabitants (whether human or not) without the need of possession, division, profit, or exchange value, or, in short, *without the need to measure* that space. Conversely, Deleuze views the *striated space* as a marked, grooved, divided, possessed, secured, defended space or, in short, a *measured* space, readymade for occupation as a territory. One is the *monadic* space of possession, the other the *nomadic* space of dispossession. While it may be an interesting question whether this transformation from a smooth space into a striated space is a secular repetition of the Eden myth, the lost paradise, that we never inhabited—because the pre-symbolic desert exhibits just the *inextricable undecidability* between reality and mirage, that is, whether one of these views is real and the other illusionary or vice versa—the bifurcation and the impossibility to just revert the ongoing processes of territorialization of desert land to its presumed Eden space is instructive, because it demonstrates the *idealism* of the affirmation of the smooth divine desert as "salvation" from the imperial forces of monotheism.

The situation is complicated by the fact that Deleuze does notice this idealism and, without giving up on it, decouples it from the ambivalence and bifurcation of the two kinds of spaces. This can be understood in two steps. The first step is to recognize the relation between these two kinds of spaces and their distributed expression of transcendence and immanence. The smooth desert space ideally is not territorialized and, hence, is one of *immanence*: there is no lack in its multiplicity; all beings are the unpossessed folds of this plane of immanence. It is by the need to territorialize, the transformation to a fear of emptiness and the sudden view of the desert as an existential threat by its (now) perceived desolation, that this lack has evaporated immanence like a fata morgana and remade the *absent* sacred unity in the image of the real reality of a transcendent *being*, the *monas* of the imperial god, the divine king of the desert territory. However, such a territorialization shocks the free flow of the smooth space. The transcendent divinity, monas, unity, power, king can only expand itself over against all other territorial claims of the walled cities, plantations, political cliques and the mutual washing of hands if it reinvents the smooth space from the perspective of the new transcendent monas. This is, for Deleuze, the birth of the "prophetic" and "theophanic" representation of the monad *as* the nomad in a new transcendence that expands (and reverts) the smooth space of the free flow of the prophetically envisioned divine forces: holy war and capitalist expansion both need this transformed smooth space.

Paradoxically, then, as it is true (on these conditions) that the "great imperial religions" expand through the smooth space—as transcendence is established and repeatedly *re-inscribed* into the flow of immanence in order to empower the flow canalizing the imperial power of the transcendent monad—*the reverse can also happen*: a potential inherent in Deleuze's proposal he did not consider! What I mean is this: In Deleuze's thought, the expansion of the religions of transcendence and the related monadic spirituality of imperial monotheism need Figures of the *inscription of the transcendent horizon within itself*: these are prophetic or mystical figures of religious expansion, figures of incarnation, and avataric presence. It is in this sense that Deleuze understands the *resistance* to such Figures of *manifest transcendence*, such as the Christ or Krishna, or more modest figures such as *mandalas* and *sephirot*, as essential in his philosophical liberation from religion, which he identifies in this sense with monotheism. The only alternative, in his view, is a philosophy of immanence the utmost "figure" of which becomes Spinoza's pantheism or non-transcendent monism or pure immanence or pure consciousness, which does discard all Figures of transcendence, and, hence, identifies the spiritual or ideal with the immanent self-creativity of the chaosmos—a kind of spiritual naturalism.

It is fascinating, seizing on the insights gained in the previous chapter, to entrain the thought that the antagonism of Moses's (and Akhenaten's) exclusive monotheism within the long-standing counter-memory of Egyptian cosmotheism, especially since the Renaissance, that eventually led to the identification of the Egyptian "cosmos" with God in Spinoza's *Deus sive natura*—that God and Nature are identical—is also the background of Deleuze's "desert monism" and maybe even for the failure of the aesthetic representatives of Moses and Akhenaten in Schönberg's and Glass's music dramas. But this is also an important icon for the *new dualism* arising from this antagonism, because it circumscribes the (still monadic) place where the paradoxical involvedness between the two spaces has transformed into an old *apocalyptic scheme of radical opposition* between immanence and transcendence, philosophy and religion, monotheism and monism. This even in contra-distinction to an old Roman tradition that, as with the Greco-Roman historian Strabo (d. 23 CE) with his Stoic bend of identifying the cosmos with god, has represented the Mosaic monotheism as a pan*en*theism based on apophatic iconoclasm, which, in the eighteenth century became recognized as the Mosaic roots of Spinozist pantheism. Contrarily, in Deleuze, his "new" *dualist* scheme must fail the intricate ambivalence of the *mutual immanence* (a Whiteheadian term) of the monad and the nomad that remains the inextricable basis for this new idealist bifurcation.

Another direction of thought and action may open up on the mutual immanence of the monad *and* the nomad—an opportunity to *counter* the use of the Figure(s) of transcendence as means of imperial expansion by the Figure(s) of the transformation of transcendence into immanence. The monad-nomad can be reconfigured into a nomad-monad if the "unifications" are not transcendent unities of being, but immanent unifications of *becoming*—this is the process view of A. N. Whitehead: Even God, as Deleuze admits in his book *The Fold* (1992), is a Process in all processes, like all other processes (the creator as creature and vice versa), manifest in all processes, but also available as manifest Figure of divine immanence, as the divine desert, within its own horizon of processuality. The Plotinic All-One, the All in the transcendent but panentheistically embracing One, can *become* the Deleuzian One-All, the immanent One *in* the All, being its creative principle of differentiation and pure consciousness, if the Figures of such transformation do not *replicate* the transcendental horizon within itself, but *pre-symbolically manifest* the all-pervasive and all-expansive immanence of the creative self-differentiation of the cosmos. Instead of an imperial representative of transcendence, such Figures would be the gap that breaks the smooth space of the reproduction of imperial transcendence for reasons of expansion *without* movements of territorializing.

Such Figures would be the shock of pure consciousness. Here, the "prophet" is not the voice of transcendence surfing smooth immanence for reasons of territorialization (the imperial religion claiming exclusive truth, inclusive law, and the final expansive boundary). Instead, the prophet would be the one *opening* the creative, chaotic, chaosmic space that *shocks* the foreclosure of imperial transcendence and its territorialization. In principle, Deleuze allows for this option if we would realize *absolute* deterritorialization, that is, do not reterritorialize, but "disappear" in a plane of immanence of pure consciousness. However, in Deleuze's idealism, he negates that this can ever be *actualized*; it must remain *virtual*.

But how about Figures of the virtual? These would be *Figures of transfiguration*, like the cosmic body of Krishna or of messianic deference of actualization (via Derrida), cyclical instead of final (via religious cosmologies), open-ended instead of apocalyptic (via multiverse cosmologies), processual instead of fixated (via Whitehead)—much like Jesus and Baháʼuʼlláh. These Figures work not as justification of transcendence, but as "kenotic" acceptance of the impermanence of the world of becoming as the *place* of pure consciousness to creatively elate its creative differentiations—much like the divine-created-creative *nous* of Plotinus, which must express fullness and desolation of the divine desert: that which, as Plotinus says, does not need anything and does not have anything! Here, monad is the becoming of the nomad and the nomad is the movement beyond any monad. Or, with Whitehead, the many become one only for that one to again become one among the many that it has left to unite and the many it has constituted by becoming one among them. Here, the inclusive *horizon* of becoming-one becomes the Figure of becoming *within* the horizon (as elaborated in the section with the same title in ch. 2). By so becoming a creative impulse of the nomadic movements, these Figures indicate and initiate the new *lateral* "transcendence" *forward* beyond any monad into the trajectories of nomads on the plane of their integration.

The cosmic Spirit is not only pure consciousness that is *not* immanent *to* anything except itself, thereby apophatically transcending cosmic becoming, but the divine immanence that explicates the luminosity or virtuality of creative differentiation by liberating them to their own nomadic actualizations *and*, simultaneously, by *perceiving, embracing and transforming* their monadic actualizations within the divine desert as/into divine nomads that again become the virtual creative impulse. This is Whitehead's *dipolar* understanding of the nature of God as the manifestation of immanence in itself (the divine Mind) *in* the world as creative impulse of its self-differentiation (becoming-nomad) and self-actualization (becoming-monad) *and* the self-transcendence *of the world* (monads) *into God* (transformed nomads). It is only in this mutuality that dualism can be avoided, as the dualism between monism and monotheism *is not overcome but based on* the Deleuzian dualism between the virtual and actual. It is *this* dualism that is the fata morgana in the divine desert.

Meditate on the following "figures" partially taken from the previous Deleuzian discourse in four phases, that is, four times over:

Read and imagine the "figures" as concepts and images. This is the phase of intellectual representation.

Feel their reality as your *own* perspectives. By doing so, you will repeat the "objective" perspective that creates the fata morgana.

Erase, by "deterritorialization," that is, by avoiding the perspective that produces the mirage, your Self into the "pure consciousness" where the differences between subject (you) and object (the content and reality of the phrases) disappear. You will become the fata morgana. It is an illusion, too!

Release the lived mirage of "pure consciousness" into the *pure perception of becoming*, a space where everything, including your Self and pure consciousness, appears as but momentary nomadic moves of self-transcendence. Now, immediacy of impermanence and permanence of immediacy is the one gate to the cosmic Spirit.

transcendental field . . .

(Only read in the first phase: *It can be distinguished from experience in that it doesn't refer to an object or belong to a subject*)

. . .

pure stream of a-subjective consciousness . . .

pre-reflexive impersonal consciousness . . .

duration of consciousness without a self...

    flow of absolute consciousness...

...

immanence of immanence...

    absolute immanence...

    complete power, complete bliss...

...

the One...

    the All-One, emanating...

    the immanent One-All complicates all beings...

...

pure luminosity without source...

...

nomadic field

Mirage

All spiritual journeys begin with the confrontation of illusions. Some, however, have said, perhaps prematurely, that the spiritual journey itself *is* the illusion. It can be an illusion on four different accounts: by the assumption that there is no Spirit (materialism or pantheism); by the conviction that there is no journey (the problem of gradualism); by the doubt that there is no one taking the journey (the problem of the reality or illusion of the Self); and by the suspicion that the claim of illusion is itself an illusion (the problem of relativism or the reality of immediacy). Yet if the spiritual journey is the confrontation of illusions, this is precisely the realization that these presumed illusions are only operative *as long as* we are *not* embarking on a serious spiritual journey. Conversely, if we do (take the journey), we will decode them (the illusions) *not* as "tactics of immunization"—a term introduced by the German philosopher Hans Albert (b. 1921)—against Spirit, spirituality and spiritualization, but as necessary *mirrors* of the hindrances to progress on this journey. If you don't realize that all four assumptions are *true* in a spiritual context, you will not "discern" the Spirit in them, but will be bound by repeating the immunizations against them, and will, as long as you do, not be able to transcend them.

There are three kinds of illusions: One kind of illusion claims a *functional* projection of a material (physiological) or neuronal (psychological) strategy of the biological organism to be a *mere* illusion, that is, with no counterpart in the objective reality of this organism. The second kind of illusion is a *structural* one, that is, it understands the illusionary complex as a symbolic reality that manifests itself in corporal entities such as individuals or societies, cultures or polities, namely, as an objective force shaping these realities, but nevertheless being just an imagination. Of course, conversely, these illusions can also be understood as creative solutions to problematic realities or deviations from reality. The third kind of illusion is *objectively* part of reality of these organisms whether they perceive it or not; they are subconsciously paradigmatic or unavoidably adaptive in the evolutionary process of the appearance of these organisms.

Regarding the *first* kind of illusion, religion is a mere mechanism of deference of deeper problems that are just projected outwardly to avoid the internal confrontation with the underlying problem: This is the general tenor or figure of thought of the atheistic "hermeneutics of suspicion" of the Critique of Religion (*Religionskritik*) of the late nineteenth century of Karl Marx (d. 1883), Friedrich Nietzsche, and Sigmund Freud. The *second* kind of illusion is embraced by sociological and cultural studies explaining religion as a structural reflection of the dynamics of these realities: for instance, in the work of the sociologists of religion Emile Durkheim (d. 1917) and Max Weber (d. 1920). The *third* kind of illusion is favored by evolutionary thinkers such as C. G. Jung (d. 1961) and Ursula Goodenough (b. 1943)—and many others, like Richard Dawkins (b. 1941) and Daniel Dennett (b. 1942), who might think more along maladaptive lines.

When I point to "mirage" instead of illusion, I don't mean either of these forms of illusion. Rather, I point to the physical (objective) reality of a "mirage" because of its *perspectival constellation* by which it "in-sists" (in, on, and) as the *reality* of these illusions only *ambivalently* being "illusions." If we, instead, assume that such *natural* constellations of many factors, and only from certain perspectives of their coming together, are not *mere* imagination, they can, perhaps, on a deeper level even awaken our understanding to the kind of realities by which we are surrounded and of which we may consist—such as events instead of substances, processes instead of particles, vibrations instead of fixed grids. What seems illusive may be profound. Then, it is not the reality of a mirage that is the illusion, but the *projections on it* of imaginative interpretations that are rather revealing of the three illusionary forms just discussed, but are not the relational, relative, perspectival reality of the mirage *itself*. To confront illusions, then, *as* the spiritual journey, means to differentiate between the perspectival mirage, its impermanence and fragility, in its hint toward spiritual reality, and the illusions that, in fear or merely for the joy of imagination, are mere projection of desires onto them.

Is religion an illusion or a mirage?

Is the Spirit an illusion or a mirage?

Is God an illusion or a mirage?

What would it mean to say that they are not illusions, but mirages? It would mean that the illusion is a way to *avoid* the perspectival ambivalence of the mirage, that is, to necessitate an absolute determination of that which cannot be determined from any limited perspective. Perhaps, we need to clear a path to the spiritual insight that spiritual reality, God and religion relate us to an *indeterminate* reality that cannot be grasped. As soon as we try to grasp it, it eludes and becomes seemingly (that is, relative to the desire of determination) illusionary. Several important symbolisms from vastly diverse religious universes explicate my meaning. Just to mention three of them: the difference between the image of God and the imagining to be like/as God (Genesis 3); the impermanent world (*samsara*) as dream of ultimate reality (*dharmakaya*); the cascade of densities of reality (or the chain of becoming) between God and the most trivial puff (an image A. N. Whitehead uses). It is worth pondering on these three variations of the same theme individually.

Think of the psychological portrait of Genesis 3 in the encounter of Eve and the serpent: the seduction, here, lies in the promise to become like God (if one gains the knowledge of good and evil). Yet Eve is said to already *be* in the image of God (Genesis 1). The image is the mirage and the promise of becoming-as-God is the illusion, the projection. So, what's the difference, then, between illusion and mirage, here? The illusion is the determination what it *means* to be-as-God, to know what it means to *be* the image of God: knowledge as determination, the use of knowledge as manipulation, hubris, self-establishment. Compare with the one who, "in the form" of God (*the* image of God), does not hold on to it as a trophy, but is aware that he can only fulfill it "in the form of" a servant in Philippians 2. Dipolar theism: in the *indeterminacy* of the apophatic, unmanifest Reality beyond any determination lies the knowledge and unknowing of the manifest divine reality, which, simultaneously—as Deleuze recognizes (in a quote cited in the section on the desert earlier in this chapter) reflecting on Plotinus—fuses God and creature. This *image* of God is thoroughly ambivalent and undetermined as to our desire to know definitively. Only in this tension is it real, a mirage, that is, *spiritual* reality. Isn't that what the temptations of Jesus in the desert teach (Luke 4)?

In certain Hindu and Buddhist contexts, we find the reasoning that the physical universe, even the feeling to be an isolated self, to be an illusion. That the act of creation, as it were, is nothing but ignorance, not individual, but collective ignorance: as the condition of the All that warrants salvation. In reality, there is only ultimate reality, be it *brahman* or *dharmakaya*, and the limited world is the illusion of separate existence. Adi Sankaracharya's nondualism (Advaita) only knows of one reality from which all else is just not separate. However, he cautiously did not *absolutely* discard of that which I have named dipolar monism, that is, there is a difference between the unmanifest *brahman* (the *brahman* without characteristics) and the manifest *brahman* (the *brahman* with characteristics), or the "subtle" consciousness (*atman-brahman*), which is independent from, but coeternal with, the universe of form and matter (*nama-rupa*), and the gross consciousness, which is somehow bound to matter (*jiva*). And the enlightened identity of us as the one universal Self (*atman*) with the indifferent Spirit (*brahman*) is, to that extent, no illusion, but, in my terminology: a mirage. Other cosmological positions within Hinduism and Buddhism tried to play on the reality of a mirage by either viewing it more like a dream, or like a process of differentiation, or as a divine power or play. Either things are only as real as the clouds of imaginations, drifting aimlessly through dreams and only become "real," that is, *illusions*, if they are reiterated; or they have a certain kind of reality from their own perspective; or they are just manifestation of divine imagination, expressions of divine powers, but in themselves illusionary. In the universe of Krishna, the cosmic powers are just divine magic, divine play, the *lila* of Krishna. In the Buddhist three body symbolism (*trikaya*), the "magical" cosmic body of the Buddha (*sambhogakaya*) is the means to bring enlightenment to every being on its own terms; it is an expression of the skillful means (*upaya*) of the Dharma. Nagarjuna goes even further and *identifies* ultimate with phenomenal reality, as the phenomenally "real" is different only by ignorant reiteration, but on its own level still (feels) "real," nonetheless. Yet, in the related Hindu and Buddhist sources, the ambivalence remains whether this appearance of the cosmos is a *fall* initiated by ignorance (reiteration of an illusion) or is the *creative play* of divine powers—it is a mirage, not an illusion.

Most of the religious traditions presuppose that there is not just a material reality. If at all, it is *not* an illusion (as in the previous thought), but allows for diverse *levels* of existence that are related to one another by a scale of relative illusion-reality perspectives. In many interesting cross-religious iterations, we find a mystical cosmology of layers of ever more integrated (or diversified) spheres of closeness (or distance) to reality. The simplest example would be the tripartite idea of earth with heaven above and a subterranean world below. Elaborate models, such as the multiple Jain, Hindu and Buddhist world-spheres, know of many moral- and consciousness-related layers of sub-human arrests and super-human expansions of powers—but they are all illusions in the sense that they are not liberating from their illusionary character; that is, even any higher approximation does not cross the "river" until you have gotten rid of the illusion that there *is* another bank to be reached—an image elaborated in chapter 3. In the perhaps clearest presentation of these layers as mirages instead of mere illusions, the Sufi monism, the ideas of the unity of being (*wahdat al-wujud*) besides its controversial pantheist tendencies, shares with more orthodox Islamic cosmological expressions the idea that God is really the only Reality, and that everything else is—a mirage. Nothing is just an illusion because everything is real on its own level of existence, but is both undetected by a lower level of existence and, simultaneously, an illusion itself for the higher levels. In the sight of God, nothing is but a cloud of becoming and perishing, but for the becoming and perishing beings, their becoming and perishing is quite real. In medieval Christian theology this relativity was expressed as one between the material and spiritual character of beings on the chain of becoming between mere matter and God. In relation to mere matter, humans were considered spiritual; but in relation to angels, humans were considered material. In relation to us, angels are spiritual, but in relation to God they are material. Again, the relative status of existence is not an illusion, but exhibits the ambivalence of a mirage.

The mirage, in the here invested meaning, then, is of apophatic (unknowable) *and* polyphilic (irreducibly complex and expressive) nature, that is, it is always *beyond* any defining determination, but appears *in* multiple ways, *in* many paths. This dipolar unity necessitates us to discern the Spirit *in* its appearance or mirage as that which is *beyond* emotional desire, conceptual limitation or fearful determination. The Spirit cannot be determined—whether as non-existent, as in naturalism, or as transcendent reality, as in theism. It might give rise to either speculation and "plays" both parties—like the *lila* of Krishna—or saves us from absolutist determinations of reality that would make it just an illusion that will bind us to its "reality" like a prison—as the *upaya* of the cosmic Buddha. Yet "in reality," Spirit always escapes our/any fixations. As the mirages of the Spirit, they always become temptations for illusionary projections, but are only *the mirrors of our illusions* that the spiritual journey must confront and transcend. It is in this sense that the Buddhist "middle way," as elaborated by Nagarjuna, establishes the necessity to hold on to the mirage of ambivalence and undecidedness: all meditation and visualization and introspection has the aim to escape any fixations in whatever directions, for instance, not to decide whether *nirvana* is a state of being (ontology) *or* of consciousness (epistemology), or whether it is formless *or* has a form (as any form is formless and any fixation onto formlessness would be a new form). And it is the final insight of the discussions about suffering in the biblical book of Job that there is no ultimate or divine perspective from which Job could determine the relational complexity and meaning of the *whole* creation, which implies that all reasons discussed regarding suffering and whether this constitutes a problem for the existence of God (the theodicies problem) are illusionary determinations of the unavailability of the "mirage" of cosmic reality.

The function of the mirage is to "place" our mind—immanent, in movement. The best way in the encounter may consist in viewing it (the mirage) as an *infinite mirror* of our particular projections, which can only be avoided if we learn that they are iterations of the *mutual reflection* of all things in all things—for which, however, *no* all-perspective, *no* God's eye view exists. It is an insight that the *Avatamsaka Sutra* and Hua Yen Buddhism formulated, as the understanding of the emptiness of all things: that all things are not Self nor even identical with themselves, but reflect the All in themselves from their perspective. However, as all perspectives are empty, that is, all-related, the whole cosmos becomes a mirage, an objective mirroring of mutual perspectives, which in their mutual immanence *are* ultimate reality—One-All, cosmic, polyphilic Spirit. Yet, as A. N. Whitehead would add, the *unity* of this infinite mirroring is *itself* a mirage, an ambivalent reality of relations. No coinherence, individually or collectively, can be real without the becoming and perishing of such perspectives, the events of making and transcending such perspectives, by which the All is moving, becoming, never finding any point of stillness in which all mirroring has lost its ambivalence and would be arrested in any final state of things. Hence, the All in All always *transcends* the All, although it is only immanent in its relations of becoming.

This brings me once more back to Deleuze's contention of the "decease of transcendence," the primordial illusionary character of transcendence, and the opposition of religion, which is always about transcendence, and philosophy, which is the "salvation" of immanence (with Spinoza as its Christ-figure). As cited in the related epigraph of Deleuze at the beginning of this chapter, because transcendence is the "original sin" of the establishment of the religious, even explicitly monotheistic mindset with all the warring, exclusivist and imperial consequences, the philosophical alternative of pure immanence is the answer to all of the involved problems: Ontologically, epistemologically, cosmologically, psychologically, and politically, we need to avoid transcendence, because it invents the construction of an imperial One that then is reinscribed into the empty (or emptied) plane as occupational power, controlled by its representatives, like authoritative prophets, priesthoods, aristocracies, or psychiatrists, and ideological constructs like Reason, Logos, or the theistic God.

We have already seen, how this is related to the pre-symbolic land of the desert and how its symbolizations have real consequences in religion- and empire-building. What is interesting in the current context of the question of illusion is that Deleuze's whole alternative "theology of the divine desert" is itself *not* materialist in its outcome or motivation, but resists all such reductionisms with a new kind of *idealism*, which, nevertheless, takes its cue from Plato and Plotinus (with an immanentist transformation attributed to Spinoza). On the face of it (but not exactly the "surface" character that Deleuze attaches to the plane of immanence, though), one still hears echoes of Ludwig Feuerbach (d. 1872) and Friederich Nietzsche, the "projection thesis" and the cry of the "death of God," respectively. Feuerbach and Nietzsche share the figure of thought that is still the basis for Deleuze's immanentist turn, as it were, namely, that in the desire for immortality, stability, security, Being, and, as a side effect or as original intention, the exertion of power over domains of thought and society, religions, and especially Christianity, in the eyes of the three thinkers, have created an atmosphere of a *lack*, of a missing fulfillment of these desires. In this "emptiness," again, religiosity came about as we (humanity under the oppression of this lack of fulfillment) began to extract the desired imaginations, projected them onto transcendent beings of immense reality (immortality, Being, power), and reinjected those beings into the emptied world of impermanence with the authority of its representatives, who now began to control humanity's creative abilities and potential for self-realization by the constraints of moral and legal codes, as well as other power mechanism of ritualistic and ideological reverence (of the king or the priest or the saint).

Transcendence, in this view, is a "projection" of humanity's creativity onto God, and the death of God is the rebirth of "the original state" of human integrity. It gives humanity back what it *is* to begin with: self-creative divergence in a cosmos of creative differentiations. Deleuze's cosmos is a "chaosmos," that is, it is meant to avoid the presupposition for thinking the character of existence with the aim of fleeing the impermanence of the world in becoming (as religions and many classical philosophies seem to desire) in the image of eternity, but, instead, to ask the question how the cosmos can be "eternally" renewing *itself*. Immanent self-creativity instead of transcendent creation was already Whitehead's reversal of thought—whom Deleuze cites as witness for his own move. But, differently from Deleuze, Whitehead *decouples* this solution from that of transcendence and immanence *as* unambivalently distributed between religion and philosophy.

However, before I go into the alternatives between these two thinkers, here, we must recognize that both thinkers relate their solution back to Plato (and Plotinus). This seems more astonishing for Deleuze, who as prophet of pure immanence—as we saw in Meditation XIII—was adamant to avoid any divine transcendence or any idealistic transcendence, as with the Platonic forms. Why? Because, even if they are not God, the Platonic forms were Plato's solution for how the world of shadows and of "perpetual perishing" (as Whitehead calls it) can have an *anchor* in a world of eternity, the *originals* of which of all beings' processes of becoming and perishing are only imperfect spatio-temporal copies or *simulacra*. In the development toward Plotinus and Neo-Platonism, these eternal forms became thoughts in the Mind (*nous*) of God. Nevertheless, although Deleuze answers transcendent eternity (of God, of Forms, originals) with self-creativity, closer to the stoic idea of an immanent Logos, Deleuze's immanent Law of self-differentiation remains essentially Platonic, because, other than the Stoics and the materialists throughout the centuries, he insists on the *ideal* character of the initiating reality of his self-differentiating universe, which he calls *virtual* reality.

Deleuze remains idealist, insofar as the virtual reality is a restatement of the *possibilities* in the Mind of God by voiding their transcendent character both as higher reality (as in Platonic philosophies) and as possibilities *of* actualization (as in Aristotelian philosophies). Platonic Forms are the actualization of all possible imperfect variations in the world of impermanence; all becoming is ephemeral, or, in Plato's poetic rendering: a moving image of eternity. Here, reality is *duplicated*, without allowing creativity to "transcend" eternity. Aristotelian possibilities, conversely, are *abstract* and lack actualization, but actual beings can only be *their* actualization, that is, they *cannot* be creative of novelties, but only be iterations of what is possible. Here, again, reality is unnecessarily *duplicated* without creative "transcendence." Now Deleuze follows Whitehead (and he acknowledges this!), avoiding both the Platonic and the Aristotelian way. Whitehead differentiates possibilities in the Mind of God (against Plato) as non-actual ideals that provide *appetite* for creative events, which, hence, are not "doubles" of their mere possibility, but the becoming of *syntheses* of other events and such ideals. However, Whitehead's ideals *cannot* become actual either (like abstract Aristotelian possibilities would), as they remain ideals *for* actualization. This is the reason that Deleuze understood the Whiteheadian possibilities as "virtualities" in his own rendering.

Moreover, in his turn to pure immanence, that is, avoiding *any* negation or lack that would indicate a hint of triggering the mechanisms of transcendence that (like Hegel's negative dialectic) feeds its reality from this negativity, Deleuze recreates philosophy in the image of pure affirmation of immanence and creative difference—which includes, in a Buddhist manner, but in a more Whiteheadian attitude, the affirmation of the world of becoming as inherently impermanent, but creatively so. Deleuze tries also to avoid the Whiteheadian Mind of God—as events or phenomena would still seem to lack existence on their own if they would need a Mind in which to be contained—situating these virtualities as *real, but not actual, ideal, but not abstract reality* in their own sphere of reality *within* the "pure pre-subjective or -reflective consciousness" or "plane of immanence" or "transcendental field." Deleuzian virtualities, then, function not as limitations (as do the Forms and possibilities in the Platonic and Aristotelian worlds), but also not as valuations of a divine Mind, as in Whitehead, but rather only as *immanent differentials* whereby all actualization is creative *self*-differentiation instead of divine law. Now, the "chaosmos" is a world of novelty instead of eternity, a world of differentiation instead of imitation. We end up with a world of nondual affirmation of becoming, without restrictive eternity of Forms or gods, close to eastern religious intimations of ultimate reality and its relation to the world, but with a generally affirmative view of its chaosmic impermanence, which does not need salvation or healing, but acceptance in the consciousness of pure immanence.

The Platonic and Plotinian basis for this transformation, however, does not disappear—and it is here that we can begin to sense the limitations and, perhaps, enveloped even an alternative, a more Whiteheadian direction of the transcendence-immanence axis of the whole discussion on eternity and creativity, and the related question of religious authenticity, that will lead us beyond the accusation of just being the manifestation of the illusion of transcendence. This for two reasons: First, since the ideal virtuals cannot be dissolved into any (future, radical, revolutionary) actualization, they remain *independent* from any actualizations, that is, in this sense, *beyond* spatio-temporal differentiation "eternal." They are still Platonic Forms or Whiteheadian "eternal objects"! Second, virtuals appear as divergences on diverse planes of immanence, not as monadic hierarchies, but as consistent nomadic distributions. These transcendental planes of consistency in pure affirmation of their divergent virtuals establish themselves only on the basis of the presupposition that *immanence is not immanent to anything*, but *only* immanent "in itself." This is, in fact, Deleuze's new "transcendence." Again, the world of Ideals of eternal suggestions for actualizations in the Mind of God remains operative in the background of this Deleuzian transformation from emanation to immanence (see Meditation XIII).

The question is whether this new "transcendence" (of virtuals and immanence) amounts to a renewal of dualism, in this case, not a monotheism or monism/monadism, but a dualistic nomadism, instead of a dipolar nomadism—falling under Deleuze's ban of *illusion* (of transcendence) and the establishment of a new religious figure of thought—*or* whether this "transcendence" escapes the reduction of the ambivalence of the *mirage*, the related complex integration of immanence and transcendence, and, even against Deleuze's intuition, between philosophy (the imperative of immanence) and religion (the imperative of transcendence). I would contend that while the "old" imperial transcendence was a negation of immanence, the "new" transcendence is one that transcends the pantheistic *identity* of God and the world, as in Spinoza. It has become (maybe even against Deleuze's intentions) a *trans-pantheistic* "transcendence" that needs another, a *dipolar* approach, in order not to fall back into patterns of the old dualistic transcendence or simple fixation as identity-monism.

Here, Whitehead may shift our perspective. The reason is that, in his understanding, it is *immanence* that must be secured against the *illusion* of transcendence, but that all realities, ideal or actual, only operate in *mutual* immanence. Mutual immanence knows of mutual transcendence of *that which cannot be abstracted from one another*: the transcendence of its elements is not an illusion, but an elusive yet necessary moment of the process of creative differentiation; and mutual immanence is not "limited" by the production of difference (which is its own transcendence), but arises from the relationality of the manifold that actually diverges only via the *synthesis* of impermanent events of unification that *transcend* themselves into ever new multiplicities. Since the *mutuality* of creative differentiations in actualizations of events with ideal appetitions appears only in movements of self-transcending syntheses, neither are two mutually exclusive worlds of the virtual and actual established (avoiding dualism), nor is a monadism of the Mind of God. The reason is that the ideals in the Mind of God are also *processes of synthesis*, of actualizations, but that what the actualizations provide is not eternal reality but *values* (Whitehead's "virtuals") for *self*-creative actualizations in the world of becoming.

And there is another reason for even supposing that Deleuze's virtual reality as creative motor of actual differentiation presupposes a Whiteheadian *actual* synthesis of the ideal and the structuring of the ideal by the actual, namely, that synthesis implies *sym-pathy*, the *feeling together of other realities by feeling their feelings*. In a sense, Deleuze's examples of virtualities as well as their linguistic implication indicating "virtues," that is, ethical habits, may reflect this. For instance, when "a life," the pre-personal, non-possessive and -possessed infinitive form of living *appears* to us in the moment where all personal traits fall away, as in a moment between life and death, the virtual triggers the virtue of *empathy* with the deadly wounded to help, whether you like the person of this "life" or not. It is in this sense that, for Whitehead, the Mind of God (the Primordial Nature of God) is not a synthesis of ideals without also to be a sympathic, empathic reception of the actualities that self-creatively activate such ideals in events (the Consequent nature of God). This Whiteheadian "dipolarity" of God is the paradigm of mutual immanence of the ideal and actual "worlds," of the Mind of God with creation, and of self-creative differentiation with the sympathic, empathic receptivity of relationality.

The test-case in differentiating illusion from mirage is the question of horizon and figure. *Illusionary* transcendence is the "emptying" of the plane of the nomadic distribution of its population (of events, concepts, beings, or affects), projecting its life onto a transcendent reality (God, state, reason) and reinsuring itself as imperial monad or monarch. Conversely, the power of the *mirage* is the *appearance* (epiphany, theophany) of the plane of immanence (the divine Mind) *as horizon "in itself"* (as *sambhogakaya, upaya, lila*), even on a human level (prophet, saint, incarnation, *avatar, nirmanakaya*), *not* as inscription of imperial power, which presupposes the identification of the horizon "in itself" as something, but as *shock of creative novelty* (the Messianic, Christ, Logos, Mind, Consciousness), *differentiating* the planes of immanence into *syntheses of becoming of new multiplicities* of events and nexuses, organisms and even universes, as ever new planes to which to connect. According to the immanentist intuition of Deleuze, this indifferentiation of God and creature, which he saw already prophetically appearing in Plotinus, is not a figure of imperial power, *but* it can only be operative if it appears as epiphany or theophany of this horizon *in itself*, much like Nietzsche's Figure of liberating immanence, the prophet Zarathustra, instead of being eliminated, as in Spinoza's divine substance. These Figures are not "figures of transcendence," but "epiphanies of immanence," not of the divine crown, scepter, and orb, but of the divine desert, where the "form of God" coincides with the "form of the evanescence," like the Christ of Philippians 2 or Plotinus's Mind, which *is and is not* God. In fact, this is how Whitehead read the history of religions in *Religion in the Making* (1926): that true religiosity appears in Figure of extraordinary creative self-differentiation and empathy (Whitehead's divine "dipolarity"), mirroring our failed projections in their solitariness and even god-forsakenness, symbolized, for instance, by the meditations of the Buddha and Muhammad, the self-less theft and punishment of Prometheus, or the Man on the cross (*ecce homo!*), and the *powerless force of peace* in the midst of polyphilic differentiations of multiplicities of becoming in an infinitely self-creative chaosmos (the here employed dipolarity of unmanifest and manifest reality). I call these manifest Figures the *in-sistence* of the divine indetermination *in* its horizon *on* indetermination (widening of the horizon) and *in* differentiation (see the Epilogue of this book).

The point, here, is not whether Deleuze or Whitehead is right, whether these are Figures of inscribed transcendence or of a divine desert of immanence. Sure, my own understanding goes with Whitehead and not with Deleuze, here, and this decision is important for the understanding of the *dipolar indifference* of the unmanifest Beyond (the Beyond as horizon) and the divine Manifestations (the appearance of the horizon "in itself"). However, the point is that if the appearance of the horizon in itself, or of immanence "in itself," cannot be definitely defeated as illusion, then the reality of the Spirit is precisely *established* by the fact that it is a *mirage*. A mirage is the appearance of the divine desert in itself in such a way that no reduction to a state of definite interpretation—such as being an imperial illusion or the reality of a theophany—can exhaust the *ambivalence* that always *apophatically escapes* these limitations and, hence, only appears in this ambivalence in *multiple* ways or paths, be they spiritual or not. The "error" of materialism, atheism or dualism, monism or monotheism, pantheism or panentheism lies only in this: that they live from the *determination* of the mirage into bifurcations of illusion and reality. Conversely, the trans-pantheism of dipolar indifference or nondual difference escapes this procedure as itself illusory imperial determination of the essential indifference and undecidability of the event of the mirage—the *true* religious event of self-transcendent synthesis and of mutual immanence, the true spiritual body (*soma pneumatikon*).

On a plane of spiritual practice, this philosophical analysis of religiosity amounts to a dipolar movement of rhythms and harmonies of ever-new manifestations of the *avoidance* of determinations of the divine desert as territories of power. A good approximation of this spiritual impulse is the attitude of never accepting anything "as God" that is delimited by *bifurcations* into truth and illusion or the acceptance of anything "definite" *as* divine. The "discerning of the spirits" is an old spiritual discipline of the ancient desert sages. Its most profound expression is the self-deferential habit (Derrida's *différance*) to *never identify oneself* with any expression of the divine that doesn't point beyond itself into the indeterminate, the apophatic, the indifferent; and to never identify anything *as* divine that does not, simultaneously reveal its penultimate, manifest *limitation* of the Beyond that cannot be determined and limited. In alteration of the Pauline warning of not confusing God with any creature (Romans 1), we may say: The Figure that Paul has himself identified with God YHWH (1 Corinthians 8:6) is, simultaneously, *neither* simply God (El Elyon, the Father) *nor* a mere creature (Philippians 2:6–7). This ambivalence reflects the "alternative" tradition that, as analyzed in chapter 5, survived from Philo of Alexandria's Logos-figure to the Bahá'í notion of the divine Manifestation (*mazhar-i-illahi*), which don't violate the apophatic nature of God Beyond (Qur'an 112). It also lives on in the Figures of Krishna, the ultimate Face of *brahman*, the cosmic Spirit, in which manifest and unmanifest aspect are *indifferentiated* "in" its own horizon. And it fits the *trikaya* cosmology of Mahayana Buddhism (the immanence of *dharmakaya* "in" the cosmos, even as a human being) as well as the dipolar nature of Samantabhadra in Vajrayana Buddhism—as elaborated in the Epilogue of the previous chapter.

In any case, as we cannot definitely identify these Figures with God, they may still be "illusions" in the sense of Deleuze's unreformed transcendence or naturalist aversion to spiritual realities or materialist reductionism to externalities of matter and energy. They remain a mirage. The great Fata Morgana of religion lies in its *ambivalence* by which its "reality" cannot be proven or determined without losing its power of indetermination and ever-new creations of relational planes of immanence. The spiritual Fata Morgana is the epiphany of the divine desert.

Epilogue and *Meditation XIV*: Vibration

Another way of describing "mirage" (in the sense employed here) is to understand it as a *vibration*. Any mirage, at sea, or in the desert, is a relational fusion of vibrations: of light and air, temperature and surfaces. All of them vibrate in their own manner and pace. But together they seem to create something that is independent from such relations, leaving the impression of "things" with their own identity. This is, however much it may have contributed to our determination of the nature of the cosmos as a collection of things or substances, an illusion, a projection onto the mirage, the vibrational nature of that which we actually encounter.

Vibrations are symbioses of patterns and nexuses of events or processes in which such patterns form, are sustained, developed, change, or from which they disappear. In this sense, Aristotelian immanence of form *in* matter—over Plato's conjecture that they exist in pre-eternal actuality for themselves—was right. However, Aristotelian forms were still the *actual* reality of which matter was only the potential to be actualized. Still, in the sense that "matter" is not "a thing" (*ens quid*: a being that/what is), but a principle (*ens quo*: that through which things are), Aristotelian based "materialism" would be right to question the assumption that it was about soulless pieces of matter hurling through empty space—much as in the ancient atomistic theories of Democritus (d. ca. 370 BCE) and Lucretius (d. ca. 55 BCE)—but that matter is rather about *potential*, the shadowy cloud of *possibilities* surrounding every event in its becoming. This "materialism" rings much truer in an age of quantum mechanic's contention that all material states are based on such non-local, non-actual, virtual, entangled probability spaces of relationships of waves, expressed in quantum wave functions. And it is here that beginning with the pioneers of quantum physics a philosophy developed that finds this virtual reality of clouds of entangled possibilities much closer to mind-like activities than dumb-dead particles of "matter."

Events and nexuses of events or processes of becoming are but such entangled fields of possibilities in the context of an actualized reality in which such spaces become decided, possibilities collapse under decisions of actualizations (some over other alternatives), and—as Deleuze relates the virtual with the actual world—the enfolded, virtual continuum of intensities unfolds, explicates itself into external things. In Whitehead's *mutual* immanence of this movement—not primarily as externalization of intensities to extensities (the process of transition), but primordially as internalization or synthesis of extensities into intensities (the process Whitehead calls "concrescence," growing together to become "concrete")—lies the avoidance of dualism, but also of the rhythmic and harmonic nature by which things are constituted as pattern of event-nexuses over generation of cyclical becoming (synthesis) and perishing (transcending, even sacrificing one's Self into externalities). Vibrations are these rhythmic and harmonic processual cycles of mutual complication (*complicatio*, folding together) and explication (*explicatio*, folding apart)—to invoke Nicolas of Cusa again, as Deleuze does—constituting the entertainment of patterns within event-nexuses that form a universe of multiple layered, nested environments and organisms, which again in their mutual immanence generate evolutions and devolutions of their interaction. From the widest context in which some "natural law" of a cosmos is entertained by the comprehensive field of *all* of its event-nexuses, being the *widest environment* of this cosmos to the laws that govern organisms in their evolutionary context, and from the epistemological rules of our engagement with the world to the character of persons—all regularities are such actually entertained patterns, that is, harmonies in rhythmic reestablishment. They are not eternal, monadic or imperial laws, but inherent relational, immanent and mutually responsive patterns that will change as the event-nexuses of all cosmic layers and magnitudes in the mutual engagement of environments and organisms *interact* in ever-new and creatively unexpected ways.

Magnitudes of vibrations (patterns in actual processes of synthesis and transition) are important for the recognition of *layers* of patterns and vibrations. Traditionally, they are viewed as spheres of inherent immanent laws and constructed as emergent levels of qualities. Think of the classical difference between material, biological, intellectual, and (for some) spiritual "realms"—within the same world. We are still puzzled by the *emergence* of life with its own inherent rules that do not dispute physical laws, but are not mere deductions from them either. The same is true for the emergence of mind in the context of life and, as some would say, of religion (the ability to recognize ultimate reality or God) or spiritual experience and insight, in the context of consciousness, intellect, as well as ethical values, virtues, and responsibilities.

Another way to look at magnitudes of vibrations is to compare the intelligible and imaginable patterns of "reality" on different *scales* of cosmic existence. On the level of elementary particles, no biological organisms exist, no humanity is visible, no spiritual reality is detectable—except you invoke the quantum space of mind-like and -entertained potentials. On the human level, we have no grasp of the world of cells that constitute us or even the brain, if we don't cut the skull, because we experience this from either the outside or the inside, whatever you prefer. And if we speed up time, our lives begin to look much like the canalized, determined and mindless flow of blood—as, for instance, demonstrated in the movie *Koyaanisqatsi* (1982) of Godfrey Reggio with the music of Philip Glass. And then, from the perspective of a galaxy, human existence is indiscernible from non-existence. From the perspective of a possible, infinite multiverse, our universe is probably to be understood as irrelevant. It is *these perspectives of magnitudes that define our reality*, and it is their vibrations in which the harmonics of the magnitudes is stabilized, that different universes seem to coexist and overlap. Yet since they are all the outcome of such *vibrational* rhythms and harmonics, their different octaves are themselves rhythmically and harmonically connected and mutually coinherent. Mind might just be a higher octave of vibration than life or physicality. And Spirit, in these harmonics of patterning vibrations, may be the very motive force of the generation, sustenance, and change of vibration, insofar as it strives for the creative realization of all of its potentials (matter) and enlightened interaction of their mutual immanence (form) in ever new manifestations of intensity (virtuality) and harmony (actuality). In this sense, not only is the cosmic Spirit the Poet of these coinherent realms of vibration, but *we* are poets of the Spirit in the spiritual mediation of all of its magnitudes and layers (see the Preamble).

Music is the vibration of patterns in events. Think of music as an aesthetic integration of the elements of vibrations, of its magnitudes, rhythms, and harmonics, as well as of diverse overlapping fields of vibrations, such as language, mathematics, matter, immanent structure, and the poetic transcendence. *Language* is a physical vibration, a phonetic production of vibrations, but also of words and sentences, symbols and grammars, whole spoken and written manifestations that exhibit the characteristics of vibrational reality, of patterned nexuses of processes of synthesis and disintegration, empathy and self-transcendence. *Mathematics* is a language of the land of connections, propositions, implications, and multiplicities in diverse fields of relationality. *Music* is an aesthetic integration of matter, mathematics, and language, adding a dimension of *immediacy* of perception, ideal and real expedience of the transcendence of all limited spaces of matter, language, and mathematics, that is unique among the arts. Music is *the art of vibration* and, in this sense, a *spiritual gate* to the mystical insight into the vibrational nature of the cosmos and the Spirit of the cosmos that vibrates over its waters, its chaosmos.

Music connects magnitude of vibrational patterns: of the matter of instruments, of the human body engaging the instruments, of the airwaves transporting the vibrations, of the human organism hearing them, of the brain assessing them, and of our inner Self *becoming* the music vibrating. There can be a symbolic representation of the temporal instantiation, a score, as in classical music, for instance, or just a mentally agreed on landscape of constraints of harmonies and rhythms, as in Jazz improvisations. But in any case, no *performance* of music, without there would be no music, will be the same.

The Austrian-British philosopher of science Karl Popper (d. 1994) developed a non-reductive theory of physicalism, differentiating three worlds, the material world (books, musical scores, ears, brains), the world of psychological states (feelings, consciousness, modes of entertainment), and the abstract world of ideas (contents of books, mathematics, musical ideas), in order to explain such phenomena as music or any other layered reality of phenomena. In his final analysis, the experience of music would be a psychological state irrelevant to the musical idea vibrating through material media to the psyche. Yet isn't it something else to experience the layers of music in an experience of immediacy that far exceeds a psychological state, but steers in the depth of our recesses vibrations of *all* magnitudes and levels in such a way that its aesthetic experience is not reducible to either of the Popperian three worlds? This *vibrational coinherence*, if it is experienced, may be one of the most *immediate sympathies* releasing the Spirit beyond the differentiation of subject and object, time and eternity, idea and material, humanly possible.

No meditation of music can be done without *actual performance* of music. Now, a score cannot substitute such a musical performance, or even suggest which kind of music will be experienced by whom to induce the state I am describing, here. Yet ever since the characterization of the world system as a musical composition of vibrating patterns with mathematical propositions and semiotic investments of Pythagorean origin, bridging vast mental spaces up to Whitehead's characterization of ultimate reality as *harmony of harmonies* and Deleuze's image the world process as a *polyphony of polyphonies*, we can "visualize" the cosmic Spirit in such rhythms and harmonies, vibrations, and polyphonies of a poetic composition in the becoming of ever-new relationships of material, expressive, and aesthetic layers of a cosmic symphony or, as

The Cosmic Spirit

Deleuze would prefer, in the form of the (divergent series of) polyphonic serialism of Pierre Boulez (d. 2016).

Settle in your silent space...

Hear in your mind a tone, arbitrarily generate it and listen to it persisting, without any change...

Try not to drift from its awareness; try to avoid any self-assertion...

You are only this listening; you are this tone...

Now, slow the tone down... until you can hear the vibration...

...

Hold on to the tone; don't lose it; don't let it fade away...

Hear its vibration as a wave, as a rocking chair, a heartbeat...

...

Hear in the vibrating tone the complete universe...

...

Slow the tone down until you hear the vibrating tone as a harmony of all beings vibrating...

...

Slow down further... and further...

Now you vibrate without time... like light vibrating only in the present...

...

Slow down further... and enter time...

...

Become the vibration that you are...

7

The Mountaineer

The wise person is always mindful. Through this alertness he discards the ways of the slothful. The wise person ascends the tower of wisdom. Once he has attained that height, he is capable of surveying the sorrowing masses with sorrowless eyes. Detached and dispassionate he sees these masses like a person atop a mountain peak, surveying the ground below.

—THE BUDDHA, *DHAMMAPADA* (VERSE 28)

When all the people witnessed the thunder and lightning, the sound of the trumpet, and the mountain smoking, they were afraid and trembled and stood at a distance . . . Then the people stood at a distance, while Moses drew near to the thick darkness where God was.

—EXODUS 20:18, 21 (NRSV)

. . . Jesus took with him Peter and James and John, and led them up a high mountain apart, by themselves. And he was transfigured before them, and his clothes became dazzling white, such as no one on earth could bleach them. And there appeared to them Elijah with Moses, who were talking with Jesus.

—MARK 9:2–4 (NRSV)

Numen

ANDES, ALPS, HIMALAYA, KARAKORAM, Rocky Mountains; K2, Eiger, Matterhorn, El Capitan, Everest, Nanga Parbat, Lhotse, Kilimanjaro, Mont Blanc. Viewing the majesty of a mountain or mountain range; scaling a mountain or a path through the bizarre formations of a ridge; approaching mythic, storied, clouded inaccessible formations; withstanding the thin air, the raw conditions, the sudden changes in weather; impatiently expecting unprecedented revelations of nature and the secrets it hides—those are all archetypical experiences, imaginations, or desires related to the motivation of becoming a mountaineer, someone who has followed this call, has not spared any energy, has left his ordinary life, has accepted the deprivation, austerities and destitution of the journey into the presence of the out-of-the-world summit of life, mounting a peak in the unexplainable feeling that it will give one's life, perhaps life as such, meaning.

The virtues of both mountains and mountaineers are legendary and revered: Majesty and strength, patience and independence, security and indifference, are as engrained in aesthetical and ethical projections sought by the mountaineer, as much as she needs strength, will, long-suffering, endurance, frugality, indifference to conditions, sharp perception, the ability to swiftly adapt to sudden changing conditions, as much as a focused mind despite bodily pains and privations. The training and test of the communal virtues of team work, mutual support, dependency on the weakest link, securing a whole group from accident, physically and symbolically being related by ropes and paths, is all as important as extensive foresight in planning and gathering all sustaining elements and gears for surviving in the wilderness.

The fascination with mastering the highest, remotest, most dangerous or most famous mountains, say, in the Himalayas, or traversing the most remote areas of storied ranges, such as the Californian Sierra Nevada on the Pacific Crest Trail or the John Muir Trail, or free climbing the tallest, vertical walls, like the Eiger North Wall, or expanding our ability to approach oxygen-deprived peaks without artificial help, like K2 or Everest—is all still much on the mind and inscribed on the bodies of those adventurers who for many are their own kind of spiritual seekers and masters. Yet even the close familiar hills and mountains in our living spaces are always welcomed images for escaping the regularities and chores, errands and routines of our lives. The ordinary mountains also invite to the extraordinary, even mysterious journey, or always lure with the possibility of such an adventure that implies and conveys spiritual elation beyond the mere physicality and regularity of our little lives in the most common circumstances.

But all of these impressions may just be bound by certain limitations of a temporal and spatial tunnel view. We just cannot see the wider spatio-temporal context of the generation and development, as well as disintegration of mountains and mountain ranges; but we can imagine them when we use our intellect and science. Geology will tell us that mountains are not timeless, and that their height is not an expression of majesty but of violent movements of the earth's crust. As tectonic plates shift and wrinkle the rocky skin of the earth, as it folds and refolds, breaks and cuts itself into pieces, rises and sinks, and creates that which from another time frame might look like fragile and evanescent figures swimming through elastic shells that encompass a hot internal core of molten or melting materials. Mountains are movements, not stabilities; mountain ranges are not glorious thrones of gods but harsh and screaming sculptures of forces of breaking under pressure and futile resistance, attested only for cosmic moments in their ongoing transformation. Mountain massifs, volcanoes, earthquakes—all indicate the continental drift that shaped not only environments for the appearance of life on Earth but human evolution and the religious landscape that, in its slow time-perception, stands before mountains as the frozen memory of the violent events after they were experienced or in fear of such experiences.

Mountains were always, as far as human memory (and perhaps archetypical symbolization) reaches, a symbol of the numinous, the encounter with the divine, harboring and releasing experiences of revelation, enlightenment, insight, power and transformation. Yet given the ambivalence or "dipolarity" of the reality symbolized, the question arises, today (since we know all that): Where should we situate mountains in a spiritual landscape—in the sphere of permanence or the sphere of flux? Traditionally, generally ignorant of the geological forces forming mountains and mountain ranges, spiritual appropriation would fall into the camp of permanence. And here spiritual reality complies to human dimensions, although incompletely: since we also know and have generational memory of the forces of unexpected flux, such as earthquakes, tsunamis, the appearance and disappearance of islands, or the forming forces of volcanoes. So, what would happen if we were not to use the "mountain" as image for spiritual paths toward liberation, but a "volcano": the closer you come, the more the underworld opens up, the belly of the earth that instantly kills?

Maybe the memory of the Moses-legends was as much about a mountain mysteriously shrouded in clouds as it was about earthquakes and volcanic activity (Deuteronomy 4:11), including a column of smoke on clear days and of fire during nights (Exodus 13:21)? Perhaps, the Sinai Peninsula and the Arabian desert were exposed to volcanic activity—why not the mythical Mount Sinai? After all, the "Glory of God" is not only invisible within the thick darkness of clouds (Exodus 20:21) but also shatters mountains (1 Kings 19:11; Qur'an 7:143). And earthquakes and volcanic activities are essential requisites of apocalypse reckoning (Deuteronomy 32:21–22; Jeremiah 10:10; Isaiah 29:6; Revelation 6:12–14), and the transformation of mountains into valleys and vice versa is not beyond such an expansive imagination (Psalm 104:6–9).

The same ambivalence between majesty and fragility, stability and flow, may well be responsible for the symbolism that relates mountains to the primordial acts of creation. In Egyptian mythology, creation arose through the appearance of the primordial mound from the receding waters of the archetypical river Nile over which the first light of the sun-god Ra shines and cosmic order, Ma'at, is established. In Greek cosmogony, Hesiod's *Theogony* (ca. 700 BCE) causes the appearance of the primordial earth with the rise of the high mountains. And the central Mount Meru of Jain, Hindu and Buddhist cosmogony and cosmology may be an island in the midst of the primordial ocean, but is the five-peaked *axis mundi* round which all cosmic entities circle. Yet it is such mountains or mountain ranges that are the mysterious, removed, lofty seat of the gods: the Olympians on Mount Olympus, the Hindu gods on Mount Meru, YHWH on Mount Sinai and Zion. Permanence and flux intersect in this vision of divine creativity that is uncontrollable, remote, and dangerous; it is a power that can even move mountains.

It is by this experience of the divine power that abides on the mountain, as it is both the stabilizing and moving expression of the divine grandeur, that everything about it can be holy or of exceptional import for, and psychological and religious impact to, the spiritual mountaineers. Mountains are the extraordinary places of divine encounter and for dramatic spiritual transformation. They are the place of past and future revelation, a revelation no one can withstand if not by divine invitation. While Moses can only see the back of God as God's Glory transits (Exodus 33:19–22), Elijah is granted the sight of its splendor and mountain-shattering power (1 Kings 19:11). No wonder that Elijah, in the face of God, was transfigured (2 Kings 2:1). While Moses needed a veil to hide the residue of this splendor (Exodus 34:29–35), the eschatological promise of salvation expands this gift to all: when God will appear on the mountain, the veil of all people will be taken away and God will wipe all tears from them (Isaiah 25:6–9). It must be by this power that Zion, in the eschatological vision (and not by current physical attribution), will be the highest mountain, as God will be dwelling on it (Micah 4:1).

Mountains are the places of the most dramatic spiritual transformations: the visitation of YHWH and the constitution of Israel by the divine Law (Exodus 19–33); the transfiguration of Jesus in the company of Moses and Elijah, the Alpha and Omega of the Israelite revelations (Matthew 17:1–8; Mark 9:2–8; Luke 9:28–36; 2 Peter 1:16–18). The exposed rock on Jerusalem's temple mount, now under the cupola of the Dome of the Rock, is traditionally said to be both the place of the almost-sacrifice of Isaac and of the ascension of Muhammad into the presence of God. However, the reverence of "the numinous" on mountains was by no means exclusive to nascent monotheism, but rather a common transreligious phenomenon of the polytheistic and cosmotheistic context of Akhenaten and Moses.

Perhaps, this is the reason that the proliferation of the reverence of spirits, holy men and deities on mountain-tops has received harsh critique from exclusive monotheism. Like the contraction of the divine reality to Aten, the sun, and Akhenaten, the son of god, and away from all deities and temples, rituals and related multiple religious authorities, so was the Mosaic iconoclasm directed against all kinds of holy mountains if they were not related to the true God (Genesis 22:2; Exodus 15:17; Deuteronomy 12:2), like Horeb/Sinai, Zion and Gerizim, Hermon and Carmel: Only Zion allows for pure worship (Psalm 24:3–4). The Canaanite Carmel had to be cleansed of the rival (and even "brother" of Yahweh in the court of the Elohim of El Elyon), Ba'al—a feat that the one who "saw" God, Elijah, accomplished (1 Kings 20). But the Roman Emperor Vespasian still received prophetic confirmation from the Zeus priests on

Mount Carmel. It is rather the Lord of the hosts (YHWH Sabaoth) who expresses divinity through Mount Tabor and Carmel (Jeremiah 46:18). And in Jewish tradition, only these four—Sinai, Zion, Tabor and Carmel—were YHWH's holy mountains. Yet for the "older" population that never left the land and went through the Exilic transformation, the Samaritans, Mount Gerizim became the new site of the presence of God after the destruction of the first temple (John 4:21–24).

Yet the desacralization in the exclusivist monotheistic context remained caught between the mountain of revelation (Sinai) and the mountain of worship (Zion)—also indicated by Akhenaten's movement of "religion" from the city of Amun (Thebes) to the city of Aten (Amarna). In the Israelite consciousness, mountains were deprived of their ancient numinal power as stable places of divine encounter and transmuted into places of unique events of revelation—a transformation from natural regularities to historical events—and eventually transferred to the column of smoke and fire, the tent of the covenant, to again be situated in the Jerusalem's temple. The destruction of the first temple transferred this presence partly or in a mode of volatile transition from all sacral objects to the sacred text, the Torah, the prophetic gaps between present announcement and future fulfillment (another representation of the divine name YHWH as the one who will be), the idea of the divine messiah, of the *shekinah* that wanders with the people into Exile, and the Christian rendering of the immanent, historically acting YHWH/*kyrios* (son of El Elyon) into the incarnation of the Christ. However, despite the re-erection of the (second) Temple and, after its destruction, the eschatological deferral of the reappearance of God in the holy city (Jerusalem), on the temple mount (Zion), in the temple in Jewish and Christian apocalyptic texts, the expectation of the numinous presence on the mountain is never suspended. Paradoxically, with the symbol of the sacred mountain, the *hybrid integration* of unique history (YHWH as exclusive) with the inclusive cosmotheism, indicated with the surrounding cultures' triangle of holy city, temple, and holy mountains, that no monotheism could overcome, seem to point *beyond* their mutual exclusion (much to the same summit to which the antagonisms of dipolar monism and dualistic monotheism is pointing).

Hence, the monotheist contraction has at no time exhausted the "natural" attraction to the numinous and transformative character of spiritual experiences related to mountains until today. Pilgrimages to holy mountains, monasteries, and living masters, or ancestral spirits, are an essential ingrediency of religious practice and central to the desired experiences of the transformation of seekers. Pilgrims of the Bon religion, Hinduism, Jainism and Buddhism revere, circumambulate and approach Mount Kailash in Tibet, often in extraneous fashion. The visit of the Wudang Mountains, Mount Longhu, Mount Qiyun and Qingcheng with their breathtaking topography, difficult ascent, multitude complexes of temples, monasteries, caves and holy spots is a magnet for Daoist seekers of the east and the west. The San Francisco Peaks for the Navaho and Hopi, the Black Hills for the Lakota, Mount Fuji, Mount

Athos, Mount Machapuchare, Mount Shasta, Mount Gerizim, Mount Carmel, and even Mount Vesuvius in ancient times—they are all still symbols and materialization of the numinous. They attract to their rarified atmosphere everyone—whether you are religious or not; everyone ready to expose herself to the numinous.

For the spiritual mountaineer, despite exclusivist claims to the contrary, expansive transreligious fluidity throughout humanity of the closeness of our body and mind, consciousness and spirit, to the divine, mystical, mythical and cosmic deep reality of existence is unbroken and indisputable one of the most common transgressions between religious and non-religious people. It is perhaps because of the feeling of the immediacy of being part of the *whole* cosmos, and not just one's small locality or limited horizon, that the thought, symbol, and experience of the sacred reality of mountains infuses an irresistible icon for the *bodily* perception of the expanse of the Spirit.

If we can trust the symbolizations in which human experience has expressed itself through the encounter with the sacred mountain, the transformations it infuses are dramatic shifts of consciousness. This eruption in the sacred presence of the mountain is inextricably interwoven with the *ambivalent character* of the divine indifferent gravitas and dangerous instability of its sphere. The mountaineers themselves become inhabitants of this physical expression of the encounter with the *mysterium tremendum et fascinans.*

The mountaineer is the seeker of the numinous that can only be acceded in two ways, by awe and by exertion. If you are in the Coachella Valley of the Southern Californian Sonoran desert, you can stop and in still awe take in the gravity of the whole massif to the west with two of the highest mountains and impressive ranges along the west coast with the two sentinels Mount San Jacinto and Mount Georginio—visible in one sweep and from the sandy and hot desert floor up to the glaringly white peaks. The other access is to try to scale such sentinels—such as the sixteen miles ascent from Palm Springs at the bottom to the peak of Mount San Jacinto. The true mountaineer is the one who exerts everything in order to withstand the trials of the ascension. If the way is chosen and in intelligent preparation the resources are applied, it is the clarity but also openness of the vision that will decide whether or not you will reach the summit. No revelation is promised. But these two paths of experience are everything for which you can ask. These are the natural feelings of the numinous that the mountain promises. The numinous is the mountain's natural spirit.

Ascent/Descent

Many of the pervasive, collective and indiscriminately recurring images of the interreligious discourse today, but also reaching back into the recesses of human memory of religious diversity and its meaning, are conveying an archetypical spiritual movement, namely, that from multiplicity to unity or from unity into multiplicity.

This archetypical double movement can be presented with the help of the profound spiritual icons of the one ocean and the many rivers, the many pathways and the one goal, and of the many ways up the one mountain. These images of unification have been utilized in times of sharpened self-reflections of the meaning of diversity in cultural and religious encounters, as long spiritually awake sages and visionaries were painfully aware that the human spiritual evolution must go beyond the general warlike clash of tribes, ethnicities, states, empires or differently structured cultural identities to some kind of mutual understanding.

Many different ways were employed, often from inherent resources of the ancient or reformed traditions from which these sages and visionaries (sometimes even people of political power) arose, thought and spoke, to explicate and manifest such a unification in thought and practice, but always with the intention to find the *ultimate unity* in the phenomenal diversity that, for this reason was divinized or, on occasion, de-divinized, as the One (*hen*), the All-One, the One-All, the One and All (*hen kai pan*) or the All in All. I have already related the axis of transformations of these thought patterns from the ancient forms of cosmotheism, dipolar nondualism, pantheism, panentheism, naturalism, and (as will explore further in the next section) trans-pantheism, to the variations of manifestations of these kinds of thought, for instance, as witnessed by as diverse figures as Philo of Alexandria, Origen, Arius, Spinoza, Whitehead and Deleuze; or Laozi, Nagarjuna, and the (XIV.) Dalai Lama, or as witnessed by the many nondual horizons of spiritual discourse within eastern and western religions and mystical traditions, as well as current naturalistic spiritualities. Not that they have, individually or by their combined efforts, eradicated the roots of warring conflicts, as far as they are based in religious or ideological motivations; but, at least, they offer alternatives of peaceful conversation and mutual understanding instead of mutual damnation, of translatability instead of antagonism, of deep conviction of being of *one* spiritual field or divine origin instead of an antagonistic dualism of a root of light and goodness and a root of darkness and evil.

The image of the sun has been instrumental as a peace-making proposition (although not unanimously, as it has also been misused as patriarchal and exclusivist image). And even in traditions that developed into exclusive, antagonistic monotheisms, such as appeared within later Christianity, these roots of the All in All and the sun that rises over good and evil have never been able to be suppressed completely. Philosophical, cosmological, and mystical discussions under the umbrella of the symbol of the sun, as in Plato, have never lost their attraction in generating new creative approaches envisioning a transcendental unity (in the sense of Deleuze) for conflicting, alternative, alienated, suppressed, complexified, or pluralistic discussions in favor of communication, relationality, mutuality, and a lasting spiritually founded place of humanity among itself and with the world. Akhenaten's iconography of the exclusivist Aten, namely, as a disc that extends its rays with hands reaching out to all creatures, cannot be deprived of such a multiplicity-unity of inclusiveness.

Another classical icon of such a peaceful relativism of religious diversity is the ancient Jain (Vidyanandi, *Tattvarthaslokavatika*, ninth century CE, and Ācārya Mallisena, *Syādvādamanjari*, thirteenth century CE), Buddhist (*Udana* 6.4), Hindu (*Chandogya Upanishad* 5.18.1) story of the one elephant that only generates diversity in the perception of as many sages that touch its body in different areas and render their insights universal: the universe or divinity or Reality is like, or is as, a trunk, a tail, a head, and so on (see the related image of the "chariot" in ch. 9). Later, smart thinkers have with super-sophisticated "arguments" heavily critiqued this image, often with petty squabbles, such as this: How could "we" as witnesses of the story be outside the sages that are in the story if there is no such outside? I cannot but shake my head in silence about the ruinous crudeness of these "oh-so-smart" arguments. In my view, these are not more than desperate attempts to cover the fear of these thinkers and related communities of religious relativity—or dare I say: relativism—that they feel undermines their security while imagining standing on the rock, or perhaps a mountain, of truth. Now, since even mountains, as we have seen, are as much about movements, tremors, and transformations as they are about effort, we will need much more excretion of sophistication in ascending their rarified heights than such cheap shots fired from some armchair philosophers. I will not address them, therefore, but, instead, explore the related images of multiplicity-unity in more depth.

It is also not true that such a relativism of peace is a new phenomenon, perhaps, of postmodern times that have lost all values and measures of truth and goodness. In fact, the most basic resource may be found in ancient tribal religions, as they know of a *deus otiosus*, an unknown god beyond all immanent divine or mundane phenomena, such as is the case for the worldwide distributed, ethnically diversified, trans-religious shamanistic spirit-universes. The same is true for the later state-based polytheistic universes that reach back to the unknown creator Godhead and allow for the mutual translation of their "phenomenal" gods into one another, as they are all names of the common cosmic realities, such as the sun, the moon and the stars—and as El Elyon in Canaan. There was no need for wars because of religion; but religion did also not contribute to peace. However, because of the religious relativity of the universe of gods and their feeling to live in a common cosmos, cultures came, at least, into *one* horizon of mutuality that laid the basis for their political and cultural negotiations.

The great "world religions," generally summarizing *revealed* religions, have become the most powerful imperial force of religious history, not only because they were universal in their claims, and not only because they were fit for the generation and sustenance of ideological unity in the emergence of imperial state constructs and the motive force for their expansions, but especially because they were not bound by such political, social, and cultural boundaries. They could help unite an empire of many cultural niches, but also overthrow it by thriving beyond the limitations of even such complex artificial unities. The crux of these religions was that they either by design or by human limitation understood unity as exclusive unification of the world population with all of its political, social, and cultural diversities in one cosmos that was defined from specific revealed truths over against "natural" insights distributed among all human populations. Instead of the immediacy of access, as was true for the cosmotheism of natural forces, even if they were culturally diverse in naming and ritually revering these forces of the one cosmos, the new exclusive monotheisms alienated all ordinary human beings from their inherent divine connection and became the gate keepers of this access by exclusive authority of a religious elite to generate, retain, harbor, renew, and administer divine reality to all others: the ones to whom are given the keys of heaven (Matthew 16:19). This is, of course, what Deleuze warned against (see ch. 6): the monadic religion of the creation of a transcendence by erasure of multiplicity and then by reoccupying the empty mental, cultural, religious or spiritual landscape with the new authorities of limitation and division.

What is the paradoxical power of division of these universally unifying religious ideologies? It is their exclusivity by which all older ecumenical cosmotheistic religions, or even older forms of shamanic rhizomatic unity among many tribal ways of life, are made deviant, evil, dark, or at least impure forms of spiritual desires, namely, only expressions of idolatry, of the reverence of images. This is the tale by which the Egyptian cosmopolitan religion, against the exclusivity of the tribal Yahwism, becomes the idolatry of the powerful oppressor, the pharaoh, against the liberating, but exclusive power of YHWH in the powerless, but faithful Moses. Yet this tale, as visible through certain layers of the Hebrew Bible (but, as we have seen in earlier chapters, never without antinomies and complex counter-discourses), was never accepted as the only way to view the "events" of the Exodus, as is attested by a long list of ancient Egyptian, Greco-Roman, and sensitive and critical commentators and historians throughout the coming centuries in their resistance to the imperial erasures even up to the point of the "revelation" of the internal traumatic events that preceded it within the Egyptian religious universe of old.

The universal power of division of the exclusive monotheisms of these "world religions" was that of the necessity of faith versus immediate insight, of elitist alienation versus empowerment of inherent potentials of spiritual evolution. It divides the world into only two groups: the faithful and the atheists, the trustworthy and the liars; and it turned them against one another: the pure versus the impure, the insider versus the outsider, the "few" determined to reach paradise versus, in the words of St. Augustine, the *massa damnata*.

In order to understand the transformation *toward* and, then, (today) also *beyond* these universal exclusive monotheisms, it is helpful to refer to the characterization given to them by the German philosopher Karl Jaspers (d. 1969), namely, to be *axial* religions. In his meaning, the great universal religious and philosophical reformulations of what it means as one humanity to exist in one cosmos, which he saw arise between the eighth and the third centuries BCE, such as that of the Buddha, Deutero-Isaiah, Socrates, Laozi, Confucius, and many others, was achieved by the shock of transience, impermanence, and the feeling that we are meant to be immortal, and the world to be heaven, while, in fact, the world is barely a cosmos, but rather a thinly veiled chaos, always endangered by evil forces of annihilation. In this context, the unanimous creator (*deus otiosus*) became the absent god (*deus absconditus*) in a world in the grip of ignorance and sin, a fallen world that needs salvation, a world that only makes sense if it could be overcome in the hope of an alternate reality either in supernatural future of this physical world or in a post-apocalyptic world of divine cleansing and purity, a world of the righteous. The axial power is one of a dualistic antagonism and the absolutist claims to authority—the monster of Deleuze's transcendence that lives from the destruction of the complex, divergent pleroma of diversity of the spiritual landscape that is innate in humanity and vital for its spiritual evolution to maturity.

Of course, neither can this axiality be reduced to the time frame Jaspers assigns to it, nor are we forced to become blind to the inherent ambivalence that always characterizes such abstract delimitations of the complex living spirit of humanity. We should not forget that not only the exclusive monotheism of Akhenaten does not fit the timeframe, and also not the soteriological tendency of the other revealed religions toward apocalyptic transcendence (as we will see in the next section). What is more, Zarathustra may have lived earlier than this timeframe (and might be even one of its inventors), and Christianity and Islam, appearing considerably after this axis-time, were, nevertheless, paradigmatic if not extreme examples of their imperial implications. What Jaspers saw in the new mind-frame of the axial universe was rather something counter-intuitive under the skin of later imperialist reconstructions of their motive force: the invitation to become a mutually coinherent and inextricably related harmony in a cosmos in which impermanence is not inherently "permanent" and ignorance or sin are not tragic necessities, but themselves inherently contingent, penultimate forces. It is not exclusivist "revelation" that is the deepest motif of these universal religions, but the awakening of the universally accessible consciousness of a deeper innate potential to trust the fundamental aesthetic integrity and ethical goodness of the world. They demand our active spiritual transformation to become activated, because this transformation is a divine gift that commands our freedom and exertion—the exertion of the effort of the spiritual mountaineer in her ascent to the summit of reality.

However, while all of the founding figures of these axial religions—whether historical or archetypical—offer this alternative to their imperialist misinterpretations, all of them have failed! In his disenchantment with these monotheisms because of the imperialist trajectories they have assumed by exploiting the universalizing soteriological desires for an alternative world, Jaspers senses to live in his time at the dawn of a *new* axial age. It promises to recover the motives of empowerment and transformation, but also clearly establishes a new paradigm in order to make sure that the old imperialist perversions cannot be repeated or, at least, are hampered by the obvious self-contradiction in the attempts of the performance of such reversals. The new paradigm builds on values, virtues, and insights of the axial religions that fundamentally underlie their *universalism*: love, peace, compassion, humble service, mutuality, forgiving, patient longsuffering of the aggressor, nondualism, and the like. The change in the background of the attitude towards spiritual existence that facilitates this new paradigm in these new axial religious movements is as important as the reference of these values, and virtues they reformulate from the old axial religious innovators. In one word, the new axial impulse is that of *affirmation* instead of negation. The affirmation of *this* world instead of its negation for another one means that the insight into the contingent construction of the constellations of our world is about the recognition of the ability for its transformation by our present ability to create this new world in light of divine empowerment.

The new "*cosmic* spirit" of this endeavor of new axial religious movements is precisely this: that all religions are *one*; that the religious diversity is not working against their divine diffusion, but wants their pleroma to be the motive force for a future transformation of this world into a harmony in which ecological, human, cosmic, and spiritual *mutuality* is the expression of the *summit of religious existence*. In our symbolism of the mountain and the mountaineer, this means that the trust of the new faith that avoids the alienations of the imperial exclusivisms is the trust that in the *ascent* toward this summit the many religious paths will *retrospectively* recover their inherent unity in *the one divine reality* that the *peak* of the mountain symbolizes. It is in *this* sense, and not in any alienating abstract discourse of arguments about the possibility or impossibility of religious relativism, that the current world-embracing impulse of spiritual sages urges humanity to explore this insight of the unity of religions.

In 1893, a highly acclaimed speech was given at the first World Parliament of Religions, at the Columbian Exhibition in Chicago, which, for the first time maybe in religious history, featured luminaries of the diverse religions of the east and the west in a climate of mutual listening and receptivity. It was the opening speech by the young Hindu sage Swami Vivekananda (1863–1902), the charismatic messenger to the west of the new understanding of Hinduism and a new world ecumene of religions as espoused by his late teacher Sri Ramakrishna (1836–86). In this speech, Vivekananda refers to a related powerful image of the unity of all religions in the combined symbolism (that I have evoked in chs. 2 and 3) of the one ocean to which all rivers lead in order to fuse in it. Relating, thereby, the diversity of religious reverence to the *one* ultimate reality, here appearing in the divine person of *Bhagavad Gita*'s Krishna, the important point is not doctrinal but deeply spiritual *and* political, mystical *and* societal: revealing the motivation for the appeal to a process of transformation with the vision of a future society of peace beyond all religious exclusivism, bigotry, warfare, and violence. A worthy aim that the spiritual seeker will not be able to avoid to not only address but to practice—if we really want to realize the cosmic Spirit, the Spirit encompassing and inhering in *all* of "its" beings, the Spirit of creative differentiation within a deep field of unifying attraction and unification! This is what Vivekananda said:

> We believe not only in universal toleration, but we accept all religions as true. I am proud to belong to a nation which has sheltered the persecuted and the refugees of all religions and all nations of the earth. I am proud to tell you that we have gathered in our bosom the purest remnant of the Israelites, who came to Southern India and took refuge with us in the very year in which their holy temple was shattered to pieces by Roman tyranny. I am proud to belong to the religion which has sheltered and is still fostering the remnant of the grand Zoroastrian nation. I will quote to you, brethren, a few lines from a hymn which I remember to have repeated from my earliest boyhood, which is every day repeated by millions of human beings: "As the different streams having their sources in different places all mingle their water in the sea, so, O Lord, the different paths which men take through different tendencies, various though they appear, crooked or straight, all lead to Thee."
>
> The present convention, which is one of the most august assemblies ever held, is in itself a vindication, a declaration to the world of the wonderful doctrine preached in the Gita: "Whosoever comes to Me, through whatsoever form, I reach him; all men are struggling through paths which in the end lead to me." Sectarianism, bigotry, and its horrible descendant, fanaticism, have long possessed this beautiful earth. They have filled the earth with violence, drenched it often and often with human blood, destroyed civilization and sent whole nations to despair. Had it not been for these horrible demons, human society would be far more advanced than it is now. But their time is come; and I fervently hope that the bell that tolled this morning in honor of this convention may be the death-knell of all fanaticism, of all persecutions with the sword or with the pen, and of all uncharitable feelings between persons wending their way to the same goal. (Sisters and Brothers)

Similar images are used by Mahatma Gandhi (1869–1948) and the fourteenth Dalai Lama: the many roads that have the same goal and the many manifestations of the same spiritual virtues, respectively. Many Hindu figures, such as Sri Ramakrishna, Sri Aurobindo (1872–1950), Rabindranath Tagore (1861–1951), Shirdi Sai Baba (1838–1918), and Meher Baba (1894–1969), in some or another way acknowledged as new divine *avatars*, present the new or truly post-axial understanding in the nineteenth century just as does Bahá'u'lláh, the founder of the Bahá'í Faith, namely, *that all religions are true*. Yet if we recede into the roots of this new axial consciousness, we must probably go back to its origins, for instance, in the orbit of the Nath movement, fusing Buddhist, Shaiva, and Yoga traditions, the Bhakti movement, uniting Vaishnavi, Shakti, and Advaita Vedanta traditions and sages like Kabir and Guru Nanak who also engaged the Islamic and Sufi traditions and led to the Sikh religion in seventeenth-century India. In the west, in Europe, North Africa and western Asia (not even considering the pre-axial spiritualities and religions of the indigenous people of the Americas, Africa, and Australia), because of the external power of the exclusivist monotheism of Christianity and Islam, we find more alienated, traumatized, and suppressed forms of alternative traditions, such as diverse mysticisms, Kabbalah, Sufism, Hermeticism, Neo-Platonism, that resisted persecution, and the pantheist and perennial philosophy that was recovered and developed in the Renaissance and Enlightenment eras of Europe in the sixteenth to eighteenth centuries.

Arguments against such acclamations of the inherent naturalness and the soteriological necessity of the unity of humanity in its religious sources and spiritual horizons has come from essentially *four alternative views* of extremely divergent orientation: exclusivism, pluralism, essentialism, and naturalism.

The *exclusivism* of axial religions insists on the universal truth of the revealed particularity of the divine monad or on the specific analysis of the human predicament and the soteriological remedy—be they theistic (Abrahamic religions) or non-theistic (Dharmic religions). There remains a trait of exclusivist exceptionalism in post-axial religions and spiritualities in so far as they insist that it is from *their* perspective that the universal truth, despite being present in all other religions and spiritualities, can be unified—such as the use of the *sanatana dharma* (the universal moral Law of the cosmos) by Mahatma Gandhi or Swami Vivekananda.

Religious *pluralism* diverges in mono- and polycentric versions, that is, in either claiming the unity of ultimate multiplicity of ultimate reality/realities or their ultimate multiplicity. Divergent from exclusivism, monistic pluralism claims the oneness of reality in the form of Plotinus's apophatic One, and not in the reiterated oneness of a mental object "one"—of which exclusivist monotheists and polycentric pluralists accuse this position. The polycentric position, however, almost inevitably presupposes such an objectification, because otherwise it would not make any sense to differentiate ultimates. In the apophatic, non-objectified, nondualist form, religious pluralism is compatible with the post-axial claim of unity. Typically, perennial positions would be close to such a dipolar nondualist understanding, even if it is, on occasion, misinterpreted in an objectified way—such as some of the most famous defenses of religious pluralism by the British writer Aldous Huxley (d. 1963) and the British theologian John Hick (d. 2012). In the reiterated form, however, this monism is incompatible with the here described post-axial unity of religions, as it becomes a new exclusivism that insists on the irrelevance or illusory character of phenomenal multiplicity of religions and reduces it to naught.

Essentialism also comes in two divergent forms: one building on the one common essence of religions, the other on an incompatible plurality of such essences. The former inclination is a version of the reiterating monocentric pluralism that understands all differences between religions as mere phenomenal epiphenomena or imaginative additions to the core characteristics of religiosity. The latter inclination is a version of polycentric pluralism, but less interested in a description of ultimate reality than in the cultural identity of the community in which religions inhere. In this manifestation, essentialist pluralism insists on the incommensurable identity of diverse cultures or related ethnic identities that can never be fully understood from another culture or ethnicity. Instead, any unification must be seen as occupation of a minority space and as suppression of diversity. Typically, postmodern pluralisms that highlight multiplicity over unity are sensitive to any violation of this diversity as an imperial move of overpowering of local identities. Hence, diverse liberation discourses and post-colonial forms of resistance against the erasure of minority identities will be tending to view any claim to "unity" as such a colonial move. But essentialized diversity will not be compatible with the fluent oscillation between unity and multiplicity of the unity of religions proposed, here.

Over against all forms of social and cultural essentialism, but also mere postmodern constructivism or relativism, *naturalism* will insist on the universality of the evolutionary relationality of humanity and understand its religions as a common factor of either adaptive or maladaptive manifestations of natural selection. Like essentialism, it knows of the unity of humanity in evolutionary terms, but denies the more than functional importance of expressions of religiosity. With constructivism it will understand diversity as essential evolutionary process, but unlike essentialism it will not presuppose any Platonic species essence of humanity (or any biological species). Certain of its spiritual versions, if they are not denying the reality of human mind, consciousness or spirit as such, are compatible physical expressions of the unity of religions.

Against these counter-argumentations, the post-axial novelty of religious unity, as that of Gandhi or Vivekananda, is meant to express a *unity in diversity* in which both are not antagonistically opposed, but *mutually inherent* in one another: the more diversity, the more unity! In other chapters, I have already invoked several thought patterns and symbolisms that purvey this complex *processual* meaning of mutual immanence: Teilhard de Chardin's "complexification," for instance, and the archetypical religious symbolizations inherent in the confluence of the ocean, the non-essentialism and processual flux of the river, or the branching diversification of the tree. I will not repeat them, here, and their deep relations to A. N. Whitehead, the *Avatamsaka Sutra* and Nicolas of Cusa.

The pluralism of this post-axial age of religious reconfiguration, as addressed in the image of the *one mountaintop and the many paths* leading up to it, is *not* a monadic reduction of diversity, but a *nomadic field of the mutuality of diversity*: without this diversity, there would be no unity and vice versa. There are no straight ways up the mountain, but maybe many meandering paths, even crossings and bifurcations. These paths run over the diversified landscapes of the mountain massif, different from one another like meadows, steep canyons, walls, thick vegetation or icy passages. Scaling mighty mountains means to traverse diverse climactic zones, temperatures, degrees of mild and rough weather and unviable surface conditions or marked traces. And these scapes are, because of the multidimensionality of a mountain, *always multiple, never one*, except from the perspective of a bird conveying the whole scape of potential fields of immanence that constitutes this mountain.

So, if the mountain is a *symbol of the cosmos* (as indicated by Mount Meru), then, the cosmic Spirit is the aura of the whole complex unity-diversity that the mountain as a whole in its diversification constitutes. The mountain is a manifold that consist *only* of diversity in mutuality, but never in the suppression of the manifold by which it is "built up" even to the top. The sacred mountain is at no point one, nor any path identical, nor any element exchangeable, without losing the image or reality of the mountain itself. The only *point* at which all converges, but which is not the mountain itself, is the *peak*. But even the peak vanishes in a dimensionless "point"—the convergence of all lines of convergence and divergence (not all ways on the mountain must lead up to the peak; in fact, more paths may miss it, but still constitute the landscape of this mountain)—that really becomes nothing more than *one* potential point of convergence, divergence, reversal, or bifurcation of all the points that make up the mountain. In this sense, the peak is not a unity that erases diversity, but a moment of the diversity itself by which the diversity remains a field instead of just one point.

In fact, in differentiation from the other images used to indicate the post-axial unity of religions, such as the rivers that empty themselves into the ocean, or the many paths that seek the same goal, or the whole elephant that can only be grasped partly by ever new attempts and partitions of touch, the unity of the paths on a mountain allows for an *inevitable diversification*. While all the paths ascending to the peak may unite at this "point," they *immediately diverge* again by just following their trajectory into the *descent* from the peak. Ascent and descent are the same process, not even reversals or mirrors of themselves, just perpetuated trajectories of continuous paths, not inclined arbitrarily to just stop at the peak. While you may change directions at the top, you may do so at any point of your ascent and descent, too. We could say, in the image of the mountain paths, the "final point" is *not* that of the convergence at the peak of the ascent, *but* the new diversification of descent into a wide field of related but divergent directions. While rivers converge at the deepest point, the ocean, mountain paths luxuriously diverge by overflowing from the mountain springs down the slopes of decent.

The multiplicity of religious identities and spiritual paths in the image of the mountain, then, needs not to feed into the reductionist four-fold field of the images of exclusivism, pluralism, essentialism, and naturalism, but, by taking up the best versions of complexity and divergence in these coordinate systems, reclaims a unity in diversity that elevates humanity from self-alienation of atomistic and mutually exclusive spiritual or religious identifies (or non-religious identities of resistance) and, instead, proposes the peace between a multiplicity of paths that always may form new planes of immanence in changing (nomadic) constellations with one another and the creative addition of new paths—a multiplicity of related but diversifies landscapes of folds in ever new foldings and, occasionally, new spiritual fabrics crossing and interweaving. The experienced spiritual mountaineer, treading the ways of the sacred mountain, which is the body of the cosmic Spirit, will eventually come to this conclusion.

Summit

The peak of the physical and spiritual mountain stands in for a diversity of related images that harbor the numinous encounter that only its summit is expected to release. It is configured in physical, mental and imaginary organizations of space that want to concentrate, elate, and amplify the presence of the numinous: Mountains become the focus of the lifting of the physical veil encountering the spirits of life (Native American contact with the ancestor and spirit-guide); of cosmic integration (Mount Meru) and eschatological divine presence (heavenly Jerusalem coming down on Zion or Carmel); of alters of sacrifice (Abraham's sacrifice) and acts of God (Elijah and the Ba'al priests on Mount Carmel); of places of theophany (Parthenon of Acropolis, Solomonic Temple on Mount Zion) and the cradle of unique prophetic missions (Moses's Sinai revelation; Mohammad's encounter with the Gabriel on Jabal al-Nur); of mystical experience, sapiential insight and spiritual transformation (meditation centers, hermitages, caves with the expectations of reaching enlightenment); of peak experiences and extraordinary alterations of perception and awareness (Jesus's transfiguration); and of transformations prescribed to, or perceived to be, the summit of cosmic consciousness.

These "peak experiences"—even if the unspeakable encounter with the numinous is clothed with the images or auditions of, or missions from, supernatural beings—express themselves in two different ways: either in natural phenomena of weather, symbolized with lightning and thunder, smoke and fire, clouds and impenetrable darkness, or as clarity of height and horizon and the sudden shift to an alternate consciousness of the surrounding nature. Two of the related epigraphs to this chapter—that on Moses and that of the Buddha—express these two facets of the numinous peak experience. Moses enters in thick darkness; the Buddha uses the peak as a new horizon of clarity, symbolizing the detachment from the world below. In a curious fusion of both kinds of experience, the famous Zen master Dogen (d. 1253) is said to have reached enlightenment when he heard the rushing rivers flowing down from Mount Lu in the dark of the night. Both aspects of this mystical encounter, as they fundamentally impact the consciousness of perception and even indicate a "transubstantiation" of the life, character, mission and meaning of the person, can express, or be expressed in, theistic or non-theistic imagery, and point again toward the relativity of all of such frameworks to fathom the numinous encounters.

As alterations in the historical adaptation of the Moses experience on Mount Sinai demonstrate, there is also a fluent transgression between public displays of the numinous and internal mystical experiences. While in the Exodus narrative Moses' experience was a public event, witnessed by the elders and Aaron, at least in its external physical representations of smoke and fire, in the later readings of this theophany it became increasingly transformed into a happening in Moses's mind. The same is true for the clarity of the peak consciousness expressed by the Buddha, as it indicates the internal awakening to a universal (selfless) horizon in the physical experience of the clarity of the view on top of a mountain and in the free range of perceiving the world around and below. This ambivalence between objective and subjective, cosmic and mystical experience reflects the undecidability between ontology (being outside the mind) and epistemology (knowing of mind)—as was already mentioned—and is just another expression of the non-conceptual nature of the peak event, which, nevertheless, only functions in resonance of both physical and mental, literal and symbolic, "planes," if they try to become the vessel of the expression of the Spirit.

The apex of consciousness is but the *boundary* of the "appearance/disappearance" of the insight and existential as well as cosmic realization of the nondual indifference of all "layers" of reality.

This peak consciousness is indicated by the experience of the spiritual mountaineer by which either the whole mountain "disappears" (becomes enfolded) into the summit as the memory of the summary of all potential approaches, or from which summit "appears" (unfolds) the whole mountain of a pleromatic manifold of self-realizing paths. In this sense, *there are no paths up the mountain that can reach the peak, but only divergent ways down the mountain luxuriantly distributing themselves like living waters flow can decent its slopes.* The unity of the enfolded mountain in its peak is but the point at which the numinous cannot be approached except as *a boundary that turns itself into the many movements* away from it in the reconstruction or rediscovery or differentiating unfolding of the mountain paths, as they *diverge away* from the top *without* ever growing further away from it, because *all of them carry the summit/summary with them* in their unique emphasis of unfolding.

A maybe unexpected but insightful way to symbolize this boundary of the peak as the *rebounding* of any access towards the unfolding of the inaccessible "point" of the convergence that is represented by the peak comes from one of the most ingenious attempts to understand the "point of beginning" of our universe in the Big Bang as a smooth curve of transitions of space-time into a rebound that does not involve a creator's intervention or a creative moment "in time" (which was, of course, already central to St. Augustine's speculation on creation). The Hartle-Hawking-theory of "imaginary" time, that is, the explanation of time with the mathematics of imaginary numbers, suggests that the quantum state close to the origin of time at the Big Bang is not a "point," a break of some sort of dimensionality out of a non-dimensional "singularity," but a *curve* that, in the theoretical retrograde movement toward the beginning, facilitates a smooth transition from the time-dimension of the Einstein universe (of the four dimensional space-time fabric) into the space-dimension such that there is no time, but only space-like convergences "at the beginning." That is, there is no "beginning" in the time-dimension, but only a bell-like boundary of space binding itself back into the expanding universe. Neither is there "any time" at which the space-bounded universe "did not exist," nor is there any state "before" or "beyond" the boundary—rather this "boundary" is itself *boundless*.

Now, if we realize that the temporally unfolding universe from this "point" diverges *like* a mountain spatially from the peak downward, and that the spatial beginning of the universe is a curved boundary *like* a peak of a mountain, we gain several important insights into the peak experiences or *the summit of spiritual consciousness*, spiritually and physically realized by the mountain and the mountaineer.

First, the mountain, indeed, can become a symbol of the *whole* space-time structure of the universe, that is, like the mythological Mount Meru (despite its otherwise mythological "flat" concentric idealization of the cosmos). The "cosmic mountain," *from* its peak, looks as (the still-life of the movement of) a *diversifying process of unfolding* and, *up toward* the peak, as that peak protruding into the sky or heaven without admitting any point at which to reach either. Rather, as the whole movement is *bound to the rebound* into differentiation, its oneness is only real in its unfolding; and there is no point at which this unity can be represented as such or beyond or without the whole mountain.

Second, the transformation of the space-like "pyramidal" structure of the mountain with the peak on top and the broadest unfoldment in the valleys around the foothills into the time-like unfoldment of the universe allows us to transform the *upward* ascent to the peak of the "pyramid" into a temporal movement *backward* to the beginning of the universe. In this sense, it transforms the processes of *ascent to mystical consciousness* as a movement backwards *into the beginning of experience itself*. Instead of understanding ourselves as seekers who extend themselves into a future of a journey, aiming at reaching the numinous peak, either as a personal encounter or as the loss of self-consciousness in the *unio mystitica*, we may realize that this is actually a journey *backward* into the beginning of all experiences—and *in any event* of our becoming (not just peak experience). Now, mystical experience is something that has unfolded into a whole complex world of our existence, physical, mental, spiritual, almost like the divergence of the cosmic forces in the development from the "unified" Big Bang into the four physical forces (gravitation, electromagnetic, strong, and weak). Reaching the mystical peak means that we must *counter-move* back into the becoming *from our spiritual nondual origin, our divine touch*, or as Meister Eckhart said, the "divine spark" at the "peak of our soul," which is always beyond reach, inaccessible, but the beginning of the manifold emanation or creation of all realities from Reality. Alternatively, in accordance with the process theology of A. N. Whitehead, one could say that we unfold in every moment of our ordinary existence *from this* creative self-differentiation of the divine unity into the plurality of self-existence; the approach of the nondual Spirit, however, would be a *converse* movement backwards into the *non-difference* of the origin of every moment of our existence.

Third, the converse transformation from the temporal peak of origin to the spatial peak on top of the universal "pyramid" of becoming and spiritual mountaineering renders another important truth evident: that of the *unity of religions*. This unity, as we have seen, is not a collection from diversity or its erasure, but the *enfolded contraction* to the summit of what it always unfolds as the whole mountain with its diverse and divergent spiritual paths. The temporal spiritual adventure is always also a spatial participation on diverse levels of unification *held together* by the summit and *radiating from* it like the rays of the sun. The creative movement of these originations is, concurrently, an *oscillation* of ascendant and descendent movements of unification and diversification. Christ appears as the symbol of both the creative and the unitive origin of diversification in the New Testament (Colossians 1:15–17); for Philo of Alexandria, the Stoics, and the Gospel of John, it is the divine Logos; for the biblical and Jewish Wisdom literature, it is divine Wisdom and Spirit; for Plato, it is the Good; for Plotinus, it is the divine Mind; for Ibn 'Arabi, it is the Muhammadan Light; for Vaishnavas, it is the divine Person of Krishna; for Adi Sankaracharya, it is the manifest Brahman; for Mahayana Buddhism, it is the Buddha-nature in which the Dharma resides; for Vajrayana Buddhism, it is the primordial Buddha Samantabhadra; and so forth.

This oscillation of plateaus, layers, zones, or planes of constancy and immanence is *not hierarchical* as in Deleuze's "arboreal" erection of imperial transcendence (as discussed in ch. 6), but is engaged in diversifications of the movements of enfolding in the ascent to the summit and their unfolding in the descent to the complexity of the phenomenal world. While they can crisscross and overlap, mutually connect and split, they can archetypically be symbolized with *diverse densities* of forms of unification and diversification between limits, of the peak and the infinitely evening out of the bottom of the mountain (physically in the sense that there is no sharp boundary at which the mountain ends or begins in its surrounding landscape). Like the symbolizations of the summit, diverse philosophical cosmologies are abound with such differentiations into *layers* of unification and diversification: the ideal and the phenomenal in Plato; the two (phenomenal and ultimate) truths of Nagarjuna; the virtual and the actual in Deleuze; the worlds of creativity and value in Whitehead; the diverse worlds between the physical and the divine in Ibn 'Arabi; the three worlds of Karl Popper and Roger Penrose (b. 1931); the four states of Plotinus (*hen, nous, psyche, hyle*); and so forth. The same complex picture arises in the religious and scientific cosmological landscapes: the many ubiquitous differentiations of non-physical dimensions into *spiritual worlds* in the vast majority of religions, as well as necessary conceptual presuppositions of the differentiations between mathematical and physical reality and, in quantum physics, the interaction between the world of limited actual states and an inclusive realm of potential and entangled states. Neither are they divorced from, and opposed to, one another as in the sharp differentiation between the physical and the mental in Rene Descartes (d. 1650), nor opposed to the point of mutual negation, as in scientific materialism and forms of spiritualism or pure idealism, or the dialectic of Hegel; and they are not mutually annihilated as in the pantheism of Spinoza. Rather they indicate mutually dependent, mutually affirming forms of concurrent counter-movements of an ascending integration of oppositional differences and the descending into multiplicities that cannot, on their level of divergency, be understood as "one."

In the "inward" spiritual journey backward and upward, these plateaus, levels, layers, zones and fields of consistency and immanence are *continuous transformations enfolding oppositions into alternatives, alternatives into coinherences, and coinherences into nondual indifferences*. In the creative journey of the unfolding of worlds, they conversely diversify even to the point of *nomadic incompossibilities*. In the "outward" context of the unity and diversity of religions and spiritual paths, these same counter-movements can explain the upward unity of all paths into the *indifference of the summit* and *the diversity or even opposition of such paths* in the phenomenal world of incompossible multiplicities. *This insight would be the summit of spiritual consciousness and the heart of all religions, the awakening to their true destiny in the image of paths on the sacred cosmic mountain: that the inward and outward counter-movement of unification and diversification in temporal and spatial mutual transformation is the mature consciousness of the awakening and wakened Reality in all religions and spiritualities.* This is their *trans-religious* truth.

This is also at the heart of the truth of the diverse approaches throughout history in articulating this unity in diversity regarding ultimate reality in the diverse eastern and western attempts of deep insight and experimental nondualism in the avoidance or overcoming of imperialistic formations of transcendence. We can discern two essential elements of such an insight. On the one hand, the strategy of *avoidance* has led into the *dissolution of transcendence into immanence*: naturalism, pantheism, even deism became identifications of God and the world in order not to allow for any space for imperial transcendence to arise. Even the oppressive monotheism of Akhenaten may have actually been such an attempt of the demythologization of all supernatural, mythological, religious figures, like deities and souls and demons and ghosts, and the like, into the affirmative and positive *identity of reality with nature*: the sun is the sun; if you revere it, you still revere nothing beyond the cosmos, but the cosmos itself in its awesome gestalt—a kind of naturalistic "revelation" or "enlightenment" of the cosmic body of God, as in Krishna's transfiguration in the *Bhagavad Gita 11*. On the other hand, the strategy of *overcoming* has always *differentiated this All in All from the apophatic One in which All is One*, but which is "One" only *by name*, as it is *beyond all names*. It "is not"—as Plato's Good and Plotinus's One, or even Deleuze's One-All—and is *not different* from that which it grants existence. Its resource is the ancient dipolar monism, for instance, of El Elion and the Elohim (see ch. 5), and it could be rescued beyond the imperial consequences of their "monotheistic" identification by the *apophatic*, mystical, nondual philosophies and cosmologies, as the mystical traditions such as Dionysian mystical practices, the Kabbalah, Sufism and the post-axial religions and spiritual paths. This twofold non-difference is their trans-pantheistic truth.

One of the maybe most fascinating examples of such an integration is the confluence of these elements in Nicolas of Cusa's cosmology. First, the approximation of the peak-boundary happens as the coincidence of opposites (*coincidetia oppositorum*) of all finite forms in the formless infinite of these forms (where, for instance, a circle becomes identical with a line—if you approximate both to infinity). Second, the boundary is the "wall of paradise" (*murus paradisi*) that no finite being can cross by holding onto its identity in opposition to any other, or only, if it becomes "identical" with all others and the infinity that is God. Third, the boundary, or peak consciousness, is the mutual translation of all-enfolding infinity (*complicatio*) and all-unfolding world (*explication*) of finite differences and oppositions. Fourth, however, the counter-movement of ascent and descent is *impossible*, as the threshold that it indicates (or populates) is the wall of coincidence (*murus coincidentiae*) that defies any rational or intellectual comprehension (*murus absurditatis*) and cannot be "crossed" if one is not *already* on both sides—in the world *and* in God (or the paradise). In fact, as in the Buddhist paradox that we cannot cross the river between *samsara* and *nirvana* (as explicated in ch. 3), we *are already always* both divergent multiplicity (of the world) and indifferent unity (in God). In Cusa's paradoxical language of nondualism: *in the world, the sun is the sun; but in the sun, God is ("contracted" as) the sun, and in God the sun is God—trans-pantheism!* The implication for Cusa, as it should be for us, is that no religion has *the* truth, or only in light of the unity in God, which Cusa presented in his book of religious relativity and unity, *De Pace Fidei* (1453 CE)—*trans-religious unity*! In this sense, at the threshold, the peak consciousness is that of concurrently "becoming God" (the ascent of *theosis*) *and* "becoming world" (becoming-minor, the descent of compassion, the universalization of love, peace-making).

As spiritual seeker, imagined in the image and the movements inherent in the image of the mountaineer, therefore, you are asked to seek the trans-religious truth of *any* spiritual path, its *trans*-pantheistic unity, and the *peace* of this summit of consciousness in all of the divergencies and nomadically shifting planes of mutual immanence.

The insight provided by the ascending and descending counter-movements performed by the spiritual mountaineer may, however, have some shocking implications that you may not be aware of to the full extent necessary to free your mind from all schemes of the conceptual intellect or the attachments to important existential ideas that give you spiritual meaning or save you from what Buddhist scripture (for instance, the *Brahmajala Sutra*) name "views." They are our limited modes of clinging to certain ideas and emotions, desires and meaning-creating mechanisms that, in the end, will hinder you from opening to the mind-blowing infinity of the consciousness promised at the peak of the mountain. With the following textual meditations from a few defining sources, I will approximate what I mean.

Meditation XV: Mirrors

Meditate on these passages in light of the images of the mountain, the ascent and descent, the multiple nomadic paths, the summit, the transformations. They will lead you to the truths of the summit of spiritual consciousness in the perceptions of the cosmic Spirit.

In the following passage, Mahatma Gandhi, in his "Spiritual Message" speech, recorded by Columbia Gramophone Company during his visit to England in 1931, opens us to this important insight, namely, that the mystical peak of the experience of the numinous is in no way world-negating, but rather, as in the image of the mountain paths, *any ascent must become another descent into the world*. While the Catholic theologian Karl Rahner prophesied that the future Christian will have to become mystical and political, Gandhi died for the realization of this visionary insight: that the unity of, and peace between, religions is, if anything, the mystical and political aim of the post-axial relevance of religions today.

> There is an indefinable mysterious power that pervades everything, I feel it though I do not see it. It is this unseen power which makes itself felt and yet defies all proof, because it is so unlike all that I perceive through my senses. It transcends the senses. . . .
>
> But it is possible to reason out the existence of God to a limited extent. Even in ordinary affairs we know that people do not know who rules or why, and how he rules. And yet they know that there is a power that certainly rules. . . .
>
> I do dimly perceive that whilst everything around me is ever changing, ever dying there is underlying all that change a living power that is changeless, that holds all together, that creates, dissolves and re-creates. That informing power of spirit is God, and since nothing else that I see merely through the senses can or will persist, He alone is. . . .
>
> . . . I gather that God is life, truth, light. He is love. He is the supreme Good. But He is no God who merely satisfies the intellect, if He ever does. God to be God must rule the heart and transform it. He must express himself in every smallest act of His votary. . . .
>
> It is proved not by extraneous evidence but in the transformed conduct and character of those who have felt the real presence of God within. Such

> testimony is to be found in the experiences of an unbroken line of prophets and sages in all countries and climes. To reject this evidence is to deny oneself....

The philosopher of mystical Islam, Henry Corbin (d. 1978), has related the important point made by the Andalusian Islamic mystic and philosopher Ibn 'Arabi, namely, that the peak of *mystical* consciousness is at the same time the consciousness of the archetypical *prophet,* the Muhammadian light, the Logos, who, as in the Gospel of John, is bound to become manifest, even human, while pervading all beings. And the great German Islamicist Annemarie Schimmel (d. 2003) writes in her book *Mystical Dimensions of Islam* (1975),

> The Perfect Man is the spirit in which all things have their origins; the created spirit of Muhammad is, thus, a mode of the uncreated divine spirit.... One can say in this context that the whole world is created from the Light of Muhammad ... (2001; p. 223)

The Eastern Church Father and theologian Gregory of Nyssa (335–94 CE), in his treaties *The Life of Moses,* reflecting on the Sinai theophany to Moses as the archetypical mystical experience mediating peak consciousness, makes the point that even the prophet (the temple of body of the presence of the Logos or Mind of God) only sees God in approaching the boundary of the inaccessible (Plotinus's One beyond the One). This summit of God-consciousness is true self-consciousness in which the utmost reachable insight reflects back onto the Self that is not identical with God, but always must in apophatic deferral detach itself from all knowledge, the act of knowing, the object of knowing and the subject of knowledge. It is a seeing that does not see, an experience of non-experience.

> Leaving behind everything that is observed, not only what sense comprehends but also what the intelligence thinks it sees, it keeps on penetrating deeper until by the intelligence's yearning for understanding it gains access to the invisible and incomprehensible, and there it sees God. This is the true knowledge of what is sought; this is the seeing that consists in not seeing, because that which is sought transcends all knowledge, being separated on all sides by incomprehensibility as by a kind of darkness. (§163)

Pseudo-Dionysius the Areopagite can be granted the title of the locus of the origination and for the justification of mystical theology unassailable by the orthodoxy of Christianity for centuries to come. In his *Mystical Theology* (ca. sixth century CE), he expresses this apex of mystical consciousness—in Mosaic terms of ascent—as "brilliant darkness," as secret silence (before the World, the Logos), prior to the intellect, but, therefore, also of utmost clarity—the two form of peak experiences.

> Direct our path to the ultimate summit of your mystical knowledge, most incomprehensible, most luminous and most exalted, where the pure, absolute and immutable mysteries of theology are veiled in the dazzling obscurity of the

secret silence, outshining all brilliance with the intensity of their darkness, and surcharging our blinded intellects with the utterly impalpable and invisible fairness of glories surpassing all beauty. (§2)

In the following two passages of the *Enneads,* Plotinus expresses the dipolar character of apophatic inaccessibility and polyphilic pervasiveness, if not identity (the pantheistic avoidance of imperial transcendence), or better, non-difference, between them (the trans-pantheistic overcoming of imperial transcendence) as the fundamental structure and the concurrent counter-movements of descent and ascent of the mystical (and prophetic) insight of the spiritual summit of consciousness and existence.

> The One is all things and no one of them; the source of all things is not all things; all things are its possession—running back, so to speak, to it—or, more correctly, not yet so, they will be (V.2, [1]). . . .
>
> [T]he One, [is] perfect because it seeks nothing, has nothing, and needs nothing, overflows, as it were, and its superabundance produces and makes something other than itself. This, when it has come into being, turns back upon the One and is filled, and becomes Intellect by looking towards it. Its halt and turning towards the One constitutes being, its gaze upon the One, Intellect. (V.2 [1], 7–11)

Finally, let me turn to a masterly symbolic characterization of the mystical peak consciousness that not only expresses the non-boundary boundary of the figure of the peak, the inaccessibility of the numinous above, beyond, or descending on it as on a mountain top, but also shakes and shocks us right into the simple precondition of its attainment. The Sufi sage and poet Farid ud-Din 'Attar (d. ca. 1220 CE), in exploring the old Persian myth of the Phoenix-like bird Simurgh, spins in *The Conference of Birds* (1177 CE) the tale of the archetypical spiritual wayfarer through "seven valleys" that, like steps and layers, are an ascent to the apex of mystical union with the formless God, in which the seeker experiences, in typical Sufi terminology, the annihilation of Self (*fana*) in order to be reborn (resurrected) to immortality, eternally living in God (*baqa*). Like the Phoenix that reconstitutes itself out of the fire of destruction, the wisdom of the Simurgh promises such resurrection to immortality in the presence of *the* Beloved, God.

Some of the seekers in this tale, represented by a flock of birds, after hearing the efforts that the seven valleys would need them to exert, want to find the legendary sage-bird Simurgh in order to gain enlightenment from it. When they, eventually, find the Simurgh after many adventures and after many birds died from stress, hunger, thirst and illness, they come to the tree of the Simurgh only to be confronted with shocking insight that the God they sought is only manifest in the *mirrors* of themselves: that *they are* the Simurgh!

And, their old selves self-knowledged and self-loathed,
And in the Soul's Integrity re-clothed,
Once more they ventured from the Dust to raise
Their Eyes—up to the Throne—into the Blaze,
And in the Centre of the Glory there
Beheld the Figure of—*Themselves*—as 'twere
Transfigured—looking to Themselves, beheld
The Figure on the Throne en-miracled,
Until their Eyes themselves and *That* between
Did hesitate which *Sëer* was, which *Seen*;
They That, That They: Another, yet the Same;
Dividual, yet One . . . (verses 1386–96)

8

Staring at Stars

And Ezra said: You are the Lord, you alone; you have made heaven, the heaven of heavens, with all their host, the earth and all that is on it, the seas and all that is in them. To all of them you give life, and the host of heaven worships you.
—NEHEMIAH 9:6 (NRSV)

Those who are wise shall shine like the brightness of the sky, and those who lead many to righteousness, like the stars forever and ever.
—DANIEL 12:3 (NRSV)

... *sic itur ad astra.*
—VIRGIL, *AENEID*, IX, VERSE 641

Two things fill the mind with ever new and increasing admiration and awe, the more often and steadily we reflect upon them: the starry heavens above me and the moral law within me.
—IMMANUEL KANT, *CRITIQUE OF PRACTICAL REASON*, CONCLUSION

Know thou that every fixed star hath its own planets, and every planet its own creatures, whose number no man can compute.
—BAHÁ'U'LLÁH, *GLEANINGS* (#82)

> The mysterious quanta of energy have made their appearance, derived, as it would seem, from the recesses of protons, or of electrons. Still worse for the concept, these quanta seem to dissolve into the vibrations of light. Also the material of the stars seems to be wasting itself in the production of the vibrations.
> —A. N. WHITEHEAD, *PROCESS AND REALITY* (78-79)

Heavens

STARS ARE THE MATTER of dreams. We are the matter of stars. Matter of light. Light is vibration. Vibration is the manifestation of the cosmic Spirit. This is the chain of thought engaging the entangled processes between cosmology and spirituality—that, throughout the centuries, unfolded in the image of the starry heavens, our companion since we became conscious of ourselves and the world. The heavens—in the form of astronomical measurements and the astrological mythologizations, in the construction of heavenly spheres and in the intuition that only the constellations of the heavenly bodies are unavoidably by their all-presence impressing on us—are the revelation of a horizon the complex patterns of which seem to tell us something important about our existence in a stunning world of diversity. The impression of the starry heavens and our unavoidable recognition of their wondrous nature is as old as human memory reaches into the recesses of history and, perchance, even deeper, to the archetypical dim cloud of collective human unconsciousness in its intuited entanglement with the rise of light and life on this earth or, for that matter, anywhere.

The appropriation of the heavenly bodies reaches from the recurrent revolution of the heavenly sphere with its orientation points of fixed stars and constellations for finding bearing on land and at sea to the coordination of the seeming or real but perceived chaos of time and history toward fundamental characters and characteristics that constitute its movements, as well as, in even a wider bold imagination, the fate of all happenings in the cosmos. In fact, the heavenly spheres with the mixture of movements and recurrent patterns that span like a tent over our heads and the world as all-encompassing horizon seem to have been the most visible presence of the majesty, inaccessibility, detachment and purposeful order, but also of unexpected events (eclipses of the sun and the moon, shooting stars, star showers) and even dangerous expressions (meteorites and asteroids) of divine or ultimate reality that virtually nothing else could rival. The heavenly bodies were a divine language in the form of constellations of light, but also of boundaries, limits and movements—calendars, important events, omens, and divine or cosmic messages—that to know in their ordering principles, which makes it a "cosmos," a *beautiful* order, would unravel the secrets of our existence in the world.

No wonder, then, that some phenomena of the heavens were early forms of what later became variations of, or divine spheres of influence in, supernatural theism and naturalism. Either their moving and fixed parts were associated with deities and demons, mythological heroes and archetypical life-forms and moral characteristics. Or, conversely, they were liberated from all of these projection to become the truly "pan*en*cosmic" Nature herself, related through causal influence or, in more sophisticated ancient astrological renderings, per proportion, sympathy, parallel movements, or translations of constellations of light into constellations of human behaviors, destiny, and meaning. While, for instance, the sun could become Amun-Ra of mythological origin, it could also become Aten of a naturalistic cosmos of light (see ch. 5). But while Ba'al and Asherah could be associated with sun, moon, Venus, and other stars, in the transmutation into Yahweh, losing his wife Asherah in post-Solomonic reforms, divinity becomes also dissociated from the heavenly bodies. Nevertheless, as the related epigraph of the biblical book of Nehemiah states (in typical Deuteronomist and Deutero-Isaiah fashion of the identification of El Elyon and YHWH in the time of the reconstruction of the temple in Jerusalem after the Exile), Yahwism, elevating Yahweh to the prince of the Elohim, dethroning the stars to the heavenly host of the heavenly king, degrading them from co-princes to servants and remaking them in the image of angels of the "Lord of hosts" (YHWH Sabaoth). While they remain messengers, expressions of divine revelation, they should never be revered as divine (Deuteronomy 4:19). While the starry heavens persist as "heavenly hosts," they have been transformed into visible manifestations *of* God Yahweh. And so, at night, Yahweh can be *seen* and *felt* as the pleromatic *Lord* of hosts. God's majesty as their creator can be intuited by the awesome nightly display of the "heaven of heavens." Now the stars are angles—immortal mediators of divine massages and manifestations of a divine realm the only form of which is light, the endurance of which is beyond space and time, and the essence of which is immortal life.

The heavenly spheres were always the expression of cosmic Wisdom, the good and beautiful order of all things, revered ("looked up" to) in the hope of the approximation of the earth to this heavenly order. She could be presented either in theistic form as the divine maid, the quasi-divine but also creaturely mediatrix of creation or, in panentheistic form, as the (dipolar) manifestation of the emanation of the world from the inaccessible apophatic Godhead, or as the pantheistic expression of the heavens as the body of divinity itself. In the cosmotheistic form, the star goddesses Ishtar/Astarte/Innana, the Queen of Heaven, developed into the pantheistic goddess Isis that embraces all beings in a purposeful and meaningful order, as visible with the starry heavens. Yet the sphere of the stars could also be transformed, in a theistic context, into the highest or first creature, the biblical Wisdom (*hokmah*, *sophia*), the mastermind or archetypical maid (Sirach 24), and, in the confluence of Isis and Sophia, come to be symbolized as the heavenly Queen. With the Virgin Mary, the Mother of Christ, in Christianity, she was revered as the cosmic Madonna, sheltering all creatures within her solar mantle and starry crown (Apocalypse 12), but also, ichnographically represented with a "cloak," *being* the starry heavens. As *Mare Stella*, she became the orientation mark for ships near the coast in the dark nights at sea. As encompassing the "dome of time," she represented the heavenly calendar, allowing the measurement and pacing of time in days, months and years. The Zodiac is her temporal body, the long-term companion of the depth of time as a form of regularity and fate, but also of the longevity of the cosmos.

Given the relativity of religious truths and identities, whether of theistic, panentheistic, pantheistic, non-theistic, naturalistic, or trans-pantheistic form, this Wisdom, in *all* of her forms, has, at one time or another, developed into an expression of the cosmic Spirit (Wisdom 9)—as long as she conveyed that the existence within this universe was not of mere haphazard randomness—at least following a natural law, if not some divine plan or intelligent (for instance, mathematical) pattern—or of motionless necessity, as the whole dome of space and time seems to vibrate in diverse frequencies and with some kind of unimaginable precision. One may, with some justification, even say that the starry order of light in the darkness of night as much as probably a few other factors (such as the impression of destiny and fate beyond human control) contributed greatly to the creation of the scientific mind as empirical correction to all kinds of fantastic myths and complex tales of creation (a privileging of astronomy that repeated itself with the scientific revolution of early Modernity); but also that the heavenly spheres made mathematics a divine discipline of space and time, of cosmic events and processes; and that it made a naturalistic spirituality more relevant than *either* haphazard stories of the gods of all-too-human character (as indicated with the ancient adventures of the Greek and Hindu gods, which were demythologized as natural forces) *or* a mere materialistic prison of mindless causality. Despite all the meaningless pirouettes of gods, one could rely on the heavens' revolution; against the dull hurling of dead particles in empty space, one could rely on the immediate feeling and security of the beauty of the open sky to be much more than random or necessary, namely, purposeful, and as having made space for *us* to live.

With the cosmological interests of the ancients, two important paradigmatic revolutions happened in the understanding on the heavenly space above us. On the one hand, the space between Earth and the sphere of the fixed stars, the Zodiac and the other patterns of light, was not just perceived as an empty space, but as a *layered space of spheres*, populated by the moving bodies of the moon, the sun, and the planets (as far as known). Since the classical sevenfold plateaus of the ancient Babylonian astronomy, the heavenly spheres became an expression not of distance, but of rarefication. Like the ascent on a mountain through climate zones (from the desert to the forest to the eternal ice), these heavenly zones were—as Aristotle imagined—made of ever more rarified matter and substances, increasingly consisting of pure disembodied light. The physical spheres, moving from space-time-matter to eternity-light-intellect, correlated with spiritual spheres of ever-higher divine character. The diverse spiritual realms, in any random sample of the world's religious or philosophical cosmologies, ancient and modern, were associated with those cosmological spheres, as was already mentioned (in ch. 7). The higher realities in this world were invisible but effective in, even directive of, the agendas of earthly matters, as well as a temporal expression of the transgressions between this life and a potential life after death. Above the layered spheres of heavens, the octo-sphere, resided the formless divine in inaccessibility.

On the other hand, another set of ancient patterns developed, that began to understand the starry sphere of heavenly bodies not as hierarchical and layered ascent to God, but as *sheer spaciousness* in which one can get lost in the depth of a perhaps finite but almost endless, even infinite, realm of lights. Now, the stars became identified as other suns, like ours. The universe was identified as utterly unfathomable expanse without any center and any circumference. While such a view, against general perception, was quite common even in the antiquity, it has, against any limitations introduced by short-time and small-space proponents with their religious desires for salvation from this world, come back with a vengeance with today's many different scenarios by which our visible physical cosmos is understood to be just a small part of a vast multiverse. From the materialist atomists of antiquity, such as Democritus, Epicurus and Lucretius, and the "demythologizing" Stoics, which know of rarified forms of matter (such as *pneuma*, in a weak sense constituting cosmic spheres), to the theistic or trans-pantheistic Nicolas of Cusa and the pantheistic Giordano Bruno to the dualists like Descartes, the monists like Leibniz, and even Immanuel Kant—the starry heavens were not higher, even spiritual or, at least, intellectual spheres, but *one* plane with an infinite wealth of suns and even planets like ours. This was a cosmos brimming with life and even worlds like ours with beings asking questions inspired by their encounter of, and insight in, this marvelous infinite universe as the very horizon of their existence, defining them as intelligent, scientific, philosophical, and religious beings.

These two models display options of understanding with enormous implications and consequences, and, although with some overlapping and surprising manifestations, all in all representing almost "hermetically" closed alternatives, perceived to be incompatible. Yet it is the *mutual transformation* of these models into one another that structures the religious questions of beginning, existence, meaning, and ends as much as the spiritual question regarding the nature of the universe and our place in it in important ways—and will be the content of the next two sections. The impression that the force for this transformation from the hierarchical and spherical to the flat and expansive model was the shift from geocentrism to heliocentrism is false. In fact, both models can coexist with any version of ancient geo- and heliocentrism (as this is an ancient alternative, and not a choice only accessible to modernity) or, more commonly today, with cosmo-centrism or multiverse non-centrism—cosmologies the spiritual importance of which will be thematized in the next chapter. Rather, the force of the transformation between the two models is one of the *counter-movements inherent to their mutuality*, not any linear replacement, for instance, triggered by a more scientific access.

The spherical system of higher intellectual or spiritual layers could be structured in such a way that it did allow for the infinite expansiveness of space-time and a decentered cosmos of many worlds-systems (suns, planets) or even universes; but it would always insist on a pervasive ethical impulse, intellectual clarity, and spiritual meaningfulness of the physical sphere in the context of any other spheres that would make these layers more obvious than the physical perception allows on its own plane. Much like the human experience of the irreducibility of layers of mind and soul, spirit and consciousness, as well as dimensions of ethics, aesthetics and logic, in ourselves, the universe appears as a "human being" (the Perfect Human Being, the Logos, the Image of God) without compromising its physical characteristics of matter and energy, space and time, quantity and dimensionality, finiteness of beings and infinity of expansion. From the hypostatic differentiation of the intelligible and soulful world of Plotinus to Kant's internal feeling of the metaphysical relevance of the starry heavens in mirroring the moral law inherent in our intellect (established by the practical reason despite the impossibility of the establishment of metaphysical entities by our theoretical reason)—as reflected in the related epigraph to this chapter—we become witness to the persistence of this mutuality.

Conversely, the flat plane of a decentered universe of matter and energy could, at no point in time, convincingly converge on the reductionisms of a postulatory or scientific materialism and succeed in denying such layers of aesthetic, ethical, intellectual, conscious and spiritual dimensions of at least human if not cosmic existence only because of the perceived infinity of the physical world. Recourses of famous scientific figures of the scientific revolution of physics in the beginning decades of the twentieth century demonstrate this fact: the recourse of Albert Einstein (d. 1955) to the cosmic intellect that does not haphazardly act (in his opposition to quantum physics); the conviction of Werner Heisenberg (d. 1976) and many other eminent quantum physicists, such as John von Neumann, Erwin Schrödinger (d. 1961), Niels Bohr (d. 1962), and Eugene Wigner (d. 1995), that the quantum reality demonstrates the mind-like more than the matter-like deep reality of the cosmos; the conjecture of John Archibald Wheeler (d. 2008) of the self-conscious universe initiated by the subject-object entanglement of consciousness and physical reality; the idea of David Bohm (d. 1992) of an "implicate order" of the (only) seemingly chaotic universe; the disappearance of matter into energy and of the new dualism of energy and information in the paradigms of cosmologies based on visions of artificial intelligence—all of these attempts to understand the fundamental structure of the physical plane in the context of a wider irreducible cosmos of a more mind- or consciousness-like character demonstrates that the multidimensionality of the ancient heavenly spheres is still alive.

The Cosmic Spirit

The decisive mutual transformation of these two models for the understanding of the cosmic spirituality, in our context, then, is not their mutual exclusiveness and linear substitution (in one direction by naturalists, in the other by occultists), but that they allow *two counter-moving mappings* onto one another. If one maps the expansive universe onto heavenly spheres, one gets a complex, layered spiritual universe of diversified levels or plateaus of existence within, but also beyond, the physical plane of existence. It is basic for religious cosmologies to explicate these worlds. The assumption that the stars are "beings" of some sort makes them the hosts of God, the Elohim, and angels. They become viewed as the place of immortalized souls of humans and perhaps other beings of the physical cosmos in their afterlife or eternal existence of light. Conversely, if one maps the complex layers of spheres onto the expansive universe, the question of alien life and alien intelligence, of other creatures on other worlds that are conscious and religious, is raised. They become the new gods or angels with the wisdom of the creator. In an unexpected turn of this combination, remythologizing the diverse spheres, our universe may even become the matrix of another dimension, maybe as the laboratory or virtual reality, a kind of text or experiment (of mad scientists?). In any case, the question of interstellar life becomes an important question of this spiritual mapping.

Before I explicate both versions of the mapping of both the layered and the expansive cosmos for our spiritual maturation, I want to at least mention another, quite different use of the starry heavens in the interest of human liberation from the demons of our devouring destructiveness and as a quite different expression of the boundary between transcendence and immanence, spirituality and political existence. The Jewish philosopher Walter Benjamin (1892–1940), writing during the time between the two world wars and of the racist madness of the time, and who finally succumbed to it, has left us with a manifesto that defies temporal succession and historical linearity by envisioning a *messianic intrusion* into the seemingly smooth world of historical continuity and ideological binding powers. In his "Theses on the Philosophy of History" (1940), he deconstructed and countered the progressive Marxist revolutionary understanding of the transformation of history into a perfect state in the future as "victor history," the history written from the perspective of the winners—whoever that may be—because they always will bury the lost ones, the forgotten ones, under their ascent. In using the painting of an Angel by Paul Klee (1879–1940), the *Angelus Novus* (1920), the New Angel, he understood progressive time as an angel fleeing time and history, looking backward, in arrested shock observing and documenting the piling up of the whole human history as one of violence, death, war and despicable inhumanity, all around and without end. Against this continuity imaged in the "angel of history" that always will destroy the dead *again* by an process of forgetting or by remembering them only in the process of their disappearance, salvation from this "continuity" could only come from a *messianic force of interruption*, of the *shock of history from the future* that *remembers* the dead, the lost, the forgotten, and the removed—a *messianic memory* that *changes the past* and transforms it into an *open space of novelty*.

Benjamin uses the astronomical term of the *star constellations* to indicate that no structure is just coherent in an air-tide logic, but must be understood as a constellation that is contingent in a specific way: open for the future to change it *in the past* into salvific structures of memory and novelty. If we understand that the zodiac is an ancient integration of relationships between unrelated stars, except that they don't change in relation to one another from the perspective of the earth, we understand also that these constellations can be used as stable patterns with inherent meaning (astrology), or as projections of human pattern recognition and imaginative abilities that can *change* meanings *if* we only activate the creative and imaginative power to do so. Then, projected meaning, seemingly inherent in the constellations we invent, transforms into *nomadic* meanings (in a Deleuzian sense), liberated to *new spaces of creative refigurations*.

Curiously, the "angel of history" resembles the failure of Orpheus to save Euridice (as presented in ch. 5): on his way out of Hades, as Orpheus looks back, Euridice disappears and remains dead! Backward, we see only death; only a messianic force from the future could overcome death. The messianic liberation *of* the past, not by overcoming the past, but by the future force of divinity to *revisit* it, resonates greatly with the archetypical Jewish "remembrance" (*anamnesis*) of the Sinai event of liberation of the people from oppressive dictatorship, where YHWH reveals "divinity" as *the essence of the novelty coming "from" the future* (Exodus 3:14–15: "I will be that or who I will be [for you])," as the one who "was, is [*estin*] and *comes* [*erchestai*]" (Revelation 1:4, 8).

It also resonates with Whitehead's "dipolar" divinity, that or who not only *is* the future of the potential of any and every event in their processes of becoming what they will be (or have become) when they will have decided to what extent to follow that which they *could* be (in divine light and lure); but God, here, is the one that or who is also the *memory* of everything that has actually happened by making its broken existence of impermanence an *inherent part of the divine experience* in which all is *transformed* in light of all becoming and the *wisdom of creative alternatives and potential for a new future to come*. In this sense, God enters *from* the future and transforms the monadic determinations *of* the past into an open space of nomadic transformation.

Actualized patterns, perpetuated throughout time, are not fixed determinations of fact and meaning, but "heavenly constellations" in the mind and memory of God that receive their meaning by *divine deconstruction* of fixed patterns and by infusion of new modes of life, *creating meaning ever anew*. Here, the image of the starry heavens binds mysticism and political engagement together in a new and unprecedented way and creatively maps the layered and expansive universe, one stratum onto the other, in quite unique form. It is not from established or past unity, nor from mystical union with the divine, that we activate world-oriented transformation, here, but from an unprecedented future to which we are never united, but which—as in Derrida's account—*defers* such unity into a *messianic event*, or, conversely, *releases* the *salvific transformations* of history in our release *from* such a (future) unity into the diversifications of this world with its incompatibilities in order to heal them. Even if we all would be or become "angels" (Mark 12:25), we would only be like the "angel of history," fleeing in to a future, leaving behind the rubble of pain and destruction. The angels are not the messianic event, but only its *absence*, its deference, *différance*—the absence of the *undeconstructable* future that, in Derrida's view, eschatologically promises and concretely and actively demands justice *now*.

More than in Kant's feeling of the correlation between moral imperative in us and the constellations of the stars above us, Benjamin's urgent *messianic shock of the past* becomes the spiritual impulse of the activation of the transformation of our Selves and humanity in light of a Spirit that conforms to nothing that "is," but always stretches the cosmic integrity beyond its smooth "planes of immanence" and breaks the "transcendental fields of consistency" in which we seek unity, liberation, and salvation, to open us to the (still lingering) *indeterminateness* of the lost past of the forgotten, the excluded, the least, and the last ones seeking healing. If this is what the starry heavens relate to us, we have already been transformed by them!

Interstellar

The movie *Interstellar* (2014), packed with the current scientific knowledge and cutting-edge hypotheses of relativity and quantum-physical theory and cosmology, reflects on questions of interstellar travel in light not only of our human curiosity, but the ecological crisis and under the assumption that we will have destroyed Earth and damned humanity to a slow but definite collective annihilation. The movie's interstellar travel is an adventure specially of and against time, about the reality or illusion of time, and the salvific importance of the paradoxical violation of linear time or the access to other forms of existence that seem to approximate to some kind of timelessness or eternity, or a block universe, in which past, present, and future are ultimately irrelevant. This knowledge becomes available because of the assumption that in an higher-dimensional hyperspace not only would temporal linearity be relieved of the assumed ultimate defining characteristic of actual facts, but also cyclical reconnections between times, future-past actions, become possible without violation of the higher-level physical laws, as they already intrude in ours space-time continuum at places of their breakdown, such as black holes and wormholes—and maybe just any quantum-physical interaction with its non-locality and indeterminacy of causal flows.

The movie, as also the bold futuristic projection of scientific potentials, even presupposes that a sufficiently developed civilization would be able to understand, control, and manipulate these higher-dimensional forces in a wider universe of which our limited dimensions are only a small realization of deeper rules; and that such a civilization would, eventually, have migrated to such a wider hyper-space—in some sense becoming indiscernible from the fantastic imaginations of ancient gods or the natural force and constellations as such. While the movie limits itself to the thesis that this civilization is the humanity of the future, acting on its own past so as to allow itself to arise and avoid premature death, current reflections and imaginations in scientific, philosophical, and literary directions highly favor the potential of the vast universe that we today know we inhabit to have incubated innumerable many other intelligent beings who, eventually, would have come to such a point of hyper-dimensional transformation.

It is this confluence of the future of humanity and potential advanced alien civilizations, on the one hand, and the mapping of the technological progress onto spiritual maturity that is the matter of dreams about the stars as the revelation of spiritual renewal. This is, of course, just another form of "spiritual materialism," a matter not of unification but of confusion. Yet not only the post-axial potential of religious movements that structurally engage alien superiority—for instance, in the emergence of UFO religions, or their integration of alien heritage in the human ancestry—but even the hope for salvation by advanced alien civilizations has some ancient precedence. We find such assumptions, for instance, in the mythologies of native cultures looking at the stars as their origin, or in the age-old theological discussion on the possibility of "another humanity" living on the other side of the world, the *antipodes*, as it were, which were not understood to be descendants of Adam—with all the consequences regarding the questions of creation, sin, and redemption through Christ—making them paradigmatic *religious* aliens.

The question of religious unity and the limitation of humanity with its religious diversity in the vast universe beyond Earth, the potential of other beings of the kind that humans would characterize as "images" of God, or as exhibiting and actively engaging Buddha-nature, or as being intelligent but perhaps in an uncontrollable, unexpected, or unexplainable way religious or irreligious—all these possibilities and many others remain inconvenient perennial questions for anyone interested in *cosmic* spirituality with its assumption of a fundamental relationality of all existants, even beyond physical connectivity: What if these beings would be of a greatly advanced civilization, but not religious at all? Conversely, what if they are of such attractive religious insight that no mundane religious identity would remain (the same or at all) if contact would be happening? What if they prove all human religious imaginations and truth claims naïve, laughable or wrong? What if they demonstrate such a spiritual depth and power that would prove all human expressions of "deep" religiosity and spiritual desires and aims just a local idiosyncrasy, a bubble of small-minded or even retarded limitation of the human mind that would also explain the inability of humanity to implement or manifest the deep spiritual values and aims of its religious traditions, prophets and mystics, teachers and warners, seers and visionaries? What if an alien civilization would be found to have escaped the evolutionary heritage of Darwinian forces of violence and mutual destruction as instruments of survival and reproduction, and had transformed itself into a profound mode of peace and unity, freedom and diversification, but only by discarding any parochial religious claims of truth and salvation—or even any relevance of spiritual questions, assumptions and presupposition of a "perfect" aesthetic, ethical, and intellectual existence? What if they had become indiscernible from nature or from whatever we would define as divine?

But why should we care? Why should religious people, religions as such, the diverse assumptions of universal spiritual identity of humanity, spiritual practitioners, and really anyone whether religious or not, take the cosmic context with the potential of other living beings who might be in a sense intelligent that we would recognize as a matter of mind and consciousness, science and philosophy, art and religion, seriously, that is, as a new and unavoidable context for their own contextualization? Is not the most reliable and as of yet unremoved fact of the scientific and visionary community, SETI, in their search for ETL, extraterrestrial intelligent life, the "Fact One": that there is *no evidence whatsoever* of any such living, intelligent alien beings? I think we ought to pay attention for several related reasons: the current scientific knowledge of astronomy, cosmology, astrobiology, evolutionary theory, on the one hand, and the ancient, deep cultural, philosophical, and religious roots of assumptions of a universe brimming with life and intelligent civilizations, on the other. Only if one could discard both areas as relevant evidence of the kind that is not better or worse than any other body of knowledge that humanity expresses, one could be claiming the advantage of any blindness to the involved questions for humanity as such and its spiritual nature and destiny in particular.

Given Fact One and the bodies of scientific and cultural knowledges, we find ourselves in the peculiar situation to envision a "Fact Two," as it were, namely: evidence, at least, of alien life forms, if not signs of intelligence, independent of the development of both life and mind on Earth, on the one hand, and the unavoidable ability of our intellect to project our current knowledges into the dark interstellar and intergalactic vastness, on the other. If we would also be prompted to avoid *simplifications*, issuing from the kind of spiritual materialism that arises in the confusion of the mapping *of* hierarchical spiritual realms of which many religions and spiritual teaches and movements are convinced to exist beyond the physical universe *onto* that physical universe, we must be careful to honor the scientific knowledge while, by harmonizing it with religious symbolisms, in no way let the religious perspective (the deep convictions, which are relative and can be wrong or incomplete or inadequate) overtake the empirical search and the open framework for the interpretations of the evidence we find for their understanding. Our religious theories may, at certain times, prompt us to investigate further scientifically, but they may also, at any time, become a roadblock for seeing the possibilities and facts and interpretations in an open enough manner so as to be able to go where our mind and the evidence might take us. I don't want to say that our religious intuitions should be excluded, but only that they must themselves be understood as "facts" of our collective, maybe universally connected existence in the universe. Yet because of their mutual transcendence, diversification, and opposition, their *relativity* is the *most basic fact* on the ground for any further discussion of their relevance for the investigation and imaginary projections that might drive the scientific establishment of evidence. This does, however, also *not* mean that the measure for a further search and interpretation of a potentially confirmed Fact Two would be scientific materialism instead of spiritual materialism—both are actually mirroring each other in their dualism of spirit and matter and their reductionism of one to the other. Rather, the fundamental assumptions of a cosmic Spirit for this endeavor must be open enough to probe the potentials of *both* that Fact One be ultimate and that Fact Two may become the new reality.

The best way to avoid such simplifications, confusions, and overstatements of the mapping process is, I think, to combine our scientific knowledge of evolution theory, physical cosmology and anthropology with the motivating pattern of diverse religions and spiritualities of a *vast universe or even multiverse*—as this is a likely or even established scientific "fact" today—and see where it takes us. That is, we *exclude* the scientific, philosophical, and religious "explanations" of a small universe that has, at times, befallen diverse of their cosmological assumptions and theological explications, as irredeemably counter-factual, without ridiculing them, and concentrate, instead, on the vastness that the human mind, as long as we can gather evidence from the past and its curiosity to investigate the universe beyond the human and even earthly spheres, has assumed as the bias and basis for, and the confirmed starting-point of, our intellectual investigations of the potential of alien intelligence, and what it would imply for cosmic spirituality in relation to human religiosity.

Beginning with the scientific predispositions for SETI, let it be said that this synthetic assumption (resonating physical with religious cosmology) reflects an alternative that is as profound in all areas of this conversation as it is defining of a religious "third space" and avoids the dualism otherwise involved: namely, that the existence of the universe, the evolution of life and mind, and the potential limitations or unlimited range of the expanse and future of the development of the cosmos (or multiverse) is either a product of *random* processes or, in some sense, a *necessity* of inherent structural and lawful progress. Curiously, on all levels, these oppositional alternatives prevail in the formation of theories and the ambivalence of gathered evidence. Either the universe, seemingly rushing into existence more than thirteen billion years ago with a Big Bang, sprang from a random quantum process, ir-repeatable in its uniqueness and singular development, *or* it followed some necessity of natural law that physics still seeks with the unification of the four fundamental physical forces, matter and energy, time and space, gravity and other fields, and the like, to one Grand Unified Theory and one world formula. No one knows; important voices diverge. It comes down to cosmological, philosophical, religious, or non-religious inclinations.

Elegant combinations of both have been found to not resolve anything, really, such as a Darwinian theory of infinite universes that would "explain" the unique characteristics of our universe to be geared toward life and mind—the so called problem of fine-tuning—but rather to confuse uniqueness with, or reduce *randomness* to, a fantastically assumed infinite number of appearances (like the throw of a dice). And if the infinite appearances of universes were *necessary*, as their contingency would self-destroy the whole argument, how do we explain this necessity except *as* a contingency, that is, as a *brute fact*? And if the ingrediencies of the production of universes were to be finite, instead, the boring repetition of the same, even if it is in the range of huge numbers beyond our mental capacity to fathom, would also end up with an infinity of replications the *fact* of which was only *the continency of this necessity*.

I will reflect more on the implications of multiverse theories for the understanding of the cosmic Spirit in the last chapter of the book, following this one, but will, here, only relate that no "solution" that holds on to this dualism of contingency and necessity has ever been able to explain or even interpret the existence of the cosmos in any more meaningful or logical or aesthetically satisfying way than any number of religious interpretations. Why? Because such religious interpretations, such as diverse forms of theism, pantheism, panentheism, trans-pantheism, and the like, have been infinitely more satisfying to counter the insufficient reductionism inherent in this dualistic alternative. Where is the evidence that a naturalism or materialism that operates by this dualism can (or ever did) cope with any of the deep religious heritage of nondualism at the heart of all religions and mature spiritual encounters, revelations, epiphanies, theophanies, manifestations, intuitions, experiences, and reasoning in any sophisticated way without falling back into the dualistic scheme? How can this materialist dualism "explain" the fundamental resonance of the awe we feel in the face of the starry heavens with our intuition that we are meant in some sense to unravel a deeper meaning to all the beauty and wholeness of this canopy above us, as a secret deposited in us, without explaining it away? Frankly, can we, *without this feeling*, even understand ourselves *as* human, *as* intelligent, *as* worthy of living beyond states of vegetation or animal impulses? The fact that we as human beings exhibit the fundamental impulses of compassion and love, justice and healing, curiosity and mindfulness, understanding and consciousness, even if we are unable to practice them to any degree of sufficiency, does not fit the dualism of randomness or necessity.

The same antagonism between randomness and necessity appears again in the evolutionary scheme, trying to explain the appearance of life on this planet: was the sudden appearance of life more the four billion years ago on Earth a random, unique effect of "historical," unrepeatable combinations of events, *or* is there a propensity toward the evolution of life built into the very fabric of the universe, even if they are not visible on the level of physical laws, but emergent laws of higher combination of forces, energies, fields, matter particles, quantum and chemical processes—one need only revisit the divergency of scientific opinions, for instance, of Stephen Jay Gould vs. Simon Conway Morris (see ch. 4).

While I see much more evidence for a probability space that favors certain islands of evolutionary convergence, given the evidence collected from the evolution of life on this earth—much like islands of stability expected in the transuranic chemical elements—fragile, but evident nevertheless, it may not be misunderstood as the determinateness of a necessary evolutionary process, like a computer program pushing the universe toward its execution. Rather, like the expression or change of expression of genes by epigenetic circuits of feedback with the environment and quickly changing constellations (too quick for natural selections to operate on diverse mutations and allele variations of genes), such "natural" places of potential evolutionary *convergences* are *not* predetermined, but *predisposed* to happen under certain conditions—for instance, the sun being the precise condition for the multiple independent developments of eyes in the evolution of life on Earth. But the precise characteristics of our sun, in relation to all possible states that stars can run through, is *contingent* at best, as well as whether there are planets, moons, and other combinations, potentially generative of life or hindering it. And then there is the utterly contingent "fact one" of evolution, namely, *that* there is life at all, that cannot be explained by the probability space of convergent evolutions, which can only operate as soon as there *is* life—as much as natural selection can only operate if there is sufficient variations and mutations from which to select.

One "solution" around this dualism that does not work, tilting the whole question towards necessity, is the theory of *panspermia*: it assumes the broad ubiquitous creation of primitive life in the cosmos, even in space, to be distributed by comets and other migrating cosmic objects, as offered already by the ancient philosopher Anaxagoras (510–428 BCE) and recently revived by Fred Hoyle (d. 2001) and Chandra Wickramasinghe (b. 1939)—not to imagine the involvement of intelligent life to have generated this process, as is the assumption in the famous novel and movie *2001: A Space Odyssey*, both 1968, by Arthur C. Clarke (d. 2008) and Stanley Kubrick (d. 1999), respectively. But this solution only *defers* the question of the origin to another unknown *contingent happening* or *mechanism* of this "fact one" of the existence of life.

The other "elegant" solution, trying to overcome the antagonistic dualism between randomness and necessity or, in a weaker sense, of contingency and regularity, that does also not work, is the often and for various reasons and to various ends invoked *principle of mediocrity*. In short, it assumes that if there is no exceptional place in the universe (as there is no center and no periphery), we cannot assume that our Earth and its evolution are exceptional either. Hence, we ought to assume the regularity of the emergence of life in the cosmos, underlined by the unimaginable huge numbers of suns in the Milky Way (about two hundred billion stars) and the huge number of galaxies just like (or even unlike) our Galaxy (about a trillion galaxies in the observable universe). Even the volume in our close proximity of about 20,000 stars in a radius of 1,200 light years from our Sun is as encouraging as the discovery of a harrowing number of planets around these suns exponentially seems to confirm the medium position we inhabit in this vast interstellar and intergalactic expanse. But the principle of mediocrity falls back onto itself and falters for several reasons. For one, its irrelevance suggests itself because of the thermodynamic unidirectionality of the "history" of our Big Bang universe, which is *not* indifferent to past and future and activates events of irreversible uniqueness—which again throws "mediocrity" into the pangs of, and the idiosyncrasies inherent in, the fundamental cosmological dualism of existence of a universe as such just mentioned above. Another reason not to trust this principle of "regularity" is that, given the vast expanses of time over which the universe has developed in its structures and appearances of matter and energy-fields, there is no way to decide whether or not any other "intelligence" out there has ever survived or whether *we* will (have) survive(d) in the case that any other life-form will appear in our future when, say, everything related to our sun system will long be gone and has without memory vanished into the remnants of a (then) nameless, burned-out sun, or, in the even further out unimaginable immensity of times passing, it will have been swallowed by a black hole, perhaps the one now growing at the center of our Galaxy.

The appearance of mind of beings in a social organization that could be called intelligent and civilizational is even more prone to be unable to escape the orbit of the gambit of favoring contingency over necessity and vice versa. All other levels of this dualism begin to interact even more on this level of our *own* existence and the question whether we are alone in the vast universe. The overwhelming arguments against the principle of mediocrity for the development of mind and consciousness, even in such a vast universe, and even if there was a convergent evolution somehow backing such mediocrity, are related to the thermodynamic rundown of order of energy states and the fast timeframe of potential developments of intelligent life in relation to the chance of its rather fast disintegration. The latter counter-assumption would be that we will never know whether there was, or is, or will be, any other civilization, as they are so rarely developing and distributed in the vast space-time expanse that even the evidence of such an existence is questionable, not even thinking yet about potential connections or visits—biological or through AI. This is the problem of the crucial last element of the famous Drake equation, called "L" (the lifetime of an advanced intelligent civilization), devised by the physicist Frank Drake (b. 1930) that tried to make a rough estimation of such civilizations in the universe and probably will bind us to a miss. Beyond that, we should not forget that the Fact One still prevails—in the famous counter-argument of the Fermi paradox, by the physicist Enrico Fermi (d. 1954): Given the age of the universe, "they" must have already visited us: so, where are they? The unviability of randomness and necessity still defines the discourse.

Religions and spiritualities *fundamentally* are *not* subject to the mechanisms of this dualism. Instead, almost as a definition of basic religious assumptions, we may say, instead, that some kind of *purpose* is seen to undergird *any* appearances of randomness and necessity, contingency and regularity. This does not mean that religious cosmologies don't apply both contingency and necessity, randomness and regularity, in their explications; but what it means is that they are not understood as ultimate or ultimately defining means of the creation, emanation or mutual immanence of divine or ultimate reality and the physical world. Of course, the concrete formulations of the religious and spiritual understanding of cosmic evolution, the appearance of intelligent life and even of ethically and religiously superior civilizations amounts to a wide spectrum that emphasizes any potential combination of these penultimate assumptions between a random and an all-determining limit. Theists may understand divine purpose as closer to randomness (using random processes as means of freedom) or necessity (defining the plan and aim of creation); pantheist may prefer the necessity of the world as it is as expression of divinity without alternative, or they may lean towards the naturalist assumption of ultimate randomness of existence.

So, elevating this variability to an important insight, here: the dualism between randomness and necessity does *not* define the difference of the *religious* positions taken by religions and spiritualities on the matter at hand, namely, whether there is intelligent life that relates to ultimate reality or God beside humanity, and whatever that implies for a specific religious or spiritual universe of discourse. One can be a religious naturalist or a theist or a pantheist or a panentheist, but still be *either* on the rare Earth side, such that we are the exception, *or* root with the principle of mediocrity for a pleroma of intelligent life in the universe other than our Earth. *Whatever* their theological persuasion, it does *not* necessitate their view to either side with the uniqueness of life and mind on this earth, which they can understand as much as a sign of the majesty of God as the opposite: that God will allow for infinitely many expressions of God's image on this and perhaps many other planets, galaxies, or even cosmic regions and epochs beyond this one.

Hence, the question of the relevance of alien life and intelligent alien civilizations for religions and vice versa is *not* whether or not religions would be transformed by the establishment of the evident definiteness of Fact One or Fact Two (although both may fail, as I said above, because we cannot trust for any definite encounter in the vastness of space and time to decide matters). The question is also *not* whether or not religions would welcome the establishment of Fact One or Fact Two, as such wishes and desires are projections of human imaginations, which in the vastness of the universe have no relevance to the potentials that it may not yet have even touched on in its unfolding expansiveness—and we still think too much of our presence in this cosmos when we assume our consciousness to be the awakening of the universe to itself.

Therefore, we need not to dive into details of the impact that either Fact One or Two would have on diverse religions—although, in the current literature on the matter, imaginations and confrontations of alien encounters with human religions are often about them. While the difference of the impact on, and details of the imaginations of, such investigations are of considerable interest for the terrestrial future of particular religions and spiritualities, as they may be quite different in their own universes of discourse, closer investigation will show that more or less all religious traditions and spiritualities harbor approaches to this question that will allow them to express both Fact One and Two in accordance with their internal resources. Instead, what we must use as a *differentiating mark* in this discussion is the *potential* of religions and spiritualities for the acceptance and meaningful expression of alien life and civilizations as *defining moment* of their cosmological character. That is, we must *discount* all attempts of religious orthodoxies to already know *either* that Fact Two is impossible *or* that Fact One is inevitable. From this assumed potentiality certain *inevitable* consequences will flow that, in fact, *are* important for any religion or spirituality to allow for both Fact One and Two to be an *inherent* expression of their truth—or, conversely, without which they would miss the opportunity to be called true. I will name only three, here, at the closure of this section.

First, only if we accept that the truth of all religions on Earth is *relative* to one another are we also open the potential of this to be the case for alien civilizations. Conversely, a religious view would be bound by its own exclusivity and incurable superiority or even finality to deny this potential, which disqualifies it from making any true statements on this matter and "relativizes" its own truth value considerably.

Second, the potential of the affirmation of alien intelligent *spiritual* beings would imply that we would be able to *recognize* them and that we can *communicate* with them. This affirmation, again, has as its presupposition that evolution in the cosmos, even if independent from that of the earth, of life and intelligence, consciousness and spirituality, despite all divergences and differences, would not be divergent to the point of being equal to the existence of different mutually exclusive worlds. In other words, if there is a possibility of *cosmic* spirituality to be *real*, then, the unity of human religiosity in all its diversity must be at least as strong, if not even much stronger (given our genetic and historical mutual dependence), such that any view of substantial cultural independence and alien identity on Earth would be detrimental to this potential; and, hence, cannot be true.

Third, the unity of humanity, its religiosity and spiritual nature, must be understood as a manifestation of a *cosmic purpose* that makes questions of randomness and necessity, contingency and mediocrity, secondary, if not irrelevant, in relation to the impression, as related in all religious traditions, that the purpose of existence cannot be reduced to particular interests and agendas of the mutual testing of Darwinian fitness for survival. In other worlds, the recognition of our *spiritual* nature means that the evolution of the universe is meant to be one of the overcoming of opposition and mutual destruction, and will reorient itself "naturally" towards relationality and cooperation, the "better life" instead of naked survival, and the realization of the *common religious values* of compassion and love, justice and mutuality, instead of mere self-preservation and beyond any special interests.

This last point, in fact, harbors one of the most exiting side-effects of the cosmological question of alien *spiritual* life: namely that, if it is meant to develop *purposefully* in the cosmos *once*, it can happen *more than once*—especially, if it happens to some such being, like humanity, that can in its own spiritual development and purpose recognize that such an evolution cannot be meant to have already come to perfection in its own peculiar path. It is exciting, indeed, to think of the purposeful evolution of the Spirit through evolutionary processes, purposing perhaps the existence of a universe as such as something that we can already understand to be under way on Earth with, besides and beyond humanity. Like the antipodes, other human species, such as the Neanderthals, as far as evidence shows, have had a spiritual nature. Even if *homo sapiens* is the only human species surviving on this planet, today, there is no necessity in this fact that *limits* the development of intelligent spiritual beings *to us*—and it does not even limit a spiritual development *beyond* humanity. In fact, isn't the transformation of humanity and life on Earth that human religions envision a sign that we are not yet the end of this evolution? How exiting to know where we might go.

Light

Light is the resident of two worlds, that of relativity and that of quantum phenomena. In the world of relativity, light is the boundary of space-time, indicating the velocity to which all beings are relative; in the world of quantum phenomena light is the face of particles and waves, discontinuity and continuity. At the boundary of temporality, light moves in spacetime, but is for everything at this boundary beyond the flow of time. Light enlightens the cosmos it flows through, and everything flows beneath its limit; and while light is collecting all information it transports, it is itself formless, but not without the life of infinite modulations of vibrations. It is movement and stillness, highest activity for all things and without any actuality of its own. If one could live in the light, one was to be timeless, immortal.

Intuitively, the strangeness of the starry umbrella of the heavens above; their regular reappearance; their zodiacal change and return; their mostly detached presence beyond an invisible boundary, but sometimes dangerous intervention; their ominous or glorious signaling of events and fate—all have been interpreted as hints towards a divine realm; a divine face toward the cosmos; even a timeless expanse of the highest rarified creatures or divine beings, gods and angels; the host of the heavens of heavens—as the related epigraph of the book of Nehemiah indicates. Intuitively, then, the starry heavens were also understood as the place of our souls, rarified, elevated, immortal, detached, and as participants of a divine realm that reflects the divine will for this earth—as expressed in the epigraph of the last prophetic book of the Hebrew Bible, the book of Daniel. Immortal like the star-lights above, being of the nature of divine light, our souls are essentially angels, light-beings, meant to exhibit our essence as immortal light-forms, of divine vibrations. In some sense, this intuition knows us as beings of Spirit-vibration, even before creation, and of being constituted by the first creative act, that of light (Genesis 1:2–3)—divine and mundane at the same time.

In this symbolic expression of the nondualism between God and the world, Spirit and the cosmos, lies the power of the mutual inherence of the "dipolar" character of everything that the immortal light-vibration can convey, but also the danger of the confusion of this dipolarity with dualisms that fuse the differences on the wrong "end," as it were: not at the "beginning" ("in the beginning . . ."), as they *diverge* by never being apart as *apophatic unity and polyphilic multiplicity*, but as "apocalyptic" *collapse* in which the dipolarity disappears by being *eliminated* in favor of one side *over* the other. In a sense, this "divergence" simulates a quantum state of energy-matter, which does not allow us to know both position and movement in space-time, because the space of potentiality is pleromatic, not exclusive. But the "collapse" of the wave-function forces one state to become (defined as) "real" over all others, particle over wave, to be expressed *in* space-time, the appearance of a subject-object contrast (an observer-constituted measurement), and the like. So, here, the "end"-fusion forces the spiritual heavens to reveal themselves as *physical equivalents*. In other words, in reversion of the movement by which the spiritual dimensionality is mapped onto the physical expanse in case of the question of alien intelligence, now, the material appearances of the physical expanse are, however subtle, projected onto the spiritual dimensions, plateaus, layers, and transcendental planes of integrity as if they were just *rarified physical states*. This "fusion" of the mapping process is, again, one of *literalism*, undermining the fundamental differences in the dipolar approach from any dualism that only works by oppositional states of the same: matter and form, information and energy, heaven and earth, lose their "superposition" and collapse to an "end-state" in which one side is erased and the other side becomes the *sole* reality. This dualism is built on a "oneness" in which one side is real and the other an illusion.

Here is a general perspective from which we can see how such a dualism operates in the mapping process of the expanse onto the spiritual planes of existence: First, soul and body are thought of being just different "beings" of some kind of similar character, such as some kind of matter or energy, or stuff or substance, or form or character, only differentiated in terms of crudeness or refinedness. Such a view appears with the materialist ideas of the soul as some kind of information or software in the body as some kind of hardware. This is not a monism, as, in fact, any such monism is based on a dualism that denies one side of reality and considers it an illusion. Such a dualism also appears with ideas of the soul to be a higher frequency of light or energy, of being a "rarified element" like all physical elements or being involved in a linear or cyclical stratification of bodies of energy. Religious beliefs that think of life after death as shadowy existence in the oblivion of Hades (as early Greek and Hebrew thinking) and the elaborated imaginations of the resurrection of the dead with or without their material body, now transformed into a heavenly body, *all* are of the same kind of dualistic "apocalyptic" mapping, because they project a prolongation, however subtle, of our phenomenal life into an afterlife or a higher plane.

Another form of such a mapping happens if we assume a dualist *mutual exclusiveness* of mind and matter, spirit and body—which is only on the surface in opposition to the phenomenal monism just mentioned! On a deeper level, however, such a dualism has already transformed the Aristotelian "duality" of principles (*ens quo*), matter and form, into beings (*ens quod*)—as already related in chapter 6—and, hence, created the subject-object dualism by which both sides are just expressions of the same, but cannot be fused without one of them to become subjugated under the other or "apocalyptically" to be erased "in the end." Even if such dualist opposition relates contrary characteristics to both sides, for instance, space-time locality on the one side and non-locality on the other, such differences are often used to map physical appearances, for instance, of quantum reality, onto spiritual immortality. For instance, when the physical body is understood to be a "projection" of the vibrating pattern of a light-body (via many New Age religions and movements), or when the material universe is understood as a three-dimensional "projection" of a two-dimensional holographic order of energy and light (via David Bohm), or as a kind of intelligent order of higher frequency than this world, the "apocalyptic" turn preserves the higher realm as a "truer" state of still another (if rarified) but same energy-information "field" that unmasks the physical world as an ephemeral illusion of such a projection process (via diverse forms of "quantum spirituality"). Theories like that often use modern physical language and insights to project it onto the symbolic language of religions and hope that this "demythologizing" literalization of religious symbolizations may either save their intelligibility in current times of quantum physics and relativity theory, or finally decode their secret *as* physical reality, or demonstrate their truth with scientific evidence. But all of them live from this "apocalyptic" mapping process.

Instead, the "dipolar" view—as elaborated in chapter 5—avoids such simplifying mapping and, instead, follows the differentiations "into their beginning" and creative release, into the vibrating Spirit and the first light of creation, as a differentiation process that cannot be reversed, that has no end, that is infinitely differentiating itself—symbolically, like the sun that gives its light away and the Sun of the Good in Plato, which overflows with goodness in pleromatic fullness without ever taking anything back. Plotinus's hypostases of the One, Mind and World-Soul (and Matter) are of his kind: they *don't imitate* one another; they *cannot be reflected* into one another (as if they were the same, but only more rarified); but they are also *not oppositional* realities (as if they were beings opposed to one another instead of principles), as they are *all released from* the One. Yet the One is *nothing like* the Mind, and so on, as all appearances are not illusions, but *ways of overflow* and an *irreversible pleroma* of multiple realizations. Cusanus's "wall of paradise," mentioned in chapter 7, is of such a character: non-imitative, a *boundary* between infinity and finiteness that does not allow for imitation of the same or of the opposition of opposites, as it is the coincidence of opposites and the movement of complication and explication of folds that are *one in their difference* in the world and *one beyond any difference* in God. Instead of the many mythical cosmic realms of *samsara*, which are only such dualist mappings, the Buddhist teaching of the impossibility of "crossing the river" of *samsara* to reach *nirvana*—as elaborated in chapter 3—is of the "dipolar" character: no mapping can reach it, no apocalyptic breakdown can erase the differences of apophatic unity and polyphilic multiplicity "between" them—as they are *one* counter-movement, much like the ascent and descent in the image of the mountaineer of the previous chapter. All of them avoid the mapping of/into the same and instead *mirror* the impossible in mutual inherence—there is no "apocalyptic" collapse of dualisms, but only *creative release of differences*; there is no reduction to illusion, but only *the mirage of the mirror*: different realities, nondually folded up in apophatic unity, but without any *essentialized* oneness or difference.

And so, our age-old quest for spiritual fulfillment in relation to the desire for immortality must be detached from the dualistic, seemingly monist or oppositional, views of mapping and be transformed into a mirroring of dipolar movements of apophatic unification and polyphilic differentiation. Instead of dualisms of opposing realities or, more so, of appearance and reality, or of the disappearance of illusions, we want to address the mirage of multiplicity, impermanence and death in light of their gift, affirmative of their reality, but enfolded and mirrored in either horizons or planes of reality that smoothly encompass some of them without any break, and are discretely enveloped by others. In this view of enfoldings of *horizons*, touched on especially in chapters 2 and 7, we can avoid to view immortality, first, as that of a "thing," a being, a soul, as one among other beings like tables and fruitcakes; second, as that of an "energy-being" that is the origin of the illusion of the body, or that even is itself an illusion of a higher refined reality (as the *pneuma* of the Stoics, the *atman* or *brahman* of Hinduism, or the common Buddha-nature); and, third, as itself being an illusion (there is no immortality!), as the discontinuity between this life and the deathless realm of God is a question of salvation and, hence, doesn't know of any continuity. Several religious views hold on to one or the other of these "rarified" reconstitutions of patterns to survive death or to be independent of physical existence or to be immortal in one way or another, either in character or in bodily existence, as the paradigm of resurrection of Zoroastrianism and the orthodoxies of Christianity and Islam have suggested, but not of Judaism, which over the centuries developed the most diversified views in these matters (without any of them becoming reduced to orthodoxy).

The closest the Jewish views on life after death came to such a view of mirroring of the mirage of realities within horizons of horizons, was the hope of the book of Daniel that the "just ones" will become "stars in heaven." While this sounds as mythological as any other view: reincarnation, resurrection, and the like, it, in fact, *excluded* the mapping of earlier desires for historical resurrections of the people of God onto the resurrection of individuals, but also any view that prolonged life "after" death as, what Ludwig Feuerbach once called, just "a change of horses." Instead, the *transfiguration into stars*, into the *host of the heaven of heavens*, takes the firmament *neither* as another physical expanse (the error of bodily resurrection imaginations) *nor* as a boundary mapping the nether life into a higher one, of the same kind but of a different level or vibration. Instead, in all symbolic intensity that it implies, this image of the "soul" as heavenly "star," uses light imagery in order to convey something *completely beyond our imagination*: namely, that *we are of the nature of the heavenly host*, of the angelic nondual origination in the pre-creation *vibration* of the Spirit, and of the *first light* of creation! *Immortality, here, means to be nondually indifferent from God in God, but as different as possible from God in the world of multiplicity and becoming.* It is this nondual "beginning" in the unity of infinity and finiteness by which we are a *discontinuous unique soul* and, concurrently, a *continuous wave* of the one Mind of God. In the language of the Wisdom literature: We are *of* the Wisdom of God, the non-different creator-creature (Proverbs 8; Wisdom 7; Sirach 24); we are *mirrors* of this Wisdom, as Wisdom is the mirror of the *apophatic* divine Reality. Because only divine Reality exists in its own reality, *nothing else exists*—all is *enfolded* to the extent and the intensity of the complete indifference from divine Reality. However, as *Wisdom is the mirror of apophatic indifference*, and, hence, is its multiplicity of creation, *our* "divine reality" is apophatically *hidden* and only mirroring itself in the *multiplicity* of the world of becoming, impermanence, bodily existence and other layers of realization. In *one* horizon we are *nonexistent*, in *another* we are waves *of* the Mind of God; at *another* level we are *unique* unisons of nexuses binding a multiplicity of composition and decompositions of events and processes, at *another* level still we are *nothing but* these compositions that for a time live and then die.

Since we live in *all* of these horizons *all* the time and *beyond* time, immortality is not a consequence, but a *presupposition* of our life—what we call "soul" is really, as already Zoroastrian psychology understood, living in this world as one of the layers of unification the highest of which, the *fravashi*, are enfolded in the divine or angelic unity with God. It is not the *highest layer of existence* in Sufi psychology, as the unity with God would mean *fana*, annihilation of Self, and *baqa*, eternal living in God, would be nondually non-different from God. However, even this "non-existence" is not the "highest" form of existence, as the unknowable apophatic Godhead beyond all unity and difference *cannot be said to exist at all* (like Plato's Good) or, is the only existence, although beyond all existence, as there in this "highest" horizon of all horizons Reality itself is *beyond all possible categories*.

The Spirit is this fullness of all horizons and the ability to pervade all of them. This Spirit is *in* all horizons *their* form or formlessness of unity and difference, the motive force of their becoming and life, but also never identical with either of them—rather always *the wider horizon in which* they can happen, *the purpose and lure* for their realization and transformation on ever wider horizons of existence. *While all beings may be mirrored in all horizons, not all live in all horizons.* So, we will say for all spiritual beings, to the extent that they have become awakened, that they are awakening to the horizons that they *are* already, just in the mode of *sleep*. And it may be the real purpose of spiritual becoming to awaken to these *highest* horizons. It may be the purpose of immortality to indicate the involvement of spiritual beings, such as humans, but probably not only humanity, even on this earth, to be in the process of awakening in *all* of these horizons. But this may not, as many religions have imperfectly, or in symbolic superabundance, realized in their imagination of cycles of reincarnation or futures of resurrection, happen at once, although this is also not excluded, but may be a *process* of more than one physical life. It may be an *infinite spiritual process in the approximation* to the Sun of Reality, the horizon in which all unifications and differentiations connect in ways that cannot be mapped one into the other with simple imaginations of unity and multiplicity. Perhaps, in this infinite spiritual journey of awakening of the horizons of horizons, we may express awareness and sleep differently at different phases such that the life that we experience in this and beyond this bodily life in the physical universe will be different for us in relation to these expressions.

Today, many reflections on these matters come from near-death experiences (NDEs) the serious collection of data of which made the matter of life after death one of increasing experimental and empirical investigation. Without going into the science and reservoir of images expressed in NDEs, the reported imaginations, visions, visualizations and conceptualizations expressed by NDEs are reflexive of that which many religious teachings, whether in eastern or western context, whether in ancient witnesses (that we can identify today as NDEs) or in modern religious movement (which take these experiences more systematically into account), relate about the question of existence beyond death: a *phase one* of the dissociation of consciousness from the body, becoming light; and a *phase two* of the transformation into other dimensions and worlds of vivid light, the encounter of light-beings, of relatives and friends, of guides, of a vast cosmos, God; but also a *phase three* of a more or less permanent transformation of a new life after the event. Yet in collective summary, they (the experiences and images) remain incoherent, varied and relative to religious and cautiously inherited forms, as well as, most importantly, *beyond* any fit to *any* religious orthodoxy. Hence, it is without a doubt a problem of their consistency that NDE-reports exhibit spectra or ranges of experiences of strongly divergent kinds that are rather bewildering as long as they are not seen in the perspective of the *diverse horizons within horizons* of the *spiritual spectral complexity* of our spiritual journey and immortal expanse of existence throughout these horizons between God (nothingness) and nothingness (mere matter).

Yet if we take this shift of perspective into account, we will be able to align experiences of darkness or absence of light with that of the many forms of light experiences; we will be able to relate experiences of dazzling darkness and of worlds populated with other beings; we will be able to concurrently accept that some "souls" experience the world as refined version of nature or civilization, others as a cosmos of formless grandeur. These are all an expression of levels of awakening in horizons of more or less imaginations, mirages, creative projections or their transcendence. It is in this sense that mystical experiences and NDEs are not only equivalent—as all of these awakenings happen in mystical experiences throughout all religions and even to people who consider themselves as mere materialists—but of the *same kind*; they are but *different intensities* of the awakening to the "immortality" that is the matrix we move through in the process of spiritual awakening. A sage once said: if you need your dog in the afterlife, it will be there. Yet, like Plotinus's One, the less you need or have, the closer you are to the *horizon* of the One that has nothing and needs nothing, but overflows in love into all horizons of the immortal spectrum of horizons of life.

Of the ancient religious symbolization of this "immortality spectrum" it is perhaps St. Paul's vision of the *soma pneumatikon*, the spiritual body, and the web of ideas it embodies (1 Corinthians 15) that comes closest to the "horizontal" spiritual integration that I am proposing, here. It comes closest by the avoidance of mapping simplifications and reductionist dualisms, be they materialist (resurrection of the body) or spiritualist (disembodies souls), individualist (personal survival throughout death and resurrection of reincarnations) or collectivist (living in the memory of children or God; dissolving in the unity with God; or being extinguished in the *nirvana* beyond Self)—by explaining the difference between bodily existence in this world of becoming and heavenly existence (as an angel, a being of light, in the divine sphere) with three characterizations: first, *no similarity, but connectivity*, like the seed and the tree are connected, but have no formal continuity; second, *no sameness* of expression of immortality between different creations, as the glory of the sun is different from that of the moon; *no life without death*, that is, without awakening to a new horizon of life that needs the encompassed horizon to "die" as the (only seemingly) "ultimate" horizon, which is always a process of death and rebirth. In this sense, the most radical expression of St. Pauls' "spiritual body" is that it has overcome the horizon of the soul-body, *soma psychikon* (1 Corinthians 15:44): it is not the "soul" that survives, the soul that is the life-principle of our movement in the horizons of our earthly existence in the evolution from matter to mind; it is the "spirit" that *is not possessed*, by any creature individually or collectively, that is "bodying" on *all* levels or in *all* horizons the existence as it is spiritually awakened on these levels or in these horizons, engrossingly dispossessed of the desires that separates it from dying to all of these horizons in order to live in the awaked ones. The process of detachment of this spiritual bodying is not aiming at the disappearance of the detached, but their appearance in another horizon as integral to it.

The cosmic Spirit is the purposive attractor of the awakening to that horizon that possesses nothing, is nothing (for itself), needs nothing, but gives everything absolutely in love, and feels everything in absolute compassion.

Finally, we ought *not* to understand this "spectral body of horizons" in which we are immortal phases of awakening as linear or hierarchical layers, but rather as multiply connected and inter-coherent webs of planes of immanence by which no individual spiritual journey is the same, and by which no religious conviction is the same. Yet all of them, all levels of awakening, are connected as in a cycle of oscillation, of mutual immanence, and of simultaneous counter-movements of ascent and descent; not by a static cycle, but always utterly and infinitely moving in counter-movements that include, but transcend beyond, space and time. Like Plotinus's "hypostases," they are not hierarchical levels, but mutually moving *mirrors of otherness* connected by movements of expansion and contraction, enfolding and unfolding. As in A. N. Whitehead's "cycle of love," the impermanent world of events and becomings cycle through the eternal Mind of God (the space and process of the imagination and valuation of potentials and values) and the realm of divine experiences in which the world's actualizations of potentials and values are transformed into all-relational transfigurations of the "all in all" in the Memory of God in order to flood back into the world of becoming, instigating creativity and renewal. As we awaken to these horizons of divine perception, that is, the divine kingdom, in the *theosis* of the world, and to the realm of primordial potentials and pure divine values, we become "horizontally" but not hierarchically, mutually but not unilaterally or linearly, awakened to horizons *far beyond* any limited views of the soul and immortality, or of resurrection or reincarnation, or of bodies and other markers of identity—but *not* in order to just disappear in God or any indifferent reality. Rather, spiritual awaking means to cycle back in self-less love *into* the world for *its* transformation.

These are the movements of the Spirit: the horizon of all horizons becomes manifest in all horizons in selfless love for the awakening in them.

Epilogue: Immolation

Of all the potential spiritual uses of the image of the starry heavens, the light, the immensity of the space, the enormity of the numbers of stars (and planets and moons and comets and asteroids, and so on), the diversity of their characters, the stunning multiplicity of forms, sizes, and colors—one fact worth thinking about is captured by the epigraph of Whitehead in this chapter: by shining, stars waste away!

While our imagination has used stars or suns to indicate eternity, greatness, warmth, life, rarified bodies, and spiritual heights, no detractor of such images will, in a scientific age as ours, at least, be convinced of the relevance of these elevating suggestions if we will not, at the same time, also acknowledge the illusion of these projections. Stars don't live eternally. In fact, they have interesting histories of becoming, and they die. They do also not hold ethereal matter, which Aristotle and the ancients understood to be of very different constitution than the sub-lunar material we live in and embody. In fact, they are the very material we are made of; what is more, they produce this material in the first place. We are—it is already a cliché—stardust, born from exploding, dying stars.

The chemical and quantum physical as well as relativistic processes and consequences are well known and make one of the most colorful stories of becoming and perishing of the great and violent realities in the cosmos, a show second to none. These light-shows perform the collective memory of violence and their outcome in explosions, compactifications, apocalyptic end-states, in their long way of dissipation into darkness. The greatest miracles of all are even invisible, as they do not emit light, but only swallow whatever comes their way: black holes are singularities, boundaries of the natural laws, strange objects of dark beauty and mind-bending, light-bending, time and space-bending extravagance. In a sense, "eternity" appears again, here, in the permanent death of all matter and energy, as its light disappears beyond the event horizon and—never disappears "beyond" it, as everything leaves its imprint on the "screen" of the flat horizon *forever*; at the horizon where time slows down to "eternal arrest." That is, as long as the sphere this horizon covers does not itself evaporate, which it does, although in painful slow motion, over 10 to the power of 100 years, maybe longer than the rest of the universe exists if it was not yet swallowed by these long-living sinks of energy-matter and primordial physical forces, space-time and gravity.

Sure, stars come in generations, the old ones show off when they die, the young ones form from what the geriatric elders leave behind. But, literally: what a colossal *waste* of matter-energy, space-time! The life cycle of stars that light up this vast universe for no reason at all, but following some strange rules of the interaction of matter-energy and space-time, is not a sign of eternity and heavenly light. If it is a sign of anything, it seems, it is one of the *immolation* of beings for the becoming of other beings, just to contribute again to their violent (exploding) or excruciatingly slow dimming, just stretching out the meaningless time of a universe that, in the end, seems to have had no reason to exist, in the first place, except to indicate (to itself) nothing more than this artistic act of disappearance. Counter to so many of the spiritual impulses that stars have held in the history of human cosmological reflection and religious veneration, the starry heavens are no divine host, but a host of scary figures. Stars are the greatest artists of death and the wonders of disintegration.

I will say more about this question of meaning in a cosmos, such as the one we happen to live in, in the following chapter. Here, I want to highlight an aspect of this change of perspective that might surprise: It is precisely in this current knowledge of the life of stars that we find reflected one of the oldest documented spiritual disciplines of humanity: that of *alchemy*. For the ancients, in the primordial great civilizations for which we still have records, the stars were related to alchemy by way of astronomy/astrology, that is, minding the heavenly constellations of the Zodiac, the movements of the planets, the rhythms of sun and moon, and of extraordinary phenomena, such as shooting stars and eclipses. All of these appearances of lights and their movements were defining imprints of events in space and time, historical singularities, but also of the inescapable destiny of the cosmic revolutions of ages and eons.

Spiritual disciplines, among them alchemy, were reflections, correlations, sympathetic movements, parallels between the heavenly movements and the mundane events as well as the universes enveloped in the mind of humanity, individually and collectively. Both the starry heavens and the alchemical processes were references to one another in the sense that they constituted the same basic elements of creation, such as the rarified and distilled pure substances of air, water, fire, and earth (for some cultures add metals and wood). As the stars were the "pure matters" of all forms (ideas), the angels were made of heavenly substances, the representative of the highest purity of the materials and forces of creation in the presence of the creator and fashioner of all of its combinations. And so was the alchemical process one of a *purification* of all the elements and a *recombination* that would *reflect the purity of the heavens*. Alchemy, although physical in its outward nature, was the process by which the human spirit was awakened *by* a process of the physical and spiritual purification, elementarization, and new, heavenly recombination of the elements into a transformed spiritual being. Alchemy was about the indifferent boundary between matter and spirit, on the one hand, and earthly and divine substances of the spiritual process, on the other.

Alchemy is the process of the *indifferentiation* between mind, soul and body, as well as matter and spirit, by way of purification. But like the *transformation of the elements* in the stars' self-immolation, the whole process rests on a *transmutation* that consists of elementary *disintegration of all elements*, material and spiritual, that is, a process of death, and a process of *recombination* of the purified elements to a new being, a *new creation*, the true human being, *theosis*, the becoming of a manifestation of God. In burning away all detachments, "spiritual alchemy" is this process of dying and reconfiguration, as the immolation of the star is the transmutation of all elements into new elements for the creation of a variegated universe of forms and substances, of diverse frequencies and landscapes. These transmutations in the heath of stars are gifts of the birth of "heavenly" beings—as we are all born into these "heavens."

There is another, deeper dimension to this "spiritual immolation" inherent to the "alchemical" nature of the Spirit expressing itself in symbolisms of light and fire: that of the unity of all light (of insight and being, reason and feeling, truth and reality) in the darkness of apophatic nonduality and its creative indifference (chs. 2 and 6). While the nondual path of embodying spiritual light means (paradoxically, alchemically) the immolation of all bodies that remain as a substrate of the difference between the manifold of light and apophatic darkness—much in the sense of the Buddhist sensitivity to the perpetuation of karmic seeds by samsaric desires, ignorance, or even the seed-consciousness (*alaya vijnana*)—the creative indifference of the revealing release of light from divine darkness is (paradoxically, alchemically) the embodiment of apophatic darkness *in* the manifold of lights (of reason, revelation, wisdom, goodness, and the like) in which the Spirit (symbolically) pervades all existence. Both forms of spiritual immolation, that of following light disappearing in, or being burned away into, ultimate darkness and that of the release of light from divine darkness, are on the deepest level expressions of the same alchemical process, namely, of that of the *nondual indifferentiation* between light and darkness—not a simple fusion, however, but the mutual movement of (pre-original) darkness into (the creative cycle of) light, in which darkness hides under light, and of (the creative processes of) lights (in their spiritual pathways) into (apophatic) darkness, in which light is hidden.

Both biblical visons of the creative process, the becoming of light at the beginning of the book of Genesis and the mystical rendering of the divine light of the Logos (Word, Wisdom, Reason, Order, Power, Spirit) in the Prologue of the Gospel of John, assume divine darkness: the Spirit hovering over the darkness in which the elements of dry wasteland and fathomless depth of the sea lie, and the Silence/Darkness from which the Word/Light/Life of the creative agent arises, respectively (ch. 2).

This has an important implication for the deeper meaning and spiritual rendering of light symbolism as such: that we must be careful to avoid or counter the dualistic simplifications of its use, which tends to further expressions of destructive dualisms and, especially, stirs up the deep-seated racist tendencies it can carry. Anti-blackness is one of the most abhorrent forms of racism and misanthropy. And it has been entangled with the division of the world into physical, psychological, spiritual, and philosophical categories of light and darkness. It is (from the perspective of the oppressor or structural elite profiting from such associations) easy to overlook the underlying simplistic and dualistic associations of light with goodness and divinity and of darkness with evil and satanic forces, or, at least, as implying some kind of superiority of the light of reason and revelation over against the darkness of stupidity and infidelity, which have accumulated around cultural arrangements that habitually and pervasively harbor racist overtones or justify racist social structures.

So, in awareness of these perversions, one of the counter measures must be the practice, in language and action, of the deeper spiritual, mystical, alchemical immolation expressed in the categorial nonduality of divine indifference that avoids, counters and even heals the problematic dualization of light and darkness. Even the duality of light and darkness in the Prologue of the Gospel of John, which—in its literal, not its mystical interpretation—assumes the association of light and life with divine reality and of darkness with ignorance, evil, and death, can be misused in this sense. However, it is a vivid image of 'Abdu'l-Bahá, the son of the prophet-founder of the Bahá'í religion, Bahá'u'lláh, that captures the paradoxical, alchemical nature of the light imagery in spiritual respects, and counters such associations or justifications head-on: Blackness is not the opposite of light, but, as the blackness of the pupil of the eye, the site of light entering the world and of the means of spiritual birth. In effect, in one of the strongest images of anti-black anti-racism, Bahá'u'lláh makes us hope that the spiritual renewal of humanity will arise from the black peoples of the world.

Meditation XVI: The Stellar Blanket

We all know, from experience, literature, or movies, that one of the most archetypical forms of the awakening to the starry heavens above is to lie down on some ground, be it in a yard or on the roof of a house, and just look straight up to the blanket that covers us and the whole earth at night. If we are lucky and seek out "dark sky" places where we can, undisturbed from the air smog and light noise of cities and industrial complexes, just enjoy the darkness between us and the universe, the Milky Way, the Zodiac, and the manifold of lights as a whole and individually, we will be stunned ever anew by the sheer uncountability of the millions and billions of stars and galaxies. Immanuel Kant, as stated by the related epigraph to this chapter, understood this experience as one of the two fundamentals in this world we can trust—the other being the ethical call of our personhood: that we are persons, aims, not means. A. N. Whitehead found this experience to be one of the "vague presences" of the "far away," the spatial and temporal past (given relativity theory) and "the other," in *this* moment, here and now.

> ... the sight at night, of the stars and nebulae and Milky Way, illustrates vague regions of the contemporary sky ... (*Process and Reality*, 122)

In *Process and Reality* (1929) and in *Adventures of Ideas* (1933), Whitehead explains this connectivity *beyond* space and time by referring to the potential of the mental *immediacy* of physically distant events, an immediacy that we can understand to be of fundamentally *spiritual* nature—as will be explored further in the next chapter. In the following quotes the "physical pole" of every event in this universe means the physical constitution of every event by other physical actualities or facts; the "mental pole," however, refers to the clouds of potentials or ideas, realized or unrealized, in the valuation process of an actuality. Insofar as every event is always a (becoming of the) tension of both poles, physicality and ideality, actualization and potentials, every new fact is the outcome of a valuation process and every fact is only a fact in a new valuation process. In this sense, immediacy of ideal, potential, mental and spiritual connectivity is not necessarily bound by the physical laws that govern their physical integration. We *can* genially feel others and distant events as immediately realizing their valuation process, their heart and ideality to us, if we become awake and perceptive.

It is not necessary for the philosophy of organism entirely to deny that there is direct objectification of one occasion in a later occasion which is not contiguous to it. Indeed, the contrary opinion would seem the more natural for this doctrine. Provided that physical science maintains its denial of "action at a distance," the safer guess is that direct objectification is practically negligible except for contiguous occasions; but that this practical negligibility is a characteristic of the present cosmic epoch, without any metaphysical generality. . . .

Indeed the contrary hypothesis is the more natural. For the conceptual pole does not share in the coordinate divisibility of the physical pole, and the extensive continuum is derived from this coordinate divisibility. Thus the doctrine of immediate objectification for the mental poles and of mediate objectification for the physical poles seems most consonant to the philosophy of organism in its application to the present cosmic epoch. This conclusion has some empirical support, both from the evidence for peculiar instances of telepathy, and from the instinctive apprehension of a tone of feeling in ordinary social intercourse. (*Process and Reality*, 307–8)

Perhaps in the mutual immanence of occasions, although the antecedence and the consequence,—the past, the present and the future—still hold equally for physical and mental poles, yet the relations of the mental poles to each other are not subject to the same laws of perspective as are those of the physical poles. Measureable [sic] time and measureable [sic] space are then irrelevant to their mutual connections. Thus in respect to some types of Appearance there may be an element of immediacy in its relations to the mental side of the contemporary world. (*Adventures of Ideas*, 248)

One of the reasons—important for the next chapter—is that the unity of ideas, potentials, as well as mental and spiritual realities is *not divisible* in the same sense as physical realities (or the physical pole of any reality): this unity cannot be physically represented, but, conversely: physical composition is only an approximation to the trans-spatiotemporal "form" of universals such as consciousness, self, mind, formless space, and the like. Yet, this also implies that there are "polar" mutual connections between the spiritual and the physical, fact and value, potential and actualization in any event and process, organism and the universe as a whole—as will be emphasized in the Epilogue to this book—by which this "cosmic epoch" seem to be a physical multiplicity *enfolding* this spiritual wholeness, but with no *metaphysical* necessity binding *all* "cosmic epochs" to be of the *same* restrictions: that means, *spiritualization can transform the universe* (this cosmic epoch) so as to unfold the spiritual pole to *envelope* the physical multiplicity, instead of just being its inherent but fragile flame (see ch. 1).

Whether, in light of this genuine immediacy of the presence of the universe as felt in view of the light-veil of stars on our face and in our heart, we meditate on the immense *spaciousness* of the heavens or the scintillating *lights*, their *plenitude* or their *endlessness*, the *darkness* embracing them and us, or whether we feel the immense *distances* between us and them or *project* on the many worlds out there the souls of the dead, of other sentient beings, or even of the heavenly court—we will immediately understand what the *Dao De Ching* (Verse 73; Star, 86) says about the heavens in relation to us, recognizing the impact on us in wisdom.

> Who can know the reasons of heaven?
>
> Who can know its endless ways?
>
> Not even the sage has an answer to this one.
>
> Heaven's way does not strive
>
> Yet it always overcomes
>
> It does not speak, yet it responds
>
> It is not summoned, yet it appears
>
> It does not hurry, yet it completes everything on time
>
> The net of Heaven spans the universe
>
> Yet not the slightest thing ever slips by

This, besides the intellectual meditations of Whitehead's text above, may be one of the most profound insights of immediate awakening to the cosmic Spirit to contemplate.

Please recite Verse 73 of the Dao De Ching *again, several times, until every phrase and the process of their progression forms a wordless, imageless imagination in your centered (folded) and decentered (universally distributed and perceiving) consciousness—that which Confucianism designates as* xin, *as heart-mind.*

. . .

As soon as you recognize that this has happened, begin again, as you have, in this moment of recognition, lost the immediacy of xin.

9

The Life of Other Days

My own true inner being actually exists in every living creature as truly and immediately as known to my consciousness only in myself.
—ARTHUR SCHOPENHAUER, *THE WORLD AS WILL AND REPRESENTATION*

Greatness no longer matters. We see now that each human being who dies is the center of a universe: a unique spark of hope and despair, hate and love, going alone into the greater darkness.
—ARTHUR C. CLARKE AND STEPHEN BAXTER, *THE LIGHT OF OTHER DAYS*

Briefly, there were many universal cycles preceding this one in which we are living. They were consummated, completed and their traces obliterated. The divine and creative purpose in them was the evolution of spiritual man, just as it is in this cycle. The circle of existence is the same circle; it returns. The tree of life has ever borne the same heavenly fruit.
—ABDU'L-BAHÁ, *PROMULGATION*, #79

Thus Peace is self-control at its widest,—at the width where the "self" has been lost, and interest has been transferred to coordinations wider than personality. Here the real motive interests of the spirit are meant, and not the superficial play of discursive ideas. Peace is helped by such superficial width, and also promotes it. In fact it is largely for this reason that Peace is so essential for civilization.
—A. N. WHITEHEAD, *ADVENTURES OF IDEAS* (285-86)

The Cosmic Spirit

Prologue: Matrix

THIS NINTH PATH IS about *time*. In spiritual contexts, this often amounts to the modes in which temporality is suspended by reference to the true reality of the present moment (*nunc stans*), reversed to experiences and concepts of timelessness and eternity, and reverse-projected onto ultimate Reality or God as non-temporal liberation from time's indignities. Yet references to these spiritual expressions of time, temporality or, rather, its suspension in experiences of timelessness, eternity, the perfect moment or a-temporal universal unity—so often reported to be of the essence of mystical experiences—have actually already had a pervasive "presence" in all of the preceding eight paths of this book: the experience of space as non-temporal spiritual emptiness or multiplicity; the diverse forms of temporal experiences of impermanence and becoming throughout the elemental explorations of water, light, fire, and their deconstruction "from behind the curtain" of the stage of temporality; the diverse forms of approaches to ultimate Reality that all need some consciousness of the mirage of temporality, the differentiations in past, present and future, or of their variability and relativity; the involvement of forms of differentiation or the unification of modes of temporality or a-temporality in the processes of self-transcendence such as altered states of consciousness; the *unio mystica* as a diversified multiplicity of experiences of complex time-suspensions; and the like.

Yet in clear differentiation from the non-temporal reductionism of temporality in such spiritual, religious, and philosophical contexts, all forms of the thematization of time in the preceding eight paths were set in a new horizon, namely, that of the access to the cosmic Spirit through forms of *becoming*—the most profound unity in multiplicity of time and timelessness in a spiritual universe. In this sense, all nine paths *are* about "spiritual time" or the Spirit-time, but not in the sense of a mere overcoming of its temporality or transitoriness by desired or imagined modes of non-temporal unity—which must be lamented as a mere flight *from* the world, which again is a spiritual deviation (or deprivation), not the "aim" of the Spirit. Rather, as should by now have become clear as one of the basic theses of this book: If the cosmic Spirit is the *unity of cosmic becoming*, then, the spiritualization *of* temporality happens as *the unison of the comic multiplicity*—always instigating, sustaining and transforming "its" (the Spirit's) cosmic manifestations as "its" own mode of insistence *on* becoming and "its" non-difference *from* it (see the epilogue to the book). Spiritual life is about time, because spiritual time is about *Life*.

I have also already, throughout the previous eight paths, referred to the material and mental poles of the unity of events of becoming, which in their process are the unification of the multiplicities of experiences of events in the context of a cloud of non-temporal possibilities. And we have seen that these sym-pathies of past and future, repetition and novelty, materiality and mentality, exteriority and interiority, space and time, are also expressions of the intricate mutual immanence of God and the world—especially in the perspective of A. N. Whitehead's understanding. We need only to remind ourselves, here, of this spiritual unison of time and eternity in this "dipolarity" of God and the world as based in the "dipolarity" of the creative nature (primordial, timeless, but instigating becoming) and the perceptive nature (consequent, everlasting and transforming becoming) of God, and, even more profoundly, of both of them in the "dipolarity" of unmanifest and manifest Reality (see ch. 5).

What will be the issue in this chapter are two elements of "spiritual time" that are not as often registered or reflected on, but which are all the more profound for the spirit-matter of *becoming*: first, the multiplicity of *magnitudes of becoming* as forming a matrix of "time" and "eternity" that explains infinitely divergent *and* unifying movements between them as the merely abstract limits of a living phenomenon; and second, the spiritual "temporality" of *cosmic multiplicity* itself in its diverse magnitudes, from "other lives" to "other universes" and their nondual, self-transcendent "materialization" in modes of becoming that *include* our Selves or in which we "become" (what we always already are, namely:) spiritual Selves.

I will reflect on *magnitudes of becoming* in a threefold manner. First, it is about magnitude in the *singular* insofar as it reverses the folds of the first chapter: what was the small flame in all things, there and then, now, in the end, becomes the universal movement of spiritual transformation enveloping the whole cosmos. Second, it is about magnitudes in the *plural*, as they concretize the global movements that they engage with universals representing fundamental dimensions of spiritual transformation. Third, it is about what it *means* to be a magnitude, namely, to indicate a spectrum of either more or less, or of emphases of something to be internal or external—but, in any case, of everything to appear on a scale or in a matrix of related scales. Let me explain these three dimensions further, individually, and how they together compose the net of ideas of this chapter.

The first way to engage magnitude, here, is by way of stating the bridge between the beginning and the ending of this book as a process of transformation from an inward foldedness of Spirit to its enveloping by *everting* the inside to the universal space itself in which all thing with their spiritual indivisibility connect. It is about the *internal* connection of all things—whether we follow ancient paradigms of universal sympathy, as in Plotinus, or the interdependent co-arising, as in the *pratitya-samutpada* of the Buddhist traditions, or the modern paradigm of holism and the holographic All, that is, the encoding of the All in every minute piece of it (whatever those pieces are: like strings or other field-particles or an infinite sea of rhythmic and harmonic vibrations). Yet, this internality is now understood as a process of transformation by which it becomes the *external* field, the *manifest* Platonic or Derridean or Whiteheadian *khora* (see ch. 1), the universal *enveloping* Spirit, manifesting itself (its Self) in the multiplicity of cosmic (and physical) appearances.

This does, of course, *not* mean, in a naïve repetition of eschatological expectations, to actually be able to *revert* this physical universe in the hope for it to become a purely spiritual one. It lies in the nature of spiritual matrix that it does avoid schemes of eschatological closure to become part of considerations about either the cosmic limitations of existence or religious imaginations regarding its future. While even physical cosmology allows for scenarios of endings, obliteration, and oblivion of the cosmic process, it has no inherent instrument to define such limitations as eschatological, but rather must always already presuppose existence as infinite process or our universe as a finite process in an open context. While eschatological timelines or goals at which the universe would "end" (but never completely, as even in such cases assumptions of other realms prevail), are often disastrous when they activate the matrix only in order to make it a means for another aim, entirely, namely, the overcoming of the cosmos, the cosmic Spirit is always creatively sustaining and newly initiating spiritual immanence. The cosmic "matrix" wants to evoke the *creative transformation* of the cosmos, not its end or overcoming. Religious images of the Spirit, referring to saturated states of divine presence, must be understood not as end-scenarios, but as expressions of the underlying motive force of the cosmic matrix. The life of "Other Days" is a life of "New Days," not of the "Last Day."

The "Last Day" would also *not* justify the image of "the Kingdom of God on Earth," as it would have obliterated the earth in a fundamentally non-ecological vision of apocalyptic forgetfulness. This would be dualism, again, that opposes spirit and matter—something that the more sophisticated versions of such a cosmic transformation process have avoided, such as the vision of Teilhard de Chardin of the infinite Omega Point, which may not be reached at any point in any becoming universe, but which may rather be understood as the point of ever-new beginnings, of the "final cause" of its very *becoming* (see, again, ch. 1). As intellectually reflected on in Meditation VXI with Whitehead's *dipolarity* of every happening—namely, to be physical and mental, objective and subjective, form and activity, creativity and receptivity, all at once—the starry heavens continue to be a symbol of the complexity of this process of transformation in which light remains enveloped by darkness harbored by which it shines in plentiful forms and constellations, although the khoric field of space is itself not only externality, but a manifestation—perhaps a mirage (see ch. 6)—of the internal connectedness of all the lights. This is the magnitude of the reversal of internality and externality by which the whole universe comes into view as polyphilic manifestation of the Spirit without obliterating, but rather emphasizing the concrete diversity, diversification, and divergence of the concreteness of such manifestations, but also by becoming visible as folds of one *khora*, field, space, continuum.

In this continuum of diverse manifestations, we can also discover a *second* sense of magnitudes pervading this process of universal cosmic spiritual transformation. These are the aspects of the transformation that *universally* and *existentially* drive the whole process. They are similar to the ontological "transcendentals" of medieval philosophy, such as unity, truth, goodness and beauty, which are of the same magnitude that is congruent with the universality of being. They are also of the magnitude of the Pauline theological virtues of faith, hope, and love (1 Corinthians 13), but an alternative version of religious virtues, independent from, although not exclusive of, the western religious context, but emphatically inclusive of the pre-axial, indigenes and Dharmic/Daoic religious contexts. Finally, they are similar in magnitude to the "existentials" of human existence (in existentialist philosophical terms not defined by categories), not abstract essential characteristics or forms, but formless, elementary processes of becoming-spiritual. These are, in the context of this book and the current chapter, as it collects them from the images and poetic symbolisms of spiritual transformation throughout, the following magnitudes: *awakening, detachment, compassion* and *peace*.

They are related as manifestations of Reality as it is itself always simultaneously non-manifest *and* manifest, apophatic *and* polyphilic (see ch. 6). Yet they are not accessible as "realities" independently from the *deep transformation* of the Self in the vast cosmic matrix inherent in the spiritual process. In fact, they are the *dimensions* of the polyphilic process of the manifestation of the non-different inner Reality of all things, the Spirit that is *the innermost, but embracing reality of the cosmos*—not its foundation (ontology), not its secret of knowledge (epistemology), but the motive force (always attempting the transformative insight) of its becoming-spiritual. This means, they are, like the "theological" virtues, not possessions, but gifts; yet, like the "transcendentals," they are also the innermost reality of *all* things in their becoming (and the spiritual direction of all becoming). Karl Rahner, in his *Foundations of Christian Faith* (1976), has elaborated on such dipolar or hybrid, transcendent-transformational existentials as "supernatural existentials" of the self-communication of God that constitute humanity as spiritual species, but are not owed or owned as possessions. This is the spiritual paradox of these magnitudes: they can never be possessed without being instantly lost; but in order to unfold their expansive magnitude, we must transcend our Selves to let them proliferate and explicate, even to become universally the manifestations of the hidden relationality of all things in the cosmic Spirit.

Still, for another, a *third*, way to state the magnitude and the magnitudes, here, namely, as a *matrix of emphases*, we need to understand the bridge that is the reversal of inside and outside from the first to this last path of this book by envisioning this transformation as one from the expansiveness, emptiness, and formless connectivity of *space* to that of the actualization of potentials, the becoming of content, the decisions of valuation and the sensible universals in the movements of *time*. Yet another image to describe the change from the first to the last path, from the (internal) beginning to the (expansive) end, is to understand it as the substitution of Light with Life. This transformation collects all the other meanings—and it *is* that of Life, of Movement itself. Light is a spiritual archetype of spatial nature, non-local and universally immanent in all that happens, as the eternal light of divinity or the inner fire of liveliness, but detached from any of its actualizations. This is the light of the Spirit immanent in all things, but it shines by being independent *from* their impermanence.

Life, on the contrary, is a movement *of* concretization, of actualization, of the valuation of that which becomes, the impermanent moments of becoming in their concrete branchings and ramifications. Light-Space becomes Life-Time.

Not only form the spiritual magnitudes of awakening, detachment, compassion, and peace such Life-processes; they are always involved an oscillating movement of enfolding and unfolding between apophatic hiddenness and polyphilic manifestations, mystical silence and many voices of articulation and phenomenal appearance—and they do so in various ways in every cosmic epoch or universe, and in every concretization of them in beings of such universes, in their own irreplaceable emphasis—something that will be approached later in the section on God as Love. But for now, we only need to understand that they form a *matrix of emphases* that transcends any individual realization. Existentially, this is a movement of spiritual transcendence of Self and cosmos, but not directed to their overcoming, but *into their eversion* or spiritualization (see also the Epilogue to the book). The universal matrix of *these* spiritual magnitudes are not a form of being, but a formless (khoric) Life-movement of any being as the becoming of their composition, and emphasizes or deemphasizes imperfections in concrete events and contexts in the universal relationality of the All that is the expression, but more so, the polyphilic and the patiently suffered release, of the *divine matrix* into its own multiplicity in the infinite process of becoming-spiritual.

Polyphilia/Multiverse

The Multiverse is a matrix of alternatives, of "other lives." What is "other life"? Is it not another's life—as there are many, and we have not created ourselves? Is it not also other *than* our lives—as there are not just human lives? May it not be the "life" of any being of the universe, a sun, a nebular, a black hole—as they all have their own life-history, typical by the laws of thermodynamics, but individual by circumstances? May we not even assume the life-history of *this* universe, from the Big Bang to one of the projected futures: Big Crunch, Big Freeze, Eternal Inflation and Proliferation of ever new Universes? And in the contrary direction of smaller magnitudes: May we not even expect every phase of our own lives to be an alternative realization of "a life"? Sure, it would be "our" life that is constituted by their continuity; but is it really a possession of my Self? Is not every event of my life becoming "other life" that I can now decide to give a continuous or different future? Are not even all of the events of our life-line throughout this universe a collection of potential alternatives that we knit together by our decisions, sensitivity of perception, will of integrity or change, and horizons of alternative futures we may imagine? And is not our religious dimension that which always calls for such alternative *futures*—be it because of the human predicament in general, the individual perceived fate, constructions of imperfections, such as sin and ignorance, or new horizons of transcending futures, and the impetus to overcome our Selves?

The "constructions" of a multiverse, although they are based on idea of cosmic expansion, are, in some sense, only an extension of all of these "other lives" we live through and often just don't recognize as such: a *matrix of alternatives*, in its becoming meandering through spaces of valuation and emphases, temporal differentiations, actual decisions; a space of ever-renewed potential alternative or branching futures, and of "living" universal horizons that cannot be reined in by any limited imagination or theory. If we understand that the life of "others" (of any magnitude) is an alternative realization of emphases of material compositions of spiritual life-histories; if we further begin to acknowledge that even in our own life-history every event becomes an Other to be reclaimed or discarded, remembered or forgotten, transcended or transformed by new events, which are "other lives" imagined and realized or contained in the realm of mere possibility—then it would not be difficult to expand our vision to the magnitude of the life-history of a complete *universe*, its peculiar becoming, its potential cloud of alternative universal life-histories, ever "other lives" of *alternative universes*.

There are legions of theories of "the multiverse" in science and philosophy, as well as in religious discourses. But, given my experimental presupposition of the infinity of "other lives," I would bet that there are not as many such theories as there are universes in a multiverse, or possible worlds which allow for multiverses. Scientifically, generally at least five kinds of models of the multiverse-context of our Big Bang universe have been devised: the roughly 10 times 500 potential solutions to string theory suggests this amount of potential physical universes with their own rules and character; the quantum Many Worlds theory of Hugh Everett lives from "decisions," that is, the observer-involved proliferation of alternative universes at any moment of what other theories would like to see as a "breakdown of the wavefunction," which, if it does *not* break down, just *diverges* at this and any other moment; the classically super-expanding universe of the Inflation Theories allows fast cosmic regions to be beyond our or any possible connection by physical causes submitting to the light-speed limit in an Einsteinian Relativity-universe of which we even don't know whether they still follow the same natural laws or a mutual relationship of parameters; Bubble Bath theories of the multiverse understand the inflation process as *eternal* creation of new universes like bubbles in a bubble bath, expanding the hyper-space of universes by quantum mechanical rules of a non-causal, non-determined breakdown of the wavefunction in the cosmic landscape; finally, the Big Bang universe may be just one cosmic epoch of a *cyclical* creation and destruction of universes, *ad infinitum*.

In the context of philosophical and religious discourses, proliferating theories of multiverse lives are not uncommon—at all times (at least as historically recorded) and in all cultures, as long as we accept that they are not limited to physical universes in a scientific way (see ch. 8). From the cyclical lives of universes, limited by birth from divine Mind or awakening and by the final "divine sleep" or "death" (for instance, of the life of Brahma) or by an all-embracing conflagration in Hindu mythology and

Stoic philosophy; from the astrological-mystical hierarchy of heavenly spheres of the Sumerian-Babylonian religious complex to the Aristotelian spheres of movement of "worlds" or their heirs in the medieval versions of multiple-layered cosmologies; from the ancient stratification of heaven, earth, and underworld in Greek and Abrahamic contexts to the Jain, Buddhist, and generally Hindu "worlds" above and below this physical universe; from the dogma of a creator God who cannot be restricted to create only one universe (as confirmed in the theses of the Theological Faculty of the University of Paris in 1277) to the infinitely many universes that are the Buddha-fields of infinitely many Buddhas in the *Lotus Sutra*—there is virtually no cultural or religious, scientific, or philosophical context in which a strict denial of any such multiplicity was ever asserted as orthodox, superior, or sole solution! And even if this *were* the case, it would just indicate the ineradicable imaginative or philosophical matrix of the multiverse ideas even at the point of its denigration.

In the philosophical discourse, two problems are prevalent: the problem of *possible* worlds and that of an infinite multiverse as *atheistic* alternative to a creator-god. The possible world assumption either states that there are infinitely many possible worlds in which all decisions taken in one universe differ such that their alternatives all realize in their own universe—similar to the quantum branching of the Everett universe—or that alternative possibilities remain only possible without being actualized in any or many universes. Roughly the first solution, of the collapse of possibility and actuality, so that all possible universes are actual in their own realm, has been taken by the modal realism of David Lewis; the second understanding has been defended by A. N. Whitehead and Gilles Deleuze—as I have shown in my book *The Divine Manifold* (2014, chs. 6–7). Without going into any of their specifics, it is interesting in our context to mention that, at least in the latter case, spiritual universes are possible or even assumed: the difference between possibility and actuality amounts to the function of the difference of a subject-object contracted world (as ours is) and a virtual world (as in Deleuze) that is nondual, trans-personal, and trans-dualistic (see ch. 6), or, as in Whitehead, the realm of pure possibilities in the Mind of God (the Primordial Nature) as erotic suggestions or attractors ingredient to the actualization of events, which are always more and different from possibilities as they always as *syntheses* of "other lives," that is, other events and actual decisions (see ch. 3).

The contentious debate on the question whether or not a multiverse substitutes a creator-god has turned in on itself in more recent years. Philosophical and theological defenses of a "theistic multiverse" have proliferated—not only against the claim of scientifically based atheism by which physicists have shown their bias for atheism (or at least an Abrahamic antipathy), but also against versions of philosophical "pantheism" that substitutes any "theistic" transcendence of divine Reality beyond the all-encompassing exclusivity of the multiverse itself. Now, in assuming the authority of religious traditions, there has been much more tolerance toward non-theistic solutions such as the Buddhist multiverse of infinite Buddha-fields, which does not necessitate any creator-god, and, in exhausting philosophical authority, the "pantheism" of infinite divine Minds of John Leslie that has based itself on Plato's axiological reason for the existence of anything in the Idea of the Good: that necessity means that something *ought* to be (see ch. 5). In any case, and as in certain definitions of analytic philosophy of religion, god, whether creator or not, or just as a necessary being, actualizing certain worlds or being the sum of all worlds, is technically understood as part of such worlds. A "world" *includes* necessity and contingency, god as necessary being and the universe or a multiverse of contingent beings, and is, hence, non-transcendent of a "world" in relation to this definition. However, both in the Buddhist as in the Platonic context, the presupposition of the multiverse is *different*: they are based on the nondual "absolute transcendence" of the *dharmakaya* and the Good, respectively, that is, the *apophatic* nature of the Reality they name.

It is by this apophatic "reserve" that we can understand the difference between both a multiverse pantheism or a pantheism of infinite divine minds and a world-including "theism" of certain analytic approaches. In case of pan*en*theism, this difference is one of the togetherness of immanence and transcendence, of the inherent divine presence in all things and an embracing transcending of any universe and world (however defined). And in a *trans*-pantheistic view (see ch. 6), which I have also called "dipolar" (see ch. 5), the apophatic in-difference of Reality *from* anything *is* the difference of God from any multiplicity, a "(non-)difference" without which there would not be any multiplicity of "worlds" or a multiverse, as it activates the love of the manifold, the *polyphilia*, by which the apophatic Reality is infinitely "overboiling" (see ch. 3). As in Plotinus, it is the apophatic inaccessibility of Reality that, here, is the *condition* of the polyphilic manifold it initiates and from which it is in-different, and in its "immanence" (which is its transcendence, the immanence "to itself") the "energy" of attraction to realize the Good, liberation, self-less perfection and spiritual maturity. This, and *not* any spiritually projected physical energy, is the cosmically "energizing" Spirit I am talking about. This Spirit is not in need of justification by any argument for or against the multiverse, as it is already the *horizon* for its very understanding.

The *matrix* of the multiverse, that is, the matrix of alternatives and emphases of the realization of characteristics constituting different metaphysical "worlds" or physical universes, can be reimagined in light of another of the spiritual imaginations evoked in this book, namely, that of the Tree. In a sense, the different imaginations of the Tree of Life as the multiverse can be differentiated into the triad of Garden, Forest, and Wilderness (see ch. 4). With the very similar conceptual distinction of the analytic philosopher Peter Forrest (b. 1948)—who is more inclined to a kind of "naturalist theism" (scientifically justifiable), but, nevertheless, in his bouquet of multiverses, as presented in his contribution to the collection *God and the Multiverse* (2015), is unavoidably involved in spiritual openings that he might not have liked to deduce from his way of differentiating them—we encounter three "scientific" options for the conceptualization of the multiverse: separate worlds, branching universes and hyper-space. They roughly can be related to Forest, Wilderness, and Garden, but without the restrictions of physical parameters in the current (merely) scientific sense—that is, allowing for the internal spiritual nature of any universe as the creation of value-facts in the inextricable unity of processual interaction and emphases.

While Peter Forrest differentiates these versions by *valuing* their worth for theism—denying parallel worlds, allowing branching (but also crossing) life-lines of universes as non-theistic favorite and suggesting hyper-space as theistic preference—the alternative symbolisms inherent in the cosmic images of Forest, Wilderness, and Garden already suggest *spiritual* alternatives in a matrix that is not in need of such a valuation, as it allows the Spirit to operate under *all* of these conditions, embracing a *field* (matrix) of emphases instead of independent alternatives (which can never be independent, as they would not be able to be "situated" in a matrix): The *many Trees* of multiverses (each tree a branching of the universe itself into a multiverse) would still be situated in the same landscape or grow ground. The *Wilderness* of nomadic developments of life-lines that amount to "worlds," which can be universes or multiverses, is itself a multiverse of alternatives in the process of fusion and divergence within a "world" that is, as Deleuze says of Whitehead's multiverse-idea in his book *The Fold* (1988), a *chaosmos* of divergences that are held together by God (the Consequent Nature) as the Process that runs through all of them. And the *Garden* unites the different trees and other plants (multiverses and unimaginable "other lives") in one *attractive* arrangement—not of fine-tuning (which would only relate to one or some or all of the individual trees), but of the integrity of the garden by the Idea of a *manifold of harmonies* that maximize one another, but are grounded in the same soil, nurtured by the same rain, enlivened by the same sun, and spirited by the same breath of air. While one might emphasize the archetype of the Garden for the idea of divine polyphilia—similar to Forrest's preference of a hyper-space that includes but partitions its regions into potentially vastly different instantiations of physical universes with their own laws, in my triad of Forest, Wilderness, and Garden—in the end, the *triad itself is the polyphilic manifestation of the apophatic divine Reality*—whether personal or transpersonal.

In fact, none of these versions of multiverses—either of Peter Forrest or of our "natural" imagery of the Tree of Life—can *necessarily exclude* non-physical instantiations of "worlds," either as part of their multiplicity or as different alternatives in the cosmic matrix—whether we call them "natural" or "supernatural" is only a matter of conceptual limitations. While they may not be in need of restating the classical differentiations of religions of a multitude of "higher" and "lower" spiritual realms, they all leave space for such variations in themselves and between themselves in *a matrix of their matrices*. Such a hyper-matrix can not only assume different physical laws, but even a "lawfulness" that includes, but transcends the vast number of physical parameters in their composition so that they end up to be what we would call "spiritual" by any meaningful account of these terms. As already mentioned in other contexts (see, for instance, ch. 8), interpretations of quantum physics by their inventors—such as Niels Bohr, Erwin Schrödinger, Werner Heisenberg, Richard Feynman, Paul Dirac, Wolfgang Pauli, David Bohm, among many others—have tended to understand them as *bridges* to, or even as expressions of, spiritual "matters" inherent in discoveries of quantum indeterminacy; the uncertainty principle; the fundamental "mentality" of quantum "matter" as virtual realm of potentials in the process of actualization and transformation into energetic vibration; non-locality and connectivity beyond space-time; consciousness or observer-bound breakdown of the wave-function; the duality of particle and wave; randomness as condition for freedom and the effect of purposes; some form of final causality (teleology); and even God. One may only point at the "entanglement" of mysticism and quantum physics in the work of the American polyglot religious thinker Catherine Keller (b. 1953), especially in her book *Cloud of the Impossible* (2015), in order to begin to acknowledge the magnitude of the co-inherence of physical and intellectual matters that make sense only if they are understood as signs of the "environment" or "field" of the universe provided by the cosmic Spirit. The Spirit, here is the grand *attractor*—but without (atheistically or pantheistically) *identifying* the physical and spiritual as in a "quantum energy field."

Whitehead's differentiation of events and possibilities, his assumption of a radical diversity of possible actualizations of collective natural laws, forces, fields, parameters, and forms of organisms in any universe, of which he always assumes a multitude, has lead him to also assert that other "worlds" (in the most universal way as paradigmatic Forests, Wildernesses, or Gardens) may be of such a *vast difference* that virtually none of these constrains are of necessary nature. Instead, he can assume "realms" that are beyond measurability (beyond science); exist beyond perishing (quasi-eternal); are in becoming, but without loss (a vision of heaven in many religions); remain as a vivid memory in God's ability to transform everything and in such transformations relate the All to All so as to be All in All (the Consequent Nature). *The multiplicity of the "worlds" is an expression of a cycle of love of this manifold in the mutual inherent transformation of God and the worlds—an expression of polyphilia.*

Classical imaginations of a multiverse consisting of realms *beyond* this physical universe, parallel or successive, are closer to such current scientific and philosophical renderings than one may suspect. NDEs and several phenomena, possibly involving non-local quantum connectivity, as well as quantum field theories have for some scientists and thinkers presupposed *mentality* that cannot be reduced to physical parameters. And even if we cannot define these forms of connectivity with scientific means, one solution favored by Whitehead's cosmology of events and processes is the immediate connections of their "mental poles," which is not necessarily exhausted by the laws that their "physical poles" obey (see ch. 8).

The ultimate question in our context, however, is another one: Has the assumption of a multiverse a *direct* spiritual impact, that is, not only an impact on the understanding of the nature of the cosmic Spirit, but also on the process of the transformation that is acknowledging this Spirit? In our context: Does the multiverse have an impact on the understanding of the four spiritual "magnitudes" of awakening, detachment, compassion, and peace? Or, asked differently: do they *presuppose* a multiverse? The answer is *yes*—and I will explain in the coming section.

Meditation XVII: Other Lives

This meditation is about a strange but seemingly quite common phenomenon: that of the *mirroring* of one's life in another one. What I mean is this:

> *Imagine, you have a chance encounter with another person, for instance, in front of you while you are waiting in line, say, at a register, or at a booth during a street fair. Someone catches your attention. You stop thinking about anything else and concentrate, for a moment, on that person—their appearance, their aura, their attitude, their movements...*
>
> *You imagine what it would be like to be that person...*
>
> *...*
>
> *When this person leaves your path...*
>
> > *...you follow their path in your mind...*
>
> *What would it be like to become that person?...*
>
> > *...and think and do and go on to live like them?...*
>
> *...*
>
> *Imagine being such a person in another part of the world...*
>
> > *...living an exotic life...*
> >
> > *...living a toxic life...*
> >
> > > *full of sorrow and inescapable poverty...*
> > >
> > > *of undeserved protection and riches...*
> >
> > *...living a life like yours, but with conditions as different from yours as you can imagine...*
>
> *...*
>
> *Imagine a life as a mountain, a tree, or a river... a plant... an animal...*
>
> *Imagine living at another time:*
>
> > *...as a mason in Babylon within the emerging agricultural civilization...*
> >
> > *...as a farmer on the ancient Nile...*

> ... *as a peasant in medieval Japan ...*
>
> ... *as a pilgrim in ancient Jerusalem during a national religious feast ...*
>
> *when rumor has it that the Messiah has appeared ...*
>
> ...
>
> *Imagine a life on another planet ...*

This ability to imagine another's life is not as strange as it may sound. In fact, this ability may be one of the most profound evolutionary acquirements of complex organisms, not only humans, to be able to mirror not only the outer world within one's own organism—whether or not you call it "mind" even in the case of other mammals or apes is irrelevant—but to *feel* the other's world from its own internal perspective. It is not intellect or reason, but the ability to *feel* the other, and to mirror such feelings in one's own body, that has allowed us to become evolved organisms. We know that the physiological basis for this ability are the mirror neurons in our brain. It is with this ability that empathy and compassion have a physiological basis.

What is more, it is this ability for empathy and compassion, the mirroring of the feeling of others, *like to be* the other, that is an inevitable condition and motive force of our becoming *human*, or—leaving the multi-species approach wide open—of becoming *spiritual beings*. This ability of emphatic mirroring is also the basis for the development of a "civilized" society, that is, a complex, dynamic inclusive emergence of social relationships that are not just built on Darwinian survival, but on mutuality, non-violence, and affirmation. It is in this sense—and not in opposition to "primitive" condition of life and technology or the classical "savage" or the superiority complex of a colonizing elite—that to become spiritual and to becoming "civilized" are one, and that "civilization" is an expression of an enlightened *cosmopolitanism* with the vision of a *future spiritualized society of peace*.

> *Now repeat the exercise again in a live situation.*
>
> *What do you feel?*
>
> *What do you learn?*

The Life of Other Days
Awakening—Detachment—Compassion—Peace

The multiverse, whatever its concrete gestalt, is the extension and expression of the manifold of "other lives," which exist, from an apophatic origination, as the polyphilic overflow of the inaccessible and, simultaneously, inexhaustible well of Reality, the Ocean from which the Rivers of existence flow, and in which everything is an ornament, a swirl, a vortex of this flow—connected and different, individual only insofar as it is also the movement of the folding of the whole of which it consists; mediated by *khora* or interrelationality; folding ever anew (and differently) space and time; perpetuating natural characteristics and realizing virtues of valuation; transforming all kinds of levels of existence.

There have been different ways of formulating this differentiation *and* connectivity of the multiplicity and the multiverse of "other lives" (in all of its forms)—which have already been evoked, but for reasons of clarity can now be named with paradigms of harmony, rhythm, or folding. The *harmonic* way is Leibniz's monadic connectivity by which the mental unity (non-deconstructibility) of the physical multiplicity (in the movement of composition or decomposition) is a pre-established divine harmonization of the spiritual realm (of eternity and simplicity without composition) with the physical composition as *its* composition. The *rhythmic* way is Whitehead's polar-processual connectivity by which every event is a process of two poles, one of inherent (mental) unity and one of external (physical) multiplicity, but, paradoxically, by making multiplicity inherent (mental) to the feeling process of an event, and making unity external (physical) as new facts for perception of new events—all as a rhythmic revolution by which nothing stays the same but changes the sides or becomes "the other life." The way of *folding* is Deleuze's nomadic connectivity by which all happenings are folds of planes of immanence, but no plane of immanence is the plane of all planes, as this "space" remains beyond such unification a *multiplicity* in which the divergence is always greater than (and the motor to overcome closed) unities. In this sense, external (physical) reality *is the same* as internal (mental) reality, only folded differently. "Other lives" are the same as my life.

Yet what is important is this: In all three solutions to diversification and unification in a multiverse of "other lives" *the multiverse "is" my life*. Or: I am but "other lives," borrowed for time as "mine," but not my possession. Rather, "I am" means—other than Descartes's *cogitio ergo sum* (I think, so I am)—that "I am" is a composition *from* and *out of* "other lives." We are reminded of the Buddhist parable of the "chariot" in the *Milinda Panha* (*The Questions of the King Milinda*) of the second century BCE, representing a historical encounter of the Hellenistic king Meander I of Bactria and the vast Greco-Indian Empire (d. 130 BCE) with the Buddhist sage Nagasena (ca. second century BCE), that consist only of parts of which none can represent the unity imagined to be the whole chariot (see the related image of the elephant in ch. 7). In the Buddhist context, this "unity" is denied and explained as a mere composition of the five *skandhas,* or aggregates (forms, sensations, feelings, perceptions, mentality, and consciousness), which have all their own "awareness"; but none of them amount to an "I" or *atman*-unity. "Other lives" *are* my life; my live is not *my* life, but (is composed of) *all* "other lives."

We must harvest three important implications of this insight. First, multiplicity is the condition of any talk about spiritual unity or modes of valuation or unification; spiritual transformation is to a great extent but the activation of this insight—as the concurrence with the divine movement of polyphilia, the love of multiplicity, of the multiverse, of the compositional and impermanent chaosmos, by initiating and syncing with movements of monadic harmonization, rhythmic unification and diversification, and nomadic foldings. Second, spiritual (and even mental) unity, here, is not a compositional component of multiplicity, but, insofar as it is "real," must be of another order than the movements of impermanence (*samsara*), namely, of the "otherness" of the timeless, deathless, indestructible (*nirvana*). In this sense, we cannot find unity *in* multiplicity, mind *in* matter, the Spirit *in* the world, but only multiplicities of multiplicities. While this second insight seems to be the stronghold of anti-religion, anti-theism, and anti-spiritual forms of materialism, scientific or ideological, practical or theoretical, postulatory or experimental, the third insight will fuse the first two to the following proposition: that the *dispossession* of the impermanent compositions, which we find in the material world, from claims of unification that misinterpret mental unity and spiritual experience as assertion of one's Self or the assertion of any atomic unity of existence and any organic or social form of unity, is an undeconstructable "presentation" of spiritual unity. *Spiritual transformation is the process of this dispossession by which unity is realized as self-transcendence.*

The four forms or virtues or magnitudes of such a spiritual transformation that I want to employ, here, as already hinted earlier, are *awakening, detachment, compassion,* and *peace*. This choice, instead of potential other lists, such as the theological virtues, follows five reasons: first, all of them are *direct expressions* of dispossessive self-transcendence or modes of selflessness; second, together they express the *process* of self-transcendence in a world of becoming as a cycle of spiritual ascent and descent; third, all of them are *forms of love*, under the umbrella of the love of the manifold, of polyphilia, the presupposition of their operation in a multiverse; fourth, they *manifest* the spiritual transformation within the multiplicity of the physical world by which it *is*, as realization of value *in* fact, transformed; and, fifth, by *manifesting* the *cosmic* Spirit as immanent attractor of the process of the multiverse, they correlate or are the internal motive forces for the realization of the fundamental *dimensions* of spiritualization of the cosmos itself, namely (essentially, but not exclusively): *consciousness, soul, civilization,* and *Reality*.

Both trajectories, that of virtues and of cosmic phenomena of the Spirit, correlate in their inherent progression and reconstruction of the process of spiritual awakening or enlightenment and of the process of cosmic expansion of spiritual transformation in the realities that carry this transformation, respectively. For the spiritual virtues of self-transcendence, this will become clear when we identify them, for instance, as a general scheme of the Buddhist enlightenment process: *Detachment* and *Compassion* are the dialectic of the disinterested overcoming of the particularizing and the desire-initiated fueling of *karma*. By detachment and, *simultaneously*, the growing ability to be compassionate we become one with all "other lives"—even up to the level of intensity at which such an existence becomes salvific, that is, that of the pure pro-existence of a *bodhisattva*. Related are *Wisdom* and *Compassion*, the two prime manifestations of *sunyata* (emptiness), the Reality that bestows (or "is") the Peace of the non-initiation of *karma* (the Buddha only "leaves" traceless *dharmas*) and the promise of its final extinguishing in death (*parinirvana*); and the "bridge" of the media of Detachment/Wisdom and Compassion to Reality/Emptiness is opened by the *Awakening to Enlightenment*.

The second series of *cosmic signs* of spiritual transformation are natural expansions of the spiritual heart beginning in *Consciousness*. Consciousness—itself "natural" to the universe, but in a sense, "super-natural," as it always transcends, or never completely reaches the point of any of its possible physical fixations and reductions—is the one pole of the spiritual "bridge" the other side of which is ultimate *Reality* itself; and these two poles of this energetic spiritual relationship that is the appearance of the cosmic Spirit are mediated with two of their cosmic intersections: the transformative progressions of *Individuation* (the Soul) and *Social-Environmental Integration* (Civilization). Both are also related dialectically, as one cannot be had without the other, although both create their own polar tension.

While psychology and sociology divide their polar sphere, spiritual transformation must unite them to an energetic sea of vibrations that must be excited to create ever-new intensive harmonies of their unified realization. Some spiritual theories and advice, such as Carl Gustav Jung's psychology of "individuation" or the "human potential movement" based on the value hierarchies and progressions of Abraham Maslow (d. 1970), often are more inclined to see through and further the process of personal development; others, such as the "integral theory" of Ken Wilber (b. 1949) and the "transpersonal psychology" of Stanislav Grof (b. 1931), and more recently of Jorge Ferrer (b. 1968), are more geared toward the integration of individual spiritual transformation with the expansive transformation of humanity in the cosmos. Yet both Soul-formation and Civilization are expansions of Consciousness—with its diverse aspects of reason, intellect, feeling, potential, decision-making, freedom, actualization, purpose, ethical and aesthetic valuation processes, and more.

These matrices of the progression or expansions of magnitudes of spiritual transformation and the magnitudes of their cosmic manifestation processes can also be understood regarding their individual correlation and resonance. *Awakening is a form or process of self-transcendence that births Consciousness.* Not only is Consciousness, here, understood as the natural attribute of sensible beings, not only humanity, that is, as an evolutionary unfolding of the spiritual purposefulness of the evolution process. What is more, it is a sign of this spiritualization of the evolutionary dynamics we find operative in our universe whether or not it exhibits its enlightened or spiritually awakened horizon. But much like the Buddhist understanding of the general participation of all sentient beings in the Buddha nature (*dharmakaya*), Consciousness is already the beginning of the Awakening that is meant to unfold to an enlightened recognition that it always was already a seed of this "nature" (*thatagatagarbha*). But we find a similar approach in Meister Eckhart's "*Seelenfunken*," the spark of God being born in the Soul—as we are always already of the nature of the "Son" (the "born God") to be born—in the Spirit (John 3:6). So, while Consciousness is an intensity of Awakening, naturally present in the evolutionary process in many species besides humanity, and of which humanity may not be seen as the final expression in the cosmos or in a multiverse of "other days," it must explicitly be recognized that, in this matrix of spiritual values and their comic manifestations, spiritual Awakening is not bound to humanity—either in this earth, this universe, or the multiverse of infinite diversity. Think of the grave implications for our understanding of the cosmic reach of the Spirit and the spiritual status of humanity in such a multiverse!

Consciousness, as related to spiritual Awakening, here, is a micro- as well as a macro-cosmic, an individual as well as a collective, and a spatial as well as temporal category. In the *microcosmic* sense, it relates to the enfolded internality of the whole cosmic process in its "spirit" in every event and process of becoming. Even if it does not lead to self-consciousness (in many sentient beings), it is based on self-transcendence or mutual inherence. In the *macrocosmic* sense, it indicates the mutual infusion of the Spirit with the cosmos as a whole, as a unison of becoming. Hence, such Consciousness must not be reduced to the marginal self-consciousness of individual organisms, as it has a *universal* "presence" in all beings, whether or not they are individually conscious, of what the ancients, such as Philo of Alexandria and Plotinus, called the World-Soul or the Mind of God. Rather, collective forms of Consciousness, such as the self-transcendence of a Civilization, is the inherent *evolutionary* potential of developments of Consciousness. As in the work of Sri Aurobindo, the individual consciousness is really surrounded by an "inconscient" and a "superconscient" expansion—something that in A. N. Whitehead's understanding relates to the sub-conscious gift of every event *to itself* by God's gift of an "initial aim" to any becoming Self of any being, on the one hand, *and* to the super-conscious Mind of God in which all possibilities are valuations of goodness, on the other. These expansions are individually connecting consciousness with the spirit-matter from which it takes its poetic material for its *theosis* and the Awakening to cosmic Consciousness. Yet they also indicate the evolution of spiritual beings through phases of subconscious Selves by self-transcendence to a widening of Consciousness that will, in the future, embrace the whole spirit-faring species. In this sense, the evolutionary "materialization" of the Spirit in a universal and collective Consciousness through phases, intensities and degrees of self-consciousness and self-transcendence can even symbolize *the whole series of the four virtues*, here, as a universalizing process of the spiritualization of the cosmos.

Detachment is a form or process of self-transcendence that relates to the concept of the Soul. This "relation" is complex, but not without immediate intuitive meaning. While our first impulse may be to either embrace or reject the concept of "the soul" because it is viewed as some kind of "substance" or "entity" that is not only different from the psychophysical unity of mind and matter, and that may be the "being" that perpetuates our individual being throughout all of the changes of this life and secures the continuity of our individuality after death, this line of thought is a highly contentious religious and philosophical matter of discussion—and it is a simplification. The two meanings of *psyche* in the Platonic-Aristotelian universe of discourse has been, first, the Platonic meaning of a *living Idea* of individual differentiation of no other, higher Ideas, except being a living manifestation of the Good, and the Aristotelian meaning of a *principle of living movement* that, even if it is the formal (structural) cause of a material being, is paradoxically the *form* of living movements and *activities* that cannot be structurally limited or deduced; that is, it names the self-activating principle of living beings (not only humanity). In neither of these meanings is the Soul a mere thing or entity or a structural characteristic. It is rather a concept that cannot be conceptually controlled, because it is, in the Platonic case, a manifestation of the self-less, apophatic Good, and, in the Aristotelian case, a placeholder for creative activity, which is per definition beyond conceptual closure.

Not forcing a decision between the Hindu meaning of *atman* and a Buddhist meaning of *anatta* regarding the Self, as the Soul indicates this conceptual *site* of this of Self/No-self-discourse, Whitehead's rendition of its meaning will be enlightening, here. I will only relate two important corrections Whitehead introduces for the understanding of the Soul: First, in *Adventures of Ideas*, "soul" does *not* indicate a soul-substance, but rather means the "self"-empty field-space of the Platonic *khora*, the *medium of cosmic intercommunication* by which the All is related to All in itself *without limitation of forms or structures*, but by the universal relationality "forming" the integrity of "a cosmos" that also allows for the polyphilic proliferation of phenomena and a multiverse of diversity. Second, in *Process and Reality* Whitehead points to the heart of the concept of the "soul" as expressing *life, originality, creativity and freedom of activation* beyond, and not limited to (but often in struggle with), structural, formal, substantial, continuous and limiting characteristics of order. The ambivalence between Self and No-Self is inherent, here, by such an appeal to life *beyond* order, as both of the Whiteheadian "pointers" of emptiness (*khora*) and the origination of creative activity express either of them *equally*, without giving in to either structural reductions of the concept of the "soul," for instance, in current discussions of machine life and its ill-formulated translation of its life into software, or the limitation of it to matters of identity and continuity, especially of individuality after death. In fact, as the Whiteheadian "soul" is a *trajectory of intense events of life in mutual processes of harmonization*; its life is not about self-preservation, but of self-transcendence. At no point is it bound to an "identity" that would obliterate its profound creativity.

Furthermore, in the context of the rather strange correlation with the virtue and transformation facilitated by Detachment, *instead* of Awakening (which one may feel to be the "natural" pairing), I am indicating the immediate connection of the concept of "the Soul" (by emphasizing the here developed sense) as one of self-*transcendence*, and not of self-assertion. While Consciousness is an *immediate experience* in which we live, as Awakening is a process by which we know of any "state before" (sleep? death? non-existence? vegetation?) only "from within" the awakened, smoothly into itself warped horizon of "having been awakened," of "already being conscious," conversely, the Soul is a *concept, always in the process of "conception,"* that points toward something inaccessible and inexpressible *beyond all experience*—like the apophatic nature of the Good and the unknowability of the creative act before it happens—that relates to a program or gradual approach for reaching the immediacy of Detachment *in the end*, although it (the Soul) is the *condition* of the whole process in the first place. You cannot "know" the spiritual state of being detached before you have experimentally tried to realize it in ever new forms—which will always be impermanent and only mysteriously hinting at a spiritual attainment as if beyond a veil. Like the Soul, Detachment is always ahead of us, unrealized, but attractive; imperative, but beyond duty; releasing, but not saturated. Detachment is a process of letting go—as indicated (in ch. 4) with the image of the intuition inherently motivating the activity of consciously (through awakening purposefully) "falling from the tree."

Finally, the Soul is already of a magnitude that has transcended merely individualistic phantasies of continuity or life, as it has always already been envisioned to indicate the universal cosmic magnitude of Life—in the concept of the World Soul, whether in Plato's *Timaeus* or Plotinus's *Enneads*. And in this conceptual function, it was meant to explain the experiential tension or polarity between physical and mental, internal and external, bodily and emotional existence, that we *perceive* (rather than project) not only of human beings. In other words, in the universal *Detachment* from mere particularity (whether there are individual souls or whether they are immortal), the cosmic Soul embraces the unity of a universe as its *internally* felt sympathy of relations (see ch. 6) and, hence, is already the universal site and expression of *Compassion*.

The World Soul is neither only Divine Mind or Divine Body, but their mutual immanence, or, with the Japanese philosopher Hajime Tanabe (d. 1962), it indicates the nexus, medium or site of Life in which all abstractions, such as universality and individuality, mind and matter, intellect and chaos *meet*—a meeting that for Tanabe and many other directions of Buddhist philosophy can be named Amida-Buddha, also called Amitabha, the Buddha of infinite Light, or Amitayus, the Buddha of infinite Life. This *middle* is for some the middle cosmic body of the *sambhogakaya*, for others the ultimate reality as the medium of "abstractions" such as *dharmakaya* and *nirmanakaya*. Similarly, for Whitehead the *nexus* of events is the concrete multiverse of which the isolated contemplations of individual events (actual occasions) and of universal characteristics (eternal objects) only reaches abstractions.

In fact, this understanding of the Soul, not in the reduction to (but also not by exclusion of) the spiritual affirmation of individual immortality, or, in the current materialist context, of an individual homunculus in our brain, or the psychological equivalent of the Freudian ego (constrained and ridden by Id and Super-ego), but as a "limitation" or "transmission" or "filter" or "valve" or "veil" or "organ" or "canalization" or "amplification" (and so on) of the universal Soul or the divine Mind, or as a subconscious connection through archetypical universals of (human) evolutionary history and common ecological existence, in individual material contexts or the universally constraining context of a world in becoming, is not the exception of a rational/intelligible cosmology, but has a long history in western and eastern religious and consciousness-philosophical reflection. From Heraclitus's "unboundedness" of the soul to Henri Bergson's universal memory beyond limiting states of matter, from Plato's and Plotinus's World-Soul in which every individual, soul-full (Buddhist would say: sentient) being participates, as it acts through the instrumentality of, and in its own expressiveness in, the body to William James's mother-sea of consciousness (see the related epigraph to ch. 2); from Plotinus's student Porphyry (d. 303 CE) with his mystical ascent to the One as recollection of the divine essence beyond color and quality, to the "hypophenomenal" Mind (in contrast to the "epiphenomenal" individual brain-inherent, emergent, ephemeral mind) of American philosopher Curt Ducasse (d. 1969); from the Neoplatonist universal "image and similarity" of the soul with the universal Mind of God of the Renaissance thinkers such as Marsilio Ficino (d. 1499) and Giovanni Pico della Mirandola (d. 1494) to the "immense intelligence" and "Over-soul" as the womb of our transcendental nature of Ralph Waldo Emerson—all of these witnesses are just detecting the *massive (unconscious) field that pervades the religious mind and its philosophical explications.* While arising during and since the "axial age" (mid-first millennium BCE), as devised by Karl Jaspers (see ch. 7), but especially as expressed in the Dharmic and Daoic religions and their cosmologies, the discovery of the trans-personal soul-fulness from which the world is understood to emanate and in which we as souls participate, not as passive receivers, but as actors in a drama, the Soul is either the "materialization" of the Spirit or the "spiritualization" of our social and natural world.

The Soul, individually as well as universally, then, is a *nexus* of concrete integration of self-transcendent but mutual immanence. And the comparativist of mythologies and religions, Joseph Campbell (d. 1987), collected a host of similar references from myths and religions as well as philosophical renderings of this insight, such as presented with the epigraph of the German Buddhism-influenced philosopher Arthur Schopenhauer (d. 1860), namely, of the universal truth of *mutual soul-full internality,* to the same effect.

Compassion is a form or process of mutual self-transcendence that inheres in any development of the Civilization of sentient, intelligent beings with spiritual maturity. The way Compassion is introduced, here, in the coordinated matrices of spiritual virtues of self-transcendence and their cosmic manifestation, is already disentangled from any individualistic misunderstanding. At this point, this collective, universal, universally integrative, but medial, nexic complexity of the term "virtue" should be emphatically recognized: "virtues" of self-transcendence are not isolations from the world, individual efforts of personal betterment, but always already co-inherent activations of the interrelations with the All and all beings—or, more imaginatively: turbulences of vortices in the flow of the river of existence (see ch. 3). So, the most basic virtue of world-relation is the Compassion that (as it is mediated by Detachment) is disinterested, that is, free from any biases and agendas, and can, thereby, sympathically and inherently relate "other lives" *as our own*, but without possessive implications (see Meditation XVIII). As such, Compassion is the "foundational" connectivity within which civilized forms of life can develop. Conversely, Compassion only can be manifested on the level of such Civilizational realizations, that is, the concrete spiritual transformation of social bodies of (and to the extent they are both) conscious and soul-full beings.

While the intensity of such Compassion will be indexed by the ability to replace evolutionary or cultural forms of opposition and violence with ever more harmonious forms of mutuality, this does not mean that all social activity will be following the same structural scheme or be of such a nature that it can be projected into only one possible structural realization of society as Civilization. On the contrary, as the Buddhist doctrine of the *upaya*, the "skillful means," demonstrates, the more Compassion is disinterested and universal, the more it will be concrete and effecting individualized transformations of the multiplicity in the diverse and differing contexts of the nexus that is the primary medium and site of Compassion—Compassion *being* the nexic Soul, as it were. Its universal tendency, without any axiological schematization in particular, will be towards non-violence and Peace, as the ideal realization of any society that deserves (and to the extent it does realize them) the name of Civilization. In this sense, we can with Whitehead speak not only of human Civilization, insofar as they realize the Spirit of Truth, Beauty, Adventure, Art and Peace, but, as Whitehead does in his last book *Modes of Thought* (1937) of a "Civilized Cosmos."

Peace is a form or process of self-transcendence that manifests apophatic Reality in the polyphilic immanence in modes of diversification, as harmonization of coincidental oppositions, alternatives or incompatibilities. I am in complete agreement with the epigraph of Whitehead to this chapter that Peace is the process of harmonization beyond the confines of Self and personality, the expression of the cosmic magnitude of spiritual self-transcendence par excellence. This also follows naturally from the internal progression of the four spiritual values and their cosmic realizations: Peace is the *point of convergence* of both being a virtue and the cosmic realization of the apophatic Reality it actualizes as the *site* of the manifestation of ultimate Reality in the multiverse, any world, and all worlds, invoking the All in All. Peace is, in translation of Teilhard de Chardin's eschatological Point of convergence between inherent messianic movements and ultimate divine plunging into the multiplicity of the cosmos, the *Omega Point of self-transformation* of the Cosmos in the Spirit. It is, in light of its enfolded modes of spiritualization of Awareness, Detachment, and Compassion beyond but integrating the alternatives of individual and collective realization, beyond but integrating the polar forces of freedom and harmony, beyond but integrating the divergent movements of differentiation and relationality. Although it is true that Peace is the highest ideal for spiritual transformation to succeed, Peace is not an empty idea, an empty promise, or an idealistic illusion, but the real, activating, teleological *attractor* inherent in the very movements toward the spiritualization of the cosmic realities over which it extends.

On an ever-deeper level, Peace is but Reality *itself*. Peace is the spiritual harmonization of space and time that—converse to Derrida's *différance: differing* (everything united throughout) space and time and *deferring* its own fulfillment (a final state of unification), but operating as such in the deconstruction of any false and oppressive unification—is *in unison with* all spaces and times and the moving attractor in all deference to follow it as the natural *eros* of its fulfillment. Peace is the intensity of beauty in which no opposition is ultimate and no alternative destructive. In the sphere of Peace, the proliferation of diversifications (the multiverse) does not fall apart, but is still of the Spirit that energizes all vibrations and flows luxuriantly into the infinite Life of the cosmos. Peace, to say it again, is, as Point Omega, *motivating, not ending*, the whole cosmic process of spiritualization as the polyphilic manifestation of apophatic Reality as One—inexhaustible and undeconstructable.

Together, the *first two* virtues, Awakening and Detachment, indicate the *ascent* from self-centeredness to Reality-centeredness; the *latter two*, Compassion and Peace, highlight the converse movement of that which could be called a process of "transcendence *within*" (see the Epilogue to the book), of manifesting polyphilic love as apophatic unity within its impermanence, and often decomposition, of/within diversity. In other words, *Consciousness and the Soul*, in our context, don't indicate notions of transcendence—being only metaphysical notions, abstractions beyond this world of becoming and perishing, composition and decomposition, dissatisfaction (*dukkha*) and impermanence (*anicca*), as they are often understood—but *natural* expressions of the spiritual character of this world, as they are not modes of self-possession (the ego-self), but processes of self-transcendence. Now, they can not only be misunderstood (as the opposite), but also misused in a way that is possessive and against which the modes of selflessness in diverse religions, but especially in the invocation of the non-self (*annata*) in Buddhism, put their weight into the arena of spiritual development. But if they are purified of such misappropriations, we may begin to see them to indicate some of the wonders of spiritual transformation: to *become awaked to the cosmic magnitude* of our Selves that are, therefore, not "our" Selves, but the Awareness of universal interrelationality. And the Consciousness of the event-character of a nexus of events the live-history of which is *purely alive*—not engaged in self-preservation, but in processes of intensification and harmonization that embrace all of the "cosmos" in its diverse areas and layers of the multiverse—can only be attained if, and to the extent which, we let go of self-closure in one's ego as an illusion and embrace the whole as "our" heritage. Now, in the Awakening to Consciousness and to the self-less life of the Soul (the life-principle) we are only what the All is: a multiverse *as expression of a divine love for this multiplicity in becoming*.

Similarly, the notions of *Compassion and Peace* are not aims one must reach or can miss, or "virtues" one must realize or can fail to attain, but they are *conditions* of the realization or manifestation of self-transcendence *within* the world of becoming at any and every moment of its becoming and existence—often despite the physical conditions opposing them. Civilization and access to ultimate Reality are such that only an *attitude of non-attainment* (there "is" no "other" river-shore) and presupposition of purpose and motivation will ever, if at all, be able to realize them.

Yoking *Civilization and Reality* together also implies that one cannot be had without the other. In other words, to restate the insight of materialist explanations of religions from Kant to Durkheim: religion and society belong together; but we can, now, reverse the intention of this relationship in their work and formulate even more radically: Civilization cannot be had without spiritual transformation! While Whitehead, in *Adventures of Ideas*, made the case for the "progress" of the understanding and potential of the attainment of Civilization to be bound to *metaphysical visions* that drive this self-transcendence, such as Truth, Beauty, Adventures, Art, Peace, he also made the case that it is only the immanence of Reality (the Great Fact) as the very beginning in the becoming of any event (as its initial Eros) and as the attractor to the realization of aesthetic value (as final Beauty) that self-forgetful transcendence essential to Civilization can be understood and actualized, although it *is* the very Reality of the movement necessary to attain to it, or approximate to some resemblance of it.

Conversely, Reality is not realized in merely individual spiritual journeys, but in the otherness of "other lives," in societies of such self-transcendent realizations as Compassion and the peaceful Awareness, actualized in habits and actions in the light of, in the midst of, and despite oppositional forces and incompatible divergences. Yet the polyphilic modes of the social "organization" manifesting Reality (*dharmakaya*) is one of conscious Awareness and detached Souls (life-principle) that in their self-transcendence only realize the *formless Life* of mutuality of relationality (*pratitya-samutpada*)—which Whitehead calls the nexus of "pure life," and which is the manifestation of the pure Life of the cosmic Spirit.

Together, all *four virtues or modes of self-transcendence* form a *matrix of emphases of the realization of types of multiverses*. As in the trifold symbolism of Forest, Wilderness, and Garden, the matrix is one of diverse matrixes that imply *diverse* multiverses of emphases that can manifest monadic parallel worlds, a nomadic crossing chaosmos, or a purposely integrate but actually (historically) open life-trajectory of ever-newly series of instantiations of intensities and harmonization of the matrix—all of them indicating possible positions in the realization of the *values* of spiritual maturation (the fourfold matrix of spiritual magnitudes) in relation to their *actualization* as the media of the spiritualization of the cosmos (the fourfold signs of the presence and attraction of the Spirit in the birth of Consciousness, Soul-fulness, Civilization, and the attainment of apophatic Reality). These processes are, as the epigraph of 'Abdu'l-Bahá to this chapter so forcefully claims, the very *reason* of the coming into existence of ever new worlds and universes in an endless and infinite (rhythmic, monadic, or nomadic) multiverse and the *telos* of spiritualization.

The cosmic Spirit seeks the spiritualization of the whole cosmos! And it *shows* in our fragile, flickering and uncertain signs of such a process. We *can* self-transcend; and we *show* characteristics of all-embracing Consciousness, of soul-full openness to Life, of the desire for a non-violent Civilization, and the experience of Reality. And this *has* become visible in the transformations of sages, prophets and holy figures as well as in momentous experiences that we can all relate to, such as sudden admission into the presence of the numinous, mystical encounters of beyond-ness, self-less acts of the disregard of self-interest, deep feeling of cosmic unity, or extraordinary boundary-experiences between life and death (for instance, NDEs, or shamanic and alchemical journey of transformation), or of sudden "otherings" in situations of extreme suffering (the Suffering Servant) and joy (ecstasies, soul-journeys).

A last thought: The matrix of emphases of the spiritual virtues and their cosmic manifestations also indicates the universal presence and attractive movements they initiate in the creation of the whole cosmos in all of its potential levels and planes of organization from universal fields of space-time and the physical forces to the nested structures of complexification of environments and organisms, from cellular life to the human mind, or, as Teilhard de Chardin so eloquently formulates: from the cosmosphere to the biosphere to the noosphere to the divine sphere.

One immediate implication is important: that the web of all phenomena in any universe, but so also in our universe, is itself the realization of a certain burst of life-lines of the emphasis of the transformational virtues and their related site of cosmic presence in the unending process of spiritualization—the axiological reason and the teleological aim of the existence of worlds. Any universe or any of its internal or more expansive multiplicities, surrounding and coinhering the universe like the quantum cloud of an electron or the virtual manifold of all the potentials of events and processes, is a *mixture* of emphases of these spiritual magnitudes and cosmic sites. *All* beings, becoming in such life-lines in the matrix of such a universe, are expressions of *all* of these spiritual virtues and their cosmic sites. This means, that it is not only humanity, but also animals, flowers and trees, and even rivers, seas, and mountains that enfold modes of Awakening and potentialize Consciousness; that live for the greater whole Detachment from self-interest and, hence, are soul-full; that are concrete nexuses of the realization of Compassion and, hence, are of a healing teleology that tends to overcome violence with gentleness; that are driven by motivations of Peace in which they become the uterus for ultimate Reality to become born in this cosmos. There is no division between us and them, humanity and the earth, self and self-transcendence—they are all gifts of the polyphilic love of the Spirit becoming cosmos, beautiful order or chaosmos, the living harmony of always overflowing intensities that never end.

Meditation XVIII: One/All No/Self

All of the five "universals" or "existentials"—polyphilia, awakening, detachment, compassion, and the "insight" (in Sufi terms: *irfan, ma'rifa*) of peace—are forms of becoming-selfless or widening the Self beyond personality, as Whitehead says. They are not only *forms* of mirroring, as in Meditation XVII, but much more: experimental processes or processes of insights into the *formlessness* of our innermost Spirit.

One of the exercises that can trigger such an insight can be built on Meditation XVII by radically widening its scope and magnitude to the utmost limit—the limit at which the difference between one Self and the All and the difference between one's Self and the insight that there is really no such thing as one's own Self disappears, and the impression of reflection (mirroring) and possession (self-referential location) vanishes completely.

This exercise *almost* engages, but really circumvents, two other potential internal paths of self-transcendence; yet it also emphasizes another important external path of selflessness, as a powerful bridge *crossing the differences* between the Self and the Other and, really, the difference between any being other than me. It may be close to the Hindu *tat tvam asi* (That art Thou) and the equation of *atman* with *brahman*, that is, of Self with Spirit, but its approach is more limited and developmental, meant to be an exercise of *becoming* rather than presupposing the sudden insight of being *that*. It also reflects the epigraph of Arthur Schopenhauer to this chapter in which the difference between the Self and the Other becomes an illusion because self-transcendence and alterity are ultimately *the same movement*.

> *Imagine, again, that other person in front of you, mirroring your Self into that person:*
>
> *what would it be like to "be" that person?*
>
> *Now, realize, if just for a moment, at first, that you are that person . . .*
>
> . . .
>
> *Imagine that all you feel to be your Self (not discriminative, but holistically, as one, your felt identity) is not like, not as, but simply "is" the other Self . . .*
>
> . . .

> *What if there is only* one *Self, mirroring itself in all of us? . . .*
>
> *What do I feel, as my I is* exactly *what anyone feels as I? . . .*
>
> . . .
>
> *Now, imagine that all inner feeling you have of your Self is just that: the feeling that anything and everything has of itself (its Self), whether human or not . . .*

In this exercise, the two approaches of selflessness engaged, but not imitated, are these: first, self-reflection—a method recommended by the Hindu sage Ramana Maharshi (d. 1950) to concentrate on the "I" and nothing else in order to realize that it does not exist as separate being but is the "I-I" (the Hebrew divine "I am"); and, second, the Buddhist mindfulness training in the Vipassana meditation, the insight (*vipassana*) of the absolute emptiness of Self. The exercise of Meditation XVIII, *instead*, only attempts to expand the mirroring beyond the self-reflective self-control of remaining "one's Self" while attempting to be *not* "one's Self." This is one of the paradoxes of the Hindu and Buddhist insight into what emptiness of Self means: that as soon as we *know*, we cannot know "it" without establishing the Self that knows it (itself) again.

The specific form of selflessness this exercise emphasizes, however, is that of the *acts* of selflessness, be it in individual or social, internal or external context. This "selflessness" of forgoing one's interest for the wellbeing of others is a central element of Jesus's message: the love of the neighbor *as* one's Self (Mark 12:31; Galatians 5:15), the sermon on the Mount (Matthew 5–7), the love of the enemy (Matthew 5:43–45), selfless service (Luke 10:29–37; Philippians 2:5–7), giving up one's will in God's name (Matthew 6:9–13; Luke 22:42) and dying for another (Mark 10:45; Galatians 2:20). Yet it also reflects the *satyagraha* of Mahatma Gandhi and, more generally, the realization of the *karma yoga* of the *Bhagavad Gita* (see chs. 4 and 12), that is, selfless acting. Such acts are religious, philosophical, ethical, or aesthetical in nature, but are always acts that cannot be substituted by merely inherent psychological or individual "spiritual" changes of attitudes or meditations. They are always "acts of dispossession" from possessiveness; liberating acts, individually and socially; or expressions of responsibilities wider than oneself, but not motivated by mere duty, psychologically imitating parameters or external social pressure (they are, in other words, neither acts of the Freudian "Id" nor of the "Super-ego").

Hence, this exercise is a preparation both *against* self-acted, reflective selflessness or the expectation of the experience of selflessness (of *anatta*) and *for* the immediate acts of selflessness that don't need differences of Self and Other to even arise. This exercise, then, does not *overcome* the feeling of Self by directly piercing into its selflessness—which would establish the Self again. Rather, this exercise widens the Self-feeling in such a way that it begins to know that the Other is *nothing but the same* Self, with the same feelings of love and hate, desire and aversion, self-preservation and doubt, self-aggrandizement and self-effacement. There is *no* difference! All *feel* the same (way). All *are* the same (way). All *is* the same (way).

Now, try again . . .

Do not imagine, know . . . *that the other person is to itself, their Self, exactly the same Self that you are to yourself, your Self* . . .

. . .

From now on, be *your Self in that manner* . . .

Love/God

A good question, at this point, is this: Why should there be another section that goes beyond the essential virtues of self-transcendence and signs of individual, social and cosmic spiritualization indicated in the previous section? It seems the potentials are exhausted. When all is said and done, an ending at the previous section may have been indicating that self-transcendence is the *essence* of spiritualization; and if that is what religion contributes to the human spirit—what is there more to say? Pause; break; period. The preceding two Meditations XVII and XVIII have also emphasized this line of thought: *selflessness* as ultimate medium of religious existence that aims at human spiritual transformation on all planes of magnitude, from quantum smallness to the unimaginable magnitude of the multiverse.

Yet something seems to be missing. What could it be? I think it is the dual insight that we only gain if we add the motley, even empty, but irreplaceable terms of *Love* and *God*. Let me explain what I mean. Self-transcendence seems to aim at some kind of universalization of Self (*atman*) or the overcoming of Self (*anatta*), self-forgetfulness (the Self of the martyr and the Suffering Servant) and self-obliteration (the death of Self, Sufi *fana*, unitive fusion with divine essence or life beyond individualization)—but what about the deeply spiritual experiences of the love of a person or the deeply personal efforts in pursuing a universal, global or common good agenda, demanding self-less or self-transcendent engagement with the world; or what about experiences of the numinous, as relating meaning by meaning *me*, personally, not any general self-less essence of my diffusion in the All or only registering generalized universals such as values and virtues instead of the ones actualizing them from their heart? I have avoided laying emphasis on these classically "personal" and "theistic" spiritual impulses and existential experiences in this chapters until now in order to, at last, regain some sense of the irreplaceability of this *personal* divine dimension in the discussion of the cosmic Spirit and the ways of spirituality. By having gone through, and, in a certain sense, by having exhausted, the transcendentalizing movements of spiritualization, I am now in the position to be able to present the missing element in the clarity of its irresistible attraction and irreplaceable necessity for a more complete understanding of the numinous in the nine ways, modes, magnitudes, layers, plateaus and virtues represented by the chapters of this book.

This does, of course, *not* mean to take anything back in the understanding of the spiritual process of self-transcendence. It does also *not* mean a late reactive strike of theism, especially of some forms of the Abrahamic variety, over and against either the postmodern interest in more trans-personal and non-theistic approaches to universal spirituality today, for instance, by evoking mysticism, perennialism, transpersonal psychology, integral theory, New Age, global interspirituality, Neo-Vedanta, eastern spirituality in general, and particularly Buddhism in its various sprawling eastern and western forms, religious pluralism, desires for a unity and unified operation of religions, de-dogmatized religion not of doctrine but of experience, and the like. It is also *not* meant as a naïve recovery of for long outworn concepts of "love" and "god" that trigger as many negative as positive reactions; that are—as the Swiss theologian Karl Barth (d. 1968) once lamented—filled with all possible justification of violence in their name, and that have become *empty, as in blind*—as Karl Rahner admits at the basis of his diagnoses of the spiritual winter today.

Rather, this move is best understood as an acknowledgement that the spiritual process of cosmic *realizations*, of "incarnational" *embodiments* and the ecological *relationality* of all existences is as much a religious and spiritual paradigm as is self-transcendence, and one that is even the inherently unfolding of its very trajectory. This was already pointed out by following the internal direction that the cosmic expansion of the four spiritual virtues has exhibited: from ascent to descent, but also from individuation to nexic all-relationality, and from directional, revisable laterality to polarity and mutual immanence. Polyphilia is the process of "bodying" (see ch. 8), of transcendence *within*, of cosmic realization; and it is already essentially what the emphasis of this section is about: divine *love*—love of the manifold. And as polyphilia is the love of ultimate Reality that, as with Plato's Good and Plotinus's One *is, has, possesses, needs nothing*—indicating emptiness and pleroma, simultaneously—so as to be without restrictions able to overflow into a multiverse, so is the "virtual" realization of this movement *into* the world through Awakening, Detachment, Compassion, as well as the cosmic sites of Consciousness, Soul-fullness, and Civilization, aiming at, and converging in, the Omega Point of Peace in which Reality *indifferentiates itself* (its "self-less Self") *from* the cosmic All.

In fact, the pair Love/God *is* the self-transcendence of the trajectory from Polyphilia/Multiverse to Peace/Reality, which can only be understood as the complete apophatic indifference between both Love and God, and as a complete restatement of the Omega Point of Conversion of self-transcendence as the Primal Point of *Origin*, of the polyphilic overflow that loves *the particular, the unique, the actual, the irreplaceable events and the nexic life-history* of such realizations. If this means to give credit to the intuitions and experiences harbored by invoking concepts of love and God, of "theistic" feelings and the depth of what we mean when we say that love is meant to be "personal"—so be it! But the point of departure of the conceptual constraints of these concepts of person, love, God, here, come from *this* framework, and not from any other possible contextualization, such as whether theism is right over non-theism, or whether Buddhist compassion is as good as Christian love. And as the trajectory of the movement from Polyphilia/Multiverse to Peace/Reality to Love/God indicates: the theistic and personal dimension of this movement is one of *divine "incarnational" self-transcendence into the world*, which is not interested in abstractions or plans or general visions or systems of morality or any other measure, but only in *unique events of actualization of this self-less gift in a resonant response of self-transcendence*—not because the Self is in some sense a bad "thing," but because it is the *only* "thing" that is established in this divine love-relation of the spiritual process and, hence, the *only* "thing" that can be given and transcended in fulfillment of its meaning, namely because it was meant *personally*.

Love and God are *without reserve indifferent from one another*—as God *is* Love (1 John 4:7–21) as much as Love as such *is* God (see the epilogue of the book)— they are not different from one another, as if God was also "something else" or love was "something else"; yet they are also *not identical* with one another, because they indicate the polyphilic movement of the overflowing expansion of and from the unique, incomparable apophatic mystery. Love/God is the apophatic mystery *in* its polyphilic love; this polyphilic love is that of the inexhaustible mystery. This mystery is both *inaccessibly* beyond any grasp by any of its creatures, expressions, expansions, actualizations and emanations, and *inexhaustible* in its accessibility to its creatures, expressions, expansions, actualizations, and emanations. With Pseudo-Dionysius the Areopagite, the mystery of Love/God indicates the always escaping Silence beyond any access of the revelatory Word, and, simultaneously, with Thomas Aquinas (1225– 74), the infinite Pleroma of self-revelation, an infinite open Book, an inexhaustible Word. It is this "dipolar" theism (see ch. 5) that is meant, here, of which the personal perspective on Love and God means: that the self-transcending apophatic Pleroma is nothing else but the polyphilic love that, because of this *unique apophatic/pleromatic mystery*, is, in its overflowing, *personal*. This is the *personal* understanding of *love*: the mutuality of the unique divine mystery with the unique mystery of life-histories of creatures, established by the divine call or erotic attraction not just into being, but into the *unique meaning* that only *it* (the creative event of God) can give and *it* (the creative event of the creature) can become. And this is the *trans-pantheistic* understanding of the *ultimate personhood* of God (see ch. 8): that it is not a mask of divine manifestation, but *the dipolar pleromatic uniqueness* in the process of polyphilic creation, revelation, elation, and mutuality.

Let me explain what this means further in relation to the three notions of Love, Person, and God. There are, of course, many different perspectives understanding and conceptualizing Love. The Greek triad of friendship (*philia*), attraction (*eros*), and self-giving (*agape*) are not the same as the Hebrew loving-kindness (*hesed*), or the Hindu worship of God (*bhakti*), or eastern and western forms of the female/male love-tensions within God's love (*shakti, hokmah, sophia*); the love of God and neighbor (in the Shema Israel and the Double Commandment in the New Testament) is not the same as the Sufi love of obliteration into the Beloved (*fana*); the magnetism of love that unites and fuses a multiplicity of beings is not the same as the Platonic ecstasy by which to self-transcend oneself and any reasonability into the rushing sea and frenzied madness of the divine unification; dying for a friend is not the same as loving an enemy or loving or dying for the whole world (of humanity, or the community of all beings of the earth, or the cosmos); familial love (to parents, children) is not the same as love for spouses or friends; sexual love is not the same as loving the beauty of a flower; the love for abstract ideas is not the same as the love of persons.

In all of these forms of love, two tendencies can be found to perform their movements, at once: self-transcending, uniting and meta-rational experimentation with, and experience of, ecstatic unity, on the one hand, as in the forms of post-philosophical madness recorded Plato's dialogue *Phaedrus* where Socrates, otherwise the philosopher of argumentative unknowing, praises the unintelligible, transpersonal states of consciences expressive of the fire of love. On the other hand, love can also, as in Teilhard de Chardin, mean *that* unification that simultaneously *differentiates*, a complication process that *personalizes* us. In other words, unification is super-personalization by which we don't become less personal but *more* personal in the sense of *uniqueness*, that is, of becoming the irreplaceable terminus of universal, interrelational connectedness.

Both movements of love can be expressed as "super-personal" in the sense of becoming *more than personal* (as restricted category of individuality) and *more personal*, as becoming more unique. As both movements are to be considered together, we can say that spiritualization is the process by which uniqueness becomes universal and universal reality become personalized.

Here, I highlight the *second* movement, that of *personalization*, because it is often degraded, equally by philosophical idealists and materialists, to a secondary epiphenomenon or to a temporary expression of bodiliness or to an ephemeral phenomenon of the material world and its physical retractions. Yet, counter to this opinion, relational *uniqueness* in all phenomena and their mutual encounters is that which Immanuel Kant has defined as transcending mere functionality, being a "purpose" and not only some "means." This is what in any phenomenon, if it happens, constitutes or reveals the *personal* in its universal connectedness and divergent embodiments (whether human or not is irrelevant, here).

In this sense, love is the *mutual immanence* of the "other life" in one another to the point that we begin to awake to our *irreplaceability* in this relation. Yet instead of shying away from the *particularity* of such a love—the Slovenian philosopher Slavoj Zizek (b. 1949) characterized it as ugly preference, and Whitehead also hesitated its use because of its limited bias of (self-)interestedness—we can understand the characteristic of uniqueness as expressing itself through polyphilic, detached, compassionate, peaceful relationality because of its apophatic/pleromatic mystery by which love is without want and need, that is, pure self-transcendence, but also irreplaceable unique relationships constituting the nexus of all relations or the connectivity of the All.

If this *dipolar* constitution of personhood is understood as originating in the *apophatic/pleromatic uniqueness* as that which is mediated in the polyphilic creativity of the multiverse, instead of being a mask (*persona*) of the inaccessible mystery, the related understanding of God as Person will a priori avoid the unfortunate duality of primary apophatic transpersonal Godhead or ultimate Reality and the secondary manifestations of it in personal faces or masks that, in the best case, are skillful means of awakening and, in the worst case, nothing but imagined or illusioned projections triggered by fundamental human limitations and ill-directed desires. The latter is the often preferred scheme by many religious and spiritual interpretations in the east and the west if they accept the mystical, apophatic and trans-personal mystery as *primary* or ultimate "characterization" (beyond any characterization), as *nirguna brahman*, as nameless Dao, as Godhead beyond God, as the apophatic One, as the *Deus absconditus*, as the *dharmakaya*, as the inaccessible and unknowable divine essence beyond existence, as Being itself, as Nothingness (*sunyata*), as the Nameless, as the Placeless, as Advaitic nondual Reality, and so forth. Yet we may not be bound by such a "hierarchical" schematization differentiating of the layers of "ultimate" and "manifest."

Although there have been counter-examples among religious traditions, such as pluralistic Jainism and nondual Kashmiri Shaivism, for instance, of Abhinavagupta (d. 1016), and philosophies such as that of the "absolute Spirit" in Hegel or the ultimate multiplicity of (spiritual) monades in Leibniz—emphasizing either the indestructability and universality of a multiplicity of liberated souls as the highest achievement of the cosmic Spirit or by understanding or making even our limited self-consciousness a moment of divine ultimacy. But, nevertheless, while "personal" in some significant sense, they often still remain in a *penultimate* position compared with the universal unity in the Spirit (either as God or as cosmos) in which they are housed or that they reflect as finite exemplars.

The unequal emphasis of the trans-personal over the personal understanding of ultimate Reality or God seems almost to be unavoidable in schemes that operate from such hierarchizations. For instance, in John Hick's pluralistic proposal, especially in the classical passages of his book *The Interpretation of Religion* (1989), the personal and non-personal approaches—divine *personae* and *impersonae*—found in diverse religions and sub-streams of even the same religious traditions only seem to collect them on an equal level, but, in fact, don't do so because Hick submits them *both* as secondary "faces" of the divine to the ultimately inaccessible, unknowable Real that, as it is beyond all categories trans-personal, that is, different from the personal, but indifferent from the impersonal divine "faces," emphasizes the impersonal "character" of ultimacy.

However, in the *dipolar* understanding (see ch. 5), the "personal" is not one equal side of two (the other being impersonal) or a secondary level (the ultimate being trans-personal), but the very *polar field or mutuality of the apophatic/pleromatic and the polyphilic/emanating pole of divine Reality*. It is the *polarity* of the mystery oscillating, circling, or vibrating between apophatic and polyphilic, or pleromatic and emanating movements—in my book *God as Poet of the World* (2003/2008), I have called this movement "in-differentiation" (§40)—that *is* itself that which *defines* a Person. And God is the Alpha and Omega of this personal dipolar field in which anything can, if at all, become personal if, and only if, it is uniquely touched by the uniqueness of the pleromatic manifesting Mystery in the mutual relation to its Self—the one Self that is *completely* Self-transcendence to the Unique that the relation manifests (see ch. 3).

Perhaps, here, one of the meanings of personhood that developed within the Christian encounter with Greek metaphysics, but later liberated itself from its substantialist categories, taking on the relational characteristics that defined even the philosophical discussions of "personhood" in Jewish and Christian personalism of the late nineteenth and early twentieth century as well as the related understanding of revelation as personal self-engagement, self-communication, and the selfless gift of God to creation, has been borne out by the ancient trinitarian discussions. In their enormous, many centuries lasting wrestling with the differentiation between, first, divine essence and personhood and, second, the mapping on it of the problem of the one and many, the one insight that became irresistible to all sides was this: that *a person is a unique but universal, irreplaceable relation.*

The theological problems inherent in this insight fill the Christian analyses of disputations for the better part of the last two millennia. They are not immediately relevant, here. But what we can take away from their insights is what Whitehead in *Adventure of Ideas* in inimitable clarity has characterized as the unfortunate dogmatic limitation of the *only* metaphysical insight improving on Plato, namely, that the ultimate Reality *in* God, *between* God and the world (all worlds), and in *any* possible "personal" incarnations is an expression of *mutual immanence*. And that *this* mutuality means also a mutual *transcendence*—not sameness, but difference; not identity, but expansion of movements of divergence; unifications, yes, unison, yes, but always as a multiplicity of such relations that are irreplaceably unique (of events) even if (and as) they are of universal import (of valuations and values), like the realization of virtues and cosmic sites of divine manifestation.

Other than Whitehead, I will add, here, that the dipolar understanding of "the personal" that I am proposing here, namely, *being the polarity itself*, manifests uniqueness not only by the contingencies of bodying (the sur/faces), but by the inexhaustibility of the apophatic pole, which is per definition indifferent from its manifestations and beyond any composition of difference and identity, impersonal and personal trajectories, or divergency and unity. As "the personal" is constituted by the indifferent *apophatic* pole (the *depth* of the sur/face), and not only (or just) by the differentiating polyphilic pole, *there is no beyond to the ultimate personality of God.*

It is in this sense that we need not shield the ultimate expression of *uniqueness* and *incomparability* of God in the Qur'an, especially as expressed in the Surah 112, from being the root of what personhood means. It is in this sense that we can, now, also assert that the ultimate Personality of Krishna in the *Bhagavad Gita* and the bhakti-oriented *Bhagavata Purana* (before the second millennium CE) in the tradition of Gaudiya Vaishnavism is not a hidden code for the trans-personal, Advaitic reinterpretation, but exactly what it indicates: that all ways end in Krishna (*Bhagavad*

Gita, ch. 12), the Supreme Divine *Person* (*Svayam Bhagavan*). We may, in this sense, also in a much stronger way emphasize that if Samantabhadra talks in term of a Person in Buddhist scriptures, or the universal Gautama Buddha in the *Lotus Sutra*, it is not just a skillful means for weak people who need such bridges for their awakening, but, rather, as several Mahayana Sutras boldly claim, the Self (*atman*) of ultimate Realty/ the Buddha-dharma "itself" expressing, revealing, awakening to "*its*" ultimately personal Reality. And it may be in this sense, then, that the trinitarian discussion on the difference between the divine Persons, the difference between God and the divine Persons, and the difference between the immanent (world-transcendent) and the economical (world-immanent) Trinity can also be understood as indicating different perspectives on the *one ultimate dipolar field of relations that is the ultimate personal Pleroma of the Mystery in the process of polyphilic manifestation*, thereby mediating its uniqueness to all that it touches and perceiving its/their unique mutuality—*from heart to heart*, as it were.

So, if we begin to see the connection between Love as *relationality* and *mutuality of the unique* that is an *inexhaustible mystery* and Personhood as this *dipolar apophatic and polyphilic Mystery of that relation*, and if Love and God are *indifferent*, then, we can say about the concept of God here invoked that it cannot be divided in personal and impersonal; that it is not penultimate in relation to an impersonal mystery beyond God; that the God beyond God is not the trans-personal ultimate of which the simple God is only a manifestation. Rather, the polar relation of Love is the *only* unique Mystery that deserves the name "God." Love that is God burns through the continuity of any conceptuality that divides and hierarchizes.

This is not implying *theism*, as this personhood self-transcends any substantialized notion of God as "a being" that happens to love; rather if Love is God, there is no "being" that loves. The uniqueness of Love is only manifest in the unique relations that it brings forth and sustains as the khoric field of intercommunication. It does not mean *pantheism*, either, as Love is not identical with anything but itself, and not different from anything insofar as it is loving relation; but love is not the universe or multiverse or creation, as the divine self-transcendence is only indifferent from acts of love, not their hindrance or opposition or ignorance or sinful denial, to which love is only patient, not affirmative or admitting. It does also not mean *pan-en-theism*, as this image presupposes, first, a being "within which" the world is (still perpetuating the classical theistic dualism of within and without, although in this case denying the world-transcendent, external without). Rather, if there is a label, Love as God may be understood in the figure of *trans-pantheism*, that is, the *indifference* that is *neither* identical with the world as love is always transcending, *nor* different from it either, as love is always seeking the unique within.

Yet as *the Self of self-transcendence* of any identity, divine Love is the Person that has no being or possesses anything and, hence, *even transcends the divinity of Love* so as to love beyond itself (its Self), to become what it loves, and to remain indifferent from that which loves it back.

Finally, on a human level: The spiritual seeker is not only a means to an aim, like a plane for the realization of virtues, or the site of becoming the expression of their cosmic realization, the playing field of divine or demonic or cosmic forces, and the like. None of us is an abstract universal, such as a conglomerate of characteristics or the summery of our acts or a list of universals or even a sum of molecules—we are unique persons, but we only awaken to this truth when we receive the gift, or offer the gift, and, hence, when we experience *the mystery of mutual love* that immediately tells us that it is *us*, our Selves, who are meant, and it is someone's "other life" that is meant. It is such experiences that relate *meaning* at least *as intensely and deeply as* experiences of self-transcendence that intend to overcome the ego-self: the way of self-purification that we have highlighted as modes of spiritual selflessness. Yet it is the same ego-self that hinders the self-transcendence of love through which the uniqueness of mutuality is born and sustained.

This is the insight that should become the companion of your spiritual search: *ultimate* meaning cannot be approached by believing that the overcoming of Self is an end in itself, at best, dissolving ours Selves in some universal Reality. Rather, ultimate meaning of one's existence can *only* reveal itself in the awakening to Reality *as Love* that manifests itself (its Self) not in abstract forms of love, but only in *concrete, irreplaceable* loving relationships that reveal the unique mystery of the ones in *this* loving relationship. *The universal is the unique,* here, and *the unique relation is the universal, self-transcendent cosmic presence of the divine*—this is the side of the personal and the revelation of the ultimate as *personal*. This, we can name "Love/God"—the universally circulating release of the comic Spirit.

Epilogue: Extinction

There are always aspects of any understanding of existence to which we feel blindness to be advantageous, or dangerous. *Ambivalence* is profound in matters of ultimate importance. Most of the Epilogues to the nine paths relate the encounter of the numinous character or aura of the journey through "the spiritual"—for the spiritualization of the cosmos recognizing some of the spiritual matter and the sensible signs of its sacredness—as they emphasize and acknowledge these blind spots of ambivalence. This Epilogue is no exception, but rather an intensification.

So, what is the "blind spot" of the spiritualization of the "dome of time," of "the life of other days"? One might be inclined to say: that which is always the thorn in any spiritual explanation or interpretation of the impermanent world, namely, the absurdity of the suffering of sentient beings, of the finiteness and mortality of conscious life, of evil intentions and the powers of nature to seemingly be an accomplice of the pursue of them, as well as of the stark violence of cosmic life. And one would not be wrong. These absurdities need to be addressed and, without explaining them away, be given at least some meaning either in the sense of their limited value in light of a greater good or as illusions of a distorted mind, or as unavoidable shadows and implications of important features of a universe that hosts consciousness and compassion, which, so one justification goes, cannot be had without some degrees of freedom and its potential destructive, collateral vortices.

So far, so good. No religious tradition was ignorant of this problem and could survive without developing some potential solutions in their understanding of the world—isn't it their business to react precisely to the existential crises that the experience of such ambivalences raises? No philosophical understanding of the cosmic realities of suffering, evil, violence, and destructiveness can afford not to consider it as part of a valuation of the physically or spiritually "ordered" integrity of the "cosmos," either. Answers are plenty. They generally begin with pre-scientific solutions that blame humanity, some evil force, a dark counter-principle or even god(s) for this predicament. Such kinds of explanation have usually, in a reflection on the origin of the universe, grouped themselves around some existential defect, of that which "ought not to be" (Plato's *me on*), either born from human or pre-human sin (Abrahamic tendency) or sentient ignorance (Dharmic tendency).

However, taking into account our current scientific knowledge, consider this: We now know that life on this earth, much more ancient than, and far beyond, any human involvement, was at least *five times* in its history exposed to *near total extinction events*! So, according to our best scientific knowledge today, such events have erased *all* life on Earth unfortunately exposed to these happenings *up to almost 100 percent*—but certainly between 78 and 96 percent, every time!

Let us meditate on this fact a while longer. Granted that humanity has a bad record of sensitivity to suffering, ethical insight into right action, and the establishment and perpetuation of the good life—but if any human being wanted to experiment with life such that it explicitly accepts the risk of extinguishing it and only *by chance fails* to eradicate all of it—this is not sin or ignorance. This is sheer madness! What? Do you think you can cook up any meaning or value important enough to defend an action that would imply the destruction of almost all of life in order to make place for humanity to appear on mother Earth—as has happened in the Cretaceous-Paleogene extinction event 65 million years ago with the Yucatan asteroid explosion that ended the reign of the dinosaurs and cleared the way for the mammals and, later, apes that, eventually, led to the rise of humanity? Or how about proposing to release sufficient volcanic waste into the atmosphere to cover the earth with a thick blanket of death and then to see how anything that *might* perchance survive will do—as has happened in the most severe extinction event and the Permian-Triassic boundary about 252 million years ago, the so-called "Great Dying" that extinguished 96 percent of all life? Or do you think that any laboratory would grant a stipend to your proposal to reduce all forms of life, say, from the dizzying variety that the soft-bodied fossils of the

Burgess Shale from 600 million years ago has revealed to the staggering 1 percent of all historic life-forms that have survived today?

Or how about the volcanic eruption of the Toba super-volcano on Sumatra 75,000 years ago that might have left us with the *genetic bottleneck* of near-identical genetic code in all human beings, possibly because only a *few dozen* humans (of the species *homo sapiens*) survived? The physicist Michio Kaku begins his considerations on *The Future of Humanity* (2018) with this event: as the basis from which to always remain alert to the *complete certainty* that such events will hit Earth again, either in the form of comets or super-volcanoes, if we don't destruct ourselves anyway by atomic war or environmental degradation. The tendency of religions to imagine eschatological end-scenarios of the world has it all wrong! Humanity doesn't need to lock into the future for an eschatology; extinction is hardwired into collective biological makeup. Human history *begins* with the memory of apocalyptic events. The widespread deluge and conflagration myths of ancient cultures, as, for instance, reported in Plato's *Timaeus*, were already in his time "ancient knowledge" (see ch. 1), and are just a faint memory of such colossal catastrophes.

Or more recently: How about the apocalyptic memory, immortalized throughout diverse cultures, of the "black death"? The bubonic plague, burning through Asia, Africa and Europe in the fourteenth century, killing, according to some estimates, in some vast swaths of land, half of the population: the streets and houses filled with corpses; no sanitation or hygiene; piles of waste and wasted bodies; the all-pervading odor of death and putrefaction; despite differences of means, social boundaries and territorial borders between classes, peoples, cultures, political powers and religions, vast and deep interruptions of social, political, cultural, religious and sheer humanitarian integrities. Chaos transgressing all boundaries and equalization in illness and death. The virus makes no distinction. The Justinian plague of the sixth century; the plague that began in Yunnan and devastated China, Mongolia, and India in 1855; the Spanish flu of 1918, with up to 50 million deaths; the bird flu, the swine flu, the diverse coronaviruses of the twentieth century; the grave global impact of the Covid-19 pandemic of 2020 . . .

Life gone rogue, splitting off mere reproduction from all other life-functions, isolating survival from environmental integrity, immortality from the interrelation of becoming like cancer cells, perpetuation from change and novelty, destructive traits from involved patterns of beauty. With viral power, we face a persistent wound not only to humanity's physical, social, and political bodies but also to any level of biological existence, and with its forces of indifferent destruction we can even anticipate a final breakdown of human civilization or even the human life form as such. We face the real possibility of an overkill that may exponentially engulf this planet and facilitate the viral death of humanity. We face the ugly disappearance of the spirit in matter, of mind in bodies of mere survival, of the beauty and expansive landscape of living, feeling organisms in merely self-regarding strings of DNA.

What does such life-destructive biology tell us about the nature of the cosmos, the harmony of life, and their spiritual character? Is it a divine punishment of humanity or the wrath of Gaia? Is it a process of self-purging, namely, of another "virus" on the face of the planet: humanity? Or is it an accident of the rules of evolution, a possibility or even necessity in the unfolding of the mechanics of life? Or is it the materialization of a spiritual rule: the all-present potential of self-regarding ego-identity, insensitive to the wider horizons of life, to invaded, pervade and undermine the patient fragility of spiritual landscapes evocative of cosmic harmonies? Perhaps, is this patience a necessity of the cosmic Spirit's ultimate avoidance of coercion and its final commitment to goodness and the attraction to beauty?

Instead of seeking out reasons for the wonder of the lucky survival of life after such repeated cataclysmic squeezes, we should ask: What is it that hindered the achievement of the ultimate aim of this scenario, namely, the successful elimination of life, eventually and completely? And this does not even take into account the cosmological environment of the massive destructive violence operating in the fundamental physical forces, creating black holes, neutron stars, supernovae, distortions of space-time, cosmic inflation, the Big Bang and potential cosmic end-scenarios such as the Big Crunch or the Big Freeze. It *is* a miracle that life survived—but life is itself not less violent in its urge for food and reproduction, mutual destruction and arms races for supremacy.

Can we really, given these facts, believe in any *purpose* within the patterns of the universe, in its intended and eventual spiritualization, or in any realistic prospect of the overcoming of Darwinian violence by cooperation, mutual immanence, relationality and peace? It seems rather obvious that only *chance* or *necessity* will survive as alternative options for an explanation of existence—and both are not less cold and absurd, if you think about their implications.

Current attempts to use versions of quantum theory proposing virtual fields of potential states, uncertainty of concurrent measurements of characteristics, indeterminacy of crossings of the threshold between virtual and actual events (if at all, as not all quantum interpretations agree on that either), and the like, to *substitute* spiritual cosmologies of world-emanation from the undifferentiated One with a *naturalized*, reductionist quantum-"materialism" (the One as the quantum field) will only heighten the impression of the inescapability of the combination of chance and necessity as the *only* "rules of the game"—not only betraying the spiritual cosmologies that they try to translate into naturalistic terms, but also the fundamental importance of the escape *beyond* chance and necessity so *essential* for these spiritual and mystical cosmologies, be it in the form of the insight into, or the salvation by, Reality/God as that which can in no way be defined by either and, hence, can liberate from their debilitating operations. Exceptions, whether or not in the end spiritually relevant, only confirm this rule. John Wheeler's and Henry Stapp's generalized or even universal claim of the breakdown of the wave-function through *consciousness* (of an observer) inevitably introduces *purpose* into the equation (see chs. 3 and 8). Yet precisely the chance of *avoiding* a "purposeless" naturalism (even with emerging characteristics of consciousness from matter/energy- or space/time-fields, rendering such purpose just an illusion) is in question here. Given the absurdity of extinction attacks of the magnitude under consideration (as well as the violent context of the physical forces in general), chance and necessity under the exclusion of purpose might be the *only* explanation left, thereby evaporating any spiritual meaning of existence.

If there was any proof of God, the extinction scenarios will blow it out of its idyllic hideaway. Teleology (the proof from guided evolution)? Are you joking? Ontology (the proof from the ground of being)? What do you mean: born to be annihilated? Intelligent design (the proof from supernatural intervention)? Frankly, which intelligent being would affirm such a scenario as acceptable and intelligible—except a delusional madman?

Spiritual and religious minds have found other coping mechanisms (than proofs of their intelligibility), neutralizing evil and existential absurdity, such as divine patience, chaos, multiplicity, or impermanence. But none of them can fit the bill, either: humans were not even on the menu, yet; and if all life on Earth had to die several times over just to produce the strange species of humans in this mediocre corner of an unexceptional galaxy among billions—this would also not be a "great" history to be proud of, only one of the perpetuation of series of explosions and of mass extinctions. How could *this* gospel be sound? "God mass-murdered almost all life *several time over* to manufacture a home for humanity on Earth." And how about Mother Earth herself: Is she a good mother that cares for her children or a raven mother who lets everything (biosphere) and everyone (noosphere) drown and burn who happens to roam her surface while she cools down, erupts, trembles and spits fire and brimstone?

Sure, we could rule out purpose—not even freedom can justify such mass-murder—and any personal god (what kind of person would such a god be, anyway?) and, if we don't want to become mere materialists, stick with some kind of insentient (or quasi-sentient) life- or spirit-force as cosmological well of existence, instead. Some "panspiritual" solutions, conjuring up something like a zero-point quantum/energy-field, as, for instance, in the work of the Hungarian system-theoretician Ervin László (b. 1932) or the American theoretical physicist Fred Alan Wolf (b. 1934), standing in a "new" tradition *equating* subtle physical realities with deep spiritual nature, present themselves a metaphysical alternative to both materialist reductionism and the idiosyncratic views of historic religious traditions. However, I have never understood the feeling of comfort related to such a concept. What is "it"? Is it unconscious or superconscious, some kind a spiritual matter or energy—some kind of *qi*, acting like lava or the electrical field? Or is it a reactive but inaccessible ocean, acting like Stanislav Lem's *Solaris*? And does it really make a difference whether we think of Reality in terms of matter and chance instead of universal consciousness and love (or for no good reason equate them) *if* both lead to the same outcome: the dissipation of uniqueness (non-possessive, but unexchangeable meaning of "being meant") as a mere phenomenal insignificance—as argued against in the previous section? So, in this case, we may do even better by *not* imagining such a force in the first place, as it can in no way live up to the aesthetic preciousness and ethical summons of conscious beings, except maybe, in the best case, as a lame body of backwater (a ghostly universal consciousness) and, in the worst case, as the monster (a ghastly general evil) that we would rather not like to encounter if we are not sadists or masochists.

More sophisticated approaches, for instance, the "panspiritual" view of Steven Taylor's book *Spiritual Science* (2018)—and potential alternative interpretations of physical-spiritual "equations" as (metaphorical) "superpositions" in Laszlo's and Wolf's work as well as that of many others, assume a deeper reality of a "spirit-force" that is neither material or physical, that is, not identical with physical (although not material) energy-fields, nor identical with mind and consciousness, at least, in their individual form appearing in human embodiments, but the root and all-harboring and -pervading pure consciousness-force that *mirrors* itself in both physicality and mentality if the right evolutionary conditions are present. Again, avoiding both materialist reductionism and religious pluralism (at last theism in favor of eastern non-theism), this view appeals to the disenchanted mind—disenchanted with the simplicity of the mechanistic exclusivity of materialism *and* the troubling infinite complexity of religious diversity. Yet while "pan-spirit" opens us to a cosmos of deep purpose and meaning to which one *might* be able to agree *if* there was not the madness of a super-destructive "intention" or "nature" that would have to come with its "essence," given the apocalyptic past of life on the earth and its projected certain future of destruction.

Some people with special experiences, such as NDEs, have on occasion imagined that their super-empirical impressions led them to understand the vast cosmos as generally good and peaceful, only in a few spots exhibiting darkness by suffering—see the case of the neurosurgeon Eben Alexander (b. 1953). But how small can the life of one whole planet be to go unnoticed as being more than exposed to a darkness that cannot be explained by local sin or ignorance?

Religious thinkers such as Keith Ward have—as in *God, Chance and Necessity* (2009)—defended the purposefulness of life and cosmos and—as in *Pascal's Fire* (2007)—relegated suffering to a necessary corollary of the evolution and self-organization of life that develops toward freedom and consciousness or aims at personal life in the community with a personal God. He even considers the Hindu image of divine self-immolation as the beginning of, and justification for, a creation in suffering (see the epilogue to ch. 8). Some philosophers, such as John Leslie in his *Immortality Defended* (2007), understand the existence of a multiverse as the expression of the overall goodness of the thoughts of such a world in the divine Mind—of which there are supposed to be infinitely many—so that all evil we may encounter must be of either some value or doesn't lower the overall goodness under a certain threshold level at which a world would become untenable to be thought by a *divine* Mind. And how about the proliferation of philosophical reflections on the implications of the multiverse to necessitate or at least not to exclude the existence of most evil worlds, as, for instance, in *God and the Multiverse* (2015)—one wonders whether a world of *such* destructiveness as the earth would not qualify as such an abandoned possibility?

Even the indigenous spiritualities, say, of Native American, global shamanic, or ancient Indic and Chinese origin, with their assumption of an all-pervading Spirit of sacredness that expresses itself through nature and the matrix of Mother Earth must take the shock of the insight of the pervasive destructiveness seriously that their "spirit-force" or "life-force" or "divine Mother" must absorb to stay relevant. Sure, there is much less blindness to the destructive side of nature in these spiritualities as their ground or divine matrix is openly able to generate or sustain both good and evil, creative and destructive powers, light and darkness. Yet, they don't escape the mirroring of "relationality" with "unilaterality," of matriarchal with patriarchal indignities. The fragmentation and madness of Tiamat mirrors the coercive power of Marduk; the Kali-aspect of the Hindu divine Mother mirrors the ambivalence of creativity and destructiveness of Shiva; the darkness of "the world," while it is pervaded by the divine Wisdom-light in the Gospel of John, mirrors the tolerance of the divine Father that rises over good and evil in the Sermon on the Mount; the White Buffalo Calf Woman of Lakota prophecies is already an answer to the perpetual violence of the tribes in their mutual destructiveness, despite the respect and the pervasive grounding of Native spirituality in natural cycles and relational spirit-worlds; the moon-goddess mirrors the sun-god. Mother Nature—wherever it was revered—remains a dangerous and mortal companion of all life she gives, mirroring not only human imperfection, sin, or ignorance, but the *mysterium tremendum* itself. Yet all this ambivalence, admitting dark, disintegrative connotations within these spiritual universes, is not designed to cope with the sheer unimaginable weight of repeated extinctions of, on, and pointed against the earth as well as its cosmological ubiquity.

I am not convinced that *any* benign or facile or seemingly logical answers can live up to the *magnitude* of the explosion- and extinction-pattern of cosmic becoming unraveling in this history of repeated near total extinction events to be able to justify even in the slightest any reasonability for this madness. If there is any *spiritual* answer to the extinction paradox, that is, one that would allow for *some* comprehension of a meaningful co-existence of the assumption of a cosmic Spirit pervading the multiverse *and* the local and global ability of such a multiverse to produce life seemingly only by the activity and under the sword of such horrid forces of extinction, it will have to become a baseline for *all* spiritual endeavors.

Where do we go from here? Perhaps, we need to look again. Isn't there an always already sensed but as of yet not fully acknowledged and rather unexplored *potential* of the nine paths, the elements they invoke, and the numinous character of the spiritual

Earth that they convey to our human level of understanding, and by way of which they implicate us in their actions, that *they themselves harbor the nucleus of these forces of extinction*? Fires burn, waters drown, saltwater and the desert parch, rivers sweep away, mountains erupt as volcanoes or are remnants of violent foldings of the crust of the earth, time kills, space admits all kinds of catastrophes and chaos, turbulences of wind, water and fire disintegrate, rain suffocates and demolishes, trees fall and crush to death, clouds pour down floods and strike by lightning, winds atomize edifices and waste landscapes, suns burn, stars explode, comets penetrate, life-forms kill each other. This all is *in* the Spirit of the Earth in the multiverse.

What this Earth-Spirit seems to imply is this: *If there is a comic Spirit—Earth being one nucleus in the matrix of this spiritual cosmos—it is this Spirit that weaves the elements of destruction into elementary forces of life.*

Perhaps, we will not understand the cosmic Spirit if we don't admit that, under its gentle veil, it *covers* these destructive forces—much like the veil that Moses carried in order to protect the people from the radiation of his face after the encounter with the Glory of God on Sinai (Exodus 34:29–35). Spirit can be violent wind and consuming fire! Maybe, "purpose" is not the opposite of "power," weakness, or lack of force, but the ability to *contain* the destructive powers by a strength that can *withstand* their chaos and *direct* their release—like the containment of the sea in ancient imaginations of divine power (Psalm 89:9)? The process theologian Bernard Loomer (d. 1985) spoke of the "size" and "stature" of God to withstand but embrace all destructiveness and suffering without either succumbing to or operating on them. Perhaps, divine creativity is divine *and* benign only by being able to *absorb* the elementary forces of existence to some measure of coordination, harmonization, and unification, but without losing the intensities that burn in them. Creation may be the divine potential of *taming*—not necessarily by fighting chaos and containing an evil principle, as in Babylonian and Manichean cosmologies, but by *vibrating* over, harmonizing, rhythmizing, *composing* the divine poem *of* the face of the deep (Genesis 1:2). Perhaps, in this sense, the ability to *spiritualize*, that is, to withstand and absorb, pervade and envelop, the explosive energies of the creative activity of the numinous elements, which are driving apart the multiverse, is the ultimate transformation of the forces that *boil over from divine essence* (Meister Eckhart's *ebullitio*). Like the sun's emanating energy, its heat and light distribute life and death, depending on the right distance.

If we envision the energetic movements of the chaosmos, its explosive nature, its forces of expansion and the magnitude of the energy hidden in their elementary manifestations, perhaps, we gain access to the meaning of the *danger* accompanying the encounter with the numinous or divine, the *mysterium tremendum*, and of the divine power as one of purpose, that is, of the *attraction* of these forces of activity to ever new forms of harmony and intensity. And maybe the emergence of the earth in the matrix of the cosmos is the precious, exceptional, or at least wondrous manifestation of this "right distance."

Perhaps, then, we *have* a possibility to cope with the extinction-problem in a *new* way: The eruptive violence of the forces operating in this chain of events may tell us about a cosmic Spirit and the Spirit of the Earth that is *not like us*—we should not project our limitations and weaknesses on it (!)—but rather that this Spirit is like a *dancer on the fire of creativity*, attracting it into transformations that must, by way of their engagement of the numinous forces of existence, harmonize their potentials into spiritual amicability. Perhaps, this is the truth of the dancing god Shiva and the *shakti*, the divine consort, the goddess, divine energy: the unity of creation and destruction—a dance where creative novelty is also transfiguration of the old. Perhaps, the cosmic Spirit is—as in the *Bhagavad Gita*—the *uncontrollable pleroma of a creative fire* in all things in the form of a *love* that attracts and tames, sympathically directs and harmonizes, its potential of destructiveness without which creativity would only be a bad imitation of life, a mere facile, virtual clone without consequences, a mere child's play.

The Spirit is tremendous! Unleash it at your own peril!

Meditation XIX: The Placeless

The last Meditation of this book wants to experiment with the sym-pathic approach to the cosmos we live in in such a way that we can begin to inherently *feel* the necessity of adding the *personal* call of Love/God to the trans-personal fusion with or dissolution in, or self-transcending movement into, Peace/Reality. The way to achieve this will need an in-depth introduction that, step by step, will build up this insight by the contrary establishment of the missing or ambivalent character of our sense of the *personal worth of existence* as the basis for an ultimate acceptance of the meaning of existence as such. Since this *ambivalence* is the reason that we will never be able to make a case that all of it is not an illusion, the resulting atheism is just another condition necessary to find that "meaning" is a matter of spiritual transformation—of the kind this book has invoked—that must lead to the insight of our existence to be meant personally, or not at all. This Meditation is about the *placelessness* of Love/God and the "missing case" of *personhood*, the Placeless.

In their novel *The Light of Other Days* (2000), science fiction authors Stephen Baxter (b. 1957) and Arthur C. Clarke (d. 2008) develop the idea of a physical revolution that establishes micro-wormholes, not only allowing far sight into other spaces but also other times. History becomes a literal affair of "viewing" the actual events, and literal religion becomes the myth that it always was: Moses is discovered to have been only a mythical invention, and Jesus, although a "spiritual" personality, did not claim any religious authority, or even founded Christianity. But as we know from contemporary history: there are no facts without interpretation, and the history of interpretation becomes part of the effects that the facts have on history. Hence, while paradoxically religious literalism is obliterated by the literal view of events as they happen(ed), no literalism of fact-views can become relevant without interpretation. This means, symbolism is so deeply entrained in the constitution of facts that it cannot be removed, but only be *exchanged* by other symbolisms, as the womb of facts to become relevant in a future history of reception and appropriation to new events, histories and times with their specifically forming *zeitgeist*.

Literalism is literally impossible and *symbolic clouds of meaning are unavoidable*, because *values are inscribed in the formation of facts* and are that which we receive and transform as their effects in the future. A. N. Whitehead philosophically circumscribed this interference of facts and values as the constitution of *events* of actual happening by the *potentials* of past facts to be perceived by actual events and in their own interpretation, that is, the *valuing process*, transported, translated, and transformed into new facts of exhausted valuation, but with the promise of future potentials of perception, appropriation, adaptation, or transformation by the ongoing process of valuation in new actual events of the *synthesis* of past facts and their valuations. Potential fictional or factual far-viewings of other spaces and times would not change anything. Religious origins would, under such conditions, not be obliterated, but only symbolized differently—according to the potentials of values still energetically lingering in them and the valuation process initiated by the viewing process itself in a different time with its limitations, biases, syntheses of views, theories and habitual characters.

"Origenism" is not an *ersatz* for the process of valuation. Religions, rather, can, through revisiting of their history, be reinvented and take a different direction—to which all religious or social reform movements are evidence. In symbolic terms, religions unfold like trees, diversifying, even if the same life-fluid flows through them; and, like the rising of the sun to its zenith, they are not exhausted by their origin, but can genuinely become more expansive and gain depth in their development (as they also can die).

Yet a more fundamental and troublesome question is lurking under the assumption of the relativism that follows from both the value-laden nature of historical facts and the interpretative nature of any historical process of restatement, recovery, or reconstruction of, and change, transformation, translation, or transcendence into, new events of life-lines or branchings of such life-trajectories: Do any historical events ever release *direct evidence* of their spiritual origin or nature? If we may become disappointed in close proximity to the life of sages, prophets, and savior figures, for instance, or change our mind when we think we have discovered their "natural" biases and physical frailties, or when we never felt susceptible to their charismatic aura or experience their volatile unsubstantiality—are we not discovering the same *disappointment* that any more substantially religious interpretation of these figures and events consciously or unconsciously tries to hide, but is verily subject to the same sudden or gradual forms of obliteration?

The nine paths of approaching the cosmic Spirit, here, are, in fact, meant to be *experimental* answers to this question: Immediate experience can only be gained by the transformation that the numinous images and symbolisms of religions, related to the earth and the multiverse, have suggested if they are *actualized* in their own way and pace through the recognition of the movements of the *formlessness of self-transcendence* (see ch. 6). As the paradoxical and often criticized heritage of the theorist of religious pluralism, John Hick, has taught us: Even when the religious spirit is the transformation from self-centeredness to Reality-centeredness, what we find Reality "to be" is mostly a projection of our approach (a form of self-centeredness) rather than the "reality" of Reality itself, which remains apophatically inaccessible. Even with a polyphilic understanding of the selfless self-giving nature of Reality, we can only reach (mystical) insight into "its" *presence* through the transformation of any construction—which, as Derrida has taught us, can always be deconstructed—toward the undeconstructable, unconstructed "messianic" (always coming, never "being") Reality that is—as the "other bank" of the river of *samsara*, namely, *nirvana*—always paradoxically *beyond any approach* (see ch. 3) a gift of the Placeless.

In any case, spiritual realities or the reality of the Spirit cannot be constructed on the physical level or the level of externality, such that no "manifestation" of Reality can take away the ambivalence in the experience to be undecidedly caught between projection and transformation. Without falling into a Cartesian dualism of mind and matter, or their reduction to one another, we may not forget the sensitive realization of modern (post-Reformation, religion-critical) philosophers with their renewed wider religious mind (than any dogmatic limitation would have handed to them in their time), such as Leibniz and Kant, (who were painfully aware) that the realm of multiplicity can be divided into ever more multiplicities of multiplicities (think of the mathematics of the differential equation of Leibniz that is based on this insight) that does *not* allow for the realization of their undivided oneness and indivisible unity. Like Aristotle's living unity (*entelechia*) of beings, expressed through the principle of their soul (*psyche*) and its actualization, which these modern philosophers don't deny, this oneness is *beyond* this (physical) realm of "natural" unities; they are unconstructed monades, as in Leibniz, or, as in Kant, part of a non-physical realm of purposes and aims, of persons and freedom, beyond the "natural" realm of means. Many of the anti-religious and anti-theistic theories or even anti-mental and -spiritual word-reductions built their denials *on* this differentiation, but by declaring such a realm of aims and purposes, persons and virtues *non-existent*. Such theories of religion, as that of the masters of suspicion, for instance, Karl Marx and Sigmund Freud, wanted such spiritual impulses to be understood as illusions of a weak psyche or punished and oppressed people. Postmodern thinkers, such as Georges Bataille (d. 1962), found such teleological insertions to be only misplaced desires of the complete closedness of the material realm of means: all aims are only "means of means," leaving us, in the end, empty of any meaning (aim, purpose, *telos*).

This is what the authors of *The Light of Other Days*, in the related epigraph to this chapter, have formulated in as sharp and clear a form as possible—meditate on that!

> Greatness no longer matters. We see now that each human being who dies is
> the center of a universe: a unique spark of hope and despair, hate and love,
> going alone into the greater darkness.

This "emptiness," this disappointment, is one of the most *critical spiritual insights* of the apophatic nature of Reality! Yet it has another side to it: that the assumption and experience of a *telos* must be sought by sounding and the treading of paths of *love*, of the *love* of the other and of God, which is always *personal* and expresses the *unique* and the inexplicably *irreplaceable* in each and the All. Its insight is, indeed, of *another* level or intensity of "transcendence within" *beyond* the movements of self-transcendence as realized by the virtues of ascension, such as Awakening and Detachment, and the virtues of descent, such as Compassion and Peace. This also includes the differentiation of such spiritual moves *beyond* the realities that these virtues initiate and, as has been shown in the previous section on Love/God, that they cannot grasp: While Polyphilia brings forth Consciousness, the Soul, Civilization, and Reality that are bound to self-transcendence, Love/God harbors and harvests *uniqueness*, which (alone) opens us to the irreplaceable *telos* of meaning, unattainable by *any* means.

The test is simple: If you feel loved, if you know you are meant personally, in your mystery of your heart, in your apophatic uniqueness, and in relation to others that in their polyphilic relations to you exhibit their apophatic mystery as a pleroma that does not indicate ending or clearing, then, do you not feel that the world makes sense, that there is meaning to it? Sure, we can, with Feuerbach affirm Love, but deny God; but, as we saw in the previous section, this is an ill-conceived alternative, rather no alternative at all, since Love and God (even in Feuerbach's own view) are *indifferent from one another*. Not to project a god into the external cosmos as a "person-thing" is not the same as turning this insight into pantheism or atheism (as Feuerbach's work was obviously generally understood). Rather, we liberate God from such projections as existence or thing-ness or being "a" (limited) person, and the like. If meaning does not touch us personally, it is abstract or general; it does not concern us in our hearts—we could be dead and nothing would change! If we experience this nihilism, we may seek our spirituality to cover the loss of meaning. We may embrace a spirituality of self-transcendence in the forms of mystical obliteration of the Self or de-personalization into the universal super-conscious immediacy of Reality—but this may actually just be a *substitute*, a *means* to an end, the end being our numbing to the "acceptance" of the meaninglessness of existence, as we personally are not meant by it in any way.

One of the boldest imaginative scenarios for such an *existential impasse pointing at the necessity to unfold Love/God from an ultimately personal perspective of eternal meaning of uniqueness* will directly lead us into the actual meditation. It is set up in the grand cosmological scheme proposed by the novel *Diaspora* (1997) of the science fiction author Greg Egan (b. 1961). Without retelling the whole story, I will rehearse its situation and how it ends, which, step by step, lead into the meditation on the precise feelings underlying this situation of the story and its ending.

Sometime in the future, probably after the "singularity" (the becoming conscious of computer programs and wars against artificial life in the form of robots) humanity has differentiated into genetic diversifications, sculptured between fish and bird, as it were, and lives in uneasy closeness to robots and societies of individualized artificial intelligence in the form of individual programs that, like the genetic variation of the evolution of life, populate societies of software individuals. These *poleis* include also transferred human patterns of individuality and produce their own artificial variations. They have developed diverse cultures, such as either only exhibiting aesthetic interests in imaginary worlds irrespective of the physical universe or committing to the curious investigation of the physical universe or some kind of combination of these impulses of *intellectuality* and *imagination*—for Whitehead the two most intense forms of "intelligent life."

After an unexpected cosmic cataclysmic event that destroys Earth and humanity, some of the *poleis* and their most curious inhabitants travel throughout the universe to find the reason for the anomaly that triggered this global disaster. Being the only survivors of the human past, these programs cannot only clone themselves and disperse into different directions of the vast universe beyond the solar system and the Milky Way. They can also clock their internal time in ways unimaginable: slow it down or speed it up, experiencing the universe in a time lapse, allowing them to cover fast cosmic distances—and they obviously do not age or die, but only move the boundaries between objective knowledge (as they all can participate in the general knowledge of the *poleis*) and subjective experience, knowledge from their "personal" perspective.

> *Imagine, your conscious integrity and your personality were transferred into a pattern of software on whatever convenient hardware medium the future might provide. You remain an individual in a society of such individuals. But you are immortal, sculpture the body you want and can imagine, and connect to the physical world, but also to the personal worlds of other individual programs, in which you can enter, or by inviting them into yours, like in your living space.*
>
> . . .
>
> *How would you furnish your personal world (you can imagine what you want and of the magnitude you can imagine: from universes to art objects, from different amounts of dimensions to not yet invented colors. . .) . . . ?*
>
> . . .
>
> *Would you isolate, invent the inhabitants of your "own" universe, or would you seek other individuals and be curious of their worlds . . . ?*
>
> . . .
>
> *Would you rather become a creator of worlds . . . ?*
>
>   *. . . or become curious about the (physical) universe . . . ?*
>
>   *. . . or travel the worlds of others . . . ?*
>
>   *. . . or find solace in the bodies of knowledge now accessible to you . . . ?*
>
> . . .
>
> *How would you feel about the infinite time you have to structure . . . ?*
>
> *How would you avoid emptiness . . . ?*

As it happens, some of the heroes of the story of this diaspora, who all have names, are individuals, have their own perspectives and outlook on their life and the meaning of existence, discover that they can transcend this universe and enter another, a parallel universe with its own natural laws and its own alien life forms, which they, still in their search for the origin of the event that destroyed humanity, contact, communicate with, and study. When they discover that the solution is less important than the fact that they are actually following a long-gone alien civilization of obvious far-advanced technology, which has traveled this other universe, but has transcended it to enter yet another one, they decide to follow these super-beings, when they discover that they have left a trace of their journey through the dimensions or the now growing magnitude of a multiverse to which they have expanded their travels. The latest split (of identical individualized programs in dispersing throughout the universe) has left two programs, Yatima and Paolo, to follow the alien civilization into ever new universes in all of which it has left a trace in a certain form. Over time, when Yatima and Paolo realize that these remnants stretch through a seemingly unending series of ever-new universes, they decide to let their vessel jump per autopilot through these unending universes and only to "awake" every thousand, ten thousand, hundred thousand of universes, to have a look around.

> *Imagine, you can let lapse vast amounts of time (by programming your memory and consciousness or by relativistic speeds of space travel) and, fast forward, could travel the Milky Way, from sun to sun, from planet to planet, in "seconds"*
>
> *. . .*
>
> *Imagine, you can let lapse vast amounts of time and, fast forward, could travel to and through the known universe from galaxy to galaxy, in "seconds" . . .*
>
> *. . .*
>
> *Imagine, you can let lapse vast amounts of time and, fast forward, could travel to and through the multiverse, from universe to universe, in "seconds" . . .*
>
> *. . .*
>
> *How does it feel . . . ?*
>
> *Does it ever become irrelevant . . . ?*
>
> *How would you battle feelings of exhaustion . . . ?*
>
> *Does liveliness and novelty ever become the repetition of the same . . . ?*
>
> *What would still convey meaning . . . ?*

After millions of millions of universes, suddenly, the track of the alien race ends. Yatima and Paolo reach a universe in which no trace of them remains. Have they left? Where? Did they stay? Give up? Disappear? What is more, in combining all the traces this race left in all of these universes, Yatima and Paolo realize that it amounts to a sculpture of the bodily form of the aliens.

> *There is nothing more to discover, no traces left, nothing to follow or do anymore . . .*
>
> *How would you react to this insight . . . ?*

The reactions of Yatima and Paolo differ because of their character—remember, they are immortal but individual software patterns or "personalities." They find themselves alone, millions of millions of universes from home, with no possible way back. What to do with their life, then, since all is said and done? Paolo loses any impulse to live on. He commits suicide—terminating his program. Yatima eventually has lost interest in the physical world, the endless repetition of the same in which all differences convert to the same over and over again. No difference can be as important or relevant or vast as to be able to overcome the irrelevance of the physicality they just run through indefinitely. He reverts to the inner world of knowledge of mathematics and formulas and the mysteries and the unknown land of discoveries it still offers when the multiverse has become a desert of vast nothingness and meaninglessness.

> *Imagine, after having seen the multiverse of millions of universes, you realize that no difference is left that can be as important or relevant or vast as to be able to overcome the irrelevance of the physicality you can run through indefinitely.*
>
> *. . .*
>
> *How would you react to this insight?*
>
> *Would you follow Paolo or Yatima . . . ?*
>
> *Have you found an alternative to both Paolo and Yatima?*
>
> *. . .*
>
> *What could still offer meaning when the multiverse has become a desert of vast nothingness and meaninglessness . . . ?*

Meaning relates to the importance of our *uniqueness*. Being meant *personally* can only be established in the *mutual immanence of persons* creating meaning in each other, from heart to heart. From the apophatic mystery of the "other life" being called—beyond Self and as condition for Self to become—was one of the central insights of Emmanuel Levinas, for instance, in his book *Otherwise than Being or Beyond Essence* (1978): the call of the other is primary, more original than the self-constitution of the Self or a metaphysics of the closed world of the Self—of which Levinas accused Heidegger. But, in the end, the "Face of the Other" is not "a person" beyond the other; rather, by the self-transcendent apophatic mystery of the Beyond, the other and you *become, in this encounter, persons* who express themselves (their selfless Self) in the Face. This Alterity is the mutuality of the Self of the Other and the Self of my Self: I am "another Life" myself! I am always beyond myself as know factor because of my own alterity (in the divine apophatic mystery being named personally), even if it comes only to light in the encounter of the mutuality with "another Life."

Why couldn't Yatima and Paolo find personal mutual awakening to meaning in their community?

. . .

Would you . . . ?

I think it is at this point that you may (or may not) have been leveling all other reasons to find meaning (not that they become meaningless; they have always been meaningless if we ultimately are meaninglessly engaging them). Yet if *you* are meant, personally, by Love/God, you count. While this insight may not be established by anything in the universe, physical or intellectual, imaginative or illusionary, it may be ultimately what spiritual transformation, the process of self-transcendence, of the spiritualization of the cosmos, is about. Can you imagine to love and to be loved—impermanently by the beloved, permanently by the Beloved?

We began the whole journey with the little flame at the heart of all things. Can you feel it . . . ?

If not, only space will remain . . .

If so, it is you, you have found . . .

Now, begin the journey . . .

Epilogue

The Great Numenaries

> I have broken the limits of embodied mind / And am no more the figure of a soul. /... I share all creatures' sorrow and content /And feel the passage of every stab and kiss.
>
> —SRI AUROBINDO (FROM THE EPIGRAPH TO THIS BOOK)

THE ONLY PROOF OF God is nature—appreciated by a conscious Self. For some, nature is enough; no God needed. For others, God is enough; nature is only an appendix of the evolutionary past of the "image of God," something to be overcome or the inherent evil opposite of divinity, the origin of all faulty desires, the beast, the monster, something to be negated and suppressed.

Yet this book is not another attempt in so many words to persuade you, us, humanity, or any religious community, which still may give some credit to spiritual impulses, to realize the fragility of our existence on Earth, our ecological dependency and the importance of ecological solidarity, the importance of the recognition of the irreplaceability of the earth for our existence and of Mother Earth for our spiritual maturation. It should be self-evident today that, as eco-theologian Thomas Berry (d. 2009) in *The Great Work* (1999) urged decades ago, we must, in expansive terms, think of and act for the integral Earth community. Or, as the socio-biologist Edward O. Wilson (b. 1929) has so forcefully proposed: Human integrity is an integrity *with* nature from which we come and in which we find the origin, archetype, and motor for human health, an ethics of justice and fairness. There is really nothing to be added.

For some, nature proves only a naturalistic reality or a non-theistic Reality and nothing beyond that. For others, it is not enough and points to an ultimate ground that is not identical with it. Yet have we not already suffered enough by the reiteration of such a differentiation between God and Reality that perpetuates the justification of religious identities, for instance, between eastern and western religions, between indigenous and colonial oppositions, or between doctrinally or experientially dualistic and monistic streams of, between, or within diverse religions? Not only the pluralism of John Hick was set against such ultimate dichotomies (and I think that no criticism of its perceived "weaknesses" is deep enough to counter the arguments from nondualism and mutual immanence, coinherence and coinhabitation). My own work on *apophatic-polyphilic* pluralism is set to overcome such resistances against these coincidences of opposites, as developed in my book *The Ocean of God* (2019).

For some, both nature and Self represent these two classes of mystical insight, namely, the impermanent processes of non-possessed interrelationality of all existents (*pratitya-samutpada*) and the pure consciousness with which Reality is supposed to be identical (and nature its limited derivative). For others, this is really not a valid dichotomy, as both are *directions* of the *same* universal process of spiritualization of the cosmos. This is much in line with Teilhard de Chardin's processual differentiation between mind and matter, and also A. N. Whitehead's process view—the rhythmical revolutions between outside and inside, perception and creativity, analysis and synthesis. I support this latter conclusion in the presentation of the nine paths.

Yet this book is also not about the establishment or defense of such or similar differentiations or oppositions within the fields of mysticism and metaphysics. This would also already be a matter of the past, as we should have already accepted the reality and value of the *noetic* quality of mystical insights beyond any empirical and logical character of knowledge, but as profoundly limited by the impossibility to coherently create a "superposition" of non-theistic and theistic tendencies without some acceptance of the unimaginability of such a solution—much like the trans-imaginative, mathematical grasp of the particle-wave dualism and the superposition of a realm of potentials in quantum physics, *together* and in transcendence of their reiterative imagination preparing accesses to both nature and Self. Similarly, it should be out of question that deep spiritual and mystical insight, whether "extravertive," gathered from sensitivity toward nature, or "introversive," approached by the formless depth of the conscious Self, reveal both nature and Self as deep resonances of *one* apophatic and pleromatic cosmic Spirit.

We must not, however, think that, thereby, everything is said and done yet. While not trusting human language to express the deep roots of our birth from the earth or nature, or, in the most expansive meaning, from the cosmos, it may still be worth mining our deep earthly and cosmic roots for the archetypical images that we inherited from them when we became human in the first place: the *adamah*, the Mother of the red dust, the natural processes and environments that we encounter and that sustain us, but that also teach us our limits and our integral relativity to the biosphere, and our inherent dependency even on the geosphere—the climates, the geographies, the topologies, the rhythms of coming and going, becoming and perishing—in which we live and from which we breath and of which we nourish one another. These root-images and -symbols—such as are, and are related to or derived from, the ocean, the river, the wilderness, the desert, the mountain, the stars, and the like—are wedded with our very humanity and express that which *makes* us human, but *is not* "human" itself *nor* a human fantasy and projection. By heightening their intensity and our inherited feelings toward them in such symbolizations, we relate our human identity on a globe in a cosmos that *transcends*—transcends us and everything we may encounter, transcends *even itself*.

What I mean is not a transcendence *of* nature, rather a transcendence *into* nature, a transcendence *within*. What is beyond, is within. It is neither about a disappearance of humanity into nature nor about a transcendence by which humanity overcomes or is defined by overcoming nature. Rather, as in ancient matriarchal and indigenous spiritualities, such a "transcendence within" means that humanity only becomes itself if it transcends itself into nature, into the nature that is the generatrix, who or that births us by being self-transcendent of its own "Self" toward the appearance of beings such as humans—as *spiritual* beings. Spirituality is this *natural* discipline of the matrix of the earth and the cosmos, which can be *cultivated* beyond its mere "natural" appearance, but is never detached from its *naturalness*—Daoist philosophy calls it ziren, naturalness, or, in the translation of Alan Watts (d. 1973), that which is "self-so." Self-transcendence, the transcendence of collective self-identity and any individual Self, is the aim of natural transcendence into that which is not nature and yet is that by which nature and we in it exist. That is meant by the cosmic Spirit: the *non-identity (the "dipolarity" that is beyond the One) of nature with itself* from which arises its *self-transcendent movement* by which it received its existence, and we ours.

Whether this Spirit is immanent or transcendent is only a matter of language and not of reality. Spirit is not identical (with anything), hence, transcendent; but Spirit is not different (from the All), hence immanent. Yet it is a matter of spirituality whether you *recognize* this subtleness of "non-identity" and "non-difference." As long as you are caught up in distorted views of an *estranged* transcendence of nature—a nature that must be controlled like Tiamat by Marduk, chaotic Mother Nature by the death-rays of the sun-god—you leave controls, such as a "god," to the institutions that represent "Him" undeconstructed (in the interaction of oppressive colonizations of gender, class, and race) in place. Conversely, however, as long as you, by intuition or disappointment, resent and resist such possessions of a god by *collapsing* nature with God (or subtracting God from nature) as the ultimate reference point of your existence and meaning to *mere* immanence without transcendence—a pan-Gaia without horizon of self-transcendence, Shakti without Shiva, Wisdom without Ein Sof, Mother Earth without Sol, and the like—you may gain a freedom from possessive (patriarchal, divisive, elitist, racialist, colonial, gendered) imperialism, but you may have traded it for anonymous orders of either mathematical nature or the red claws of Darwinian survival. You may begin to revere either nature's hidden mathematical propositions and abstract laws or act on its evolutionary impulse to be, become, and hunt food ("we are what we eat," from the German "*Der Mensch 'ist' was er 'isst'*"). The spiritual insight into *naturalness*, instead, that is, the non-identity *and* non-difference, of the Spirit of/from the earth and the cosmos, is meant to avoid these alternatives and their related strategies to remodel the earth either in *their* image (of the law and survival) or the distorted or even destructive images of a religion, an ideology, a state, a powerful family, a corporation, and the like. What is more, sensing and instilling the naturalness of *your* being, becoming and activation of your whole humanity in body and mind, heart and soul, again, means to become the *place of* the earth and the cosmos, of nature and of the whole community of beings, *to arise*, to become "itself," by transcending its limiting "self" toward the immanent Spirit in the All that it enlivens.

In several contexts since the beginning of this century, systematically collected in my book *The Becoming of God* (2017), I have conceptualized this inward transcendence or expansive immanence as the *in-sistence* of the Spirit (see ch. 6)—or of the Godhead or nondual Reality of the mystics *beyond* the difference of God and the world—*on* and *in* the cosmos. The Beyond or transcendence, here, means immanence, the movement of the infusion *into its differentiation*. This term, originally appearing in Gilles Deleuze's philosophy of immanence and difference (see ch. 4), indicates that Spirit is not about a god that *exists*—much like the projection of "a being" beyond all beings or the world into a realm beyond, like a thing—but about *Reality that is nothing beyond everything, but neither identical with it* (monism, pantheism, naturalism, atheism), *nor different from it* (dualism, personalism, theism, panentheism). Rather, Reality is the *movement* of *in-differentiation*—which I have explored in my book *God as the Poet of the World* (2003/2004 and 2008)—of both differentiation *and* identification, as well as of both non-differentiation *and* non-identification.

Spirit does not exist, but in-sists.

This means, while Spirit is in-different from anything, Spirit is not identical with anything, either; but as Spirit is not a neutral reality or a being, it *in-sists* only *in* the valuation processes that *are* the activities of the cosmos: elements and consciousness, compassion and love, harmony and rhythm, matter and form, patience and activity, perception and creativity, valuation and transformation. In-sistence means the *activity* of in-differentiation, of being/becoming *in-different* from Earth and the All, but only *in (generating, sustaining and transforming) the differences* of the multiplicity that is the becoming of the Earth and the All. It is in this sense, then, that Spirit *is not* the earth or the cosmos, as it "is" (exists) not at all (!), but *in-sists on* the becoming of the earth and the matrix of the cosmos and *in-sists in* it as its motive force.

I have called this movement *trans-pantheism*—beyond monism, but not dualism—while Karl Rahner embraces it even as the heart of theism (see ch. 2). Hence, it is not fitting the hardened differentiation between dualism and monism, theism and atheism, impersonal Reality and personal divinity. Such a use of "in-sistence" of the reality of the Spirit *in* and *on* the life of the earth and the weird and beautiful "coherence" of the cosmos (despite the chaotic destructiveness that pervades it) does not void the concept of "existence," however, but rather recovers a *radical* version of the medieval rendering of the meaning given to it by medieval monk and theologian Richard of St. Victor (d. 1173). While he reserved its use for the inner-trinitarian relations of the Christian God, we will, in sync with Whitehead, as generally characterized in his book *Adventures of Ideas*, use it in a *universal cosmic* sense, indicating *universal relationality* and *mutual immanence: ex-sistence*, being born *from the relationship to* everything else. Mutual ex-sistence.

This is where the *conscious Self* comes into focus: It is the *site* of this mutual ex-sistence at which not only nature becomes conscious of itself, but also God is reflected as the Self of nature. I don't mean a pantheistic identity of Mother Nature or the All, but that "God" as the All in All is the *trans-pantheistic Self of (Mother) Nature*, of the transcendence within. This "Self" is the self-transcendent in-sistence of God *in* nature, the apophatic mystery *within* from which nature emanates itself (its Self)—as the *polyphilic* manifestation of "its" (the mystery's) inexhaustible *pleroma* generating all beings that she can harbor. Religious and philosophical cosmology has sensed this *inherent universal "Self"* at the *sacred heart* of nature and all natural beings with images such as, different as, the imaginative divine Mind, commanding Will, expressive Word, but even more so with the sensitive World-Soul and the providing Mother Earth. But these images reflect the mysteries of the mind, will, word, soul, and of the immanent Goddess at the heart of the undivided *human Self as its awakening to divine awareness*, to the *recognition of being a sign of Reality/God*, to be called by Reality's/God's Self to become Reality's/God's mystery. In our communication with the apophatic nature of Reality's/God's pleromatic Self, we become *Selves* in the light of Reality's/God's mystery of apophatic-polyphilic revelation. It is in this sense that the Qur'an speaks of nature *and* Self as the *signs* of God (Surah 41:53) and the *Upanishads* of the equation of *atman* with *brahman*. At these sites of the signs of Reality/God, where Reality/God appears as the Self of nature and as the mystery of our Selves, no proof (of Reality's/God's existence) is possible and any demonstration is experiential (but not logical, as in Thomas Aquinas's *quinque viae*). We need to *awaken* to "her/his/its" truth as our *own* reality—the reality of the Spirit *of* the Earth/cosmos *and* Self.

This is what the nine spiritual paths of this book are about: not Nature *or* God/Self as alternatives of an integrative image for humanity's existence and future, but *Spirit*, which is both Nature and God/Self, and neither, as it is neither external to nature nor its essence. This is also what I understand Sri Aurobindo to convey in his poem "The Comic Spirit" in the epigraph to this book: the integrative but simultaneously diverging foldedness of the earth and the cosmos in the Spirit; and the unfolding of the earth and the cosmos in this Spirit, as the Spirit enfolds in the earth and the cosmos—one in the other in mutual immanence that also means mutual transcendence or transcendence within. Hence, it is *not* about ecology and awareness of our human integrity in the global community that is Earth—as this should be the self-evidently "natural" condition in which to view *all things religious and spiritual* today *in any case*.

And it is *not* about a transcendent God/Self who or that looks inward from afar (the masculine limitation), or even an immanent God/Self who or that considers (or of whom or which we consider) the world as "God's body" (the feminine limitation)—as this is always already a distorted image of a mystery that cannot be described in human terms and by means of human conceptual degenerations, hardened to "realities" apart from one another as if they were things. Rather both extremes or alternatives of a more monistic (pantheist or atheist) and a more dualistic (theist or panentheist) view are, in fact, only *variations* of the *polyphilic* "brooding presence" of the nondual reality of the Spirit "in relation to" the cosmos (see the Preamble). In fact, *there is no* "relation," either, as this would presuppose dualistic differentiation; but there is also not "*no* relation," as this could be misinterpreted as absolute dualism or absolute monism. *Spirit and cosmos are non-different, but polyphilically differentiating in the loving brooding of/over/on/in multiplicity.*

The nine paths of accesses, experiences, perceptions, and transformations of a spirituality of the cosmic Spirit are such non-differentiations of nature and Self, cosmos and Mind, the earth and the sun, multiplicity and the One. They are the apophatic and the polyphilic sensible images of that which I call *Numenaries—the poetic materializations of the spiritual indifferentiation of nature and Self*. When Rudolf Otto in his book *The Idea of the Holy* defined the Holy as the *numinous*, he referred to the Latin term *numen*, which goes back to ancient Roman religious experiences, their poetic renderings and philosophical conceptualizations—from Cicero (106–43 BCE) to Virgil (70 BCE–19 CE)—as encounters with the divine Mind, Will or Power. Indicating the ancient *idea of the presence* of the divine or the Spirit at a sacred place or in a sacred time or as a sacred event or through a sacred person, the numinous also refers to the whole *process of the encounter* with the Holy as the transcendent and inaccessible, creative and axiological, quasi-supernatural and superimposing power of the divine, but in diverse modes of *immanence* in the natural and cosmic multiplicity of sensible, local and material phenomena.

In an unsurpassed way, Otto characterized the encountered numinous as a *mysterium tremendum et fascinans* (see ch. 1)—as twofold experience: that of fascination and attraction (although not necessarily intimacy) and that of tremor, of holy terror, because of the concurrent experience of our undeserved and even impure approach of the Holy. In its core, this experience of "presence" is not one of tensionless satisfaction or saturation, of a restless and total clearing and absolute quieting of questions or of a mere fulfillment without more intriguing depth to come, but that of an *insoluble mystery* that, in principle, is beyond any grasp. It is this "wholly Other" that became central to the lines of research and thought of the Rumanian ethnologist of religion Mircea Eliade (d. 1986) and of the perennialist Aldous Huxley on underlying cross-religious fields of spiritual, mystical and symbolic integration of humanity with divinity. However, much in line with Derrida (but contrary to Derrida's assumptions), they importantly understood this divine alterity as the *immanent* spiritual power of the *deconstruction* of any creaturely mode of approach, especially if it closes itself off from the transformation inherent in the modes of self-transcendence and love. And even theoretical atheists, such as Christopher Hitchens (d. 2011), in his book *God Is Not Great* (2007), allow for this experience of the numinous: as a general, non-illusionary human characteristic of the awareness that the world cannot be reduced to dead matter. Twist: "Matter" of the Spirit it is!

The Numenaries of the nine paths relate to the sensible matters that since ancient times are understood as the most simple or basic and powerful elements of creation or formation of the material world and its beauty—as the powerful spiritual expressions of Mother Nature in the matrix of the forces of the near and far cosmos. Yet these Numenaries are *not identical* with the traditional "elements." In antique cosmology, the simplest (irreducible) and most universal elements (applicable without exception)—like water, air, fire, and earth (and sometimes also iron and wood)—were the physical and chemical but also psychological and divine bases of earthly and cosmic existence. They were, in sophisticated ways, revered as expression of the spiritual Earth (indigenous religions), analyzed (natural philosophy), sought out for predictions of fate and future (astrology), manipulated for physical gain and spiritual transformation (alchemy) and minded as powers of the saints (miracles), angels (theurgy), and spirits (shamanism), but also feared as susceptible to the manipulation of dark forces (sorcery). And they remained sensible reminders of the non-conceptual, material (infinitely potential) nature of "universals" besides the so-called "transcendentals" (applicable to all beings beyond any differentiation), such as unity, being, truth, goodness, and beauty. What is more, they were always maintained as "sacramentals" of religions—as universal "presentations" or "real symbols" for the pervading but uncontrollable presence of divine reality.

Numenaries are foldings of elements and consciousness. They are not externalities, but integrate nature and Spirit. In this integration, they give birth to the increasing *public* spiritualization of the cosmos or materialization of the Spirit. In an everting process of re-folding, the enfolded inwardness becomes the envelope of the unfolded physical plane, which, in its own turn, becomes, in the same movement, enfolded in the Spirit. The Numenaries are neither pure elements—as, for instance, both sea and river are water—nor pure consciousness—as symbols like the "finger" of God indicate. They are neither simply material nor energetic—as space and time are rather horizons—nor simply conscious mind—as patterns of construction are relations of matter and energy. They are not passive universals waiting to be manipulated or surfed on, nor are they mere activities without form—as they include the activation of value, ethically and aesthetically. And they cannot be divided in either male or female, feminine and masculine, Earth-based and sun-based religiosity. Rather, they are in-differentiations of *all* of these divergent multiplicities—elements, consciousness, universals, activities, horizons, energies, forms and patterns, as well as gendered representations of nature and Self, immanence and transcendence—or their *releasing unison*, which *is* what *becoming*-Spirit means: the becoming that is the spiritualization of the earth and the cosmos *from within* and *toward itself.*

It is through this peculiar spiritual movement that we can avoid becoming stuck in the paradox of the variously engaged elements and their psychophysical, synergetic relationality: that they are uncontrollable, but can be manipulated; that they transcend all interests, but offer themselves to their ambivalent activation. Even if we thought them to be alive, they seem to indicate a kind of paradigm of *alien* life, as in the novel *Solaris* of Stanisław Lem (see ch. 2), of which we can only gain external insight, really mere projections, but remain forever oblivious of their inherent essence. In this perspective, they seem totally detached but not compassionate, disinterested but without any awareness and awakened participation in the transformation they facilitate. They seem, again, to favor an *impersonal* ultimate reality—if not of monism so of a kind of naturalism over and against supernatural characteristics of the Spirit such as compassion and love.

Yet Numenaries avoid this aporia by appearing as a *composition* of elements *and* consciousness, activity *and* form, nature *and* value, impersonal harmony *and* personal love and compassion. They are, in fact, meant to describe their indescribable unison that releases them as multiple folds of itself. They name the unnamable, invoking the Dao of the *Dao De Jing* (see ch. 1)—being the movement from the in-difference in the (immanent) Numen to the multiplicity of the (self-transcending) Numenaries. They cannot be reached, except by the human awakening to detachment and conscious personal or "soulful" engagement in aesthetic and ethical processes of valuation (see ch. 9), of activating events of decision-making and by purposefully directing the numinous activities toward a peaceful harmonization of the indirections and even bifurcations of unconscious and mal-conscious activities of nature and consciousness. In other words, one has to become a *saint* (always imperfectly so, but not shying away from the task) in order to activate the Numenaries in oneself and universally in nature and consciousness by perceiving one's Self as being reborn in *their* creative, but compassionate space.

In a sense, as I have tried to demonstrate in my book *The Divine Manifold* (ch. 11), if we really want to access the "personal" essence of Reality as *Love*, we might not only need to become prepared to lose our particular idiosyncratic ego-self, but also *to give up on any version of possessiveness*: that Love was possessed by any god! It is one of the striking arguments of Ludwig Feuerbach in his book *The Essence of Christianity* (1841) that the combination of Love with "God" is an *antinomy*: that if God is fully and exhaustibly Love, then, God is not the possessor of Love; but if God is also "something else" besides Love, then, God not only possesses Love, but can also decide to be or do even the opposite. The question is: If Love is personal, what does "personal" mean? Is it the possession of characteristics such as "love," or is it established *by* Love? If the former, dualism is unavoidable, or: the difference between theism and dualism is vanishingly slim, if not obliterated, here. If the latter, then "personality" is the multiplication of the polyphilic nature of the nondual Reality of Love. It is in this sense that Love as ultimate Reality is *personal, but not a person*, in any creaturely limited sense that we cannot, it seems, escape to project onto this Reality of personal Love. Yet if understanding Reality always also means to become detached, it will be the saints who may provide us with a meaningful language; and their insights, reflecting on the experiences of their mystical unison with/within the sacred and ultimate, become often expressed in *both* ways, non-reductively disinterested (impersonal) and compassionate (personal)—even if always in different degrees or variations of emphases.

The nine paths don't want to limit the Numenaries in any taxative sense, but rather open a space for their multiplication, their different folding, the many ways in which to compose their complexity or decompose or re-compose their unison in ever-new ways. Yet all of them, as presented in these paths, can be said to be found within *all* religions, and even *beyond* them *universally* in the non-religious, "naturalistic" reference to, and the reverence of, (the aesthetic or ethical value of) nature, the sensation of the Spirit in nature or of nature in the Spirit. They are not a matter of allegiance in the sense of parochial aims or dogmatic exclusions essential to certain religious mindsets and many historical hostile claims of superiority of one religion over another. Rather, they are "matters" of *universal allegiance to the earth and the cosmos in the Spirit*, of "its" inexhaustible becoming, of ever-new harmonizations as movements of Love, but also of earthly, cosmic and divine *patience* that sustains even the freedom of "its" denial.

Spirit is the sym-pathy that pervades and envelops the becoming of the earth, the cosmos and the All—and they are always in the *form* of becoming—that "matters" (is relevant and materializes) in all of its phenomenal multiplicity, but "forms" (flows together to) their unity as *unison of becoming*—without beginning and end, but with many beginnings and endings. In the end, beginning—Spirit; in the beginning, end—cosmos. In the impermanent fragility of their togetherness—Earth. Oscillation. Rhythm. In-differentiation. In-sistence. Polyphilia.

Bibliography

THE FOLLOWING COLLECTION OF references to books, articles, and websites reflects direct citations and indirect allusions relating to names, titles, thought patterns and movements mentioned in the corpus of the book. Meditation instructions and actual meditation texts are presented in italics. All of the rare direct quotations appearing in the text and integrated in the Meditations, even if not written in italics, also indicate their meditative use.

Abbate, Carolyn, and Roger Parker. *A History of Opera*. New York: Norton, 2012.
Abdullah, Arif Kemil. *The Qur'an and Normative Religious Pluralism: A Thematic Study of the Qur'an*. London: International Institute of Islamic Thought, 2014.
Abe, Masao. "God and Absolute Nothingness." In *God, Truth and Reality: Essays in Honour of John Hick*, edited by Arvind Sharma, 33–45. 1993. Reprint, Eugene, OR: Wipf & Stock, 2011.
———. "Kenotic God and Dynamic Sunyata." In *The Emptying God: A Buddhist-Jewish-Christian Conversation*, edited by John Cobb and Christopher Ives, 3–65. Maryknoll, NY: Orbis, 1990.
———. *A Study of Dogen: His Philosophy and Religion*. Edited by Steve Heine. Albany: State University of New York Press, 2000.
———. *Zen and Western Thought*. Honolulu: University of Hawaii Press, 1985.
Adams, Michael. *The Mythological Unconscious*. New York: Springer, 2010.
Adamson, Peter. *Medieval Philosophy*. A History of Philosophy without Any Gaps 4. Oxford: Oxford University Press, 2019.
Addas, Claude. *Ibn 'Arabi: The Voyage of No Return*. Translated by David Streight. Cambridge, UK: Islamic Text Society, 2000.
Affifi, A. E. *Mystical Philosophy of Ibn al-'Arabi*. Lexington, KY: Apex, 1979.
Agassiz, Louis. *A Journey in Brazil: A Travel Diary of Rio de Janeiro, Manaus, the Amazon River and Rainforests, Featuring Brazilian History, Food, Culture and the Native Peoples*. 1st ed. 1868. Reprint, Pantianos Classics, 2018.
Aho, Kevin. *Existentialism: An Introduction*. Malden, MA: Polity, 2014.
Albert, Hans. *Traktat über die kritische Vernunft*. Tübingen: J. C. B. Mohr, 1975.
Alexander, Eben. *Proof of Heaven: A Neurosurgeon's Journey into the Afterlife*. New York: Simon & Schuster, 2012.

BIBLIOGRAPHY

Angus, Ian. *Facing the Anthropocene: Fossil Capitalism and the Crisis of the Earth System*. New York: Monthly Review Press, 2016.

Appiah, Kwame Anthony. *Cosmopolitanism: Ethics in a World of Strangers*. New York: Norton, 2006.

Apuleius. *The Golden Ass*. Translated by P. G. Walsh. Oxford: Oxford University Press, 1994.

Arasteh, A. Reza. *Rumi the Persian, the Sufi*. Abingdon, UK: Routledge, 2008.

Aristotle. *Poetics*. Translated by Anthony Kenny. Oxford: Oxford University Press, 2013.

Armour, Ellen T. *Deconstruction, Feminist Theology, and the Problem of Difference: Subverting the Race/Gender Divide*. Chicago: University of Chicago Press, 1999.

Armstrong, Karen. *Fields of Blood: Religion and the History of Violence*. New York: Anchor, 2015.

———. *The Great Transformation: The Beginnings of Our Religious Traditions*. New York: Anchor, 2007.

———. *A History of God: The 4,000-Year Quest of Judaism, Christianity and Islam*. New York: Random House, 1993.

———. *Muhammad: A Prophet for Our Time*. New York: HarperCollins, 2006.

Arnold, Denis. *Monteverdi*. Oxford: Oxford University Press, 2000.

Aronson, Ronald. *Camus and Sartre: The Story of a Friendship and the Quarrel That Ended It*. Chicago: University of Chicago Press, 2004.

Ashkenazi, Michael. *What We Know about Extraterrestrial Intelligence: Foundations of Xenology*. Cham, Switzerland: Springer, 2017.

Assmann, Jan. *Moses the Egyptian: The Memory of Egypt in Western Monotheism*. Cambridge: Harvard University Press, 1998.

———. *The Price of Monotheism*. Stanford: Stanford University Press, 2010.

———. *The Search for God in Ancient Egypt*. Ithaca: Cornell University Press, 2001.

Athanassakis, Apostolos N., and Benjamin M. Wolkow, eds. *The Orphic Hymns*. Baltimore: Johns Hopkins University Press, 2013.

Attar, Farid ud-Din. *Bird Parliament*. Translated by Edward Fitzgerald. London: Macmillan, 1889.

Augustine. *Confessions*. Translated by Henry Chadwick. Oxford: Oxford University Press, 2008.

Aurobindo, Sri. *The Essential Aurobindo*. Edited by Robert McDermott. Herndon, VA: Lindisfarne, 2001.

———. *The Life Divine*. Pondicherry, India: Sri Aurobindo Ashram Press, 2006.

Aurobindo, Sri, and The Mother. *The Hidden Forces of Life*. Pondicherry, India: Sri Aurobindo Ashram Press, 2005.

Auyang, Sunny Y. *How Is Quantum Field Theory Possible?* Oxford: Oxford University Press, 1995.

Aveni, Anthony. *Empires of Time: Calendars, Clocks, and Culture*. New York: I. B. Taruris, 2000.

Ayala, Francesco J., and Camilo J. Cala-Conde. *Processes in Human Evolution: The Journey from Early Hominins to Neanderthals and Modern Humans*. Oxford: Oxford University Press, 2017.

Aziz, Muhammad Ali. *Religion and Mysticism in Early Islam: Theology and Sufism in Yemen*. London: I. B. Tauris, 2011.

Badiou, Alan. *Being and Event*. New York: Continuum, 2005.

———. *Deleuze: The Clamor of Being*. Minneapolis: University of Minnesota Press, 2000.

———. *Infinite Thought: Truth and the Return to Philosophy*. New York: Continuum, 2003.

———. *Logics of Worlds: Being and Event II*. New York: Continuum, 2009.

Badiou, Alain, and Giovanbattista Tussa. *The End: A Conversation*. Translated by Robin Mackay. Medford, MA: Polity, 2019.

Bahá'u'lláh. *Gems of Divine Mysteries*. N.p.: Aeterna, 2010.

———. *Gleanings from the Writings of Bahá'u'lláh*. Wilmette, IL: Bahá'í Publishing, 1976.

———. *The Kitab-i Iqan: The Book of Certitude*. Wilmette, IL: Bahá'í Publishing, 1974.

———. *The Seven Valleys and the Four Valleys*. Translated by Marziah Gail. Wilmette, IL: Bahá'í Publishing, 1991.

———. *Tabernacle of Unity*. Haifa: Bahá'í World Center, 2006.

Baker, Gordon, and Catherine Morris. *Descartes's Dualism*. New York: Routledge, 1996.

Balyuzi, H. M. *Bahá'u'lláh, the King of Glory*. Oxford: George Ronald, 1991.

———. *Muhammad and the Course of Islam*. Oxford: George Ronald, 1976.

Barbour, Ian. *Religion in an Age of Science: The Gifford Lectures, Volume 1*. New York: HarperCollins, 1990.

———. *When Science Meets Religion: Enemies, Strangers, or Partners?* New York: HarperCollins, 2000.

Barker, Margaret. *The Great Angel: A Study of Israel's Second God*. Louisville: Westminster John Knox, 1992.

———. *The Lost Prophet: The Book of Enoch and Its Influence on Christianity*. Sheffield: Sheffield Phoenix Press, 2005.

———. *The Mother of the Lord: Volume 1, The Lady in the Temple*. New York: Bloomsbury, 2012.

———. *The Older Testament: The Survival of Themes from the Ancient Royal Cult in Sectarian Judaism and Early Christianity*. Sheffield: Sheffield Phoenix Press, 2005.

Barnard, G. William. *Living Consciousness: The Metaphysical Vision of Henri Bergson*. Albany: State University of New York Press, 2011.

Barnes, Burton V., et al. *Forest Ecology*. 4th ed. New York: Wiley, 1998.

Barrow, John. *The Origin of the Universe: To the Edge of Space and Time*. New York: Basic Books, 1997.

Barrow, John, and Frank Tipler. *The Anthropic Cosmological Principle*. Oxford: Oxford University Press, 1986.

Barrow, John, Paul Davies, and Charles Harper, eds. *Science and Ultimate Reality: Quantum Theory, Cosmology, and Complexity*. Cambridge: University of Cambridge, 2004.

Barth, Karl. *A Unique Time of God: Karl Barth's WWI Sermons*. Translated by William Klempa. Louisville: Westminster John Knox, 2016.

Bassuk, Daniel. *Incarnation in Hinduism and Christianity: The Myth of the God-Man*. London: Macmillan, 1987.

Bateson, Gregory. *Mind and Nature: A Necessary Unity*. Advances in System Theory, Complexity, and the Human Sciences. Creskill, NJ: Hampton, 2002.

———. *Steps to an Ecology of Mind: Collected Essays in Anthropology, Psychiatry, Evolution, and Epistemology*. Chicago: University of Chicago Press, 2000.

Bauckham, Richard. *Gospel of Glory: Major Themes in Johannine Theology*. Grand Rapids: Baker Academic, 2015.

———. *Jesus and the God of Israel: "God Crucified" and Other Studies on the New Testament's Christology of Divine Identity*. Grand Rapids: Eerdmans, 2008.

Bausani, Alessandro. *Religion in Iran: From Zoroaster to Bahá'u'lláh*. Winona Lake, IN: Bibliotheca Persica Press, 2000.

Beauregard, Mario, and Denyse O'Leary. *The Spiritual Brain: A Neuroscientist's Case for the Existence of the Soul*. New York: HarperOne, 2007.

Beierwaltes, Werner. *Der verborgene Gott: Cusanus und Dionysius*. Trier: Paulinus, 1997.

———. *Identität und Differenz*. Frankfurt: Klostermann, 1980.

Bekkum, Koert van, et al., eds. *Playing with Leviathan: Interpretation and Reception of Monsters from the Biblical World*. Leiden: Brill 2017.

Bell, Jeffrey. *Philosophy at the Edge of Chaos: Gilles Deleuze and the Philosophy of Difference*. Toronto: University of Toronto Press, 2006.

Bellah, Robert, and Hans Joas, eds. *The Axial Age and Its Consequences*. Harvard: Belknap Press of Harvard University Press, 2012.

Bender, Courtney, and Pamela Klassen, eds. *After Pluralism: Reimagining Religious Engagement*. New York: Columbia University Press, 2010.

Benjamin, Walter. "Theses on the History of Philosophy." In *Illuminations: Essays and Reflections*, edited by Hannah Arendt, 253–64. New York: Schocken, 1968.

Bennett, Michael. *Reassessing the Theatre of the Absurd: Camus, Beckett, Ionesco, Genet, and Pinter*. New York: Palgrave Macmillan, 2011.

Berger, Peter L., ed. *Between Relativism and Fundamentalism: Religious Resources for a Middle Position*. Grand Rapids: Eerdmans, 2010.

———. *The Many Altars of Modernity: Toward a Paradigm for Religion in a Pluralistic Age*. Boston: de Gruyter, 2014.

Bergson, Henri. *Matter and Memory*. Tunbridge Wells, UK: Solis, 2014.

Berndt, Guido, and Roland Steinacher, eds. *Arianism: Roman Heresy and Pagan Creed*. New York: Routledge, 2014.

Berry, Mark. *Arnold Schoenberg*. Critical Lives. London: Reaktion, 2019.

Berry, Thomas. *The Dream of the Earth*. Berkeley, CA: Counterpoint, 2015.

———. *The Great Work: Our Way into the Future*. New York: Bell Tower, 1999.

———. *The Sacred Universe: Earth, Spirituality, and Religion in the Twenty-First Century*. Edited by Mary Evelyn Tucker. New York: Columbia University Press, 2009.

Best, Steven, and Douglas Kellner. *Postmodern Theory: Critical Interrogation*. New York: Guilford, 1991.

Bhaskar, Roy. *The Possibility of Naturalism: A Philosophical Critique of the Contemporary Human Sciences*. New York: Routledge, 2015.

Biernacki, Loriliai, and Philip Clayton, eds. *Panentheism across the World's Traditions*. Oxford: Oxford University Press, 2014.

The Bhagavad Gita according to Gandhi. Translation and commentary by John Strohmeier. Berkeley, CA: North Atlantic, 2009.

Biechler, James, ed. *Nicolas of Cusa on Religious Harmony: Text, Concordance, and Translation of De Pace Fidei*. Lewiston, NY: Mellen, 1991.

Bloom, Alfred, ed. *Living in Amida's Universal Vow: Essays in Shin Buddhism*. Bloomington, IN: World Wisdom, 2004.

———. "Shin Buddhism in the Encounter with a Religiously Plural World." *The Pure Land*, n.s., 8–9 (1992) 17–31.

Boesel, Chris, and Wesley Ariarajah, eds. *Divine Multiplicity: Trinities, Diversities, and the Nature of Relation*. New York: Fordham University Press, 2014.

Boesel, Chris, and Catherine Keller, eds. *Apophatic Bodies: Negative Theology, Incarnation, and Relationship*. New York: Fordham University Press, 2010.

Boff, Leonardo. *Trinity and Society*. 1988. Reprint, Eugene, OR: Wipf & Stock, 2005.

Bohm, David. *Wholeness and the Implicit Order*. London: Routledge, 1980.

Bolton, Robert. *The Order of the Age: The Hidden Laws of World History*. Kettering, OH: Angelico, 2015.

Bondarenko, Dimitri. "The Second Axial Age and Metamorphoses of Religious Consciousness in the 'Christian World.'" *Journal of Globalization Studies* 2 (2011) 113–36.

Bonneuil, Christophe, and Jean-Baptiste Fressoz. *The Shock of the Anthropocene: The Earth, History and Us*. Translated by David Fernbach. London: Verso, 2016.

Bonting, Sjoerd L. *Creation and Double Chaos: Science and Theology in Discussion*. Minneapolis: Fortress, 2005.

Borsch, Frederick. *The Son of Man in Myth and History*. Philadelphia: Westminster, 1967.

Boss, Jack. *Schoenberg's Atonal Music: Musical Idea, Basic Image, and Specters of Tonal Function*. Cambridge: Cambridge University Press, 2019.

Botha, Marc. *A Theory of Minimalism*. New York: Bloomsbury, 2017.

Bowman, Donna, and Clayton Crockett, eds. *Cosmology, Ecology, and the Energy of God*. New York: Fordham University Press, 2012.

Boyarin, Daniel. *The Jewish Gospel: The Story of the Jewish Christ*. New York: New Press, 2012.

Boyce, Mary. *Zoroastrians: Their Religious Beliefs and Practices*. London: Routledge, 2003.

The Brahmajala Sutta: The Discourse on the All-Embracing Net of Views. Translated by Bhikkhu Bodhi. Kandy, Sri Lanka: Buddhist Publication Society, 2013.

Brannen, Peter. *The Ends of the World: Volcanic Apocalypses, Lethal Oceans, and Our Quest to Understand Earth's Past Mass Extinctions*. New York: Ecco, 2018.

Bråten, Stein, ed. *On Being Moved: From Mirror Neurons to Empathy*. Amsterdam: John Benjamins, 2007.

Brecht, Berthold. *Brecht on Theater: The Development of an Aesthetic*. Edited by Steve Gilles, Marc Silberman, and Tom Kuhn. New York: Hill and Wang, 1992.

Brockman, John, ed. *What to Think about Machines That Think*. New York: HarperCollins, 2015.

Broek, R. van den, and M. J. Vermaseren, eds. *Studies in Gnosticism and Hellenistic Religions: Presented to Gilles Quispel on the Occasion of His 65th Birthday*. Leiden: Brill, 1981.

Brown, Joseph Epes. *Teaching Spirits: Understanding Native American Religious Traditions*. Oxford: Oxford University Press, 2001.

Brown, Keven. "Hermes Trismegistus and Apollonius of Tyana in the Writings of Bahá'u'lláh." In *Revisioning the Sacred: New Perspectives on a Bahá'í Theology*, edited by J. A. McLean, 153–88. Los Angeles: Kalimát, 1997.

Brown, Tom. *Awakening Spirits: A Native American Path to Inner Peace, Healing and Spiritual Growth*. New York: Berkeley, 1994.

Brown, Vahid. "The Beginning that Hath No Beginning: Bahá'í Cosmogony." *Lights of Irfan* 3 (2002) 21–40.

Brunnhölzl, Karl, trans. *A Lullaby to Awaken the Heart: The Aspiration Prayer of Samantabhadra and Its Tibetan Commentaries*. Somerville, MA: Wisdom Publications, 2018.

Bruno, Giordano. *On the Infinite, the Universe, and the Worlds: Five Cosmological Dialogues*. Translation and introduction by Scott Gosnell. Port Townsend, WA: Huginn, Munnin, 2014.

Bruntrup, Godehard, and Ludwig Jaskolla, eds. *Panpsychism: Contemporary Perspectives*. Oxford: Oxford University Press, 2017.

Bryant, Edwin. *The Yoga Sutras of Patanjali: A New Edition, Translation, and Commentary*. New York: North Point, 2009.

Bryden, Mary, ed. *Deleuze and Religion*. London: Routledge, 2001.

Buber, Martin. *I and Thou*. Translated by Walter Kaufmann. New York: Touchstone, 1996.

Buck, Christopher. "Native Messengers of God in Canada? A Test Case for Bahá'í Universalism." *Bahá'í Studies Review* 6 (1996) 97–133.

———. *Symbol and Secret: Qur'an Commentary in Bahá'u'lláh's Kitab-i Iqan*. Los Angeles: Kalimát, 1995.

———. "A Unique Eschatological Interface: Bahá'u'lláh and Cross-Cultural Messianism." In *In Iran*, edited by Peter Smith, 157–80. Studies in Bábí and Bahá'í History 3. Los Angeles: Kalimát, 1986.

Buel, Laurence, ed. *The American Transcendentalists: Essential Writings*. New York: Modern Library, 2006.

Bulgakov, Sergei. *Sophia: The Wisdom of God*. Herndon, VA: Lindisfarne, 1993.

Burgos, Juan. *An Introduction to Personalism*. Washington, DC: Catholic University of America Press, 2018.

Burkert, Walter. *Ancient Mystery Cults*. Cambridge: Harvard University Press, 1987.

———. *Babylon, Memphis, Persepolis: Eastern Contexts of Greek Culture*. Cambridge: Harvard University Press, 2004.

———. *Greek Religion*. Cambridge: Harvard University Press, 1985.

———. *Structure and History in Greek Mythology and Ritual*. Berkeley: University of California Press, 1979.

Burrus, Virginia. *Ancient Christian Ecopoetics: Cosmologies, Saints, Things*. Philadelphia: University of Pennsylvania Press, 2018.

Burton, Simon J. G., Joshua Hollmann, and Eric M. Parker, eds. *Nicolas of Cusa and the Making of the Early Modern World*. Leiden: Brill, 2019.

Butler, Judith. "Critique, Coercion, and Sacred Life in Benjamin's 'Critique of Violence.'" In *Political Theologies: Public Religions in a Post-Secular World*, edited by Hent de Vries and Lawrence E. Sullivan, 201–19. New York: Fordham University Press, 2006.

Buxton, Richard. *The Complete World of Greek Mythology*. London: Thames & Hudson, 2004.

Byassee, Jason. *An Introduction to the Desert Fathers*. Eugene, OR: Cascade, 2007.

Campbell, Joseph. *The Hero with a Thousand Faces*. Novato, CA: New World Library, 2008.

———. *The Inner Reaches of Outer Space: Metaphor as Myth and as Religion*. Novato, CA: New World Library, 2002.

Campion, Nicholas. *Astrology and Cosmology in the World's Religions*. New York: New York University Press, 2012.

———. *A History of Western Astrology*. 2 vols. New York: Bloomsbury, 2008–9.

Capra, Fritjof. *The Tao of Physics*. Boston: Shambhala, 2000.

———. *The Turning Point: Science, Society, and the Rising Culture*. New York: Simon & Schuster, 1982.

Capra, Fritjof, and David Steindl-Rast. *Belonging to the Universe: Explorations of Science and Spirituality*. New York: HarperCollins, 1991.

Caputo, John. *Deconstruction in a Nutshell: A Conversation with Jacques Derrida*. New York: Fordham University Press, 1997.

———. *Heidegger and Aquinas: An Essay on Overcoming Metaphysics*. New York: Fordham University Press, 1982.

———. *The Mystical Element in Heidegger's Thought*. New York: Fordham University Press, 1986.

———. *The Prayers and Tears of Jacques Derrida: Religion Without Religion*. Bloomington: Indiana University Press, 1997.

———. *The Weakness of God: A Theology of the Event*. Bloomington: Indiana University Press, 2006.

Carabine, Deirdre. *John Scottus Eriugena*. New York: Oxford University Press, 2000.

———. *The Unknown God: Negative Theology in the Platonic Tradition; Plato to Eriugena*. 1995. Reprint, Eugene, OR: Wipf & Stock, 2015.

Caragounis, Chrys. *The Son of Man: Vision and Interpretation*. 1986. Reprint, Eugene, OR: Wipf & Stock, 2011.

Carelbach, Elisheva. *Palaces of Time: Jewish Calendar and Culture in Early Modern Europe*. Cambridge: Harvard University Press, 2011.

Carr, Bernard, ed. *Universe or Multiverse?* Cambridge: Cambridge University Press, 2007.

Carter, Chris. *Science and the Near-Death Experience: How Consciousness Survives Death*. Rochester, VT: Inner Traditions, 2010.

Casti, John. *Complexification: Explaining a Paradoxical World through the Science of Surprise*. New York: HarperPerennial, 1995.

Chalmers, David. *The Character of Consciousness*. Oxford: Oxford University Press, 2010.

———. *The Conscious Mind: In Search of a Fundamental Theory*. Oxford: Oxford University Press, 1996.

Chatterjee, Margaret. *Gandhi and the Challenge of Religious Diversity: Religious Pluralism Revisited*. New Delhi: Promilla, 2005.

Chew, Phyllis. *The Chinese Religion and the Bahá'í Faith*. Oxford: George Ronald, 1993.

———. "Religious Pluralism in the Chinese Religion and the Bahá'í Faith." *Word Order* 34 (2002) 27–44.

Chittick, William C. "Ibn 'Arabi on the Ultimate Model of the Ultimate." In *Models of God and Alternative Ultimate Realities*, edited by Jeanine Diller and Asa Kasher, 915–30. Dordrecht: Springer, 2013.

———. *Imaginal Worlds: Ibn 'Arabi and the Problem of Religious Diversity*. Albany: State University of New York Press, 1994.

———. "Rumi and Wahdat al-Wujud." In *Poetry and Mysticism in Islam: The Heritage of Rumi*, edited by Amin Banani et al., 70–111. Cambridge: Cambridge University Press, 1995.

———. *The Sufi Path of Love: The Spiritual Teachings of Rumi*. Albany: State University of New York Press, 1983.

Chopra, Deepak. *Life after Death: The Book of Answers*. London: Rider, 2008.

Churchland, Paul. *Matter and Consciousness: A Contemporary Introduction to the Philosophy of Mind*. Cambridge: MIT Press, 2013.

Clarke, D. S., ed. *Panpsychism: Past and Recent Selected Readings*. Albany: State University of New York Press, 2004.

Clarke, Ernest. *The Wisdom of Solomon*. Commentary by Ernest Clarke. Cambridge: Cambridge University Press, 1973.

Clarke, J. J. *The Tao of the West: Western Transformation of Taoist Thought*. New York: Routledge, 2000.

Clayton, Philip. *God and Gravity: A Philip Clayton Reader on Science and Theology.* Edited by Bradford McCall. Eugene, OR: Cascade, 2018.

———. *The Problem of God in Modern Thought.* Grand Rapids: Eerdmans, 2010.

———. *Religion and Science: The Basics.* New York: Routledge, 2019.

Clayton, Philip, and Paul Davies, eds. *The Re-emergence of Emergence: The Emergentist Hypothesis from Science to Religion.* Oxford: Oxford University Press, 2006.

Clayton, Philip, and Arthur Peacocke, eds. *In Whom We Live and Move and Have Our Being: Panentheistic Reflections on God's Presence in a Scientific World.* Grand Rapids: Eerdmans, 2004.

Clayton, Philip, and Wm. Andrew Schwartz. *What Is Ecological Civilization? Crisis, Hope, and the Future of the Planet.* Claremont, CA: Process Century Press, 2019.

Clayton, Philip, and Zachary Simpson, eds. *The Oxford Handbook of Religion and Science.* Oxford: Oxford University Press, 2006.

Cleary, Thomas, trans. *The Flower Ornament Scripture: A Translation of the Avatamsaka Sutra.* Boston: Shambhala, 1993.

Cobb, John B., Jr. *Beyond Dialogue: Toward a Mutual Transformation of Christianity and Buddhism.* Philadelphia: Fortress, 1982.

———. *Christ in a Pluralistic Age.* Philadelphia: Westminster, 1975.

———. *A Christian Natural Theology: Based on the Thought of Alfred North Whitehead.* Louisville: Westminster John Knox, 1974; 2007.

———, ed. *Religions in the Making: Whitehead and the Wisdom Traditions of the World.* Eugene, OR: Cascade, 2012.

———. *Sustainability: Economy, Ecology, and Justice.* 1992. Reprint, Eugene, OR: Wipf & Stock, 2007.

Cobb, John B., Jr., and David Ray Griffin. *Process Theology: An Introductory Exposition.* Louisville: Westminster John Knox, 1976.

Cobb, John B., Jr., and Christopher Ives, eds. *The Emptying God: A Buddhist-Jewish-Christian Conversation.* Maryknoll, NY: Orbis, 1990.

Coffey, Maria. *Explorers of the Infinite: The Secret Spiritual Lives of Extreme Athletes—and What They Reveal about Near-Death Experiences, Psychic Communication, and Touching the Beyond.* New York: Tarcher/Penguin, 2008.

Cohen, Mitchell. *The Politics of Opera: A History from Monteverdi to Mozart.* Princeton: Princeton University Press, 2017.

Cole, Juan. "The Concept of Manifestation in the Bahá'í Writings." *Bahá'í Studies* 9 (1982). http://bahai-library.com/cole_concept_manifestation.

Cole-Turner, Ronald, ed. *Transhumanism and Transcendence: Christian Hope in an Age of Technological Enhancement.* Washington, DC: Georgetown University Press, 2011.

Collins, Adela Yarbro, and John J. Collins. *King and Messiah as Son of God: Divine, Human, and Angelic Messianic Figures in Biblical and Related Literature.* Grand Rapids: Eerdmans, 2008.

Connolly, William E. *Pluralism.* Durham: Duke University Press, 2005.

Conway Morris, Simon. *The Crucible of Creation: The Burgess Shale and the Rise of Animals.* Oxford: Oxford University Press, 1998.

———. *Life's Solution: Inevitable Humans in a Lonely Universe.* Cambridge: Cambridge University Press, 2003.

———. *The Runes of Evolution: How the Universe Became Self-Aware.* West Conshohocken, PA: Templeton Foundation Press, 2015.

Conway Morris, Simon, and Stephen Jay Gould. "Showdown on the Burgess Shale." *Journal of Natural History* 107 (1998) 48–55.
Cooke, G. A. *The History and Song of Deborah: Judges IV and V*. 1892. Reprint, London: Andesite, 2017.
Coole, Diana, and Samantha Frost, eds. *New Materialisms: Ontology, Agency, and Politics*. Durham: Duke University Press, 2010.
Cooper, John W. *Panentheism, the Other God of the Philosophers: From Plato to the Present*. Grand Rapids: Baker Academics, 2006.
Coppes, Christophor. *The Essence of Religions: A Glimpse of Heaven in the Near-Death Experience*. New York: SelectBooks, 2013.
Corbin, Henry. *Alone with the Alone: Creative Imagination in the Sufism of Ibn 'Arabi*. Princeton: Princeton University Press, 1997.
Cotter, Christopher, Philip Quadrio, and Jonathan Tuckett, eds. *New Atheism: Critical Perspectives and Contemporary Debates*. Cham, Switzerland: Springer, 2017.
Coward, Harold, ed. *Modern Indian Responses to Religious Pluralism*. Albany: State University of New York Press, 1987.
Cracknell, Kenneth. *In Good and Generous Faith: Christian Responses to Religious Pluralism*. London: Epworth, 2005.
Crisp, Oliver, and Fred Sanders, eds. *Advancing Trinitarian Theology: Explorations in Constructive Dogmatics*. Grand Rapids: Zondervan, 2014.
Crosby, David, and Jerome Stone, eds. *The Routledge Handbook of Religious Naturalism*. New York: Routledge, 2018.
Cross, Charlotte, and Russell Berman, eds. *Political and Religious Ideas in the Works of Arnold Schoenberg*. New York: Garland, 2000.
Cross, Richard. *The Metaphysics of the Incarnation: Thomas Aquinas to Duns Scotus*. Oxford: Oxford University Press, 2002.
Crowe, Michael J. *The Extraterrestrial Life Debate, 1750–1900*. Mineola, NY: Dover, 1999.
Crowell, Steven, ed. *The Cambridge Companion to Existentialism*. Cambridge: Cambridge University Press, 2012.
The XIV Dalai Lama (Tenzin Gyatso). *The Universe in a Single Atom: The Convergence of Science and Spirituality*. New York: Morgan Road, 2005.
Dalela, Ashish. *Mystic Universe: An Introduction to Vedic Cosmology*. Pasadena, CA: Shabda, 2016.
Dalley, Stephanie. *Myths from Mesopotamia: Creation, the Flood, Gilgamesh, and Others*. Devised edition. Oxford: Oxford University Press, 2000.
Daly, Herman E., and John Cobb, Jr. *For the Common Good: Redirecting Economy toward Community, the Environment, and a Sustainable Future*. 2nd ed. Boston: Beacon, 1994.
Dante, Alighieri. *Inferno*. Translated by John Ciardi. New York: Random House, 1996.
———. *Paradiso: A Verse Translation*. Translated by Allen Mandelbaum. New York: Bantam, 1986.
Daoud, Yousef. *The Rose and the Lotus: Sufism and Buddhism*. N.p.: Xlibris, 2009.
Darwin, Charles. *On the Origin of Species*. London: Penguin, 2002.
Davies, Paul. *God and the New Physics*. New York: Simon & Schuster, 1983
———. *The Goldilocks Enigma: Why Is the Universe Just Right for Life?* London: Penguin, 2006.
———. *The Last Three Minutes: Conjectures about the Ultimate Fate of the Universe*. New York: Basic Books, 1994.

———. *The Mind of God: The Scientific Basis for a Rational World.* New York: Touchstone, 1992.
Davies, Paul, and John Gribbin. *The Matter Myth: Dramatic Discoveries That Challenge Our Understanding of Physical Reality.* New York: Simon & Schuster, 1992.
Davis, Andrew M., and Philip Clayton, eds. *How I Found God in Everyone and Everywhere: An Anthology of Spiritual Memoirs.* Rhinebeck, NY: Monkfish, 2018.
Davis, Colin. *Levinas: An Introduction.* Cambridge: Polity, 1996.
Davis, Heather, and Etienne Turpin. *Art in the Anthropocene: Encounters among Aesthetics, Politics, Environments and Epistemologies.* London: Open Humanities Press, 2015.
Davis, Jeremy. *The Birth of the Anthropocene.* Berkeley: University of California Press, 2016.
Dean, Thomas, ed. *Religious Pluralism and Truth: Essays on Cross-Cultural Philosophy of Religion.* Albany: State University of New York Press, 1995.
Deleuze, Gilles. *Bergsonism.* Brooklyn, NY: Zone, 1988.
———. "Conclusions on the Will to Power and the Eternal Return." In *Desert Islands and Other Texts, 1953–1974,* edited by David Lapoujade, 117–27. Los Angeles: Semiotext(e), 2004.
———. *Desert Islands and Other Texts, 1953–1974.* Edited by David Lapoujade. Los Angeles: Semiotext(e), 2004.
———. *Expressionism in Philosophy: Spinoza.* New York: Zone Books, 1992.
———. *The Fold: Leibniz and the Baroque.* Minneapolis: University of Minnesota Press, 1992.
———. *Kant's Critical Philosophy.* Minneapolis: University of Minnesota Press, 1993.
———. *The Logic of Sense.* New York: Columbia University Press, 1990.
———. *Negotiations, 1972–1990.* New York: Columbia University Press, 1995.
———. *Nietzsche and Philosophy.* New York: Columbia University Press, 2006.
———. "On Spinoza." *Lectures by Gilles Deleuze* (blog). http://deleuzelectures.blogspot.com/2007/02/on-spinoza.html.
———. *Pure Immanence: Essays on a Life.* Brooklyn, NY: Zone, 2005.
———. *Two Regimes of Madness: Texts and Interviews, 1975–1995.* New York: Semiotext(e), 2006.
Deleuze, Gilles, and Félix Guattari. *A Thousand Plateaus.* Minneapolis: University of Minnesota Press, 1987.
———. *What Is Philosophy?* New York: Columbia University Press, 1994.
Deleuze, Gilles, and Claire Parnett. *Dialogues.* New York: Columbia University Press, 1997.
Deloria, Vine, Jr. *God Is Red: A Native View of Religion.* New York: Putnam, 2003.
DeLoughrey, Elizabeth M. *Allegories of the Anthropocene.* Durham: Duke University Press, 2019.
Dennett, Daniel. *Breaking the Spell: Religion as Natural Phenomenon.* New York: Penguin, 2006.
Denton, Michael. *Evolution: A Theory in Crisis.* Chevy Chase, MD: Adler & Adler, 1985.
———. *Evolution: Still a Theory in Crisis.* Seattle: Discovery Institute, 2016.
———. *Nature's Destiny: How the Laws of Biology Reveal Purpose in the Universe.* New York: Free Press, 1998.
Derrida, Jacques. "Différance." In *Margins in Philosophy,* translated by Alan Bass, 1–28. Chicago: University of Chicago Press, 1984.
———. "Jacques Derrida, 1930–2004: The Last Interview." *Le Monde,* August 19, 2004.
———. *Of Grammatology.* Baltimore: Johns Hopkins University Press, 1997.

———. *Of Spirit: Heidegger and the Question*. Chicago: University of Chicago Press, 1989.

———. *Margins of Philosophy*. Translated by Alan Bass. Chicago: University of Chicago Press, 1984.

———. *Writing and Difference*. London: Routledge, 2001.

Desai, Gaurav, and Supriya Nair, eds. *Postcolonialisms: An Anthology of Cultural Theory and Criticism*. New Brunswick: Rutgers University Press, 2005.

Descartes, René. *Discourse on Method and Meditations on First Philosophy*. Translated by Donald Cress. Indianapolis: Hackett, 1998.

Deutsch, Eliot. *Advaita Vedānta: A Philosophical Reconstruction*. Honolulu: University of Hawaii Press, 1980.

Deutsch, Eliot, and Rohit Dalvi, eds. *The Essential Vedanta: A New Source Book of Advaita Vedānta*. Bloomington, IN: World Wisdom, 2004.

Devamata, Sister. *Sri Ramakrishna and His Disciples*. La Crescenta, CA: Ananda Ashrama, 1928.

Devettere, Raymond. *Introduction to Virtue Ethics: Insights of the Ancient Greeks*. Washington, DC: Georgetown University Press, 2002.

Dibb, Andrew. *Servetus, Swedenborg and the Nature of God*. Washington, DC: University Press of America, 2005.

Dick, Steven J. *The Biological Universe: The Twentieth-Century Extraterrestrial Life Debate and the Limits of Science*. Cambridge: Cambridge University Press, 1996.

———. "Cosmotheology: Theological Implications of the New Universe." In *Many Worlds: The New Universe, Extraterrestrial Life, and the Theological Implications*, edited by Stephen Dick, 191–210. Philadelphia: Templeton Foundation Press, 2000.

———, ed. *The Impact of Discovering Life beyond Earth*. Cambridge: Cambridge University Press, 2015.

———, ed. *Many Worlds: The New Universe, Extraterrestrial Life, and the Theological Implications*. Philadelphia: Templeton Foundation Press, 2000.

———. *Plurality of Worlds: The Origins of the Extraterrestrial Life Debate from Democritus to Kant*. Cambridge: Cambridge University Press, 1982.

Diessner, Rhett. *Psyche and Eros: Bahá'í Studies in a Spiritual Psychology*. Oxford: George Ronald, 2007.

Dolan, Jill. *Utopia in Performance: Finding Hope at the Theater*. Ann Arbor: University of Michigan Press, 2005.

Dollimore, Jonathan. *Radical Tragedy: Religion, Ideology and Power in the Drama of Shakespeare and His Contemporaries*. London: Red Globe, 2010.

Donaldson, Brianne. *Creaturely Cosmologies: Why Metaphysics Matters for Animal and Planetary Liberation*. Lanham, MD: Lexington, 2015.

Doniger, Wendy. *The Hindus: An Alternative History*. New York: Penguin, 2010.

Donington, Robert. *Opera and Its Symbols: The Unity of Words, Music and Staging*. New Haven: Yale University Press, 1990.

Donner, Fred M. *The Early Islamic Conquests*. Princeton: Princeton University Press, 1981.

———. *Muhammad and the Believers: At the Origins of Islam*. Cambridge: Belknap Press of Harvard University Press, 2010.

Dowman, Keith. *Spaciousness: The Radical Dzogchen of the Vajra-Heart; Longchenpa's Precious Treasury of the Dharmadhatu*. Translated by K. Dowman. Kathmandu: Vajra Publications, 2013.

Drees, William. *Religion, Science and Naturalism*. Cambridge: Cambridge University Press, 1996.

Dreyer, J. L. E. *A History of Astronomy from Thales to Kepler*. Revised with a foreword by W. H. Stahl. 2nd ed. Mineola, NY: Dover, 1953.

Ducasse, Curt. *A Critical Examination of the Belief in a Life after Death*. Springfield, IL: Charles C. Thomas, 1961.

Duffy, Kathleen. *Teilhard's Mysticism: Seeking the Inner Face of Evolution*. Maryknoll, NY: Orbis, 2014.

Duhem, Pierre. *Medieval Cosmology: Theories of Infinity, Place, Time, Void, and the Plurality of Worlds*. Edited and translated by Roger Ariew. Chicago: University of Chicago Press, 1987.

Dumoulin, Henrich. *Zen Buddhism: A History*. 2 vols. Bloomington, IN: World Wisdom, 2005.

Dunn, James D. G. *Christology in the Making: A New Testament Inquiry into the Origins of the Doctrine of the Incarnation*. 2nd ed. Grand Rapids: Eerdmans, 1996.

Dupuis, Jacques. *Christianity and the Religions: From Confrontation to Dialogue*. Maryknoll, NY: Orbis, 2002.

———. *Toward a Christian Theology of Religious Pluralism*. Maryknoll, NY: Orbis, 2001.

Durkheim, Émile. *The Elementary Forms of the Religious Life*. 1915. Reprint, N.p.: Pantianos Classics, 2016.

Dutton, Richard, Alison Findlay, and Richard Wilson, eds. *Theatre and Religion: Lancastrian Shakespeare*. Manchester: Manchester University Press, 2004.

Easwaran, Eknath, trans. *The Upanishads*. Tomales, CA: Blue Mountain Center of Meditation, 2007.

Ebeling, Florian. *The Secret History of Hermes Trismegistus: Hermeticism from Ancient to Modern Times*. Ithaca: Cornell University Press, 2011.

Edwards, Paul. *Immortality*. Amherst, NY: Prometheus, 1997.

Ehrman, Bart. *How Jesus Became God: The Exaltation of a Jewish Preacher from Galilee*. New York: HarperOne, 2014.

Eliade, Mircea. *Shamanism: Archaic Techniques of Ecstasy*. Princeton: Princeton University Press, 1963.

Ellis, Erle. *Anthropocene: A Very Short Introduction*. Oxford: Oxford University Press, 2018.

Elverskog, Johan. *Buddhism and Islam on the Silk Road*. Philadelphia: University of Pennsylvania Press, 2010.

Emerson, Ralph Waldo. *The Essential Writings of Ralph Waldo Emerson*. Edited by Brooks Atkinson. New York: Random House, 2000.

———. *Nature and Selected Essays*. New York: Penguin, 2003.

Emilsson, Eyjólfur K. *Plotinus*. New York: Routledge, 2017.

Epperson, Michael. *Quantum Mechanics and the Philosophy of Alfred North Whitehead*. New York: Fordham University Press, 2004.

Equale, Tony. *Arius and Nicaea: Science and Religion in a Material Universe*. Willis, VA: Boundary Rock, 2014.

Esack, Farid. *Qur'an, Liberation and Pluralism: An Islamic Perspective of Interreligious Solidarity against Oppression*. Oxford: Oneworld, 1996.

Esslemont, J. E. *Bahá'u'lláh and the New Ear: An Introduction to the Bahá'í Faith*. Wilmette, IL: Bahá'í Publishing Trust, 2006.

Esslin, Martin. *The Theatre of the Absurd*. 3rd ed. New York: Vintage, 2004.

Fabel, Arthur, and Donald Patrick St. John, eds. *Teilhard in the 21st Century: The Emerging Spirit of Earth*. Maryknoll, NY: Orbis, 2003.

Faber, Roland. *The Becoming of God: Process Theology, Philosophy, and Multireligious Engagement*. Eugene, OR: Cascade, 2017.

———. "Becoming Intermezzo: Eco-theopoetics after the Anthropic Principle." In *Theopoetic Folds: Philosophizing Multifariousness*, edited by Roland Faber and Jeremy Fackenthal, 212–38. New York: Fordham University Press, 2013.

———. "De-ontologizing God: Levinas, Deleuze and Whitehead." In *Process and Difference: Between Cosmological and Poststructuralist Postmodernism*, edited by Catherine Keller and Anne Daniell, 209–34. Albany: State University of New York Press, 2002.

———. "Ecotheology, Ecoprocess, and *Ecotheosis*: A Theopoetical Intervention." *Salzburger Zeitschrift für Theologie* 12 (2008) 75–115.

———. *The Garden of Reality: Transreligious Relativity in a World of Becoming*. Lanham, MD: Lexington, 2018.

———. *God as Poet of the World: Exploring Process Theologies*. Louisville: Westminster John Knox, 2008.

———. "God in the Making: Religious Experience and Cosmology in Whitehead's *Religion in the Making* in Theological Perspective." In *L'experience de Dieu: Lectures de "Religion in the Making" d'Alfred N. Whitehead (=Aletheia)*, edited by Michel Weber and Samuel Rouvillois, 179–200. Janvier: Ecole Saint-Jean, 2005.

———. "God's Advent/ure: The End of Evil and the Origin of Time." In *World Without End: Christian Eschatology from Process Perspective*, edited by Joseph Bracken, 91–112. Grand Rapids: Eerdmans, 2005.

———. "Immanence and Incompleteness: Whitehead's Late Metaphysics." In *Beyond Metaphysics? Conversations on A. N. Whitehead's Late Thought*, edited by Roland Faber, Brian Henning, and Clinton Combs, 91–110. Amsterdam: Rodopi, 2010.

———. "'Indra's Ear'—God's Absence of Listening." In *The Presence and Absence of God*, edited by Ingolf U. Dalferth, 161–86. Tübingen: Mohr Siebeck, 2010.

———. "Introduction: Negotiating Becoming." In *Secrets of Becoming: Negotiating Whitehead, Deleuze, and Butler*, edited by Roland Faber and Andrea M. Stephenson, 1–50. New York: Fordham University Press, 2010.

———. "Khora and Violence: Revisiting Butler with Whitehead." In *Butler on Whitehead: On the Occasion*, edited by Roland Faber, Michael Halewood, and Deena Lin, 105–26. Lanham, MD: Lexington, 2012.

———. "Laozi: A Lost Prophet? The Challenge of the Dao De Jing for the Bahá'í Universe of Discourse." *Lights of Irfan* 19 (2018) 34–110.

———. "Messianische Zeit: Walter Benjamins 'mystische Geschichtsauffassung' in zeittheologischer Perspektive." *Münchner Theologische Zeitschrift* 54 (2003) 68–78.

———. "'The Infinite Movement of Evanescence'—The Pythagorean Puzzle in Plato, Deleuze, and Whitehead." *American Journal of Theology and Philosophy* 21 (2000) 171–99.

———. "Multiplicity and Mysticism: Toward a New Mystagogy of Becoming." In *The Lure of Whitehead*, edited by Nicholas Gaskill and A. J. Nocek, 187–206. Minneapolis: University of Minnesota Press 2014.

———. "'Must "religion" always remain as a synonym for "hatred"?' Whiteheadian Meditations on the Future of Togetherness." In *Living Traditions and Universal Conviviality: Prospects and Challenges for Peace in Multireligious Communities*, edited by Roland Faber and Santiago Slabodsky, 167–82. Lanham, MD: Lexington, 2016.

———. "The Mystical Whitehead." In *Seeking Common Ground: Evaluation and Critique of Joseph Bracken's Comprehensive Worldview*, edited by Marc Pugliese and Gloria Schaab, 213–34. Milwaukee: Marquette University Press, 2012.

———. *The Ocean of God: On the Transreligious Future of Religions*. New York: Anthem, 2019.

———. "On the Unique Origin of Revelation, Religious Intuition and Theology." *Process Studies* 28 (1999) 273–89.

———. "Organic or Orgiastic Metaphysics? Reflections on Whitehead's Reception in Contemporary Poststructuralism." *Japanese Journal of Process Thought* 14 (2010) 203–22.

———. "Process, Progress, Excess: Whitehead and the Peace of Society." In *Recent Advances in the Creation of a Process-Based Worldview: Human Life in Process*, edited by Łukasz Lamża and Jakub Dziadkowiec, 6–20. Newcastle upon Tyne: Cambridge Scholars, 2016.

———. *Prozeßtheologie: Zu ihrer Würdigung und kritischen Erneuerung*. Mainz: Matthias Grünewald, 2000.

———. *Der Selbsteinsatz Gottes: Grundlegung einer Theologie des Leidens und der Veränderlichkeit Gottes*. Würzburg: Echter, 1995.

———. "The Sense of Peace: A Para-doxology of Divine Multiplicity." In *Polydoxy: Theology of Multiplicity and Relation*, edited by Catherine Keller and Laurel Schneider, 36–56. London: Routledge, 2011.

———. "Surrationality and Chaosmos: A More Deleuzean Whitehead (and a Butlerian Intervention)." In *Secrets of Becoming: Negotiating Whitehead, Deleuze, and Butler*, edited by Roland Faber and Andrea M. Stephenson, 157–77. New York: Fordham University Press, 2010.

———. "Touch: A Philosophic Meditation." In *The Allure of Things: Process and Object in Contemporary Philosophy*, edited by Roland Faber and Andrew Goffey, 47–67. New York: Bloomsbury Academic, 2014.

———. "Whitehead at Infinite Speed: Deconstructing System as Event." In *Schleiermacher and Whitehead: Open Systems in Dialogue*, edited by Christine Helmer et al., 39–72. Berlin: de Gruyter, 2004.

Faber, Roland, Jeffrey Bell, and Joseph Petek, eds. *Rethinking Whitehead's Symbolism: Thought, Language, Culture*. Edinburgh: Edinburgh University Press, 2017.

Faber, Roland, and Jeremy Fackenthal, eds. *Theopoetic Folds: Philosophizing Multifariousness*. New York: Fordham University Press, 2013.

Faber, Roland, and Andrew Goffey, eds. *The Allure of Things: Process and Object in Contemporary Philosophy*. New York: Bloomsbury Academic, 2014.

Faber, Roland, Brian Henning, and Clinton Combs, eds. *Beyond Metaphysics? Conversations on A. N. Whitehead's Late Thought*. Amsterdam: Rodopi, 2010.

Faber, Roland, Henry Krips, and Daniel Pettus, eds. *Event and Decision: Ontology and Politics in Badiou, Deleuze, and Whitehead*. Cambridge: Cambridge Scholars Press, 2010.

Faber, Roland, and Andrea M. Stephenson, eds. *Secrets of Becoming: Negotiating Whitehead, Deleuze, and Butler*. New York: Fordham University Press, 2010.

Farag, Lois. *Balance of the Heart: Desert Spirituality for Twenty-First-Century Christians*. Eugene, OR: Cascade, 2012.

Fazel, Seena. "Bahá'í Approaches to Christianity and Islam: Further Thoughts on Developing an Inter-religious Dialogue." *Bahá'í Studies Review* 14 (2008) 41–53.

———. "Interreligious Dialogue and the Baháʼí Faith: Some Preliminary Observations." In *Revisioning the Sacred: New Perspectives on a Baháʼí Theology*, edited by J. A. McLean, 127–52. Los Angeles: Kalimát, 1997.

———. "Is the Baháʼí Faith a World Religion?" *Journal of Baháʼí Studies* 6 (1994) 1–16.

———. "Religious Pluralism and the Baháʼí Faith." *Interreligious Insight* 1 (2003) 42–49.

———. "Understanding Exclusivist Texts." In *Scripture and Revelation: Papers Presented at the First Irfan Colloquium*, edited by Moojan Momen, 239–82. Oxford: George Ronald, 1997.

Ferguson, Niall. *Civilization: The West and the Rest*. New York: Penguin, 2012.

Ferngren, Gary, ed. *Science and Religion: A Historical Introduction*. Baltimore: Johns Hopkins University Press, 2002.

Ferrando, Francesca. *Philosophical Posthumanism*. London: Bloomsbury Academic, 2019.

Ferrer, Jorge N. "The Future of World Religion: Four Scenarios, One Dream." *Tikkun* 27 (2012) 14–16, 63–64.

———. *Participation and the Mystery: Transpersonal Essays in Psychology, Education, and Religion*. Albany: State University of New York Press, 2017.

———. *Revisioning Transpersonal Theory: A Participatory Vision of Human Spirituality*. Albany: State University of New York Press, 2002.

Ferrer, Jorge N., and Jacob H. Sherman. "The Participatory Turn: Spirituality, Mysticism, Religious Studies." In *The Participatory Turn: Spirituality, Mysticism, Religious Studies*, edited by Jorge Ferrer and Jacob Sherman, 1–78. Albany: State University of New York Press, 2007.

———, eds. *The Participatory Turn: Spirituality, Mysticism, Religious Studies*. Albany: State University of New York Press, 2007.

Feuerbach, Ludwig. *The Essence of Christianity*. Translated by George Eliot. Amherst, NY: Prometheus, 1989.

Fideler, David. *Restoring the Soul of the World: Our Living Bond with Nature's Intelligence*. Rochester: VT: Inner Traditions, 2014.

Flanagan, Owen. *The Real Hard Problem: Meaning in a Material World*. Cambridge: MIT Press, 2009.

Fletcher, Jeannine Hill. *Monopoly on Salvation? A Feminist Approach to Religious Pluralism*. New York. Continuum, 2005.

Foltz, Richard. *Religions of the Silk Road: Premodern Patterns of Globalization*. New York: Palgrave Macmillan, 2010.

Forman, Robert K. C. *Mysticism, Mind, Consciousness*. Albany: State University of New York Press, 1999.

———, ed. *The Problem of Pure Consciousness: Mysticism and Philosophy*. New York: Oxford University Press, 1990.

Forrest, Peter. *Developmental Theism: From Pure Will to Unbounded Love*. Oxford: Clarendon, 2008.

———. "The Multiverse: Separate Worlds, Branching, or Hyperspace? And What Implications Are There for Theism?" In *God and the Multiverse: Scientific, Philosophical and Theological Perspectives*, edited by Klaas Kraay, 61–91 New York: Routledge, 2015.

Fox, Mark. *Spiritual Encounters with Unusual Lights: Lightforms*. Cardiff: University of Wales Press, 2008.

Fox, Matthew. *Meister Eckhart: Mystic-Warrior for Our Time*. Novato, CA: New World Library, 2014.

Frankfort, Henri. *Ancient Egyptian Religion: An Interpretation.* New York: Columbia University Press, 1975.

Frankfort, Henri, et al. *The Intellectual Adventure of Ancient Man: An Essay on Speculative Thought in the Ancient Near East.* Chicago: University of Chicago Press, 1977.

Fredericks, James. *Buddhists and Christians: Through Comparative Theology to Solidarity.* Maryknoll, NY: Orbis, 2004.

Freke, Timothy, and Peter Gandy. *The Hermetica: The Lost Wisdom of the Pharaohs.* New York: Penguin, 1999.

Freud, Sigmund. *The Ego and the Id.* Edited by James Strachey. New York: Norton, 1989.

———. *The Future of an Illusion.* 1927. Reprint, N.p., Pacific Publishing Studio, 2010.

———. *Moses and Monotheism.* New York: Vintage, 1955.

Frisch, Wolfgang, Martin Meschede, and Ronald Blakey. *Plate Tectonics: Continental Drift and Mountain Building.* Berlin: Springer, 2011.

Fung, Yu-Lan. *A Short History of Chinese Philosophy: A Systematic Account of Chinese Thought from Its Origins to the Present Day.* New York: Free Press, 1948.

Garber, Daniel. *Leibniz: Body, Substance, Monad.* Oxford: Oxford University Press, 2009.

Geldard, Richard, ed. *The Essential Transcendentalists.* New York: Tarcher/Penguin, 2005.

Geraci, Robert. *Apocalyptic AI: Visions of Heaven in Robotics, Artificial Intelligence, and Virtual Reality.* Oxford: Oxford University Press, 2010.

Gerould, Daniel, ed. *Theatre/Theory/Theatre: The Major Critical Texts from Aristotle and Zeami to Soyinka and Havel.* New York: Applause Theatre & Cinema Books, 2003.

Gharavi, Lance. *Religion, Theatre, and Performance: Acts of Faith.* New York: Routledge, 2012.

Gieschen, Charles A. *Angelomorphic Christology: Antecedents and Early Evidence.* Leiden: Brill, 1998.

Gill, Sam. *Native American Religions: An Introduction.* Belmont, CA: Wadsworth, 2005.

Gilloch, Graeme. *Walter Benjamin: Critical Constellations.* Cambridge: Polity, 2002.

Glass, Philip. *Words Without Music.* New York: Liveright, 2015.

Glassé, Cyril. *The New Encyclopedia of Islam.* Rev. ed. Walnut Creek, CA: AltaMira, 2001.

Glasenapp, Helmuth von. *Jainism: An Indian Religion of Salvation.* Delhi: Motilal Banarsidass, 1999.

Gleick, James. *Chaos: Making a New Science.* New York: Penguin, 1987.

Godwin, Jocelyn. *Harmonies of Heaven and Earth: Mysticism in Music.* Rochester, VT: Inner Traditions, 1995.

Goldstein, Joseph. *Insight Meditation: The Practice of Freedom.* Boston: Shambhala, 1993.

———. *Mindfulness: A Practical Guide to Awakening.* Boulder, CO: Sounds True, 2016.

Golitzin, Alexander. "'Suddenly, Christ': The Place of Negative Theology in the Mystagogy of Dionysius Areopagites." In *Mystics: Presence and Aporia*, edited by Michael Kessler and Christian Sheppard, 8–37. Chicago: University of Chicago Press, 2003.

Goodenough, Ursula. *The Sacred Depths of Nature.* Oxford: Oxford University Press, 1998.

Goodman, Lenn. *Religious Pluralism and Values in the Public Sphere.* New York: Cambridge University Press, 2014.

Goswami, Amit. *Physics of the Soul: The Quantum Book of Living, Dying, Reincarnation and Immortality.* Newburyport, MA: Hampton Roads, 2001

———. *The Self-Aware Universe: How Consciousness Creates the Material World.* New York: Tarcher, 1995.

Goswami, Amit, and Maggie Goswami. *Science and Spirituality: A Quantum Interpretation.* New Delhi: Project of History of Indian Science, Philosophy, and Culture, 1997.

Gottlieb, Anthony. *The Dream of Enlightenment: The Rise of Modern Philosophy.* New York: Liveright, 2017.

Gould, Stephen Jay. *The Panda's Thumb: More Reflections in Natural History.* New York: Norton, 1992.

———. *The Structure of Evolutionary Theory.* Cambridge: Belknap Press of Harvard University Press, 2002.

———. *Wonderful Life: The Burgess Shale and the Nature of History.* New York: Norton, 2007.

Gowans, Christopher. *Philosophy of the Buddha.* London: Routledge, 2003.

Green, Brian. *The Elegant Universe. Superstrings, Hidden Dimensions, and the Quest for the Ultimate Theory.* New York: Norton, 2003.

———. *The Fabric of the Cosmos: Space, Time, and the Texture of Reality.* New York: Vintage, 2005.

———. *The Hidden Reality: Parallel Universes and the Deep Laws of the Cosmos.* New York: Vintage, 2012.

Gregorios, Paulos Mar, ed. *Neoplatonism and Indian Philosophy.* Albany: State University of New York Press, 2002.

Gregory, Andrew. *Ancient Greek Cosmogony.* New York: Bloomsbury, 2013.

Gregory, of Nyssa. *The Life of Moses.* Translated by Abraham J. Malherbe and Everett Ferguson. San Francisco: HaperSanFrancisco, 2006.

Griffin, David Ray, ed. *Deep Religious Pluralism.* Louisville: Westminster John Knox, 2005.

———. *Evil Revisited: Responses and Reconsiderations.* Albany State University of New York Press, 1991.

———. *God, Power, and Evil: A Process Theodicy.* Philadelphia: Westminster, 1976.

———. *Panentheism and Scientific Naturalism: Rethinking Evil, Morality, Religious Experience, Religious Pluralism, and the Academic Study of Religion.* Claremont, CA: Process Century Press, 2014.

———. *Parapsychology, Philosophy and Spirituality: A Postmodern Exploration.* Albany: State University of New York Press, 1997.

———. *Process Theology: On Postmodernism, Morality, Pluralism, Eschatology and Demonic Evil.* Claremont, CA: Process Century Press, 2017.

———. *Reenchantment without Supernaturalism: A Process Philosophy of Religion.* Ithaca: Cornell University Press, 2001

———. *Unsnarling the World-Knot: Consciousness, Freedom, and the Mind-Body Problem.* 1998. Reprint, Eugene, OR: Wipf & Stock, 2007.

Griffin, David Ray, et al., eds. *Founders of Constructive Postmodern Philosophy: Peirce, James, Bergson, Whitehead, and Hartshorne.* Albany: State University of New York Press, 1993.

Griffith, Bede. *A New Vision of Reality: Western Science, Eastern Mysticism and Christian Faith.* London: Collins, 1989.

Grigg, Ray. *The Tao of Zen.* Edison, NJ: Alva, 1994.

Grimm, John. "Native North American Worldviews and Ecology." In *Worldviews and Ecology: Religion, Philosophy, and the Environment*, edited by Mary Evelyn Tucker and John Grimm, 41–54. Maryknoll, NY: Orbis, 1994.

Grindheim, Sigurd. *God's Equal: What Can We Know about Jesus' Self-Understanding in the Synoptic Gospels?* London: T&T Clark, 2011.

Grof, Stanislav. *Beyond the Brain: Birth, Death and Transcendence in Psychotherapy.* Albany: State University of New York Press, 1985.

———. *The Cosmic Game: Explorations from the Frontiers of Human Consciousness*. Albany: State University of New York Press, 1998.

Grummet, David. *Teilhard de Chardin: Theology, Humanity and Cosmos*. Leuven: Peeters, 2005.

Gunton, Colin *The Promise of Trinitarian Theology*. London: T&T Clark, 1997.

Guthrie, Kenneth Sylvan, trans. *The Pythagorean Sourcebook and Library*. Edited by David R. Fideler. Grand Rapids: Phanes, 1988.

Guthrie, William. *Orpheus and Greek Religion*. Princeton: Princeton University Press, 1993.

Gutting, Gary. *French Philosophy in the Twentieth Century*. Cambridge: Cambridge University Press, 2001.

Habermas, Jürgen. *Between Naturalism and Religion: Philosophical Essays*. Malden, MA: Polity, 2008.

Hagan, John C., ed. *The Science of Near-Death Experiences*. Columbia: University of Missouri Press, 2017.

Haight, Roger. *Jesus: Symbol of God*. Maryknoll, NY: Orbis, 1999.

Haisch, Bernard. *The God Theory: Universes, Zero-Point Fields and What's Behind It All*. San Francisco: Weiser Books, 2006.

Hallamish, Moshe. *An Introduction to the Kabbalah*. Albany: State University of New York Press, 1999.

Hamerton-Kelly, R. G. *Pre-existence, Wisdom, and the Son of Man*. 1973. Reprint, Eugene, OR: Wipf & Stock, 2000.

Hamid, Idris Samawi. "The Metaphysics and Cosmology of Process according to Shaykh Ahmad al-Ahsa'i: Critical Edition, Translation, and Analysis of Observations in Wisdom." PhD diss., State University of New York at Buffalo, 1998.

Hamilton, Edith. *Mythology: Timeless Tales of Gods and Heros*. Boston: Little, Brown, 1942.

Hamilton, James M., Jr. *With the Clouds of Heaven: The Book of Daniel in Biblical Theology*. Downers Grove, IL: IVP Academic, 2014.

Hand, Seán. *Emmanuel Levinas*. New York: Routledge, 2009.

Hankins, James, ed. *The Cambridge Companion to Renaissance Philosophy*. Cambridge: Cambridge University Press, 2007.

Hannity, Vincent. *From Savagery to Civilization: The Power of Greek Mythology*. Boise, ID: Hector, 2018.

Hansen, Chad. *A Daoist Theory of Chinese Thought: A Philosophical Interpretation*. Oxford: Oxford University Press, 1992.

Harari, Yuval. *Homo Deus: A Brief History of Tomorrow*. New York: HarperCollins, 2017.

———. *Sapiens: A Brief History of Humankind*. New York: HarperPerennial, 2018.

Hardt, Michael. *Gilles Deleuze: An Apprenticeship in Philosophy*. Minneapolis: University of Minnesota Press, 1993.

Harkin, Michael, and David Lewis, ed. *Native Americans and the Environment: Perspectives on the Ecological Indian*. Lincoln: University of Nebraska Press, 2007.

Harman, Willis W. *Global Mind Change: The Promise of the 21st Century*. 2nd ed. San Francisco: Berrett-Koehler, 1998.

Harmless, William. *Desert Christians: An Introduction to the Literature of Early Monasticism*. Oxford: Oxford University Press, 2004.

Harrington, Joel. *Dangerous Mystic: Meister Eckhart's Path to the God Within*. New York: Penguin, 2018.

Harris, Errol E. *Fundamentals of Philosophy: A Study of Classical Texts*. Atlantic Highlands, NJ: Humanities Press, 1994.

———. *The Restitution of Metaphysics*. Amherst, NY: Humanity Books, 2000.

Harrison, Paul. *Elements of Pantheism*. Dorset, UK: Element Books, 2004.

Hart, William. *The Art of Living: Vipassana Meditation*. New York: HarperCollins, 1987.

Hartshorne, Charles, and William Reese. *Philosophers Speak of God*. Chicago: University of Chicago Press, 1976.

Harvey, Peter. *Buddhism*. New York: Continuum, 2001.

———. *The Selfless Mind: Personality, Consciousness and Nirvana in Early Buddhism*. London: Routledge, 1995.

Harvey, Van A. *Feuerbach and the Interpretation of Religion*. Cambridge: Cambridge University Press, 1995.

Hauck, Dennis. *Spiritual Alchemy: Metamorphosis of Body, Mind, and Soul*. N.p.: CreateSpace, 2017.

Haught, John. *God After Darwin: A Theology of Evolution*. Boulder, CO: Westview, 2007.

———. *God and the New Atheism: A Critical Response to Dawkins, Harris, and Hitchens*. Louisville: Westminster John Knox, 2008.

———. *Is Nature Enough? Meaning and Truth in the Age of Science*. Cambridge: Cambridge University Press, 2006.

———. *The New Cosmic Story: Inside Our Awakening Universe*. New Haven: Yale University Press, 2017.

———. *Science and Religion: From Conflict to Conversation*. New York: Paulist, 1995.

Hawking, Stephen. *Brief Answers to the Big Questions*. New York: Bantam, 2018.

———. *A Brief History of Time*. New York: Bantam, 1998.

Hawley, John Stratton. *A Storm of Songs: India and the Idea of the Bhakti Movement*. Cambridge: Harvard University Press, 2015.

Hayes, Terrill G., et al., eds. *Peace: More than an End to War*. Wilmette, IL: Baháʼí Publishing, 2007.

Hazini, Nima. "Neoplatonism: Framework for a Baháʼí Metaphysics." Presented at the Texas Regional Baháʼí Studies Conference, Austin, Texas, November 1995. https://bahai-library.com/hazini_neoplatonism_framework_metaphysics.

The Heart Sutra: The Womb of Buddhas. Translated by Red Pine Berkeley, CA: Counterpoint, 2004.

Hegel, Georg Wilhelm Friedrich. *The Phenomenology of Spirit*. Translated and edited by Terry Pinkard. Cambridge: Cambridge University Press, 2018.

Heidegger, Martin. *Basic Writings: From "Being and Time" (1927) to The Task of Thinking" (1964)*. Edited by David Farrell Krell. New York: HarperCollins, 1993.

———. *The Essence of Truth: On Plato's Cave Allegory and Theaetetus*. Translated by Ted Sadler. New York: Continuum, 2009.

———. *Heraclitus: The Inception of Occidental Thinking and Logic; Heraclitus's Doctrine of the Logos*. London: Bloomsbury, 1994.

———. *Parmenides*. Translated by André Schuwer and Richard Rojcewicz. Bloomington: Indiana University Press, 1992.

Heim, S. Mark. *The Depth of the Riches: A Trinitarian Theology of Religious Ends*. Grand Rapids: Eerdmans, 2001.

———, ed. *Grounds for Understanding: Ecumenical Resources for Responses to Religious Pluralism*. Grand Rapids: Eerdmans, 1998.

———. *Salvations: Truth and Difference in Religion.* Maryknoll, NY: Orbis, 1995.

Heine, Steven, and Dale Wright, eds. *Zen Classics: Formative Texts in the History of Zen Buddhism.* Oxford: Oxford University Press, 2006.

Heisenberg, Werner. *Physics and Philosophy: The Revolution in Modern Science.* New York: Penguin Classics, 2000.

Held, David. *Cosmopolitanism: Ideals and Realities.* Malden, MA: Polity, 2017.

Held, David, and Anthony McGrew. *Globalization/Anti-globalization: Beyond the Great Divide.* 2nd ed. Cambridge: Polity, 2013.

———, eds. *Globalization Theory: Approaches and Controversies.* Cambridge: Polity, 2007.

Heller, Ruth. *A Sea within a Sea: Secrets of the Sargasso.* New York: Gosset & Dunlap, 2000.

Heraclitus. *Fragments.* Translated by Brooks Haxton. New York: Penguin, 2001.

Herbert, Nick. *Elemental Mind: Human Consciousness and the Human Mind.* New York: Plume, 1994.

Herman, Arthur. *The Cave and the Light: Plato versus Aristotle, and the Struggle for the Soul of Western Civilization.* New York: Random House, 2013.

Herrick, James. *The Making of the New Spirituality: The Eclipse of the Western Religious Tradition.* Downers Grove, IL: InterVarsity, 2003.

———. *Scientific Mythologies: How Science and Science Fiction Forge New Religious Beliefs.* Downers Grove, IL: IVP Academic, 2008.

Herzogenrath, Bernd, ed. *An (Un)Likely Alliance: Thinking Environment(s) with Deleuze/Guattari.* Newcastle upon Tyne: Cambridge Scholars Press, 2008.

Hetherington, Norris, ed. *Cosmology: Historical, Literary, Philosophical, Religious and Scientific Perspectives.* New York: Routledge, 2008.

Hewitt, Harold, ed. *Problems in the Philosophy of Religion: Critical Studies of the Work of John Hick.* New York: St. Martin's, 1991.

Hick, John. *Death and Eternal Life.* Louisville: Westminster John Knox, 1994.

———. *An Interpretation of Religion: Human Responses to the Transcendent.* New Haven: Yale University Press, 2005.

———. *The Metaphor of God Incarnate: Christology in a Pluralistic Age.* Louisville: Westminster John Knox, 2005.

———. *The New Frontiers of Science and Religion: Religious Experience, Neuroscience, and the Transcendent.* New York: Palgrave Macmillan, 2006.

Hick, John, and Paul Knitter, eds. *The Myth of Christian Uniqueness: Toward a Pluralistic Theology of Religions.* Maryknoll, NY: Orbis, 1987.

Highland, Chris, ed. *Meditations of John Muir: Nature's Temple.* Berkeley, CA: Wilderness Press, 2011.

Hines, Brian. *Return to the One: Plotinus's Guide to God-Realization.* Salem, OR: Andrasteia, 2004.

Hobbes, Thomas. *Leviathan.* 1651. Reprint, Whithorn, UK: Anodos, 2019.

Hoffman, Edward. *The Way of Splendor: Jewish Mysticism and Modern Psychology.* Lanham, MD: Rowman & Littlefield, 2007.

Hoffmeier, James. *Akhenaten and the Origins of Monotheism.* Oxford: Oxford University Press, 2015.

Holden, Janice, Bruce Grayson, and Debbie James, eds. *The Handbook of Near-Death Experiences.* Santa Barbara, CA: Praeger, 2009.

Holland, Glenn. *Gods in the Desert: Religions of the Ancient Near East.* Lanham, MD: Rowman & Littlefield, 2009.

Holt, Jim. *Why Does the World Exist? An Existential Detective Story*. New York: Liveright, 2012.

Honen-shonin. *The Promise of Amida Buddha: Honen's Path to Bliss*. Translated by Jōji Atone and Yōko Hayashi. Somerville, MA: Wisdom Publications, 2011.

Horgan, John. *The End of Science: Facing the Limit of Knowledge in the Twilight of the Scientific Age*. New York: Broadway, 2015.

———. *The End of War*. San Francisco: McSweeney's, 2012.

———. *Rational Mysticism: Spirituality Meets Science in the Search for Enlightenment*. New York: Mariner, 2004.

———. *The Undiscovered Mind: How the Human Brain Defies Replication, Medication, and Explanation*. New York: Touchstone, 1999.

Hornung, Erik. *Akhenaten and the Religion of Light*. Translated by David Lorton. Ithaca: Cornell University Press, 2001.

Hosinski, Thomas. *Stubborn Fact and Creative Advance: An Introduction to the Metaphysics of Alfred North Whitehead*. Lanham, MD: Rowman & Littlefield, 1993.

Houston, Jean. *The Passion of Isis and Osiris: A Gateway to Transcendent Love*. New York: Ballantine, 1995.

Howard, Veena R., ed. *Dharma: The Hindu, Jain, Buddhist and Sikh Traditions of India*. London: I. B. Tauris, 2017.

Hoyle, Fred, and Chandra Wickramasinghe. *Evolution from Space: A Theory of Comic Creationism*. New York: Touchstone, 1984.

Hudson, Nancy. *Becoming God: The Doctrine of Theosis in Nicolas of Cusa*. Washington, DC: Catholic University of America Press, 2007.

Huff, Toby. *The Rise of Early Modern Science: Islam, China, and the West*. Cambridge: Cambridge University Press, 1992.

Humphreys, David. *Logjam: Deforestation and the Crisis of Global Governance*. London: Earthscan, 2006.

Hurtado, Larry W. *One God, One Lord: Early Christian Devotion and Ancient Jewish Monotheism*. London: Bloomsbury, 2015.

Huxley, Aldous. *The Perennial Philosophy*. New York: HarperPerennial, 2009.

Hyman, Arthur, James Walsh, and Thomas Williams, eds. *Philosophy in the Middle Ages: The Christian, Islamic, and Jewish Traditions*. Indianapolis: Hackett, 2010.

Iacoboni, Marco. "Imitation, Empathy, and Mirror Neurons." *Annual Review of Psychology* 60 (2009) 653–70.

Iraqi, Shahabuddin. *Bhakti Movements in Medieval India: Social and Political Perspectives*. New Delhi: Manohar Publishers, 2009.

Irigaray, Luce. *This Sex Which Is Not One*. Translated by Catherine Porter and Caroline Burke. Ithaca: Cornell University Press, 1985.

Irvin, Lee, ed. *Native American Spirituality: A Critical Reader*. Lincoln: University of Nebraska Press, 2000.

Islam, Sirajul. *Sufism and Bhakti: A Comparative Study*. Washington, DC: Council for Research in Values and Philosophy, 2004.

Ivakhiv, Adrian. *Shadowing the Anthropocene: Eco-realism for Turbulent Times*. Goleta, CA: Punctum, 2018.

Izutsu, Toshihiko. *Sufism and Taoism: A Comparative Study of Key Philosophical Concepts*. Berkeley: University of California Press, 1984.

Jackson, Leslie. *Isis: The Eternal Goddess of Egypt and Rome*. London: Avalonia, 2016.

James, E. O. *The Ancient Gods: The History and Diffusion of Religion in the Ancient Near East and the Eastern Mediterranean.* Edison, NJ: Castle, 2004.

James, William. *Essays in Psychical Research.* Cambridge: Harvard University Press, 1986.

———. *A Pluralistic Universe.* Lincoln: University of Nebraska Press, 1996.

———. *The Principles of Psychology.* Mineola, NY: Dover, 1950.

———. *The Varieties of Religious Experience: A Study in Human Nature.* New York: New American Library, 1958.

Jammer, Max. *Einstein and Religion: Physics and Theology.* Princeton: Princeton University Press, 1999.

———. *The Philosophy of Quantum Mechanics.* New York: Wiley, 1974.

Jasper, David. *The Sacred Desert: Religion, Literature, Art, and Culture.* Malden, MA: Blackwell, 2004.

Jaspers, Karl. *The Great Philosophers.* Vol. 1, *Socrates, Buddha, Confucius, Jesus, Plato, Augustine, Kant.* Edited by Hannah Arendt. San Diego: Harcourt Brace, 1962.

———. *The Great Philosophers.* Vol. 2, *Anaximander, Heraclitus, Parmenides, Plotinus, Lao-Tzu, Nagarjuna.* Edited by Hanna Arendt. San Diego: Harcourt Brace, 1966.

———. *The Origin and Goal of History.* Translated by Michael Bullock. New Haven: Yale University Press, 1953.

———. *Philosophy of Existence.* Translated by Richard F. Grabau. Philadelphia: University of Pennsylvania Press, 1971.

———. *Way to Wisdom: An Introduction to Philosophy.* Translated by Ralph Manheim. 1951. Reprint, Eastford, CT: Martino, 2015.

Johnson, Todd E., and Dale Savidge. *Performing the Sacred: Theology and Theatre in Dialogue.* Grand Rapids: Baker Academic, 2009.

Johnston, John. *The Allure of Machinic Life: Cybernetics, Artificial Life, and the New AI.* Cambridge: MIT Press, 2008.

Jones, Alexander, and Liba Taub, eds. *The Cambridge History of Science.* Vol. 1, *Ancient Science.* Cambridge: Cambridge University Press, 2018.

Jones, Allen. *Soul Making: The Desert Way of Spirituality.* New York: HarperCollins, 1985.

Jones, Richard H. *Curing the Philosopher's Disease: Reinstating Mystery in the Heart of Philosophy.* Lanham, MD: University of America Press, 2009.

———. *Mystery 101: An Introduction to the Big Questions and the Limits of Human Knowledge.* Albany: State University of New York Press, 2018.

———. *Philosophy of Mysticism: Raids on the Ineffable.* Albany: State University of New York Press, 2016.

———. *Piercing the Veil: Comparing Science and Mysticism as Ways of Knowing Reality.* New York: Jackson Square, 2014.

Johnston, Ronald. *Religion in Society: A Sociology of Religion.* New York: Routledge, 2007.

Joyce, Paul M., and Dalit Rom-Shiloni, eds. *The God Ezekiel Creates.* New York: Bloomsbury, 2016.

Jung, Carl Gustav. *The Archetypes and the Collective Unconscious.* Translated by R. F. C. Hull. 2nd ed. Collected Works of C. G. Jung 9/1. Princeton: Princeton University Press, 1980.

———. *Psychology and Alchemy.* Translated by R. F. C. Hull. 2nd ed. Collected Works of C. G. Jung 12. Princeton: Princeton University Press, 1980.

———. *Synchronicity: An Acausal Connecting Principle.* New York: Routledge, 2008.

Kaku, Michio. *The Future of Humanity: Our Destiny in the Universe.* New York: Anchor, 2018.

Kalkavage, Peter. *The Logic of Desire: An Introduction to Hegel's "Phenomenology of Spirit"*. Philadelphia: Paul Dry, 2007.

Kallenbach, Ulla. *The Theatre of Imagination: A Cultural History of Imagination in the Mind and on the Stage*. New York: Palgrave Macmillan, 2018.

Kaplan, Stephen. *Different Paths, Different Summits: A Model for Religious Pluralism*. Lanham, MD: Rowman & Littlefield, 2002.

Kärkkäinen, Veli-Matti. *Pneumatology: The Holy Spirit in Ecumenical, International, and Contextual Perspective*. Grand Rapids: Baker Academic, 2018.

———. *Trinity and Revelation*. Grand Rapids: Eerdmans, 2014.

Karlberg, Michael. *Beyond the Culture of Contest: From Adversarialism to Mutualism in an Age of Interdependence*. Oxford: George Ronald, 2004.

Katō, Bunnō, Yoshirō Tamura, and Kōjirō Mirasaka, trans. *The Threefold Lotus Sutra*. Tokyo: Kōsei, 2005.

Katz, Steven. *Mysticism and Philosophical Analysis*. New York: Oxford University Press, 1978.

Kaufmann, Walter. *The Critique of Religion and Philosophy*. Princeton: Princeton University Press, 1990.

Kearns, Laurel, and Catherine Keller, eds. *Ecospirit: Religions and Philosophies of the Earth*. New York: Fordham University Press, 2007.

Keel, Othmar. *The Symbolism of the Biblical World: Ancient Near Eastern Iconography and the Book of Psalms*. Translated by Timothy J. Hallett. New York: Seabury, 1977.

Keil, Gerald. *Time and the Bahá'í Era: A Study of the Badi Calendar*. Oxford: George Ronald, 2008.

Keller, Catherine. "The Cloud of the Impossible: Embodiment and Apophasis." In *Apophatic Bodies: Negative Theology, Incarnation, and Relationship*, edited by Christian Boesel and Catherine Keller, 25–44. New York: Fordham University Press, 2010.

———. *Cloud of the Impossible: Negative Theology and Planetary Engagement*. New York: Columbia University Press, 2015.

———. *Face of the Deep: A Theology of Becoming*. New York: Routledge, 2003.

———. *God and Power: Counter-Apocalyptic Journeys*. Minneapolis: Fortress, 2005.

———. *Intercarnations: Exercises in Theological Possibility*. New York: Fordham University Press, 2017.

———. "Process and Chaosmos: A Whiteheadian Fold in the Discourse of Difference." In *Process and Difference: Between Cosmological and Poststructuralist Postmodernism*, edited by Catherine Keller and Anne Daniell, 55–72. Albany: State University of New York Press, 2002.

———. "Theopoetics and the Pluriverse: Notes on a Process." In *Theopoetic Folds: Philosophizing Multifariousness*, edited by Roland Faber and Jeremy Fackenthal, 179–94. New York: Fordham University Press, 2013.

Keller, Catherine, and Anne Daniell, eds. *Process and Difference: Between Cosmological and Poststructuralist Postmodernism*. Albany: State University of New York Press, 2002.

Keller, Catherine, Michael Nausner, and Mayra Rivera, eds. *Postcolonial Theologies: Diversity and Empire*. St. Louis: Chalice, 2004.

Kelly, Edward F., Adam Crabtree, and Paul Marshall, eds. *Beyond Physicalism: Toward Reconciliation of Science and Spirituality*. Lanham, MD: Rowman & Littlefield, 2015.

Kessler, Michael, and Christian Sheppard, eds. *Mystics: Presence and Aporia*. Chicago: University of Chicago Press, 2003.

Khan, Inayat. *The Soul's Journey*. New Lebanon, NY: Omega, 2001.

Khan, Maulana Wahiduddin. *The Prophet of Peace: Teachings of the Prophet Mohammad.* New Delhi: Penguin, 2009.

Kim, Grace Ji-Sun. *The Grace of Sophia.* Cleveland: Pilgrim, 2002.

———. *The Holy Spirit, Chi, and the Other: A Model of Global and Intercultural Pneumatology.* New York: Palgrave Macmillan, 2011.

———. *Reimagining Spirit: Wind, Breath, and Vibration.* Eugene, OR: Cascade, 2019.

King, Richard. *Indian Philosophy: An Introduction to Hindu and Buddhist Thought.* Edinburgh: Edinburgh University Press, 1999.

———, ed. *Religion, Theory, Critique: Classical and Contemporary Approaches and Methodologies.* New York: Columbia University Press, 2017.

King, Ursula. *Spirit of Fire: The Life and Vision of Teilhard de Chardin.* Maryknoll, NY: Orbis, 2003.

———. *Towards a New Mysticism: Teilhard de Chardin and Eastern Religions.* New York: Seabury, 1980.

Kirsch, Jonathan. *God Against the Gods: The History of the War between Monotheism and Polytheism.* New York: Penguin, 2004.

Kisak, Paul, ed. *Religious Cosmology: Religious Explanations for the Origin of the Universe.* N.p.: CreateSpace, 2016.

Kline, Meredith G. *Images of the Spirit.* 1980. Reprint, Eugene, OR: Wipf and Stock, 1999.

Knepper, Timothy D. *Negating Negation: Against the Apophatic Abandonment of the Dionysian Corpus.* Eugene, OR: Cascade, 2014.

Knitter, Paul. "Can Christian Theology Be Only Christian? A Dialogical Theology for the Third Millennium." In *Theology toward the Third Millennium: Theological Issues for the Twenty-First Century*, edited by David Schultenover, 83–102. Lewiston, NY: Mellen, 1991.

———. *Introducing Theologies of Religion.* Maryknoll, MI: Orbis, 2007.

———. "My God Is Bigger than Your God: Time for Another Axial Shift in the History of Religion." *Studies in Interreligious Dialogue* 17 (2007) 100–118.

———, ed. *The Myth of Religious Superiority: Multifaith Explorations of Religious Pluralism.* Maryknoll, NY: Orbis, 2015.

———. *No Other Name? A Critical Survey of Christian Attitudes toward the World Religions.* Maryknoll, NY: Orbis, 1986.

———. *One Earth, Many Religions: Multifaith Dialogue and Global Responsibility.* Maryknoll, NY: Orbis, 1995.

———. *Without Buddha I Could Not Be a Christian.* Oxford: Oneworld, 2009.

Knoppers, Gary. *Jews and Samaritans: The Origins and History of Their Early Relations.* New York: Oxford University Press, 2013.

Koestler, Arthur, and J. R. Smythies. *Beyond Reductionism: New Perspectives in the Life Sciences.* London: Hutchinson, 1969.

Kohn, Livia, ed. *Daoism Handbook.* Leiden: Brill, 1999.

———. *The God of Dao: Lord Lao in History and Myth.* Ann Arbor: Center for Chinese Studies, University of Michigan, 1998.

———. *Taoist Mystical Philosophy: The Scripture of Western Ascension.* Albany: State University of New York Press, 1991.

Kohn, Michael. *Lama of the Gobi: How Mongolia's Mystic Monk Spread Tibetan Buddhism in the World's Harshest Desert.* Hong Kong: Blacksmith, 2010.

Kolbert, Elisabeth. *The Sixth Extinction: An Unnatural History.* New York: Henry Holt, 2014.

Kraay, Klaas, ed. *God and the Multiverse: Scientific, Philosophical and Theological Perspectives.* New York: Routledge, 2015.

Kraus, Elisabeth. *The Metaphysics of Experience: A Companion to Whitehead's Process and Reality.* New York: Fordham University Press, 1998.

Kripal, Jeffrey, et al. *Comparing Religions: Coming to Terms.* Malden, MA: Wiley-Blackwell, 2014.

Krishna, Sankaran. *Globalization and Postcolonialism: Hegemony and Resistance in the Twenty-First Century.* Lanham, MD: Rowman & Littlefield, 2009.

Krishnananda, Swami. *Mandukya Upanishad: An Exposition.* Rishikesh, India: Divine Life Society, 1996.

Krumholz, Mark R. *Star Formation.* Singapore: World Scientific Publishing, 2017.

Kumar, Raj. *Know the Vedas at a Glance.* Delhi: Pustak Mahal, 2008.

Kunin, Seth D., and Jonathan Miles-Watson, eds. *Theories of Religion: A Reader.* New Brunswick: Rutgers University Press, 2006.

Künrig, Rongtön Sheja. *Adorning Maitreya's Intent: Arriving at the View of Nonduality.* Translated by Christian Bernert. Boulder, CO: Snow Lion, 2017.

Kurzweil, Ray. *The Age of Spiritual Machines: When Computers Exceed Human Intelligence.* New York: Penguin, 2000.

———. *The Singularity Is Near: When Humans Transcend Biology.* New York: Penguin, 2005.

Lachman, Gary. *The Quest for Hermes Trismegistus: From Ancient Egypt to the Modern World.* Edinburgh: Floris, 2011.

LaCugna, Catherine. *God for Us: The Trinity and Christian Life.* New York: HarperCollins, 1991.

LaFave, Kenneth. *The Sound of Ontology: Music as Model for Metaphysics.* Lanham, MD: Lexington, 2018.

Lake-Thom, Bobby. *Spirits of the Earth: A Guide to Native American Nature Symbols, Stories, and Ceremonies.* New York: Plume, 1997.

Lakshman Jee, Swami. *Kashmir Shaivism: The Secret Supreme.* Edited by John Hughes. Albany: State University of New York Press, 2007.

Lambden, Stephen. "The Background and Centrality of Apophatic Theology in Bábí and Baháʼí Scripture." In *Revisioning the Sacred: New Perspectives on a Baháʼí Theology*, edited by J. A. McLean, 37–78. Los Angeles: Kalimát, 1997.

———. "Dimensions of Abrahamic and Babi-Baháʼí Soteriology: Some Notes on the Baháʼí Theology of the Salvific and Redemptive Role of Bahá'-Alláh." Last updated June 3, 2018. http://hurqalya.ucmerced.edu/node/3451.

———. "The Mysteries of the Call to Moses: Translation and Notes on a Tablet of Baháʼuʼlláh Addressed to Jinab-i Khalil." *Baháʼí Studies Bulletin* 4 (1986) 33–78.

———. "The Sinaitic Mysteries: Notes on Moses/Sinai Motifs in Bábí and Baháʼí Scripture." In *Studies in Honor of the Late Hasan M. Balyuzi*, edited by Moojan Momen, 65–184. Los Angeles: Kalimát, 1988.

———. "Some Aspects of Isrāʼīliyyāt and the Emergence of the Bābī-Baháʼí Interpretation of the Bible." PhD diss., Newcastle University, 2002.

———. "The Tafsir Hadith al-Haqiqah: Its Shiʻi Origins and Commentators." Presented at the Irfan Colloquia Session #48 (English), Center for Baháʼí Studies, Acuto, Italy, July 10–13, 2003. https://hurqalya.ucmerced.edu/node/684.

———. "The Word Bahá: Quintessence of the Greatest Name." *Baháʼí Studies Review* 3 (1993) 19–42.

Lambert, Yves. "Religion in Modernity as a New Axial Age: Secularization or New Religious Forms." *Sociology of Religion* 60 (1999) 303–33.

Lampe, Geoffrey. *God as Spirit: The Bampton Lectures 1976*. Oxford: Oxford University Press, 1977.

Lane, Belden. *The Solace of Fierce Landscapes: Exploring Desert and Mountain Spirituality*. Oxford: Oxford University Press, 1998.

Lang, Bernhard. *The Hebrew God: Portrait of an Ancient Deity*. New Haven: Yale University Press, 2002.

Lanzetta, Beverly. *Emerging Heart: Global Spirituality and the Sacred*. Minneapolis: Fortress, 2007.

———. *Radical Wisdom: A Feminist Mystical Theology*. Minneapolis: Fortress, 2005.

Laszlo, Erwin. *Science and the Akashic Field: An Integral Theory of Everything*. Rochester, VT: Inner Traditions, 2007.

———. *The Self-Actualizing Universe: The Akasha Revolution in Science and Human Consciousness*. Rochester, VT: Inner Traditions, 2014.

Latour, Bruno. *Politics of Nature: How to Bring Sciences into Democracy*. Cambridge: Harvard University Press, 2004.

Lawson, Todd. "The Báb's Epistle on the Spiritual Journey toward God." In *The Bahá'í Faith and the World's Religions*, edited by Moojan Momen, 231–47. Oxford: George Ronald, 2003.

Lee, Hyo-Dong. *Spirit, Qi, and the Multitude: A Comparative Theology for the Democracy of Creation*. New York: Fordham University Press, 2014.

Leibniz, G. W. *Discourse on Metaphysics, and The Monadology*. Translated by George Montgomery. Mineola, NY: Dover, 2005.

Lele, Jayant, ed. *Tradition and Modernity in Bhakti Movements*. Leiden: Brill Academic, 1997.

Lem, Stanislav. *Solaris: A Novel*. New York: Faber & Faber, 1970.

Leslie, John. *Immortality Defended*. Malden, MA: Blackwell, 2007.

———. *Universes*. London: Routledge, 1996.

Leslie, John, and Robert Kuhn, eds. *The Mystery of Existence: Why Is There Anything at All?* Malden, MA: Wiley-Blackwell, 2013.

Leslie, Michael, and John Hunt, eds. *A Cultural History of Gardens*. 6 vols. London: Bloomsbury Academic, 2016.

LeValley, Paul. *Seekers of the Naked Truth: Collected Writings on the Gymnosophist and Related Shramana Religions*. Delhi: Motilal Banarsidass, 2018.

Levinas, Emmanuel. *Alterity and Transcendence*. New York: Columbia University Press, 1995.

———. "God and Philosophy." In *The Levinas Reader*, edited by Seán Hand, 166–89. Oxford: Blackwell, 1994.

———. *Otherwise than Being or Beyond Essence*. Translated by Alphonso Lingis. Dordrecht: Kluwer Academic, 1978.

———. *Totality and Infinity*. The Hague: Kluwer Academic, 1981.

Levine, Michael P. *Pantheism: A Non-theistic Concept of Deity*. London: Routledge, 1994.

———. *A Weak Messianic Power: Figures of a Time to Come in Benjamin, Derrida, and Celan*. New York: Fordham University Press, 2014.

Lewels, Joe. *The God Hypothesis: Extraterrestrial Life and Its Implications for Science and Religion*. Mill Spring, NC: Wild Flower, 2005.

Lewis, David. *Counterfactuals*. Malden, MA: Blackwell, 2001.

———. *On the Plurality of Worlds*. Malden, MA: Blackwell, 2001.

———. "Possible Worlds." In *Contemporary Readings in the Foundations of Metaphysics*, edited by Stephen Laurence and Cynthia Macdonald, 96–102. Malden, MA: Blackwell, 1998.

Lewis, Simon, and Mark Maslin. *The Human Planet: How We Created the Anthropocene*. London: Penguin, 2018.

Lewisohn, Leonard, ed. *Hafez and the Religion of Love in Classical Persian Poetry*. London: I. B. Tauris, 2015.

———, ed. *The Heritage of Sufism* Vol. 1, *Classical Persian Sufism from Its Origins to Rumi (700–1300)*. Oxford: Oneworld. 1999.

Lichtheim, Miriam. *Ancient Egyptian Literature: A Book of Readings*. Vol. 2, *The New Kingdom*. Berkeley: University of California Press, 1976.

Lieberman, Daniel. *The Story of the Human Body: Evolution, Health, and Disease*. New York: Vintage, 2014.

Lindberg, David. *The Beginning of Western Science: The European Scientific Tradition in Philosophical, Religious, and Institutional Context; Prehistory to A.D. 1450*. Chicago: University of Chicago Press, 2007.

Lingan, Edmund. *The Theatre of the Occult Revival: Alternative Spiritual Performance from 1875 to the Present*. New York: Palgrave Macmillan, 2014.

Lings, Martin, and Clinton Minnaar, eds. *The Underlying Religion: An Introduction to the Perennial Philosophy*. Bloomington, IN: World Wisdom, 2008.

Llewellyn, John. *The Hypocritical Imagination: Between Kant and Levinas*. London: Routledge, 2000.

Loewer, Barry, and Jonathan Schaffer, eds. *A Companion to David Lewis*. Malden, MA: Blackwell, 2015.

Loke, Andrew Ter Ern. *The Origin of Divine Christology*. Cambridge: Cambridge University Press, 2017.

Long, Jeffrey. *God and the Afterlife*. New York: HarperOne, 2016.

Long, Jeffrey, and Paul Perry. *Evidence of the Afterlife: The Science of Near-Death Experiences*. New York: HarperOne, 2011.

Long, Jeffrey D. "Anekanta Vedanta: Toward a Deep Hindu Religious Pluralism." In *Deep Religious Pluralism*, edited by David Ray Griffin, 130–45. Louisville: Westminster John Knox, 2005.

———. *Jainism: An Introduction*. New York: I. B. Tauris, 2009.

———. "Tentatively Putting the Pieces Together: Comparative Theology in the Tradition of Sri Ramakrishna." In *The New Comparative Theology: Interreligious Insights from the Next Generation*, edited by Francis X. Clooney, 151–70. New York: T&T Clark, 2010.

———. "Truth, Diversity, and the Incomplete Project of Modern Hinduism." In *Hermeneutics and Hindu Thought: Toward a Fusion of Horizons*, edited by Rita Sherma and Arvind Sharma, 179–210. Dordrecht: Springer, 2008.

Loomba, Ania. *Colonialism/Postcolonialism*. London: Routledge, 2015.

Loomer, Bernard. "The Size of God." In *The Size of God: The Theology of Bernard Loomer in Context*, edited by William Dean and Larry E. Axel, 20–51. Macon, GA: Mercer University Press, 1987.

Lopez, Donald. *Buddhism and Science: A Guide for the Perplexed*. Chicago: University of Chicago Press, 2008.

———. *The Story of Buddhism: A Concise Guide to Its History and Teachings*. New York: HarperSanFrancisco, 2001.

Lorraine, Tamsin. *Irigaray and Deleuze: Experiments in Visceral Philosophy*. Ithaca: Cornell University Press, 1999.

Losensky, Paul, trans. *Farid ad-Din 'Attār's Memorial of God's Friends: Lives and Sayings of Sufis*. New York: Paulist, 2009.

Lossky, Vladimir. *The Mystical Theology of the Eastern Church*. Crestwood, NY: St. Vladimir's Seminary Press, 1997.

Louth, Andrew. *The Origins of the Christian Mystical Tradition: From Plato to Denys*. Oxford: Oxford University Press, 2007.

Lovejoy, Arthur. *The Great Chain of Being*. Cambridge: Harvard University Press, 2001.

Lovelock, James. *Gaia: A New Look at Life on Earth*. 3rd ed. Oxford: Oxford University Press, 2000.

Lovelock, James E., and Lynn Margulis. "Atmospheric Homeostasis by and for the Biosphere: The Gaia Hypothesis." *Tellus* 26 (1974) 2–10.

Löwith, Karl. *From Hegel to Nietzsche: The Revolution in Nineteenth-Century Thought*. New York: Columbia University Press, 1991.

Loy, David. *Non-duality: A Study in Comparative Philosophy*. Amherst, NY: Humanity Books, 1988.

Lucretius. *On the Nature of Things*. Translated by Martin Ferguson Smith. Indianapolis: Hackett, 2001.

Lumpkin, Joseph. *The Books of Enoch: The Angels, The Watchers and The Nephilim (With Extensive Commentary on the Three Books of Enoch, the Fallen Angels, the Calendar of Enoch, and Daniel's Prophecy)*. Blountsville, AL: Fifth Estate, 2011.

Lycan, William. "Possible Worlds and Possibilia." In *Contemporary Readings in the Foundations of Metaphysics*, edited by Stephen Laurence and Cynthia Macdonald, 83–95. Malden, MA: Blackwell, 1998.

Lyotard, Jean-Francois. *The Postmodern Condition: A Report on Knowledge*. Minneapolis: University of Minnesota Press, 1984.

Macauliffe, Max. *The Sikh Religion: Its Gurus, Sacred Writings and Authors*. 6 vols. Oxford: Oxford University Press, 1909.

Maharshi, Sri Ramana. *Be as You Are*. Edited by David Godman. New York: Arkana, 1985.

Malin, Shimon. *Nature Loves to Hide: Quantum Physics and the Nature of Reality; a Western Perspective*. New York: Oxford University Press, 2001.

Manderson, Desmond. *Essays on Levinas and Law: A Mosaic*. New York: Palgrave Macmillan, 2009.

Manring, Rebecca J. *Reconstructing Tradition: Advaita Acarya and Gaudiya Vaisnavism at the Cusp of the Twentieth Century*. New York: Columbia University Press, 2005.

Mansfield, Vic. *Tibetan Buddhism and Modern Physics: Toward a Union of Love and Knowledge*. West Conshohocken, PA: Templeton Foundation Press, 2008.

Marks, John. *Gilles Deleuze: Vitalism and Multiplicity*. London: Pluto, 1998.

Marlene, Cheryl. *Many Paths, One Mountain: The Five Steps of the Spiritual Journey*. Portland, OR: Essential Knowing, 2016.

Marmion, Declan, and Mary E. Hines, eds. *The Cambridge Companion to Karl Rahner*. Cambridge: Cambridge University Press, 2005.

Marshall, Ian, and Danah Zohar. *Who's Afraid of Schrödinger's Cat? An A-to-Z Guide to the All the New Science Ideas You Need to Keep Up with the New Thinking*. New York: Morrow, 1997.

Marshall, Paul. *Mystical Encounters with the Natural World: Experiences and Explanations.* Oxford: Oxford University Press, 2005.
Maslow, Abraham. *The Farther Reaches of Human Nature.* New York: Penguin, 1993.
———. "A Theory of Human Motivation." *Psychological Review* 50 (1943) 370–96.
———. *Toward a Psychology of Being.* 1962. Reprint, Floyd, VA: Sublime, 2014.
Mason, David. *The Performative Ground of Religion and Theatre.* New York: Routledge, 2019.
———. *Theatre and Religion on Krishna's Stage: Performing in Vrindavan.* New York: Palgrave Macmillan, 2009
Ma'súmián, Farnaz. *Life After Death: A Study of the Afterlife in World Religion.* Los Angeles: Kalimát, 1995.
Matt, Daniel. *The Essential Kabbalah: The Heart of Jewish Mysticism.* San Francisco: HarperSanFrancisco, 1996.
Matthews, Caitlin. *Sophia: Goddess of Wisdom, Bride of God.* Wheaton, IL: Quest, 2009.
Matthiessen, Peter. *The Snow Leopard.* New York: Penguin Classics, 2016.
Maturana, Humberto, and Francesco Varela. *The Tree of Knowledge: The Biological Roots of Human Understanding.* Boston: Shambhala, 1992.
Maxwell-Steward, P. G. *The Chemical Choir: A History of Alchemy.* New York: Continuum, 2008.
May, Gerhard. *Creatio ex nihilo: The Doctrine of "Creation out of Nothing" in Early Christian Thought.* Edinburgh: T&T Clark, 1994.
Mbiti, John. *Introduction to African Religion.* London: Heinemann, 1975.
McBride, William, ed. *Sartre and Existentialism: Sartre's French Contemporaries and Enduring Influences.* New York: Routledge, 2011.
McCagney, Nancy. *Nagarjuna and the Philosophy of Oneness.* Lanham, MD: Rowman & Littlefield, 1997.
McCort, Dennis. *Going Beyond the Pairs: The Coincidence of Opposites in German Romanticism, Zen, and Deconstruction.* Albany: State University of New York Press, 2001.
McDaniel, Jay. *Gandhi's Hope: Learning from Other Religions as a Path to Peace.* Maryknoll, NY: Orbis, 2005.
McFague, Sallie. *The Body of God: An Ecological Theology.* Minneapolis: Fortress, 1993.
———. *Models of God: Theology for an Ecological, Nuclear Age.* Philadelphia: Fortress, 1987.
McFarland, James. *Constellation: Friedrich Nietzsche and Walter Benjamin in the Now-Time of History.* New York: Fordham University Press, 2013.
McGaa, Ed. *Mother Earth Spirituality: Native American Paths to Healing Ourselves and Our World.* New York: HarperCollins, 1990.
McGinn, Bernard, ed. *The Essential Writings of Christian Mysticism.* New York: Random House, 2006.
———. "The God beyond God: Theology and Mysticism in the Thought of Meister Eckhart." *The Journal of Religion* 61 (1981) 1–19.
———. *Meister Eckhart: Teacher and Preacher.* Mahwah, NJ: Paulist, 1986.
———. *The Mystical Thought of Meister Eckhart: The Man from Whom God Hid Nothing.* New York: Crossroad, 2001.
McGinn, Colin. *Shakespeare's Philosophy: Discovering the Meaning behind the Plays.* New York: HarperCollins, 2007.
McGrath, Alister. *The Foundations of Dialogue in Science and Religion.* Oxford: Blackwell, 1998.
———. *Science and Religion: An Introduction.* Oxford: Blackwell, 1999.

McGrath, James. *The Only True God: Early Christian Monotheism in Its Jewish Context.* Urbana: University of Illinois Press, 2009.

McGuckin, John Anthony, trans. *The Book of Mystical Chapters: Meditations on the Soul's Ascent, from the Desert Fathers and Other Early Christian Contemplatives.* Boston: Shambhala, 2002.

McIntosh, Mark A. *Mystical Theology: The Integrity of Spirituality and Theology.* Malden, MA: Blackwell, 1998.

McLeod, W. H. "The Influence of Islam on the Thought of Guru Nanak." *History of Religions* 7 (1968) 302–16.

Medina, John Fitzgerald. *Faith, Physics and Psychology: Rethinking Society and the Human Spirit.* Wilmette, IL: Baha'i Publishing Trust, 2006.

Meher Baba. *Discourses.* Ahmednagar, India: Sheriar Foundation, 2000.

———. *God Speaks.* New York: Dodd, Mead, 1997.

Mehrotra, L. L., ed. *Science, Spirituality, and the Future: A Vision for the Twenty-First Century.* New Delhi: Mudrit, 1999.

Meillassoux, Quentin. *After Finitude: An Essay on the Necessity of Contingency.* New York, Continuum, 2010.

Mendis, N. K. G., ed. *The Questions of the King Milinda: An Abridgement of the Milinda Panha.* Sri Lanka: Buddhist Publication Society, 1993.

Merton, Thomas. *A Course in Desert Spirituality: Fifteen Sessions with the Famous Trappist Monk.* Edited by Jon M. Sweeney. Collegeville, MN: Liturgical, 2019.

———. *New Seeds of Contemplation.* New York: New Directions, 2007.

———, trans. *The Wisdom of the Desert: Saying from the Desert Fathers of the Fourth Century.* New York: New Directions, 1960.

Mettinger, Tryggve N. D. *The Eden Narrative: A Literary and Religio-historical Study of Genesis 2–3.* Winona Lake, IN: Eisenbrauns, 2007.

Meyer, Marvin, ed. *The Ancient Mysteries: A Sourcebook of Sacred Texts.* Philadelphia: University of Pennsylvania Press, 1999.

Miller, Patrick D. *The Religion of Ancient Israel.* Louisville: Westminster John Knox, 2009.

Mizuno, Kogen. *Essentials of Buddhism: Basic Terminology and Concepts of Buddhist Philosophy and Practice.* Tokyo: Kōsei, 1996.

Moltmann, Jürgen. *The Coming of God: Christian Eschatology.* Minneapolis: Fortress, 1996.

———. *God in Creation: A New Theology of Creation and the Spirit of God.* Minneapolis: Fortress, 1993.

———. *The Trinity and the Kingdom: The Doctrine of God.* Minneapolis: Fortress, 1993.

Momen, Moojan. *Bahá'u'lláh: A Short Biography.* Oxford: Oneworld, 2007.

———. "The God of Bahá'u'lláh." In *The Bahá'í Faith and the World's Religions*, edited by Moojan Momen, 1–38. Oxford: George Ronald, 2003.

———. *Understanding Religion: A Thematic Approach.* Oxford: Oneworld, 2009.

Monahan, Susanne C., William A. Mirola, and Michael O. Emerson, eds. *Sociology of Religion: A Reader.* New York: Routledge, 2011.

Moor, Johannes C. de. *The Rise of Yahwism: The Roots of Israelite Monotheism.* Leuven: Leuven University Press, 1997.

Moore, Norah. *The Sound of Bells: Meher Baba, Carl Gustav Jung and Eastern Mysticism; Spiritual Progress and Psychological Blocks.* Bloomington, IN: AuthorHouse, 2013.

Moran, Dermot. *The Philosophy of John Scottus Eriugena: A Study of Idealism in the Middle Ages.* Cambridge: Cambridge University Press, 2004.

More, Max, and Natasha Vita-More. *The Transhumanist Reader: Classical and Contemporary Essays on the Science, Technology, and Philosophy of the Human Future.* Oxford: Wiley, 2014.

Moritz, Joshua M. *Science and Religion: Beyond Warfare and toward Understanding.* Winona, MN: Anselm Academic, 2016.

Mounier, Emmanuel. *Personalism.* London: Routledge, 2017.

The Mountaineers. *Mountaineering: The Freedom of Hills.* Shrewsbury, UK: Quiller, 2017.

Muir, John. *Essential Muir: A Selection of John Muir's Best Writings.* Edited by Fred White. Berkeley: Heyday, 2006.

Mullan, David George, ed. *Religious Pluralism in the West: An Anthology.* Malden, MA: Blackwell, 1998.

Muller-Ortega, Paul Eduardo. *The Triadic Heart of Shiva: Kaula Tantricism of Abhinavagupta in the Non-dual Shaivism of Kashmir.* Albany: State University of New York Press, 1989.

Munitz, Milton K. *Cosmic Understanding: Philosophy and Science of the Universe.* Princeton: Princeton University Press, 1986.

———. *The Question of Reality.* Princeton: Princeton University Press, 1990.

Murdoch, Iris. *The Sea, the Sea.* Introduction by Mary Kinzie. New York: Penguin, 2001.

Murphy, Roland. *The Tree of Life: An Exploration of Biblical Wisdom Literature.* 3rd ed. Grand Rapids: Eerdmans, 2002.

Nagasawa, Yujin, and Benjamin Matheson, eds. *The Palgrave Handbook of the Afterlife.* New York: Palgrave Macmillan, 2017.

Nagel, Thomas. *Mind and Cosmos: Why the Materialist Neo-Darwinian Conception of Nature Is Almost Certainly False.* Oxford University Press, 2012.

Nah, David S. *Christian Theology and Religious Pluralism: A Critical Evaluation of John Hick.* Eugene, OR: Pickwick, 2012.

Nayar, Pramod K. *Postcolonialism: A Guide for the Perplexed.* London: Continuum, 2010.

Needham, Joseph. *Science and Civilization in China.* Vol. 2, *History of Scientific Thought.* Cambridge: Cambridge University Press, 1991.

Needleman, Jacob. *The New Religions.* New York: Tarcher/Penguin, 2009.

Neighbour, Oliver, Paul Griffiths, and George Perle. *The New Grove Second Viennese School: Schoenberg, Webern, Berg.* New York: Norton, 1983.

Nerburn, Kent, ed. *The Wisdom of the Native Americans.* Novato, CA: Now World Library, 1999.

Neusner, Jacob. *The Incarnation of God: The Character of Divinity in Formative Judaism.* Philadelphia: Fortress, 1988.

Nicholson, Helene. *Theatre, Education and Performance.* New York: Palgrave Macmillan, 2011.

Nicolescu, Basarab. *From Modernity to Cosmodernity: Science, Culture, and Spirituality.* Albany: State University of New York Press, 2014.

Niehaus, Jeffrey J. *God at Sinai: Covenant and Theophany in the Bible and Ancient Near East.* Grand Rapids: Zondervan, 1995.

Nietzsche, Friedrich. *Thus Spoke Zarathustra: A Book for All and None.* Edited by Adrian Del Caro and Robert B. Pippin. Translated by Adrian Del Caro. Cambridge: Cambridge University Press, 2006.

Nisargadatta, Maharaj. *I Am That: Talks with Sri Nisargadatta Maharaj.* Translated by Maurice Frydman et al. Richfield, CT: Acorn, 2012.

Nisbett, Richard. *The Geography of Thought: How Asians and Westerners Think Differently . . . and Why*. New York: Free Press, 2003.

Nishitani, Keiji. *Religion and Nothingness*. Translated by Jan Van Bragt. Berkeley: University of California Press, 1983.

Norbu, Chögyal Namkhai. *The Supreme Source: The Kunjed Gyalpo, the Fundamental Tantra of Dzogchen Semde*. Ithaca, NY: Snow Lion, 1999.

North, John. *Cosmos: An Illustrated History of Astronomy and Cosmology*. Chicago: University of Chicago Press, 2008.

Nouwen, Henri. *The Way of the Heart: The Spirituality of the Desert Fathers and Mothers*. New York: HarperOne, 1991.

Nowak, Martin A., and Sarah Coakley, eds. *Evolution, Games, and God: The Principle of Cooperation*. Cambridge: Harvard University Press, 2013.

Öcalan, Abdullah. *Manifesto for a Democratic Civilization*. Vol. 1. Porsgrunn, Norway: New Compass, 2015.

Oderberg, David S. *Real Essentialism*. New York: Routldge, 2007.

Odin, Steve. *Process Metaphysics and Hua-Yen Buddhism: A Critical Study of Cumulative Penetration vs. Interpenetration*. Albany: State University of New York Press, 1982.

Odom, Glenn. *World Theories of Theatre*. New York: Routledge, 2017.

Okello, Joseph B. Onyango. *A History and Critique of Methodological Naturalism: The Philosophical Case for God's Design of Nature*. Eugene, OR: Wipf & Stock, 2016.

O'Meara, Thomas. *Vast Universes: Extraterrestrials and Christian Revelation*. Collegeville, MN: Liturgical, 2012.

Oord, Thomas. *Defining Love: A Philosophical, Scientific, and Theological Engagement*. Grand Rapids: Brazos, 2010.

———. *The Nature of Love*. St. Louis: Chalice, 2010.

Oppy, Graham. *Naturalism and Religion: A Contemporary Philosophical Investigation*. New York: Routledge, 2018.

O'Regan, Cyril. *The Heterodox Hegel*. Albany: State University of New York Press, 1994.

Osman, Ahmed. *Moses and Akhenaten: The Secret History of Egypt at the Time of the Exodus*. Rochester, VT: Inner Traditions, 2002.

Overzee, Anne Hunt. *The Body Divine: The Symbol of the Body in the Works of Teilhard de Chardin and Ramanuja*. Cambridge: Cambridge University Press, 1992.

Ozaki, Makoto. *Introduction to the Philosophy of Tanabe*. Amsterdam: Rodopi, 1990.

Palmer, David A., and Elijah Siegler. *Dream Trippers: Global Daoism and the Predicament of Modern Spirituality*. Chicago: University of Chicago Press, 2017.

Palmer, Michael. *Freud and Jung on Religion*. New York: Routledge, 1997.

Pals, Daniel L. *Nine Theories of Religion*. 3rd ed. New York: Oxford University Press, 2015.

———. *Seven Theories of Religion*. New York: Oxford University Press, 1996.

Panikkar, Raimon. *The Experience of God: Icons of the Mystery*. Minneapolis: Fortress, 2006.

———. "The Pluralism of Truth." *World Faiths Insight* 26 (1990) 7–16.

———. *The Silence of God: The Answer of the Buddha*. Maryknoll, NY: Orbis, 1989.

———. *The Trinity and the Religious Experience of Man: Icon—Person—Mystery*. Maryknoll, NY: Orbis, 1973.

Parmenides. *Parmenides of Elea: Fragments*. Translated by David Gallop. Toronto: Toronto University Press, 1991.

Parrinder, Geoffrey. *Avatar and Incarnation: The Divine in Human Form in the World's Religions*. New ed. Oxford: Oneworld, 1997.

Parry, Robin. *The Biblical Cosmos: A Pilgrim's Guide to the Weird and Wonderful World of the Bible*. Eugene, OR: Cascade, 2014.

Patomäki, Heikki. "Cosmological Sources of Critical Cosmopolitanism." *Review of International Studies* 36 (2010) 181–200.

Patton, Paul. *Between Deleuze and Derrida*. New York: Continuum, 2003.

———, ed. *Deleuze: A Critical Reader*. Oxford: Blackwell, 1996.

Peacocke, Arthur R. *Paths from Science toward God: The End of All Our Exploring*. Oxford: Oneworld, 2002.

———. *Theology for a Scientific Age: Being and Becoming—Natural, Divine, and Human*. Minneapolis: Fortress, 1993.

Penrose, Roger. *The Emperor's New Mind: Concerning Computers, Minds, and the Laws of Physics*. New York: Penguin, 1989.

Penrose, Roger, et al. *The Large, the Small and the Human Mind*. Edited by Malcolm Longair. Cambridge: Cambridge University Press, 1999.

Perry, David A., Ram Oren, and Stephen C. Hart. *Forest Ecosystems*. 2nd ed. Baltimore: Johns Hopkins University Press, 2008.

Peters, Ted. *God as Trinity: Relationality and Temporality in Divine Life*. Louisville: Westminster John Knox, 1993.

Peters, Ted, and Gaymon Bennett, eds. *Bridging Science and Religion*. London: SCM, 2002.

Phan, Peter, and Jonathan Ray, eds. *Understanding Religious Pluralism: Perspectives from Religious Studies and Theology*. Eugene, OR: Pickwick, 2014.

Pieper, Josef. *Enthusiasm and Divine Madness: On the Platonic Dialogue "Phaedrus"*. South Bend, IN: St. Augustine's Press, 2018.

Pinch, Geraldine. *Egyptian Mythology: A Guide to the Gods, Goddesses, and Traditions of Ancient Egypt*. Oxford: Oxford University Press, 2012.

Plantinga, Alvin. *God, Freedom and Evil*. Grand Rapids: Eerdmans, 2001.

———. *Where the Conflict Really Lies: Science, Religion and Naturalism*. New York: Oxford University Press, 2011.

Plato. *Complete Works*. Edited by John Cooper and D. S. Hutchinson. Indianapolis: Hackett, 1997.

———. *The Last Days of Socrates (Euthrypho, Apology, Crito, and Phaedo)*. Translated by Hugh Tredennick and Harold Tarrant. New York: Penguin Classics, 2003.

———. *The Republic of Plato*. Translated and with an interpretive essay by Allen Bloom. New York: Basic Books, 2016.

Plotinus. *Enneads*. Edited by Lloyd Gerson. Translated by George Boys-Stones et al. Oxford: Oxford University Press, 2018.

Plumptre, Constance. *General Sketch of the History of Pantheism*. 2 vols. Cambridge: Cambridge University Press, 2011.

Polkinghorne, John. *The Faith of a Physicist*. Princeton: Princeton University Press, 1994.

———. *Science and Religion: An Introduction*. Minneapolis: Fortress, 1998.

———, ed. *The Work of Love: Creation as Kenosis*. Grand Rapids: Eerdmans, 2001.

Popper, Karl. *Knowledge and the Body-Mind Problem: In Defence of Interaction*. New York: Routledge, 2000.

———. *The Open Universe: An Argument for Indeterminism from the Postscript to "The Logic of Scientific Discovery"*. New York: Routledge, 2007.

———. "Three Worlds." Tanner Lecture on Human Values, delivered at the University of Michigan, April 7, 1978. https://tannerlectures.utah.edu/_documents/a-to-z/p/popper80.pdf.

Popper, Karl, and John C. Eccles. *The Self and Its Brain: An Argument for Interactionism*. New York: Routledge, 1983.

Post, John F. *Metaphysics: A Contemporary Introduction*. New York: Paragon, 1991.

Potter, Keith. *Four Musical Minimalists: La Monte Young, Terry Riley, Steve Reich, Philip Glass*. Cambridge: University of Cambridge, 2000.

Poythress, Vern. *Interpreting Eden: A Guide to Faithfully Reading and Understanding Genesis 1–3*. Wheaton, IL: Crossway, 2019.

———. *Theophany: A Biblical Theology of God's Appearing*. Wheaton, IL: Crossway, 2018.

Prabhu, Joseph, ed. *The Intercultural Challenge of Raimon Panikkar*. Maryknoll, NY: Orbis, 1996.

———. "Religious Identity in an Emergent Second Axial Age." Lecture given at the Berkley Center for Religion, Peace & World Affairs, Georgetown University, April 11, 2011. https://berkleycenter.georgetown.edu/events/religious-identity-in-an-emergent-second-axial-age.

Prance, Ghillean T. *That Glorious Forest: Exploring the Plants and Their Indigenous Uses in the Amazonia*. Bronx, NY: New York Botanical Garden Press, 2014.

Prothero, Stephen. *God Is Not One: The Eight Rival Religions That Run the World—and Why Their Differences Matter*. New York: HarperOne, 2010.

Pseudo-Dionysius, the Areopagite. *On the Divine Names, and The Mystical Theology*. Reprint, Whitefish, MO: Aeterna, 2015.

Pui-lan, Kwok. *Postcolonial Imagination and Feminist Theology*. Louisville: Westminster John Knox, 2005.

Purdom, C. B. *The God-Man: The Life, Journeys and Works of Meher Baba with an Interpretation of His Silence and Spiritual Teaching*. London: Allen & Unwin, 1964.

Purdy, Jedediah. *After Nature: A Politics of the Anthropocene*. Cambridge: Harvard University Press, 2018.

Quammen, David. *The Tangled Tree: A Radical New History of Life*. New York: Simon & Schuster, 2018.

Quincey, Christian de. *Consciousness from Zombies to Angels: The Shadow and the Light of Knowing Who You Are*. Rochester, VT: Park Street, 2009.

Quispel, Gilles. *Gnostica, Judaica, Catholica: Collected Essays of Gilles Quispel*. Edited by Johannes van Oort. Leiden: Brill, 2008.

Race, Alan. *Thinking about Religious Pluralism: Shaping Theology of Religions for Our Time*. Minneapolis: Fortress, 2015.

Radin, Dean. *The Conscious Universe: The Scientific Truth of Psychic Phenomena*. New York: HarperOne, 1997.

———. *Supernormal: Science, Yoga, and the Evidence for Extraordinary Psychic Abilities*. New York: Deepak Chopra, 2013

Rahner, Karl. *Foundations of Christian Faith: An Introduction to the Idea of Christianity*. New York: Crossroad, 2005.

———. *The Trinity: Milestones in Catholic Theology*. New York: Herder & Herder, 1997.

———. "The Unity of Spirit and Matter in the Christian Understanding of Faith." In *Theological Investigations*, vol. 6, *Concerning Vatican Council II*, 153–77. Baltimore: Helicon, 1969.

Rajchman, John. *The Deleuze Connections.* Cambridge: MIT Press, 2000.

Ramadan, Tariq. *The Quest for Meaning: Developing a Philosophy of Pluralism.* London: Penguin, 2010.

Ramos, Alice M. *Dynamic Transcendentals: Truth, Goodness, and Beauty from a Thomistic Perspective.* Washington, DC: Catholic University of America Press, 2012.

Rapp, Friedrich, and Reiner Wiehl, eds. *Whitehead's Metaphysics of Creativity.* Albany: State University of New York Press, 1990.

Ravindra, Ravi, ed. *Science and Spirit.* New York: Paragon House, 1991.

Reaoch, Stacy. *Wilderness Wanderings: Finding Contentment in the Desert Times of Life.* Hudson, OH: Cruciform, 2017.

Red Star, Nancy. *Star Ancestors: Extraterrestrial Contact in the Native American Tradition.* Rochester, VT: Bear and Company, 2012.

Redmond, Geoffrey. *Science and Asian Spiritual Traditions.* Westport, CT: Greenwood, 2008.

Redner, Harry. *Totalitarianism, Globalization, Colonialism: The Destruction of Civilization Since 1914.* New York: Routledge, 2014.

Reeves, Marjorie. *Joachim of Fiore and the Prophetic Future.* Stroud, UK: Sutton, 1999.

Remes, Pauliina, and Svetla Slaveva-Griffin, eds. *The Routledge Handbook of Neoplatonism.* New York: Routledge, 2014.

Renard, John, ed. *Fighting Words: Religion, Violence, and the Interpretation of Sacred Texts.* Berkeley: University of California Press, 2011.

Restivo, Sal. *The Social Relations of Physics, Mysticism, and Mathematics: Studies in Social Structure, Interests, and Ideas.* Boston: D. Reidel, 1983.

Ribi, Alfred. *Turn of an Age: The Spiritual Roots of Jungian Psychology in Hermeticism, Gnosticism and Alchemy.* Translated by Mark Kyburz. Los Angeles: Gnosis Archive Books, 2019.

Ricard, Matthieu, and Trinh Xuan Thuan. *The Quantum and the Lotus: A Journey to the Frontiers Where Science and Buddhism Meet.* New York: Crown, 2001.

Richards, E. G. *Mapping Time: The Calendar and Its History.* Oxford: Oxford University Press, 2000.

Richardson, John. *Singing Archeology: Philip Glass's Akhnaten.* Hanover, NH: University Press of New England, 1999.

Richerson, Peter J., and Robert Boyd. *Not by Genes Alone: How Culture Transformed Human Evolution.* Chicago: University of Chicago Press, 2006.

Ridley, Ronald. *Akhenaten: A Historian's View.* Cairo: American University in Cairo Press, 2019.

Rigtsal, Tulku Pema. *The Great Secret of Mind: Special Introductions on the Nonduality of Dzogchen.* Translated and edited by Keith Dowman. Boston: Snow Lion, 2012.

Rinpoche, Kyabje Kalu. *Luminous Mind: The Way of the Buddha.* Boston: Wisdom Publications, 1993.

Rizzato, Mattheo, and Davide Donelli. *I Am Your Mirror: Mirror Neurons and Empathy.* Translated by Stafano Cozzi. Turin: Blossoming Books, 2014.

Robbins, Bruce, and Paulo Lemos Horta, eds. *Cosmopolitanisms.* New York: New York University Press, 2017.

Robinet, Isabelle. *Taoism: Growth of a Religion.* Stanford: Stanford University Press, 1997.

———. *Taoist Meditation: The Mao-Shan Tradition of Great Purity.* Albany: State University of New York Press, 1993.

Robinson, Keith, ed. *Deleuze, Whitehead, Bergson: Rhizomatic Connections.* New York: Palgrave Macmillan, 2008.

Rodinson, Maxime. *Muhammad: Prophet of Islam.* New York: New Press, 2002.

Rodriguez-Pereyra, Gonzalo. *Leibniz's Principle of Identity of Indiscernibles.* Oxford: Oxford University Press, 2014.

Roemischer, Jessica. "A New Axial Age: Karen Armstrong on the History—and the Future—of God." *What Is Enlightenment?*, December 2005–February 2006.

Rohr, Richard. *The Universal Christ: How a Forgotten Reality Can Change Everything We See, Hope For, and Believe.* New York: Convergent, 2019.

Rolland, Romain. *The Life of Ramakrishna.* Translated by E. F. Malcolm-Smith. Calcutta: Advaita Ashram, 1929.

Roscoe, John. *A History of the Quest for Philosophical Clarity from Descartes to Wittgenstein.* Lewiston, NY: Mellen, 2011.

Rose, Kenneth. *Knowing the Real: John Hick on the Cognitivity of Religions and Religious Pluralism.* New York: Peter Lang, 1996.

———. *Pluralism: The Future of Religion.* New York: Bloomsbury, 2013.

Rose, Philip. *On Whitehead.* Belmont, CA: Wadsworth, 2002.

Rosenblum, Bruce, and Fred Kuttner. *Quantum Enigma: Physics Encounters Consciousness.* New York: Oxford University Press, 2006.

Rothblatt, Martine. *Virtually Human: The Promise—and the Peril—of Digital Immortality.* New York: St. Martin's, 2014.

Rothman, Tony, and George Sudarshan. *Doubt and Certainty.* Reading, MA: Perseus, 1998.

Rowland, Christopher, and Christopher R. A. Morray-Jones. *The Mystery of God: Early Jewish Mysticism and the New Testament.* Leiden: Brill, 2009.

Rowland, Ingrid D. *Giordano Bruno: Philosopher/Heretic.* New York: Farrar, Straus and Giroux, 2008.

Roy, Louis. *Mystical Consciousness: Western Perspectives and Dialogue with Japanese Thinkers.* Albany: State University of New York Press, 2003.

Rubenstein, Mary-Jane. *Worlds Without End: The Many Lives of the Multiverse.* New York: Columbia University Press, 2004.

Rubin, Charles T. *Eclipse of Man: Human Extinction and the Meaning of Progress.* New York: New Atlantis, 2014.

Rue, Loyal. *Nature Is Enough: Religious Naturalism and the Meaning of Life.* Albany: State University of New York Press, 2011.

———. *Religion Is Not about God: How Spiritual Traditions Nurture Our Biological Nature and What to Expect if They Fail.* New Brunswick: Rutgers University Press, 2005.

Runyan, Christiane, and Paolo D'Odorico. *Global Deforestation.* New York: Cambridge University Press, 2016.

Russell, Robert, Nancey Murphy, and Arthur R. Peacocke, eds. *Chaos and Complexity: Scientific Perspectives on Divine Action.* Vatican City: Vatican Observatory Foundation, 1995.

Sadakata, Akira. *Buddhist Cosmology: Philosophy and Origins.* Translated by Gaynor Sekimori. Tokyo: Kōsei, 1999.

Sagan, Carl. *The Varieties of Scientific Experience: A Personal View of the Search for God.* Edited by Ann Druyan. New York: Penguin, 2006.

Said, Edward. *Culture and Imperialism.* New York: Vintage, 1994.

Saiedi, Nader. *Gate of the Heart: Understanding the Writings of the Báb.* Waterloo, ON: Wilfrid Laurier University Press, 2010.

Saint-Exupéry, Antoine de. *The Wisdom of the Sands.* Chicago: University of Chicago Press, 1984.

Sankaracharya, Sri. *The Bhagavad Gita: With the Commentary of Sri Sankaracharya.* Chennai, India: Samata, 2004.

Satprem. *Sri Aurobindo or the Adventure of Consciousness.* New York: Discovery, 2015.

Savi, Julio. "The Baha'i Faith and the Perennial Mystical Quest: A Western Perspective." *Baha'i Studies Review* 14 (2007) 5–22.

———. "Religious Pluralism: A Bahá'í Perspective." *World Order* 31 (1999–2000) 25–41.

———. *Towards the Summit of Reality: An Introduction to the Study of Baha'u'llah's Seven Valleys and Four Valleys.* Oxford: George Ronald, 2008.

Savino, John, and Marie Jones. *Supervolcano: The Catastrophic Event That Changed the Course of Human History.* Franklin Lakes, NJ: Career Press, 2007.

Schewel, Benjamin. "Religion in an Age of Transition." In *Religion and Public Discourse in an Age of Transition: Reflections on Bahá'í Practice and Thought,* edited by Geoffrey Cameron and Benjamin Schewel, 1–12. Waterloo, ON: Wilfrid Laurier University Press, 2018.

Schimmel, Annemarie. *Mystical Dimensions of Islam.* Chapel Hill: University of North Carolina Press, 2001.

———. *As through a Veil: Mystical Poems in Islam.* Oxford: Oneworld, 2001.

Schmid, Konrad, and Christoph Riedweg, eds. *Beyond Eden: The Biblical Story of Paradise (Genesis 2–3) and Its Reception History.* Tübingen: Mohr Siebeck, 2008.

Schmidt-Leukel, Perry. *Buddhism, Christianity and the Question of Creation: Karmic or Divine?* Burlington, VT: Ashgate, 2006.

———. *Religious Pluralism and Interreligious Theology: The Gifford Lectures—an Extended Edition.* Maryknoll, NY: Orbis, 2016.

Schmidt-Leukel, Perry, and Joachim Gentz, eds. *Religious Diversity in Chinese Thought.* New York: Palgrave Macmillan, 2013.

Schoenberg, Arnold. *Style and Idea: Selected Writings.* Edited by Leonard Stein. Translated by Leo Black. Berkeley: University of California Press, 2010.

Scholem, Gershom. *Major Trends in Jewish Mysticism.* New York: Schocken, 1995.

Schopenhauer, Arthur. *The Essential Schopenhauer: Key Selections from "The World as Will and Representation" and Other Writings.* Edited by Wolfgang Schirmacher. New York: HarperPerennial, 2010.

Schroeder, Jonathan, Anna Westerstahl Stenport, and Eszter Szalczer, eds. *August Strindberg and Visual Culture: The Emergence of Optical Modernity in Image, Text, and Theatre.* New York: Bloomsbury, 2018.

Schrödinger, Erwin. *What Is Life? The Physical Aspect of the Living Cell, with Mind and Matter and Autobiographical Sketches.* Cambridge: Cambridge University Press, 2008.

Schuon, Frithjof. *The Transcendent Unity of Religions.* Wheaton, IL: Quest, 2005.

Schwab, Gustav. *Gods and Heroes of Ancient Greece.* New York: Pantheon, 1974.

Schwarz, Hans. *Eschatology.* Grand Rapids: Eerdmans, 2000.

Schweig, Graham, trans. *Dance of Divine Love: India's Classic Sacred Love Story; the Rasa Lila of Krishna.* Princeton: Princeton University Press, 2005.

Scott, Mark. *Pathways in Theodicy: An Introduction to the Problem of Evil.* Minneapolis: Fortress, 2015.

Scruton, Roger. *Modern Philosophy: An Introduction and a Survey*. New York: Penguin, 1994.
———. *The Soul of the World*. Princeton: Princeton University Press, 2014.
———. *Spinoza: A Very Short Introduction*. Oxford: Oxford University Press, 2002.
Seager, Richard. *The World's Parliament of Religions: The East/West Encounter, Chicago, 1893*. Bloomington: Indiana University Press, 2009.
Segal, Alan F. *Life after Death: A History of the Afterlife in Western Religion*. New York: Doubleday, 2004.
———. *Two Powers in Heaven: Early Rabbinic Reports about Christianity and Gnosticism*. Waco: Baylor University Press, 2012.
Segal, Robert. "Jung's Psychologizing of Religion." In *Beyond New Age: Exploring Alternative Spirituality*, edited by Steven Sutcliffe and Marion Bowman, 65–79. Edinburgh: Edinburgh University Press, 2000.
Seland, Torrey, ed. *Reading Philo: A Handbook to Philo of Alexandria*. Grand Rapids: Eerdmans, 2014.
Selbie, Joseph. *The Physics of God: Unifying Quantum Physics, Consciousness, M-Theory, Heaven, Neuroscience, and Transcendence*. Newburyport, MA: New Page, 2018.
Sellars, John. *Stoicism*. New York: Routledge, 2014.
Sells, Michael A. "Apophasis in Plotinus: A Critical Approach." *Harvard Theological Review* 87 (1985) 47–65.
———. *Mystical Languages of Unsaying*. Chicago: University of Chicago Press, 1994.
Shakespeare, William. *The Tempest*. Edited by Barbara Mowat and Paul Werstine. New York: Simon & Schuster, 2015.
Sharma, Arvind, ed. *God, Truth and Reality: Essays in Honor of John Hick*. 1993. Reprint, Eugene, OR: Wipf & Stock, 2011.
———. *The Philosophy of Religion and Advaita Vedanta: A Comparative Study in Religion and Reason*. University Park: Pennsylvania State University Press, 1995.
———. *A Primal Perspective on the Philosophy of Religion*. Dordrecht: Springer, 2006.
———, ed. *The World's Religions: A Contemporary Reader*. Minneapolis: Fortress, 2011.
Sharma, Arvind, and Kathleen M. Dugan, eds. *A Dome of Many Colors: Studies in Religious Pluralism, Identity, and Unity*. Harrisburg, PA: Trinity Press International, 1999.
Shastri, J. L., ed. *Shiva Purana*. 4 vols. Delhi: Motilal Banarsidass, 2014.
Shaviro, Steven. *The Universe of Things: On Speculative Realism*. Minneapolis: University of Minnesota Press, 2014.
———. *Without Criteria: Kant, Whitehead, Deleuze, and Aesthetics*. Cambridge: MIT Press, 2009.
Sherazi, Mariam Aisha. *The Fantastic in the Plays of August Strindberg*. N.p.: CreateSpace, 2011.
Sheridan, Daniel P. *The Advaitic Theism of the Bhagavata Purana*. Delhi: Motilal Banarsidass, 1986.
Sherma, Rita, and Arvind Sharma, eds. *Hermeneutics and Hindu Thought: Toward a Fusion of Horizons*. Dordrecht: Springer, 2008.
Shook, John. *The God-Debates: A 21-Century Guide for Atheists and Believers*. Chichester, UK: Wiley, 2010.
Siegfried, Tom. *The Number of the Heavens: A History of the Multiverse and the Quest to Understand the Cosmos*. Cambridge: Harvard University Press, 2019.
Simmons, Brian, and Candice Simmons. *The Wilderness: Where Miracles Are Born*. Racine, WI: BroadStreet, 2016.

Simms, Brian. *Schoenberg, Berg, and Webern: A Companion to the Second Viennese School.* Santa Barbara, CA: Greenwood, 1999.

Sinnerbrink, Robert. "Deconstructive Justice and the 'Critique of Violence': On Derrida and Benjamin." *Social Semiotics* 16 (2006) 485–97.

Sjöö, Monica, and Barbara Mor. *The Great Cosmic Mother: Rediscovering the Religion of the Earth.* 2nd ed. San Francisco: HarperSanFrancisco, 1991.

Skrbina, David. *Panpsychism in the West.* Cambridge: MIT Press, 2017.

Smart, Ninian. *Dimensions of the Sacred: An Anatomy of the World's Beliefs.* Berkeley: University of California Press, 1996.

———. *The Phenomenon of Religion.* New York: Macmillan, 1973.

———. *World Philosophies.* Edited by Oliver Leaman. 2nd ed. New York: Routledge, 2008.

Smith, Cyprian. *The Way of Paradox: Spiritual Life as Taught by Meister Eckhart.* London: Darton, Longman and Todd, 2004.

Smith, Huston. *Forgotten Truth: The Common Vision of the World's Religions.* San Francisco: HarperSanFrancisco, 1992.

———. *Why Religion Matters: The Fate of the Human Spirit in an Age of Disbelief.* New York: HarperCollins, 2001.

Smith, Mark. *The Early History of God: Yahweh and the Other Deities in Ancient Israel.* Grand Rapids: Eerdmans, 2002.

———. *The Genesis of Good and Evil: The Fall(out) and Original Sin in the Bible.* Louisville: Westminster John Knox, 2019

———. *The Origins of Biblical Monotheism: Israel's Polytheistic Background and the Ugaritic Texts.* Oxford: Oxford University Press, 2001.

Smith, Paul, trans. *The Quartet of Great Sufi Master Poets: 'Attar, Rumi, Sadi and Hafez.* Essays and introductions by Hazrat Inayat Khan and Paul Smith. Campbells Creek, VIC: New Humanity Books, 2016.

Smith, Peter. *The Bábí and Bahá'í Religions: From Messianic Shi'ism to a World Religion.* Cambridge: Cambridge University Press, 1987.

Smith, William C. *The Meaning and End of Religion.* Minneapolis: Fortress, 1991.

Smith, Wolfgang. *Theistic Evolution: The Teilhardian Heresy.* Tacoma, WA: Angelico, 2012.

Sodargye, Khenpo. *Haven of Peace: Finding Our True Home in the Mind and Heart.* N.p.: Bodhi Institute of Compassion and Wisdom, 2013.

Sölle, Dorothee. *Thinking about God: An Introduction to Theology.* Philadelphia: Trinity Press International, 1990.

Solomon, Robert. *Dark Feelings, Grim Thoughts: Experience and Reflection in Camus and Sartre.* Oxford: Oxford University Press, 2006.

———. *Existentialism.* Oxford: Oxford University Press, 2004.

Spaemann, Robert. "Which Experiences Teach Us to Understand the World? Observation on the Paradigm of Whitehead's Philosophy." In *Whitehead's Metaphysics of Creativity*, edited by Friedrich Rapp and Reiner Wiehl, 152–66. Albany: State University of New York Press, 1990.

Spivak, Gayatri Chakravorty. *A Critique of Postcolonial Reason: Toward a History of the Vanishing Present.* Harvard: Harvard University Press, 1999.

———. *Death of a Discipline.* New York: Columbia University Press, 2003.

Sprintzen, David, and Adrian van den Hoven, eds. and trans. *Sartre and Camus: A Historic Confrontation.* Amherst, NY: Humanity Books, 2004.

Srinivas, Tulasi. *Winged Faith: Rethinking Globalization and Religious Pluralism through the Sathya Sai Movement*. New York: Columbia University Press, 2010.

Stace, Walter. *Mysticism and Philosophy*. London: Macmillan, 1951.

Stambaugh, Joan. *The Formless Self*. Albany: State University of New York Press, 1999.

Stang, Charles. "'Being Neither Oneself Nor Someone Else': The Apophatic Anthropology of Dionysius the Areopagite." In *Apophatic Bodies: Negative Theology, Incarnation, and Relationship*, edited by Christian Boesel and Catherine Keller, 59–78. New York: Fordham University Press, 2010.

Stapp, Henry. *Mindful Universe: Quantum Mechanics and the Participating Observer*. Berlin: Springer, 2011.

———. "A Quantum-Mechanical Theory of the Mind/Brian Connection." In *Beyond Physicalism: Toward Reconciliation of Science and Spirituality*, edited by Edward F. Kelly, Adam Crabtree, and Paul Marshall, 157–94. Lanham, MD: Rowman & Littlefield, 2015.

Stark, Rodney, and William Bainbridge. *The Future of Religion: Secularization, Revival, and Cult Formation*. Berkeley: University of California Press, 1985.

Stavish, Mark. *The Path of Alchemy: Energetic Healing and the World of Natural Magic*. Woodbury, MN: Llewellyn, 2006.

Stcherbatsky, Theodore. *Buddhist Logic*. 2 vols. Mineola, NY: Dover, 1984.

———. *The Conception of Buddhist Nirvana*. Delhi: Motilal Barnasidass, 2003.

Stein, Robert H. *Jesus, the Temple and the Coming Son of Man: A Commentary on Mark 13*. Downers Grove, IL: IVP Academic, 2015.

Stenger, Victor. *God and the Multiverse: Humanity's Expanding View of the Cosmos*. Amherst, NY: Prometheus, 2014.

———. *The New Atheism: Taking a Stance for Science and Reason*. Amherst, NY: Prometheus, 2009.

———. *The Unconscious Quantum: Metaphysics in Modern Physics and Cosmology*. Amherst, NY: Prometheus, 1995.

Stern, Tom. *Philosophy and Theatre: An Introduction*. Abingdon, UK: Routledge, 2014.

Stevens, Anthony. *Archetypes Revisited: An Updated Natural History of the Self*. New York: Routledge, 2007.

Stevens, Don E., et al. *Meher Baba's Gift of Intuition: Fifteen Essays*. London: Companion Books, 2006.

Stockman, Robert. *The Bahá'í Faith: A Guide for the Perplexed*. New York: Bloomsbury Academic, 2013.

Stone, Jerome A. *Religious Naturalism Today: The Rebirth of a Forgotten Alternative*. Albany: State University of New York Press, 2008.

Stonier, Tom. *Beyond Information: The Natural History of Intelligence*. London: Springer, 1992.

Stordalen, Terje. *Echoes of Eden: Genesis 2–3 and Symbolism of the Eden Garden in Biblical Hebrew Literature*. Leuven: Peeters, 2000.

Storl, Wolf-Dieter. *Shiva: The Wild God of Power and Ecstasy*. Rochester, VT: Inner Traditions, 2004.

Strickland, Edward. *Minimalism*. Bloomington: Indiana University Press, 1993.

Strindberg, August. *Julie and Other Plays*. Translated by Michael Robinson. Oxford: Oxford University Press, 1998.

———. *Selected Essays*. Edited by Michael Robinson. New York: Cambridge University Press, 1996.

Strong, John S. *The Experience of Buddhism: Sources and Interpretations*. Belmont, CA: Wadsworth, 1995.
Stroumsa, Guy. *A New Science: The Discovery of Religion in the Age of Reason*. Cambridge: Harvard University Press, 2010.
Studstill, Randall. *The Unity of Mystical Traditions: The Transformation of Consciousness in Tibetan and German Mysticism*. Boston: Brill, 2005.
Suchocki, Marjorie. *Divinity and Diversity: A Christian Affirmation of Religious Pluralism*. Nashville: Abingdon, 2003.
Suchocki, Marjorie, and Joseph Bracken, eds. *Trinity in Process: A Relational Theology of God*. New York: Continuum, 1997.
Susskind, Leonard. *The Cosmic Landscape: String Theory and the Illusion of Intelligent Design*. New York: Back Bay, 2006.
Susskind, Leonard, and Art Friedman. *Quantum Mechanics: The Theoretical Minimum*. New York: Perseus, 2014.
Sutcliffe, Steven, and Marion Bowman, eds. *Beyond New Age: Exploring Alternative Spirituality*. Edinburgh: Edinburgh University Press, 2000.
Sutcliffe, Steven, and Ingvild Saelid Gilhus, eds. *New Age Spirituality: Rethinking Religion*. Abingdon, UK: Routledge, 2013.
Sutton, Florian. *Existence and Enlightenment in the Lankavatara-Sutra: A Study in the Ontology and the Epistemology of the Yogacara School of Mahayana Buddhism*. Albany: State University of New York Press, 1991.
Suzuki, Daisetz Teitaro. *Outlines of Mahayana Buddhism*. London: Luzac, 1907.
Swidler, Leonard, ed. *For All Life: Toward a Universal Declaration of a Global Ethics; an Interreligious Dialogue*. Ashland, OR: White Cloud, 1999.
———, ed. *Muslims in Dialogue: The Evolution of a Dialogue*. Lewiston, NY: Mellen, 1992.
Swidler, Leonard, et al., eds. *Trialogue: Jews, Christians, and Muslims in Dialogue*. New London, CT: Twenty-Third Publications, 2007.
Swinburn, Richard. *The Coherence of Theism*. Oxford: Oxford University Press, 2016.
———. *Is There a God?* Oxford: Oxford University Press, 2010.
Taft, Michael. *Nondualism: A Brief History of a Timeless Concept*. Berkeley, CA: Cephalopod Rex, 2014.
Tagore, Rabindranath. *The Essential Tagore*. Edited by Fakrul Alam and Radha Chakravarty. Cambridge: Harvard University Press, 2014.
———. *The Heart of God: Prayers by Rabindranath Tagore*. Edited by Herbert Fetter. North Clarendon, VT: Tuttle, 1997.
Tanabe, Hajime. *Philosophy as Metanoetics*. Berkeley: University of California Press, 1986.
Tanahashi, Kazuaki, ed. *Moon in a Dewdrop: Writings of Zen Master Dogen*. Translated by Robert Aitken et al. San Francisco: North Point, 1995.
———, ed. *Treasury of the True Dharma Eye: Zen Master Dogen's "Shobo Genzo"*. Boston: Shambhala, 2013.
Tarn, W. W. *The Greeks in Bactria and India*. Cambridge: Cambridge University Press, 2010.
Tart, Charles. *The End of Materialism: How Evidence from the Paranormal Is Bringing Science and Spirit Together*. Oakland: New Harbinger, 2009.
Taylor, Bonnie. *One Reality: The Harmony of Science and Religion*. Wilmette, IL: Bahá'í Publishing, 2013.
Taylor, C. C. W. *The Atomists: Leucippus and Democritus; Fragments*. Translation with commentary by C. C. W. Taylor. Toronto: University of Toronto Press, 2010.

Taylor, Steve. *Spiritual Science: Why Science Needs Spirituality to Make Sense of the World.* London: Watkins, 2018.

Teasdale, Wayne. *The Mystic Heart: Discovering a Universal Spirituality in the World's Religions.* Novato, CA: New World Library, 1999.

Teilhard de Chardin, Pierre. *Christianity and Evolution: Reflections on Science and Religion.* San Diego: Harcourt, 1971.

———. *The Divine Milieu.* Brighton, UK: Sussex Academic, 2004.

———. *The Phenomenon of Man.* New York: HarperCollins, 2002.

———. *Science and Christ.* New York: Harper & Row, 1965.

Thanissaro Bhikkhu, trans. "Alagaddupama Sutta: The Water-Snake Simile (MN 22)." *Access to Insight (BCBS Edition)*, December 17, 2013. https://www.accesstoinsight.org/tipitaka/mn/mn.022.than.html.

Thiselton, Antony. *Systematic Theology.* Grand Rapids: Eerdmans, 2015.

Thomassen, Bjørn. "Anthropology, Multiple Modernities and the Axial Age Debate." *Anthropological Theory* 10 (2010) 321–42.

Thorne, Kip. *Black Holes and Time Warps: Einstein's Outrageous Legacy.* New York: Norton, 1994.

———. *The Science of "Interstellar".* New York: Norton, 2014.

Thurman, Robert. *Infinite Life: Awakening the Bliss Within.* New York: Penguin, 2004

Tierno, Michael. *Aristotle's "Poetics" for Screenwriters: Storytelling Secrets from the Greatest Mind in Western Civilization.* New York: Hyperion, 2002.

Tinker, George. *American Indian Liberation: A Theology of Sovereignty.* Maryknoll, NY: Orbis, 2008.

Tipler, Frank. *The Physics of Immortality. Modern Cosmology, God, and the Resurrection of the Dead.* New York: Doubleday, 1997.

Tiso, Francis. *Rainbow Body and Resurrection: Spiritual Attainment, the Dissolution of the Material Body, and the Case of Khenpo A Chö.* Berkeley, CA: North Atlantic, 2016.

Tompkins, Ptolemy. *The Modern Book of the Dead: A Revolutionary Perspective on Death, the Soul, and What Really Happens in the Life to Come.* New York: Atria, 2012.

Townshend, George. *Christ and Bahá'u'lláh.* London: George Ronald, 1966.

Tracy, David. *The Analogical Imagination: Christian Theology and the Culture of Pluralism.* New York: Crossroad, 1998.

Trinkaus, Charles. *In Our Image and Likeness: Humanity and Divinity in Italian Humanist Thought.* Notre Dame: University of Notre Dame Press, 1995.

Trungpa, Chögyam. *Cutting Through Spiritual Materialism.* Boulder, CO: Shambhala, 2002.

Tucker, Mary, and John Grim, eds. *Thomas Berry: Selected Writings on the Earth Community.* Maryknoll, NY: Orbis, 2014.

Underhill, Evelyn. *Mysticism: A Study in the Nature and Development of Spiritual Consciousness.* Mineola, NY: Dover, 2002.

Uždavinis, Algis. *Orpheus and the Roots of Platonism.* London: Matheson Trust, 2001.

———. *Philosophy and Theurgy in Late Antiquity.* Kettering, OH: Philosophia Perennis, 2010.

———. *Philosophy as a Rite of Rebirth: From Ancient Egypt to Neoplatonism.* Westbury, Wiltshire, UK: Prometheus Trust, 2008.

Vandermeer, John, and Ivette Perfecto. *Breakfast of Biodiversity: The Political Ecology of Rain Forest Destruction.* 2nd ed. Oakland: Food First, 2013.

Vander Weg, John D. *Serial Music and Serialism: A Research and Information Guide*. New York: Routledge, 2001.

Vanhoozer, Kevin, ed. *The Cambridge Companion to Postmodern Theology*. Cambridge: Cambridge University Press, 2003.

Varma, Pavan. *Adi Shankaracharya: Hinduism's Greatest Thinker*. Chennai, India: Tranquebar, 2018.

Versluis, Arthur. *Perennial Philosophy*. Minneapolis: New Cultures, 2015.

———. *Platonic Mysticism: Contemplative Science, Philosophy, Literature, and Art*. Albany: State University of New York Press, 2017.

Vilenkin, Alex. *Many Worlds in One: The Search for Other Universes*. New York: Hill & Wang, 2006.

Vince, Gaia. *Adventures in the Anthropocene: A Journey to the Heart of the Planet We Made*. Minneapolis: Milkweed, 2014.

Vivekananda, Swami. *Bhakti-Yoga: The Yoga of Love and Devotion*. Hollywood: Vedanta Press, 1978.

———. *Complete Works*. Vol. 1. Hollywood: Vedanta Press, 2003.

———. *Complete Works*. Vol. 7. Hollywood: Vedanta Press, 1972.

———. *Complete Works*. Vol. 8. Hollywood: Vedanta Press, 1947.

———. *Sisters & Brothers of America: Swami Vivekananda's Speech at World's Parliament of Religions, Chicago, 1893*. Edited by Sankar Srinivasan. India: LeoPard, 2017.

Von Neumann, John. *Mathematical Foundations of Quantum Mechanics*. Translated by Robert T. Beyer. Princeton: Princeton University Press, 1955.

Walbridge, John. *The Wisdom of the Mystic East: Suhrawardi and Platonic Orientalism*. Albany: State University of New York Press, 2001.

Waldenfels, Hans. *Absolute Nothingness: Foundations for a Buddhist-Christian Dialogue*. New York: Paulist, 1980.

Waldrop, M. Mitchell. *Complexity: The Emerging Science at the Edge of Order and Chaos*. New York: Simon & Schuster, 1992.

Walker, Theodore, Jr., and Chandra Wickramasinghe. *The Big Bang and God: An Astrotheology*. New York: Palgrave Macmillan, 2015.

Wallace, B. Allen. *Choosing Reality: A Contemplative View of Physics and the Mind*. Boston: New Science Library, 1989.

———. *Mind in the Balance: Meditation in Science, Christianity, and Buddhism*. New York: Columbia University Press, 2009.

Wallace, B. Allen, and Brian Hodel. *Embracing Mind: The Common Ground of Science and Spirituality*. Boston: Shambhala, 2008.

Wallace, David. *The Emergent Multiverse: Quantum Theory according to the Everett Interpretation*. Oxford: Oxford University Press, 2014.

Wallace, Edward, ed. *Theatre Symposium*. Vol. 21, *Ritual, Religion, and Theatre*. Tuscaloosa: University of Alabama Press, 2013.

Wallace, Robert M. *Philosophical Mysticism in Plato, Hegel, and the Present*. London: Bloomsbury Academic, 2020.

Walton, John H. *The Lost World of Genesis One: Ancient Cosmology and the Origins Debate*. Downers Grove, IL: InterVarsity, 2009.

Ward, Keith. *Christ and the Cosmos: A Reformulation of Trinitarian Doctrine*. Cambridge: Cambridge University Press, 2017.

———. *God, Chance and Necessity*. Oxford: Oneworld, 2009.

———. *In Defense of the Soul*. Oxford: Oneworld 1998.

———. *Pascal's Fire: Scientific Faith and Religious Understanding*. Oxford: Oneworld, 2007.

Ward, Peter D. *Rivers in Time: The Search for Clues to Earth's Mass Extinctions*. New York: Columbia University Press, 2000.

Ward-Thompson, Derek, and Anthony P. Whitworth. *An Introduction to Star Formation*. Cambridge: Cambridge University Press, 2015.

Wardhaugh, Jesssica. *Popular Theatre and Political Utopia in France, 1870–1940: Active Citizens*. London: Palgrave Macmillan, 2017.

Warren, Marianne. *Unraveling the Enigma: Shirdi Sai Baba in the Light of Sufism*. New Delhi: Sterling, 2004.

Watts, Alan. *The Way of Zen*. New York: Pantheon, 1985.

———. *What Is Tao?* Novato, CA: New World Library, 2000.

Weber, Max. *The Sociology of Religion*. Boston: Beacon, 1993.

Weeks, Andrew. *Boehme: An Intellectual Biography of the Seventeenth-Century Philosopher and Mystic*. Albany: State University of New York Press, 1991.

Weinberg, Steven. *Dreams of a Final Theory*. New York: Pantheon, 1992.

Weintraub, David. *Religions and Extraterrestrial Life: How Will We Deal with It?* Cham, Switzerland: Springer, 2014.

Weis, Eric. *The Long Trajectory: The Metaphysics of Reincarnation and Life after Death*. Bloomington, IN: iUniverse, 2012.

Wertheim, Margaret. "Space and Spirit." In *When Worlds Converge: What Science and Religion Tell Us about the Story of the Universe and Our Place in It*, edited by Clifford N. Matthews, Mary Evelyn Tucker, and Philip Hefner, 187–206. Chicago: Open Court, 2002.

Wheeler, John Archibald. "The 'Past' and the 'Delayed-Choice' Double-Slit Experiment." In *Mathematical Foundations of Quantum Theory*, edited by A. R. Marlow, 9–48. New York: Academic Press, 1978.

Whenham, John. *Claudio Monteverdi: Orfeo*. Cambridge: Cambridge University Press, 1994.

Whenham, John, and Richard Wistreich, eds. *The Cambridge Companion to Monteverdi*. Cambridge: Cambridge University Press, 2007.

Whitehead, Alfred N. *Adventures of Ideas*. New York: Free Press, 1967.

———. *Modes of Thought*. New York: Free Press, 1968.

———. *Process and Reality: An Essay in Cosmology*. Edited by David Ray Griffin and Donald W. Sherburne. Corrected ed. New York: Free Press, 1978.

———. *Religion in the Making: Lowell Lectures, 1926*. New York: Fordham University Press, 1996.

———. *Science and the Modern World*. New York: Free Press, 1967.

———. *Symbolism: Its Meaning and Effect*. New York: Fordham University Press, 1985.

Wickramasinghe, Chandra, and Robert Bauval. *Cosmic Womb: The Seeding of Planet Earth*. Rochester, VT: Bear and Company, 2017.

Wilber, Ken, ed. *Quantum Questions: Mystical Writings of the World's Greatest Physicists*. Rev. ed. Boston: Shambhala, 2001.

———. *The Religion of Tomorrow: A Vision for the Future of the Great Traditions*. Boulder, CO: Shambhala, 2017.

———. *The Spectrum of Consciousness*. Wheaton, IL: Quest, 1993.

Wilde, Marc de. "Violence in the State of Exception: Reflections on Theo-political Motifs in Benjamin and Schmitt." In *Political Theologies: Public Religions in a Post-secular*

World, edited by Hent de Vries and Lawrence E. Sullivan, 188–200. New York: Fordham University Press, 2006.

Wiles, Maurice. *Archetypical Heresy: Arianism through the Centuries*. Oxford: Oxford University Press, 1996.

Wilkinson, David. *Science, Religion, and the Search for Extraterrestrial Intelligence*. Oxford: Oxford University Press, 2013.

Williams, Delores S. *Sisters in the Wilderness: The Challenge of Womanist God-Talk*. Maryknoll, NY: Orbis, 1995.

Williams, Michael. *Deforesting the Earth: From Prehistory to Global Crisis*. Chicago: University of Chicago Press, 2006.

Williams, Paul. *Mahayana Buddhism*. The Doctrinal Foundations. New York: Routledge, 2008.

Williams, Paul, and Anthony Tribe. *Buddhist Thought: A Complete Introduction to the Indian Tradition*. New York: Routledge, 2000.

Williams, Rowan. *Arius: Heresy and Tradition*. Grand Rapids: Eerdmans, 2001.

Wills, Christopher. *Children of Prometheus: The Accelerating Pace of Human Evolution*. Reading: MA: Perseus, 1998.

Wilson, E. O. *The Meaning of Human Existence*. New York: Liveright, 2014.

———. *On Human Nature*. Cambridge: Harvard University Press, 2004.

Wilson, Richard. *Secret Shakespeare: Studies in Theatre, Religion and Resistance*. Manchester: Manchester University Press, 2004.

Winston, David. *The Wisdom of Solomon*. A New Translation with Introduction and Commentary by David Winston. New York: Doubleday, 1979.

Witherington, Ben. *Jesus the Sage: The Pilgrimage of Wisdom*. Minneapolis: Fortress, 1994.

Witteveen, H. J. *Universal Sufism*. Arcata, CA: Wild Earth, 2013.

Wohlleben, Peter. *The Hidden Life of Trees: What They Feel, How They Communicate—Discoveries from a Secret World*. Vancouver, BC: Greystone, 2016.

Wolf, Fred Alan. *The Dreaming Universe: A Mind-Expanding Journey into the Realm Where Psyche and Physics Meet*. New York: Simon & Schuster, 1994.

———. *The Spiritual Universe: How Quantum Physics Proves the Existence of the Soul*. New York: Simon & Schuster, 1996.

Wolfe, Cary. *What Is Posthumanism?* Minneapolis: University of Minnesota, 2010.

Wolfson, Elliot R. *The Duplicity of Philosophy's Shadow: Heidegger, Nazism, and the Jewish Other*. New York: Columbia University Press, 2018.

Wolin, Richard. *Heidegger's Children: Hannah Arendt, Karl Löwith, Hans Jonas, and Herbert Marcuse*. Princeton: Princeton University Press, 2001.

———. *The Seduction of Unreason: The Intellectual Romance with Fascism from Nietzsche to Postmodernism*. 2nd ed. Princeton: Princeton University Press, 2019.

Woods, Richard. *Meister Eckhart: Master of Mystics*. London: Continuum, 2011.

Woolley, Benjamin. *Virtual Worlds: A Journey in Hype and Hyperreality*. London: Penguin, 1994.

Wootton, David. *The Invention of Science: A New History of the Scientific Revolution*. New York: HarperPerennial, 2015.

Wortley, John. *An Introduction to the Desert Fathers*. Cambridge: Cambridge University Press, 2019.

Wright, N. T. *History and Eschatology: Jesus and the Promise of Natural Theology*. Gifford Lectures 2018. Waco: Baylor University Press, 2019.

Xing, Guang. *The Concept of the Buddha: Its Evolution from Early Buddhism to the* Trikāya *Theory*. New York: RoutledgeCurzon, 2010.

Yamada, Koun. *The Gateles Gate: The Classic Book of Zen Koans*. Somerville, MA: Wisdom Publications, 2004.

Yates, Frances. *Giordano Bruno and the Hermetic Tradition*. Chicago: University of Chicago Press, 1991.

Young, Robert. *Colonial Desire: Hybridity in Theory, Culture, and Race*. London: Routledge, 1995.

———. *Postcolonialism: A Very Short Introduction*. Oxford: Oxford University Press, 2003.

Yount, David. *Plato and Plotinus on Mysticism, Epistemology, and Ethics*. New York: Bloomsbury Academic, 2017.

Zajonc, Arthur, ed. *The New Physics and Cosmology: Dialogues with the Dalai Lama*. New York: Oxford University Press, 2004.

Zengotita, Thomas de. *Postmodern Theory and Progressive Politics: Toward a New Humanism*. Cham, Switzerland: Palgrave Macmillan, 2019.

Zizek, Slavoj. "Love Is Evil." https://www.youtube.com/watch?v=hg7qdowoemo.

Zohar, Danah, and Ian Marshall. *The Quantum Self: A Revolutionary View of Human Nature and Consciousness Routed in the New Physics*. London: Bloomsbury, 1993.

———. *The Quantum Society: Mind, Physics, and the New Social Vision*. New York: Quill, 1994.

Index

2001: Odyssey in Space (movie), 239

A Dream Play (drama), 135
A Pluralistic Universe, 11
A Thousand Plateaus, 24, 50
'Abdu'l-Bahá, 113, 253, 257, 281
Abe, Masao, 168
Abraham (patriarch), 94, 149, 174–75, 216
Adam (archetype), 108, 235, 312
adamah, 84, 312
Adittapariyaya Sutta, 35
Advaita Vedanta, 59, 177, 188, 212
adventure, 25, 53, 56, 66, 77, 92, 96, 201, 219, 224, 229, 234, 278
Adventures of Ideas, 33, 254, 257
Aeneid, 226
aesthetics, 107, 231
Africa, 116, 174, 212–13, 295
Akhenaten (pharaoh), 37, 150–56, 160, 162, 180, 204–7, 210, 220
Akhnaten (opera), 132, 150, 154, 158
Akko, 118
Agnes (Daughter of god Indra), 135
Alagaddupama Sutta, 76
Albert, Hans, 186
Alexander, Eben, 298
algorithm, 115, 120
'Ali ibn Abu Talib, 40
aliens, 173, 307
    plant-based, 125
    religious, 235
All in all, 12–13, 35, 41–46, 156, 159–60, 163–64, 167, 175, 190, 207, 220, 230, 250, 267, 269, 315
All-One, the, 45, 177–78, 183, 185, 207
Allegory of the Cave, 166
alterity, 47, 53, 72, 283, 308, 316
Amazonas, 96–97

America(s), 11, 65, 78, 94, 116–17, 163, 174, 181, 213, 216, 267, 277, 297, 299
Amida-Buddha, 276
Amitabha-Buddha, 276
Ananta Nirdesa Sutra, 165
anatta, 166, 168, 275, 284, 286
Anaxagoras, 239
angel(s), 38–9, 79, 95, 99, 120, 124, 189, 232, 234, 243, 247, 249, 252, 317
    burning, 38
    flaming, 37
    fire-, 36, 124
    of death (and hellfire), 38, 83
    of divine love, 124
    of God, 145, 175
    of history, 232–34
    of the Lord of hosts, 228
    of the name of God, 121
    of the throne, 38, 124
Angelus Novus (picture), 232
Anthony of Alexandria, St., 174
Anthropocene, the, 173–74
anthropology, 237
Apollo (god), 37, 39, 122, 125, 141
Apology (of Socrates), 27
apophasis, 34, 41, 50, 120, 179–89, 195–96, 213, 220–28, 244–47, 252–53, 261–66, 271, 275–81, 287–92, 304–5, 308, 312, 315–16
Aquinas, Thomas, 288, 315
Arabia, 173, 203
Arianism, 147, 163
Aristotle, 12, 34, 102, 137, 229, 250, 304
Arius, 207
Arjuna, 31–33
As You Like It (comedy), 131
Asia, 116, 212, 295
Assmann, Jan, 151, 161
astrobiology, 236

Index

astrology, 108, 110, 233, 251, 317
astronomy, 61, 108, 110, 229, 236, 251
atheism, 60–61, 65, 105, 153, 163, 186, 195, 209, 264, 267, 302, 305, 314–17
    New, 101, 176
Aten (god), 27, 158, 160–61, 204–5, 207, 228
    Great Hymn of, 151, 158, 161
atman, 21–22, 31, 33, 94, 130, 164, 177, 188, 272, 275, 286, 292
atman-brahman, 4, 188, 246, 283, 315
'Attar, Farid ud-Din, 224
attributes, 43
    creative, 80
    divine, 22, 42
Augustin of Hippo, 31, 209, 217
Aurobindo, Sri, v, 4, 212, 274, 311, 315
Auschwitz, 47
Australia, 213
avatar, 30, 40, 165, 182, 194, 212
awakening, 105, 220, 261, 263, 271–74, 276, 279–80, 283, 287, 292, 305, 318
    beyond any dogmatic limitation, 22
    conscious, 155, 210
    cosmic, 25
    forms of, 254
    intensities of, 249
    levels of, 248, 250
    magnitudes of, 262, 268
    mode of, 59
    moment of, 112
    mutual, 309
    of life in nature, 141
    of the Buddha, 119
    of the universe to itself, 241
    phases of, 250
    power of, 49
    process of, 248–49
    skillful means of, 290
    spiritual (journey of), 133, 139, 248–49, 272, 274
    to a universal horizon, 217, 248
    to consciousness, 280–81
    to divine awareness, 315
    to enlightenment, 273
    to Reality, 293
    to the cosmic Spirit, 114, 256
    to the deathless, 21
Axial Age, 277
    New, 210–12, 214

Báb, the, 93–94

Bábí religion, 178
Bactria, 271
Bahá'í religion, 3, 9, 40, 58, 93, 95, 102, 110, 113, 118, 178, 196, 212, 253
Bahá'u'lláh, 7, 9, 33, 41, 83, 94–95, 113, 121, 183, 212, 262, 253
Baker, Richard St. Barb, 99, 116
baqa, 47, 83, 111, 224, 247
Bataille, George, 304
Bateson, Gregory, 111
Baxter, Stephen, 257, 302
becoming-God, 12–13, 221
Benjamin, Walter, 232–34
Berg, Alban, 143
Bergson, Henri, 44, 277
Berry, Thomas, 311
Bhagavat Gita, 121, 129–30, 211–12, 220, 284, 291–92, 301
Bhagavata Purana, 291
bhakti, 40, 212, 288, 291
Bodhi-Tree, 110, 119
bodhisattva, 112, 165, 273
body, 35, 50–51, 56, 59, 65, 70, 87, 100, 114, 120, 125, 128, 157, 188, 199, 206, 208, 223
    cosmic, 122, 166, 176, 183, 220
    divine, 74
    heavenly, 244
    material/physical, 244–45
    nondual, 147
    of God/divinity, 130, 220, 228
    of resonance, 10
    of the Earth, 174
    of the (cosmic) Spirit, 123, 216
    of transcending movements, 21
    -space, 114, 117
    spectral, 250
    spiritual, 74, 122, 195
    temporal, 229
    universal, 31–32
    without organs, 50
body and consciousness, 85
body and soul, xi, 244, 252
body and space, 117
Bohm, David, 231, 245, 267
Boyarin, Daniel, 145
brahman, 11–12, 21–22, 31, 33, 58, 79, 94, 130, 147, 164, 178, 188, 196, 219, 290
brain, 102, 198–99, 270, 277
Brecht, Berthold, 131, 136
Broad, C. D., 111
Buber, Martin, 17

Index

Buddha, the, (Siddhartha Gautama), 35, 64, 94, 119, 147, 165–66, 195, 201, 209, 216–17, 292
Buddha(s), 33, 164, 166, 168, 264, 273
   -body, 33
   cosmic, 147, 188–89
   -dharma, 292
   -field, 264
   -nature, 33, 47, 58, 164, 219, 235, 246, 274
   primordial, 166, 219
Buddha-dharma, 292
Buddhism, 188, 205, 277, 279, 286
   Hua Yen, 190
   Mahayana, 16, 196, 219
   Theravada, 94, 168
   Vajrayana, 166, 196, 219
   Zen, 118, 168–70, 216

Campbell, Joseph, 277
Camus, Albert, 64, 136
Canaanites, 148, 152, 160–62, 180, 204, 208
Caputo, John, 85
Carmel (mount), 204–6, 216
Caruso, Enrico, 97
chaosmos, 85–86, 114, 117, 172, 182, 191–95, 199, 266, 272, 281–82, 300
Cherubim, 36, 38, 108, 120–22, 124
China, 165, 259
Christ (Jesus), 22, 31, 39, 73, 121, 159, 182
Christianity, 22, 39–40, 58, 62, 65, 73, 85, 142, 146–47, 162, 174–75, 191, 207, 210, 213, 223, 228, 246, 302, 318
Christology, 160
   Logos-, 22
   Spirit-, 22
Cerberus, 140
Cicero, 316
civilization, 53, 77, 114, 116–17, 136, 173–74, 180, 221, 234, 249, 257, 270, 272, 295
   alien, 235–36, 240–42, 307
   global, 144
   primordial, 251
   spiritual, 25, 273–74, 278, 280–81, 287, 305
Clarke, Arthur C., 257, 203, 239
Cloud of the Impossible, 267
classism, 72, 54
Cobb, John, 111
coherence, 110, 314

coincidence, 8, 110, 245
coincidentia oppositorum, 30, 221, 312
coinhabitation, 86, 312
coinherence, 85, 190, 199, 220, 312
community, 147, 214, 298, 309
   Bahá'í, 113
   global, 315
   integral Earth, 311
   of being, 73, 288, 314
   of conscious and awakened freedom, 74
   of light, 67
   of Qumran, 175
   scientific, 236
   religious, 311
   the good of, 103
   universal, 73
compassion, 4, 35, 46–47, 50, 71–73, 93–94, 112–13, 135, 137, 166, 211, 221, 238, 242, 249, 261–62, 268, 270–73, 276–83, 287, 289, 294, 305, 314, 318–19
composition, 8, 40, 142–43, 168, 255, 262, 271–72, 291
   impermanent, 272
   musical, 199
   of elements, 218
   of spiritual life-histories, 263
   (theo)poetic, 151, 199
composition and decomposition, 247, 271, 279
Confucianism, 81, 256
Confucius, 209
conscience, 44, 289
consciousness, 25, 30, 44, 60–1, 64, 67, 73, 77, 85, 91, 96, 102, 105, 111, 113, 115–16, 122–23, 164, 189–90, 194, 198–99, 206, 210, 214, 223, 231, 236, 238, 240–42, 248
   altered, 47, 50, 216, 255, 257–58, 267, 272–82, 287, 294, 296–98, 305, 314, 317–18
   axial, 121
   collective, 100, 274
   cosmic, 3, 21, 52, 153, 216, 274
   emergence of, 127, 138
   expansion of, 41
   formless, 61
   God-, 223
   human, 53, 101, 175, 227
   infinite, 63
   interstellar, 129
   global, 14
   indigenous, 15

mystical, 218, 223
consciousness (*continued*)
    pattern of, 97
    peak, 216–17, 221, 223–24
    pure, 176, 178–9, 182–4, 193, 298, 312, 317
    reflexive, 192
    religious, 277
    seed-, 252
    self-, 218, 223, 274, 290
    spiritual, 3, 78, 120, 218, 220–22
    stream of, 79, 177
    subtle, 188
    transcendental, 61–63
    universal, 297–98
consciousness and body, 85
constructivism, 214
convergence, 20, 54, 215, 217, 239, 278–79
conviviality, 79
Conway Morris, Simon, 111–12, 239
Copernican turn, 61
Corbin, Henry, 13, 223
Corpus Hermeticum, 110, 153
cosmic epoch, 80, 86, 255, 262–63
cosmo-centrism and non-centrism, 230
cosmogony, 53, 203
cosmology, xii, 104, 164, 178, 196, 203, 221, 227, 234, 236, 267, 277, 317
    mystical, 189
    philosophical, 86, 315
    physical, 237, 260
    religion and, 153–54
    religious, 237
cosmos, 2, 8, 15, 24, 31, 57, 66, 80, 101, 109, 114, 152, 188, 210, 215, 218, 220, 248, 274, 278, 293, 302, 314, 317
    alternative, 69
    community of, 288
    conflagration of, 35
    creative, 23, 177, 241, 260, 281
    decentered, 213
    divine, 102, 164, 182, 243
    evolution of, 14, 74, 120, 237, 242
    harmony in, 210, 227
    immanent reality of, 3
    infinite, 63
    living, 79, 117, 122, 230, 239, 243, 273, 298
    longevity of, 229
    matrix of, 21, 25, 300, 313–14, 317
    mind-like reality of, 231
    moral, 213
    multiplicity of, 279–80
    naturalistic, 228
    nature of, 196–97, 199, 296
    numinous, 15, 314–15
    one, 208–9, 243, 290
    physical, 230, 232, 305
    renewal of, 19
    resurrection of, 43
    self-differentiation of, 178, 183, 191
    spiritual, xi, 3–4, 25, 95, 100, 107, 113, 199, 232, 244, 261, 274, 290, 294, 298, 300, 314–15
    spiritualization of, xi, 5, 11, 34, 41, 102, 262, 272, 275, 281–82, 293, 309, 312, 317–18
    transformation of, 4, 259, 273, 279, 313
    violent realities of, 251
cosmosphere, 281
cosmotheism, 152–3, 161, 183, 205, 207, 209
Cratylus, 76
creativity, 4, 11, 32–33, 36–37, 54, 71, 73, 78–79, 85–86, 92, 95, 129, 137, 191, 193, 219, 250, 260, 275–76, 299, 301, 312, 314
    cosmic, 144, 179
    cultural, 112
    divine, 43, 46, 98, 104–5, 123, 204, 300
    energy/power of, 80, 154
    polyphilic, 289
    self-, 176, 182, 191–92
Creatrix, 160
Critique of Religion, 186
Cutting Through Spiritual Materialism, 101
cycle of love, 93–95, 250, 267

Daniel (prophet), 109
Dao De Jing, 34, 82, 147, 318
Daoism, 80–81
Darwin, Charles, 104
Davies, Paul, 110
Dawkins, Richard, 187
De Pace Fidei, 221
deconstruction, 68, 168, 258, 279, 317
    divine, 233
Deleuze, Gilles, 24, 34, 44, 50, 81, 104–6, 124, 171–72, 176–83, 188, 190–200, 207–10, 219–20, 264, 266, 271, 314
Democritus, 197, 230
Dennett, Daniel, 187

Denton, Michael, 111–12
Derrida, Jacque, 23, 72, 168, 183, 234, 279, 304, 316
Descartes, René, 61, 219, 230, 271
detachment, 111, 216, 227, 252, 261, 262, 268–83, 287, 305, 318
    -compassion, 4, 268, 271
    process of, 249
Deutero-Isaiah (prophet) 209, 144, 159, 228
Deuteronomist, 159
Dhammapada, 201
Dharma, the, 94, 147, 165, 168, 187–8, 219
dharmakaya, 4, 33, 94, 147, 166, 196, 265, 274, 276, 280, 290
dharmas, 273
Diaspora (novel), 305
Dionysus, 37, 141, 161, 220
dipolarity of God, 194, 259
discourse, 72, 137, 153, 155, 184, 209, 211, 240
    interreligious, 206
    liberation, 214
    philosophical, 264
    religious, 263
    spiritual, 207, 241
    universe(s) of discourse, 241–42, 275
Discourse on Metaphysics, 34
distribution,
    nomadic, 193–94, 214
divergence, 22, 193, 215, 242, 244, 260, 266, 271, 280
    cosmic, 218, 266
    movements of, 291
    self-creative, 191
Divine Milieu, 29
Dogen, 170, 216
dualism, xii, 60, 111, 117, 138, 165, 179–80, 182, 184, 193–97, 207, 231, 237–53, 260, 293, 304, 314, 316, 318
    wave-particle, 312
Duns Scotus, John, 58, 176
Durkheim, Emile, 168, 280
Dzogchen, 33, 61

Earth, the, 4, 15, 24, 55, 63, 66, 71, 84, 95–96, 100, 114–18, 123, 173–75, 202–3, 228, 232, 242, 260, 282, 288, 294, 298–301, 303, 311–14, 316–19
    -organism, 71
    Spirit of, 4, 21, 25, 74, 300–301, 315

ecophobia, 72
Eddington, Athur, 110
Egan, Greg, 305
Egypt, 36–7, 69, 132, 141, 143, 150–54, 160–62, 171, 173, 180, 182, 203, 209
Ein Sof, 58, 111, 313
Einstein, Albert, 231
El Elyon, 145, 152, 158–59, 196, 204–5, 208, 220, 228
elements, the, xi, 14–15, 20, 22, 49, 54, 57, 161, 172, 198, 239, 244, 252–53, 299–300, 314, 317–18
Eliade, Mircea, 316
emanation, 45, 58, 80, 98, 167, 177, 193, 218, 228, 241, 288, 296
emergence, 105, 127, 138, 208, 270
    of consciousness, 127, 138
    of life, 198, 239
    of mind, 198
    of religions, 144, 245
    of the Earth, 300
    of the spirit, 25, 123
    of the universe, 105
Emerson, Ralph Waldo, 117, 277
empiricism, 176–77
emptiness, 18, 20, -4, 48, 63–65, 81–83, 101, 166, 169, 173–74, 179, 181, 190–91, 258, 261, 273, 275, 284, 287, 304
energy, xi, 78, 85, 106–7, 113, 115, 118, 148, 196, 202, 231, 244–45, 265, 300
    -being, 246
    creative, 23
    divine, 301
    -field, 297–98
    fire-, 36, 41
    free, 138
    of transfer, 81
    overflowing/overboiling, 25, 80
    quanta of, 227, 267
    states, 86, 240
Enlightenment (era), 153, 213
enlightenment, 57, 101, 110, 113, 155, 168, 170, 188, 203, 216, 220, 224, 272–73
Enneads, 45, 224, 276
Enoch (patriarch), 109–10
    Second Book of, 38
Enuma Elish, 54
environment, 18, 21, 23, 46, 70, 86, 90–91, 104–7, 112–17, 138, 175, 197, 203, 239, 267, 281, 295–96, 312

Epicurus, 230
epiphany, 38, 164–70, 175, 180, 194–96
    event of, 168
    Moses-, 152, 168
epistemology, 61, 112, 190, 217, 261
equality, 143, 149, 149
Ernani (opera), 97
eschatology, 295
esoterism, 163
Essays in Psychical Research, 52
essence, 1, 19, 33, 57–65, 79, 83, 90, 136, 233, 298, 315, 318
    divine, 79, 277, 290–91, 300
    human, 42, 114, 214
    of God/Reality, 11, 33, 121, 168
    of immortal life-forms, 243
    of spiritualization, 286
    of the mystical experience/journey, 112, 258
    of the universe, 1
Essenians, 175
essentialism, 213–5
eros, 46–47, 279–80, 288
eternity, 8, 11, 19, 35, 40, 43, 45, 78–79, 83, 93, 107, 111, 144, 191–93, 199, 229, 234, 250–51, 258, 271
    pre-, 173
eternity-light-intellect, 229
ethnocentrism, 72, 177
Euridice, 139–41, 154, 233
Europe, 7, 96, 116, 141, 155, 212–13, 295
Eve (archetype), 108
event(s), 12, 25, 34, 42, 46, 80–86, 89–90, 92–93, 101, 127, 129, 138, 144, 155, 172, 187, 190, 194, 197, 217, 229, 240, 247, 252–55, 267, 271, 274, 277, 294, 198, 203, 303, 307, 318
    actual, 194, 296, 301, 303
    apocalyptic, 295, 306
    (of) becoming (of), 218, 250, 258, 280
    creative, 192, 288
    deep reality of, 206
    historical, 205, 238, 303
    natural, 53
    nexus of, 50, 280, 299
    of God, 192, 288
    of life, 275, 262–64, 287, 303
    of togetherness, 9
    potentials of, 281
    religious, 91, 143–44, 148, 165, 168–69, 195, 209, 211
    sacred, 119, 316
    spiritual, 211
    unique, 205, 287, 291
    virtual, 296
Everett, Hugh, 85, 263–64
evolution, 2, 14–15, 17, 20, 43–44, 53, 60, 67, 73–74, 89, 100, 102–7, 111–24, 127–28, 155, 165, 186, 197, 203, 214, 236–43, 249, 270, 274, 277, 296–99, 305, 311, 313
    spiritual, 207, 209–10, 257
exceptionalism, 54
    exclusivist, 213
exclusivism, 152, 160, 163, 211, 213, 215
existence, 9, 11, 34, 55, 60, 68, 77, 79, 92, 103, 107–8, 119, 127, 130–32, 136, 144, 157, 168–69, 188, 220, 224, 230, 233, 237, 249, 252, 295–96, 299, 311, 313, 315
    absurd, 176
    beyond (death), 167, 248, 290
    character of, 191
    circle of, 257
    cosmic, xi, 3, 45, 198, 229, 231, 237–38, 317
    cosmological well of, 297
    ecological, 277
    elementary forces of, 300
    elements of, 15
    eternal, 232
    event of, 129
    experience of, 64
    genesis of, 53
    horizon of, 247
    heart(beat) of, 36, 43
    human, 1–2, 13,15, 17, 24, 52, 64–66, 70, 86, 100, 108, 113, 115, 117, 120, 124, 135, 137, 139, 198, 218, 227, 240, 246, 261, 265, 280–81, 315
    in between, 67
    infinite horizon/points of, 40, 129
    layers/ levels of, 189, 247, 271
    limitation of, 260
    material of, 12, 16
    meaning of, 15, 44, 105, 138, 293, 297, 302, 305, 307
    mutuality of, 42
    mystery of, 15, 96, 105
    nature of, xi, 89, 103
    noetic character of, 111
    numinous forces of, 301
    of a multiverse, 298
    of God, 190, 222, 315
    of the world, 64, 164, 242
    origin of, 104

pains of, 48
personal worth of, 302
plane/plateau of, 81, 232, 244, 247
potency of, 63
pro-, 81, 273
randomness of, 241
religious, 211, 286
rivers of, 271, 278
self-, 167, 218
shadows of, 18
Spirit of, 93, 133
spiritual (nature of), 31, 81
spontaneous arising of, 81
teleological aim of, 281
theatre of, 138
unity of, 272
universally connected, 237
wonder of, 134
existentials, 261, 283
experience, 21, 35, 69, 76–79, 93, 113, 130, 148, 217, 231, 294, 316
immediate, 61, 169, 175, 178, 199
mystical, 120, 289
of a telos, 304
of an open-ended ex-sistence, 64
of divine light-fire, 40
of emptiness, 48
of God/Reality, 40, 86, 144, 173, 204, 281
of life, 100
of mutual inherence, 33
of non-experience, 223
of numinous/sacred reality, 206, 222, 317
of selflessness, 284
of the Spirit, 9, 31
peak, 216, 218, 223
spiritual, 217, 258
extinction, 115, 149, 293–301
extinction-level events, 114, 214, 299
Ezekiel (prophet), 38, 145, 164

Face of the Deep, 54
fallacy of misplaced concreteness, 30
fana, 47, 83, 111, 224, 247, 286, 288
fanaticism, 212
Fata Morgana, 17, 171, 173, 175, 179, 181, 183–85, 187, 189, 191, 193, 195–97, 199
feeling, 49, 73, 92–3, 96, 102, 105, 119, 123, 175–76, 188, 194, 199, 206, 208, 210, 212, 229, 231, 234, 238, 252, 255, 270–73, 281, 284, 287, 295, 313

aesthetic, 53, 138–39, 307
oceanic, 58
Fermi, Enrico, 240
Ferrer, Jorge, 273
Feuerbach, Ludwig, 191, 247, 305, 318
field, 75, 84, 157, 198, 277
Buddha-, 264
khoric, 260, 275, 292
nomadic, 185, 214
of action, 100
of bones, 9
of energy, 81, 240, 245
of event-nexuses, 197
of immanence, 215, 220
of information, 245
of multiplicity, 12
of possibilities, 197
of pure consciousness, 178
of relationality, 199
of the universe, 267, 281
of unification, 212
(di)polar, 290, 292
quantum/energy-, 267, 296–98
physical, 12, 106, 111, 237–38, 259, 281
space/time-, 297
spiritual, 107, 207, 266–67, 293
transcendental, 177, 180, 184, 192, 234
virtual, 296
visual, 8
finger, 126
in the flow (of water), 16, 76, 85, 87
of God, 76, 84–86, 317
finite, the 19, 293
moments of becoming, 58, 106
firdaus, 95
fire, 15, 20, 35–42, 45, 50–51, 104, 108, 135, 158, 203, 205, 216–17, 252, 258, 297, 300, 317
a world of, 35
angels of divine love, 124
creative, 35, 46, 301
divine, 32, 55, 57, 122
elementary/elemental, 14–15
eternal, 35
Heraclitan, 72
inner, 261
life as, 16
logos-, 77
of a thousand suns, 32
of desire, 35
of destruction, 234
of hell, 35

of life, 46
fire (*continued*)
    of love, 289
    of purification, 108
    of revelation, 35
    of the infinity of the heart, 57
    river of, 93–94
    sea, 35–36
fire/light, 122
Fire Sermon (of the Buddha), 35
Fitzcarraldo (movie), 97
forest, 17, 71, 96–97, 107, 115–19, 229
form(s), 2, 16, 31, 34, 46, 48, 50, 61, 83, 105, 147, 153, 157, 160, 190, 198, 207, 212, 220, 228–29, 238, 247, 258, 260, 272–73, 275, 283, 317–18
    abstract, 22, 55, 261
    aesthetic, 117, 138
    angelic, 124
    apophatic, 213
    Aristotelian, 196–97
    beyond, 68
    divine, 32, 131, 156
    eternal, 192–93, 252, 255
    finite, 221
form and matter, 12, 188, 196, 230, 244–45, 252, 275, 307
    human, 39, 124, 129, 145
    imaginative, 175
    infinite, 31
    law-like, 62
    magical, 164
    manifest, 40
    multiplicity of, xii, 1, 21, 32, 57, 61, 250, 258, 286, 288
    mystical, 40
    mythological, 154
    non-dualist, 213
    of alternative traditions, 213
    of awakening, 254
    of becoming, 55, 258, 283, 319
    of being, 78, 262
    of connectivity, 267
    of consumerism, 24
    of (religious) consciousness, 2, 61, 123, 274
    of cosmic harmony, 127
    of differentiation, 80
    of evolutionary unity, 123
    of existence, 234, 247
    of experience, 40
    of exploitation, 116
    of extinction, 115, 149, 303, 305
    of evanescence, 195
    of fields, 12
    of God, 61, 124, 129, 188, 195
    of goodness, 80
    of harmony and intensity, 300
    of illusion, 187
    of imagination, 13, 21
    of impermanence, 258
    of love, 272, 289, 293, 301
    of materialism, 272
    of mutuality, 278
    of nature, 15
    of nondual unity, 159
    of oppression and violence, 23, 278
    of organisms, 267
    of post-philosophical madness, 289
    of racism and misanthropy, 253
    of relationality, 49
    of religious paths, 54, 59, 180
    of selflessness, 284
    of self-transcendence, 275, 278
    of shamanic rhizomatic unity, 209
    of simplification, 136
    of (the) spiritual (desire), 29, 32, 209
    of spiritual immolation, 253
    of the becoming of spiritual beings, 107
    of the interiority of the Spirit, 31
    of theatre, 132, 136
    of thought, 104
    of unity/unification, 219, 272, 319
    of universals, 33, 255
    of virtues, 272
    Platonic, 191–93
    post-colonial, 214
    primordial, 115
    ritual, 141
    symbolic, 120
    the formless infinite of, 221
    theory of, 166–67
    universal, 31
    universe of, 252
formlessness, 22, 40, 53, 56, 156, 190, 246, 283, 303
formula, 177
    mathematical, 308
    world-, 237
Foundations of Christian Faith, 261
fragmentation, 24, 299
Freud, Sigmund, 151, 186, 304
future, 218, 233, 298
    aesthetic, 73
    alternative, 136
    of the cosmos, 237

Index

of evolution, 107, 113
of humanity, 73, 114, 118, 120, 235
of the multiverse, 129
of the physical world, 210
of religious identity, 24
terrestrial, 242

Gandhi, Mahatma, 130, 212, 213–14, 222, 284
galaxy, 27, 66, 198, 239–40, 297, 307
garden, 17, 99, 102–3, 108, 117–22, 135, 266
    divine, 95
    Earth, 114
    of Amaravati, 110
    of Eden, 13, 95
    of Reality, 113, 115, 122
    Persian, 95
Garden/Forest/Wilderness, 115, 265–67, 280–81
Gerizim (mount), 204–6
German Sermons, 171
Glass, Philip, 132, 198
Gleanings, 33, 226
globe, the, 25, 27, 60, 62
glory, 121–22, 225, 249
    human, 131
    in the form of a human being, 109
    of cosmic conflagration, 41
    of the divine presence, 122
Glory of God, the, 38–39, 121, 145–46, 158, 203–4, 300
    Manifestation of, 145
Gnosticism, 110
God, 17, 38, 42, 46, 59, 63–9, 79, 146, 148, 189, 193, 204, 216, 241, 289, 292
    as fire, 39
    as goodness and wisdom, order and light, life, 37, 40, 58
    as infinite sea, 52, 57
    as infinitely near, 29, 31
    as mother, 160
    as space, 34–35
    as open horizon, 60, 62
    as infinite Spirit, 17, 39, 60
    as trans-personal reality, 20
    becoming of, 259
    biblical images of, 40
    body of, 130, 220
    city of, 135
    coming of, 174
    court of, 38
    creative act/event/presence, 11, 56, 288
    death of, 191
    deathless realm of, 246
    eternity of, 83
    eye of, 33
    -figure, 33
    hidden in the fire of love, 39
    image and likeness of, 108–9, 113, 124, 147–48, 187–88, 231, 235, 311
    immanence of, 258
    in all things, 47
    in human form, 121
    in the form of Krishna, 58
    incomparability of, 291
    incomprehensible concept of, 147
    indifference of, 175, 194
    invisible, but all-engaged, 38–39
    king-, 54, 110
    kingdom of, 120–21, 159, 260
    memory of, 86, 253, 250
    nameless, 45
    nature/essence of, 12, 57, 184, 194, 196
    new people of, 148, 246
    personality/personhood of, 32, 288, 291
    plurality of, 149
    presence of (the powers of), 11, 122, 147, 205, 222
    poet of the Spirit, 12
    proof of, 297, 311
    punctiform, 35
    self(less) gift of, 13, 291
    self-communication of, 261
    self-transcendent in-sistence of, 315
    song of, 149
    spark of, 274
    spirit-breath of, 108
    sun-, 37, 122
    the eye of, 33
    the face of, 47
    the heart of, 49
    the One, 45
    the personality of, 32, 58
    throne of, 38–39, 99, 109–10, 120–23
    voice of, 16
    worship of, 288
God and the Multiverse, 299
God and the world, 57–59, 65, 92, 121, 162, 193, 220, 244, 259, 267, 291, 314
God, Chance and Necessity, 298
goddess, 54, 153, 160–61, 228, 299, 301, 315

Godhead, 45–46, 58
God/Self, 215–16
Good, the, 138, 154, 167–68, 219, 228, 245, 265, 275–76, 294
good and evil, 17, 38, 45, 48–49, 73, 83, 104, 108, 167, 175, 187, 207, 299
Goodenough, Ursula, 186
Gospel of John, 9, 38–39, 82, 219, 223, 253, 299
gradualism, 101, 186
Greece, 4, 37–38, 54–55, 69, 83–84, 93, 102, 108, 136, 139–40, 144, 161, 177, 203, 229, 244, 264, 288, 291
Greenaway, Peter, 134
Gregory of Nazianzus, 52, 57
Gregory of Nyssa, 223
Grof, Stanislav, 273
Guattari, Felix, 24, 50, 124, 171, 178–80

Hades, 55, 60, 105, 139–40, 233, 244
Hagar, 174
Haight, Roger, 22
haqq, 40
haqiqah, 40
harmony, 4, 46, 86, 105–7, 117, 119, 127, 137, 148, 150, 154, 198, 200, 210–11, 271, 279, 282, 296, 300, 314, 318
harmony and intensity, 300
harmony of harmonies, 45, 72, 199
Hartle, James, 217
Haught, John, 111
Hawking, Stephen, 217
heart, xii, 1, 4, 12, 16, 33, 37, 48–49, 118, 168, 220, 275
  of all beings/existence/things, 15–16, 21, 42–49, 57, 64, 77, 159, 309
  of all religions, 2, 15, 21, 120, 220, 238
  of God, 49
  of the Spirit(-space), 42, 49
  sacred, 315
Hebrew Bible, 102, 109, 173, 209, 243
Hegel, Georg F. W., 73, 177, 192, 220, 290
Heidegger, Martin, 23, 63–64, 72–73, 167, 177, 308
Heisenberg, Werner, 110, 231, 267
Hellenism, 144, 146, 152, 160, 271
hen, 45, 151, 207, 219
henotheism, 151
Heraclitus, 34–35, 44–45, 57, 72, 76–78, 85, 277
Hermes Trismegistus, 108, 110
Hermeticism, 213
Hermon (mount), 204

Herzog, Werner, 97
Hick, John, 111, 213, 290, 303, 312
Hinduism, 11, 188, 205, 211, 246
Hitchens, Christopher, 317
Hobbes, Thomas, 56
Homer, 140
Horeb (mount), 204
horizon, 62–64, 85, 96, 129, 183, 208, 216, 230, 249, 276, 313
  infinite, 16, 62–65, 69, 72, 129
  of all horizons, 247, 250
  open, 56, 60
Hoyle, Fred, 239
Huxley, Aldous, 213, 316
Hyksos, 152
hyle, 219
hypostasis, 39, 245, 250

Ibn ʿArabi, Muhammad, 39, 219, 223
idea(s), 33, 78–9, 89, 103, 137, 150, 167, 199, 221, 244, 249, 252, 254–55, 257, 264, 275, 289
identity, 188, 214, 315
  of creativity and nihilism, 73
  of God and the world, 193
  of reality with nature, 220
  religious, 15, 24, 235
  spiritual, 236
ideology, 152, 180, 314
idolatry, 153, 209
image, 10, 13, 22, 26, 30, 41, 43, 45, 55, 57, 73, 94–95, 98, 103, 122, 149–50, 174, 181, 191, 199, 202, 206–9, 216, 228, 248, 253, 260, 271, 276, 312, 314–16
  -clouds, 14, 23
  divine, 93, 124
  event-, 102
  humanity as, 124
  immortal, 68
  moving, 78
  multiplicity of, 66
  mystical, 65
  mythic, 102
  numinous, 303
  of deep secrets and desires, 70
  of divine inapproachable alterity, 53
  of divine self-immolation, 298
  of eternity, 78, 191–92
  of (life as) fire, 16–17, 36
  of forest, wilderness, and garden, 266
  of the ocean, 57–58, 67
  of oceanic chaos, 55
  of one like a son of man, 39

of one mountaintop and many paths, 214–15
of pure affirmation of immanence and creative difference, 192
of pure flow, 79, 83, 92
of space, 34
of the Spirit-ocean, 73
of spiritual/divine light-fire, 40
of the chaotic, 54
of the cosmic Phoenix, 37
of the desert, 173
of the divine chariot, 69
of the essence of being as spaciousness, 33
of the freedom of the journey through the open sea, 63
of the genesis of existence, 53
of the horizon, 60, 62
of the invisible infinity/God, 14, 38
of the mountain, 215, 220–22, 246
of the ocean, 100
of the (flowing) river, 8, 140–41
of the soul as heavenly star, 247
of the starry heavens, 227, 233, 250
of the sun, 38, 154, 156, 166
of the tree (of life), 100, 106, 113, 121–22, 129–30, 266
of the unity of all religions, 211, 215
of the winged creature, 36
of transcendence, 60
-pattern, 14
poetic, 9, 21, 48, 78, 85, 261
polysemic, 8
prophetic, 120
rarified, 77
secular, 102
spiritual, 25, 93
symbolic, 116, 118, 147–48
transreligious, 79
imagination, 13–5, 19, 26, 32, 39–40, 60, 71, 77, 79, 100, 147, 156, 172–76, 179, 187, 191, 202–3, 227, 235, 241, 247–50, 260, 263, 300, 306
apocalyptic, 49
binocular, 158
cauldron of, 37
clouds of, 13, 188
imageless, 256
mythic, 101
of multifariousness, 21
of reality, 95
of the cosmic Spirit, 23
self-imposed limitations of, 134
spiritual, 101, 265

theopoetic, 24–25
transcendentalizing, 180
immanence, 98, 105, 145, 159, 168, 175, 177, 185, 193, 219–20, 280
divine, 62–63, 83, 102, 183–84, 313
epiphanies of, 195
fields of, 215
flow of, 182
mutual, 46, 86, 120, 172, 180, 182, 190, 193–95, 197–98, 214, 221, 241, 250, 255, 258, 276–77, 285, 289, 291, 296, 308, 312, 315–16
of personal and transpersonal divine reality, 167
of the cosmic Spirit, 92
of the *dharmakaya*, 196
of the transcendent God, 160
philosophy of, 172, 182, 314
plane of, 171, 178, 181, 183, 191–94, 196, 215, 234, 250, 271
polyphilic, 278
pure, 177–78, 182, 191–94
sacred, 179
spiritual, 260
universal, 46
Immanence: A Life, 176
immanence and transcendence, 45, 66, 151, 179, 181–83, 191, 193, 220, 232, 265, 317
immolation, 250
divine self-, 298
sacrificial self-, 36, 48
immortality, 36–38, 70, 83, 92, 108–12, 117, 120, 140–41, 191, 224, 246–50, 277, 295
spiritual, 102, 245–53
Immortality (movie), 100, 112, 140
Immortality Defended, 298
impermanence, 17, 19, 36–37, 47, 121, 183, 18, 210, 237, 246–47, 261, 279, 297
chaosmic, 193
cosmic, xii
cycles of, 71
fear of, 81
flow/flux of, 77
movements of, 272
suffering/dread of, 35, 78
temporal experience of, 258
world of, 191–92
impermanence and permanence, 184
impersonae, 290
incarnation(s), 141, 148, 182, 194, 246, 248–49, 250, 287, 291

incarnation(s) (*continued*)
  endless repeating, 41
  memories, 96
  of matter in spirit, 13
  of the Christ, 205
  of the divine horizon in itself, 165
  of the Logos, 22, 40
  of the meaning of the cosmic Spirit, 2
inclusivism, 162
incompossibilities, 220
indetermination, 187, 195–96, 234
India, 59, 132, 165, 212, 271, 295
indifference, 16, 22, 60, 73, 175, 202, 220, 292
  apophatic, 247, 287
  creative, 252
  dipolar, 195
  divine, 253
  experience of, 175
  nondual, 217, 220
  of God, 175
  of suffering, 176
  of the divine desert, 176
  of the infinite and the finite, 177
  pluripotential, 56
indistinction, 53
Indra (king of gods), 110, 135
infinite, the, 63, 106
  appearances of the universe, 238
  expansiveness of space-time, 231
  flow, 80, 123
  horizon, 16, 62–65, 69, 72, 148
  life of the cosmos, 279
  movement, 12, 61
  Omega Point, 260
  One, 107
  place, 33
  Pleroma of self-revelation, 288
  points of existence, 40
  potentials, 13
  process (of becoming), 44, 106, 262
  reality, 63
  sea, 52, 65, 79
  sphere, 34
  suns of the Spirit, 47
  time, 306
  unfolding, 43
  universes/worlds, 129, 264
infinite, the, and the finite, 177
infinity, 14, 23, 32, 50, 56, 62–64, 71, 122, 221, 231, 238
  all-enfolding, 221
  of creative power, 47
  of cycles of becoming, 95

  of other lives, 263
  of reality, 61
  of the consciousness, 221
  of the heart of all things, 57
infinity and finiteness, 19, 245, 247
infinity and indefiniteness, 43
initial aim, 274
in-sistence, 195, 258, 314–15, 319
intellect, 37, 69, 127, 202, 221–24, 229, 231, 236, 270, 273, 276
  cosmic, 231
intellect and consciousness, 127, 198
intensification, 106, 280, 293
interrelationality, 34, 271, 280, 312
intersectionality,
  feminist, racial and postcolonial, 14
intercommunication,
  cosmic, 275
  khoric field of, 292
  medium of, 33
intermezzo, 173
interspirituality, 286
Interstellar (movie), 284
'*irfan*, 33, 111, 283
Irigaray, Luce, 14
Isaiah (prophet), 38, 109, 121, 145, 174, 209
Ishmael, 174
Ishvara, 58, 147, 164
Isis, 141, 153, 160–62, 164, 228
Islam, 13, 38, 40, 58, 93, 95, 110, 147, 149, 153, 162, 175, 189, 210–13, 223, 246

Jainism, 205, 290
James, William, 11, 44, 52, 64, 78, 110,
Jaspers, Karl, 209–10, 277
Jeans, James, 111, 277
Jerusalem, 39, 92, 119–20, 145, 152, 173, 204–5, 216, 228, 270
Jesus, 10, 22, 39, 42, 68, 73, 84, 94, 146–50, 159–60, 175, 183, 188, 201, 204, 216, 284, 302
John of Damascus, 52, 57
Josephus, Flavius, 152
Judaism, 73, 84, 92, 95, 120, 145–46, 121, 124, 142, 145–49, 152, 160–63, 175, 205, 219, 232–33, 246, 291
Jung, C. G., 100–102, 186, 273
Justin Martyr, 146

Kabbalah, 36, 58, 110–11, 121, 133, 142, 147, 163, 213, 220
Kabir, 212

Index

kabod, 39, 145, 148, 158
Kafka, Franz, 124
Kaku, Michio, 295
Kali, 105, 299
Kant, Immanuel, 61, 63, 226, 230–31, 234, 254, 280, 289, 304
Keller, Catherine, 15, 54, 267
khora, 33–34, 107, 259–60, 271, 275
Kinski, Klaus, 97
Kitab-i-Iqan/The Book of Certitude, 7, 42
Klee, Paul, 232
knowledge, 1, 7, 42, 62, 102, 107–15, 133, 188, 223, 261
    ancient, 295
    cultural, 236
    empirical/external, 164
    empirical and logical character of, 312
    mystical, 223
    objective/subjective, 306
    of good and evil, 187
    of mathematics, 308
    of navigation, 70
    of the life of stars, 251
    of the secrets of creation, 95
    of truth and goodness, 69
    scientific, 234, 236–37, 294
    self-, 225
    spiritual, 15
    superstition hiding in, 40
    transcendental, 61
Koyaanisqatsi (movie), 198
Krishna, 30–33, 35, 40–41, 43, 47, 58, 94, 105, 121–22, 129–30, 182–83, 188–89, 196, 211, 219–20, 291
Kubrick, Stanley, 239
Kumayl ibn Ziyad al-Nakha'i, 40

La Gioconda (opera), 97
Lampe, Geoffrey, 22
Laozi, 207, 209
László, Ervin, 297
Leibniz, Gottfried W., 34, 44, 58, 176, 230, 271, 290, 304
Lem, Stanislav, 69
Leslie, John, 167, 176, 265, 298
level(s), 23, 25, 127, 129, 187–88, 194, 234, 237–38, 240, 245, 247, 249–50, 253, 278–79, 281, 290, 293, 295, 299–300, 304–5
    emergent, 198
    of elementary particles, 107, 198
    of existence, 189, 271
    of divergency, 220, 232
    of intensity, 273
    of the One, 177
    of unification, 219
    of universes, 107
Leviathan, 56
Levinas, Emmanuel, 167, 308
Lewis, David, 264
liberation, 8, 47, 63, 81–82, 95, 143, 154, 173, 203, 214, 232–34, 265
    desert, 179
    desire for, 54
    eternal, 94
    event of, 233
    experience, 144
    from religion, 182
    messianic, 233
    new age of, 73
    non-temporal, 258
    process of, 68
Lichtheim, Mariam, 156
life, 11, 19, 48, 92, 113, 124, 239, 247, 262, 296
    -blood, 123
    cosmic magnitudes of, 276
    divine, 13, 40, 102, 111, 120
    existence of, 239
    -flow/fluid/stream, 102, 122, 126, 130, 303
    -force, 103, 181, 297, 299
    formless, 280
    -functions, 295
    -history, 262–63, 287–88
    immortal, 108, 110, 123, 218
    -lines, 262, 266, 281, 303
    -matters, 14
    -movements, 25, 262
    of Brahman, 263
    of flowing waters, 77, 87
    of God, 47, 92
    of infinite modulations of vibrations, 234
    of one whole planet, 298
    of other days, 260, 293
    of others, 263
    of sages, prophets, and savior figures, 303
    of the deathless Spirit, 95
    of the earth, 314
    of the ocean, 57
    pleroma of, 44
    -principle, 249, 280
    -processes, 262
    pure, 50
    spiritual, 107, 243, 258, 263
    stars, 251

life (*continued*)
 the good, 294
 -time, 262
 -trajectories, 281, 303
 -veins of the earth, 95
 wheel of, 41
 womb of, 68
 -worlds, 102
life-form, 14, 55, 58, 69, 96, 103–4, 106,
 128, 130, 194, 228, 236, 240, 271,
 275, 294–95, 300
 alien, 307
 artificial, 305
 civilized, 278
 intelligent, 306
 khoric, 262
life and death, 37–9, 45, 59, 70, 86, 90, 93,
 103–7, 110, 140–41, 151, 156, 175,
 194, 281, 300
light, 38, 75, 251
 -beings, 243, 248
 -body, 245
 -emitting bodies, 36
 -form, 19, 38, 42, 243, 248
 -fire, 39–42
 -life, 37
 -intellect, 229
 -love, 45
 -space, 262
 -speed, 263
 -symbolic, 39
 -veil, 255
 -vibration, 244
lila, 188–9, 194
Liszt, Franz, 143
literalism, 101–2, 244, 302
Logos (*logos*), 22, 38–40, 45–6, 58, 82, 92,
 94, 102, 109, 111, 121, 146, 148,
 160, 176, 190, 192, 194, 219, 223,
 231, 253
 Logos-figures, 196
 Logos-fire, 77
Logos/Wisdom, 160
Longchenpa, 33
Loomer, Bernard, 111, 300
L'Orfeo (opera), 132, 139, 142, 154
Lotus Sutra, 33, 165–66, 264, 292
love, 43, 46, 113, 139, 286, 289
 divine, 40, 124, 287–88
 of everything beyond limitation, 42
 of God, 38, 42, 47, 288, 305
 of the enemy, 284
 of the manifold/multiplicity, 265, 267,
 272, 287

 of the neighbor, 284
 of the other, 305
 of the Spirit, 282
 of ultimate Reality, 287
 paths of, 304
 polyphilic, 279, 282, 288
Lovelock, James, 15
Lucretius, 197, 230
Lyotard, Jean-François, 24

Madhyamika, 170
magnitude, 16, 20, 44, 129, 143, 176, 197,
 198–99, 253, 261–63, 267–68,
 272–73, 276, 278, 280–81, 283,
 286, 297, 299–300, 306–7
Mahler, Gustav, 143
Maitreya, 166
Manaus, 95–97
Manichaeism, 300
manifestation, 34, 37, 43, 300, 304, 315
 of a cosmic purpose, 242
 of all gods and goddesses, 161
 of divine imagination, 188
 of immanence, 184
 of self-transcendence, 280
 of the apophatic divine Reality, 266
 of the apophatic Reality as One, 279
 of the cosmic Spirit, 227, 260
 of the divine manifold, 121
 of the emanation of the world, 228
 of the Glory of God, 145
 of the Good, 275
 of the illusion of transcendence, 193
 of the inaccessible Godhead, 93
 of the infinite unfolding and refolding
 of the divine values, 43
 of the invisible God/Reality, 38–39, 41
 of the invisible Spirit-Light, 43
 of the Mind of God, 39
 of the non-different inner reality of all
 things, 261
 of the pure life of the cosmic Spirit,
 280
 of the ultimate Reality, 279
Manifestation of God, the, 58, 102, 121,
 252
manifold, 4, 11, 20, 35, 41, 103, 119, 122,
 194, 215, 217–18, 252, 252, 265–
 67, 271–72, 281, 287
 divine, 32, 39, 121, 149, 161
Marduk, 54, 56, 105, 299, 313
Marx, Karl, 186, 304
Maslow, Abraham, 273
Master Ch'ing, 170

materialism, 101–2, 177, 195, 197, 238, 272, 298
  quantum-, 296
  scientific, 61, 218–19, 231, 237
  spiritual, xii, 30, 101, 107, 176, 235–37
matter and energy, 85, 111, 196, 231, 237, 240, 244, 251, 295, 317
matrix, xi, 4, 232, 249, 258–66, 274, 280–81
  of a universe, 281
  of alternatives, 262–63, 265
  of becoming Spirit, 12
  of emphases, 261–62, 266, 280–81
  of generation, 4
  of matrices, 266
  of spiritual magnitudes, 262, 281
  of spiritual values, 274
  of the (spiritual) cosmos, 21, 25, 300, 314, 317
  of the earth and the cosmos, 313
  of the Mother Earth, 299
  of the multiverse, xi, 4, 264–65
  of time, 259
Maturana, Humberto, 112
mazhar-i-ilahi, 58, 196
Meander I (king), 271
Mecca, 173, 175
Medina, 173
meditation, 158, 190, 216, 284
  act of, 166, 174
  intellectual, 256
  Muhammad's, 175, 195
  of music, 199
  of the Buddha, 195
  textual, 221
  Vipassana, 284
Meher Baba, 212
Meister Eckhart, 13, 58, 79, 169, 171, 175–77, 218, 274, 300
Melinda (king), 122
memory, 2, 90, 93, 95, 118–9, 152–3, 160, 182, 203, 206, 217, 249, 251, 295
  of God, 86, 233
  of sacred events, 119
  of the existential fall, 107
  of the Spirit, 92
Merkabah mysticism, 120
Meru (mount), 204
Messiaen, Olivier, 119
metanoia, 48, 68, 120
metaphysics, 312
  Greek, 291
  of the closed world of the Self, 308
Metatron, 109

Michelangelo, 84
Milky Way, 27, 239, 254, 306–7
mind, 1, 14, 25, 37, 48, 57, 65, 74, 100–101, 202, 217, 236, 240, 245, 252, 277, 316
  conscious, 57, 274, 317
  nonmaterial, 85
  -ocean, 70
  religious, 277
mind and body, 25, 57, 206, 314
mind and brain, 85
mind and consciousness, 60, 111, 123, 127, 206, 236, 240, 298
Mind and Cosmos, 127
mind and intellect, 127
mind and life, 15, 67, 94, 100, 105, 122, 236–38, 241
mind and light, 74
mind and matter, xi, 4, 25, 65, 92, 106, 111, 117–18, 127, 178, 245, 275–76, 304, 312
mind and reason, 127
mind and soul, 231, 314
mind and spirit, 206
Mind of God, the, 39, 80, 178, 192–93, 194, 223, 233, 247, 250, 264, 274, 277, 298–99
minimalism, 150
minority, 24
  identities, 214
  perspective, 24
  space, 214
  symbolic, 136
mirror, 3, 17–18, 21, 58, 46, 55, 80, 90, 137, 144, 156, 167, 179, 186, 222–25, 246–47, 269, 283, 298
  infinite, 190
  mirage of the, 246
  -neurons, 270
  of apophatic indifference, 247
  of illusions, 189
  of otherness, 250
misogyny, 54
Modes of Thought, 273
monad, 181–84, 290, 304
  divine, 213
monadism, 193–94
monism, xii, 177, 182, 193, 195, 213, 244–45, 314, 316, 318
  desert, 182
  dipolar, 162, 165, 178, 180, 188, 205, 220
  non-transcendent, 182
  panentheistic, 159

monism (continued)
    pantheistic, 61
    Sufi, 189
monism and dualism, xii, 165, 314
monism and monotheism, 172, 179, 182, 184, 193, 195, 205
monism and pluralism without dualism, 180
monotheism, 144, 146, 150–54, 172, 205
    Abrahamic, xii, 149
    abstract, 150
    all-embracing/inclusive, 153, 161
    antagonistic, 207
    dipolar, 156, 159–60
    dualistic, 146, 150, 159–60, 162, 165, 205
    exclusive/exclusivist, 152–53, 156, 160, 182, 204, 209–10, 213
    historic, 180
    immanent, 156
    imperial, 177–82
    Mosaic, 182
    nascent, 204
    oppressive, 220
    rabbinic, 146
    transcendent, 156
    universalist, 144
monstrosity, 54–55, 72, 173
Monteverdi, Claudio, 132, 139, 142
Morgan le Fay, 171
Moses, 31, 39, 47, 94, 132, 143–54, 164, 168, 175, 182, 201–4, 209, 216–17, 223, 300, 302
Moses and Monotheism, 151
Moses und Aron (opera), 132, 142, 154, 168
Mother Earth, 4, 12, 294, 297, 299, 311, 313, 315
Mother Nature, 299, 313, 315, 317
mountain, xii, 18, 20, 30, 39, 87, 89, 91, 96, 116, 119, 147, 158, 160, 169, 172–75, 201–25, 229, 246, 269, 218, 300, 313
mountaineer, xii, 18, 201–23, 246
movement, 26–7, 44–5, 49–50, 52, 58, 62, 66, 72, 80, 94, 98, 144, 150–51, 156–57, 180, 202, 207–8, 217–18, 227–28, 243–45, 269, 280–83, 287, 289
    chaotic, 55, 84–85
    Christ-, 74
    coinhering, 81
    converse, 218, 279
    cosmic, 20

    counter-, 220–21, 224, 230, 246, 250
    creative, 219
    dipolar, 195, 246
    divine, 74, 121, 272
    emanating, 290
    everlasting, 77
    external, 101
    global, 59, 259
    God as, 62
    heavenly, 69, 252
    immanent, 64, 190, 197
    inclusivist, 160
    infinite, 12, 30, 61, 63
    liberation, 54
    messianic, 279
    monastic, 174
    multifarious, 58
    mutual, 81, 197, 253
    nomadic, 181, 183
    of complication and explication, 246
    of composition and decomposition, 271
    of concretization/actualization/valuation, 262
    of creation, 74
    of enfolding, 219, 271
    of expansion and contraction, 250
    of flux, 77
    of impermanence, 272
    of in-differentiation, 314
    of letting-be, 60
    of life, 35, 45, 262, 275
    of love, 319
    of reality, 93
    of self-less love, 63
    of self-transcending synthesis, 194, 302, 305, 313
    of the chaosmos, 300
    of the formlessness of self-transcendence, 303
    of the immanent One-All, 179
    of transcending, 2, 17, 21, 180
    of unification, 219, 259, 291
    of worlds, 264
    oscillating, 262
    polyphilic, 288
    religious, 211, 248
    shadows of, 68
    spiritual, 20, 206, 236, 279, 318
    spontaneous, 81
    substantial, 80, 82
    surreal, 34
    sympathetic, 252
    temporal, 218, 261

the permanence of/as, 19, 78
transcendentalizing, 286
transhumanist, 115
transreligious, 147
undetermined, 63
universal, 259
Muhammad (prophet), 38, 58, 94, 110, 175, 195, 204, 219, 223
Muir, John, 117
multiplicity, 2–4, 20, 25, 35, 37, 66, 156, 209, 213, 215, 250, 290–91
    cosmic, 4, 279, 288, 316
    field of, 12
    in mutuality, 34
    infinite, 34
    of beautiful harmonies, 149
    of composition and decomposition, 247
    of experiences of complex time-suspension, 258
    of infinite potentials of actualization, 12
    of magnitudes of becoming, 259
    of (spiritual) monads, 290
    of natural forces and their mutual immanence, 180
    of (self-transcending) Numenaries, 318
    of oppressed voices, 168
    of relations, 46
    of spiritual transformation, 41
    of stratified realms of knowledge, 110
    of the multiverse, 272
    of the universe/world, 42, 247, 272
    of time and timelessness, 258
    of ultimate Reality, 213
    of world phenomena/natural appearances, 153, 259
    of worlds, 265, 269
    punctiform, 37, 47
multiplicity and becoming, 247
multiplicity and multiverse, 271
multiplicity and the One, 316
multiplicity and unity, 31, 153, 214, 248
multiverse, xi–xii, 20, 66–67, 85, 122, 129–30, 164, 183, 230, 262–68, 271–72, 274, 277, 279–80, 287, 298–300, 303, 308
    diverse, 281
    infinite, 107, 198, 230
    magnitude of, 286, 307
    matrix of, 4
    monadic, 281
    nomadic, 281
    of unending cyclical or branching realizations, 123, 129
    rhythmic, 281
    theories, 238
    types of, 280
multiverse(s) and universe(s), 107, 237, 292
Murdock, Iris, 131, 134
mutuality, 12, 33–34, 45–46, 184, 207, 231, 242, 270, 288, 291–92, 308
    diversity in, 215
    formless life of, 280
    harmonious forms of, 278
    medium of, 138
    nomadic/polar field of, 214, 290
    of creative differentiations, 194
    of existence, 42
    one horizon of, 208
    spiritual, 211
    uniqueness of, 292–93
mystery, 40, 66, 70, 172, 288, 290, 316
    apophatic/pleromatic, 288–89, 305, 308, 315
    divine, 22, 43, 288
    of existence, 15, 96, 105
    of God, 57, 305
    of life, 102
    of mutual love, 293
    of our Selves, 315
    of powerlessness and poverty, 48
    pleromatic manifesting, 291–92
    polyphilic, 292
    religion, 141
    trans-personal, 290
Mystical Dimensions of Islam, 223
Mystical Theology, 223
mysticism, 163, 213, 233, 286
    Islamic, 39–40
    Merkabah, 110, 121
    Persian, 67
    Sufi, 33
    throne, 110
mysticism and metaphysics, 312
mysticism and quantum physics, 267

Nagarjuna, 33, 94, 170, 177, 188–89, 207, 219
Nagasena, 271
Nagel, Thomas, 127
Nanak, Guru, 212
Nath, 212
naturalism, xii, 165, 172, 182, 189, 207, 213–15, 220, 228, 238, 297, 314, 318

nature, 72, 79, 156, 253
  apophatic, 315
  beauty of, 10
  divinity, 84
  of all beings/things, 67, 101
  of Christ, 58
  of existence, xi, 81, 89
  of experience, 164
  of oceanic life, 55, 57, 69, 71
  of (nondual) Reality, 265, 319
  of Reality's/God's pleromatic Self, 315
  of the chaosmos, 117
  of the cosmos, 4, 196, 199, 296
  of the divine reality, 37
  of the drive to exist, 138
  of the Good, 84, 89, 276
  of the heavenly host, 247
  of the Logos, 58
  of the peak event, 217
  of the Son, 274
  of the (cosmic) Spirit (Brahman), 58, 252, 267
  of (the reality of) the Spirit, 64, 119
  of the universe, 230
  of this world, 77
  of theatre, 137
  of universals, 317
  polyphilic, 319
  religious paths, 90
  spiritual, 81, 101, 107, 109, 117, 119, 132, 137–38, 236, 242–43, 254, 266, 297
  symbolic, 101–2
Neo-Platonism, 147, 163, 192, 213
Neo-Vedanta, 286
nephesh, 84
New Age, 163, 245, 286
New Testament, 9, 11, 16, 42, 146, 159–60, 219, 288
nexus, 276–78, 282
  entirely living, 50
  of all relations, 289
  of events, 50, 86, 196–97, 277, 280
  of processes of synthesis, 198
  of pure life, 280
  unique unisons of, 247
Nicolas of Cusa, 13, 34, 46, 176, 178, 197, 214, 221, 230, 245
Nietzsche, Friedrich, 62–3, 63, 78, 81, 176, 186, 191, 195
nirmanakaya, 166, 194, 277
nirvana, 3, 30, 33, 94, 111, 140, 164, 166, 168, 177, 190, 221, 246, 249, 272–73, 304

Nishitani, Keiji, 48
nomad, 173, 175, 179, 180–85, 193
nomadism, 193
non-attachment, 280
non-being, 168
non-boundary boundary, 224
non-centrism, 230
non-constructability, 271
non-difference, 59, 73, 169, 180, 218, 211, 224, 247, 258, 261, 265, 313–14, 316
non-differentiation, 314, 316
nondualism, 61, 153, 175–77, 188, 207, 211, 220–21, 238, 244, 312
non-ego, 169
non-existence, 81–82, 140, 192, 198, 247, 276
  beyond, 167
non-experience, 223
non-essentialism, 214
non-identification, 314
non-identity, 138, 213–14
non-locality, 245, 261, 267
non-object, 169
non-place, 140
non-self, 168–69, 275, 279
non-theism, xii, 1, 287, 289, 311–12
non-violence, 270, 278, 281
nothingness, 18, 63–65, 73, 77–78, 83, 166, 175–76, 284, 290, 308
nous, 45, 48, 167, 178, 183, 192, 219
novelty, 46, 78, 86, 105, 107, 233, 258, 295, 307
  apocalyptic, 54
  creative, 85, 194, 301
  God of, 144
  open space of, 233
  orgiastic, 106
  post-axial, 214
  unity of, 83
  world of, 193
Nuages Gris/Gray Clouds (music), 143
numen, 21, 201, 316, 318
Numenaries, the, 21, 311, 316–19
numinous, the, xi, 20–22, 47, 203–4, 206, 216–17, 222, 224, 286, 300, 316–17
  spirituality of, 15
nunc stans, 258
nur Muhammadiyah, 58

ocean, 10, 16, 53–55, 59, 65–67, 69, 71, 98, 100, 166, 207, 214
  mind-, 70

of a complex community, 74
of light, 74
of matter, 74
of simple manyness, 74
of suffering, 74
of the starry heavens, 20
primordial, 84
ocean of God, the, 71, 58–59, 69–70, 72, 82
Odyssey (Homer), 140
Of Spirit, 23, 72
Omega Point, 43, 74, 104, 260, 279, 287
On the Origin of Species, 103
One, the, 42, 45, 58, 107, 153, 159, 163, 167, 176–78, 185, 207, 223–24, 245, 249, 277, 296, 313, 316
One-All, the, 176–79, 183, 185, 190, 207, 220
oneness, 19, 32, 151, 244, 206, 218
    divine, 40
    of reality, 213
    originating, 35
    undivided, 304
openness, 30, 60–64, 72, 206
    soul-full, 281
organism(s), 35, 70, 102–7, 112, 115, 136, 138, 186, 194, 197–99, 255, 281
    complex (social), 122, 270
    evolved, 270
    feeling, 295
    forms of, 267
    human, 199
    intelligent, 104
    living, 24, 105
    of mutual implication, 45
    organism of, 107
    sym-pathic, 45
    symphony of, 119
Origen of Alexandria, 146, 207
Orpheus, 139–41, 233, 154, 161
Orpheus and Euridice (myth), 139–40, 154
Orphic Mysteries, 141
oscillation, 3, 82, 219, 319
    cycle of, 250
    eternal, 149
    fluent, 214
    of mutual immanence, 250
    spheres of, 20
Osiris, 141
other(s), the, 47, 82, 254, 270–71, 283–84, 308
otherness, 46, 175
    moving mirrors of, 250
    mutual, 83
    of other lives, 280

of reality, 16
of the timeless, deathless, indestructible, 272
relation of, 45
Otherwise than Being or Beyond Essence, 308
Otto, Rudolf, 47, 316

Palestine, 173
Pali-canon, 35, 168
Pallas Athena, 54
panentheism, xii, 62, 65–66, 107, 161–62, 165–66, 176–78, 182, 195, 207, 258, 265, 314
pantheism, xii, 12, 59–60, 65, 66, 107, 153, 155, 165, 176–78, 182, 186, 195, 207, 220–21, 238, 264–65, 292, 305, 314
paradox(es), 117, 142, 173, 234, 252–53, 318
    Buddhist, 221
    Cusa's, 221
    extinction, 299
    Fermi's, 240
    of Buddhist and Hindu insight, 284
    of limits in the midst of infinities, 55
    of magnitudes, 261
    temporal, 46
Parmenides, 44
participation, 89, 318
    in the suffering of God, 49
    of all sentient beings in the Buddha-nature, 274
    spatial, 219
Pascal's Fire, 298
passage, 14, 21, 87, 89–95, 159, 214, 311
    through matter, 11
    visionary, 120
patriarchalism, 54
Paul, St. (apostle), 16, 29, 101, 109, 249
Pauli, Wolfgang, 102, 110, 267
peace, xi, 7, 16, 119, 125, 127, 175, 208, 215, 221–22, 257, 261–62, 268, 270–83, 287, 296, 305
    convergence in, 20
    future (spiritualized) society of, 211, 270
    powerless force of, 195
    profound mode of, 236
    sphere of, 279
    spiritual, 2
Peace/Reality, 287, 302
Peneus (river god), 125
Penrose, Roger, 219

perennialism, 286
Persephone, 140–41
Persian Bayan, 93
person, 20, 72, 90, 92, 131, 166, 194, 201, 212, 216, 254, 269, 283, 285–89, 290, 292–93, 297, 304, 308, 319
    character of, 187
    divine, 176, 211, 219, 292
    God as, 189
    in Buddhist scriptures, 292
    of Jesus, 150
    of Krishna, 41, 219
    primordial divine, 36, 41
    sacred, 316
    supreme divine, 31, 292
    -thing, 305
    three, 149
persona(e), 298–90
personalism, 314
    Christian, 291
personality, 31, 77, 176, 257, 278, 306, 308, 319
    beyond, 283
    of God, 291
    of Krishna, 291
    spiritual, 302
    ultimate, 58
personalization, 289
    de-, 305
personhood, 254, 289, 291–92, 302
    of God, 288
Phaedrus, 289
Philo of Alexandria, 92, 121, 147–48, 196, 207, 219, 274
philosophy, 135, 138, 182, 190, 197, 236, 263
    Benjamin's, 232
    Buddhist, 4, 61, 276
    Daoist, 313
    Deleuze's, 192, 314
    Existentialist, 136
    Greek, 44
    Hegel's, 73, 177
    Heidegger's, 73, 177
    Hindu, 31
    Kant's, 61
    medieval, 260
    natural, 317
    of nonduality, 177
    of the Spirit, xii
    origins of, 73
    perennial, 213
    Plato's, 68
    Stoic, 265
    Whitehead's, 4
philosophy and religion, 182, 191, 193
philosophy of immanence, the, 172, 182, 314
philosophy of organism, the, 255
Phoenix (mythological bird), 42
physicalism, 101, 199
Plank, Max, 110
Plato, 13, 33–37, 68–69, 73, 76–79, 102, 122, 124, 141, 147, 154, 166, 176–78, 177, 191–92, 196, 207, 219–20, 245, 247, 265, 276–77, 287, 289, 291, 294–95
plenitude, 98, 106, 145, 256
pleroma, the 11, 30, 111, 149, 211, 245, 287, 305, 315
    apophatic, 288
    divergent, 210
    infinite, 288
    oceanic, 55
    of all creative fire, 301
    of all things, 33, 42
    of divine multiplicity, 43
    of (intelligent) life, 44, 241
    of modes of beauty, 55
    of spiritual pathways, 175
    of the becoming of spiritual beings, 107
    of the mystery, 292
    spiritual, 119
Plotinus, 44–45, 102, 107, 147, 167–67, 178, 181, 183, 188, 191–92, 195, 213, 219–20, 223–4, 231, 245, 249–50, 259, 265, 274–78
pluralism, 175, 213, 215, 312
    apophatic-polyphilic, 312
    essentialist, 214
    monistic, 213
    monocentric, 213
    of the post-axial age, 214
    polycentric, 213
    postmodern, 214
    religious, 119, 213, 286, 298, 303
plurality,
    of essences, 213
    of God, 149
    of self-existence, 218
pluralization, 106
pluriform, 29, 34–35, 37, 47
Plutarch, 35
pneuma, 12, 22, 57, 70, 102, 230, 246
    zoopoioun, 84
pneumatology, 21
poet, 7–17, 141, 137, 198, 314

of the Spirit of life, 12–13
of the world, 7, 137
poetics, 13, 17, 25
Polkinghorne, John, 110
polyphilia, 262–68, 272, 283, 287, 305, 319
polyphony, 199
polytheism, 147, 151, 153
Ponchielli, Amilcare, 97
Popper, Karl, 199, 219
Porphyry, 277
prajna, 168
pratitya-samutpada, 33, 46, 101, 259, 280, 312
principle, 197, 227, 245, 294, 300, 304
    life-, 36, 49, 249, 275, 280
    of creative differentiation, 178, 183
    of mediocrity, 66, 239–41
    of regularity, 240
    spiritual, 36
    ultimate, 4
    uncertainty, 267
process, 45, 68, 81, 83, 90–91, 93, 95, 81, 104, 111–12, 143, 187, 197, 211, 227, 237–38, 248, 251, 259, 262, 271–72, 279, 296, 316
    aesthetic, 4, 46
    alchemical, 252
    by which uniqueness becomes universal, 289
    creation/creative, 46, 80, 84, 109–10, 133, 138, 253
    divine, 43, 135
    enlightenment, 273
    eternal, 37
    evolutionary/emergent, 74, 100, 102, 105, 127, 186, 214, 239, 243, 274
    mapping, 244–45
    mental, 14
    natural, 85, 312
    of actualization and transformation, 267
    of becoming and perishing, 13, 36, 45–46, 106–7, 122, 144, 192, 233
    of bodying, 287
    of cosmic expansion, 272
    of cosmic impermanence, xii
    of cosmic realization, 287
    of differentiation and unification, 177, 188, 194, 218, 245
    of eternal inflation, 85
    of fusion and divergence, 266
    of intensification and harmonization, 44, 46, 106, 124, 197, 275–76, 278, 280
    of life, 36, 86, 90
    of non-possessive interrelationality, 312
    of permanent transformation, 41
    of polyphilic creation, 288
    of polyphilic manifestation, 292
    of processes, 90, 133, 283
    of purification, 109, 111, 133
    of en/re/unfolding, 47, 218, 317
    of renewal, 36–37
    of (mutual) self-transcendence, 3, 258, 272–73, 275, 278–79, 286, 309
    of spiritualization, xi, 5, 11, 23, 41–42, 47, 60, 109, 120, 249, 272, 281, 312, 252, 261, 275
    of synthesis and transition, 198
    of territorialization, 188
    of the Spirit, 37
    of uncontrollable movements of life, 35
    of unification, 42–43, 46
    of valuation, 105, 250, 254, 273, 303, 314, 318
    polyphilic, 261
    quantum, 237
    spiritual, 288
    temporal, 103
    universal cosmic, 37, 44, 92, 100–101, 260–61, 274, 279
Process and Reality, 7, 46, 76, 254
process philosophies, 34, 44, 183, 197–98
process theology, 218
Prometheus, 108, 152, 195
Promulgation of Universal Peace, 257
prophet(s), 9, 31, 38–39, 53, 55, 58, 70–71, 77, 93, 95, 108–10, 113–14, 120, 124, 141, 143, 145, 151, 154, 160, 164, 174–75, 179, 181–83, 190–91, 194–95, 204–5, 216, 223–24, 235, 243, 253, 281, 303
Prospero, 133–34, 154–55, 164, 172
Prospero's Books (movie), 134
Protagoras, 68
Pseudo-Dionysius, the Areopagite, 109, 147, 223, 288
psyche, 45, 100, 199, 219, 275, 304
purpose, 18, 53, 55, 85, 102, 127, 241, 243, 247, 267, 273, 280, 289, 296–97, 300
    creative, 257
    cosmic, 242

purpose (*continued*)
  dark depth of, 19
  deep(er), 155, 298
  non-physical realm of, 304
  of evolution, 120
  of existence, 242
  of human existence, 120
  of immortality, 248
  of spiritual becoming, 248
  of the spiritual nature of evolution, 107
  sacred, xi
  spiritual, 120, 142, 248
  teleological, 114
  without any, 104
purposefulness,
  of life, 298
  spiritual, 274
Pythagoras, 44, 154
Pythagoreans, 141, 199

qalb, 47
qi, 81, 297
Qumran, 175
Qur'an, 40, 47, 93, 110, 121, 291, 315

racism, 72–73, 253
  anti-, 253
Rahner, Karl, 24, 58–65, 60, 222, 261, 287, 314
Ramakrishna, Sri, 211–12
Ramanuja, 31
rationality, 7, 66
reality, 16, 42, 52, 107, 135, 139, 165, 167, 169, 186–87, 197–99, 206, 214, 280, 314
  apophatic, 41, 265, 278–79, 281
  divine, 2, 22, 30, 37, 40, 42, 61, 63, 83, 148, 151, 167, 188, 204, 209, 211, 247, 253, 264, 266, 290, 317
  immanent, 3
  intangible, 15
  nondual, 290, 314, 316, 319
  of a mirage, 187–88
  of a spirit-force, 298
  of a theophany, 195
  of a transcendent being, 181
  of evolution, 44
  of divine fire/light, 122
  of love, 319
  of Reality, 304
  of relations, 190
  of suffering, perishing, and violence, xii
  of the cosmos, 3, 44–45, 94, 190, 231, 261
  of the Forms and Ideas, 167
  of the present moment, 258
  of the self-differencing universe, 192
  of the (cosmic) Spirit, 12, 41, 115, 119, 195, 304, 314–16
  spiritual, xi, 3, 11, 15, 60, 95, 101, 187–88, 198, 203
  transcendent, 20, 30, 61–63, 151, 166, 189, 194
  ultimate, xii, 3, 22, 30–31, 39, 59, 61, 72, 81–82, 98, 127, 130, 135, 147–48, 154, 169, 187–88, 190, 193, 198–99, 211, 213, 220, 227, 241, 258, 273, 276, 279–80, 282, 287, 289–91, 318–19
Reality/God, 213, 273, 296, 315
realm(s), 55
  cosmic, 246
  of a controlling ego, 101
  of desire, 140
  of divine experience, 230
  of experience, 165
  of God, 246
  of knowledge, 110
  of lights, 230
  of mere/pure possibility, 263–64
  of multiplicity, 304
  of mystical experience, 13
  of natural unities, 304
  of permanent forms, 78
  of potential and entangled states, 219, 312
  of (primordial) potentials, 250, 267
  of purposes and aims, 304
  of the small and the large, 16
  of vibration, 198
  of the Spirit, 73
  spiritual, 236
reconciliation, 94, 119, 148
  of spiritual interiority with cosmic adventures, 25
redemption, 109, 179, 235
reductionism, 101–2, 191, 231, 237–38
  Eurocentric, 62
  materialist, 11, 198, 297–98
  naturalist, 127
  non-temporal, 258
Regio, Godfrey, 198
relationality, 11, 33, 35, 64, 66, 92, 207, 242, 275, 279, 292, 296, 299
  all-, 35, 262, 287
  God of, 49

ecological, 287
empathic receptivity of, 194
evolutionary, 214
field of, 199
mutual, 32, 280
of all existents, 235, 261
of multiplicity, 35, 194
peaceful, 289
synergetic, 318
universally transgressive, 21
universal, 262, 275, 315
ultimate, 20
relativism, 163, 165, 186, 208, 214, 303
    religious, 211
relativity, 55, 84, 164, 189, 216, 237, 258, 312
    of infinite spiritual paths, 167, 172
    of infinite worlds, 167
    of religious truth, 229
    philosophy of, 62
    religious, 208, 221
    sacred, 23
    theory, 234, 243, 245, 254, 263
Religion in the Making, 195
religions, 11, 15, 21, 23, 40, 73, 78, 80, 90–91, 110, 119–20, 191, 211–12, 220, 222, 238, 240–43, 248–49, 277, 280, 287, 295, 303, 319
    Abrahamic, 151, 173, 213
    ancient, 141
    axial, 209–11, 213
    classical differentiation of, 266
    common essence of, 213
    cosmotheistic, 209
    Daoic, 277
    death of, 92
    desert, 179
    Dharmic, 213, 277
    diversity of, 220, 236–37, 241, 279, 290, 312
    ecumene of, 211
    history of, 151, 195
    imperial, 182
    indigenous, 213, 317
    multiplicity of, 213
    Near Eastern, 144
    new, 3, 41
    New Age, 245
    post-axial, 213, 221
    primordial, 2, 77
    renewal of, 41
    revealed, 153, 208, 210
    symbolism of, 303
    tribal, 208

UFO, 235
unity of, 211, 213–15, 219
universal, 210
western, 207, 311
world, 208–9
religions and spiritualities, 2, 11, 41, 91, 213, 220–21, 236–37, 240–42
Religionskritik, 186
religiosity, xi, 154, 173, 181, 191, 195, 237, 242
    characteristics/dimensions of, 2, 213
    deep, 173, 235
    essential features of, 3
    expressions of, 214
    new, 2
    sun-based, 317
Republic, 141
resonances, 21–22, 88, 151, 161, 312
    between macro-and micro-realities, 3–4
    body of, 10
    of everything in every moment of movement, 82
revelation, 36, 38–9, 47, 50, 83, 90, 97, 109, 129–30, 149–52, 164, 173, 175, 202–3, 209–10, 227–28, 235, 238, 252–53, 291, 293
    apophatic-polyphilic, 315
    events of, 205
    extraordinary scenes of, 174
    flow of, 80
    future, 204
    Israelite, 204
    Naturalistic, 220
    new, 41
    of Spirit, 63
    self-, 288
    Sinai, 216
    the fire of, 35
    YHWH-, 144
revolution, 44, 63, 118, 136, 150, 174, 193
    French, 118
    Industrial, 61
    Marxist, 232
    musical, 142–43, 150
    religious, 151–52
    scientific, 229, 231
rhizome, 103–4, 106
Ridvan (realm), 95
Ridvan Garden, 118
river, xii, 17, 18, 36, 71, 76–100, 140, 157, 160, 168–69, 189, 203, 207, 211, 214–16, 221, 246, 269, 280–81, 300, 313, 317

river (*continued*)
    flow of, 20
    of existence, 271, 278
    of life, 16, 122–23
    of *samsara*, 304
Rohr, Richard, 41
Roman Empire, 91, 125, 146

Saddharma Pundarika Sutra, 165
sages, 12, 207–8, 211, 232, 281, 303
    desert, 196
    spiritual, 211
Saint-Exupéry, Antoine de, 67
salvation, 41, 78, 94–95, 100, 109, 123, 139, 181, 188, 190, 193, 210, 234–36, 242, 296
    Abrahamic, 43
    desires for, 230
    divine powers of, 166
    eschatological promise of, 204
    pattern of, 93
    secular, 140
    ultimate, 60
    universal, 37
Samantabhadra (Buddha), 165–66, 196, 219, 292
Samantabhadra Meditation Sutra, 165, 167
sambhogakaya, 164, 166, 188, 194, 276
samsara, 33, 35, 94, 111, 140, 164, 177, 187, 221, 246, 272, 304
Samyutta Nikaya, 35
sanatana dharma, 213
Sankaracharya, 177, 188, 219
satchitananda, 178
Schimmel, Annemarie, 223
Schopenhauer, Athur, 257, 277, 283
Schrödinger, Erwin, 110, 231, 267
science, 101, 138, 202, 248, 255, 267
    ancient, 106, 108
    new, 110
    space-, 150
Science and Christ, 43
science and philosophy, 127, 199, 236, 263
science and religion, 74, 110–11
Science and the Modern World, 4
science fiction, 302, 305
scriptures, 2, 109
    Baháʼí, 3
    Buddhist, 94, 221, 292
    Hebrew, 11, 39, 160–61, 173, 212, 226, 253, 300
sea, the, 18, 32, 58, 60, 62–63, 67–73, 158
    of God, 68, 79, 81–82
    open spaces of, 16
    of the heavens, 69
Self, the, 21, 97, 166–67, 176, 186, 223, 261, 275, 283–84, 286–87, 305, 308
    beyond, 96
    dying of, 83
    of all things, 31
    of nature, 315
    of God, 13
    of self-transcendence, 292
    of the Prophet Muhammad, 58
sephirot, 121, 182, 36, 58, 111
Seraphim, 38, 42, 121, 122, 124
sexism, 54, 72
Shakespeare, William, 131, 133, 135–36, 154
shakti, 212, 288, 301, 313
Shambhala, 95
shekinah, 39, 102, 205
Shirdi Sai Baba, 212
Shiva, 105, 299, 301, 313
Shiva Purana, 105
Sidrat al-Muntaha, 110
Sidrat bridge, 93
Sikhism, 164, 212
silence, 83, 87, 157, 161, 174, 208, 288
    listening, 4
    mystical, 148, 262
    of graves, 23
    of hopelessness, 48–49
    secret, 223–24
silence/darkness, 253
Simurgh, 224
Sinai (mount), 31, 39, 47, 143–44, 151, 173, 175, 203–5, 216, 223, 233, 300
singularity, 114–15, 120, 217, 305
sirr, 47
skillful means, 94, 188, 278, 290, 292
Socrates, 37–38, 289
Solaris (movie), 69
soma pneumatikon, 195, 249
soma psychikon, 249
Son of God, 121, 145–46, 204
Son of Man, 39, 41, 109, 121, 124, 145–46
sophia, 102, 228, 288
soul, 69, 79, 102, 225, 249–50, 273–80, 305
    -formation, 273
    -fullness, 277–78, 281–82, 287
    -journey, 38, 109, 114, 120–21, 161, 164, 281
    -life, 108

materialist ideas of, 244
   of the dead, 256
   -substance, 275
space, 4, 12, 20, 26–7, 29–35, 48–9, 57, 71,
      81, 107, 118, 181, 184, 199–200,
      202, 216, 250, 258–60, 263, 275,
      300, 302–3, 306–7, 309
   abstract, 129
   all-embracing, 16
   apophatic, 50
   awakened conscious, 47
   chaosmic, 183
   compassionate, 318
   connectivity of, 261
   creative, 50, 178, 318
   deep, 60
   desert, 181
   -dimension, 217
   divine, 119
   empty, 51, 82, 121, 179, 197, 229
   exploration, 150
   external, 43–44
   flat, 18
   formless, 255
   heavenly, 229
   hyper-, 234–35, 263, 266
   immediate, 61
   imperial, measured, 181, 220
   infinite, 51, 60, 62
   inner, 57
   layered, 229
   minority, 214
   nomadic, 181
   of divine revelation, 50
   of emptiness, 18
   of existence, 119
   of indirection, 56
   of liberation, 173
   open, 16, 40, 180, 233
   primordial, 175
   probability, 84–85, 112, 129, 197, 239,
      244
   public, 41
   quantum, 198
   sacred, 117
   smooth, 181–83
   spiritual, 37, 40, 43
   stochastic, 84
   striated, 181
   theophanic, 129
   third, 55, 237
space and time, xi-xii, 8, 11, 78, 90, 111,
      228–29, 231, 241, 250–52, 254,
      258, 271, 279, 297, 317

spacetime, 243, 296
Spinoza, Baruch, 61, 154, 176–77, 178,
      182, 190–95, 207, 220
Spirit (spirit), 4, 7, 9, 117, 319
   of awakening, 13
   of a cosmos, 107, 199, 314–15
   of creative differentiation, 221
   of God, 2, 39, 56–57, 91, 149–50, 173
   of existence, 133
   of freedom, 179
   of life, 2, 8–12, 23–24, 62, 84–85, 90,
      100, 106, 114, 122
   of the All, 16
   of the earth, 4, 300–301, 314–15
   of the universe, 91
   of transformation, 4
   of truth, beauty, adventure, art and
      peace, 278
   seeker, xi, 10
   -space, 36–37, 40, 42–43, 46–47, 49,
      57, 85
   -substance, 12
   -time, 258
   -universes, 208
   -worlds, 299
Spirit-Light-Love, 43, 45
Spiritual Science, 298
spirituality, 14, 21, 24–25, 29, 38, 68, 73,
      131, 142, 172, 174, 176, 186, 227,
      286, 305, 313
   bodied, 172
   -counter, 160
   cosmic, xii, 232, 235, 237, 242
   eastern, 286
   ecological, xii
   free, 2
   matriarchal, 163
   monadic, 182
   native, 299
   naturalistic, 229
   non-theistic, 1
   of the numinous, xi, 15
   of the Mother Earth, 4
   origins of, 172
   quantum, 245
   transformation of, 316
   universal, 286
Stevenson, Robert Louis, 124
Strabo, 182
Strange Case of Dr. Jekyll and Mr. Hyde
      (novel), 124
Stoics, 12, 35, 37–38, 45, 57, 82, 102, 182,
      192, 219, 230, 246, 264
Strindberg, August, 135

Styx (river), 140
substance, 52, 58–59, 74, 80, 90, 187, 196, 229, 244, 275
    divine, 69–71, 79, 195, 252
    heavenly, 252
    moving, 81
    primordial, 57
    psychophysical, 69
    pure, 252
    spiritual, 109
Sufism, 47, 147, 163, 213, 220
summit, 205–6, 216–24
    of life, 202
    of many religious paths, 211
    of reality, 210
    of religious existence, 211
sunyata, 16, 33, 101, 107, 166, 273, 290
superiority, 73, 80, 179, 253
    alien, 235
    claims of, 319
    complex, 270
    incurable, 242
    of Christianity, 22, 62, 73
    thinking, 177
Susskind, Leonard, 86
Sutra of Infinite Meanings, 165
symbiosis, 104, 114, 131
symbol,
    of a pleroma, 55
    of animal weakness, 108
    of divine and anti-divine forces, 53–54
    of divine defense against human attacks, 108
    of evolution, 103
    of gentle beginnings of the flow, 98
    of life, 17
    of the civilized nature of a society, 118
    of the complexity of the process of transformation, 260
    of the cosmos, 215
    of the creative and unitive origin of differentiation, 219
    of the creative Spirit, 84
    of the diversified nature of existence, 103
    of the Garden of Reality, 119
    of the gratitude of overflowing, 98
    of the knowledge of healing, 108
    of the numinous, 203
    of the sacred mountain, 205
    of the sun, 207
    of the transcendent divine reality, 154
    of the tree (of life), 100, 103
    of the warlike chaos, 56
    of the warring Word of God, 108
    of the whole space-time structure, 218
    of universal salvation, 37
symbolism, 37, 101–3, 108, 110, 113, 120, 132, 134–35, 138–39, 165, 187–88, 203, 211, 214, 236, 252–53, 261, 266, 280, 302–3
sym-pathy, 45–47, 67, 73, 101, 104–7, 114, 194, 319
    mutual 46
Syria, 173
system, 71, 215, 231
    Hindu, 130
    many worlds-, 231
    of energy, 115
    of life, 18
    of morality, 286
    of the religious, spiritual universe, 90
    planetary, 32
    star, 44, 114
    sun/solar, 240, 306
    theory, 297
    world, 199, 231

Tagore, Rabindranath, 212
tat twam asi, 125
Taylor, Steven, 298
Teatro Amazonas, 96
Teilhard de Chardin, Pierre, 29–30, 34, 42–43, 64, 74, 104, 224, 260, 279, 281, 289, 312
teleology, 85, 267, 282, 297
telos, 281, 304–5
thatagatagarbha, 274
The Becoming of God, 314
The Conference of Birds, 224
The Creation of Adam (fresco), 84
The Divine Manifold, 264, 318
The Essence of Christianity, 318
The Fold, 183, 266
The Future of Humanity, 295
The Great Work, 311
The Idea of the Holy, 47, 316
The Life of Moses, 223
The Light of Other Days (novel), 257, 302, 304
The Interpretation of Religion, 290
The Metamorphosis, 124
The Ocean of God, 312
The Phenomenon of Man, 43
The Principles of Psychology, 78
The Sea, The Sea (novel), 131
The Tempest (drama), 131
The Tree of Knowledge, 111

The Wisdom of Crocodiles (movie), 100, 112
The Wisdom of the Sands, 67
The World as Will and Representation, 257
theism, 65–66, 165, 176, 189, 238, 265–66, 286–87, 292, 298, 314, 318
    anti-, 272
    dipolar, 146, 159, 162, 188, 288
    dualistic, 177
    existential, 176
    naïve, 176
    naturalist, 265
    supernatural, 228
theology, 135, 223
    Christian, 162, 189
    mystical, 109, 223
    of the divine desert, 191
theophany, 31–32, 38, 149, 164, 180, 194–95
    primordial, 34
    of YHWH, 146
    of the Spirit, 35–36
    places of, 216
    Sinai, 151, 175, 217, 223
theopoetics, 13, 18
theory, 2, 263
    complexity, 84
    Darwinian, 238
    Everett's, 85
    Evolution(ary), 103, 112, 186, 236–37
    Grand Unified, 237
    Hartle-Hawking, 217
    Integral, 273, 286
    Many Worlds, 263
    mathematical-physical, 84
    of Forms, 166
    of imaginary time, 217
    of panspermia, 239
    of physicalism, 199
    of synchronicity, 102
    quantum, 234, 296
    relativity, 245, 254
    social contract, 56
    string, 263
    Susskind's, 86
    Vilenkin's, 85
Theses on the Philosophy of History, 232
Tiamat, 54, 105, 299, 313
Timaeus, 33, 36, 267, 295
time, 7, 10, 78, 80, 90, 103, 109, 119, 125, 128, 144, 151, 161, 198, 200, 232, 234, 240, 247, 252, 258–59, 271, 300, 302, 307
    axis-, 210, 217
    chaos of, 227
    depth of, 229
    -dimension, 217–18
    dome of, 229, 293
    flow of, 78, 232, 243
    imaginary, 217
    immensity of, 240
    infinite, 306
    internal, 306
    life-, 157, 240, 262
    linear, 234
    medieval, 13
    moment in, 10, 217, 261
    multiplicity of, 258
    Neolithic, 163
    of becoming, 78
    -perception, 203
    sacred, 316
    sanctification of, 123
    spiritual (unison of), 258–59
    -suspensions, 258
time and eternity, 92, 199, 259
timelessness and eternity, 258
Torah, 83, 205
transcendence, 57, 59, 63, 110, 168, 171, 178, 183, 191, 194, 209, 220, 249, 287, 303, 311, 313
    absolute, 265
    apocalyptic, 210
    apophatic, 179
    creative, 192
    decease of, 190
    Deleuze's, 210
    dissolution of, 220
    divine, 175, 191
    dualistic, 193
    engaged, 313
    experience of, 199
    Figures of, 182, 195
    idealistic, 191
    image of, 60
    imperial, 183, 193, 219–20, 224
    God's, 62
    illusionary, 190, 193–94
    lateral, 184
    manifest, 182
    mutual, 237, 291, 315
    new, 182, 193
    of absence, 175
    of nature, 313
    poetic, 198
    process of, 279
    religious of, 182

transcendence (*continued*)
   self-, 20, 82, 111, 117, 125, 184, 199, 258, 272–89, 291–93, 303, 305, 309, 313, 317
   self-forgetful, 280
   spiritual, 262
   theistic, 264
   trans-pantheistic, 193
   unreformed, 196
   within/inward, 271, 279–80, 287, 305, 313–15
transformation, 41, 49, 63, 105, 107–9, 112, 137, 143, 159–60, 181, 193, 205, 207, 209, 211, 218, 243, 247–50, 261, 267–68, 272, 301, 303–4, 309, 314, 316–18
   alchemical journey of, 281
   algorithmic, 120
   apocalyptic, 41, 47
   burning desire of, 49
   continuous, 220
   converse, 219
   cosmic, 74, 260
   creative, 74, 260
   deep, 261
   ecological, 114
   future, 211
   hype-dimensional, 235
   immanentist, 191
   intermezzo of, 173, 230, 232
   mutual, 220, 267
   nomadic, 233
   of heart/mind/body, 25
   of society, 25
   of the cosmos, 4
   of the elements, 252
   of sages, prophets, and holy figures, 281
   of transcendence into immanence, 183
   panentheistic/monistic, 159
   salvific, 234
   self-, 4, 279
   spiritual, 22, 24, 40–41, 90, 109, 114, 204, 210, 216, 259–61, 272–73, 278–80, 286, 302, 317
   theomorphic, 109
   ultimate, 300
   universal, 43, 260
translucency, 20, 85
transmutation, 159, 179, 228, 252
   spiritual, 92
   traumatic, 152

trans-pantheism, xii, 66, 177–78, 195, 207, 221, 238, 292, 314
trans-religious, 15, 160, 204
   approach, 21
   flows/fluidity, 110, 206
   images, 79, 93
   movements, 147
   mutation, 146
   nature of religious paths, 90
   poetic pattern, xi
   reality, 41
   shamanic spirit universe, 208
   truth, 220
   unification/unity, 161, 221
tree, 17, 20, 36, 52, 87, 97, 99, 100–130, 174, 214, 224, 249, 265–66, 269, 281, 295, 300, 303
   falling from, 114, 276
   neither from the eats nor from the west, 40
   of Abrahamic religious traditions, 39
Tree of Existence, 122, 127
Tree of Good and Evil, 73
Tree of Knowledge, 107–17, 120, 123, 133
Tree of Life, 17, 36–37, 99–117, 120–24, 127–30, 257, 265–66
Tree of Universes, 130
Trees, two, 108, 114–15, 120–21
Trinity, the, 22, 162, 176, 292
tritheism, 149
Trungpa, Chögyam, 101, 176
truth, 7, 69, 90, 108, 112, 119, 129, 138, 196, 208, 221, 260, 278, 280, 301, 315, 317, 231, 242, 252, 260, 280, 293, 315, 317
   claims, 235–36
   Darwinian theory of infinite, 238
   exclusive, 122, 162, 183
   modes of, 16
   moment of, 134
   nontrivial, 77
   of all religions, 242
   of the Spirit, 19, 208
   of the summit od spiritual consciousness, 222
   phenomenal, 219
   religious, 229
   revealed, 209
   spiritual, 33, 156, 166–67
   sword of, 121
   symbolic, 135
   trans-pantheistic, 221
   trans-religious, 220–21
   ultimate, 77, 219

universal, 213, 277
Turangalila Symphony, 119

Udana, 168, 208
ultimacy, 79, 290
ultimate, the, 18, 290, 293
unification(s), 31, 42–43, 46, 74, 104, 164, 177, 183, 212, 214, 219, 235, 237, 247–48, 258, 271–72, 279, 289, 291, 300
    apophatic, 246
    artistic, 138
    divine, 288
    events of, 194
    exclusive, 208
    false, 179
    images of, 207
    intercultural, 161
    movements of, 219–20
    mystical, 109
    of all symbolic senses, 139
    of the two Trees, 114
    oppressive, 279
    ultimate, 159
unio mystica, 13, 218, 258
uniqueness, 107, 237–38, 240, 289, 291, 298, 305, 308
    apophatic/pleromatic, 289, 291, 305
    divine, 40
    of life and mind on this earth, 241
    of love, 292
    of mutuality, 293
    of Reality, 41
    of the YHWH-revelation, 144
    pleromatic, 288
    relational, 289
unison,
    of becoming, 274, 319
    of physical and spiritual dimensions, 101
    of the cosmic multiplicity, 258
    of time and eternity, 259
unity, 43, 69, 190, 217, 252, 266, 272
    dipolar, 167
    nondual, 159
    of a universe, 276
    of being(s), 189, 314
    of cosmic becoming, 258
    of creation and destruction, 301
    of emptiness and creativity, 33
    of events of becoming, 258
    of detachment-compassion, 4
    of God, 104
    of human religiosity, 242
    of humanity, 213–14, 242
    of ideas and potentials, 255
    of infinity and finiteness, 247
    of inner Self with the All, 164
    of life and knowledge, 113–15, 122
    of love, 42
    of mind and matter, 275
    of novelty, 83
    of opposites, 17
    of Reality, 41
    of religions, 211, 213–15, 219–20, 222
    of the cosmos/world, 4, 82
    of transcendence and immanence, 161, 169
    of ultimate multiplicity, 213
    of unmanifest Reality and its Manifestations, 180
universality, 60, 73, 153, 214, 260, 272, 290
universe(s), the, 12, 27, 31–32, 28, 42, 45, 51, 53, 58, 66–67, 70, 81–82, 84, 87, 89, 95, 102, 119, 194, 198, 200, 208, 229–31, 235–43, 251–67, 281, 294, 296, 304, 309
    alternative, 263
    axial, 210
    Big Bang, 240, 263
    birth and death in, 85, 263
    block, 234
    branching, 265–66
    causeless eruption of, 86
    chaotic, 231
    complex, 150, 263
    collapse of, 92
    creativity of, 37
    cyclical lives of, 263
    decentered, 231
    differentiation of, 85, 198
    Einstein, 217, 263
    essence of, 1
    Everett, 264
    ever-evolving, xi, 4, 105, 107, 242
    expanding/expansive, 218, 232–33, 263
    freezing death of, 92
    infinite (process of), 44, 60, 230, 238, 264, 307
    intelligent life in, 241
    lattice of connected, 129
    many/multiple, 129, 264
    mutual, 208
    new, 85–86, 92, 130, 263, 307
    Newtonian, 61
    observable, 239

universe (continued)
   of collision, 12
   of multiple layered, nested environments, 197
   other, 259, 307
   parallel, 85, 129, 267, 307
   physical/material, 188, 236, 245, 248, 259, 263–67, 306
   Platonic-Aristotelian, 275
   polytheistic, 208
   possible, 129, 264
   quartering of, 92
   religious, 187, 208–9
   self-conscious, 231, 273
   self-differing, 192
   space of/space-bounded, 43, 218, 263
   spiritual (aspects/nature of), 53, 90, 232, 241, 264, 266–67, 296
   strangers in, 91
   successive series of, 129, 267
   symbolic, 137, 141–42
   unfolding, 218
   unity of, 276
universes and multiverses, 107, 237, 266, 274, 281, 292, 307–8
unknowability, 115, 276
unknowing, 38, 69, 188, 289
Upanishads, 12, 32, 208, 315

valuation(s), 95, 263, 266, 274, 291, 294, 303, 314
   aesthetic, 272
   decisions of, 261
   divine, 86
   modes of, 272
   of potentials and values, 250
   of that which becomes, 262
   of the Mind of God, 192
   process of, 105, 254, 303, 318
   virtues of, 271
values, 67, 80, 92–93, 104, 109, 208, 250, 281, 286, 291, 302–3
   divine, 250
   ethical, 127
   for self-creative actualizations, 194
   divine, 43, 84
   of universal ecological awareness, 67
   religious, 242
   spiritual, 235, 274, 278
values and virtues, 42, 198, 211, 271, 286
Varela, Francesco, 112
variation, 71, 104, 207, 228, 239, 266
   allele, 239
   artificial, 306

   fields of, 198
   genetic, 305
   imperfect, 192
   infinite living, 4
   internal infinity of, 23
   of eternal ideas, 78
   of the polyphilic presence of the Spirit, 316
Vendidad, 93
Verdi, Giuseppe, 97
Vespasian, 204
vibrations, 3–4, 10, 187, 196–97, 199, 227, 279
   divine, 243
   harmonic, 259
   inherent/internal, 14, 44
   magnitudes of, 198
   material, 139
   modulations of, 243
   of inclusiveness, 14
   of Spirit-Light, 45
   proportions of, 44
   relational fusion of, 196
   sacred, 49
   sea of, 273
Vilenkin, Alexander, 85
violence, xi, 23, 25, 211–12, 232, 278, 282, 287, 294, 296, 301
   collective memory of, 251
   cycle of, 133
   Darwinian (forces of), 236, 296
   of cosmic life, 293
   of the impersonal law, 149
   perpetual, 150, 299
   psychological forms of, 23
   slow-motion, 70
Virgil, 316
virtuality, 184, 198
virtues, 202, 272, 275, 279–80, 291, 293, 304–5
   of self-transcendence, 286
   religious, 261
   spiritual, 20, 66, 194, 212, 273, 278, 281, 287
   theological, 261, 272
   transformational, 281
vision, 121, 138–39
   Ezekiel's, 9
   of a divine garden of delight, 95, 120
   of a future (spiritualized) society of peace, 211, 270
   of heaven, 267
   of a paradise, 93
   of a state of altered consciousness, 50

of a unifies and cultures humanity,
119
of any perfect ion of being human,
108
of apocalyptic forgetfulness, 260
of divine creativity, 204
of Moses, 147
of Teilhard de Chardin, 260
of the *Bhagavad Gita*, 31
of the creation, 115
of the divine manifestation of the
invisible God, 39
of the divine wisdom, 46
of the future (of humanity), 108, 118
of the future integration of matter and
mind, 118
of the Good, Beauty and Truth, 138
of the throne(s) of God, 109, 139
poetic, 138
prophetic vision, 108
St. Paul's, 249
vivacity, 10, 16
Vivekananda, Swami, 211–14

wahdat al-wujud, 189
Ward, Keith, 176, 298
waves, 10, 30, 55–59, 67–70, 75, 79,
81–82, 197, 199, 243, 247
Weber, Max, 186
Webern, Anton, 143
What Is Philosophy?, 171
Whitehead, Alfred N., 4, 7, 12, 33, 33–34,
44–46, 50, 64, 72–73, 76, 79–81,
86, 92, 104–6, 110, 127, 137–38,
153, 155, 167, 176, 180–84, 187,
190–99, 207, 214, 218–19, 227,
233, 250, 254, 256–60, 264–67,
271–80, 283, 289, 291, 302, 306,
312, 315
wholeness, 19, 33, 238, 255
manifest, 35
Wickramasinghe, Chandra, 239
Wilber, Ken, 273
wilderness, 17, 115–19, 171–72 174, 202,
313
Wilson, Edward O., 311
wisdom (Wisdom), 17, 38, 53–54, 77–78,
81, 93–95, 100, 102–3, 111, 201,
224, 252, 256
ancient, 36
cosmic, 228
biblical, 228
Buddhist, 111, 168

divine, 38, 46, 85, 92, 109, 121, 127,
146, 148, 158, 219, 229, 247, 253,
299, 313
God as, 37–38
House of, 95
Jewish, 219
Lady, 160
-light, 299
literature, 48, 148, 160, 247
of creative alternatives, 233
of the creator, 232
of the flow, 82
of the mariner, 70
prophet of, 160
religion, 2, 163
sun of 166
revelation of, 50
teacher, 29, 174
wisdom and compassion, 93–94, 111,
113, 273
Wisdom of Crocodiles, The
word (Word), 299
of God, 56, 108–9
of truth, 212
words/worlds, 4
Wordsworth, William, 4
world(s), 80, 91–93, 114–15, 119, 129–30,
161, 230, 248, 264–67, 281
actual, 164, 176, 178, 194
all, 30, 164, 167, 265, 279, 281
-apple 65
-construction, 147
creator of, 306
destroyer of, 108
different/differentiating, 60, 91
different metaphysical, 265
-emanation, 296
Hindu, 264
ideal, 194
imaginary, 306
infinite, 167
interval between, 92
life-, 102
many, 111, 231, 256, 263
material, 92, 121
most evil, 299
multiplicity of, 265 267
multiverse of, 107
mutually exclusive, 194, 242
new, 231
non-physical, 266
of becoming, 107
of creativity and value, 219
of vivid light, 248

world(s) (*continued*)
   other, 172, 232
   parallel, 266, 281
   personal, 306
   possible/potential, 107, 164, 178, 263–64
   Platonic and Aristotelian, 192
   -relation, 278
   small, 72
   -spheres, 189
   spiritual, 92, 191, 219
   three, 199
   two, 243
   unconnected, 91
   unfolding of, 220
   unnumberable, 66
   upon worlds, 88
World Parliament of Religions, 211
World-Soul, 45, 79, 245, 274, 277, 315

xenophobia, 72
xin, 256

Yahweh, 31, 39, 105, 145, 204, 209, 228
Yanomami, 97
Yasna, 93
Yatima and Paolo (figures of *Diaspora*), 307–9
Yggdrasil, 110
YHWH, 39, 142–60, 168, 173–74, 196, 204–5, 209, 228, 233
YHWH Sabaoth, 205, 228
Yogananda, Paramahansa, 58

Zeus, 55, 105, 204
Zion (mount), 204
Zoroaster, 35, 94, 151
Zoroastrism, 37, 93, 95, 212, 246–47

www.ingramcontent.com/pod-product-compliance
Lightning Source LLC
Chambersburg PA
CBHW081533300426
44116CB00015B/2614